Advances in Theory and Practice of Emerging Markets

Series Editor

Yogesh K. Dwivedi
EMaRC, School of Management
Swansea University Bay Campus
Swansea, United Kingdom

Series Regional Editors

David Brown, Lancaster University, UK
Regions: China and UK

Lemuria Carter, Virginia Commonwealth University, USA
Region: North America

Marijn Janssen, TU Delft, The Netherlands
Region: Europe

Samuel Fosso Wamba, Toulouse Business School, France
Region: Africa

More information about this series at http://www.springer.com/series/15802

Yogesh K. Dwivedi • Nripendra P. Rana
Emma L. Slade • Mahmud A. Shareef
Marc Clement • Antonis C. Simintiras
Banita Lal
Editors

Emerging Markets from a Multidisciplinary Perspective

Challenges, Opportunities and Research Agenda

Springer

Editors
Yogesh K. Dwivedi
EMaRC, School of Management
Swansea University
Swansea, UK

Emma L. Slade
EMaRC, School of Management
Swansea University
Swansea, UK

Marc Clement
EMaRC, School of Management
Swansea University Bay Campus
Swansea, UK

Banita Lal
Nottingham Trent University
Nottingham Business School
Nottingham, UK

Nripendra P. Rana
EMaRC, School of Management
Swansea University
Swansea, UK

Mahmud A. Shareef
School of Business & Economics
North South University
Dhaka, Bangladesh

Antonis C. Simintiras
Gulf University for Science and Technology
Mubarak Al-Abdullah, Kuwait

ISSN 2522-5006 ISSN 2522-5014 (electronic)
Advances in Theory and Practice of Emerging Markets
ISBN 978-3-030-09128-6 ISBN 978-3-319-75013-2 (eBook)
https://doi.org/10.1007/978-3-319-75013-2

Printed on acid-free paper

This Springer imprint is published by the registered company Springer International Publishing AG part of Springer Nature.
The registered company address is: Gewerbestrasse 11, 6330 Cham, Switzerland

To all my classmates and friends from Saraswati Sishu Mandir Pratapgarh, Government Inter College Pratapgarh, the University of Allahabad, the Indian Agricultural Research Institute (IARI), National Bureau of Plant Genetic Resources (NBPGR) and Brunel University London. You have all supported and inspired me in various ways and at different stages of my journey, which I often remember fondly. I am truly thankful for all your support and trust in me and for the inspiration that I constantly drew from you at different junctures

Yogesh K. Dwivedi

To my parents, wife, and two lovely children, Shambhavi and Shashwat, for their never-ending love, unwavering and continued support, and belief in me

Nripendra P. Rana

To my godparents, Linda and Peter, with all my love

Emma L. Slade

To my father Late Md. Murshed Ali and mother Mrs. Lutfunnahar

Mahmud A. Shareef

To all my family members and friends who have given me such support

Marc Clement

To my wife Mary and our son Constantine

Antonis C. Simintiras

To Maya, Maanvi, Yuvraj, and Erol – the epitomes of "joy"

Banita Lal

Foreword

Emerging Markets Research: Opportunities and Challenges for Conceptualizing, Researching and Theorizing

Emerging Markets (EMs) growth and advanced economies slow down have encouraged business actors to explore and take up opportunities in this new and different context. Not surprisingly, EMs have not escaped the interest of academic scholars. Research is constantly picking up since EMs serve as "laboratories" and "thought trials" (Weick, 1989 p. 522) for the testing of established theories and the development of new theoretical lenses. EMs research is challenging the current theoretical and methodological status quo paving the way to context-sensitivity and interdisciplinarity. This is especially evident in this intellectual effort that aims at filling a critical void EMs scholarship. Drawing upon the Preface, the authors' contributions, and my own research experiences, this Foreword discusses challenges and opportunities of *conceptualizing*, *researching*, and *theorizing* EMs phenomena. It provides an overarching framework for contemplating and appreciating the rich mosaic of themes and approaches hosted in this edited book.

EMs research poses conceptual challenges associated with the inconsistency and plethora of country classification schemes of the term "emerging markets." Despite the commonalities, EMs manifest significant diversity in terms of population characteristics, cultural idiosyncrasies, institutional environments, governance and state ownership, and network structures inviting for context-specific definitions and posing the dilemma of contextualization vs. generalization of empirical evidence. In addition, the useful nuances generated by comparative research (emerging vs. advanced economies) have limited the potential of EMs scholarship to develop and flourish as a standalone field. Despite these challenges, EMs offer notable possibilities to problematize our conventional understanding of theories, concepts, constructs, variables, and their relationships and account for contextual variations (Wright, Filatotchev, Hoskisson, & Peng, 2005). This requires moving away from the prevalent gap-spotting strategies that add to the existing literature, "not identifying and challenging its underlying assumptions" (Alvesson & Sandberg, 2011, p. 249), and embracing problematization as an approach to formulating research questions. This approach not only questions assumptions of existing literature but also challenges one's own theoretical position through "dialectical interrogation" (Alvesson & Sandberg, 2011, p. 249), allowing the emergence of new theories and cross-fertilization.

The complexities of EMs research expand beyond conceptualization to include methodological challenges associated with "serious engagement in deep contextualization, novel questioning, and innovative theorizing" (Tsui, 2007, p. 1353). In light of difficulties in defining sampling frames and availability of accurate secondary data, emic qualitative research holds a critical role in contributing to contextualized theory building and testing (Welch, Piekkari, Plakoyiannaki, & Paavilainen-Mäntymäki, 2011). Echoing Buchanan and Bryman (2007, p. 483), the "choice of methods is shaped not only by the research aims, norms of practice, epistemological concerns but also by a combination of organisational, historical, political, ethical, evidential and personally significant characteristics of the field of research." The tension between scientific explanation and context is a concern for any research, particularly visible in EMs not only due to the crossborder nature of the field but also to the unproblematic applicability of universal theories (Welch et al., 2011). Viewed in this light, EMs serve as a site for methodological pluralism and innovation. For instance, visual methodologies (e.g., observation, videography, photoelicitation), largely underutilized in international business/management, can pave the way for inquisitive and context-sensitive thinking of EMs phenomena connecting the researchers to their empirical setting, defying linguistic boundaries, making the intangible tangible, and allowing phenomenon-driven research to take place (Belk et al., forthcoming). It is refreshing to see this methodological discourse embedded in this book as different contributions seek to illuminate EMs phenomena adhering to emic and etic approaches, with the purpose of engaging participants and strengthening trustworthiness of empirical evidence.

Methodological diversity invokes alternative modes of understanding, knowing, and theorizing the field. EMs truly encapsulate the notion that theories are not free-floating statements but are always based on and bounded by researchers' assumptions and the complexity of the research context (Bacharach, 1989). Transparency and clarity in theorizing call, among others, for a reflexive approach that challenges the assumptions and identity of the researcher and research participants. Especially in EMs, it is impossible to separate the theorizing process from reflexivity, not only as practiced by the researcher but also by research participants (See Michailova et al. 2014), as richer meanings that explain and unravel context complexity are a joint cumulative effort.

This discussion suggests that EMs scholarship poses *conceptualizing*, *researching*, and *theorizing* challenges, but most importantly exciting opportunities that need to be further explored and exploited by the academic community. Joint enterprises such as this edited book, entitled *Emerging Markets from a Multidisciplinary Perspective: Challenges, Opportunities and Research Agenda*, offer a fresh and rigorous view of EMs embracing diversity of contexts (e.g., Brazil, India, China, Pakistan, Bangladesh, Saudi Arabia, Jordan, Tanzania, Kuwait, Iraq, UAE, Mexico, and Oman) while *conceptualizing*, *researching*, and *theorizing* intriguing research questions. As an IB scholar, I was impressed by the diverse and thought-provoking topics, contexts, theoretical lenses, and methodologies discussed by the authors. I am grateful to the editors for the invitation to write this Foreword, but most importantly for the opportunity to be part of this topical dialogue that they substantially enrich with this work.

Leeds University Business School
Leeds, UK
Emmanuella Plakoyiannaki

References

Alvesson, M., & Sandberg, J. (2011). Generating research questions through problematization. *Academy of management Review*, *36*(2):247–271

Bacharach, S. B. (1989). Organizational theories: Some criteria for evaluation. *Academy of Management Review*, *14*:496–515.

Belk, R., Kozinents, R., Eckhardt, G., Henry, P., Devinney, T., Caldwell, L., & Plakoyiannaki, E. Envisioning consumers: How videography can contribute to marketing knowledge. *Journal of Marketing Management*, Forthcoming.

Buchanan, D. A., & Bryman, A. (2007). Contextualizing methods choice in organizational research. *Organizational Research Methods*, *10*, 483–501.

Michailova, S., Piekkari, R., Plakoyiannaki, E., Ritvala, T., Mihailova, I., & Salmi, A. (2014). Breaking the silence about exiting Fieldwork: A relational approach and its implications for theorizing. *Academy of Management Review*, *39*(2), 138–161.

Tsui, A. S. (2006). Contextualization in Chinese management research. *Management and Organization Review*, *2*(01): 1–13.

Weick, K. E. (1989). Theory construction as disciplined imagination. *Academy of Management Review*, *14*:516–531.

Welch, C., Piekkari, R., Plakoyiannaki, E., & Paavilainen-Mäntymäki, E. (2011). Theorising from case studies: Towards a pluralist future for international business research. *Journal of International Business Studies*, *42*(5):740–762.

Wright, M., Filatotchev, I., Hoskisson, R. E., & Peng, M. W. (2005). Strategy research in emerging economies: Challenging the conventional wisdom. *Journal of Management Studies*, *41*(1):1–33.

Preface

"Emerging Markets" (EMs) can be broadly described as markets that are developing and yet to attain their final shape and size (Hoskisson, Wright, Filatotchev, & Peng, 2013; Thomas & Ambrosini, 2015; Yamakawa, Peng, & Deeds, 2008). According to the World Bank classification, they include countries that fall within the categories of "middle income" and "low income" (Burgess & Steenkamp, 2006). Geographically, EMs are present across almost all continents, from "the transition economies of the former Soviet Union, the Eastern Bloc, and Asia, and the so-called 'developing countries' of Africa, Asia, the Middle East, and Latin America" (Burgess & Steenkamp, 2006, p. 339). As these markets continue to grow, it is clear to see the increasingly vital role they play in the global economy and society.

Being unsaturated in nature in terms of growth, EMs exhibit a number of unique characteristics (i.e., unique challenges and opportunities) that are socioeconomic, demographic, cultural, political, and regulatory in nature. Examples of such unique challenges and opportunities (i.e., unique characteristics) include diversity and fragmentation of markets, differential market growth rate in terms of urban vs rural and Tier 1 vs Tier 2 cities, evolution of institutions and business ecosystems, leapfrogging in the absence of resistance from legacy systems, political instability, distinct cultural heritage, inherent corruption, relatively young demographic composition, and unusual technological diffusion trends (Roberts et al., 2015). Such differences and uniqueness of EMs have implications for both theory and practice.

Some recent studies (Hoskisson et al., 2013; Luo & Tung, 2007; Xu & Meyer, 2013; Yamakawa et al., 2008; Yamakawa, Khavul, Peng, & Deeds, 2013) have begun to explore challenges, opportunities, and other distinct characteristics to theorize the EM paradigm by enriching existing theories related to consumer behavior, promotional marketing, consumer relationship marketing, strategy development, and information and communication technology (ICT). Marketing managers, economists, and ICT experts are also striving to explore EMs as there are enormous opportunities hidden in such markets in terms of investment, development, product proliferation, and enhanced market share, which again offer opportunities and contexts for undertaking research that is specific to EMs.

Existing studies on EMs (Hoskisson et al., 2013; Luo & Tung, 2007; Xu & Meyer, 2013) assert that such markets are characterized by uncertainty due to various socio-economic and political conditions that are dynamic in nature. Rules and regulations are not well established yet and are subject to constantly changing political landscapes. Hence, streamlining opportunities in these markets are not only challenging but also risky as information regarding structure, process, suppliers, and stakeholders is not readily available (Hoskisson et al., 2013; Yamakawa et al., 2013). Rapid and disruptive technological evolution is another challenge for EMs as it is difficult to realize and implement emerging technologies due to resource constraints (Agnihotri et al., 2012; Chandwani, De, & Dwivedi, 2017; Chandwani & Dwivedi, 2015; Dwivedi, Sahu, Rana, Singh, & Chandwani, 2016; Yamakawa et al., 2008), yet they offer unique opportunities in the form of technology-mediated development.

Based on the discussions, it can be concluded that EMs offer enormous opportunities but realizing them is both challenging and risky due to inherent uncertainties of such markets. Relatively difficult access and, in many instances, lack of availability to relevant information and infrastructure pose further complexity and challenges not only to organizations for establishing and growing businesses but also to researchers for conducting rigorous research. Yet, challenges and complexities inherent in EMs can be translated as opportunities by both practitioners and researchers through attending to the large number of unexplored issues awaiting attention (Hoskisson et al., 2013; Trainor, Rapp, Beitelspacher, & Schillewaert, 2011; Xu & Meyer, 2013).

Unique characteristics of EMs and developing countries make this context different from developed countries, causing implications for both theory and practice. It necessitates substantial adaptations of theories developed (Dwivedi et al. 2017; Dwivedi, Shareef, Simintiras, Lal, & Weerakkody, 2016; Kapoor, Dwivedi, & Williams, 2015; Rana, Dwivedi, Lal, Williams, & Clement, 2017; Rana, Dwivedi, Williams, & Weerakkody, 2016) and approaches employed in the Western world for investigating problems specific to such markets, such as identifying new theoretical constructs, (re)developing hypotheses, emphasizing institutional contexts, deciding how to collect data and validate measurements, and interpreting results (Burgess & Steenkamp, 2006). As such, doing research in the EM context for establishing new conceptual and theoretical paradigms from multidisciplinary perspectives is vital for making the global economy more equitable and sustainable.

This book, entitled *Emerging Markets from a Multidisciplinary Perspective: Challenges, Opportunities and Research Agenda*, aims to bring together a variety of disciplines and a community for the advancement of knowledge regarding issues prominent in EMs. Theoretical, conceptual (including position papers), and empirical papers are included in this inaugural multidisciplinary edited volume under the *Advances in Theory and Practice of Emerging Markets*[1] book series. In line with the aim of the series, this particular edited volume covers topics from various subject areas focusing on a number of EMs such as Brazil, India, China, Pakistan, Bangladesh, Saudi Arabia, Jordan, Tanzania, Kuwait, Iraq, UAE, Mexico, and Oman. The 30 chapters are organized into six sections in this book.

---

[1] http://www.springer.com/series/15802

We hope these chapters outline a rich tapestry of research issues related to emerging markets. Since most chapters are from different areas of business, management, finance, and economics, they provide a window into the multidisciplinary view of EMs. Considering the breadth and depth of the content, we hope this book will become a trusted resource for readers wishing to learn more about the various aspects and dimensions of EMs, as well as those interested in finding out diverse research issues pertinent in the context of EMs.

Swansea, UK — Yogesh K. Dwivedi
Swansea, UK — Nripendra P. Rana
Swansea, UK — Emma L. Slade
Bashundhara, Dhaka, Bangladesh — Mahmud A. Shareef
Swansea, UK — Marc Clement
Kuwait City, Kuwait — Antonis C. Simintiras
Nottingham, UK — Banita Lal

References

Agnihotri, R., Kothandaraman, P., Kashyap, R., & Singh, R. (2012). Bringing "social" into sales: The impact of salespeople's social media use on service behaviors and value creation. *Journal of Personal Selling and Sales Management*, *32*(3), 333–348.

Burgess, S. M., & Steenkamp, J. B. E. (2006). Marketing renaissance: How research in Emerging Markets advances marketing science and practice. *International Journal of Research in Marketing*, *23*(4), 337–356.

Chandwani, R., De, R., & Dwivedi, Y. K. (2017). Telemedicine for low resource settings: Exploring the generative mechanisms. *Technological Forecasting and Social Change*. Available at http://www.sciencedirect.com/science/article/pii/S0040162517307965

Chandwani, R. K., & Dwivedi, Y. K. (2015). Telemedicine in India: current state, challenges and opportunities. *Transforming Government: People, Process and Policy*, *9*(4), 393–400.

Dwivedi, Y. K., Rana, N. P., Janssen, M., Lal, B., Williams, M. D., & Clement, R. M. (2017). An Empirical Validation of a Unified Model of Electronic Government Adoption (UMEGA). *Government Information Quarterly, 34*(2), 211–230.

Dwivedi, Y. K., Sahu, G. P., Rana, N. P., Singh, M., & Chandwani, R. K. (2016). Common Services Centres (CSCs) as an approach to bridge the digital divide: Reflecting on challenges and obstacles. *Transforming Government: People, Process and Policy*, *10*(4), 511–525.

Dwivedi, Y. K., Shareef, M. A., Simintiras, A. C., Lal, B., & Weerakkody, V. (2016). A generalised adoption model for services: A cross-country comparison of mobile health (m-health). *Government Information Quarterly*, *33*(1), 174–187.

Hoskisson, R. E., Wright, M., Filatotchev, I., & Peng, M. W. (2013). Emerging multinationals from mid-range economies: The influence of institutions and factor markets. *Journal of Management Studies*, *50*(7), 1295–1321.

Kapoor, K. K., Dwivedi, Y. K., & Williams, M. D. (2015). Examining the role of three sets of innovation attributes for determining adoption of the interbank mobile payment service. *Information Systems Frontiers, 17*(5), 1039–1056.

Luo, Y., & Tung, R. (2007). International expansion of Emerging Market enterprises: A springboard perspective. *Journal of International Business Studies*, *38*(4), 481–498.

Rana, N. P., Dwivedi, Y. K., Lal, B., Williams, M. D., & Clement, M. (2017). Citizens' adoption of an electronic government system: towards a unified view. *Information Systems Frontiers, 19*(3), 549–568.

Rana, N. P., Dwivedi, Y. K., Williams, M. D., & Weerakkody, V. (2016). Adoption of online public grievance redressal system in India: Toward developing a unified view. *Computers in Human Behavior, 59*, 265–282.

Roberts, J., Kayande, U., & Srivastava, R. (2015). What's different about Emerging Markets and what does it mean for theory and practice? *Customer Needs and Solutions, 2*(4), 245–250.

Thomas, L., & Ambrosini, V. (2015). Materializing strategy: The role of comprehensiveness and management controls in strategy formation in volatile environments. *British Journal of Management, 26*(S1), S105–S124.

Trainor, K. J., Rapp, A., Beitelspacher, L. S., & Schillewaert, N. (2011). Integrating information technology and marketing: An examination of the drivers and outcomes of e-Marketing capability. *Industrial Marketing Management, 40*(1), 162–174.

Xu, D., & Meyer, K. E. (2013). Linking theory and context: "Strategy research in emerging economies" after Wright et al. (2005). *Journal of Management Studies, 50*(7), 1322–1346.

Yamakawa, Y., Khavul, S., Peng, M. W., & Deeds, D. L. (2013). Venturing from emerging economies. *Strategic Entrepreneurship Journal, 7*(3), 181–196.

Yamakawa, Y., Peng, M. W., & Deeds, D. L. (2008). What drives new ventures to internationalize from emerging to developed economies. *Entrepreneurship Theory and Practice, 32*(1), 59–82.

Contents

Part I Economics and Finance

1 **The Political Economy of Financial Development: A Review** 3
Sumon Kumar Bhaumik

2 **Grievance Redressal in the Indian Financial Regulatory Space: The Unified Approach** 17
Parimala Veluvali

3 **Role of Intermediaries in Providing Financial Access: Current and Future Research Trends** 27
Rajesh Chandwani and Vaibhavi Kulkarni

4 **The UK Economy and Brexit** 37
David Blackaby

Part II Financial Technology

5 **Digital Technologies and Pro-poor Finance** 49
Silvia Masiero and M. N. Ravishankar

6 **Identifying Critical Success Factor (CSFs) for the Adoption of Digital Payment Systems: A Study of Indian National Banks** 61
G. P. Sahu and Naveen Kumar Singh

7 **Mobile Banking Adoption: Key Challenges and Opportunities and Implications for a Developing Country** 75
Sujeet Kumar Sharma and Saeed Al-Muharrami

Part III Digital Business

8 **Hyper-localizing e-Commerce Strategy: An Emerging Market Perspective** 89
Nitish Singh and Brendan M. Keating

9 **Exploring E-Business in Indian SMEs: Adoption, Trends and the Way Forward** 95
Vishnupriya Raghavan, Marya Wani, and Dolphy M. Abraham

10 **Opportunities and Challenges of Augmented Reality Shopping in Emerging Markets** 107
Salma S. Abed

11 **The Impact of Social Media on Internal Communications in the Tanzanian Telecom Industry** 119
Shirumisha Kwayu, Banita Lal, and Mumin Abubakre

Part IV Information Systems and Communication Technologies

12 **Social Media Research in and of India: A Snapshot** 135
P. Vigneswara Ilavarasan

13 **Evaluating the Current Situation of Mobile Services (M-Services) in the Kingdom of Saudi Arabia** 149
Abdullah Mohammed Baabdullah, Ali Abdallah Alalwan, and Naim Salameh Al Qadi

14 **An Examination of the Role of National IT Development and Infrastructure in Models for Smartphone Adoption and Use: The Cases of Iraq, Jordan and the UAE** 161
Nisreen Ameen and Robert Willis

15 **Factors Influencing the Adoption of E-Ticketing in Arabic Frontier Markets: Conceptual Extension of UTAUT** 195
Zainah Qasem

16 **Internet of Things (IoT) in Agriculture Supply Chain Management: A Developing Country Perspective** 209
Sunil Luthra, Sachin K. Mangla, Dixit Garg, and Anil Kumar

17 **Readiness of Smart City: Emerging Economy Perspective** 221
Sheshadri Chatterjee and Arpan Kumar Kar

18 **Integration of Public Sector Healthcare Information Systems with Private Sector Healthcare Providers in Pakistan: Challenges, Opportunities and Solutions** 233
Khalil Khoumbati, Munir Abbasi, Syed Ghulam Sarwar Shah, and Lampros K. Stergioulas

Part V Marketing

19 **Adoption of Pro-poor Innovations in the Context of the Base of the Pyramid and Subsistence Marketplaces: Challenges, Opportunities and Research Agenda** 243
Ben Lowe and Md. Rajibul Hasan

20 Branding for Bottom of the Pyramid: A Case of Branded Footwear Consumer in Indian Rural Setting 255
Ashish Gupta and Anushree Tandon

21 Rurality in Flux: A Perspective on Rural Tourism Enterprise 273
Gunjan Saxena

22 Factors Affecting Jordanian Consumers' Attitudes Towards Facebook Advertising: Case Study of Tourism 285
Dina Hesham Abu-Ghosh, Hani Al-Dmour, Ali Abdallah Alalwan, and Rand Hani Al-Dmour

23 Factors Affecting Consumers' Pro-environmental Behaviours in Saudi Arabia 303
Hawazin Alzubaidi

24 Do you Like to be an Aspirational Referee to Promote a Product? Act Like a Celebrity in Emerging Market 315
Mahmud A. Shareef, Vinod Kumar, Uma Kumar, and Mohammad Abdallah Ali Alryalat

Part VI Management and International Business

25 Institutional Export Barriers on Exporters from Emerging Markets: Evidence from China 331
Jia Li and Ling Liu

26 What Caused the Shortage of Labour: Examining the Recruitment and Selection in the Internet Financial Industry in China 339
Jingyi Liu and Yujie Cai

27 Advances in Talent Management Research: A Review of Extant Literature 359
Adel Alferaih

28 Networking and Entrepreneurial Activity in Kuwait 381
Antonis C. Simintiras and Yusif M. Al-Hajji

29 The Ethics and Governance of an Emerging Technology in an Emerging Market: The Case of Private Umbilical Cord Blood Banking in India 391
Shashank S. Tiwari

30 Institutional Voids and Indian Automotive Industry: Challenges and Reflection 405
Maneesh Kumar

Index 415

About the Editors

Yogesh K. Dwivedi is a Professor of Digital Marketing and Innovation, and Director of the Emerging Markets Research Centre (EMaRC) in the School of Management at Swansea University, Wales, UK. His research interests are in the area of Information Systems (IS), including the adoption and diffusion of emerging ICTs, electronic/digital government, and digital marketing, particularly in the context of emerging markets. He has published more than 250 articles in several leading academic journals and conferences. He has coedited/coauthored more than 20 books on technology adoption, e-government, IS theory, eWOM, and social media, which have been published by international publishers such as Chandos Publishing (an imprint of Elsevier), Springer, Chapman and Hall/CRC Press, Routledge, and Emerald. He has acted as coeditor of fifteen journal special issues; organized tracks, minitracks, and panels in leading conferences; and served as program cochair of the 2013 IFIP WG 8.6 Conference on *Grand Successes and Failures in IT: Public and Private Sectors* and as Conference Chair of the IFIP WG 6.11 I3E2016 Conference on *Social Media: The Good, the Bad, and the Ugly*. He is an Associate Editor of the *European Journal of Marketing* and *Government Information Quarterly*, and Senior Editor of the *Journal of Electronic Commerce Research*. He is the founding editor of the recently established Springer Book Series on *Advances in Theory and Practice of Emerging Markets* (http://www.springer.com/series/15802). More information about Professor Dwivedi can be found at http://www.swansea.ac.uk/staff/som/academic-staff/y.k.dwivedi/.

Nripendra P. Rana is an Associate Professor in the School of Management at Swansea University, UK. With an academic and professional background in Mathematics and Computer Science and with PhD in Information Systems, his current research interests focus primarily upon adoption of emerging and cutting-edge technology, e-government, m-government, e-commerce, and m-commerce systems. His work has been published in leading academic journals, including *European Journal of Marketing*, *Information Systems Frontiers*, *Government Information Quarterly*, *Production Planning & Control*, *Journal of Business Research*, *Public Management Review*, *Annals of Operations Research*, *International Journal of*

Production Research, and *Computers in Human Behavior*. He has also presented his research in some of the prominent international conferences of information systems across the world.

Emma L. Slade is a Lecturer in Management at the University of Bristol. She is working on a variety of research topics across marketing and information systems, including consumer/public engagement on social media and adoption of new financial technologies. Emma has published articles in a number of highly regarded journals such as *Public Management Review*, *Psychology & Marketing*, *Information Systems Frontiers*, and *Computers in Human Behaviour*. In 2016, Emma was selected for participation in the inaugural Digital Economy Crucible funded by EPSRC through the CHERISH-DE multidisciplinary research center. Emma was also Program Cochair of the 15th IFIP I3E Conference on "Social Media: The Good, the Bad, and the Ugly" (#I3E2016).

Mahmud A. Shareef is a Professor in the School of Business and Economics, North South University, Bangladesh. He was a visiting faculty in the DeGroote School of Business, McMaster University, Canada. He gained his PhD in Business Administration from the Sprott School of Business, Carleton University, Canada. He received two graduate degrees: one from the Institute of Business Administration, University of Dhaka, Bangladesh, in Business Administration; and the other from Carleton University, Ottawa, Canada, in Civil Engineering. His research interest is focused on online consumer behavior and virtual organizational reformation. He has published more than 100 papers addressing consumers' adoption behavior and quality issues of e-commerce and e-government in a range of refereed conference proceedings and international journals. He was the recipient of more than ten academic awards including three Best Research Paper Awards in the UK and Canada.

Marc Clement is a Full Professor and the Dean of School of Management in Swansea University. He graduated with a first-class honours degree in Physics from Swansea University and a PhD in Laser Physics from Swansea University with the research undertaken at the Rutherford Laboratory. Marc then gained a fellowship from the Royal Society to study at the Centre d'etudes Nucléaires de Saclay, Paris. He has held several senior academic positions and is currently Executive Chairman in the Institute of Life Science at the College of Medicine, Swansea University. As well as being an eminent academic, Marc is an attempted entrepreneur having founded several businesses and is the named inventor of many patents in the field of medical devices. He has also developed a number of projects and initiatives in supercomputing and big data. Marc was a Founding Director of High Performance Computing Wales and established the original Blue C supercomputer at the Institute of Life Science, Swansea University. Marc has supervised dozens of research degrees and is particularly keen to apply the latest developments in network and relationship science to the medical profession for the improvement of human health and the development of knowledge economies globally.

Antonis C. Simintiras is the Dean of the College of Business Administration, Gulf University for Science and Technology, Kuwait, and PT Research Professor of Marketing at the School of Management, Swansea University, UK. Over the years, he held visiting professorial appointments in France, Spain, Austria, Greece, Finland, USA, and China. His main research interests are in the areas of personal selling and sales management, consumer behavior, and crosscultural research methodology. Part of his work has appeared in the *Journal of International Business Studies*, *Journal of Business Research*, *European Journal of Marketing*, *Industrial Marketing Management*, *Psychology & Marketing*, *Journal of Managerial Psychology*, and *Journal of Small Business Management.* He has also coauthored a book on *Global Sales Management* and two monographs.

Banita Lal is a Senior Lecturer in Information Studies at the Nottingham Business School, Nottingham Trent University. She gained her PhD in Information Systems from Brunel University, London. Her research interests revolve around the adoption and diffusion of technology, including mobile and e-Government technology, social media technology, and ICT for development. She has published in several leading peer-reviewed conferences and journals in the field of Information Systems, which include *Information Systems Frontiers*, *Government Information Quarterly*, and *Information Technology and People*.

Part I
Economics and Finance

Chapter 1 The Political Economy of Financial Development: A Review

Sumon Kumar Bhaumik

Abstract The importance of financial development for economic growth is well understood, and hence there is a demand for policies that facilitate financial development in emerging market economies and, more generally, in developing economies. This paper reviews the literature on the political economy of financial development which suggests that relevant policies are shaped, in large measure, by the interplay between the governments and interest groups that benefit from or lose rent on account of financial development. It draws some conclusions about formulation of financial policies and highlights possible ways in which the literature can be meaningfully extended.

Keywords Financial Development · Financial Policies · Political Economy · Emerging Market Economies · Developing Economies

1.1 Introduction

It is now stylized in policy circles that financial development and economic growth are correlated. Indeed, despite differences of opinions among economists (see discussion in Levine, 1997), and some evidence that financial development may not be a panacea in so far as growth is concerned (e.g., Demetriades & Hussein, 1996), the

The author thanks seminar/workshop participants at Swansea University, UK, and the Leibniz Institute for East and Southeast European Studies (IoS), Regensburg, Germany, for their helpful comments. The paper was partly developed when the author was a visiting scholar at IoS in August 2017. He remains responsible for all remaining errors.

S. K. Bhaumik (✉)
Sheffield University Management School, University of Sheffield, Sheffield, UK

IZA – Institute of Labor Economics, Bonn, Germany

Global Labor Organization
e-mail: s.k.bhaumik@sheffield.ac.uk

Y. K. Dwivedi et al. (eds.), *Emerging Markets from a Multidisciplinary Perspective*, Advances in Theory and Practice of Emerging Markets,
https://doi.org/10.1007/978-3-319-75013-2_1

popular wisdom is that financial development promotes or *causes* growth (e.g., Christopoulos & Tsionas, 2004; King & Levine, 1993).[1] This happens, in part, by averting market failures that prevent mobilization of resources from savers to entrepreneurs which facilitates capital formation and, in part, by ensuring that capital is better (or more efficiently) allocated among competing projects.

In emerging market contexts, this requires both creation of markets for financial resources, in a move away from financial repression, and reduction in transactions and information costs that can lead to market failure.[2] The latter involves strengthening creditors' rights, better contract enforcement, and reduction in information costs through better financial disclosures by firms (Demirguc-Kunt & Maksimovic, 1998; Levine, 1999). This focus on factors such as investor and creditor protection and contract enforcement, in turn, has spawned a large literature on the legal origins of countries and how legal origin influences structure of the financial sector – e.g., bank based vs equity market based – and financial development, in general (Beck, Demirguc-Kunt, & Levine, 2003; La Porta, Lopez-de-Silanes, Shleifer, & Vishny, 1997, 1998).

However, the basis for the legal origin-based explanations for extent and nature of financial development has since been questioned (Roe & Siegel, 2009), and perhaps the most important of the criticisms is that there are considerably more changes in the direction of financial development of countries – indeed, financial reversals – than what the legal origin approach would predict.[3] In some cases, policy reversals can be directly traced back to political events; e.g., the decline of the bond market

[1] Evidence suggests that there is a two-way causality between financial development and growth (e.g., Calderon & Liu, 2003). The rationale for the causality running from financial development to economic growth is discussed below, and the rationale for the causality running in the other direction is that growth "provides the means to implement costly financial structures" (Greenwood & Jovanovic, 1990: pp. 1076).

[2] The source of information cost is well understood in the context of financial markets. Firm managers typically know more about the project portfolio of the firms than outsider investors. This creates two different problems, namely, the ex ante problem of adverse selection and the ex post problem of moral hazard. In addition, in primary equity markets, some investors may be better informed than other investors, thereby adding another dimension to the information asymmetry problem. In the credit market, the adverse selection problem is overcome using mechanisms such as relationship banking, collateral, credit ratings, and debt covenants, while the moral hazard problem is mitigated using other mechanisms such as a credible threat to liquidate borrowers' assets in the event of default and/or breach of covenants. In the equity market, the existence of adverse selection can lead to non-issuance of equity by firms or underpricing of equity during IPOs, and, subsequent to issue of equity, external investors mitigate the moral hazard problem using corporate governance mechanisms such as the board of directors. For discussion of these issues, see, for example, Myers and Majluf (1984), Rock (1986), Bhattacharya and Thakor (1993), Rajan and Winton (1995), Boot (2000), Garleanu and Zwiebel (2009), and Oshry, Hermalin, and Weisbach (2010).

[3] Other criticisms include, for example, the presumption about the de facto ability of courts in common law countries to adapt the laws to a changing economic environment. Armour and Lele (2009) use data to demonstrate that in the Indian context, the courts are so overburdened, with a very high volume of pending cases, that the judiciary may not have significant ability to rapidly adapt laws to the changing economic environment.

in Brazil can perhaps be traced back to a politically motivated bankruptcy law reform in 1945 which prioritized workers' rights over creditors' rights (Musacchio, 2008). There is, therefore, the need to examine the process of financial development through a different prism. In particular, since the publication of a seminal paper by Rajan and Zingales (2003), there is considerable interest in political economy forces that shape financial development.[4]

In this paper, we briefly discuss the growing literature on the political economy of financial development – in particular, on the development of financial markets and factors such as investors' rights that underpin these markets – that facilitate greater access to external finance to a wide range of private agents. On the basis of this discussion, we draw some conclusions about the implications of this literature for financial development in emerging market economies. We shall start with a view of political economy in which private interest groups act to influence government policies to generate or protect rent. Subsequently, we shall expand the discussion to consider the government itself as an active player that acts in its own interest, using its unique power to grant and expropriate economic rights.

1.2 Political Economy of Seeking and Protecting Rent

Using a range of indicators of financial development, Rajan and Zingales (2003) observe that the trend of financial development over time is not linear and monotonic. In particular, they note the following: First, the extent of financial development in countries does not increase monotonically over time; countries were, by and large, more financially developed in 1913 than in 1980, and they caught up with their 1913 level of financial development only toward the end of the century. Second, trends in financial development across countries are not necessarily consistent with the conclusions that one can draw from the legal origin literature. For example, France (a French civil code country) had a higher level of market capitalization (as a percentage of GDP) than the United States (a common law country) in 1913.[5] More importantly, the relative levels of financial development – in this case, equity market development – changed over time, bringing into question structural explanations for financial development. Specifically, market capitalization in the United States overtook France by quite a margin by 1980, and in 1999 the two countries had comparable levels of market capitalization. An important implication for these observations is that the level and pace of financial development may not be deter-

[4] There has always been considerable interest among economists about political economy of financial crises and government's regulatory response to these crises, e.g., Haggard (2000), Congleton (2009), Coffee Jr. (2012), and Wolfson and Epstein (2013). However, as we have mentioned above, in this paper, we focus more on the process of financial development that is characterized by greater access to external finance by a wide range of private agents, including nonincumbents.

[5] It is stylized in the legal origin literature that common law countries provide better investor protection than French civil law countries (La Porta et al., 1998).

mined entirely by structural factors such as legal origin and that variable factors such as the political economy of lawmaking and institutional building may affect the aforementioned level and pace.[6]

Recapitulate that financial development facilitates economic growth by way of, among other things, better or more efficient allocation of resources. A corollary of this line of argument is that in the absence of financial development, given high information and transactions costs, incumbent firms with proven track record and relationships with financial institutions and investors will have an advantage over potential new entrants at accessing financial resources. This advantage can restrict competition from new firms and thereby generate rent for the incumbent firms. In the economics literature, it is well understood that where rents exist, incumbent firms compete for these rents and devote significant resources toward this competition (Krueger, 1974). It follows that incumbent firms will lobby for protection from competition to protect rent, and the government will oblige with suitable restrictions that protect this rent, either to seek the political support of these firms and their stakeholders (Chari & Gupta, 2008; Hillman, 1982) or because incumbents who are already earning rent can make a more credible promise to share this rent than potential incumbents who may earn (close to) zero economic profit in a more competitive post-entry environment (see, e.g., Djankov, 2009 and the references therein).

In light of this discussion, the political economy of financial development is easy to understand. Financial development, which involves improvement in protection of property rights, disclosure and (more generally) corporate governance quality, and ease of contract enforcement, can facilitate entry by new firms. It is, therefore, in the interest of rent-earning incumbent firms to lobby to preserve the status quo and prevent reforms that facilitate financial development. Indeed, this rent-based argument is applicable to a wide range of contexts. For example, Benmelech and Moskowitz (2007) demonstrate that in the United States, in the nineteenth century, usury laws "were used by incumbents with political power to control entry and hamper competition as well as lower their own cost of capital" (p. 2). Specifically, by limiting the maximum interest rate that could be charged, these incumbents were able to cause credit rationing which disproportionately disadvantages potential new entrants.[7]

However, the rent-seeking argument does not suggest that it is always in the interest of the incumbents to thwart financial development, which is consistent with the nonlinear and non-monotonic trends of financial development discussed above. If there are other disruptions that affect rents, for example, liberalization of trade

[6] Financial development is by no means the only sphere of policymaking that is influenced by a country's political economy. As discussed by Persson and Tabellini (2000), political economy (and the political process that underpins it) influences policies about a wide range of issues such as fiscal policy, provision of public goods, and redistributive policies.

[7] Since firms are able to mitigate the asymmetric information problem in financial markets better with age and size turnover (Berger & Udell, 1998), lending to (or investing in) incumbents is likely to carry less risk than lending to (or investing in) potential entrants. Hence, to the extent that interest rates are positively correlated with risk, an upward limit on interest rates will disproportionately affect the ability of potential entrants to access external finance.

and capital flows to meet international obligations, it may be in the interest of the incumbents to lobby for financial development. If trade and capital flows are liberalized, the rent-seeking ability of incumbent domestic firms will be reduced, irrespective of whether there is market entry by new domestic firms. At the same time, these incumbent firms will require access to finance to compete with the imports and foreign multinationals and also to take advantage of opportunities associated with overseas markets. The better firms may be able to raise capital overseas at lower costs, if they can signal good disclosure and corporate governance quality and if the overseas creditors and investors are not wary about property rights protection and contract enforcement in the country. This disruption of existing banking relationships, together with the competition posed by cross-border capital flows, will induce domestic financial institutions to seek out new clients and, without long-term relationships to mitigate the problems associated with adverse selection and moral hazard, it would be in their interest to have clarity about property rights associated with collateral and ease of enforcement of contracts. In other words, if current and capital accounts of the balance of payments are simultaneously liberalized, it may be in the interest of both the incumbent firms and financial institutions to lobby for financial development.[8]

Braun and Raddatz (2008) use an interesting research design to demonstrate the relevance of political economy for financial development. To begin with, using price-cost margin (PCM) as a proxy for product market competition (and hence rent), they estimate the impact of financial development on PCM at the country-industry level, for the 1980–2000 period. They then use the estimated sensitivity of PCM to financial development "to distinguish between those industries that favor (in relative terms) policies conducive to the development of the financial system (henceforth the "*Promoters*") and those industries that oppose these policies (henceforth the "*Opponents*") (p. 1479). The relative strength of promoters of financial development in a country can, therefore, be computed as the value-added weighted average of PCM of promoter industries less the similarly weighted average of PCM or opponent industries. Correspondingly, the change in the relative strength of promoters can be computed as the value-added weighted change in PCM of promoter industries less the similarly weighted average of PCM of opponent industries. Finally, the event of trade liberalization in the cross section of countries in the sample is used to estimate the relationship between the change in financial development and the change in the relative strength of the promoters.[9] The regression estimates (see Table IV of the paper on p. 1491) suggest that, in the event of trade liberalization,

[8] However, liberalizing only trade or only capital flows may not have the desirable impact on financial development. For example, as argued by Rajan and Zingales (2003), in the event of only trade liberalization, incumbent firms experiencing greater import competition may actually see greater financial repression to reduce competition from domestic sources, and incumbent financial institutions may also find strengthening of the relationship-based businesses with incumbent firms less challenging than facing additional competition that may arise from financial development, by way of entry of new financial institutions.

[9] For details about the windows over which the changes in financial development and relative strength of the promoters are computed, refer to Braun and Raddatz (2008).

an increase in the relative strength of industries that benefit from financial development has a positive, statistically significant, and economically meaningful impact on the change in financial development.

In other words, there is a compelling case in favor of the argument that financial development is influenced by the political economy of the country but that this influence is not deterministic and, instead, depends on both the distribution of winners and losers following any disruption that affects the creation and distribution of rent, the ability of these winners and losers to form coalitions, and the relative strengths of these coalitions to influence government policy. Since some disruptions are exogenous, for example, on account of a country's external commitments or on account of economic crises, this process is dynamic (see, e.g., Fig. 1 in Pagano & Volpin, 2001) and thereby provides a prima facie explanation for shifts in government policy related to financial development. The nonlinear and non-monotonic trends in financial development over time can similarly be explained.

1.3 Government as an Active Player

Thus far, we have discussed a scenario in which private economic agents, firms in particular, lobby the government and influence the direction and pace of financial development in large measure to protect the rent that they earn in the absence of such liberalization. These private agents can also lobby in favor of financial development under certain circumstances, but the disruptions that can induce them to actively seek financial development are viewed as being exogenous to the political economy process. This, however, is unrealistic, especially in the context of emerging market economies that – to use the nomenclature of North, Wallis, and Weingast (2009) – are more likely to be "limited access" states than "open access" states. In limited access states, groups of elites control or have privileged access to various resources, and they earn rent on the basis of this control or privileged access, usually with tacit or explicit support of the state. In return, they share some of this rent with the state or political elites who are de facto embodiment of the state.

Calomiris and Haber (2014) describe the political economy of financial development in such a context, specifically, Mexico. Between 1821 and 1876, Mexico witnessed a series of coups, and political instability was palpable. In 1876, Porforio Diaz started his tenure as the president of the country, and his reign lasted till 1911. Diaz granted rent-seeking power to a handful of banks such as the Banco Nacional de Mexico by exempting them from the tax on issue of bank notes, by removing the authority of state or regional governments to issue bank charters, and by imposing high capital requirements on new banks. In return, these banks lent money to the government at low rates of interest to finance military and other expenditures that were necessary to politically stabilize the country. Private sector lending by these banks were largely directed at insiders such as board members and major industrialists, in effect protecting these incumbent entrepreneurs from competition from potential entrants. Variations of this arrangement were used by subsequent Mexican governments well into the twentieth century. The legacy of this arrangement was an underdeveloped banking sector; in 1960, domestic credit to the private sector amounted to only 20.5% of the GDP (source: The World Bank).

The argument that governments in emerging market economies – more generally, developing economies – repress financial development to finance their expenditures is not new. It is well understood that governments with large fiscal deficits (and/or high public debt to GDP ratios) often adopt policies that reduce their cost of borrowing (Reinhart, Kirkegaard, & Sbrancia, 2011). These policies include preempting credit disbursal to the private sector by way of mechanisms that channel a significant share of available financial resources to the government,[10] implicit or explicit cap on interest rates, and (in the presence of an excess private sector demand for financial resources) use of nonmarket mechanisms for disbursal of credit. In the context of emerging market economies, it is reasonable to assume that political connections of private agents influence the disbursal of credit (and financial resources, in general) through nonmarket mechanisms (Claessens, Feijen, & Laeven, 2008; Faccio, Masulis, & McConnell, 2006; Khwaja & Mian, 2005; Li, Meng, Wang, & Zhou, 2008). Since incumbent private agents/firms are more likely to have the necessary political connections, we see shades of the Rajan and Zingales (2003) paradigm, with an additional factor in the form of the direct involvement of governments (and political elites who form governments).

To be fair, this political economy process can also lead to outcomes that are associated with (unexpected) benefits. Consider, for example, the case of the seventeenth-century England. As noted by Andrianova, Demetriades, and Xu (2011), until 1688, crown borrowing was short term, and there was a persistent gap between the government's revenues and expenditures, thereby limiting military expenditure and, in turn, England's military power. Evidence suggests that the government's ability to raise long-term credit rose significantly between 1693 and 1698, and much of this borrowing was funded by the New East Indian Company (NEIC) and the Bank of England (BoE). In return, the NEIC was granted exclusive rights over the trading route to India, and the BoE was granted a monopoly license. The economic rent accruing to a limited number of joint stock companies such as NEIC with monopoly over trade routes made investment in these companies lucrative for investors, especially when their risk could be spread over multiple voyages. Together with better protection of property rights, which was clearly in the interests of the joint stock companies and those who invested in them, and which was an ex ante commitment mechanism to prevent ex post expropriation of monopoly rent by the government, this "created the pre-conditions for the financial markets to emerge and flourish in the second half of the 17th century" (p. 690). It is unclear, however, to what extent

[10]Arguably, the statutory liquidity requirement (SLR) that Indian banks have to meet is an example of such preemption. Prior to the start of the economic liberalization process in India, in 1991, the SLR for Indian banks was 38.5%, i.e., 38.5% of their deposits in liquid assets, government securities being the dominant form of such assets. For more detailed discussion of initial conditions of the Indian banking sector in 1991 and the changes thereafter, see Bhaumik and Dimova (2004) and Bhaumik and Piesse (2009).

these such benevolent outcomes, unexpected or otherwise, can be replicated in emerging market contexts.[11]

One limitation of the above characterization of the interplay between the government and private agents is that in our examples governments operated in environments of limited suffrage, such that a small group of elites had to be co-opted to put in place the arrangements that were mutually beneficial for the government and the private agents.[12] As we have discussed above, in such contexts, financial repression may well be observed in equilibrium, since the benefits of rent generated for the political and economic elites by an underdeveloped financial system may outweigh the private (as opposed to social) benefits of economic expansion that are brought about by financial development (Girma & Shortland, 2007). The question, therefore, is how the political coalitions required to perpetuate or end rent-seeking activities are formed in contexts that have democratically elected government and, however, flawed the quality of the democracy.[13] Intuition suggests that as suffrage expands, such that the median voter is no longer part of the economic and political elites, the laws and regulations that influence the level, pace, and nature of financial development would be influenced by the socioeconomic identity of the median voter.[14] For example, Degryse, Lambert, and Schwienbacher (2013) argue that a wealthy median voter is more likely to result in greater shareholder protection, while a poorer median voter is likely to lead to greater banking sector development.

Pagano and Volpin (2005) demonstrate that the electoral system itself can have an impact on factors that influence the pace of financial development, for example, corporate governance. They consider a game involving three players: *entrepreneurs* who want weak shareholder protection once they have raised capital, *rentiers* who are minority (or dispersed) shareholders and therefore want strong investor protection, and *employees* who are interested in strong employment protection. The political space is dominated by two parties, each of which commit to a policy plat-

[11] For example, cost of contract enforcement is high in emerging market contexts, and, as a consequence, concentrated ownership structures for firms, often by way of family control, is the optimal way to mitigate agency conflicts between insider managers and outsider investors (Bhaumik & Dimova, 2014; Young, Peng, Ahlstrom, Bruton, & Jiang, 2008). However, where ownership is concentrated in the hands of controlling families, there is significant risk of expropriation of minority shareholders by majority shareholders, and this could reduce the firms' ability to raise external equity capital.

[12] Available evidence suggests that, prior to 1832, only about 3% of the total population of England had the right to vote, and in Scotland, the proportion of males with suffrage was 2.6% of the population (source: http://www.nationalarchives.gov.uk/pathways/citizenship/struggle_democracy/getting_vote.htm). The first Reform Act of 1832 sought to expand suffrage, but it was extended only to men who occupied property with annual value of £10, which excluded about 60% of males from the voting process. Despite two other Reform Acts, in 1867 and 1884, universal suffrage, which granted voting rights to women, albeit not to those under the age of 30, did not arrive until 1918.

[13] According to the Economist Intelligence Unit's democracy index, as of 2016, a large number of emerging market economies including Argentina, Brazil, Chile, Colombia, India, Indonesia, Mexico, Peru, and South Africa are (flawed) democracies.

[14] For a discussion of median voter models, see Congleton (2004).

form before the election. The entrepreneurs and the employees have homogeneous political preference and, therefore, have a bias toward one or the other of the two parties, depending on their policy platform. The rentiers (and sundry others such as the unemployed and the self-employed) do not have strong preference for any one party. In a proportional electoral system, in (what one might call an "corporatist") equilibrium, there is weak shareholder protection and strong employment protection because in this system electoral benefits are higher when a party's policy platform is closely aligned with a group that has homogeneous preferences. In a majoritarian electoral system, by contrast, it is rational to solicit the support of the ideologically uncommitted voters in key electoral districts.[15] Hence, in a majoritarian system, in equilibrium, there is strong shareholder protection and weak employment protection. In Pagano and Volpin's (2005) study, this prediction finds empirical support in a sample of 45 countries that includes both OECD and developing countries. It follows that share market development is more likely in contexts that have majoritarian electoral systems than in contexts that have proportional electoral systems.

The above discussion suggests that any analysis of the political economy of financial development is enriched when one moves away from (what I call) a quasi-Beckerian paradigm in which interest groups compete for political influence (Becker, 1983), such that the pace and nature of financial development depends on the relative balance of power between winners and losers from financial development, to one in which the political parties have to take into consideration the views of the wider electorate. There may also be significant mileage in moving away from Downs-Hotelling models of spatial (political) equilibrium to scenarios in which interest groups have to trade off their ideological affinity with political parties with the expected private benefits (viz., rent) accruing from financial sector rule-making that is inconsistent with the ideology (Dixit & Londregan, 1996).[16] Further, in the age of economic populism, it would also be interesting to consider scenarios in which vote-maximizing populist parties can credibly threaten to disrupt a two-party system (Palfrey, 1984).

Finally, given that large political parties are "big tent" organizations with heterogeneous views about policy platforms within each political party, and given that in emerging market economies like India votes may be split among multiple federal and regional political parties, it may be meaningful to examine the interplay between intraparty heterogeneity and the party system concentration (Zhang, 2007). The leadership of "big tent" parties has to be accountable to broad constituencies and hence might find it difficult to formulate policies that favor a narrow interest group.

[15] Evidence of such tactical positioning by political agents, albeit at the legislature rather than at the party level, can be found in Cox and McCubbins (1986) and Gerber and Lewis (2004).

[16] Examples of such trade-offs in the context of other policy issues can arguably be found in the trade-off between the expected economic benefits of remaining in the European single market and the ideological benefits of a "hard" Brexit for a section of the UK electorate. Where ideological benefits are certain and immediate, while expected economic benefits lie in the future, the choice may depend on the extent to which the economic benefits are state contingent and the extent to which the contract about ex post rent (or benefit) sharing is incomplete.

By contrast, in a fragmented party system, each political party is likely to be aligned with a narrow interest group, some of whom would favor financial repression. The final outcome is dependent not only on the policy platform of the political party in power but also on its ability to deliver on the promised policy platform with the latter depending on intraparty unity. This framework can potentially be extended to (more formally) encompass issues such as trade-offs between electoral coalitions and policy coalitions of political parties (Gibson, 1997) and factors such as the executive's constitutional authority that may (or may not) enable it to gather support beyond its partisan support in the legislature (Shugart, 1998). This, therefore, is a promising line of inquiry for future research.

1.4 Summing Up

The above discussion confirms that the process of enactment of laws and formulation of policies that facilitate financial development is, indeed, influenced by a country's political economy. The policy implication of this observation is twofold. First, any expectation that governments can adopt and implement policies that are consistent with financial development on a top-down basis is perhaps unrealistic; governments have to (and do) take into consideration how policies would be viewed by their key constituents, whether economic elites or voters. Second, the objectives of financial development may be facilitated by simultaneously pursuing other policies such as liberalization of current and capital accounts of balance of payments that disrupt the ability of interest groups to earn rent even in the absence of financial development.

However, an important issue related to financial development remains largely unexplored. The literature consistently distinguishes between the government and private agents that favor financial repression or financial development. As we have discussed above, in such cases, the outcome depends on the relative strength of the group(s) that favor financial development, whether through lobbying or through the ballot box. In many contexts, however, this separation may de facto not exist, i.e., there could be state capture such that incumbent political agents in government and incumbent economic agents in the industrial-financial landscape work together to maximize joint rent, with some agreement about rent sharing.[17] In such a case, the level and pace of financial development may be the choice variable(s) in a framework

---

[17] It is possible to argue that there is a thin line between this world and the Mexican case discussed earlier in this paper. In the Mexican case, however, there is a distinction between the political elite and the economic elite, such that policy choice is an outcome of bargaining between these two groups. In many emerging market contexts, however, the separating line between these two types of elites is blurred; many powerful politicians (or their families) have strong business interests and, by the same token, people hailing from powerful business families find it in their interests to participate in electoral politics. Further, as noted earlier in the paper, many emerging countries of today are democratic and hence electoral considerations have to be taken into account.

that maximizes the joint rent of these agents.[18] While "capture" is discussed in the context of financial sector regulation (Levitin, 2014),[19] there is little discussion about the implications for state capture on financial development. The relevant policy questions are how state capture interacts with electoral politics and hence with factors such as political awareness of the voters (Bardhan & Mookherjee, 2000) and how (or whether) the dominant interest groups can be incentivized to pursue policies that facilitate financial development. Developing appropriate frameworks and building an evidence base about contexts with (different degrees of) may be the next step in the exploration of the political economy of financial development.

References

Andrianova, S., Demetriades, P., & Xu, C. (2011). Political economy origins of financial markets in Europe and Asia. *World Development*, *39*(5), 686–699.

Armour, J., & Lele, P. (2009). Law, finance and politics: The case of India. *Law & Society Review*, *43*(3), 491–526.

Auty, R. M., & Gelb, A. H. (2000). *Political economy of resource abundant states*. Paper prepared for the Annual Bank Conference on Development Economics, Downloadable from http://documents.worldbank.org/curated/en/926361468781759170/pdf/28750.pdf

Bardhan, P., & Mookherjee, D. (2000). Capture and governance at local and national levels, *American Economic Review*. Papers and proceedings of the one hundred and twelfth annual meeting of the Annual Economic Association, pp. 135–139.

Beck, T., Demirguc-Kunt, A., & Levine, R. (2003). Law and finance: Why does legal origin matter? *Journal of Comparative Economics*, *31*(4), 653–675.

Becker, G. S. (1983). A theory of competition among pressure groups for political influence. *Quarterly Journal of Economics*, *98*(3), 371–400.

Benmelech, E., & Moskowitz, T. (2007). *The political economy of financial regulation: Evidence from U.S. state usury laws in the 19th century* (Working paper no. 12851), Cambridge, MA: National Bureau of Economic Research.

Berger, A. N., & Udell, G. F. (1998). The economics of small business finance: The roles of private equity and debt markets in the financial growth cycle. *Journal of Banking & Finance*, *22*(6–8), 613–673.

Bhattacharya, S., & Thakor, A. V. (1993). Contemporary banking theory. *Journal of Financial Intermediation*, *3*(1), 2–50.

Bhaumik, S. K., & Dimova, R. (2004). How important is ownership in a market with a level playing field? The Indian banking system revisited. *Journal of Comparative Economics*, *32*(1), 165–180.

Bhaumik, S. K., & Dimova, R. (2014). *How family firms differ: Structure, strategy, governance and performance*. Basingstoke, UK: Palgrave Macmillan.

Bhaumik, S. K., & Piesse, J. (2009). Does lending behavior of banks in emerging economies vary by ownership? Evidence from the Indian banking sector. *Economic Systems*, *31*(4), 375–390.

[18] State capture is largely discussed in the context of Central and Eastern Europe (e.g., Hellman, Jones, & Kaufmann, 2003; Innes, 2013), but there is discussion of state capture in other contexts as well (e.g., Auty & Gelb, 2000; Rijkers, Freund, & Nucifora, 2014), with considerably more anecdotal evidence about contexts that are not discussed in the academic literature.

[19] For a theory of regulatory capture, see Laffont and Tirole (1991).

Boot, A. (2000). Relationship banking: What do we know? *Journal of Financial Intermediation, 9*(1), 7–25.

Braun, M., & Raddatz, C. (2008). The politics of financial development: Evidence from trade liberalization. *Journal of Finance, 63*(3), 1469–1508.

Calderon, C., & Liu, L. (2003). The direction of causality between financial development and economic growth. *Journal of Development Economics, 72*(1), 321–334.

Calorimis, C. W., & Haber, S. H. (2014). *Fragile by design: The political origins of banking crises and scarce credit*. Pronceton, NJ: Princeton University Press.

Chari, A., & Gupta, N. (2008). Incumbents and protectionism: The political economy of foreign entry liberalization. *Journal of Financial Economics, 88*(3), 633–656.

Christopoulos, D. K., & Tsionas, E. G. (2004). Financial development and economic growth: Evidence from panel unit root and cointegration tests. *Journal of Development Economics, 73*(1), 55–74.

Claessens, S., Feijen, E., & Laeven, L. (2008). Political connections and preferential access to finance: The role of campaign contributions. *Journal of Financial Economics, 88*(3), 554–580.

Coffee, J. C., Jr. (2012). Political economy of Dodd-Frank: Why financial reforms tends to be frustrated and systematic risk perpetuated. *Cornell Law Review, 97*(5), 1019–1082.

Congleton, R. D. (2004). The median voter model. In C. K. Rowley & F. Schneider (Eds.), *The encyclopedia of public choice* (pp. 707–712). Springer, New York, NY.

Congleton, R. D. (2009). On the political economy of the financial crisis and bailout of 2008-2009. *Public Choice, 140*(3–4), 287–317.

Cox, G. W., & McCubbins, M. D. (1986). Electoral politics as a redistributive game. *Journal of Politics, 48*(2), 370–389.

Degryse, H., Lambert, T., & Schwienbacher, A. (2013). *The political economy of financial systems: Evidence from suffrage reforms in the last two centuries* (CESifo working paper no. 4527), Ludwig.

Demetriades, P. O., & Hussein, K. A. (1996). Does financial development cause economic growth? Time-series evidence from 16 countries. *Journal of Development Economics, 51*(2), 387–411.

Demirguc-Kunt, A., & Maksimovic, V. (1998). Law, finance, and firm growth. *Journal of Finance, 53*(6), 2107–2137.

Dixit, A., & Londregan, J. (1996). The determinants of success of special interests in redistributive politics. *Journal of Politics, 58*(4), 1132–1155.

Djankov, S. (2009). The regulation of entry: A survey. *World Bank Research Observer, 24*(2), 183–203.

Faccio, M., Masulis, R. W., & McConnell, J. J. (2006). Political connections and corporate bailouts. *The Journal of Finance, 61*(6), 2597–2635.

Garleanu, N., & Zwiebel, J. (2009). Design and renegotiation of debt covenants. *Review of Financial Studies, 22*(2), 749–781.

Gerber, E. R., & Lewis, J. B. (2004). Beyond the median: Voter preferences, district heterogeneity, and political representation. *Journal of Political Economy, 112*(6), 1364–1383.

Gibson, E. L. (1997). The populist road to market reform: Policy and electoral coalitions in Mexico and Argentina. *World Politics, 49*(3), 339–370.

Girma, S., & Shortland, A. (2007). The political economy of financial development. *Oxford Economic Papers, 60*, 567–596.

Greenwood, J., & Jovanovic, B. (1990). Financial development, growth, and the distribution of income. *Journal of Political Economy, 98*(5), 1076–1107.

Haggard, S. (2000). *The political economy of the Asian financial crisis*. Washington, DC: Institute for International Economics.

Hellman, J. S., Jones, G., & Kaufmann, D. (2003). Seize the state, seize the day: State capture and influence in transition economies. *Journal of Comparative Economics, 31*(4), 751–773.

Hillman, A. L. (1982). Declining industries and political-support protectionist motives. *American Economic Review, 72*(5), 1180–1187.

Innes, A. (2013). The political economy of state capture in Central Europe. *Journal of Common Markets Study, 52*, 88–104.

Khwaja, A. I., & Mian, A. (2005). Do lenders favor politically connected firms? Rent provision in an emerging financial market. *Quarterly Journal of Economics, 120*(4), 1371–1411.
King, R. G., & Levine, R. (1993). Finance, entrepreneurship and growth: Theory and evidence. *Journal of Monetary Economics, 32*(3), 513–542.
Krueger, A. O. (1974). The political economy of the rent-seeking society. *American Economic Review, 64*(3), 291–303.
La Porta, R., Lopez-de-Silanes, F., Shleifer, A., & Vishny, R. (1997). Legal determinants of external finance. *Journal of Finance, 52*(2), 1131–1150.
La Porta, R., Lopez-de-Silanes, F., Shleifer, A., & Vishny, R. (1998). Law and finance. *Journal of Political Economy, 106*(6), 1113–1155.
Laffont, J.-J., & Tirole, J. (1991). The politics of government decision-making: A theory of regulatory capture. *Quarterly Journal of Economics, 106*(4), 1089–1127.
Levine, R. (1997). Financial development and economic growth: Views and agenda. *Journal of Economic Literature, 35*(2), 688–726.
Levine, R. (1999). Law, finance and economic growth. *Journal of Financial Intermediation, 8*(1–2), 8–35.
Levitin, A. J. (2014). The politics of financial regulation and the regulation of financial politics: A review essay. *Harvard Law Review, 127*, 1991–2068.
Li, H., Meng, L., Wang, Q., & Zhou, L.-A. (2008). Political connections, financing and firm performance: Evidence from Chinese private firms. *Journal of Development Economics, 87*(2), 283–299.
Musacchio, A. (2008). Can civil law countries get good institutions? Lessons from the history of the creditors rights and bond markets in Brazil. *Journal of Economic History, 68*(1), 80–108.
Myers, S. C., & Majluf, N. C. (1984). Corporate financing and investment decisions when firms have information that investors do not have. *Journal of Financial Economics, 13*(2), 187–221.
North, D. C., Wallis, J. J., & Weingast, B. R. (2009). *Violence and social order: A conceptual framework for interpreting recorded human history*. Cambridge, UK: Cambridge University Press.
Oshry, B., Hermalin, B. E., & Weisbach, M. S. (2010). The role of boards of directors in corporate governance: A conceptual framework and survey. *Journal of Economic Literature, 48*(1), 58–107.
Pagano, M., & Volpin, P. (2001). The political economy of finance. *Oxford Review of Economic Policy, 17*(4), 502–519.
Pagano, M., & Volpin, P. (2005). The political economy of corporate governance. *American Economic Review, 95*(4), 1005–1030.
Palfrey, T. R. (1984). Spatial equilibrium with entry. *Review of Economic Studies, 51*(1), 139–156.
Persson, T., & Tabellini, G. (2000). *Political economics: Explaining economic policy*. Cambridge, MA: The MIT Press.
Rajan, R., & Winton, A. (1995). Covenants and collateral as incentives to monitor. *Journal of Finance, 50*(1), 1113–1146.
Rajan, R., & Zingales, L. (2003). The great reversals: The politics of financial development in the twentieth century. *Journal of Financial Economics, 69*, 5–50.
Reinhart, C. M., Kirkegaard, J. F., & Sbrancia, M. B. (2011). Financial repression redux. *Finance & Development, 48*(1), 22–16. Downloadable from http://www.imf.org/external/pubs/ft/fandd/2011/06/Reinhart.htm
Rijkers, B., Freund, C., Nucifora, A. (2014). *All in the family: State capture in Tunisia* (Policy research working paper no. 6810), Washington, DC: The World Bank.
Rock, K. (1986). Why new issues are underpriced. *Journal of Financial Economics, 15*(1–2), 187–212.
Roe, M. J., & Siegel, J. I. (2009). Finance and politics: A review essay based on Kenneth Dam's analysis of legal tradition in "the law-growth nexus". *Journal of Economic Literature, 47*(3), 781–800.
Shugart, M. S. (1998). The inverse relationship between party strength and executive strength: A theory of politicians' constitutional choices. *British Journal of Political Science, 28*(1), 1–29.

Wolfson, M. H., & Epstein, G. A. (Eds.). (2013). *The handbook of the political economy of financial crises*. New York, NY: Oxford University Press.
Young, M. N., Peng, M. W., Ahlstrom, D., Bruton, G., & Jiang, Y. (2008). Corporate governance in emerging economies: A review of the principal-principal perspective. *Journal of Management Studies*, *45*(1), 196–220.
Zhang, X. (2007). Political parties and financial development: Evidence from Malaysia and Thailand. *Journal of Public Policy*, *27*(3), 341–374.

Sumon Kumar Bhaumik has a PhD in Economics from the University of Southern California. At present, he is Chair in Finance at the University of Sheffield. He is also a research fellow at IZA, Institute of Labor Economics, and a fellow at the Global Labor Organization. His research interests are eclectic and span a wide range of areas such as corporate governance, banks and credit markets, development economics, and multinational enterprises.

Chapter 2
Grievance Redressal in the Indian Financial Regulatory Space: The Unified Approach

Parimala Veluvali

Abstract Retail consumer protection has always been one of the guiding factors for financial regulation in India. Access to a simple and effective consumer grievance redressal mechanism has been considered vital in this pursuit of consumer protection. The financial sector regulation in India has witnessed a major reform with the conceptualization of the Indian Financial Code (IFC) based on the recommendations of the Financial Sector Legislative Reforms Commission (FSLRC). The setting up of the Financial Redressal Agency (FRA) that would serve as a one-stop redressal machinery spanning all the financial entities in India has been the upshot of the recommendations of the FSLRC. The present study provides a narrative on the case for setting up of the FRA by synthesizing the extant literature in the nature of policy reports. The findings of this paper may serve to provide the base for further thought on the subject of unified financial regulation.

Keywords Retail consumers · Consumer Protection · Grievance Redressal · FRA · Regulatory framework

2.1 Introduction

The basic premise of consumer protection law in India has been the protection of consumers at the grassroot level. Globally, it is well accepted that retail consumers who are the end users of any product or service are vulnerable considering that they are often misled by unfair market practices and in view of informational asymmetries are at a higher risk of experiencing negative outcomes in the market (Cartwright, 2015). Consumer protection in India has progressed from the age-old common law

P. Veluvali (✉)
Symbiosis Centre for Management Studies, Symbiosis International (Deemed University), Pune 400014, Maharashtra, India
e-mail: Parimala.veluvali@scmspune.ac.in

Y. K. Dwivedi et al. (eds.), *Emerging Markets from a Multidisciplinary Perspective*, Advances in Theory and Practice of Emerging Markets,
https://doi.org/10.1007/978-3-319-75013-2_2

maxim of "caveat emptor" where the onus of exercising caution while buying a product or hiring a service is entirely on the buyer to "caveat venditor" wherein accountability is also thrusted on the seller or the service provider. This transition signifying growing consumerism in India has been strengthened over a period due to constant regulatory interventions according greater protection to the consumer.

Consumer protection in the context of the financial sector merits greater care in view of certain attributes unique to financial products and services. Apart from being complex and intangible, they are difficult to value and deliver returns mostly in the distant future. The sale and distribution of financial products and services therefore involves a huge amount of trust. Financial consumer protection is more emphasized in emerging countries like India, where retail investors have been elusive and financial literacy is low (Chandrasekhar, Malik, & Akriti, 2016).

Traditionally the market for financial services in India has been riddled with anomalies in the nature of lack of transparency, hidden costs, penalties, product misselling, and unsolicited advice. Empirical evidence (Veluvali, 2014) suggests that such irregularities undermine consumer confidence and in the long run would contribute to lack of retail participation in the market.

Retail investor protection has always been one of the guiding factors for financial regulation in India with various reforms having been brought in to incentivize retail participation in the market. The Nachiket Mor Committee Report on the provision of comprehensive financial services for small businesses and low-income households (Nachiket Mor Committee Report, 2013) outlines consumer protection as a wide range of measures encompassing disclosure requirements, code of conduct with respect to product design, and suitability along with the provision of an institutional mechanism to implement such protection measures. The committee has stressed on effective redressal of consumer grievances as an integral part of the consumer protection.

India has been on the reform path in the recent past especially in the financial sector. Fueled by the need to remove certain inconsistencies in the existing financial regulatory structure in the nature of regulatory overlaps and regulatory arbitrage, the Financial Sector Legislative Reform Commission (FSLRC) was constituted by the Ministry of Finance in the year 2011. The product of the deliberations of the commission has been the conceptualization of the Indian Financial Code (IFC), a new framework to regulate the financial sector. The setting up of the Financial Redressal Agency (FRA) that would serve as a one-stop redressal machinery spanning all the financial entities has been one of the recommendations of the FSLRC.

In this backdrop, it is relevant to explore the role of the Financial Redressal Agency (FRA) in catering to the needs of the retail consumers through a simplified resolution process. The present study traces the genesis of the Unified Redressal Agency as envisaged by the FSLRC. The nature of the study is descriptive and theoretical. By examining and interpreting existing policy documents and reports, the study examines the grievance redressal mechanism as it transcends the sectorial approach to a unified redressal mode. The chapter is divided in three parts. The first part reviews the financial regulatory structure and the existing redressal mechanism on the eve of reforms. The second part builds the case for unified redressal of grievances. The third part provides an overview of the operational design of the

FRA as envisaged by the task force on the FRA. The debate on the efficacy of a unified approach to financial regulation and grievance redressal has already begun. The present paper intends to contribute to the body of literature on the unified financial redressal with special focus on the retail financial consumer.

2.2 An Overview of Financial Regulation in India

Historically financial regulation in India has been slanted toward product-specific and sectorial regulation with clearly demarcated contours segregating the regulators and their regulatory dominions. The financial regulatory framework in India is currently comprised of the Reserve Bank of India (RBI) regulating the banking products and services, the Securities and Exchange of India regulating the capital market and its intermediaries, and the Insurance Regulatory and Development Authority (IRDA) for the insurance sector and pension funds being regulated by the Pension Fund Regulatory Authority. The Forward Markets Commission (FMC) is the regulatory body for the commodity markets. The existing structure is the culmination of various enactments and multiple laws legislated at a time when the financial system in India was at its nascent stage.

The existing regulatory structure has been subject to considerable academic scrutiny (Patnaik & Shah, 2015; Shah & Patnaik, 2011). Many of the legislations have been noted as archaic[1] and not in touch with the requirements of the emerging economy. In addition, with the growing sophistication of the financial system, the existing framework was mended with many intermittent regulations that have been drafted in response to changes in the market design. Consequently, the financial regulatory landscape in India has been characteristic of regulatory gaps and oversight. Instances of financial products either falling into the regulatory ambit of more than one regulator[2] or cases of conflict of interest, shadow financial services which are unregulated[3] have been the offshoots of such sectorial framework. Empirical evidence (Monica, Sane, & Thomas, 2014) demonstrates that retail consumers have suffered colossal losses[4] owing to misselling of expensive products by service providers thriving on gaps caused by regulatory arbitrage. Such a framework was also not conducive for leveraging economies of scale as a wide range of financial services that could have been easily grouped and offered by one financial firm have to be necessarily spread across multiple firms to adhere to regulatory compliances

[1] A reference in the literature is always made to the RBI Act enacted in 1935 during the colonial rule.

[2] This has been evident in case ULIPS, equity-linked insurance investment products which have come under the purview of SEBI and IRDA.

[3] Ponzi schemes that have periodically surfaced in India and for want of regularity clarity have been able to operate in the system unregulated.

[4] The study estimates that consumers have lost Rs 1.5 trillion over a 7-year period from 2004 to 2012 due to misselling of ULIPS, an investment-linked insurance policy.

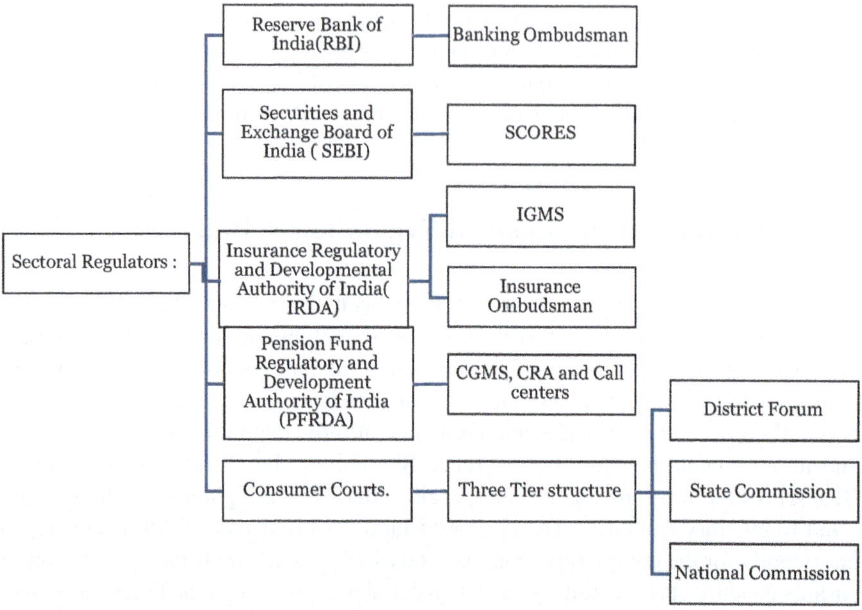

Fig 2.1 Existing redressal mechanisms under the sectorial regulation (Compiled from "Current Redress Mechanisms" as given in the Report of the Task Force on FRA (2016) at p. 26)

2.3 Grievance Redressal in the Financial Sector in India on the Eve of the Reform

Grievance redressal under the existing financial structure is sectorial with sector specific redressal mechanism of receiving and resolving disputes. The Fig. 2.1 above depicts the current redressal mechanism under the product specific regulation. Studies conducted elsewhere (Ajit et al., 2015; Report of the Task force on FRA, 2016; Yadav & Mohania, 2014) have reviewed the performance of the individual redressal agencies. The existing redressal agencies appear to have a satisfactory rate of disposal of grievances. Arbitration and mediation appear to the preferred mechanisms of dispute resolution. A growing preference to an online mechanism of lodging complaints is also noted. The number of complaints being referred to the individual redressal agencies has also shown an increasing rate[5] which is an indication of the growing users of financial services and the increased awareness regarding redressal opportunities.

A review of the procedures of the different sectorial agencies reveal certain inconsistencies that may not be in tandem to serve the larger purpose of comprehensive consumer protection. While the objective of all the existing mechanisms is fair transparent and speedy redressal, owing to divergence in the approach, manner of

[5] See Report of the Task Force (2016) under the "Complaints received and their disposal" at p. 151.

Table 2.1 Inconsistencies in the current redressal practices

S. no.	Current redressal mechanisms: certain inconsistencies
1.	Physical presence of the redressal agencies only in select locations and mostly in major cities
2.	Onus of approaching the appropriate redressal agencies within whose jurisdiction the grievance falls is on the retail consumer.
3.	Manner of resolving complaints is not uniform across all the agencies. However, screening of the complaints at the initial stage to decide on the admissibility or otherwise is the first step toward grievance redressal for all the agencies
4	A common reason for non-admissibility of the compliant across the regulators is due to the complaint being addressed at the wrong forum and hence falling outside the jurisdiction of the redressal agency
5	Varying timelines and capacity and powers of redressal of grievances
6	Legislative power to award compensation not available with all the redressal agencies. This compels retail consumers to resort to the regular courts to seek compensation defying the spirit of redressal as a simple and speedy mechanism for seeking justice
7	Owing to regulatory gaps, cases of complaints not tenable with the redressal agencies have resulted in losses to investors for want of timely correction in the regulations to address the gap. The absence of a feedback mechanism about the nature of the complaints has delayed the process of reforming the law to fill the gap
8.	Independent functioning of the redressal agencies without coordination with others has denied them the benefit of sharing expertise and best practices
9.	Experts are also of the view that combining the role of the regulator with the redressal function raises the question of accountability of the redressal agency
10	Owing to different sets of personnel who handle the same type of complaints, expertise is not acquired by the personnel

Source: Compiled from the Report of the Task Force (2016) on the Current redress practices

redressal, and remedies offered by the different redressal mechanisms, the current framework offers only suboptimal outcomes to retail consumers who may be accessing these agencies separately due to product variation (Report of the Task Force, 2016). Table 2.1 outlines the inconsistencies in the existing redressal framework.

2.4 The Case for Unified Financial Redressal

The consensus on revamping the financial landscape in India has been constructed over a period of time based on the collective wisdom of various committees[6] mooting for increased market integration, strengthening regulatory infrastructure, and

[6]The earliest reference to market integration can be found in the report of the committee on "Making Mumbai the International Financial Centre" (2007). The other committees include the Committee on Financial Sector Reforms (2008) led by Raghuram Rajan and the Committee on Investor Awareness and Protection (2009) led by Dhirendra Swarup, Former Secretary, MOF, and the Chairman of the Task Force on Financial Redressal Agency.

protecting the consumers against unfair market practices. The case for market integration has been argued not only for increasing domestic participation in the financial markets but also for boosting foreign investments in India.[7] The constitution of the Financial Sector Legislative Reform Commission (FSLRC) by the Ministry of Finance, Government of India, signifies the culmination of the momentum to rethink and redraft the law with central focus on consumer protection resulting in the drafting of the Indian Financial Code (IFC).[8]

Consumer protection framework under the unified approach is designed to be preventive as well as curative. While effective regulations and enforcement actions would avert the incidence of fraud against consumers, a simple and speedy redressal mechanism would provide relief to retail consumers. The Report of the Task Force on establishing the Financial Redressal Agency (2016) submitted an extensive review of the current redressal mechanism while elaborating on the design and structure of the FRA.

Central to the inception of the FRA is the provision of simple resolution process for the benefit of retail consumers spread across the country. Stemming from the curative aspects of consumer protection, the FRA is designed to be a one-stop shop for retail consumers to redress their grievances against all financial services providers. The design of the FRA also allows the regulator to harness the complaints data to strengthen consumer protection. The complaints data with the FRA would serve to be rich source of information for the unified regulator to work on the areas of improvement in regulation and supervision. Whether such a unified structure for redressal of consumer grievances would be in the interests of the consumers or not has been explored by Dev (2013). Dev (2013) maintains that the grievance redressal by a unified agency would accord more accountability in view of the fact that the dispute resolution forum and the regulator are delineated removing any bias. All issues arising from regulatory arbitrage are expected to be eliminated under the unified model.

2.5 Operational Design of the FRA: An Overview

Traditionally the road toward seeking justice and redressal has been daunting to retail consumers who are gullible and less informed when compared to institutional investors or high-net-worth individuals. The FRA is structured to be consumer friendly and accessible. A notional representation of the FRA model is depicted in Fig. 2.2.

---

[7] The committee chaired by UK Sinha, Former Chairman SEBI, worked on reviewing the policies regulating foreign direct investment in India. The committee recommended rationalizing the capital account regulation aligning the regulations for foreign investment in India in line with the international practices.

[8] The IFC as drafted on the basis of the FSLRC recommendations has been initially submitted to the Government on March 2013. Subsequently a revised IFC code has been submitted for review and awaits legal sanctions.

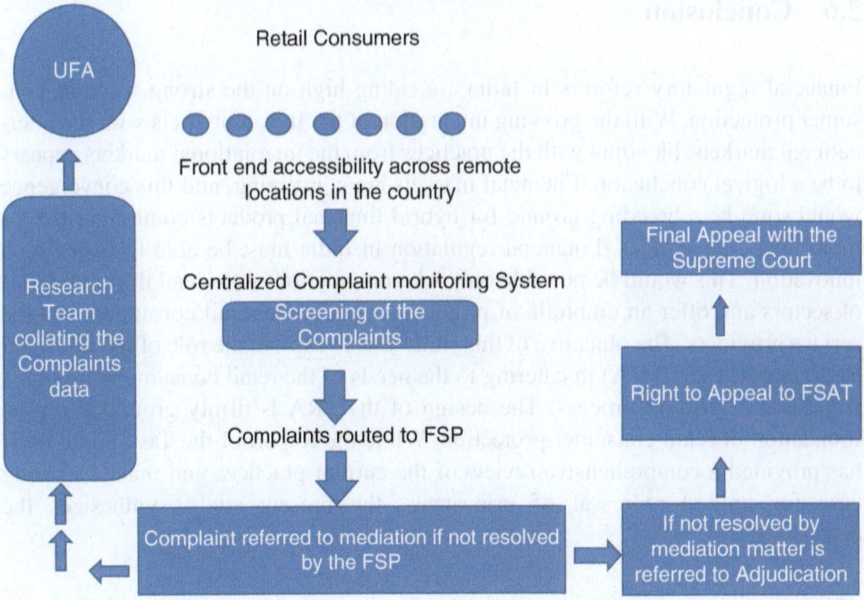

Fig. 2.2 Author's perception of the flow of the grievance redressal process of the proposed FRA (Adapted from the FRA model as envisaged by the task force (Report of the Task Force at p. 26))

A close inspection of the design and structure of the FRA reveals the proposed FRA would facilitate a uniform manner of grievance redressal without any product-wise differentiation. The mechanism of dispute resolution as envisaged for FRA is systematic and time bound. The ultimate beneficiary of the unified financial redressal is the retail consumer who hitherto could not seek timely redressal at the appropriate forum due to informational asymmetries. As a departure from the current redressal mechanisms which have been limited to certain locations or by jurisdictional constraints, the FRA is designed to be accessible through a front end presence to all the retail consumers who are dispersed across the country. All financial service providers would now be covered by the FRA doing away with the need to identify the appropriate redressal forum. Adhering to international practices,[9] the FRA relies heavily on mediation to resolve consumer grievances, and recourse to adjudication is only contemplated as a last resort.

Regulatory gaps have been the cause of financial losses to retail investors in India. This ambiguity in the regulation is now addressed with the provision of a feedback mechanism embedded into the structure of the FRA to make corrections in the regulations in a timely manner to arrest the ramifications of any loop holes in the law. Recourse to a speedy redressal is made available to retail consumers without the intervention of a lawyer.

[9] The task force has adopted a consultative approach while conceptualizing the design of the FRA by reviewing the redressal practices of the UK Financial Services Ombudsman and the Australian Financial Ombudsman Services which have moved toward the unified way of redressal.

2.6 Conclusion

Financial regulatory reforms in India are riding high on the strong wave of consumer protection. With the growing integration of the Indian markets with the international markets, blending with the practices from the international markets appears to be a logical conclusion. Financial markets are converging, and this convergence would soon be a breeding ground for hybrid financial products combining two or more financial services. Financial regulation in India must be able to foster such innovation. This would be possible only when regulations transcend the boundaries of sectors and offer an umbrella of protection both to the retail consumers and the service providers. The objective of this study was to explore the role of the Financial Redressal Agency (FRA) in catering to the needs of the retail consumers through a simplified resolution process. The design of the FRA is firmly grounded on the foundation of retail consumer protection. While the Report of the Task Force itself has provided a comprehensive review of the current practices and makes a strong case for unified redressal of grievances, the present study synthesizes the discussion.

References

Ajit, D., Malik, S., & Nautiyal, S. (2015). Effectiveness of SEBI's Complaints Redress System (SCORES) in India. Available at http://www.sebi.gov.in/sebi_data/DRG_Study/DRG_II_Scores_15092015.pdf. Last accessed on 13 Sept 2017.

Cartwright, P. (2015). Understanding and protecting vulnerable financial consumers. *Journal of Consumer Policy, 38*(2), 119–138.

Chandrasekhar, C. P., Malik, S., & Akriti. (2016). The elusive retail investor: How deep can (and should) India's stock markets be? Available at http://www.sebi.gov.in/sebi_data/DRG_Study/elusiveretailinvestor.pdf. Last accessed on 08 Sept 2017.

Dev, S. (2013). Unified financial agency – Axe on sectoral decentralization? Available at http://www.simplydecoded.com/2013/04/07/unified-financial-agency-axe-on-sectoral-decenteralization/. Last accessed on 10 Sept 2017.

Monica, H., Sane, R., & Thomas, S. (2014). The case of missing billions: Estimating losses to customers due to mis-sold life insurance policies. *Journal of Economic Policy Reform, 17*, 285–302.

Nachiket Mor Committee Report. (2013). Committee on comprehensive financial services for small businesses and low income households at p 167 Available at https://rbidocs.rbi.org.in/rdocs/PublicationReport/Pdfs/CFS070114RFL.pdf. Last accessed on 30 Aug 2017.

Patnaik, I., & Shah, A. (2015). Fundamental redesign of financial law: The Indian approach. *India Review, 14*(1), 91–110. https://doi.org/10.1080/14736489.2015.1004257.

Report of the High Powered Expert Committee on Making India an International Financial Centre. (2007). Available at http://dea.gov.in/sites/default/files/mifcreport.pdf. Last accessed on 07 Feb 2018.

Report of the Committee on Financial Sector Reforms. (2008). Available at http://planningcommission.nic.in/reports/genrep/rep_fr/cfsr_all.pdf. Last accessed on 07 Feb 2018.

Report of the Committee on Investor Awareness and Protection. (2009). Available at http://www.finmin.nic.in/sites/default/files/D%20Swarup%20Committee%20Report.pdf. Last accessed on 07 Feb 2018.

Report of the Task Force on Financial Redressal Agency. (2016). Available at http://dea.gov.in/sites/default/files/Report_TaskForce_FRA_26122016.pdf. Last accessed on 13 Sept 2017.
Shah, A., & Patnaik, I. (2011). Chapter 67: India's financial globalization. In J. Capiro (Ed.), *Encyclopedia of financial globalization*. New Delhi, India: Elsevier.
Veluvali, P. (2014). *Regulatory framework relating to investor protection with specific reference to retail investors in initial public offerings* (Doctoral thesis). Symbiosis International University, Pune, India. Available at http://shodhganga.inflibnet.ac.in:8080/jspui/handle/10603/38115. Last accessed on 13 Sept 2017.
Yadav, R. K., & Mohania, S. (2014). Role of Insurance Ombudsman and Grievance Management in Life Insurance Services in Indian perspective. *International Letters of Social and Humanistic Sciences, 20*, 9–13.

Dr. Parimala Veluvali is an Assistant Professor and Deputy Director of Symbiosis Centre for Management Studies, Symbiosis International (Deemed University), Pune, India. Her research interests are in the field of retail investor protection in the financial markets. As an academician, her teaching interests are in the areas of Financial regulation and Corporate laws. She believes in collaborative research and is open to receiving feedback on her work. She can be reached at Parimala.veluvali@scmspune.ac.in.

Chapter 3
Role of Intermediaries in Providing Financial Access: Current and Future Research Trends

Rajesh Chandwani and Vaibhavi Kulkarni

Abstract Access to financial products and services is considered to be an important determinant of development, as it has been linked to poverty alleviation. Policymakers in the emerging economies design and implement various solutions to overcome barriers to financial access. Mobile phones have been highlighted as the potential means to extend financial services, especially in countries like India, where mobile penetration is high. However, gaps in digital literacy and financial literacy need to be overcome to realize the potential of mobile phones in enabling financial access. Scholars and practitioners have highlighted the role of 'intermediaries' who can bridge these gaps and provide the last mile connectivity between ICT initiatives and the user community. Traditionally, 'intermediaries' refer to the human intermediaries. We do, however, have some initiatives that use technology itself to bridge gaps related to financial literacy as well as digital literacy. For instance, user-friendly interactive systems that provide information about the use of mobile phones for payment as well as about financial products and services. In this chapter, we describe such initiatives where intermediation through both human intervention and technology was used for enabling financial access. Further, we outline potential research directions that can further illuminate the role of intermediation in enabling financial access.

Keywords Intermediaries · Financial inclusion · Access · ICT4D · Digital literacy

3.1 Introduction

The ease and convenience of financial transactions is directly linked to the economics of transactions and hence to the 'development'. Several empirical studies across various countries have shown that investment in 'financial development' perpetuates country-level growth (Claessens, 2006). A well-developed financial system

R. Chandwani (✉) · V. Kulkarni
Indian Institute of Management, Ahmedabad, India
e-mail: rajeshc@iima.ac.in; vaibhavik@iima.ac.in

Y. K. Dwivedi et al. (eds.), *Emerging Markets from a Multidisciplinary Perspective*, Advances in Theory and Practice of Emerging Markets,
https://doi.org/10.1007/978-3-319-75013-2_3

entails several benefits related to individual well-being, and evidence suggests that financial inclusion can lead to reduction in poverty as well as income inequality (Beck, Demirgüç-Kunt, & Levine, 2004; Clarke, Xu, & Zou, 2003).

In the emerging markets, financial access has been generally found to be skewed towards those who are financially better off (Rajan & Zingales, 1998; Sundaram & Sriram, 2016). The lack of financial access to the poor and the needy impedes their growth prospects and subjects them to financial vulnerabilities, thus affecting their well-being. Studies have described several barriers to financial inclusion such as lack of awareness with regard to banking products, inability to produce documents needed for a bank account, high transaction costs and, most importantly, illiteracy as cause for financial exclusion (Ghosh, De, & Mahanti, 2014).

With about 48% of the citizens devoid of access to formal banking system in India, the problem of financial inclusion is significant and acute (Allen, Demirgüç-Kunt, Klapper, & Martinez Peria, 2012). Illiteracy, absence of required documentation, fear of approaching financial institutions and inaccessibility of banking systems have led to financial exclusion of about half of the adult population in India reference. In an effort to move towards financial inclusion, the Government of India has made it a policy objective, defining financial inclusion as the *process ensuring access to financial services and timely and adequate credit where needed by vulnerable groups such as weaker sections and low income groups at an affordable cost* (Ghosh et al., 2014). It has introduced the 'Jan Dhan Yojana' scheme, which entrusts public sector banks with the responsibility of opening zero balance accounts for the underprivileged population and educating them about the various financial products and services. The Reserve Bank of India (RBI), the central bank of India, has also undertaken several initiatives to bring about comprehensive financial inclusion.

The Indian banking sector, consisting of the central bank, public sector banks, private sector banks, their branches, automated teller machines (ATMs), etc., constitutes the *formal* financial system in the country. However, studies suggest that the reach of the formal systems in India is limited, especially with regard to provision of services to the underprivileged sections. One of the ways of overcoming infrastructural and manpower constraints in extending financial services to the nooks and corners of India is through mobile banking. According to a study by Consultative Group to Assist the Poor (CGAP), within the developing country context, the underprivileged have limited financial access to banking services because there is considerably less deployment of formal banking infrastructure, including bank branches and ATM machines (Ignacio & Kumar, 2008). The report advocates tapping the potential of mobile phones to reach out to this population. A branchless banking channel with mobile phones is more likely to attract the poor people rather than the rich as they do not have access to formal banking infrastructure. Mobile banking presents a better opportunity for smaller banking organizations and microfinance institutions which handle transactions of smaller value and have customers dispersed over a larger geographical area. The key benefits have been identified as increased penetration, selling of more services, retaining customers and reducing the cost of providing services (Ignacio & Kumar, 2008).

With India's subscriber base for mobile phones having crossed 1 billion as per Telecom Regulatory Authority of India (TRAI, 2015), the use of mobile technology for banking holds promise. However, there are some key constraints when it comes to the reach and financial access provided by mobile banking within the Indian context. Studies have found that lack of literacy prevents mobile phone users from using features such as text messaging and exploring functionalities beyond voice calls (Sambasivan & Smyth, 2010). According to Kumar, Martin, and O'Neill (2011), factors such as perceived low self-efficacy, fear of making a mistake while using mobile phones, fear of incurring additional payments and lack of confidence prevent low-income communities from engaging in mobile banking. Thus, though low-literate communities are faced with unavailability of financial infrastructure and can benefit greatly from mobile banking, access to phones does not translate into financial access. In order to be successful, such technology-based interventions need to take into account issues of non-literacy, lack of technology-related skills and low self-efficacy of the end users.

Another key challenge in introducing mobile banking to the marginalized community members is their lack of knowledge regarding the financial products and services. Exposure to mobile banking and financial infrastructure can lead to financial access only when the end users are able to make sense of the products and services and make an informed decision in using these services. Unfortunately, due to lack of knowledge and exposure to financial services, these community members are oftentimes unable to make use of mobile banking applications. Financial literacy, therefore, has been identified as another factor that serves as a barrier to financial inclusion reference.

3.2 Overcoming Barriers to Financial Access: The Role of Intermediaries

As noted in the earlier section, there are two broad categories of barriers to the use of mobile phone for financial inclusion – lack of financial literacy and the gaps in digital literacy. Overcoming these barriers, and providing 'access' to financial system, hence, entails a multipronged approach. Oxford dictionary defines access as 'a way of approaching, reaching or entering a place, as the right or opportunity to reach, use or visit'. Access, thus, has both processual and outcome aspects. One of the ways to achieve the inclusion and provide access is the use of intermediaries to address the specific barriers. In order to successfully make use of mobile phones for financial access, these intermediaries need to address both the gaps – digital literacy and financial literacy.

Scholars have advocated the role of intermediaries in extending the reach of the formal systems. According to Cutrell (2011), 'In intermediated interactions, we break apart the traditional notion of user into at least two people. First is the beneficiary user who instigates the interaction and derives direct value from it. Second are intermediary users who directly interact with the device or service to achieve some outcome for the beneficiary user. Intermediaries "constitute an important part of information and communication technologies for global development (ICT4D) projects, because they transfer technological benefits to grassroots levels, ensure that projects run smoothly, and contribute to their sustainability"' (Sambasivan & Smyth, 2010, p. 2584). Several initiatives have reported the important role of intermediaries in enabling access. For example, there has been considerable support for linkages between self-help groups (SHGs) and banks (reference). Scholars have also highlighted the role of microfinance institutions in educating the consumers about the financial products and services and in provision of these services at the community level (Cole, Sampson, & Zia, 2009). These microfinance institutions, being nearer to the grass root, are aware of the sociocultural and economic nuances of the communities and hence are effective in bridging the gap between the formal financial system and the citizens.

According to Toyama (2010), the role of human intermediaries in technology-based interventions has become a common phenomenon in developing countries where the 'notion of a single technology "user" splits into two or more people fulfilling roles as either technology beneficiaries or technology manipulator' (p. 60). The manipulator, also referred to more commonly as the intermediary, handles the device to perform tasks such as entering data or dialling numbers, while the system is geared towards providing goods/services to the beneficiary. This has led to increasing number of studies focusing on the role of community members as intermediaries.

Use of such intermediaries for financial access entails several aspects, including access to the technology that links the community members to the services (e.g. Internet kiosks and mobile banks), access to the knowledge about the available financial solutions in terms of products and services (e.g. the variety of insurance policies available for crops), and the skills as well as capabilities to make use of the technology (e.g. understanding the process of making payment through the application). Thus, technology-based intermediaries such as Common Services Centres (Dwivedi, Sahu, Rana, Singh, & Chandwani, 2016) can play a key role in creating awareness and reducing knowledge-based barriers (Toyama, 2010).

While the term 'intermediaries' have largely been used for 'human intermediary', the rise of technology-based solutions and machine learning has paved the way for designing digital intermediaries. We conceptualize 'digital intermediary' as a technology that enables the 'user' to make sense of the financial services and products and also facilitates the use of technology itself. For instance, this can take a form of a video clip, which could be used for several purposes, including knowledge sharing, trust building, smooth onboarding of the user, etc. In these cases, technology-based intervention itself attempts to bridge the gaps in financial literacy as well as digital literacy. The major advantage of using a digital intermediation is that it can achieve scale rapidly as it subverts the need of 'employing' human intermediaries for last mile connectivity to the users. Technology-based intermediaries can potentially increase access and lead to financial inclusion, provided they are designed keeping in mind the existing community ecosystems, sociocultural context and lack of digital literacy of the end users.

In this section, we describe three ICTs for development initiatives that enable financial access and explicate how these intermediaries act as enablers of access.

3.2.1 *Samwad*

Digital intermediaries can play a significant role in helping the farmers understand and choose appropriate financial products, provided they take into consideration lack of skills, lack of affordability and low literacy in the design of their platform. Samwad, a digital learning platform aimed at increasing financial literacy of the underprivileged section of the society through the use of basic mobile phones, falls under such a category and could possibly be classified as an instance of digital intermediary.

Scholars have noted that providing financial infrastructure is not enough to achieve financial access – oftentimes, marginalized sections of the society are unable to engage with formal financial institutions due to lack of knowledge and perceived low self-efficacy. Financial access, therefore, also needs to translate into appropriate usage of financial products, which in turn necessitates imparting of financial education. Strategies for increasing financial literacy can lead to increase in usage of formal services and lessen the dependency on costly informal alternatives. Samwad attempts to empower the users so that they are able to make the right choices based on accurate understanding of their own needs as well as the risks associated with the financial products. In an attempt to reach out to low-literate users with limited exposure, Samwad primarily uses images and engages in storytelling via videos. Stories embedded in the cultural context of the users enable them to easily grasp information regarding financial products and services. Multilingual content in case of storytelling as well as IVR further increases the reach of this platform.

3.2.2 *Awaaz.De*

In a similar vein, Awaaz.De, a venture engaged in providing voice-based solutions to organizations working in the social sector, combines digital as well as human intermediation to provide financial information to the community members. The goal of financial literacy is accomplished through audio lessons on the cell phone, along with interactive quizzes, shared at regular intervals. Users can avail the required information by dialling a designated number and responding to simple voice-automated prompts through the touch-tone keys on their phones (Patel, Klemmer, & Parikh, 2011). Since there is no reading or writing involved, Aawaz.De is accessible to all communities, including those that are low literate, as long as they are able to recognize and dial numbers on a basic phone.

In case of Awaaz.De, interactive quizzes and FAQs can be regarded as digital intermediation. Community members need to dial a phone number and respond to automated prompts through their touch-tone keys, which will allow them to browse through FAQs and navigate through interactive quizzes. Human intermediation takes place in the form of community managers, who facilitate response to specific queries made on community boards. Community members are expected to dial in and choose the relevant community board through touch-tone keys, and if they are unable to find a pre-existing response to their query, they can select the 'audio record' option and pose their question. The role of the community manager is to go through these questions and assign subject matter experts who respond to them and, at the same time, post appropriate answers on the community board.

3.2.3 Eko

Eko is an example an alternative design system that uses mobile phone-based technology for reaching out to those below the poverty line, with a local community member – usually a shopkeeper or vendor – as the human intermediary. Eko identifies, trains and mentors local shopkeepers for the role of Customer Service Point (CSP) agents, till they manage to engage with 50–100 beneficiaries. In order to open an account with the State Bank of India through Eko – India's largest government-owned bank – the beneficiaries require a cell phone and a visit to a neighbourhood CSP they trust. For deposit, transfer or withdrawal of money, the CSP dials certain predetermined numbers on the cell phone, and the customer receives a confirmation text message, which is often saved by them as a proof of their transaction. For every new account, a CSP earns a commission of US$0.6. Eko, thus, makes use of existing social infrastructure by employing community members as intermediaries to achieve financial inclusion. This marks a significant departure from the traditional banking practices to tap unreached customer base, since the customer does not need to enter a bank, operate an ATM or use online banking for any of the basic functions, including opening a bank account.

Geographically, Eko currently operates across eight states in India but is most active in the National Capital Region (NCR), Bihar and Jharkhand. There is a large segment of population that relocates from Bihar and Jharkhand to the NCR region in search of jobs and livelihood; thus, NCR has a large immigrant population. Poverty, illiteracy and lack of local support result in a large section of the migrant population being completely or partially cut off from the large-scale benefits of formal banking and financial services. Eko's daily transaction volume exceeds Rs 50 million ($ 1 million) and is considered one of the most successful examples of branchless banking.

The three different initiatives described above use either human or digital intermediation to address the gaps in digital as well as financial literacy. While the scholarship has largely explored the design, implementation, pros and cons of human intermediaries, extant literature has not yet examined the role and design of digital intermediaries. Both types of intermediation processes have their advantages and disadvantages. Digital intermediation can be rapidly scaled up; indeed, it can follow the penetration of mobile phones itself. On the other hand, the human intermediation has a 'personal touch' by definition and hence may have higher acceptability. Furthermore, human intermediaries can be assigned according to the sociocultural nuances, as in the case of Eko. However, these two types of intermediation need not be mutually exclusive. Further research is needed to explore how to take advantages of both types of intermediation for design and implementation of ICT for financial inclusion. The following section highlights the directions for future research that can inform scholarship and policymakers on these aspects.

3.3 Directions for Future Research

While human intermediation has limitation in terms of scaling up, digital intermediation can be rapidly scaled up. However, as the arena of digital intermediation has recently evolved, researchers and policymakers need to understand the process of intermediation in greater detail. The future researchers should explore various dimensions of digital intermediation, for example, what are the design elements of an appropriate digital intermediary? What processes are involved in designing a context sensitive digital intermediary? How do the community members make sense of the digital intermediation process? The 'learning process' is a highly context-specific and culturally embedded phenomenon. Does the learning from digital intermediation differ from culture to culture, if so how? For example, in a high context culture, the use of 'voice' in the intermediation process may be preferred over text, as it might give an 'impression' of a 'person' behind the digital platform. Similarly, video might be a preferred mode of learning of some communities. It would be interesting to investigate the links between the communities' conceptualization of learning process and the culturally appropriate aspects of intermediation design.

Studies focusing on the use of human intermediaries in technology-based interventions usually examine the way in which beneficiaries make use of such systems or the way in which these systems enhance access. From the systems perspective, these studies examine how social infrastructure affects technology design and implementation. However, we have little knowledge of how intermediation impacts the intermediaries themselves. This question is of some significance because sustainability and scalability of these initiatives hinges predominantly on involvement of community members as intermediaries. Future research can delve into questions such as: How are intermediaries affected by their role in such initiatives? Does it impact their standing within the community? How does it shape their relationship with the beneficiaries?

Prior research has also emphasized the importance of processes and systems for creating trust (Moloney, 2009). The issue of trust becomes salient especially in case of multiple users (community member as well as the intermediary) operating the same technology (mobile phone) and accessing sensitive information related to financial matters. What are the design features that can facilitate trust in technology as well as the human intermediary? Can blending the two different types on intermediaries enhance trust? Is there a difference in trust levels in case of intermediaries who are members of the local community as compared to intermediaries such as business correspondents who are formal representatives of the financial institution?

Further, the researchers need to compare the two types of intermediation, human and technological. Is one more effective than the other? If so why and how? While the effect of the two types of intermediation will depend upon cultural understanding of the learning process, the context and the related content also might play an important role. For example, the requirements of content design for financial literacy about crop insurance products might be different from those of health insurance products for the family members. In other words, the cultural understanding of the targeted behaviour should also be taken into account for designing digital intermediaries.

References

Allen, F., Demirgüç-Kunt, A., Klapper, L. F., & Martinez Peria, M. S. (2012). *The foundations of financial inclusion: Understanding ownership and use of formal accounts* (World Bank Policy Research Working Paper, (6290)).

Beck, T., Demirgüç-Kunt, A., & Levine, R. (2004). *Finance, inequality and poverty: Cross- country evidence* (Policy Research Working Paper, 3338). Washington, DC: World Bank.

Claessens, S. (2006). Access to financial services: A review of the issues and public policy objectives. *The World Bank Research Observer, 21*(2), 207–240.

Clarke, G., Xu, L. C., & Zou, H. (2003). *Finance and income inequality: Test of alter- native theories* (Policy Research Working Paper, 2984). Washington, DC: World Bank.

Cole, S. A., Sampson, T. A., & Zia, B. H. (2009). *Financial literacy, financial decisions, and the demand for financial services: Evidence from India and Indonesia* (pp. 09–117). Cambridge, MA: Harvard Business School.

Cutrell, E. (2011). Technology for emerging markets at MSR india. In *Proceedings of the ACM 2011 conference on computer supported cooperative work* (pp. 9–16), March 17-23, 2011, Hangzhou, China.

Dwivedi, Y. K., Sahu, G. P., Rana, N. P., Singh, M., & Chandwani, R. K. (2016). Common Services Centres (CSCs) as an approach to bridge the digital divide: Reflecting on challenges and obstacles. *Transforming Government: People, Process and Policy, 10*(4), 511–525.

Ghosh, A., De, J. S., & Mahanti, A. (2014). A mobile banking model in the cloud for financial inclusion in India. In *Proceedings of the 32nd ACM international conference on the design of communication CD-ROM* (p. 3), September 27-28, 2014, Colorado Springs, USA.

Ignacio, M., & Kumar, K. (2008). *Banking on mobiles: Why, how, for whom? Consultative group to assist the poor* (Focus Note No. 48). Washington DC.

Kumar, D., Martin, D., & O'Neill, J. (2011). The times they are a-changin': Mobile payments in india. In *Proceedings of the SIGCHI conference on human factors in computing systems* (pp. 1413–1422), May 07-12, 2011, Vancouver, Canada.

Moloney, T. (2009). Carving a niche: ICT, social capital, and trust in the shift from personal to impersonal trading in Tanzania. *Information Technology for Development, 15*(4), 283–301.

Patel, N., Klemmer, S. R., & Parikh, T. S. (2011). An asymmetric communications platform for knowledge sharing with low-end mobile phones. In *Proceedings of the 24th annual ACM symposium adjunct on user interface software and technology* (pp. 87–88). ACM.

Rajan, R., & Zingales, L. (1998). Financial development and growth. *The American Economic Review, 88*(3), 559–586.

Sambasivan, N., & Smyth, T. (2010). The human infrastructure of ICTD. In *Proceedings of the 4th ACM/IEEE international conference on information and communication technologies and development* (p. 40), December 13-16, 2010, London, UK.

Sundaram, N., & Sriram, M. M. (2016). Financial inclusion in India: A review. *International Journal of Applied Engineering Research, 11*(3), 1575–1578.

Toyama, K. (2010). Human–computer interaction and global development. *Foundations and Trends® in Human–Computer Interaction, 4*(1), 1–79.

TRAI Press Release. (2015). Highlights of Telecom subscription data as on 31st October, 2016. Retrieved 1 Aug 2017 from http://www.trai.gov.in/sites/default/files/Telecom%20Sub_Eng_pr.03_09-01-2017_0.pdf

Rajesh Chandwani is an Assistant Professor in the human resource management area at the Indian Institute of Management (IIM), Ahmedabad. He is a Fellow of IIM Bangalore and has also completed his MD (Paediatrics) from Baroda Medical College. He has wide-ranging interest in HRM issues and challenges in the Indian healthcare sector. Specifically, research interests include the use of information technology to enhance the effectiveness of healthcare personnel and healthcare delivery, scaling up of affordable and quality healthcare services for the underprivileged.

Vaibhavi Kulkarni is a faculty member at the Indian Institute of Management, Ahmedabad, in communication area, with a doctoral degree from the School of Communication and Information, Rutgers University, USA. Her research focuses on the significance of discourse in organizational and societal contexts, including implementation of technology-enabled change and the role of new entrepreneurial ventures in facilitating development.

Chapter 4
The UK Economy and Brexit

David Blackaby

Abstract This paper reviews some important literature on the likely implications of Brexit on the UK economy, including that from some of the large forecasting organisations in the UK. Most of these forecasts suggest that the economy will be smaller than it would have been had the UK remained in the EU going forward, though the extent will depend on the trading arrangements which are put in place following Brexit. The paper also reviews research on the implications of Brexit on different household types and areas within the UK. Implications for foreign direct investment (FDI), emerging markets as well as SMEs are discussed, including the potential to damage important supply chains and just-in-time production methods.

Keywords Brexit · Emerging Markets · EU · Impact · UK

Brexit is likely to involve dramatic adjustment costs for the UK economy, but these costs may still not be fully understood, despite many attempts to estimate them. During the referendum campaign, the cost of the UK contribution to the EU played an important role including the claim that the UK could save around £350 m a week if it left the EU that could be used in other areas such as the NHS. However, this claim was shown, though perhaps not accepted by many, to be false. As revealed in Table 4.1, after the UK receives its rebate, the UK pays £275 m a week into the EU budget; however, much of this comes back to the UK through programmes such as agricultural support and structural fund spending to support poorer areas, and the final contribution is estimated at around £150 m per week. However, it wasn't clear that this contribution figure to the EU (from one of the EU's richest countries) got through clearly to the electorate during campagning at the time of the referendum.

D. Blackaby (✉)
Department of Economics, School of Management, Swansea University, Bay Campus, Swansea, UK
e-mail: d.h.blackaby@swansea.ac.uk

Y. K. Dwivedi et al. (eds.), *Emerging Markets from a Multidisciplinary Perspective*, Advances in Theory and Practice of Emerging Markets,
https://doi.org/10.1007/978-3-319-75013-2_4

Table 4.1 UK EU financial contribution (2013–2014) (gross and net effect)

	Per annum	Per week
Ignoring UK's rebate	£18.8bn	£350 m
With rebate	£14.4bn	£275 m
Taking out money that comes back through programmes	£8bn	£150 m

Source: Emmerson, Johnson, Mitchell, and Phillips (2016)

Table 4.2 Assessment of 2030 economic impact of Brexit

Organisation	Scenario	Estimated GDP (%)	Range
HM Treasury	EEA	−3.8	(−3.4 to −4.3)
	FTA	−6.2	(−4.6 to −7.8)
	WTO	−7.5	(−5.4 to −9.5)
NIESR	EEA	−1.8	(−1.5 to −2.1)
	FTA	−2.1	(−1.9 to −2.3)
	WTO	−3.2	(−2.7 to −3.7)
	WTO+	−7.8	
CEP	Dynamic EEA/FTA	−7.9	(−6.3 to −9.5)
	Static EEA	−1.3	
	Static WTO	−2.6	
PwC/CBI	FTA	−1.2	
	WTO	−3.5	
Economists for Brexit	WTO	+4.0	

Source: Emmerson et al. (2016)

If getting across clearly, the difference between gross and net contributions to the EU budget was difficult, explaining the likely second-round financial effects of a Brexit decision was much more difficult. It was estimated that the net contribution of £8bn per year, for example, would be lost to the government if the growth of the economy slowed down such that the economy was 0.6% smaller than expectedly it would have been following Brexit. Slow growth would lead to lower tax receipts leading to less money to be spent on public services. The vast majority of the forecasts before the referendum suggested the economy would be reduced in size by more than 0.6% following Brexit (see Table 4.2). As noted by Emmerson et al. (2016) of the IFS, 'assuming WTO rules, NIESR, CEP and HM Treasury found that GDP would be more than 7% less in the long run than it would otherwise have been'. A reduction in the size of the economy of this amount would have led to large falls in tax receipts and so have important implications for the public finances and so public expenditure.

A further complication is that when making forecasts, estimates of the likely falls in the size of the economy and growth rates are uncertain due to the uncertainty over the possible trading arrangements after an EU exit. The Treasury in their research discussed three possible alternatives, and their estimates of the likely falls in the level of GDP predicted in 2030 with Brexit compared with remaining in the EU are again shown in Table 4.2 (with confidence levels given around GDP predictions). Their assumed alternative scenarios were:

- Membership of the European Economic Area (EEA) like Norway
- A negotiated bilateral agreement, such as between the EU and Switzerland, Turkey or Canada
- World Trade Organization (WTO) membership without any form of specific agreement with the EU, like Russia or Brazil

Falls in growth occur because following Brexit under whatever trading arrangements that are likely to be adopted it was assumed that trade would fall and economic theory suggests that increasing trade barriers reduces world output and freer trade increases world output. Following the referendum result, economic forecasters came in for criticism as the economy didn't immediately begin to contract, and so it was suggested forecasters shouldn't be trusted. However, forecasts from economic models are predictions based on knowledge we have at the time forecasts are made, and if for any reason the world changes, such as unforeseen demand or supply shocks take place, forecasts will have errors. Economic models also are dramatic simplifications of the world in which we live, and many unforeseen shocks will hit the economy. So forecasts from economic models are predictions based on knowledge we have at the time forecasts are made; we call them conditional forecasts. Therefore, economic models are better at giving an estimate of the direction of change following a policy change rather than a precise estimate.

For example, medics/doctors can tell you smoking is bad for you, increases your chances of getting cancer and reduces your life expectancy but can't tell you the date you might get cancer. They will tell you your chances of getting cancer might also depend on other lifestyle choices and environmental factors. The same is true with economic models, and it is difficult to be precise about the exact economic outcomes of Brexit; however, economists are more confident about the direction of travel. Why? Because it is agreed that freer trade, through enabling countries to specialise, increases world output.

Forecasts are also influenced by unforeseen policy responses for example, the UK economy was supported after the referendum result by a delay in triggering Article 50 and a monetary policy stimulus, seen in a reduction in the interest rate and a boost in quantitative easing. Both responses were designed to boost economic growth in the short run. The government also loosened its deficit reduction programme, its fiscal stance, which again supported the economy in the short run.

For most individuals GDP is a fairly abstract concept. What does Brexit mean for individual households? The Treasury estimated the loss of income to the economy under its three alternative scenarios, as shown in Table 4.2. However, there are likely to be important distribution effects, and these were estimated by the NIESR (Armstrong, Lisenkova, & Lloyd, 2016). The NIESR estimated that because of the fall in income following Brexit if the government was to maintain its deficit reduction programme, public expenditure would need to be further reduced. Table 4.3 shows potential reductions in household income for different family types following

Table 4.3 Estimated loss of tax credit and benefit receipts of low-income household 2014

Claimant type	Loss if 25% of cuts fall on welfare budget	Loss if 50% of cuts fall on welfare budget
Single, working age, no children	£600	£1200
Couple, working age, no children	£465	£930
Couple, working age, two children	£1211	£2422
Lone parent, working age, two children	£1386	£2771
Single, unemployed, no children	£558	£1116

Source: Armstrong et al. (2016)

two different scenarios, where the welfare benefits cut account for 25% and 50% of the expenditure cuts, respectively. This NIESR research shows costs of Brexit are likely to fall disproportionately on low-income households, with the biggest losers a lone parent working age household with two children. They state, 'After 15 years even with savings from reduced contributions to the EU, receipts would be £20bn a year lower (EEA), £36bn a year lower (bilateral agreement) and £45bn a year lower for the WTO alternative'. They note, '£36bn is more than a third of the NHS budget and equivalent to 8p on the basic rate of income tax'.

Despite large drops in predicted income, the NIESR weren't predicting large increases in unemployment mainly due to relatively flexible labour markets found in the UK; so they forecast unemployment would not be perceptively higher by 2030 following a Brexit decision. However, they did suggest wages could be between 4.6% and 7.0% lower (in real figures) following a decision to leave the EU. The IFS (Emmerson et al., 2016), using NIESR GDP forecasts estimated that the public figures could be between £20bn and £40bn worse by 2019–2020 than currently forecasted. They suggested this would extend the 'austerity programmes' and deficit reduction plan by an additional 1 or 2 years. Also as a result, government debt would be higher than originally estimated requiring additional debt interest payments.

Table 4.2 shows that one group of forecasters, Economists for Brexit, estimate that GDP would be 4% higher by 2030 (than estimated if the UK remained) following a decision to leave the EU. As noted by Sampson, Dhingra, Ottaviano, and Van Reenen (2016), this is surprising as the vast majority of forecasters predict a negative outcome on the economy of leaving the EU. They put this down to the use of a theory-based computable general equilibrium (CGE) model and the assumption of perfect competition and lack of a gravity equation. The lack of a gravity equation is important as they argue 'Geography matters – the further apart countries are, the less they trade'. Their model also assumes the UK will revert to World Trade Organization (WTO) rules after Brexit and the UK will unilaterally eliminate all trade barriers to imports. Minford, Gupta, Le, and Mahambare (2016) note that this would likely eliminate large sections of manufacturers in the UK leaving mainly design, marketing and hi-tech industries, but this shouldn't concern us as these industries are part of the high-growth sectors. He also claims if we left the EU we would no longer be bound by EU safety standards and this could benefit trade and reduce prices in the UK. Sampson et al. also (2016) suggest that the Minford forecasting model is not an appropriate model for estimating the effects of Brexit on the economy, as it ignores important recent empirical data on trade flows. They also find no evidence of a developed country unilaterally dropping tariffs against other countries, which they believe would be extremely damaging to the economy and also lead to a further increase in wage inequality. A unilateral move to free trade they argue would mean the UK would lose an important bargaining position and result in tariffs still being present on UK exports to other countries.

Exit from the single market could also have implications for foreign direct investment (FDI) inflow into the UK. A significant proportion of FDI into the UK particularly from countries like the USA and Japan was undertaken to avoid the EU common external tariff barriers. The relatively depressed areas of the UK like Wales benefitted significantly from such investment and so helped address the problem of growing regional inequalities in economic performance. Wales not only provided a tariff-free base to foreign investors from which to exploit the large EU market but also offered financial incentives and relatively low labour costs. Despite having only approximately 0.5% of the EU population, Wales accounted for almost 5% of total foreign investment into the EU between 1982 and 1994. By 1992 30% of all employees in the manufacturing sector were employed by foreign companies.

Foreign direct investment is thought to bring with it a number of advantages. Firstly, by attracting foreign-owned firms, the economy increases its economic capacity and so provides more employment. Secondly, they are thought to bring with them more advanced products and processes; their production systems are more likely to be at the frontier of available technology in order to be able to overcome the additional costs associated with entering foreign markets, and generally their plants are more productive than domestic firms. Thirdly, there are thought to be positive economic spillovers to domestic plants that are located near (either geographically or sectorally) to foreign plants. From the labour market perspective, foreign firms are thought to pay higher wages, tend to be located in sectors with high growth rates, have a higher probability of exporting and are more capital and R&D intensive when compared to domestic firms. All of these factors suggest that FDI is beneficial to an economy, and indeed UK industrial policy has in the past been directed at attracting foreign investment into the UK, especially to relatively less prosperous areas, such as Wales as a means of increasing and safeguarding employment.

Dhingra, Ottaviano, Sampson, and Van Reenen (2016) conclude 'that leaving the EU will reduce FDI inflows to the UK by around 22%', which could lower real incomes by as much as 3.4% following reductions in investment and lower productivity effects. They estimate that the impact on the UK car industry could be particularly dramatic with production falling by 12% and prices rising by 2.5%. Also given that the financial services sector is currently the largest beneficiary of FDI and concerns over the loss of 'single passporting' benefits to the City of London, losses in this sector could be substantial.

A recent working paper by Sands, Balls, Leape, and Weinberg (2017) published by the Harvard Kennedy School moved the focus from multinational firms and focused on domestic SMEs noting that this group was perceived to see greater benefits from Brexit and noted the importance of these firms to the UK economy, where they employ around 14.5 million individuals and are responsible for almost 50% of the country's GVA. They suggest that much of the current rhetoric around Brexit is a legacy of the referendum campaign where 'leavers' tended to exaggerate opportunities and downplay risks and 'remainers' tending to overstate threats to businesses and the economy. Their research involved interviews with 50 SMEs and their trade associations to assess the challenges and opportunities to businesses. Their findings emphasised the importance of outcomes on SMEs in achieving a good trade deal with the EU, the importance of the regulatory burden not increasing after Brexit and other important concerns raised by particular industrial sectors.

They note that given over half of the UK's current trade is with the EU generally, firms see the importance of and wish to remain in the single market and customs union and not default to WTO rules, which would lead to a sharp increase in tariffs and non-tariff barriers. Whilst they note that companies welcome the increased trading opportunities which could result following Brexit, they also observe that 'the UK's major export markets outside the EU, which are the US, Canada, Switzerland and Korea already have low or no tariffs as a result of EU FTAs and other trade facilitation arrangements'. They note that trade opportunities outside of the EU are often exaggerated; for example, Germany currently exports four times more to China than the UK; so trade is often restricted by a lack of products to trade from the UK arising from structural and competitiveness issues which have nothing to do with being a member of the EU. Taking advantage of many opportunities outside of the EU would require changes in product ranges, innovation, substantial new investment and increases in competitiveness all of which could take many years to achieve.

Concerns were also expressed about the ability to negotiate new trade deals with the fastest-growing economies in the world such as China and India as well as Commonwealth countries. Current exports to Commonwealth countries amount to less than a quarter of that which the UK exports to the EU. Sands et al. (2017) calculate, for example, 'to compensate for a 5% reduction in trade with the EU, the UK would have to increase trade volumes with the top ten Commonwealth trading partners by around 28%...trade with India would have to increase by more than 170%'. They also suggest that completing a trade agreement could be difficult, given that despite the EU being India's largest trading partner, free trade negotiations have 'stalled repeatedly'.

Sands et al. (2017) also find that firms don't expect a regulatory 'windfall' after Brexit and are generally happy with current regulatory procedures; a fear is that the regulatory burden could increase if UK and EU regulations diverge. Concerns were also expressed over the loss of UK engagement in EU rule-making, which they believe had been helpful in the implementation of appropriate regulations particularly in financial services, energy and creative industries. A number of industries such as pharmaceuticals noted whether in or out of the EU they will still be heavily influenced by EU regulations, such as drug approval. Important sectors such as finance and the creative industries will also be constrained by EU rules when trading in the EU post Brexit.

Anxiety was also expressed over the potential damage to complex supply chains which have developed over many years, following the UK entry in the EU and the single market, in industries such as automotive, aviation and the chemical sectors, where unregulated and tariff-free movement of components is seen as critical. Many sectors, for example, have complex just-in-time production methods with components moving across many boarders in Europe; tariff increases, potential delays at border crossings and increased bureaucracy associated with trading with the UK could damage the efficiency of current supply chains leading to production leaving the UK. Other sectors such as agriculture and fishing outlined their dependence on EU protection and subsidies. Many sectors also revealed the importance of the need for continued access to EU labour both skilled and unskilled and the benefits of the free movement of labour from an operation's view point.

After the referendum result, studies also began to look at the likely regional/area impacts within the UK of Brexit. Clayton and Overman (2017), for example, estimated that 'every local authority area is predicted to be negatively affected but cities are likely to be hit harder than non-urban areas' even though they may recover quicker. They also predict that cities with relatively high employment shares in private sector knowledge-intensive services will be the hardest hit. Dhingra, Machin, and Overman (2017) also predict a North-South divide, with nine of the top ten worst affected local authorities being located in the South; these areas 'have high employment shares in Business Activities or Financial Intermediation (or both)'. The only area in the North, in the top 10 group, is Aberdeen City. The ten areas predicted to be least affected show more geographical dispersion but are overly concentrated in the North. They noted their results are different to earlier studies, such as Los, McCann, Springford, and Thissen (2017), and suggest that this difference arises due to that study not modelling non-tariff barrier affect which they argue could be particularly costly under a hard Brexit scenario. They also find that the areas predicted to be most harmed economically by Brexit were also more likely to vote to remain in the EU, consistent with a rational voting model.

In summary as a result of Brexit, the UK economy faces many challenges and uncertainties, especially as the UK trading arrangements after Brexit are still to be agreed. Opportunities exit as potentially new markets will be opened up after negotiating new trade deals. The UK does have a comparative advantage in business and financial services; these sectors also account for a relatively large proportion of the economy, and this type of trade is growing relatively quickly and has the potential for further growth (as the digital economy continues to grow in importance), especially if the relatively high trade barriers facing many business and financial services can be reduced. Growth prospects in these areas may also be higher in many emerging markets which are forecast to grow quicker than many advanced countries. However, as shown earlier, geography matters and when it comes to trade the EU will still be the UK's major trading destination as it currently accounts for just under half of our exports and just over half of our imports. So getting the best possible trade deal in terms of access to the single market following Brexit will be critically important. The implications of a no deal could be very damaging for the UK economy, complex international supply chains and just-in-time production methods could be badly damaged, and multinational companies could cut back on FDI, with important implications for growth, jobs and living standards. Negotiating new trade agreements with other countries and trading blocs will be particularly important, though on past evidence these could take up to 5–10 years to negotiate with the possibility of important failures along the way. Deals may also have to be renegotiated with countries where EU trade deals currently exit. Trying to negotiate many deals simultaneously will put substantial pressures on UK trade negotiators, where success will be critical if the worst predictions for the economy after Brexit aren't to come true.

Acknowledgements The author is grateful to those who took part in the Emerging Markets and Brexit, EMaRC workshop, 3 July 2017, Swansea University for helpful comments. Financial support from the Economic and Social Research Council (ESRC) grant number ESL009099/1 is gratefully acknowledged.

References

Armstrong, A., Lisenkova, K., & Lloyd, S. P. (2016). The EU referendum and fiscal impact on low income households. National Institute of Economic and Social Research, 9 June 2016. London, UK.

Clayton, N., & Overman, H. G. (2017). Brexit, trade and the economic impacts on UK cities, centreforcities, London.

Dhingra, S., Machin, S., & Overman, H. G. (2017). The local economic effects of Brexit. Centre for Economic Performance, Brexit analysis, No. 10. LSE. London.

Dhingra, S., Ottaviano, G., Sampson, T., & Van Reenen, J. (2016). The Impact of Brexit on foreign investment in the UK. Centre for Economic Performance, Brexit analysis, No. 3, LSE.

Emmerson, C., Johnson, P., Mitchell, I., & Phillips, D. (2016). Brexit and the UK's public finances, Institute for Fiscal Studies, Report 116. London.

Los, B., McCann, P., Springford, J., & Thissen, M. (2017). The mismatch between local voting and the local economic consequences of Brexit. *Regional Studies, 51*(5), 786–799.

Minford, P., Gupta, S., Le, V. P. M., & Mahambare, V. (2016). *Should Britain leave the EU? An economic analysis of a troubled relationship* (Second ed.), Institute of Economic Affairs, London.

Sampson, T., Dhingra, S., Ottaviano, G., & Van Reenen, J. (2016). Economists for Brexit: A critique. Centre for Economic Performance, Brexit Analysis, No. 6 LSE.

Sands, P., Balls, E., Leape, S., & Weinberg, N. (2017). Making Brexit work for British Businesses, Harvard Kennedy School.

David Blackaby is a Professor of Economics. His main areas of research are labour markets, regional economics and public policy, and he has published papers in *The Economic Journal, Oxford Economic Papers and Oxford Bulletin of Economics and Statistics*. From 1996 to 2005, he was the Head of Economics, 2005–2008 the Deputy Head of the School of Business and Economics and 2012–2013 the Director of Research, College of Business, Economics and Law. He was a Member of the Royal Economic Society Committee for Women in Economics (2002–2011), and from 1991 to 1995, he was a Convenor of the Labour Economics Study Group. He was a Member of the Business and Management Panel and Economics and Econometrics Panel for REA2008 and REF2014. In 1999, 2006 and 2014, he was a Member of the QAA Panel, responsible for writing the Benchmark Statement for Economics. He was also a Member of the ABS Panel producing *Academic Journal Quality Guide* (2008–2011). David's ESRC responsibilities include being a Member of the Research Resources Board (2006–2010), Senior Examiner (Economics) for PhD Competition (2003–2006), Chair of Postgraduate Training Recognition Panel for Economics (2007) and Deputy Chair in 2005. He was a Member of CHUDE Steering Group (2001–2010) and NHS Pay Review Body (2009–2015). David has attracted research grant income from a number of areas including the ESRC, European Social Fund, Welsh Government, WDA, HEFCW, Equal Opportunities Commission, Equalities and Human Rights Commission, SIGOMA and BP. He is currently the Director of Welsh Economy Labour Market Evaluation and Research Centre (WELMERC) and Co-director of the Wales Institute of Social and Economic Research Data and Methods (WISERD).

Part II
Financial Technology

Chapter 5
Digital Technologies and Pro-poor Finance

Silvia Masiero and M. N. Ravishankar

Abstract Social enterprises need to be ambidextrous, i.e. simultaneously pursue social and financial goals. In this paper we focus on how digital social entrepreneurs at the base of the pyramid implement ambidextrous strategies. We draw on a case study of Rang De, India's first platform for the delivery of credit to the poor, whose ecosystem involves multiple intermediaries and thousands of borrowers all over India. The paper identifies key actor-technology mechanisms leading to the achievement of social and financial goals, finding that the platform is instrumental to building trust amongst the social investor community and, at the same time, delivering loans at the base of the pyramid. The study contributes to a deeper understanding of pro-poor finance in the Indian context and also adds to the literature on digitally driven financial inclusion.

Keywords India · Digital entrepreneurship · Financial inclusion

5.1 Introduction

Across the developing world, an estimated 2.5 billion adults lack access to basic formal financial services, which are costly or not well suited to their needs (Mas & Radcliffe, 2010). Financial inclusion is important for improving the living conditions of poor farmers, rural enterprises and other vulnerable groups. In their seminal work on the functioning of entrepreneurship at the base of the pyramid, Prahalad and Hammond (2002) have suggested that digital technologies could alleviate at least some of the issues related to access and that they need to be tailored in order to provide safe and affordable finance options for below-poverty-line households.

However, it is operationally difficult for digital enterprises to do so. Organisations engaging in finance for the poor encounter multiple issues, ranging from technical viability to social and political complexities of many sorts (Banerjee, Duflo, Glennerster, & Kinnan, 2015). In particular, the traditional model of microfinance is

S. Masiero (✉) · M. N. Ravishankar
School of Business and Economics, Loughborough University, Loughborough, UK
e-mail: s.masiero@lboro.ac.uk; m.n.ravishankar@lboro.ac.uk

Y. K. Dwivedi et al. (eds.), *Emerging Markets from a Multidisciplinary Perspective*, Advances in Theory and Practice of Emerging Markets,
https://doi.org/10.1007/978-3-319-75013-2_5

criticised for its high cost of credit, resulting in an unsustainable model of service provision. As technologies are incorporated in financial services for the poor, it is paramount that they are tailored to guaranteeing affordability and effectiveness of finance.

Over the last decade, digital technologies have been incorporated in base-of-the-pyramid financial service provisions. However, the outcomes of such efforts have not yet been the object of systematic study. In particular, challenges on the technical and political front make it hard for organisations to become effective financial service providers and call for 'ambidextrous' approaches that pursue competing goals at the same time (Gibson & Birkinshaw, 2004). Looking at digital entrepreneurship at the base of the pyramid, in this chapter we frame ambidexterity as the simultaneous pursuit of social as well as more instrumental or financial goals (Hahn, Pinkse, Preuss, & Figge, 2016).

This chapter studies Rang De, the first digital platform for the delivery of affordable credit in India. Rang De, based in Bangalore, has built a strong financial ecosystem involving thousands of social investors and provides credit to thousands of borrowers all over India. Rang De provides a strong example of harmonisation of social and commercial goals and constitutes a good case to explore the processes behind such harmonisation. In this chapter, building on the Rang De case, we address the question: how do digital entrepreneurs at the base of the pyramid implement ambidextrous strategies?

The chapter explores and identifies key actor-technology mechanisms that undergird the achievement of social and financial goals. Based on empirics collected during fieldwork with the Rang De team in Bangalore, we identify two enabling mechanisms, respectively centred on trust-building (the digital platform is instrumental to mobilising the trust of social investors) and smooth delivery of loans (the platform is essential for building solid and continuative relations with borrowers and intermediaries). The two mechanisms are mutually reinforcing, and the chapter illustrates how their combination allows the simultaneous pursuit of contrasting goals, leading to Rang De's strikingly impactful results.

The chapter's theorising around ambidexterity and digital pro-poor finance has implications at two levels. First, it helps explain pro-poor finance especially in the Indian context, where multiple failures of the traditional model demand urgent innovation. Second, it contributes to explaining how models of digital finance for the world's poor and marginalised communities could be constructed.

5.2 Theory

5.2.1 Organisational Ambidexterity

The concept of organisational ambidexterity represents 'an organisation's ability to pursue two disparate things at the same time' (Gibson & Birkinshaw, 2004: 210). The notion of competing acts is important because it points to the paradox achieved by ambidextrous organisations, whose ability lies in balancing goals of natures that are not only different, but often come across to the external observer as mutually exclusive (Gupta, Smith, & Shalley, 2006; Raisch & Birkinshaw, 2008).

It is significant that existing literature frames ambidexterity mainly as means to achieve financial performance, observing how the simultaneous pursuit of exploration and exploitation is functional to the achievement of greater profits. Against this backdrop, in a nascent stream, a distinction is made between *commercial* goals, aimed at profit sustenance or maximisation, and *social* goals, aimed at the pursuit of value-laden social objectives. Hahn et al. (2016) explore the coexistence of a moral and an instrumental rationale, both of which are essential to corporate social responsibility (CSP) for firms. Pache and Santos (2010) similarly examine the demands imposed by firms' institutional environments, observing the apparent 'collision of worlds' between goals of greater social value (e.g. global poverty reduction) and objectives of a commercial nature.

5.2.2 Ambidexterity for Digital Enterprises at the Base of the Pyramid

Seminal work by Prahalad and Hammond (2002) suggests that firms can serve the poor profitably, meaning they can make a sustainable and successful business by serving communities below the poverty line. They also make the argument that digital technologies play a substantial role in such effort, by connecting marginalised communities and enabling new business models. In this respect, the role of digital technologies as instrumental in serving the poor has generated a wide literature on digital entrepreneurship at the base of the pyramid (e.g. Foster & Heeks, 2013; Hart & Christensen, 2002; Kuriyan, Nafus, & Mainwaring, 2012; Prahalad, 2012).

Digital entrepreneurs at the base of the pyramid need to balance goals of a social and a financial nature. These ambidextrous goals are common to different types of digital enterprises working with poor and marginalised communities. Telecentres, i.e. shared premises where information technologies of diverse types can be accessed, need to make a difference for the poor and be financially sustainable at the same time (Madon, 2005; Kuriyan, Toyama, & Ray, 2006; Masiero, 2011). Impact sourcing ventures, seeking to extend the benefits of outsourcing to marginalised communities, need to engage the poor as service producers and at the same time make sustained profit (Heeks & Arun, 2010; Sandeep & Ravishankar, 2015). Digital platforms for farmers' services, such as m-Farm in Kenya or eKutir in India, need to balance the ability to serve vulnerable farmer groups with that of financially sustaining their own work (Jha, Pinsonneault, & Dubé, 2013).

The coexistence of social and commercial objectives hence emerges as a strong shared objective of digital entrepreneurs operating with the poor. The ability to pursue such goals simultaneously is a crucial factor for survival and success of this particular type of entrepreneurship. This leads us to ask, how do digital entrepreneurs at the base of the pyramid implement ambidextrous strategies?

5.3 Research Setting

Digital entrepreneurs providing financial services at the base of the pyramid are subject to particular pressure due to the need to provide credit to communities below the poverty line. In particular, some digital finance providers seek to innovate on traditional microfinance, criticised for the dire consequences that its high cost of credit imposes on the poor (Banerjee et al., 2015). Prahalad and Hammond (2002) illustrate the existence of a 'poverty premium', meaning much higher costs of credit to the poor result from informational asymmetry and low bargaining power. As 'fintech' social enterprises start proliferating in developing nations, the need to provide effective pro-poor financial services is combined with that of remaining commercially sustainable.

Rang De is India's first Internet platform for delivering affordable credit through peer-to-peer lending. It is based on a network of 41 intermediary NGOs and social enterprises (referred to as 'impact partners') working in 18 Indian states and operates a digital platform with the objective to lower the cost of credit. Rang De was co-founded in 2006 by digital entrepreneurs Ramakrishna (Ram) NK and his wife Smita, whose business model was inspired by Muhammad Yunus's Grameen Bank. The purpose was that of leveraging the Internet for lowering the cost of credit, by enabling social investors from all over the world to invest in borrowers from poor communities of India.

In the Rang De model, social investors can use the website (www.rangde.org) to browse stories of borrowers, understand their personal history and reasons why they need a loan and then invest in them. Interest rates charged to borrowers vary, from a minimum of 4.50% for higher education loans to a maximum of 10% for microbusiness and special loans. These rates are far more competitive than what is offered by private moneylenders and other microfinance organisations. Borrowers repay their loans on a monthly basis, normally over a period of 1–2 years. As repayments occur, Rang De pays a fee to the impact partner, retaining 2% of the total amount. Finally, Rang De pays social investors an interest of 2%, plus the original amount they had invested. The interest rate breakup of borrower repayments and the yield for each stakeholder are illustrated in Tables 5.1 and 5.2.[1]

A small organisation when it started and in its first years, Rang De expanded very quickly from 2009 to 2010, when it evolved from a platform to an ecosystem of social investors, intermediaries and borrowers all over the nation. Its goal of impacting the lives of borrowers all over India is currently combined with a focus on scale: as founder Ram declared in an interview, the idea is that of becoming 'India's public distribution system for loans', running computerised kiosks from which potential

[1]As the table shows, interest is not paid to social investors on primary and higher education loans.

Table 5.1 Interest rate breakup for borrower repayments (for each loan type)

Loan product	Impact partner (%)	Rang De (%)	Social investor (%)	Contingency (%)	Total (flat) (%)	Total (APR)[a] (%)
Business	5.50	2.00	2.00	0.50	10.00	17.97
Higher education	2.00	2.00	–	0.50	4.50	8.41
Primary education	4.00	2.00	–	0.50	6.50	11.79
Microventure	2.00	2.00	2.00	1.00	7.00	12.60
Working capital for artisans	–	2.00	2.00	1.00	5.00	8.98
Special loans	5.00	2.00	2.00	1.00	10.00	17.97

Source: www.rangde.org
[a]APR interest rates are calculated on a monthly repayment schedule

Table 5.2 Interest rate breakup of the yield to each stakeholder

Loan product	Impact partner (%)	Rang De (%)	Social investor (%)	Contingency (%)	Total (APY)[a] (%)
Business	9.88	3.59	3.59	0.90	17.97
Higher education	3.74	3.74	–	0.93	8.41
Primary education	7.25	3.63	–	0.91	11.79
Microventure	3.60	3.60	3.60	1.80	12.60
Working capital for artisans	3.59	3.59	1.80	5.00	8.98
Special loans	8.96	3.58	3.58	1.79	17.92

Source: www.rangde.org
[a]APY interest rates are calculated on a monthly repayment schedule

borrowers can apply directly for a loan. This project, known as *Swabhimaan*, has been successfully piloted in a rural village of Karnataka and accompanied by financial literacy training which enabled borrowers, mainly female, to use the kiosk. An instrument called a *bioscope*, allowing interaction between the user and the digital content, has been built to enable the application process.

Rohit Parakh, a member of the Rang De team, details the rationale of the shift to Swabhimaan:

> While [the current] model works, there are a few challenges. People who are not associated with a self-help group are excluded from the financial system. We want to reach out to the sections of the population who are truly excluded. What we are trying to achieve with *Rang De Swabhimaan* is to allow individuals to seek loans at low interest rates. The money will directly be transferred to their bank accounts.

To pursue its scaling project, Rang De leverages innovations, both financial and technological, that the Indian government has engaged with at multiple levels. The first one, known as the *Pradhan Mantri Jan Dhan Yojana*, is a programme aimed at enabling even the poorest of the poor to have a bank account: since borrowers need a bank account to receive their loans, the existence of Jan Dhan is instrumental for them to do so. The presence of *Aadhaar* and the identification scheme that provides a unique 12-digit number to all those enrolled and captures their biometric details is also important. All Rang De borrowers need an Aadhaar number to verify their identity, and they will need one to use the Swabhimaan kiosk. Finally, payment banks – a bank model tailored for low-income households – have started operating in 2017 and will be utilised for Swabhimaan's diffusion.

5.4 Methods

To understand the social worlds of human actors in their contextual setting (Ravishankar, 2013), we conducted an interpretive case study (Mayasandra, Pan, & Myers, 2006; Walsham, 1995), meaning a type of case study in which the multifaceted views of respondents are taken to represent reality. Data collection has been carried out from November 2016 to April 2017 on the ecosystem around Rang De, starting from exploratory interviews with the platform's founders and social investors. Fieldwork has been conducted with the Rang De team in Bangalore, the technologists supporting financial innovation and two of the impact partners that mediate the organisations' relation with borrowers. More data have been collected through a virtual ethnography of the Rang De website and the many blogs, online journals and social media on which Rang De's experience of digital pro-poor finance is recounted.

Data analysis has been informed by the concept of generative mechanisms, seen as the underlying and often unobservable causal structures that lead to events (Mingers, 2004). More specifically, we focused on seeking the generative mechanisms that lie behind the empirically observed ability of Rang De to pursue financial and social objectives at the same time. In the first stage of our analysis, a collection of all our data was compiled, in order to find themes related to Rang De's ambidexterity and code the data accordingly (Strauss & Corbin, 1998). In the second stage, themes have been mapped and related to each other in order to formulate possible explanations, which have then been validated with respondents. This process has been chosen in virtue of its suitability to answer an explanatory research question, centred on the causal structures behind phenomena (Gregor, 2006).

5.5 Findings

Our analysis answers the question on how digital entrepreneurs implement ambidextrous strategies by illustrating two actor-technology mechanisms enacted through Rang De's digital platform. This creates a virtuous cycle in which the effective delivery of loans feeds the trust of social investors in the organisation, and such trust generates the capital needed for sustainability and further scaling.

5.5.1 Effective Delivery of Loans

Timely and efficient disbursement of loans to recipients is crucial for the Rang De model. Having been developed in direct opposition to the more costly model of microfinance, delivery of loans from Rang De needs to be cheaper to the borrower and sustainable, in a context ridden with technical hurdles (e.g. lack of financial infrastructure) and political ones (e.g. influence of exploitative moneylenders). In spite of these hurdles, Rang De distinguishes itself for a strong record of loan delivery.[2]

In the pursuit of this record, Rang De leverages digital technologies in two ways. The first is the construction of long-term relations with intermediaries, resulting into a system of trusted NGOs that spans a large part of the nation. Our field data reveal that impact partners share reports with Rang De, in which they detail the borrowers' situation and justify any case of missing repayment. What is crucial, in the relation with intermediaries, is the importance of nondigital contact, which consists in field visits where Rang De's impact team directly appraises the situation of borrowers and consolidates the relation with key individuals in the partner organisation.

The second way, enhanced through the recent Swabhimaan project, lies in multiple disintermediation activities. As suggested above, the Swabhimaan project embodies the goal of directly reaching communities whose marginalisation prevents them from even accessing self-help groups. To do so, technology is used to operate kiosks where financial literacy courses are imparted, a test is taken by borrowers and loan applications by previously financially illiterate women take place. After a successful pilot in Bangalore's Kolar district, the Swabhimaan project is to be scaled up to the rest of Rang De's states.[3]

It is the blending of intermediation and direct contact with borrowers, only recently shifted towards the latter, that allows Rang De to deliver loans in an effective and transparent way. The main finding coincides with the blending of digital and nondigital organisation and highlights the interdependence of these two forms of action in Rang De's work. In the absence of a digital platform, low-cost loan delivery would not be possible, but in the absence of face-to-face contact, a network of intermediaries would not exist. The combination of the two leads to financially and socially sustainable loan delivery.

[2] At our latest check (29 August 2017), 59,905 loans had been disbursed by Rang De since its establishment.

[3] https://www.rangde.org/swabhimaan, accessed 29 August 2017.

5.5.2 Building Trust of Social Investors

A precondition for the good functioning of Rang De is a large number of social investors, but it is difficult to reach the credibility needed for individuals to engage. As a current social investor details:

> I came across Rang De through a post on The Better India website and my reaction was SCAM, FRAUD! After all, what seems too good to be true is more often than not, just that – too-good-to-be-true. After what seemed like a lifetime of hearing about such initiatives that went wrong, I had low trust to start off with.

Our interviews reveal that suspicion is often the first reaction of those encountering Rang De. This requires the organisation to engage in systemic operations of trust-building, which are again supported by the digital platform and especially by the web interface. In particular, three actions – detailing of narratives, operations and impact – are performed through the web presence.

Detailing of narratives refers to provision of synoptic recounts on the borrowers' life stories. Browsing the website a list of borrowers appears, classifiable by state and type of activity. For each borrower a synthetic story of the emerging business is provided; this is often matched by photos and/or videos taken during the impact team's visit to the field. As witnessed during one of these visits, the impact team collects detailed narrative data on each borrower, and two members of the marketing team come along to convert such information into words and pictures which are then shared online.

Detailing of operations also happens on the website. A blog section, curated primarily by the impact team, is functional to inform prospective and current investors of the day-to-day workings of the organisation. In addition, social investors receive detailed reports on their loan repayments, which increases transparency of the key phases of the repayment process. Furthermore, the organisation's transaction reports are detailed in a specific section of the website, to abide by the principle of transparency that has been developed against widespread mistrust.

Finally, *detailing of impact* is both in terms of figures (reported on the website's home page) and in terms of life changes resulting from borrowers' access to a Rang De loan. Careful documentation of impact on borrowers is conducted during the field visits and reported on the website through short videos and written narratives of the changes reached. This helps developing empathy in the social investors, generating a mechanism of digital construction of emotive connections with the borrower. The use of social media, which Rang De pursues through a dedicated team, complements the website by diffusing awareness of this alternative financial model.

Rang De's twofold pursuit of an ambidextrous strategy is summarised in Fig. 5.1. This is what allows the simultaneous pursuit of social and commercial objectives, which are sustained by mutually reinforcing mechanisms. On the one hand, effective loan delivery feeds social investors' trust in the organisation, as it is reflected in the narratives, operations and impact that the website details. On the other hand, trust of increasing numbers of investors allows loan delivery to continue and is the

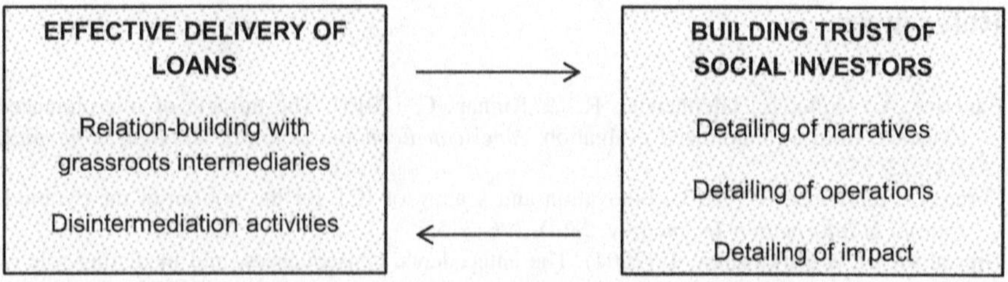

Fig. 5.1 Mechanisms informing Rang De's ambidextrous strategy

basis on which the recent scaling strategy, based on Swabhimaan's diffusion, has been developed.

5.6 Discussion

Social enterprise literature discusses the tensions emerging between social and financial logics, but the role of digital technologies in handling such tensions has not been the focus of systematic research. Our analysis fills the gap by revealing two coexisting actor-technology mechanisms, which explain how Rang De uses digitality in the pursuit of its twin goals. The virtuous cycle illustrated above, explaining effective loan delivery in spite of hurdles, also explains the presence of a wide pool of social investors and the high rate of retention of the existing ones.[4]

While based on a single case study, implications of this research are at two levels. First, it helps explain pro-poor finance in the Indian context, where many problems have emerged with the cost of microfinance. Our analysis reveals that, with a digital strategy aimed at transparency and trust-building, providers can reach a mass of investors that is functional to cost reduction for loans at large. If financial sustainability is pursued, an ambitious project like that of Swabhimaan may be possible, even if limitations dictated by cost and exogenous political factors may emerge.

Second, the study adds to the existing knowledge on pro-poor models of digital finance. In particular, strategic blending of digital and nondigital actions turns out to be crucial for sustainability. As the analysis reveals, the platform is not sufficient for an ambidextrous strategy to work well, and its success still requires face-to-face engagement with intermediaries. Furthermore, the ecosystem's harmony is essential for the model to work, and the importance of the virtuous cycle outlined here lies also in its ability to hold actors together. If so, a platform alone is not sufficient for financial inclusion, but an ecosystem lens (Jha et al., 2016) is crucial to build real life-changing systems.

[4]As of August 2017 Rang De had a total of 12,768 social investors. A total of £7.7 million has been disbursed as loans.

References

Banerjee, A., Duflo, E., Glennerster, R., & Kinnan, C. (2015). The miracle of microfinance? Evidence from a randomized evaluation. *American Economic Journal: Applied Economics, 7*(1), 22–53.

Foster, C., & Heeks, R. (2013). Innovation and scaling of ICT for the bottom-of-the-pyramid. *Journal of Information Technology, 28*(4), 296–315.

Gibson, C. B., & Birkinshaw, J. (2004). The antecedents, consequences, and mediating role of organizational ambidexterity. *Academy of Management Journal, 47*(2), 209–226.

Gregor, S. (2006). The nature of theory in information systems. *MIS Quarterly, 30*(3), 611–642.

Gupta, A. K., Smith, K. G., & Shalley, C. E. (2006). The interplay between exploration and exploitation. *Academy of Management Journal, 49*(4), 693–706.

Hahn, T., Pinkse, J., Preuss, L., & Figge, F. (2016). Ambidexterity for corporate social performance. *Organization Studies, 37*(2), 213–235.

Hart, S. L., & Christensen, C. M. (2002). The great leap: Driving innovation from the base of the pyramid. *MIT Sloan Management Review, 44*(1), 51.

Heeks, R., & Arun, S. (2010). Social outsourcing as a development tool: The impact of outsourcing IT services to women's social enterprises in Kerala. *Journal of International Development, 22*(4), 441–454.

Jha, S. K., Pinsonneault, A., & Dubé, L. (2016). The evolution of an ICT platform-enabled ecosystem for poverty alleviation: The case of eKutir. *MIS Quarterly, 40*(2), 431–445.

Kuriyan, R., Nafus, D., & Mainwaring, S. (2012). Consumption, technology, and development: The "poor" as "consumer". *Information Technologies & International Development, 8*(1), 1–12.

Kuriyan, R., Toyama, K., & Ray, I. (2006). Integrating social development and financial sustainability: The challenges of rural computer kiosks in Kerala. Proceedings of the International Conference on *Information and Communication Technologies and Development*, Berkeley (CA), 25-26 May 2006.

Madon, S. (2005). Governance lessons from the experience of telecentres in Kerala. *European Journal of Information Systems, 14*(4), 401–416.

Mas, I., & Radcliffe, D. (2010). *Mobile payments go viral: M-PESA in Kenya*. Working Paper for the Bill and Melinda Gates Foundation, November 2010.

Masiero, S. (2011). Financial vs social sustainability of telecentres: Mutual exclusion or mutual reinforcement? *The Electronic Journal of Information Systems in Developing Countries*, 45(1), 1–23.

Mayasandra, R., Pan, S. L., & Myers, M. D. (2006). Viewing information technology outsourcing organisations through a postcolonial lens. In E. Trauth, D. Howcroft, T. Butler, B. Fitzgerald, & J. De Gross (Eds.), *Social inclusion, societal and organisational implications for information systems*. Berlin, Germany: Springer.

Mingers, J. (2004). Realizing information systems: Critical realism as an underpinning philosophy for information systems. *Information and Organization, 14*(2), 87–103.

Pache, A. C., & Santos, F. (2010). When worlds collide: The internal dynamics of organizational responses to conflicting institutional demands. *Academy of Management Review, 35*(3), 455–476.

Prahalad, C. K. (2012). Bottom of the pyramid as a source of breakthrough innovations. *Journal of Product Innovation Management, 29*(1), 6–12.

Prahalad, C. K., & Hammond, A. (2002). Serving the world's poor, profitably. *Harvard Business Review, 80*(9), 48–59.

Raisch, S., & Birkinshaw, J. (2008). Organizational ambidexterity: Antecedents, outcomes, and moderators. *Journal of Management, 34*(3), 375–409.

Ravishankar, M. N. (2013). Public ICT innovations: A strategic ambiguity perspective. *Journal of Information Technology, 28*(4), 316–332.

Sandeep, M. S., & Ravishankar, M. N. (2015). Social innovations in outsourcing: An empirical investigation of impact sourcing companies in India. *The Journal of Strategic Information Systems, 24*(4), 270–288.

Strauss, A., & Corbin, J. (1998). *Basics of qualitative research techniques*. New York, NY: Sage Publications.

Walsham, G. (1995). Interpretive case studies in IS research: Nature and method. *European Journal of Information Systems, 4*(2), 74.

Silvia Masiero is a Lecturer in International Development at the School of Business and Economics, Loughborough University, UK. Her research focuses on the use of information and communications technologies (ICTs) in the field of socio-economic development. Silvia holds a PhD in Information Systems and an MSc in Development Management from the London School of Economics and Political Science. Her research has appeared in scholarly outlets such as ***World Development***, ***Oxford Development Studies***, ***Information Technology for Development*** and the ***Economic and Political Weekly***.

M. N. Ravishankar is Professor of Globalisation and Emerging Markets and Head of the International Business, Strategy and Innovation (IBSI) Discipline Group in the School of Business and Economics, Loughborough University, UK. He conducts interdisciplinary research on the digital economy of emerging markets and their social and economic impacts. Ravi regularly contributes to international conferences and has published over 30 refereed journal articles on globalisation and emerging markets, management of digital technologies, social innovations and global sourcing. He is a Senior Editor of *Information Systems Journal* and is a Member of *IEEE Transactions on Engineering Management*'s editorial board.

Chapter 6
Identifying Critical Success Factor (CSFs) for the Adoption of Digital Payment Systems: A Study of Indian National Banks

G. P. Sahu and Naveen Kumar Singh

Abstract Global Internet connectivity and updated and latest electronic devices increase in the availability of digital payment (e-payment) system according to your choice. Previous research showed that there are few variables which are important to implement digital payment system. But no study has been undertaken to understand the interaction/interrelationship between the selected variables and to develop the hierarchy of digital payment adoption variable. This paper aims to investigate the critical success factors (CSFs), through interpretive structural modelling (ISM). To identify the contextual relationships between the variables, experts from banking personnel and academia were consulted. The CSFs may ensure the customer adoption of digital payment. The research study mainly uses the deductive approach to consider secondary and primary sources of data. An extensive literature review was conducted to identify the ten CSFs, namely, compatibility, complexity, customer support management, top management support, infrastructure, expert selection, security, cultural factor, government policies and awareness. With the help of model development, these ten variables are interrelated and prioritised for digital adoption system. Moreover this paper explores sustainability and adoptability issue to digital payment. This study will assist researchers and policymakers in relevant fields.

Keywords Digital payment system · Critical Success Factors (CSFs) · e-Payment · Interpretive structural modelling (ISM)

G. P. Sahu · N. K. Singh (✉)
School of Management Studies, Motilal Nehru National Institute of Technology Allahabad, Allahabad, UP, India

Y. K. Dwivedi et al. (eds.), *Emerging Markets from a Multidisciplinary Perspective*, Advances in Theory and Practice of Emerging Markets,
https://doi.org/10.1007/978-3-319-75013-2_6

6.1 Introduction

The Internet, globally known as "network of networks", provide the global connectivity to the world (Rogers & Shoemaker, 1971). The worldwide range of the Internet led to the birth of the electronic transfer of information through the electronic medium like computers, cellphones, etc. However, at a general level, the term "payment system" refers to the complete set of instruments, intermediaries, rules, procedures, processes and interbank fund transfer systems which facilitate the circulation of money in a country or currency area (ISACA, 1990). The method of noncash payments includes payment of goods and services to an individual or an entity without involvement of exchange of cash. Shon & Swatman (1998) define e-payment as an exchange of funds through electronic communication channels, while Gans and Scheelings (Fortune & White, 2006) define it as the payment made digitally through electronic channels directly linked with bank accounts.

> *"Non-cash payments are not accomplished merely by exchanging the payment instrument between payer and payee, but transferring deposit money between the payer's bank and the payee's bank. Non-cash payment instruments provide the mechanism for this bank-to-bank transfer. Non-cash payment instruments, such as cheques, must specify the payment amount, the names of the payer and the payee and their banks"* (Kokkola, 2010)

Electronic commerce (EC) is built upon e-payment systems (EPS). It becomes an important component of business operations for many organisations; e-payment has become one of the key issues of the most critical success issues for successful business and financial services. EC offer direct sales through direct channels, i.e. the Internet, via electronic medium or other innovative formats (Singh & Kant, 2008). In digital payment (e-payment), the drawee can easily transfer the amount to the bank account of the drawer. It requires customer, merchant, infrastructure, security and authenticity. Organisations have better chance to gain competitive advantage through adoption of Internet-based systems (Gargeya & Brady, 2005).

In this context, conceptual academic studies on how to enhance the understanding of the adoption and implementation of Internet-based system are lacking. There is a gap between information system and the mode of payment (Jennex, Amoroso, & Adelakun, 2004). This study intends to find the success factors influencing the implementation of digital payment through extensive literature review and in-depth personal interview of bank personals. With the help of a case study, ten CSFs are identified, namely, compatibility, complexity, customer support management, top management support, infrastructure, expert selection, security, cultural factor, government policies and awareness. To know the barriers and difficulties while using digital payment option, interpretive structural modelling (ISM) is used to determine relationship among these CSFs and to develop a model.

6.1.1 Digital Payment Options in India

EC is the platform which accelerates the e-payment services from traditional cash-based instruments. E-payment is defined as transfer of an electronic value of payment from a payee to a payer through an e-payment medium. It allows customers to manage and access bank accounts remotely through an electronic device (Kander, 1985; Somers & Nelson, 2001). E-payment represents any kind of noncash payment that does not involve a paper cheque (Grover, 1993). E-payment promotes the activity of digital transaction of money and reduction in the transaction of cash. Arnone & Bandiera (2004) stated that e-banking strengthens monetary policy effectiveness and that the current level of e-money usage does not pose an intimidation to the stability of the financial system.

There are lots of payment options available in India. According to previous studies the total digital payments of India in the year 2016 are $32.5379 billion, while the topmost country with the collection amount of $635,462.5 was the USA (Lim, 2008), and the current digital payment options are listed below:

1. *M-wallets*: Popular digital payment mode via smartphones; enable easy payments to vendors with cash back facility. Wallets include SBI Buddy, HDFC PayZapp, ICICI Pocket, Paytm and Mobikwik. Interoperability is a challenge in this form of payment.
2. *NEFT and RTGS*: National Electronic Fund Transfer (NEFT) and real-time gross settlement (RTGS) help one-to-one and business-to-business fund transfer. Both operate only during banking hours. Anyone can transfer large amounts with the help of this method.
3. *IMPS*: Immediate Payment Service (IMPS), a real-time electronic fund transfer system using mobile phones 24/7.
4. *Plastic money*: According to the RBI annual report, 750 million cards are in circulation, less than 400 million are used, 250–300 million debit cards are used mainly at ATMs to withdraw cash and 27 million credit cards are in use. Most merchants insist on transaction fees between 2 percent and 20 percent and annual interest (on outstanding card dues) between 36 percent and 40 percent.
5. *Mobile banking*: Access and operate your bank account via the banks' app or browser, with the help of smartphone, laptops, desktop, etc.
6. *UPI*: Unified Payments Interface (UPI) interconnects banks to help transfer funds. Both the money sender and receiver need a UPI identity. Most of the nationalised and private banks offer this payment system in India.
7. *AEPS*: Aadhaar Enabled Payment System (AEPS) is a complete payment system using biometric authentication.
8. *BHIM*: Bharat Interface for Money (BHIM) is an UPI-based application to enable money transfer using just a mobile number.
9. *USSD:* Unstructured Supplementary Service Data (USSD) is a GSM-based payment system to help money transfer for featured phone users. The USSD platform, which is hosted by the National Payment Corporation of India (NPCI), allows transactions to be conducted on the cheapest phones without the need for

an Internet connection. Available round-the-clock, users can make peer-to-peer payments, generate ministatements and carry out other transactions by dialling *99# on GSM phones.

In addition to methods of digital payment, there are few partners working not only wallets but also payment banks which provide the facility to transfer money from one place to another with easy steps. Payment bank is a quite new term in this industry; the best examples of payment banks are Bharti Airtel Ltd. and Paytm. Airtel has launched India's first live payment bank (Hord, 2005).

This paper contributes to filling the gap by providing the relevant and important variables for successful adoption of digital payment system in India. The core aspect of the paper is to describe the primary variables of digital payment system using ISM. The characteristics of the paper are as follows:

1. Variables were selected through secondary source of data. The extensive literature review has been done to verify the variable and merged few variables which are of same type.
2. With the help of expert from banking industry and academicians, the interpretive structural modelling (ISM) was used to map the contextual relationships between variables.
3. ISM offers to prioritise the important variables to set up a network model.

Primary objectives of this research paper are as follows:

1. To identify the significant variables for adoption of digital payment system
2. To prioritise the variables
3. To discover the relationship between the distinguished variables
4. To develop the structural model using ISM technique

The further part of the paper provides the review of literature, research methodology, model development through ISM, discussion and conclusion of the suggested variables. Discussion of research follows the sections and provides the result of development of the model using ISM.

6.2 Literature Review

The amount collected from offline merchants such as unorganised retailers, fast food corners and transport which is around 60 percent of total transaction amount (Arnone & Bandiera, 2004). Electronic payment medium which include cards, ATMs, POS terminals, mobile phones etc. are not only provide a transparent system but also provide a safe, cheap and easy way to global transaction (Ein-Dor & Segev, 1982; http://moneyfinanceideas.com/airtel-payments-bank/; ISACA, 1990; Lee & Kim, 2007; Listfield & Montes-Negret, 1994; Shah et al. 2016; Spiller & Lohse, 1997).

Payment system is one of the substantial change policies all over the world. Barter system is used for transaction initially (Achor & Robert, 2013). But the concept of digital payment is completely different; here the transaction is made through digital medium. Current digital transaction and the usage of electronic banking strengthen monetary policy of India which provides stability of the financial system (Arnone & Bandiera, 2004). Digital mode of transaction reduces the risk of cash handling, theft by pickpocket, etc. (Munro & Wheeler, 1980; Noor, 2011; Premkumar & Roberts, 1999). During 2010 digital payment methods became well established in most of the countries, and people like to use digital transactions. Different types of digital payment medium like Paytm, Smartcards, mobile wallet, QR code, etc. are available in India (Rogers, 1995). Earlier online tools like PayPal, NFC payments by smartphone or cards, digital wallet system by Apple and bill payment systems helped users towards cashless transactions online.

As far as banks are concerned, it provide the platform to make digital payment (ie. ready money) to make transaction on the virtual channel. It helps the customer to make payment through their bank deposit or through credit card. Before the modern banking system, there are traditional and manual system that are available for transaction (Rogers, 1995). Traditional banking or manual banking takes lots of time which involves "book-keeping". The posting of entries from one ledger to journal book without using any machine is called book-keeping (Das & Agarwal, 2010). Computer and electronic machines were used only for figure or counting of money (ISACA, 1990). Banks have no or very few numbers of computers at that time to improve the crawling working condition. Those banks having more than one computer were like "triton among the minnows". At the end of this paper we'll find the factors that are essential for the adoption of digital payment system. Another study (Davis, 1989) told that there are multiple success factor which provide the platform in adoption of digital payment systems, each factor are the predictor of economy and environment of the particular country.

6.3 Research Methodology

The method used to conduct this study is the interpretive structural modelling (ISM), which is an established approach to examine interrelationships between various concepts related to a particular problem domain (Dwivedi et al., 2017; Hughes, Dwivedi, & Rana, 2017; Hughes, Dwivedi, Rana, & Simintiras, 2016; Janssen, Rana, Slade, & Dwivedi, 2017; Sahu & Singh, 2016). The factors were examined and prioritised which were collected through extensive literature. A questionnaire was designed on the basis of factors extracted from literature review for adoption of digital payment system, and feedback from experts (banking professionals and academicians) were used to design the initial version of the questionnaire.

After deep and wide searches, based on secondary data, the ultimate list of articles reviewed for this paper covers articles published in reputed referred scholarly journals on digital payment and were not found on any paper on the modelling of digital payment system using ISM. The approach of research is exploratory in nature. There were lots of variables that have been found through various search engines like Emerald, Google Scholar, Springer Link, etc. with the help of primary keywords such as ISM and digital payment system. Ten variables were selected from all on the basis of expert's opinion from banking professionals and academicians. At the end of the study, ISM was used to develop the model of CSFs of digital payment system.

6.3.1 Critical Success Factors (CSFs) of Digital Payment System

The concept of critical success factor (CSF) was developed in 1979 to help managers define the key information needed by top-level management by John F. Rockart of MIT. Rockart (Premkumar & Ramamurthy, 1995) further stated that the executives tried to determine the most critical factor so they could take the necessary actions and correct any problems that had arisen. CSFs can be used as strategic plans for development of an organisation (Kwak, 2002), it can be used as guidelines for monitoring a corporation's activities (Dickinson, Ferguson, & Sircar, 1985), and it can also be used by higher authority of organisations to achieve high performance (Dwivedi et al., 2017).

> *Critical success factors will insure successful competitive performance for the organisations, if they are satisfactory. The factors belongs to few key areas where "things must go right" for the better future of the business. If inadequate result found in selected areas, the organisations' efforts for the periods for the period will be less than desired. (p.85)*

6.4 Model Development Through Interpretive Structural Modelling (ISM)

ISM modelling is an interactive learning process which determines interdependency and direction and provides priority among the selected variables of the system. This model enables a researcher to build up a structure to establish relationship between the variables (Bolanos, Fontela, Nenclares, & Pastor, 2005). With the help of structured questionnaire, data are collected from banking experts and academicians to build a model. For better understanding of interdependency, this model is used to interpret the relationship and direction between the variables relevant to specific problem (Sahu & Singh, 2016). Hence, ISM model is used to develop a model for adoption of digital payment system. The model consisted of several steps:

(i) Identified CSFs from literature review and expert opinion (Table 6.1).
(ii) Development of structural self-interaction matrix (SSIM) which provides pairwise relationship among variables.

Table 6.1 CSFs for adoption of digital payment system

Sl. no.	CSFs	Definition	Reference
1	Compatibility	Compatible with changes caused by adoption of digitalisation	Alaskari, Ahmad, Dhafr, and Pinedo-Cuenca (2013), Listfield and Montes-Negret (1994), Munro and Wheeler (1980), Noor (2011), Premkumar and Roberts (1999), Spiller and Lohse (1997)
2	Complexity	Requires skill, IT knowledge, digital awareness, etc.	Lee and Kim (2007), Listfield and Montes-Negret (1994), Nasir and Sahibuddin (2011), Shah et al. (2016), Spiller and Lohse (1997)
3	Customer support management	Continuous connection with customers, frequent performance and quick responses help to fulfil customer need and research	Alaskari et al. (2013), Dwivedi et al. (2017), Ein-Dor and Segev (1982), Gans and Scheelings (1999), Hughes et al. (2016, 2017), Lee and Kim (2007), Listfield and Montes-Negret (1994), Premkumar, Ramamurthy, and Nilakanta (1994), Shon and Swatman (1998)
4	Top management support	Top management vision is the benefit of new technologies that leads to development and operation of digital infrastructure	Alaskari et al. (2013), Ein-Dor and Segev (1982), Gans and Scheelings (1999), Gonsalves, Lederer, Mahaney, and Newkirk (1999), Hughes et al. (2017), Janssen et al. (2017), Lee and Kim (2007), Listfield and Montes-Negret (1994), Munro and Wheeler (1980), Shah et al. (2016), Shon and Swatman (1998)
5	Infrastructure	Internet connectivity between seller and buyer, customer and banks, etc. existence of good connectivity, applications, network services, large-scale data processing facilities and widespread services needed for better infrastructure	Alaskari et al. (2013), Cockburn and Wilson (1996), Gans and Scheelings (1999), Gonsalves et al. (1999), Hughes et al. (2017), Lee and Kim (2007), Munro and Wheeler (1980), Shah et al. (2016), Shon and Swatman (1998), Spiller and Lohse (1997)
6	Expert selection	Existence of experts of IS to resolve the issue of digitalisation	Soliman and Janz (2004)
7	Security	Security is concern with safe money transaction through the online channels. Reduction of risk, trust building and improve customer loyalty are factors for a safe digital infrastructure	http://moneyfinanceideas.com/airtel-payments-bank/, Ein-Dor and Segev (1982); Lee and Kim (2007), Listfield and Montes-Negret (1994), Shah et al. (2016), Spiller and Lohse (1997)
8	Cultural factor	Habit of cash makes the barrier during adoption of digital mode of transaction	Alaskari et al. (2013), Gans and Scheelings (1999), Hughes et al. (2017), Janssen et al. (2017), Lee and Kim (2007)

(continued)

Table 6.1 (continued)

Sl. no.	CSFs	Definition	Reference
9	Government policies	Unexpected changes in government, absence of regulation system, rates and methods of taxation, role of local courts, etc. are included in government policies	Alaskari et al. (2013), Gans and Scheelings (1999), Janssen et al. (2017)
10	Awareness	Understanding of digital payment as a means of cashless transaction	Ein-Dor and Segev (1982), Gonsalves et al. (1999), Lee and Kim (2007), Munro and Wheeler (1980), Shah et al. (2016), Shon and Swatman (1998)

Table 6.2 Reachability, antecedent and intersection set and level of factors

Sl. no.	Factors	Reachability set	Antecedent set	Intersection set	Level
1	Compatibility	1,5,8,10,11	1,3,4,5,6,7,10	1,5,10	III
2	Complexity	2,3,4,6,7,11	2,5,7,10	2,7	V
3	Customer support management	1,3,4,5,6,10	2,3,4,6,7,9,11	3,4,6	IV
4	Top management support	1,3,4,5,6,7,10,11	2,3,4	3,4	V
5	Infrastructure	1,2,5,7,8,9,10,11	1,3,4,5,8,10	1,5,8,10	V
6	Expert selection	1,3,6,7	2,3,4,6,7,11	3,6,7	IV
7	Security	1,2,3,6,7	2,4,5,6,7,10,11	2,6,7	V
8	Cultural factor	5,8,9,11	1,5,8,10	5,8	II
9	Govt. policies	3,9,10,11	5,8,9	9	II
10	Awareness	1,2,5,7,8,10,11	1,3,4,5,9,10	1,5,10	VI
11	Digital payment adoption	11	1,2,4,5,8,9,10,11	11	I

(iii) Development of reachability matrix with the help of SSIM to check the transitive matrix, e.g. if factor 1 is related to factor 2 and factor 2 is related to factor 3, it means, according to ISM assumption, factors 1 and 3 are related to each other (Table 6.2).

(iv) Development of antecend set from SSIM which provides the relationship between variables in another axis.

(v) Development of intersection set from intersecting variables of reachability matrix and antecedent set.

Based on the result of intersection set, i.e. step 5, a hierarchal graph is drawn by removing transitive relationship (Fig. 6.1).

It is evaded from Table 6.2 that all ten factors influencing the adoption of digital payment system are categorised into six levels from I to VI. Table 6.2 also shows the antecend set and reachability matrix with different factors. With the help of Table 6.2, a model is developed (Fig. 6.1) for better understanding of interdependency on each other. The developed model is called ISM model of CSFs.

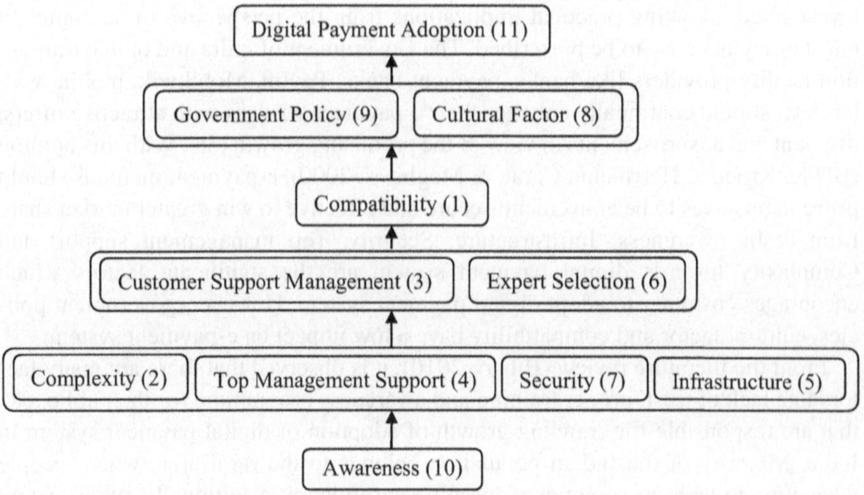

Fig. 6.1 Model for CSFs for digital payment adoption

The developed model represents a systematic direct-indirect relationship among the CSFs which is categorised into six levels. Model shows "bottom-up" approach where factor 10 (i.e. awareness), at level VI, is the predictor of factors 2, 4, 7 and 5 (i.e. complexity, top management support, security and infrastructure, respectively) at level V. These factors again are predictors and interrelated to factors 3 and 6 (i.e. customer support management and expert selection) at level IV. Similarly, these two factors are predictors of next interdependent interrelated factor 1 (i.e. compatibility) at level III. Further, factor 1 is predictor of factors 9 and 8 (i.e. government policy and cultural factor). At level I, the objective factor of this study is directly predicted by government policy and cultural factor (i.e. factors 9 and 8) and indirectly with all the rest of the eight factors. Therefore, this ISM model provides a clear hierarchal direction vision of interdependent CSFs of digital payment system.

6.5 Discussion

By closely reviewing the main body of literature of the digital payment system, researchers were able to notice that there are ten important success factors covered. Interpretive structural modelling (ISM) has been used in order to identify the most important factor for e-payment. This paper is divided into six sections, in which first section introduces the meaning and methods of digital payment in India, second section contains the literature of the study, third section is about the methodology of the research with critical success factors of digital adoption system by various studies and fourth section is about the development of ISM model with the help of analysis of suggested variables. Fifth and sixth sections are about the discussion and conclusion of the study. The findings confirm the salience of all ten CSFs investigated, allowing practical implications from the perspective of strategies to boost e-payment use to be prescribed. The Government of India and online transaction facility providers like banks, payment banks, Paytm, Mobikwik, mobile wallets, etc. should continually enhance their e-payment services with attractive offers, discount and advertisements in view of the promising growth rate. With this opinion (Böhle, Krueger, Herrmann, Carat, & Maghiros, 2000), e-payment methods should prove themselves to be convenient, secure and effective to win greater market share from cash. Awareness, Infrastructure, Security, Top management support and Complexity towards digital payment system are the significant factors which encourages customer to adopt digital payment system. However, government policies, cultural factor and compatibility have a low impact on e-payment system.

From the literature review (Bihari, 2010), it is observed that there are many factors like lack of trust, proper training and awareness programme for the public, etc. that are responsible for crawling growth of adoption of digital payment system in India. Majority of the Indian population belongs to the rural area, where people takes time to learn or sometimes doesn't want to learn. Additionally, other factors are insufficient sources to implement the digital system, insufficient Internet connectivity, lack of communication, undefined goal, lack of digital awareness, etc. (Rockart, 1978). As fas as limitations of the study is concern, there are limited literature data has been used to prepare the ISM model. This problem could be solved in the next phase of study where larger literature will be targeted. This study can serve as an eye-opener for the current payment system; organisations can make better management through more research and experts.

The main contribution of this research includes an attempt to identify the significant variables for successful adoption of digital payment system. Though few researches are available on digital payment adoption variables, no study is taken to understand the interaction among these significant variables. Also, there is no research on the development of ISM on variables of digital payment system. The present ISM-based model helps managers and policymakers to understand the relationship crux.

6.6 Conclusion

This study aims to improve understanding of critical factors affecting digital payment system in India. A principal conclusion of this research provides "awareness" as a significant variable. On the basis of ISM model, it is observed that "awareness" is at the bottom level of the hierarchy which means it implies a higher driving power. So the government and other payment partners should focus on the digital literacy and awareness of the digital method of the transactions. Variables belong to lower level (level I), maintaining high driving power in the adoption of digital payment systems i.e. complexity, top management support, security, infrastructure, etc. Thus, the systematic framework proposed in this study has broad practical application and also can be used to improve the performance, ability to payment online and effectiveness of the organisation.

References

Achor, P. N., & Robert, A. (2013). Shifting policy paradigm from cash-based economy to cashless economy: The Nigeria experience. *Afro-Asian Journal of Social Sciences, 4*(4), 1–16.

Alaskari, O., Ahmad, M. M., Dhafr, N., & Pinedo-Cuenca, R. (2013). *Critical successful factors (CSFs) for successful implementation of lean tools and ERP systems*. London, UK: WCE.

Arnone, M. M., & Bandiera, M. L. (2004). *Monetary policy, monetary areas, and financial development with electronic money* (No. 4–122). International Monetary Fund.

Bihari, S. C. (2010). Green banking-towards socially responsible banking in India. *International Journal of Business Insights & Transformation, 4*(1).

Böhle, K., Krueger, M., Herrmann, C., Carat, G., & Maghiros, I. (2000). *Electronic payment systems-Strategic and technical issues*, Background paper Nr. 1 of the EPSO. Institute for Prospective Technological Studies.

Bolanos, R., Fontela, E., Nenclares, A., & Pastor, P. (2005). Using interpretive structural modelling in strategic decision-making groups. *Management Decision, 43*(6), 877–895.

Cockburn, C., & Wilson, T. D. (1996). Business use of the world-wide web. *International Journal of Information Management, 16*(2), 83–102.

Das, A., & Agarwal, R. (2010). *Cashless payment system in India-A roadmap*, 1-104. Indian Institute of Technology Bombey.

Davis, F. D. (1989). Perceived usefulness, perceived ease of use, and user acceptance of information technology. *MIS Quarterly, 13*, 319–340.

Dickinson, R., Ferguson, C., & Sircar, S. (1985). Setting priorities with CSFs. *Business Horizons, 35*(2), 44–47.

Dwivedi, Y. K., Janssen, M., Slade, E., Rana, N., Weerakkody, V., Millard, J., … Snijders, D. (2017). Driving innovation through big open linked data (BOLD): Exploring antecedents using interpretive structural modelling. *Information Systems Frontiers, 19*(2), 197–212.

Ein-Dor, P., & Segev, E. (1982). Organizational context and MIS structure: Some empirical evidence. *MIS Quarterly, 6*, 55–68.

Fortune, J., & White, D. (2006). Framing of project critical success factors by a systems model. *International Journal of Project Management, 24*(1), 53–65.

Gans, J. S., & Scheelings, R. (1999). Economic issues associated with access to electronic payments systems. *Australian Business Law Review*, 1–27

Gargeya, V. B., & Brady, C. (2005). Success and failure factors of adopting SAP in ERP system implementation. *Business Process Management Journal, 11*(5), 501–516.

Gonsalves, G. C., Lederer, A. L., Mahaney, R. C., & Newkirk, H. E. (1999). A customer resource life cycle interpretation of the impact of the World Wide Web on competitiveness: Expectations and achievements. *International Journal of Electronic Commerce, 4*(1), 103–120.

Grover, V. (1993). An empirically derived model for the adoption of customer-based interorganizational systems. *Decision Sciences, 24*(3), 603–640.

Hord, J. (2005). How electronic payment works. Online]. HowStuffWorks. Available: http://money.howstuffworks.com/personal-finance/onlinebanking/electronic-payment1.htm.

http://moneyfinanceideas.com/airtel-payments-bank/

Hughes, D. L., Dwivedi, Y. K., & Rana, N. P. (2017). Mapping IS failure factors on PRINCE2® stages: An application of interpretive ranking process (IRP). *Production Planning & Control, 28*(9), 776–790.

Hughes, D. L., Dwivedi, Y. K., Rana, N. P., & Simintiras, A. C. (2016). Information systems project failure–analysis of causal links using interpretive structural modelling. *Production Planning & Control, 27*(16), 1313–1333.

ISACA, E. (1990). Control guide, EDI Council of Australia, Sydney chapter. *Information Systems Audit and Control Association*.

Janssen, M., Rana, N., Slade, E., & Dwivedi, Y. K. (2017). Trustworthiness of digital government services: deriving a comprehensive theory through interpretive structural modelling. *Public Management Review*. Available at https://doi.org/10.1080/14719037.2017.1305689

Jennex, M. E., Amoroso, D., & Adelakun, O. (2004). E-commerce infrastructure success factors for small companies in developing economies. *Electronic Commerce Research*, *4*(3), 263–286.

Kander, S. L. (1985). *The relations between an innovation strategy and success of telecommunications implementation in organizations*. UMI.

Kokkola, T. (2010). The payment system. Payments, securities and derivatives, and the role of the eurosystem. *Frankfurt am Main: ecB.*

Kwak, Y. H. (2002). Critical success factors in international development project management. In *Proceedings of 10th international symposium construction innovation & global competitiveness*. Cincinnati, OH.

Lee, S., & Kim, K. J. (2007). Factors affecting the implementation success of internet-based information systems. *Computers in Human Behavior*, *23*(4), 1853–1880.

Lim, A. S. (2008). Inter-consortia battles in mobile payments standardisation. *Electronic Commerce Research and Applications*, *7*(2), 202–213.

Listfield, R., & Montes-Negret, F. (1994). *Modernizing payment systems in emerging economies* (Vol. 1336). World Bank Publications. Washington D. C.

Munro, M. C., & Wheeler, B. R. (1980). Planning, critical success factors and management's information requirements. *MIS Quarterly*, *4*(4), 27–38.

Nasir, M. H. N., & Sahibuddin, S. (2011). Critical success factors for software projects: A comparative study. *Scientific Research and Essays*, *6*(10), 2174–2186.

Noor, M. M. (2011). Determining critical success factors of mobile banking adoption in Malaysia. *Australian Journal of Basic and Applied Sciences*, *5*(9), 252–265.

Premkumar, G., & Ramamurthy, K. (1995). The role of inter-organizational and organizational factors on the decision mode for adoption of inter-organizational systems. *Decision Sciences*, *26*(3), 303–336.

Premkumar, G., Ramamurthy, K., & Nilakanta, S. (1994). Implementation of electronic data interchange: An innovation diffusion perspective. *Journal of Management Information Systems*, *11*(2), 157–186.

Premkumar, G., & Roberts, M. (1999). Adoption of new information technologies in rural small businesses. *Omega*, *27*(4), 467–484.

Rockart, J. F. (1978). Chief executives define their own data needs. *Harvard Business Review*, *57*(2), 81–93.

Rogers, E. M. (1995). Diffusion of Innovations: modifications of a model for telecommunications. In Die Diffusion von Innovationen in der Telekommunikation (pp. 25-38). Springer, Berlin, Heidelberg.

Rogers, E. M., & Shoemaker, F. F. (1971). Communication of innovations: A cross-cultural approach, *Royal Anthropological Institute of Great Britain and Ireland*, *9*(2), 331–332.

Sahu, G. P., & Singh, M. (2016). Green information system adoption and sustainability: A case study of select Indian Banks. In *Conference on e-Business, e-Services and e-Society* (pp. 292–304). Springer International Publishing. Switzerland.

Shah, A., et al. (2016). *Digital payments 2020: The making of a $500 billion ecosystem in India*. The Boston Consulting Group.

Shon, T. H., & Swatman, P. M. (1998). Identifying effectiveness criteria for internet payment systems. *Internet Research*, *8*(3), 202–218.

Singh, M. D., & Kant, R. (2008). Knowledge management barriers: An interpretive structural modeling approach. *International Journal of Management Science and Engineering Management*, *3*(2), 141–150.

Soliman, K. S., & Janz, B. D. (2004). An exploratory study to identify the critical factors affecting the decision to establish internet-based inter-organizational information systems. *Information Management*, *41*(6), 697–706.

Somers, T. M., & Nelson, K. (2001). The impact of critical success factors across the stages of enterprise resource planning implementations. In *System sciences, 2001. Proceedings of the 34th annual Hawaii international conference on* (p. 10). IEEE. Maui, HI, USA.

Spiller, P., & Lohse, G. L. (1997). A classification of Internet retail stores. *International Journal of Electronic Commerce*, *2*(2), 29–56.

G. P. Sahu is a Professor of Motilal Nehru National Institute of Technology Allahabad, India. He has more than 19 years of teaching and research experience. He completed his 1-year postdoctoral fellowship programme from the California State University, Monterey Bay, California, USA, and PhD in Management from the Indian Institute of Technology Delhi, India. His research interests are in the areas of MIS, e-governance and green information systems. Dr. Sahu has published around 80 research papers in international journals and conferences. He has edited six books in the area of e-governance. Dr. Sahu has acted as a reviewer for international journals.

Naveen Kumar Singh is a PhD Research Scholar in the School of Management Studies, Motilal Nehru National Institute of Technology Allahabad, India. He worked on financial inclusion and mutual fund during his master's programme. He is doing research on digital payment system during his doctoral programme. His research interest is in the area of e-commerce and m-payment systems.

Chapter 7
Mobile Banking Adoption: Key Challenges and Opportunities and Implications for a Developing Country

Sujeet Kumar Sharma and Saeed Al-Muharrami

Abstract Technology adoption is one of the promising and growing research domains as new technology emerges continuously. Mobile banking is one of the latest technological innovations and offers multiple benefits and challenges to users and financial institutions. This chapter highlights the recent trends in the banking industry and establishes a relationship between mobile technology and traditional banking systems. Major benefits offered and main challenges faced by mobile banking adoption are discussed in detail. In addition, integration of latest technologies such as big data and cloud computing in the context of banking industry is also discussed. By exploring various dimensions of mobile banking adoption, this chapter provides theoretical and practical implications for researchers and decision-makers from a developing country perspective.

Keywords Mobile banking · Technology adoption · m-Banking benefits · m-Banking challenges

7.1 Introduction

The fast developments in the mobile technologies are the key reasons behind the higher penetration of handheld devices into our daily lives. The subscription of mobile phone users is much higher than fixed line users at global level (International Telecommunication Union, 2014). The latest mobile/handheld devices such as

S. K. Sharma (✉)
Department of Operations Management and Business Statistics, Sultan Qaboos University, Muscat, Oman
e-mail: drsujeet@squ.edu.om

S. Al-Muharrami
Department of Economics and Finance, Sultan Qaboos University, Muscat, Oman
e-mail: muharami@squ.edu.om

Y. K. Dwivedi et al. (eds.), *Emerging Markets from a Multidisciplinary Perspective*, Advances in Theory and Practice of Emerging Markets,
https://doi.org/10.1007/978-3-319-75013-2_7

personal digital assistants (PDA), smartphones, and tablets are not only used for phone calls but as sophisticated device, which enables Internet access along with high-speed data transfer and many value-added services (Alalwan, Dwivedi, & Rana, 2017; Alalwan, Dwivedi, Rana, & Simintiras, 2016; Kapoor, Dwivedi, & Williams, 2015a, 2015b, 2014a, 2014b; Liebana-Cabanillas, Marinkovic, & Kalinic, 2017; Shareef, Dwivedi, & Kumar, 2016; Slade, Dwivedi, Piercy, & Williams, 2015; Slade, Williams, Dwivedi, & Piercy, 2015). Mobile banking (m-banking) is defined by Barnes and Corbitt (2003) as "as a channel whereby the customer interacts with a bank via a mobile device, such as a mobile phone or personal digital assistants." Mobile banking (m-banking) is considered as pioneer banking technology comprising of novelty and innovativeness in comparison with other banking forms such as telebanking and automated teller machines (Püschel, Afonso Mazzon, & Hernandez, 2010). It is expected to increase the number of mobile phone subscribers around the globe that will enhance scope for mobile banking market and hence will provide greater facilities to banking customers and banks (Alalwan et al., 2016; Sharma, Govindaluri, Al-Muharrami, & Tarhini, 2017). Further, mobile banking is also considered as one of the recent mobile technological wonders. In the strict definition of mobile banking, telebanking and Internet banking are not considered as part of it. m-Banking offers a variety of services starting with the most traditional transactions such as fund transfer, payment of school fees, bill payments, trading, or loans to more advanced ones such as automatic check payments, virtual advisory/sales agent, personal savings plan, mobile recharges or predictive cross-selling of products, online booking, and various other financial services. (Baptista & Oliveira, 2016). In spite of having multiple benefits, the use of mobile devices is not at it was expected (Dineshwar & Steven, 2013; Shaikh & Karjaluoto, 2015). In 2013, Juniper Research stated that m-banking services will be used by more than 1 million users around the globe by the end of 2017. Further, Juniper Research in 2017 predicted that there would be more than 3 billion users of digital banking by the end of 2021. These numbers motivate us to explore and understand the mobile banking adoption from users and technological point of view.

m-Banking offers two key features such as anytime and anywhere for flexibility in banking systems. The integration of mobile devices and latest mobile and web technologies has changed Internet banking to mobile banking. This chapter provides an overview of the integration of banking system and mobile technology. Further, it discusses the key benefits and challenges of mobile banking adoption from a developing country perspective. In addition, it also discusses the trust and security issues of mobile banking adoption and its economic impact in Oman. This chapter is developed on the basis of philosophical and argumentative approach. Finally, this paper integrates banking sector with two latest web technologies: big data and banking sector and cloud computing and banking sector.

7.2 Banking System and Mobile Technology

Information and communication technology have revolutionized the way things were done earlier. It has spread across every fields of our day-to-day life making things convenient and easy. The banking industry too is no exception. In fact, ICT in the banking sector is the most widespread and acceptable medium that has brought radical changes in the conduct of banking transactions. One such glaring development of ICT is the innovation of mobile technology. Mobile communication technology combined with high-speed Internet in the form of 3G and 4G services is changing the way companies do business, transforming public service delivery and democratizing innovation.

"The mobile platform is emerging as the single most powerful way to extend economic opportunities and key services to millions of people," says Christine Zhen-Wei Qiang, World Bank economist and editor of a new Bank Group report on information technology and development (World Bank, 2009). Mobile technology has taken hold in everything from media to food service to health care to banking sector and a lot more. Integration of mobile technology is bringing multiple opportunities to banking sector as well as customers. Multiple mobile applications have become integral part of smartphones and connect consumers to service providers directly. The main purpose of mobile applications is to provide services at ease and save time. The GigaOM survey for European Commission estimated that 63 billion euros would be generated in EU economy by the development of mobile applications by 2018 in addition to the creation of 4.8 million jobs. Zamfiroiu (2014) discussed a number of key factors influencing quality of mobile applications from user's perspective and found that mobile phone storage, mobile device battery life, CPU processing power, and command rapidity are among the key factors. Isac (2013) explored the potential of mobile applications in the banking sector in the context of Romania. Isac found that the number of mobile application users is increasing rapidly, and it can generate substantial amount of funds to Romanian economy and can create a large number of jobs to its people. In Oman, there are mainly five banks offering mobile services to customers. Bank Muscat is the flagship financial service provider in Oman and offers multiple financial services to its customers through mobile devices. Mobile application offered by Bank Muscat in Oman is the serving 350,000 registered customers (TOO, 2015). Mobile banking services complement the vision of supreme leadership to create digital society. In addition, mobile banking services provide by Bank Muscat are in English and Arabic to cater national and international customers.

7.3 Benefits of m-Banking Adoption

The rise of mobile technology has changed the way of conducting banking transactions. Across industries, mobile technology has reduced paperwork and processing times by allowing the instant exchange of digital information. Various services such as balance inquiry, fund transfer, bill payments, credit/debit alerts, transaction history, minimum balance alerts, etc. can be accessed from mobile devices. The following are the main benefits offered through m-banking services:

- *Saves time and money*: m-Banking saves time and money as customers no longer need to visit bank branches or wait in queue and worry about the banking hours to perform banking transactions (Chong, Chan, & Ooi, 2012).
- *Provides instant access*: m-Banking facilitates anytime, anywhere access and instant conduct of transactions. With m-banking customers can transfer funds, pay utility bills, perform balance checks, apply for credit and debit card, and perform a host of other banking transactions all from the pinnacle of their comfort zone and in their convenient time at any hour of the day.
- *Provides enhanced data security*: Banking through mobile reduces the risk of fraud as customers will receive an SMS whenever there is any activity in their account such as deposits, cash withdrawals, fund transfer, etc. Also before conducting any transactions, customers have to provide their user ID and password, which are confidential and are known only to the user. Further, banks use encryption in the form of codes, which can be accessed only by authorized personnel. In addition, banks send onetime password (OTP) on the registered mobile number before conducting any financial transaction. Therefore, m-banking safeguards and protects privacy, identity, and financial information of the customers.
- *Increases efficiency*: As consumers switch to mobile banking services, financial institutions will strive to improve their overall efficiency because huge costs are incurred in maintaining and running of an ATM branch or an on-site bank branches, whereas the costs associated with a mobile transaction are much lower than that. Therefore, this offers a unique opportunity to banks to increase their efficiency as well as lower operating costs.
- *Provides improved access to products and services*: Mobile banking appeals to the consumer on the go; this facilitates its speedy adoption by the public. As mobile banking apps become more advanced and widely available, customers will have a greater opportunity to consider all of their financial options when making any purchase. Moreover, it would give banks the ability to engage with their customers in real time (Brooks, 2014).

7.4 Challenges of m-Banking Adoption

Significant revolutions in the Internet and communication technology over the past few decades have forced banks and financial institutions to embrace m-banking as a strategy for their sustainable growth in an expanded and competitive environment. However, despite the increased use of smartphones and tablets, m-banking application is not much popular among the customers. There are various challenges in developing a sophisticated mobile banking application. Some of these are:

- *Privacy and security concerns*: Security of financial transactions is the most complicated challenge that needs to be addressed jointly by mobile application developers, wireless network service providers, and the bankers to offer a secure infrastructure for financial transaction over wireless network. There should be authentication of the device with service provider before initiating a transaction. This would ensure that unauthorized devices are not connected to perform financial transactions and customer's information is safeguarded. Moreover, security and privacy is on the top of the people priority in developing country like Oman as mobile technology has not reached at the mature level.
- *Scalability and reliability*: Another challenge for the banks is to scale up the mobile banking infrastructure to handle exponential growth of the customer base. With mobile banking, the customer may be sitting in any part of the world (anytime, anywhere banking), and hence banks need to ensure that the systems are up and running in a true 24 × 7 fashion.
- *User-friendly*: Banks need to ensure that their m-banking app is easy to use and is user-friendly. Even though m-banking provides instant access to banking transaction, people often choose to visit bank branches to perform their transactions as they believe payment by cash is easy. Further, payment by cash involves no transaction charge. Therefore, banks should ensure that payment via mobile devices involves no extra transaction charge so that a large number of populations could adopt and use this application.
- *Quality of infrastructure*: Quality of Internet connectivity and other basic services is seen to be an important component of any mobile-based application. Fast, reliable, and speedy Internet connection is the base on which customers will adopt and use m-banking. Without a strong Internet access, customers can distract transactions leading to withdrawal of m-banking app. Therefore, for proper delivery of m-banking app use, a country should first focus on developing its Internet connectivity to a great extent.

7.5 Security and Trust Issues in m-Banking

Mobile banking involves high degree of uncertainty and risk due to its virtual nature (Zhou, 2011). Similar to online banking, mobile banking is built on mobile networks and may be more prone to hacker's attack due to its protocol translation.

Through WAP (Wireless Application Protocol), different types of devices can be used to access the Internet. WAP is vulnerable to hacker's attacks and compression of contents, which are insecure. Therefore, mobile service providers need to build initial trust among users to help them overcome their perceived risk. Trust facilitates users to believe that mobile service providers have enough ability and benevolence to protect their interest by providing them fair and transparent services (Maroofi, Kahrarian, & Dehghani, 2013). Some of the security areas that could be found problematic in building consumers initial trust are:

- *Confidentiality*: Issues such as identity theft, information disclosure to unauthorized individual or systems, replay attacks, and exploits on mobile devices which could disclose personal information to attackers are some of the risk factors on payment via mobile phones. m-Banking should ensure highest priority in maintaining customer's confidential information.
- *Authentication*: It is necessary to ensure that the transaction is being carried out by the person authorized or registered to carry it out. In mobile banking transactions, it is fundamental for users to have the guarantee that the process is carried out by a valid and official bank, not to a fake institution (or individual). Use of two-factor authentication will contribute to more effective identity protection for the consumer and higher identity assurance to the merchant.
- *Data protection and privacy*: Many banks outsource their facilities of handling m-banking customer service to third-party service provider. These result in security issues and minimize the trust of customers in m-banking service. Mobile banking should ensure protection of elements such as GPS location, phone conversation, and exchange of messages or e-mails, passwords, and others. Another risk is the loss of mobile phones; mobile devices can be lost or stolen (more often than PCs). There is increased risk that stolen or lost phones' information could be accessed by unauthorized users who could view sensitive information such as password from the cached memory or auto-fill settings of m-banking app and misuse mobile devices (Chong, 2013).
- *Virus attack and SMS spoofing attack*: Users generally don't install antivirus on mobile phones very often. With no such detection system, a malware won't be detected and other vulnerabilities can be exploited. Viruses like Trojan horses can easily take up password on the web browser or any cached information on operating systems and cause misuse of data. SMS spoofing attack is another such dangerous attack where an attacker can send messages on network by manipulating sender's number (Goyal, Pandey, & Batra, 2012). As most of the banks offer SMS-based mobile banking, building users trust in m-banking would be very difficult if a proper authenticated platform to perform banking transaction is not established.
- *Network security*: Network security is another major concern in m-banking application. Identification of network users, applications, and services to allow only authorized users, maintaining confidentiality, and protecting information from eavesdropping or tampering using encryption technologies are some of the security areas in which m-banking has to work upon (Kaya, 2013).

Risk for the participants in the mobile payment ecosystem depends largely on the role of the entity user, network or communication provider, or payment service provider (ISACA, 2011). Furthermore, ISACA (2011) summarized a brief idea of the type of threats and risks that may crop up across the mobile payment environment.

7.6 Cloud Computing and Banking Sector

Cloud computing was defined by the National Institute of Standards and Technology (NIST) as "a model for enabling convenient, on-demand network access to a shared pool of configurable computing resources (i.e., networks, servers, storage, applications, and services) that can be rapidly provisioned and released with minimal management effort or service provider interaction" (Mell & Grance, 2011; Sharma, Al-Badi, Govindaluri, & Al-Kharusi, 2016). The resource pooling is considered one of the most prominent features of cloud computing services. Avram (2014) discussed the four key characteristics of cloud computing such as virtual resources, pay-per-use, unlimited resources, and self-service. The usage of cloud computing is transforming the role of the Internet at workplaces. Banks are using cloud computing services to create flexible banking environment as per the need of customers (Asadi, Nilashi, Husin, & Yadegaridehkordi, 2017). Smaller banks can use cloud computing services to save cost by only paying for the services they are using. Benton (2010) discussed two domains where bank customers may use cloud computing applications such as (1) by providing ample opportunities to customers to interact with banks and (2) commonly used cloud-based application, namely, software as service (SaaS), to assist banking users to perform financial activities with banks more easily and effectively without downloading and installing software applications on their devices. Further, banks can use cloud computing services to customer segmentation as well.

There are several advantages of using cloud computing services in the banking sectors. However, there are some considerable concerns with respect to the emerging cloud computing technology. Confidentiality, security, and trust are on the top of these concerns.

7.7 Big Data and Banking Sector

Big data is one of the latest and hotspot technologies of the recent times, which is attracting great attention of researchers from academia, industry, and government sector across the globe. Some experts believe that the big data can be considered as the "new petroleum that will power the future information economy" (Jin et al., 2015). There is no universally accepted and final definition of big data. In Wikipedia, big data is defined as "an all-encompassing for any collection of data sets so large and complex that it becomes difficult to process using traditional data processing applications." In comparison with the traditional data sets, big data is being explained with the help of 5Vs, namely, volume, velocity, variety, veracity, and value.

In the banking sector, huge amount of data is being stored since several decades in the databases, and very limited useful information was extracted. Big data can help banks in various ways such as understanding the secrets of money movement and customer behavior. Furthermore, big data can help in extracting meaningful information from large data sets for banks as well as for customers. Big data can be used to understand the customer behavior in the number of domains such as customer life event analysis, next best offer, micro segmentation, real-time allocation-based offerings, and sentiment analysis and enable sales forecasting (Srivastav & Gopalkrishnan, 2015).

The explosion of data is due to the introduction of open-source data technologies in almost all business domains. Gulf News (2017) reported the banks ready to embrace the data revolution would get edge over those that are not. It is right time to review the working of banks in the context of the adoption of new big data technologies. Standard Chartered in Gulf region have put data assets on the key priority. Big data technologies help banking sector in understanding their customers and assure better service quality. Big data technologies are very powerful and can be used to segregate potential cases of money laundering and financial crimes in the context of huge mobile data.

7.8 Economic Impact of m-Banking in Oman

The proliferation of mobile data services supported by increasing 3G and 4G services in recent years has led to the emergence of Internet and m-banking services among customers and businesses. Mobile banking by facilitating anytime, anywhere access has helped not only in reducing the cost of delivering financial services but have also helped in the free flow of money in the economy by making markets and financial transactions more efficient and unleashing entrepreneurship. With the use of m-banking services, banks will need to hire fewer employees, as customers will no longer visit bank branches other than few occasions (Goyal et al., 2012). All this has a direct impact on economic growth of a developing country. As per the GSMA, 2012 report, "For a given level of total mobile penetration, a 10 per cent substitution from 2G to 3G penetration increases GDP per capita growth by 0.15 percentage points" and "a doubling of mobile data use leads to an increase in GDP per capita growth of 0.5 percentage points." Waverman et al. (2005) by enumerating on the positive economic impacts of mobile telephony services have concluded that "10 more mobile phones per 100 people would increase GDP per capita growth by up to 0.6 percentage points. Studies focusing on developing countries found this impact to be longer, between "0.8 and 1.2 percentage points." This shows that m-banking would have a great economic impact particularly for countries like Oman, which is in a developing stage in the 3G and 4G markets. m-Banking also helps in extending the client reach of banks and covers more populations from remote areas to use the service for performing monetary transaction as mobile phones are readily available in every individual household and is a more cheaper medium than Internet banking.

7.9 Conclusion

The information and communication technology is shifting paradigm to individual banks as well as banking sector. Mobile technology will have greater impact on the future economy of developing countries, resulting in multiple benefits for customers, individual banks, and banking sector as a whole. A number of challenges are expected while integrating mobile technology with banking industry. This chapter attempted to explore various facets of mobile banking adoption in order to get familiar with the background of the multiple benefits and challenges of the same from a developing country perspective. The impact of mobile technology on banking sector was discussed. Furthermore, the relationship of the latest mobile technology and banking sector was reviewed. The key benefits and challenges of mobile banking adoption were summarized on the basis of the available literature on the integration of latest technologies and banking sector. In addition, the economic impacts of mobile banking adoption were discussed. Finally, the impact of big data technologies and cloud computing technologies on banking sector were also discussed. Future research lies in the identification of key issues and requirements of banking customers as well as banking industry with respect to mobile banking adoption from developing countries perspective, as substantial literature is available in the context of the developed world. Recently, Sharma (2017) examined mobile banking adoption using technology acceptance model. In line with that, the role of additional antecedents from other established theories (see, e.g., Dwivedi, Rana, Jeyaraj, Clement, & Williams, 2017; Venkatesh, Morris, Davis, & Davis, 2003) should be examined to gain a more comprehensive understanding of factors influencing consumer adoption of mobile banking in the context of developing countries. In addition, future researchers may focus on the development of policies and guidelines to ensure effective and successful mobile banking adoption.

References

Alalwan, A. A., Dwivedi, Y. K., & Rana, N. P. (2017). Factors influencing adoption of mobile banking by Jordanian bank customers: Extending UTAUT2 with trust. *International Journal of Information Management, 37*(3), 99–110.

Alalwan, A. A., Dwivedi, Y. K., Rana, N. P., & Simintiras, A. C. (2016). Jordanian consumers' adoption of telebanking: Influence of perceived usefulness, trust and self-efficacy. *International Journal of Bank Marketing, 34*(5), 690–709.

Asadi, S., Nilashi, M., Husin, A. R. C., & Yadegaridehkordi, E. (2017). Customers perspectives on adoption of cloud computing in banking sector. *Information Technology and Management, 18*(4), 305–330.

Avram, M. G. (2014). Advantages and challenges of adopting cloud computing from an enterprise perspective. *Procedia Technology, 12*, 529–534.

Baptista, G., & Oliveira, T. (2016). A weight and a meta- analysis on mobile banking acceptance research. *Journal of Computers in Human Behaviour, 63*, 480–489.

Barnes, S. J., & Corbitt, B. (2003). Mobile banking: Concept and potential. *International Journal of Mobile Communications, 1*(3), 273–288.

Brooks, S. (2014). Five positive aspects of M-banking. Retrieved from http://www.banking.com/2014/08/13/5-positive-aspects-of-mobile-banking #.WAcXH9xOVx8

Benton, D. 2010. "How Cloud Computing Will Influence Banking Strategies in the Future", 15/5/2014, fromwww.accenture.com/banking.

Chong, A. Y. L. (2013). A two-staged SEM-neural network approach for understanding and predicting the determinants of m-commerce adoption. *Expert Systems with Applications, 40*(4), 1240–1247.

Chong, A. Y. L., Chan, F. T. S., & Ooi, K. B. (2012). Predicting consumer decisions to adopt mobile commerce: Cross country empirical examination between China and Malaysia. *Decision Support System, 53*(1), 34–43.

Dineshwar, R., & Steven, M. (2013). An investigation on mobile banking adoption and usage: A case study of Mauritius. In *Proceedings of the 3rd Asia-Pacific Business Research Conference*, Kuala Lumpur, Malaysia.

Dwivedi, Y. K., Rana, N. P., Jeyaraj, A., Clement, M., & Williams, M. D. (2017). Re-examining the unified theory of acceptance and use of technology (UTAUT): Towards a revised theoretical model. *Information Systems Frontiers*. Available at https://link.springer.com/article/10.1007/s10796-017-9774-y

Goyal, V., Pandey, S. U., & Batra, S. (2012). Mobile banking in India: Practices, challenges and security issues. *International Journal of Advanced Trends in Computer Science and Engineering, 1*(2), 56–66.

GSMA. (2012). What is the impact of mobile telephony on economic Growth? A report for the GSM Association, November 2012. Available at http://www.gsma.com/newsroom/press-release/gsma-and-deloitte-release-comprehensive-research-into-the-impact-of-mobile-telephony-on-economic-growth/. (Retrieved on November 20, 2012).

Gulf News (2017). Accessed on 11 June 2017 http://gulfnews.com/business/sectors/banking/the-big-databanking-security and privacyrevolution-1.2041732.

Isac, A. (2013). Use of mobile technology in banking services. *Annals of the University of Petrosani, Economics, 13*(2), 109–116.

ISACA. (2011). *Mobile payments: Risk, security and assurance issues*, An ISACA Emerging Technology White Paper, November 2011. www.isaca.org

ITU (2015). Global ICT developments. [internet] Retrieved from:www.itu.int/en/ITUD/Statistics/Pages/stat/default.aspx.

Juniper Research. (2013). Mobile banking handset & tablet market strategies 2013–2017. Available at http://www.juniperresearch.com/reports/mobile_banking. Accessed 1 Jan 2014).

Juniper Research. (2017). https://www.juniperresearch.com/researchstore/commerce-fintech/worldwide-digital-banking. Accessed on 28 Apr 2017.

Jin, X., Wah, B. W., Cheng, X., & Wang, Y. (2015). Significance and challenges of big data research. *Big Data Research, 2*(2), 59–64.

Kapoor, K. K., Dwivedi, Y. K., & Williams, M. D. (2014a). The interbank mobile payment acceptance in an Indian context. *International Journal of Indian Culture and Business Management, 8*(4), 473–494.

Kapoor, K. K., Dwivedi, Y. K., & Williams, M. D. (2014b). Conceptualizing the role of innovation-attributes for examining consumer adoption of mobile innovations. *The Marketing Review, 14*(4), 407–430.

Kapoor, K. K., Dwivedi, Y. K., & Williams, M. D. (2015a). Examining the role of three sets of innovation attributes for determining adoption of the interbank mobile payment service. *Information Systems Frontiers, 17*(5), 1039–1056.

Kapoor, K. K., Dwivedi, Y. K., & Williams, M. D. (2015b). An empirical examination of the role of three sets of innovation attributes for determining adoption of the IRCTC mobile ticketing service. *Information Systems Management, 32*(2), 153–173.

Kaya, M. M. (2013). Trust and Security Risks in Mobile Banking (Doctoral dissertation, University of Oxford, UK).

Liébana-Cabanillas, F., Marinković, V., & Kalinić, Z. (2017). A SEM-neural network approach for predicting antecedents of m-commerce acceptance. *International Journal of Information Management, 37*(2), 14–24.

Maroofi, F., Kahrarian, F., & Dehghani, M. (2013). An investigation of initial trust in mobile banking. *Internet Journal of Academic Research in Business and Social Sciences, 13*(9), 394–403.

Mell, P., Grance, T. (2011). The NIST definition of cloud computing (draft), NISTGoogle Scholar.

Püschel, J., Afonso Mazzon, J., & Hernandez, J. M. C. (2010). Mobile banking: Proposition of an integrated adoption intention framework. *International Journal of Bank Marketing, 28*(5), 389–409.

Shaikh, A. A., & Karjaluoto, H. (2015). Mobile banking adoption: A literature review. *Telematics and Informatics, 32*(1), 129–142.

Shareef, M. A., Dwivedi, Y. K., & Kumar, V. (2016). *Mobile marketing channel: Online consumer behavior*. Springer International Publishing, USA.

Sharma, S. K. (2017). Integrating cognitive antecedents into TAM to explain mobile banking behavioral intention: A SEM-neural network modeling. *Information Systems Frontiers*, 1–13. Available at https://link.springer.com/article/10.1007/s10796-017-9775-x

Sharma, S. K., Al-Badi, A. H., Govindaluri, S. M., & Al-Kharusi, M. H. (2016). Predicting motivators of cloud computing adoption: A developing country perspective. *Computers in Human Behavior, 62*, 61–69.

Sharma, S. K., Govindaluri, S. M., Al-Muharrami, S., & Tarhini, A. (2017). A multi-analytical model for mobile banking adoption: A developing country perspective. *Review of International Business and Strategy, 27*(1), 133–148.

Slade, E., Dwivedi, Y. K., Piercy, N. L., & Williams, M. D. (2015). Modeling consumers' adoption intentions of remote mobile payments in the UK: Extending UTAUT with innovativeness, risk and trust. *Psychology & Marketing, 32*(8), 860–873.

Slade, E., Williams, M., Dwivedi, Y. K., & Piercy, N. (2015). Exploring consumer adoption of proximity mobile payments. *Journal of Strategic Marketing, 23*(3), 209–223.

Srivastav, U., & Gopalkrishnan, S. (2015). Impact of big data analytics on banking sector: Learning for Indianbanks. *Procedia Computer Science, 50*, 643–652.

TOO. (2015). Bank Muscat launches all-new, feature-rich mobile banking app. http://timesofoman.com/article/73867/Business/Bank-Muscat-launches-all-new-feature-rich-mobile-banking-app

Venkatesh, V., Morris, M. G., Davis, G. B., & Davis, F. D. (2003). User acceptance of information technology: Toward a unified view. *MIS Quarterly, 27*(3), 425–478.

World Bank. (2009). *Information and communications for development 2009: Extending reach and increasing impact*. Retrieved from http://live.worldbank.org/information-communications-technology-development

Waverman, L., Meschi, M., & Fuss, M. (2005). The impact of telecoms on economic growth in developing countries. *The Vodafone policy paper series, 2*(3), 10–24.

Zamfiroiu, A. (2014). Factors influencing the quality of mobile applications. *Informatica Economica, 18*(1), 131–139.

Zhou, T. (2011). An empirical examination of initial trust in mobile banking. *Internet Research, 21*(5), 527–540.

Sujeet Kumar Sharma is an Assistant Professor in the Department of Operations Management and Business Statistics in Sultan Qaboos University, Oman. Dr. Sharma earned his PhD in Statistics. His teaching and research interests include the areas of Business Analytics, Business Statistics, Structural Equation Modeling, Multivariate Data Analysis, Data Mining, Technology Acceptance Model, and Cricket Statistics. His research has been published in journals including ***Behavior and Information Technology, Information Systems Frontiers, Computers in Human Behavior, Management Research Review, Journal of Enterprise Information Management, INFO, Review of International Business and Strategy, Journal of Modeling in Management, Measurement, Journal of Indian Business Research, European Journal of Sports Science, and other reputed journals***. He has authored a book on computer-based numerical and statistical techniques.

Saeed Al-Muharrami is an Associate Professor of Banking and Finance at Sultan Qaboos University. He received his BSc in 1988 from University of Arizona, USA, his MBA in 1994 from Oregon State University, USA, and his PhD in 2005 from Cardiff University, UK. He has written three books and has published several scientific papers and publications. Besides his teaching and research duties, he was the Director of Humanities Research Center and the Dean of the College of Economics and Political Science. He was previously appointed as Fulbright Visiting Scholar at the International Monetary Fund in Washington, D.C., USA.

Part III
Digital Business

Chapter 8
Hyper-localizing e-Commerce Strategy: An Emerging Market Perspective

Nitish Singh and Brendan M. Keating

Abstract With the rise of global competition, multinationals are facing a decline in sales outside of their home regions as startups chip away at their dominance. One method of countering this trending decline is to embrace a hyper-localization e-commerce strategy, wherein unique locale-specific consumer segments are identified and then targeted to meet hyper-local needs and consumer demands. This piece identifies how organizations are developing hyper-localized strategies and leveraging local resources to deliver their product, services, and communications to the targeted emerging economies.

Keywords Hyper-localization · Globalization · Global e-commerce · Internet-based companies · Emerging market multinationals

8.1 Introduction

Today the forces of globalization and integration of global economies are creating a counter-trend toward burgeoning nationalism and are unleashing ethnocentric tendencies. This phenomenon is most visible on the international stage in the form of nationalist political movements, consumer ethnocentric demands, and countervailing currents of economic nationalism. A recent article in *The Economist* documents the decline of multinationals and cross-border trade activity (The Economist, 2017). The article shows that in 2016 multinationals' cross-border trade/investment declined by about 10–15%; this trend is further confirmed by the declining sales of Western multinationals outside their home regions (ibid). Many multinationals are

N. Singh (✉)
Department of International Business John Cook School of Business, Saint Louis University, Saint Louis, MO, USA
e-mail: nitish.singh@slu.edu

B. M. Keating
IntegTree LLC, Saint Louis, MO, USA
e-mail: Brendan.Keating@IntegTree.com

Y. K. Dwivedi et al. (eds.), *Emerging Markets from a Multidisciplinary Perspective*, Advances in Theory and Practice of Emerging Markets,
https://doi.org/10.1007/978-3-319-75013-2_8

struggling with enhancing and maintaining their global market share. Western multinationals, in particular, are facing tough competition from their local counterparts in several emerging economies. The rise in global competition is not only attributable to the rising consumer nationalistic feelings, but also to the leveling of the playing field between the established Western multinationals and the new multinationals from the emerging markets.

The Internet and its facilitation of global e-commerce are perhaps the greatest equalizer of power between established multinationals and their emerging market counterparts. The Internet reduces information asymmetry, weakens the barriers of market entry, and serves as a medium to help companies internationalize rapidly (Singh, 2012). In fact, the Internet-based companies or e-commerce companies (ECCs) are by their very nature global and can harness the power of the Internet to conduct global e-commerce from their inception (Shareef, Dwivedi, Williams, & Singh, 2009; Singh, Bartikowski, Dwivedi, & Williams, 2009; Singh & Kundu, 2002). Today Internet-based companies from emerging markets such as India, China, and Russia are thriving and have a strong hold in their local markets, with some examples including WeChat, Baidu, Alibaba, Flipkart, and Graband. These emerging market multinationals (ECCs) are seeing success, growing market share due to their hypersensitivity to local consumer needs and preferences. In India, ECCs such as Shaadi.com and BharatMatrimony.com are burgeoning because they cater to locale-specific marriage and matchmaking preferences unique to many Indian consumers; and Utrarichmatch.com goes even further by exploiting the niche to fulfill matrimonial expectations of the elite Indian class across the globe. If Western multinationals want to effectively compete with the growing number of emerging market ECCs, then they need to redefine their global strategy and think in terms of hyper-localization.

Hyper-localization (or extreme localizing) is an approach that moves beyond standardized marketing approaches and localization based on broad national market characteristics. Hyper-localization aims to identify, understand, and target unique locale-specific consumer segments or subcultures, within a country or region, and to then localize product/service, communications, and business models in order to deliver customized solutions to meet hyper-local needs and consumer demands. Hyper-localization also encompasses finding unique solutions to locale-specific business challenges and then delivering value in a local platter. Hyper-localization, in the e-commerce context, means going beyond merely translating the digital content to adapting the substance and style of the content/product/services to meet locale-specific needs of within-country niche markets; it entails appropriate considerations to geopolitical, cultural, social, economic, technical, and other business challenges. Uber recently adopted the hyper-localized approach when it redesigned its app icon to reflect the culture and style of countries and locales within which it is operating, with the goal to create unique designs not only for countries but also hundreds of sites across the world. Now Uber's app design for Mexico is inspired by Mexican pink and the patterns in the local tiles, while for Ireland, the design is inspired from Georgian architecture and the lush greens; and the app icon Uber uses in China incorporates red, while in India it is colored turquoise (Travis, 2016).

Another example of the hyper-localization trend is how Google India not only localizes in Hindi (the national language of India) but also in various regional languages. By leveraging neural machine translation, Google Translate technology can now translate between English and several regional Indian languages such as Bengali, Marathi, Tamil, Telugu, Gujarati, Punjabi, Malayalam, and Kannada (Mathur, 2017).

In this thought-piece, we specifically investigate how hyper-localization as a strategy can help marketers tap the huge market potential in emerging economies. While geopolitical barriers to market entry still loom large in emerging economies, companies can leverage the power of the Internet and e-commerce to develop hyper-localized strategies and gain market share. However, marketers need to appreciate within-country differences to identify and satisfy the needs of unique country-specific market niches and thus implement a successful hyper-localized marketing strategy. We attempt to provide insights on how ECCs from emerging economies are leveraging their local knowledge to develop products, services, communications, and business models to serve within-country niches. We specifically focus our analysis on emerging economies of Asia, with the hope it will help global marketers gain insights into how best to think of hyper-localization when targeting emerging economies.

8.2 Leveraging Local Resources

Flipkart, an Indian ECC, is currently battling Amazon.com by introducing new delivery practices, fulfillment robots, and the utilization of local repair technicians to fix smartphones, rather than absorb return costs (Rai, 2016). Competition enhancers aside, two major problems for businesses engaging in commerce in India are the shipping and handling expenses, with "[l]ast mile deliveries account[ing] for 30% of all logistics costs…" (Porwal, 2016). Hyper-localization may provide a solution – Flipkart has leveraged a hyper-localized delivery solution, with intimate knowledge of Mumbai, *dabbawallas*. These Indian hot lunch delivery providers are now also serving as Flipkart package delivery persons (Rai, 2016).

8.3 Mobile Apps

Technology and tech startups are often described as "disruptive" in relation to their seismic effect on markets and the ways in which individuals engage in one activity or another. In emerging markets, however, some tech startups are not so much market disrupting as they are market creating – hyper-localized market creating in particular. While companies like Flipkart vie against larger multinational e-commerce retailers for space in the emerging e-commerce market in a top-down approach, other companies are seizing the growing opportunity in emerging markets in more unique ways. Multiple tech companies are attempting to break into the mobile commerce market by leveraging the ubiquity of cell phones to tap into the hyper-localized commerce niche, centered around mobile platforms utilizing real-time location tracking via GPS.

Facebook Marketplace and Alipay in China allow individuals to list products for sale on a map nearby. While Facebook's application focuses on used goods, similar to Craigslist, Alipay allows individuals to sell items, and buyers can request services and make payments right from their app, similar to the popular app WeChat (Griffiths, 2016). ECCs centered around these hyper-localized apps are able to avoid logistical concerns entirely – they create a market, rather than directly sell goods or services.

Meanwhile, other companies tackle logistical concerns head on – Indian tech startup Dunzo leverages independent contractors who serve the client as concierge shoppers, to handle the burdens of fulfillment (Rao, 2016). From their app, customers can order and pay for goods or services, and Dunzo's contractors will then find, purchase, and deliver the product to the customer's doorstep (Bagchi, 2016). Dunzo is hyper-localized, being Bangalore focused, although the company plans to expand over time (ibid).

Each of these business models masterfully illustrates the ways in which businesses in emerging markets can tap into the emerging smartphone and e-commerce markets while leveraging local knowledge, consumer preferences, consumption patterns, and markets to compete with multinational retailers via the magic of hyper-localization.

8.4 A Unique Chinese Holiday: Singles' Day

Emerging markets with unestablished consumer bases provide a unique *tabula rasa* for retail experimentation. In more mature markets, holiday sales cycles are established and engrained into the fabric of society (e.g., Black Friday in the USA and Canada). However, in emerging markets, as new channels of commerce open up, forward thinking businesses are quickly capitalizing on their ability to mold consumer trends. Innovative ECCs that are able to leverage their marketing prowess and capitalize on culture-specific trends will find rich openings to create new sales opportunities in these emerging markets before consumer attitudes and patterns solidify as individuals settle into more patterned consumer behavior, something characteristic of more mature markets. One such example of this phenomenon is China's Singles' Day, November 11. As its name suggests, Singles' Day serves as a polar opposite of the commercial understanding of Valentine's Day – on Singles' Day, proud single Chinese celebrate their unattached status. Although the holiday has existed in smaller, less-commercialized respects for several decades (e.g., on university campuses), ECCs like Alibaba capitalized on its profit potential and turned Singles' Day into a sales jackpot. As the holiday has ballooned in size, in part due to Alibaba's efforts, the company even went so far as to file for six trademarks related to the term "Double 11," to hamstring its competitors' ability to actively participate in the holiday by limiting their marketing options (Reuters, 2014). In 2016 retailers selling on Alibaba were able to record $17.8 billion in gross merchandise volume, the growth of more than 32% from previous years (Ming, 2016). Now, thanks to the nurturing of Alibaba, this once uniquely Chinese holiday has spread, with consumers in 207 different countries taking advantage of the holiday sales (ibid).

8.5 Conclusion

Even a cursory analysis of emerging markets reveals a host of logistical, technological, and cultural issues associated with the advancement of e-commerce companies. Yet these issues need not be viewed as mere problems – as John Adams famously stated: "[e]very problem is an opportunity in disguise." And emerging markets allow businesses and entrepreneurs unprecedented opportunities to co-develop new consumer patterns, alongside a rapidly expanding customer base. In these markets, consumers are being exposed to a multitude of competing e-commerce options – no one retailer or even method (e.g., online versus mobile, concierge versus warehouse) is ubiquitous or dominant, while in more mature markets, there is something of an uphill battle to innovate. Consider, for example, that Amazon accounts for 43% of all US online retail sales according to Business Insider (BI Intelligence, 2017). Such logistical backbone, name recognition, and purchasing power create a kind of entry barrier in the e-commerce marketplace, and each year more "mom-and-pop" stores in the USA fall to the pricing and logistical might of Amazon.

But in emerging markets, consumers are now able to dip their toes into the water of e-commerce and develop their tastes and preferences, as a host of companies and technologies cater to them, and begin to tackle the logistical and technological hurdles of these locales. Clearly hyper-localization is a very powerful tool in this endeavor. Until the "problems" associated with emerging markets are resolved, consumers will benefit from the massive competition that gathers to vie for and to capture their consumer base – which only grows day by day as increasing numbers of their population make their way online.

References

Bagchi, S. (2016, August 30). Dunzo! How a hyperlocal concierge app is killing it in Bengaluru. *FactorDaily.com*. Accessed June 6, 2017, from https://factordaily.com/dunzo-hyperlocal-concierge-app-killing-bengaluru/

BI Intelligence. (2017, February 3). Amazon accounts for 43% of US online retail sales. *BusinessInsider.com*. Accessed June 5, 2017, from http://www.businessinsider.com/amazon-accounts-for-43-of-us-online-retail-sales-2017-2

Griffiths, T. (2016, October 17). Trend: hyper-localisation in 3 major apps. Facebook, Alipay and WeChat. *Medium.com*. Accessed June 4, 2017, from https://medium.com/half-a-world/trend-hyper-localisation-in-3-major-apps-facebook-alipay-and-wechat-4236eb195cc1

Mathur, N. (2017, April 25). Google Translate for 9 Indian languages, 11 more get keyboard support. *Livemint.com*. Accessed May 29, 2017, from http://www.livemint.com/Industry/XOK0qZSXHwJGPgFYbDN8bI/Google-launches-translator-for-9-Indian-languages-expands-s.html

Ming, C. (2016, November 11). Singles' day: Alibaba smashes records at world's largest online shopping event. *CNBC.com*. Accessed June 7, 2017, from http://www.cnbc.com/2016/11/11/singles-day-news-alibaba-poised-to-smash-records-at-worlds-largest-online-shopping-event.html

Porwal, M. (2016). 3 Major challenges faced by E-commerce companies in India. *LoginNextSolutions.com*. Accessed Jan 13, 2017, from https://loginextsolutions.com/blog/3-major-challenges-faced-by-e-commerce-companies-in-india/

Rai, S. (2016, July 18). India's Flipkart has an Amazon problem. *Bloomberg.com*. Accessed Jan 9, 2017, from https://www.bloomberg.com/news/articles/2016-07-18/india-s-flipkart-has-an-amazon-problem

Rao, M. (2016, August 31). A concierge startup steps in where Amazon and other ecommerce giants failed. *TechinAsia.com*. Accessed June 6, 2017, from https://www.techinasia.com/dunzo-goes-hyperlocal

Reuters. (2014, October 30). Alibaba plays trademark card to protect lead as China's $8 billion e-commerce spree nears. *Reuters.com*. Accessed June 4, 2017, from http://www.reuters.com/article/us-alibaba-group-jd-com-idUSKBN0IJ1KE20141030

Shareef, M. A., Dwivedi, Y. K., Williams, M. D., & Singh, N. (2009). *Proliferation of the Internet economy: E-Commerce for global adoption, resistance, and cultural evolution* (p. 263). Hershey, PA: Information Science Reference, IGI Global.

Singh, N. (2012). *Localization strategies for global e-business*. Cambridge, UK: Cambridge University Press.

Singh, N., Bartikowski, B. P., Dwivedi, Y. K., & Williams, M. D. (2009). Global megatrends and the web: Convergence of globalization, networks and innovation. *The DATA BASE for Advances in Information Systems, 40*(4), 14–27.

Singh, N., & Kundu, S. (2002). Explaining the growth of e-commerce corporations (ECCs): An extension and application of the eclectic paradigm. *Journal of International Business Studies, 33*(4), 679–697.

The Economist. (2017, January 28). The retreat of the global company. *Economist.com*. Accessed May 26, 2017, from http://www.economist.com/news/briefing/21715653-biggest-business-idea-past-three-decades-deep-trouble-retreat-global

Travis. (2016, February 2). Celebrating cities: A new look and feel for Uber. *Uber.com*. Accessed June 12, 2017, from https://newsroom.uber.com/celebrating-cities-a-new-look-and-feel-for-uber/

Nitish Singh is a professor of international business at St. Louis University, USA. He holds a Ph.D. in international business and marketing from St. Louis University, USA. He has published more than 60 academic papers in journals, such as JIBS, JBR, IMR, JIM, etc., and 4 books. His research spans cross-cultural issues, global e-business strategies, and sustainability.

Brendan M. Keating is vice president at IntegTree LLC, an ethics, compliance, and sustainability consulting company. He partnered with Dr. Singh in building the Certificate and Certification in Global Digital Marketing and Localization, offered by the University of North Carolina at Wilmington, and The Localization Institute, respectively. He serves as co-instructor for that program.

Chapter 9
Exploring E-Business in Indian SMEs: Adoption, Trends and the Way Forward

Vishnupriya Raghavan, Marya Wani, and Dolphy M. Abraham

Abstract We identify the key factors that influence the adoption and use of E-Business technologies by small and medium enterprises. Amongst the key influencers are owner-manager characteristics, technology factors, organizational factors and institutional influences. While the capabilities of technologies are an important driver, the other influencers play a key role as well. Owner-managers are the key facilitators. Organizational readiness reflects a firm's technological capabilities. SMEs also adopt technologies due to the pressure exerted by their key customers, competitors, government regulations, industry standards or suppliers. These institutional pressures are classified as mimetic, coercive and normative. Mimetic pressures cause SMEs to react to competitors' actions. Coercive pressures are those exerted by firms on which the SME is dependent. Normative pressures arise from the need to keep up with industry standards. We analyse these factors in the context of a rapidly growing E-Business sector in India.

Keywords E-Business · Institutional Influences · SME · Owner-Manager · Organizational Readiness

V. Raghavan (✉)
Manipal Global Education Services, Bangalore, India

M. Wani
Institute of Product Leadership, Bangalore, India

D. M. Abraham
Alliance University, Bangalore, India
e-mail: dolphy.abraham@alliance.edu.in

Y. K. Dwivedi et al. (eds.), *Emerging Markets from a Multidisciplinary Perspective*, Advances in Theory and Practice of Emerging Markets,
https://doi.org/10.1007/978-3-319-75013-2_9

9.1 Introduction

Businesses can reap significant benefits by adopting E-Business practices catalysed by modern technologies. It will help transform business models, gain competitive advantages and help reach out to a wider market. However, there seems to be little evidence that SMEs (*small and medium enterprises*) have used E-Business practices beyond basic functionalities like email. Two tectonic changes in the Indian economy will act as catalysts in the adoption of E-Business practices and technologies. One was the sudden demonetization of certain currency denominations. This caused a temporary shortage of physical currency forcing large-scale adoption of electronic payment modes (Dwivedi, 2016; Dwivedi, Slade, Rana, & Tamilmani, 2016) – almost 86% of cash in circulation was nullified (Rowlatt, 2016). The players in the mobile wallet business were the most profitable as they saw a traffic increase of 435 % and a 250 % increase in overall transactions and transaction value (Chakravorti, 2017). Second is the GST act that came into force from July 2017 with two primary intentions: to enable a transparent tax structure throughout the country and to enable seamless movement of goods and services across India (Nair, 2017). An implication of this is that a robust digital payment infrastructure must be present. It is important for SMEs to adopt E-Business technologies as digital payments can deliver a significant uplift to the profitability and growth for the sector. Improved customer service, cost reduction and the ability to service overseas markets are a few of the many benefits that the SMEs can experience with E-Business technologies.

E-Business assimilation and the resultant digitization of the economy are an important initiative in developing economies. In India, for example, SMEs contribute about 37.5% of the GDP (KPMG, 2017). The benefits of E-Business adoption and assimilation for SMEs are well known. A study of 504 SMEs (KPMG, 2017) in India found that E-Business assimilation leads to a higher profit growth (about two times faster than other SMEs who do not use E-Business), expansion across the country and city boundaries and higher rate of employment (SMEs using E-Business services employed five times more people compared to those that did not).

Even after measures to digitize India, a staggering 68% SMEs have still not adopted E-Business technologies, and these businesses are completely offline (KPMG, 2017). What plagues the adoption of E-Business technologies is a question that needs further investigation and a strong intent from the government to implement such a policy. This chapter looks into some of the key factors that influence the adoption and use of E-Business technologies amongst SMEs and the road ahead.

9.2 Small and Medium Enterprises (SMEs)

There are varying definitions of SME across the world. Definitions of SME can vary from country to country and within the same country. For instance, in a country like India as per the Micro, Small and Medium Enterprises Development Act 2006, enterprises are broadly classified into micro units, small units, medium units and large units depending on the investment in plant and machinery (Paramasivan & Selvam, 2013).

Different countries use different measures for defining small and medium enterprises (SMEs). Criteria to define SME include employment, investment or sales (Ayyagari, Beck, & Demirguc-Kunt, 2007). Some countries use employment as the measure, and some use this criterion and an additional criterion based on either the value of the firm's assets or the size of the revenues, typically denominated in the local currency (e.g. Nigeria, European Union, India, Malaysia). A notable exception is Cambodia where the revenue is measured in US dollars. With no formal consensus or categorization of what constitutes a SME (Curran & Blackburn, 2000) and with definitions that can change over a period, SME studies have employed varying definitions including employment, turnover and assets.

9.3 E-Business and SMEs

SMEs constitute between 96 and 99% of the total number of businesses in most *Organization for Economic Cooperation and Development* (*OECD*) countries (Scupola, 2002). The sector is considered as an important source of flexibility and innovation (OECD, 2002). The role of SMEs is further stressed in studies by Bharati & Chaudhury (2009) and Bharati (2010) that highlight that SMEs produce more patents per employee than large patenting firms and these patents are so significant that they are likely to be cited twice as many times as those of the patents of the large firms.

With the Indian economy expected to emerge as one of the leading economies in the world (expected to become a $5 trillion economy by 2025), there have been a number of initiatives by governments and associations alike to strengthen the backbone of the economy – the SME sector. The sector is touted to be a $ 25 billion market for emerging technologies by 2020. The SME council set up by NASSCOM and several policy interventions by the government are examples of initiatives to improve the business environment for the sector.

Much of the technology advances in the last two decades have been in the ability to process information and integrate business processes with the help of Internet and web-based technologies (Chen & Dwivedi, 2007; Chen, Papazafeiropoulou, & Dwivedi, 2010; Dwivedi & Papazafeiropoulou, 2009). Technology associated with E-Business practices in particular has enabled e-commerce practices such as online procurement and selling. It is viewed as an important tool in cost reduction, increasing customer satisfaction and building good relationships with business partners. Despite the many benefits, technology penetration has been low in the SME sector. This is particularly true of the Indian SME sector where less than 2% of the small-medium businesses are digitally engaged[1] (KPMG, 2017). E-Business capabilities across the four main aspects of business – communication, intelligence, commerce

[1] Digitally engaged: small and medium businesses using digital technology actively to enable business online by either selling on e-commerce websites or advertising online or listing on third-party portals.

and collaboration (Raymond & Bergeron, 2008) – can help reap maximum benefits for the firm.

- "E-communication" refers to the use of Internet and E-Business technologies to promote the firm and its products/services and includes online catalogues and websites designed to communicate amongst employees or with customers, suppliers, vendors and other business partners.
- "E-intelligence" refers to the ability by which the firm can scan its business environment to explore new product-market opportunities and to improve its operations and decision-making.
- "E-commerce" refers to the activities that are transactional in nature, i.e. encompassing all the activities of buying and selling via Internet and web-based technologies.
- The fourth form of E-Business capability is "e-collaboration" that helps the firm to link with its upstream and downstream business partners. It enables the firm in exchange of information with its trading partners and business partners to collaborate in the design and development of products and services through the different stages of their life cycle.

In general, organizations realize increased benefits with higher levels of integration (Daniel & Grimshaw, 2002) because of increased assimilation of E-Business technologies. Limited use or penetration prevents organizations from reaping the full benefits of an innovation, particularly true of E-Business (Eikebrokk & Olsen, 2007). Staged models of adoption of innovations suggest that the organizational assimilation of E-Business technologies follows a sequence of stages that begin with email for communication and progress through transactional processing for online banking and online buying, e-commerce and finally transformation of the organization. Contingent role models have been viewed as a better alternative to staged models and have been used to study technology adoption. Contingent role models are of the premise that E-Business can be approached in many ways depending on the specific business processes as required by the organization (Alonso-Mendo & Fitzgerald, 2005). This perspective assumes that an organization determines the combination of applications that best suits its particular business context and strategy (ibid). Such approaches see change as a reaction to market demands and external pressure and not as a predetermined end point as viewed by the staged models.

However, the adoption of E-Business does not guarantee continued deployment or mean widespread or intense use across different business functions of the organizations. SMEs tend to leap over one or several stages in e-commerce adoption (Lefebvre, Lefebvre, Elia, & Boeck, 2005), and some abandon following a short period of adoption despite growing functionality and benefits (Molla et al. 2006). This raises the question if technology adoption follows a linear fashion and affirms that these models do not take into the account the heterogeneity of the sector. It is worth noting that in the context of SMEs, many firms do not progress beyond the initial levels.

The true potential of E-Business technologies can be realized only when firms recognize the need for business transformation and understand all the benefits that E-Business practices can bring about. In the context of SMEs, the owner-manager plays an important role in technology adoption decisions, in addition to forces external to the organization. Increased levels of assimilation are also largely associated with the strategic intent of the firm (Ramsey & McCole, 2005). SMEs may be expending their limited resources to implement applications without a complete understanding of strategic role of the technology within their organizations (Chong & Pervan, 2007). Opportunities for E-Business transformation must be within the context of long-term vision for improved business performance.

9.4 Influencing Factors

A range of factors may affect SMEs' decisions to invest in E-Business technologies. Implementation and successful management of technology and progression occur with the appropriate combination of both exogenous and endogenous factors of the firm (Ramsey & McCole, 2005). Adopting of E-Business practices largely depends on the support provided by the owner-manager of the firm. This support is not merely an approval for adoption or implementation of new technologies but an active support with a long-term vision that will transcend throughout all levels of the firm. The influence from the external environment on E-Business decisions cannot be underestimated. It is imperative that studies include a combination of factors including owner-manager characteristics and technological, organizational and environmental characteristics to investigate the drivers and inhibitors of E-Business in SMEs.

9.4.1 Owner-Manager Characteristics

Organizations that scan their business environment for technology-related practices are more likely to adopt and try out innovations. For many SMEs, decision to exploit a new technology is dependent upon how well the owner-manager is aware of the changes that happen in the industry, captures the demands of the customers and interprets and reacts to signals from the technological as well as environmental contexts (Uwizeyemungu & Raymond, 2011). This requires two enabling conditions to exist:

1. Hashim (2007) opines that the decision to adopt technologies earlier or later depends mostly on the IS knowledge of the owner-managers. Owner-managers may not be keen on adopting sophisticated technologies if they are unfamiliar with the basic ones (Reynolds & Bopaya, 1994). Also, their levels of knowledge and experience of IS have a positive impact on perceptions, attitudes and behavioural intentions that would provide the needed push to make use of the technology (Mao & Palvia, 2008).

2. The willingness of the owner-manager to make available financial resources, technical support, employee training, and removal of any other barriers is key to promoting organizational capability. Organizational capability is found to have a significant effect on E-Business implementation success (Lin, 2008), and this wholly depends upon the owner-manager who should develop and nurture a climate that is conducive to learning so that E-Business activities that are initiated can get routinized and accelerate further development.

In short, it is the owner-manager that provides and ensures the "facilitating conditions" (Uwizeyemungu & Raymond, 2011) for technology adoption and use.

9.4.2 Technological Factors

Technological factors are considered important for assimilation of E-Business technologies. Diffusion of innovation theory (DOI) (Rogers, 1995) identifies five factors as influencing the rate of diffusion of an innovation. They are:

- The relative advantage over present ways of meeting the need
- Its compatibility with the current practices and values
- Its complexity (the degree to which the new technology is easy to use and learn)
- Its trialability referring to adopting the technology on a trial basis if it can be tried out before the actual commitment and implementation
- Its observability indicating as to how well the features of the technology including its benefits can be communicated

All of these five factors have been studied extensively in E-Business studies as the DOI framework encompasses innovations, adoption decision-making processes and the social context in which adoption occurs (Parker & Castleman, 2009).

Since E-Business is a type III innovation (Swanson, 1994), considered to be a continuous process of incorporating e-enablement of business activities thereby bringing organizational transformation, organizational and environmental factors cannot be ignored (Lee & Cheung, 2004). Focusing only on the technological features of an innovation may not be sufficient to explain subsequent assimilation and continued use, especially in the case of E-Business technologies.

9.4.3 Organizational Factors

For an innovation such as e-enabling of businesses, it is important that the organization has the necessary attributes to ensure sustained use after initial adoption. Organizational factors include financial readiness, technological readiness and external support. E-Business technologies provide a wide range of functionalities from online business processes to sharing databases with external partners. Assessing an organization's readiness becomes much more important when firms plan to implement E-Business technologies to link with its customers and business partners. Organizational readiness reflects a firm's technological capabilities and is a significant influencer of assimilation of E-Business technologies and practices (Alam, Ali, & Jani, 2011).

9.4.4 Institutional Influences

The influence of the macroenvironment should not be underestimated. Environmental uncertainty does exert some pressure on SMEs to e-enable their business functions. Most SMEs adopt technologies due to the pressure exerted by their key customers, competitors, government regulations, industry standards or suppliers (Chwelos, Benbasat, & Dexter, 2001).

It seems rational to believe that organizations exert influences on each other as they operate in the business environment consisting of other entities (e.g. trading partners, vendors, suppliers, customers, agencies, governments). This is especially true of SMEs that are forced to comply with demands of their larger partners who may pursue different strategies to induce adoption of E-Business technologies.

The three types of isomorphic pressures exerted on organizations are, namely, coercive, normative and mimetic pressures. Mimetic pressure can be attributed to competitors in uncertain environments (Basaglia, Caporarello, Magni, & Pennarola, 2009). Organizations react to competitors' actions to survive and maintain competitive advantage. Mimetic pressures cause the structures and actions of an organization to change over time and adjust to the structures and actions of other organizations, which are at a similar position in the common environment. Competitive pressure has been found to be a significant predictor of adoption of E-Business practices and technologies in both developed countries such as the UK (Daniel & Grimshaw, 2002) and South Korea (Joo & Kim, 2004) and developing countries such as Vietnam (Van Huy, Rowe, Truex, & Huynh, 2012), Thailand (Lertwongsatien & Wongpinunwatana, 2003) and Brunei (Looi, 2005).

Coercive pressure is the pressure exerted on the organization by those on which the firm is dependent. This includes government, professional regulatory agencies (Harcourt, Lam, & Harcourt, 2005), governmental entities, suppliers (Zorn, Flanagin, & Shoham, 2011), customers, parent corporations and other key constituents (Teo, Wei, & Benbasat, 2003). The regulatory environment is one of the important factors of e-commerce adoption in developing countries (Zhu, Dong, Xu, & Kraemer, 2006). The role played by the government and the support extended by governments have been found to significantly influence E-Business technology adoption in developing countries (Sanayei & Rajabion, 2009; Van Huy et al., 2012).

Trading partners could be a dominant customer or a supplier pushing the firm to implement or increase the use of relationship-specific information systems. Adoption of ERP in many manufacturing companies across India and China stands as evidence to pressure from trading partners/parent body. Larger organizations or parent body can exert pressure on its smaller suppliers to follow a specific technology for increased efficiency and to streamline operations. The small sector may become marginalized and lose business if they do not keep pace with the changes in technology. With suppliers or trading partners already using E-Business practices, there is motivation for the SME sector to make adequate investments needed for adoption and continued use. The impetus for adopting E-Business-related technologies is a combination of choosing to be innovative while maintaining competitive advantage.

Normative pressure can stem from the need to keep up with industry norms, competitor's moves and the fear of being "singled out" amongst peer firms. The need to follow the other firms that use E-Business practices and the need to have a cutting-edge image in front of its competitors and stakeholders push the organization to adopt E-Business technologies. Researchers have termed these phenomena as bandwagon theories (Abrahamson & Rosenkopf, 1993) and theories of fads (Abrahamson, 1991). In short, the need to maintain legitimacy and stakeholder support can lead organizations to adopt E-Business technologies. However, this copying or imitation does not seem coerced by any larger organization or superior power, nor is it conscious. Attitudes, behaviours and practices demonstrated for a long time by most actors in the same social context become so legitimized as the "right" way things are done that individuals often come to believe that these practices and behaviours indicate the "only" way to do things (Jan, Lu, & Chou, 2012).

The decisions of SMEs to adopt E-Business technologies are also largely dependent on the benefits they might obtain. It is important for the user to feel that the technologies are essential to complete a particular task and appreciate the benefits from using them. In addition to the owner-manager being a prime driver, other potential influencing factors are the customers, suppliers, competitors, government and regulatory bodies.

9.5 Lessons for SMEs and Researchers

For technologies to be adopted and diffused, determinants and barriers of technology adoption have to be well understood not only by the owner-managers of firms and governments but also by those who innovate, make and implement such technologies (Oliveira & Martins, 2008). First, the owner-manager of the firm is the driver of change and has to champion adoption of E-Business practices. Second, the greatest benefits of adopting E-Business practices come with a strategic intent that views technologies as an investment rather than a cost.

New research will help shed light on the current E-Business practices, particularly in emerging markets such as India, and provide guidelines on the future development of E-Business technologies. Studies on how E-Business assimilation will help the governments and SMEs to understand barriers of such technology adoption and help understand ways in which such barriers can be removed to pave the way for complete digitization of the economy in the long run. Such studies will help the SME sector to make informed decisions about the "combination" of E-Business applications that are appropriate for them and will help the supply side of E-Business technology companies to customize products to better suit the specific context and business needs of the sector. While noting that there is a significant opportunity in adopting E-Business technologies by the SME sector, further collaboration is needed amongst researchers, policy makers, supply side of the technologies, SMEs and industry practitioners to bridge the gap. It is also important to explore what role is played by adoption of new technologies and applications such as social media and social commerce (Abed, Dwivedi, & Williams, 2015a, 2015b; Abed, Dwivedi, & Williams, 2016) on E-Business and e-commerce adoption and use by SMEs.

9.6 Conclusion

SMEs form the backbone of a country's economy, especially the emerging economies. A research report published by McKinsey & Company suggests that digital finance alone, which is just one element of E-Business technology, can increase the GDPs of all emerging economies by 6%, which amounts to $3.7 trillion dollars by the year 2025 (Manyika, Lund, Singer, White, & Berry, 2016). The non-participation of SMEs in e-finance, for instance, results in expensive and scarce credit sources. This affects SMEs' performance and that of the economies that they are a part of. Financial non-inclusion makes the economy as a whole suffer.

One positive sign for assimilation of E-Business practices in the emerging economies is that governments of these countries are now using interventions to expedite the adoption of E-Business and digital technologies using both mandatory and persuasive methods. In India, the government is implementing mandatory and voluntary efforts to digitize businesses especially in the SME sector. Amongst the non-mandatory procedures are training students in digital and E-Business skills, awareness campaigns and easier tax filing procedures, thus making it easy to access government services.

As SMEs begin to see the benefit from this initiative, the adoption of such practices and technologies will only accelerate.

Acknowledgements The authors would like to acknowledge the valuable contribution of Bhaskaran Srinivasan, Director Academics, Manipal Global Education Services. We highly appreciate his review towards improvement of quality, coherence and content presentation in the chapter.

References

Abed, S., Dwivedi, Y. K., & Williams, M. D. (2015a). Social media as a bridge to E-commerce adoption in SMEs: A systematic literature review. *The Marketing Review, 15*(1), 39–57.

Abed, S., Dwivedi, Y. K., & Williams, M. D. (2015b). SMEs' adoption of e-commerce using social media in a Saudi Arabian context: A systematic literature review. *International Journal of Business Information Systems, 19*(2), 159–179.

Abed, S., Dwivedi, Y. K., & Williams, M. D. (2016). Social commerce as a business tool in Saudi Arabia's SMEs. *International Journal of Indian Culture and Business Management, 13*(1), 1–19.

Abrahamson, E. (1991). Managerial fads and fashions: The diffusion and rejection of innovations. *Academy of Management Review, 16*(3), 586–612.
Abrahamson, E., & Rosenkopf, L. (1993). Institutional and competitive bandwagons: Using mathematical modeling as a tool to explore innovation diffusion. *Academy of Management Review, 18*(3), 487–517.
Alam, S. S., Ali, M. Y., & Jani, M. F. M. (2011). An empirical study of factors affecting electronic commerce adoption among SMEs in Malaysia. *Journal of Business Economics and Management, 12*(2), 375–399.
Alonso-Mendo, F. A., & Fitzgerald, G. (2005). A multidimensional framework for SME e-business progression. *Journal of Enterprise Information Management, 18*(6), 678–696.
Ayyagari, M., Beck, T., & Demirguc-Kunt, A. (2007). Small and medium enterprises across the globe. *Small Business Economics, 29*(4), 415–434.
Basaglia, S., Caporarello, L., Magni, M., & Pennarola, F. (2009). Environmental and organizational drivers influencing the adoption of VoIP. *Information Systems and e-Business Management, 7*(1), 103–118.
Bharati, P. (2010). IT Adoption in Small and Medium-Sized Enterprises: The Role of Knowledge Acquisition, in Proceedings of the 16th Americas Conference on Information Systems, D. E. Leidner and J. J. Elam (eds.), Lima, Peru, August 12-15.
Bharati, P. and Chaudhury, A. (2009), SMEs and competitiveness: the role of information systems, *International Journal of E-Business Research, 5*(1), 1–9
Chakravorti,B.(2017,March14).EarlylessonsfromIndia'sdemonetizationexperiment.RetrievedJune 28, 2017, from https://hbr.org/2017/03/early-lessons-from-indias-demonetization-experiment
Chen, H., & Dwivedi, Y. K. (2007). Conceptualising the relationship between integration needs and integrations technologies adoption: Comparing a case of SME with a large organization. *International Journal of Management and Enterprise Development, 4*(4), 459–476.
Chen, H., Papazafeiropoulou, A., & Dwivedi, Y. K. (2010). Maturity of supply chain integration within small and medium size enterprises (SMES): Lessons from the Taiwan IT manufacturing sector. *International Journal of Management and Enterprise Development, 9*(4), 325–347.
Chong, S., & Pervan, G. (2007). Factors influencing the extent of deployment of electronic commerce for small-and medium sized enterprises. *Journal of Electronic Commerce in Organizations (JECO), 5*(1), 1–29.
Chwelos, P., Benbasat, I., and Dexter, A. S. Empirical Test of an EDI Adoption Model (2001), *Information Systems Research, 12*(3), 304–321.
Curran, J., & Blackburn, R. (2000). *Researching the small enterprise*. Sage. London
Daniel, E. M., & Grimshaw, D. J. (2002). An exploratory comparison of electronic commerce adoption in large and small enterprises. *Journal of Information Technology, 17*(3), 133–147.
Dwivedi,Y.K.(2016).Indiatakingastepontheroadtocashlesseconomy.*TheConversation*.Available at https://theconversation.com/india-taking-a-step-on-the-road-to-cashless-economy-70309
Dwivedi, Y. K., & Papazafeiropoulou, A. (2009). Editorial: Knowledge management and enterprise systems adoption by SMEs. *Journal of Enterprise Information Management, 22*(1/2), 5–9.
Dwivedi, Y. K., Slade, E., Rana, N. P., & Tamilmani, K. (2016). How getting rid of 'black money' has driven a digital treasure hunt in India. *The Conversation*. Available at https://theconversation.com/how-getting-rid-of-black-money-has-driven-a-digital-treasure-hunt-in-india-69013
Eikebrokk, T. R., & Olsen, D. H. (2007). An empirical investigation of competency factors affecting E-business success in European SMEs. *Information Management, 44*(4), 364–383.
Harcourt, M., Lam, H., & Harcourt, S. (2005). Discriminatory practices in hiring: Institutional and rational economic perspectives. *The International Journal of Human Resource Management, 16*(11), 2113–2132.
Hashim, J. (2007). Information communication technology (ICT) adoption among SME owners in Malaysia. *International Journal of Business and Information, 2*(2), 221–240.
Jan, P. T., Lu, H. P., & Chou, T. C. (2012). The adoption of e-Learning: An institutional theory perspective. *Turkish Online Journal of Educational Technology-TOJET, 11*(3), 326–343.
Joo, Y. B., & Kim, Y. G. (2004). Determinants of corporate adoption of e-marketplace: An innovation theory perspective. *Journal of Purchasing and Supply Management, 10*(2), 89–101.

KPMG. (2017, January). Impact of internet and digitisation on SMBs in India. Retrieved June 28, 2017, from https://home.kpmg.com/in/en/home/insights/2017/01/impact-of-internet-and-digitisation.html

Lee, M. K., & Cheung, C. M. (2004). Internet retailing adoption by small-to-medium sized enterprises (SMEs): A multiple-case study. *Information Systems Frontiers, 6*(4), 385–397.

Lefebvre, L. A., Lefebvre, É., Elia, E., & Boeck, H. (2005). Exploring B-to-B e-commerce adoption trajectories in manufacturing SMEs. *Technovation, 25*(12), 1443–1456.

Lertwongsatien, C., & Wongpinunwatana, N. (2003). E-commerce adoption in Thailand: An empirical study of small and medium enterprises (SMEs). *Journal of Global Information Technology Management, 6*(3), 67–83.

Lin, H. F. (2008). Empirically testing innovation characteristics and organizational learning capabilities in E-Business implementation success. *Internet Research, 18*(1), 60–78.

Looi, H. C. (2005). E-commerce adoption in Brunei Darussalam: A quantitative analysis of factors influencing its adoption. *Communications of the Association for Information Systems, 15*(1), 3.

Manyika, J., Lund, S., Singer, M., White, O., & Berry, C. (2016, September). How digital finance could boost growth in emerging economies. Retrieved June 28, 2017, from http://www.mckinsey.com/global-themes/employment-and-growth/how-digital-finance-could-boost-growth-in-emerging-economies

Mao, E., & Palvia, P. (2008). Exploring the effects of direct experience on IT use: An organizational field study. *Information Management, 45*(4), 249–256.

Molla, A., Heeks, R., & Balcells, I. (2006). Adding clicks to bricks: a case study of E-Commerce adoption by a Catalan small retailer. *European Journal of Information Systems, 15*(4), 424–438.

Nair, A. (2017, January 11). GST coupled with digitisation will make Indian economy cleaner, bigger: Arun Jaitley. Retrieved June 28, 2017, from http://indianexpress.com/article/business/economy/gst-coupled-with-digitisation-will-make-indian-economy-cleaner-bigger-arun-jaitley-4469211/

OECD. (2002). *OECD small and medium enterprise outlook*. Paris, France: Author.

Oliveira, T., & Martins, M. F. O. (2008). Determinants of information technology diffusion: A study at the firm level for Portugal. *The Electronic Journal Information Systems Evaluation, 11*(1), 27–34. available online at www.ejise.com.

Paramasivan, C., & Selvam, P. M. (2013). Progress and performance of micro, small and medium Enterprises in India. *International Journal of Management Studies, 2*(4), 11–22

Parker, C. M., & Castleman, T. (2009). Small firm E-business adoption: A critical analysis of theory. *Journal of Enterprise Information Management, 22*(1/2), 167–182.

Ramsey, E., & McCole, P. (2005). E-business in professional SMEs: The case of New Zealand. *Journal of Small Business and Enterprise Development, 12*(4), 528–544.

Raymond, L., & Bergeron, F. (2008). Enabling the business strategy of SMEs through E-Business capabilities: A strategic alignment perspective. *Industrial Management & Data Systems, 108*(5), 577–595.

Reynolds, A., & Bopaya, B. (1994). Challenges facing information technology to support world class manufacturing. *Computers in Industry, 28*, 163–165.

Rogers, E. M. (1995). *Diffusion of innovations*. Simon and Schuste. New York.

Rowlatt, J. (2016). *Why India wiped out 86% cash overnight?* Retrieved from http://www.bbc.com/news/world-asia-india-37974423

Sanayei, A., & Rajabion, L. (2009). Critical successful factors contributing to E-Commerce adoption among Iranian SMEs. *International Journal of Information Science and Management, 7*(2), 57–66A.

Scupola, A. (2002). Adoption issues of business-to-business internet commerce in European SMEs. Proceedings of the 35th annual Hawaii International conference on systems sciences (HICSS). Hawaii, USA

Swanson, E. B. (1994). Information systems innovation among organizations. *Management Science, 40*(9), 1069–1092.

Teo, H. H., Wei, K. K., & Benbasat, I. (2003). Predicting intention to adopt interorganizational linkages: An institutional perspective. *MIS Quarterly, 27*(1), 19–49.

Uwizeyemungu, S., & Raymond, L. (2011). Information technology adoption and assimilation: Towards a research framework for service sector SMEs. *Journal of Service Science and Management, 4*(2), 141–157.

Van Huy, L., Rowe, F., Truex, D., & Huynh, M. Q. (2012). An empirical study of determinants of E-Commerce adoption in SMEs in Vietnam: An economy in transition. *Journal of Global Information Management, 20*(3), 23–54.

Zhu, K., Dong, S., Xu, S. X., & Kraemer, K. L. (2006). Innovation diffusion in global contexts: Determinants of post-adoption digital transformation of European companies. *European Journal of Information Systems, 15*(6), 601–616.

Zorn, T., Flanagin, A., & Shoham, M. D. (2011). Institutional and non-institutional influences on information and communication technology adoption and use among non-profit organizations. *Human Communication Research, 37*(1), 1–33.

Vishnupriya Raghavan has a PhD in Information Systems and Operations. She also holds Master's degrees in Mathematics and Information Systems. Her research interests lie in e-business, user experience design and interaction, social media and e-Learning. Prior to joining as Head of programs in Manipal Global Academy of Information Technology, she was the Director of rograms Programs at Institute of Product Leadership. She has worked with Omnikron Systems, Chicago and Calisys, India.

Marya Wani has a PhD in Information Systems and Operations. She also holds a Master's in Business Administration. She is the director of research and head of programmes at the Institute of Product Leadership. Her research interest lies in the areas of information systems strategy, user experience design and measurement, social media, social network analysis and e-Learning. Prior to joining Institute of Product Leadership, Dr. Wani was on the faculty at International School of Management Excellence, Bangalore Management Academy and Alliance University.

Dolphy Abraham earned his PhD from the Joseph M. Katz Graduate School of Business, University of Pittsburgh. His research interests are in the area of knowledge management, social network analytics and information systems strategy. Prior to joining Alliance University, Dr. Abraham was on the faculty at Loyola Marymount University, Los Angeles, and St. Joseph's College of Business Administration, Bangalore.

Chapter 10
Opportunities and Challenges of Augmented Reality Shopping in Emerging Markets

Salma S. Abed

Abstract Augmented reality (AR) is one of the newly emerging technologies that has ability to completely revolutionise the world as we see it and the manner in which the products are sold and purchased. It has a wide range of applications from entertainment and education through to the healthcare sector, architecture and more. The technology began to be used in applications in the 1990s but was first developed in the 1960s. Over the years, especially with the penetration of smartphone devices, AR has seen far higher use in applications. The major advantage of AR is in the field of the shopping experience of online product buyers. In this study, an overview of the field of AR is presented, comprising definitions of AR, a historical overview of AR and the presence of AR in emerging markets and shopping and marketing in emerging markets with the help of AR tools and the applications. This study also discusses the opportunities and the challenges faced by augmented reality in these emerging markets.

Keywords Augmented reality · Virtual reality · Emerging markets · Shopping

10.1 Introduction

New computer applications are developing rapidly as computing power increases and the size of computers decreases, allowing access to online resources at all times (Abed, Dwivedi, & Williams, 2015). This development has helped the development and spread of novel applications like augmented reality. Through augmented reality (AR), it is possible to incorporate virtual information in the physical environment of an individual in the form of the existing information in the individual's

S. S. Abed (✉)
Department of Management Information Systems, College of Business (COB), King Abdulaziz University, Rabigh, Saudi Arabia
e-mail: sabid@kau.edu.sa

Y. K. Dwivedi et al. (eds.), *Emerging Markets from a Multidisciplinary Perspective*, Advances in Theory and Practice of Emerging Markets,
https://doi.org/10.1007/978-3-319-75013-2_10

surroundings (Brohm, Domurath, Glanz-Chanos, & Grunert, 2017). This process is achieved by software that supplies the real world with objects generated by the computer, which appear in the surroundings just as real objects do. This allows an individual to interact with these objects to gain information, collaborate with other individuals and resolve queries. Through AR, it is possible to create next-generation reality-based interfaces (Alimamy, Deans, & Gnoth, 2017). AR is in fact already in use in laboratories, industries and the consumer markets of the world.

Augmented reality has been employed in many diverse fields, including advertising campaigns, education, video gaming and the arts (Brohm et al., 2017). One of the main applications of the technology is in the field of commerce, where it can be used to develop virtual previews of products so customers may review what they can buy before making purchasing decisions, as in, for example, IKEA's product catalogue (Raska & Richter, 2017). Another example is that of Botta Design, which has taken up AR to allow previews of their Botta 24 model watch by utilising an iOS application. In another project, *National Geographic* utilised augmented reality to bring to life thousands of animal species that have gone extinct, placing them in modern locations such as shopping centres to give people the chance to interact with virtual dinosaurs in familiar contexts. Using the same kinds of ideas and concepts, augmented reality is enriching the experience of shopping.

In this chapter, a detailed introduction to augmented reality has been provided. In the next section, augmented reality is defined before a historical overview of augmented reality is presented along with a description of augmented reality in emerging markets. After this, an overview of shopping and marketing with augmented reality in emerging markets is given, as well as a description of the applications of augmented reality in the commercial context. Finally, opportunities and challenges for augmented reality shopping in emerging markets are explored and conclusions drawn.

10.2 Augmented Reality: Definitions

The definition of augmented reality is based on the concept of virtual reality (VR). Through the virtual reality concept, it is possible to create an artificial environment which an individual can explore with the help of technology that stimulates the senses (Sapientnitro: Virtual Reality: Taking an Emerging Technology Mainstream, 2016). Augmented reality is also based on developing an interactive environment, but it aims to add to the existing environment rather than developing a completely artificial environment (Alimamy et al., 2017). Several researchers have defined augmented reality from different perspectives. Though there is conformity among international research communities regarding the different aspects that are part of augmented reality, arrived at after a series of international conferences, there remain differences between researchers in terms of opinion and the nomenclature related to this technology. For the purposes of this study, the definitions provided by (Azuma, 1997; Azuma et al., 2001) are followed, which indicate that AR combines real information with computer-generated information in a real environment in real time, combining virtual objects with physical ones. AR could also be explained as the broader concept of 'mixed reality', in which simulations predominately take place in the virtual domain and not in the real world (Yim, Chu, & Sauer, 2017).

It has been indicated (Klopfer & Sheldon, 2010) that it is not possible to define AR in a restricted way. The term could be utilised for any technology that purposefully blends real and virtual environments. Thus, AR has been defined (Klopfer & Squire, 2008; p. 205) as 'a situation in which a real world context is dynamically overlaid with coherent location or context-sensitive virtual information'. Thus, augmented reality could provide a technology-mediated immersive user experience, in which virtual and real worlds are blended (Klopfer & Sheldon, 2010) and user engagement and interactions are augmented. It is important to define AR in a broad sense for educators and designers, as it can be created and implemented utilising a wide range of technologies including desktop computers, handheld devices, head-mounted displays, etc. (Brohm et al., 2017): AR is not restricted to any single form of technology. It exploits the affordances that are present in the real world by supplying additional information which is contextual in nature and augments the user's experience of reality (Klopfer & Sheldon, 2010).

In this section, the definitions and concept of AR have been presented. In the following section, a historical overview of the complete technology is provided.

10.3 Historical Overview

Though the term 'augmented reality' was first coined in the early 1990s, functional AR systems date back to the 1960s, when a mechanically tracked 3D see-through head-worn display was first developed by Ivan Sutherland and colleagues in 1968. Through this display, it was possible for the user to see information generated by the computer mixed with physical objects like, in this case, the signs present on the walls of the laboratory. Over the following few years, research was carried out which aimed to generate graphical information from computers, and the field of computer graphics flourished (Furness, 1986). In the late 1970s, photorealistic computer-generated images became the main centre for research, and with the advancements that were made in tracking, hopes for the development of the perfect environment for simulation ran high.

Over the last few decades, several works have been produced in the field of AR as a research activity. In 1997, the field was defined (Azuma, 1997) along with explanation of its problems, summarising the advancements that had been made in this technology up to that point. Since then, the growth and progress of AR have been remarkable. Several workshops started to take place in the late 1990s, such as the International Workshop and Symposium on Augmented Reality, the International Symposium on Mixed and Augmented Reality and the Designing Augmented Reality Environments workshop. Further, it was during the late 1990s that well-funded organisations were formed which focused on the development of this technology, like the Mixed Reality Systems Lab (Zhang, Navab, & Liou, 2000).

In this section, a brief historical review of AR has been presented. In the next section, developments that have taken place in AR technology in emerging markets are described.

10.4 Augmented Reality in Emerging Markets

In 2016, a global study was conducted regarding evaluation of the interest and awareness of consumers as related to augmented reality, comprising more than 2500 people spread across five different countries. The study indicated that the user base of existing platforms has a high level of interest, comprising predominantly young consumers, suggesting that the younger generation will guide AR adoption. The survey found that 47% of the respondents felt they were very or extremely excited to utilise AR technologies. In emerging economies like India and China, consumers are extremely happy and excited, as 64% and 66% of the respondents expressed their desire to use the technology (Sapientnitro: Virtual Reality: Taking an Emerging Technology Mainstream, 2016). In fact, the democratisation of technologies is expected to grow not just in affluent and mature markets but also in emerging economies where the penetration of the smartphone technologies has been very high (Wilson, 2017).

Early signs of a bright future for this technology can be witnessed in China. The Chinese government is heavily invested in large technology companies, and there has been a dramatic rise in this technology in certain consumer segments (Koytcheva, 2017). A study that took place in 2016 (Virtual Reality Technology in China, 2016) found that AR-related revenues in China grew by 372.2% in the year 2016 to RMB850 million ($136.5 million), reaching a peak of RMB2 billion ($321.1 million) in 2017. Furthermore, shipments of AR and VR devices from China have reached as high as 480,000 units in the year 2016, and this is projected to grow through 2017 and 2018 (Virtual Reality Technology in China, 2016). As the Chinese government is eager to increase domestic consumption and assist the development of home-grown technologies, it is moving fast to develop the domestic AR industry and set the country on the course of those nations that can be considered early adopters of the technology. For this purpose, major players in Chinese industry have scaled up investment in AR technologies, including development of AR hardware, software and platforms upon which AR technology could be installed. According to surveys, young Chinese people, mainly those born in the 1980s and 1990s, are most interested in utilising AR technology (Virtual Reality Technology in China, 2016).

The worldwide revenues from the AR/VR market are assumed to reach $162 billion by the year 2020, as per the findings of the Worldwide Semi-Annual Augmented and Virtual Reality Spending Guide, published by International Data Corp. (IDC). In recent years, AR and VR technology has made developments in different sectors including health care, gaming, education, media and online shopping (Violino, 2016).

This section contained an overview of augmented reality in emerging markets. A brief description of shopping and marketing with augmented reality in emerging markets will be presented in the next section.

10.5 Shopping and Marketing with Augmented Reality in Emerging Markets

There has been rapid development in shopping that utilises AR, with huge growth in the markets in terms of advertisements and marketing. However, there are problems faced by the technology as it is still in the early stages of development and regular changes are still being made. In India and China, it has been found that personal and daily use of AR could support routine activities like sending e-mails and communicating through mobile phones (Greenwood et al., 2016). Further, with the help of location-aware overlays, it is possible to provide navigational guidance and allow individuals to store personal information related to specific locations. Furthermore, it is possible to get a unified control interface for the different types of applications that are present in the home. Such personal platforms could have great benefits for direct marketing agencies. Additionally, with the help of this technology, it will be possible for stores to offer virtual coupons to passing consumers, and the development of virtual billboards that advertise products based on personal choices would be easier, and virtual 3D product prototypes could pop up in the consumers' eyewear (Raska & Richter, 2017). Moreover, AR could be built to integrate with the retailer's portal, allowing them to leverage product visualisation, which provides value to shoppers (Greenwood et al., 2016).

This section has given a background in shopping and marketing with augmented reality in emerging markets. An overview of the applications of augmented reality in the commercial context will be presented in the next section.

10.6 Applications of Augmented Reality in the Commercial Context

There are a number of applications of augmented reality in the commercial context, some of which can be summarised as follows:

10.6.1 Mobile Coupons

Mobile coupons have recently become a propensity among clients: previously, it was an impractical dream to be able to go to a retail location and have all applicable coupon bargains sent straight to their cellphones. Now, the portable coupon has become an essential instrument. With the improvement of AR innovation, clients are noticeably equipped for getting great local deals around their specific location (Jackson, Angermann, & Meier, 2011).

10.6.2 Product Shopping

AR applications give clients important content that may provide information, advantages and characteristics of a product, as well as data that helps clients compare different products and services and guide them to make the best shopping decisions. For instance, when a purchaser needs to purchase grains, yet there are many brands to browse, he can tap an AR application to receive all relevant information to compare the choices and pick the most suitable (Alkhamisi & Monowar, 2013).

10.6.3 Garment Shopping

Web-based business is considered one strategic use of AR applications, particularly online clothing shopping as online shoppers cannot forecast whether outfits will be suitable for them or not. With AR, buyers can interface with their electronic outfit shopping, overcoming the greatest obstacle they face when choosing outfits. This development would enhance the quality level of this business to new strategic levels (Pereira, Silva, & Alves, 2011).

10.6.4 Browsing Through Different Product Reviews

Many purchasers depend mainly on online social content, such as product ratings, reviews and recommendations before purchasing items. Recent studies on retail business indicated that web-based social content is the primary component buyers depend on before making a purchasing decision. These days, this web-based social content is reachable by PCs distant from the shopping experience itself. A mobile AR app spreads this social content from the PC to the real world by mobile devices, providing clients with item-related information that encourages them to understand the appropriate considerations when making purchasing decisions (Guven et al., 2009).

10.7 Opportunities for Augmented Reality Shopping in Emerging Markets

Several factors have been shown to contribute to purchasing decisions, and AR can create three key opportunities that resolve buyer uncertainty in online shopping.

10.7.1 Creation of an Engaging Buyer Experience

With the help of AR technology, it will be possible to overcome the challenges faced by online buyers that help them transform imagination into reality. With this technology, the customer can see how the product will look and feel in their environment (Blázquez, 2014).

10.7.2 Modifying or Customising Selections

By utilising AR technology, it will be possible for shoppers to explore several options and make customised modifications to products in terms of colour and other features. Shoppers will be able to change the colour of the product and apply it in their environment to get a feel for how that product will actually look (Lau, Lee, & Lau, 2014).

10.7.3 Visualise or Understand Products and Features

Augmented reality enables shoppers to understand the working and functioning of complex products with the help of animation. In addition, AR technology is able to make the complete shopping experience personalised and interactive (Pachoulakis & Kapetanakis, 2012).

10.8 Challenges Faced by Augmented Reality Shopping in Emerging Markets

Similar to other new technologies, AR faces several challenges in its early adoption period. Some of these challenges are illustrated as follows:

10.8.1 Environmental Challenges

- The first challenge faced by this technology is the environmental challenge, whereby perceptual matters within the environment can cause a problem in the utilisation of this technology (Kruijff, Swan, & Feiner, 2010), such as lighting and weather conditions in outside environments that may affect the localisation quality (Arth & Schmalstieg, 2011).

- The diversity of the colour scheme in the environment can cause major harm to light conditions. There are also challenges presented by hardware and software technologies that are used in handheld display devices, such as colour quality and fidelity (Kruijff et al., 2010).

10.8.2 Content Management Challenges

Most of the present AR systems lack the technique of attaching new content. Generally, a small number of professional domains control these systems. Application developers are the only authorised group to add new content due to the need of programming skills to create a link between data sources and present systems. In AR systems, regular users should be able to add special content without the need for serious technical effort. Furthermore, in these systems, there is a user-created feature that provides an easy way for all users to combine the content they have created from different sources to the same AR view (Kurkovsky, Koshy, Novak, & Szul, 2012).

10.8.3 Display Device Challenges

- Poor camera sensor quality in bad lighting conditions seriously affects the quality of an AR experience. Pictures become fuzzy and colours begin to experience major aberration (Arth & Schmalstieg, 2011).
- Colour fidelity in outside environments is an extremely challenging issue. Changing outside environments significantly affects the visual presentation of AR. In video see-through presentations, both real world and overlays are displayed on similar colour scales (Kruijff et al., 2010).

10.8.4 User Challenges

User concern is one of the challenges of AR. The location of the user is the key element in the utilisation of the AR system (Arth & Schmalstieg, 2011), so user acceptance and adoption of AR in emerging markets could face some challenges surrounding privacy.

10.9 Conclusion

Although augmented reality is an important technology that has been around for several years, it is still in its developmental infancy, particularly in emerging markets such as China and India. There are several kinds of AR products that have been developed and presented in different parts of the world, such as a completely new shopping experience obtained from the layering of 3D spaces, and this supports the broader transitions that are taking place in online shopping. In this study, a complete overview of the field of AR has been presented, comprising definitions of AR, a historical overview of AR and a description of the presence of AR in emerging markets, shopping and marketing in emerging markets with the help of AR tools and the applications that are presented by AR for commercial purposes. Furthermore, this study also presented the opportunities and challenges faced by the AR today.

The field of augmented reality is increasing rapidly with the help of a greater quantity of research that has taken place in this field, and emerging markets such as China and India have an important contribution to make in this field. However, there are also certain challenges that are faced in the adoption of this technology, like those of technical issues and issues related to the availability of content. Thus, it will take some time before AR becomes a normal feature of the shopping experience. When used to its full potential, it can be said that AR will have a huge impact on the way the world operates. In order to enhance understanding of antecedents influencing consumer attitude and behaviour towards AR use, theories and models that are well tried and tested (see, e.g. Dwivedi et al., 2017; Dwivedi, Rana, Jeyaraj, Clement, & Williams, 2017; Rana, Dwivedi, Lal, Williams, & Clement, 2017; Rana, Dwivedi, Williams, & Weerakkody, 2016; Shareef, Dwivedi, Kumar, & Kumar, 2016) in the context of emerging markets (such as India) should be adapted to empirically examine AR-related aspects.

References

Abed, S. S., Dwivedi, Y. K., & Williams, M. D. (2015). Social media as a bridge to E-commerce adoption in SMEs: A systematic literature review. *The Marketing Review, 15*(1), 39–57.

Alimamy, S., Deans, K. R., & Gnoth, J. (2017). Augmented reality: Uses and future considerations in marketing. In *Leadership, innovation and entrepreneurship as driving forces of the global economy* (pp. 705–712). Springer International Publishing, Cham, Switzerland.

Alkhamisi, A., & Monowar, M. (2013). Rise of augmented reality: Current and future application areas. *International Journal of Internet and Distributed Systems, 1*(04), 25–34.

Arth, C., & Schmalstieg, D. (2011). *Challenges of large-scale augmented reality on smartphones* (pp. 1–4). Graz, Austria: Graz University of Technology.

Azuma, R., Baillot, Y., Behringer, R., Feiner, S., Julier, S., & MacIntyre, B. (2001). Recent advances in augmented reality. *IEEE Computer Graphics and Applications, 21*(6), 34–47.

Azuma, R. T. (1997). A survey of augmented reality. *Presence: Teleoperators and Virtual Environments, 6*(4), 355–385.

Blázquez, M. (2014). Fashion shopping in multichannel retail: The role of technology in enhancing the customer experience. *International Journal of Electronic Commerce, 18*(4), 97–116.

Brohm, D., Domurath, N., Glanz-Chanos, V., & Grunert, K. G. (2017). Future trends of augmented reality. In *Augmented reality for food marketers and consumers* (pp. 1681–1685). Wageningen Academic Publishers, Wageningen, The Netherlands.

Dwivedi, Y. K., Rana, N. P., Janssen, M., Lal, B., Williams, M. D., & Clement, R. M. (2017). An empirical validation of a unified model of electronic government adoption (UMEGA). *Government Information Quarterly, 34*(2), 211–230.

Dwivedi, Y. K., Rana, N. P., Jeyaraj, A., Clement, M., & Williams, M. D. (2017). Re-examining the unified theory of acceptance and use of technology (UTAUT): Towards a revised theoretical model. *Information Systems Frontiers*. https://doi.org/10.1007/s10796-017-9774-y

Furness III, T. A. (1986). The super cockpit and its human factors challenges. In *Proceedings of the Human Factors Society Annual Meeting*. Sage CA: Los Angeles, CA: SAGE Publications, *30*(1), 48–52.

Greenwood, K., Morris, R., Smith, V., Jones, A., Pearman, D., & Wykes, T. (2016). Virtual shopping: A viable alternative to direct assessment of real life function? *Schizophrenia Research, 172*(1), 206–210.

Guven, S., Oda, O., Podlaseck, M., Stavropoulos, H., Kolluri, S., & Pingali, G. (2009). Social mobile augmented reality for retail. pervasive Computing and Communications, 2009. PerCom 2009. *IEEE International Conference on Pervasive Computing and Communications*, (pp. 1–3). IEEE. doi:10.1109/PERCOM.2009.4912803.

Jackson, T., Angermann, F., & Meier, P. (2011). Survey of use cases for mobile augmented reality browsers. In *Handbook of augmented reality* (pp. 409–431). Springer, New York, NY.

Klopfer, E., & Sheldon, J. (2010). Augmenting your own reality: Student authoring of science-based augmented reality games. *New Directions for Student Leadership, 128*, 85–94.

Klopfer, E., & Squire, K. (2008). Environmental detectives—The development of an augmented reality platform for environmental simulations. *Educational Technology Research and Development, 56*(2), 203–228.

Koytcheva, M. (2017). Augmented and virtual reality devices to become a $4 billion-plus business in three years. [online]. http://www.ccsinsight.com/press/company-news/2251-augmented-and-virtual-reality-devices-to-become-a-4-billion-plus-business-in-three-years. Accessed 15 June 2017.

Kruijff, E., Swan, J., & Feiner, S. (2010). Perceptual issues in augmented reality revisited. mixed and augmented reality (ISMAR). In *2010 9th IEEE international symposium* (pp. 3–12), IEEE, Seoul, Korea.

Kurkovsky, S., Koshy, R., Novak, V., Szul, P. (2012). Current issues in handheld augmented reality. In *Communications and information technology (ICCIT), 2012 international conference on* (pp. 68–72).

Lau, K. W., Lee, P. Y., & Lau, H. F. (2014). Shopping experience 2.0: An exploration of how consumers are shopping in an immersive virtual reality. *Advances in Economics and Business, 2*(2), 92–99.

Pachoulakis, I., & Kapetanakis, K. (2012). Augmented reality platforms for virtual fitting rooms. *The International Journal of Multimedia & Its Applications, 4*(4), 35.

Pereira, F., Silva, C., & Alves, M. (2011). Virtual fitting room augmented reality techniques for E-commerce. In *International conference on ENTERprise information systems* (pp. 62–71).

Rana, N. P., Dwivedi, Y. K., Lal, B., Williams, M. D., & Clement, M. (2017). Citizens' adoption of an electronic government system: Towards a unified view. *Information Systems Frontiers, 19*(3), 549–568.

Rana, N. P., Dwivedi, Y. K., Williams, M. D., & Weerakkody, V. (2016). Adoption of online public grievance redressal system in India: Toward developing a unified view. *Computers in Human Behavior, 59*, 265–282.

Raska, K., & Richter, T. (2017). *Influence of augmented reality on purchase intention: The IKEA case* (Master Thesis). Jonkoping University.

Sapientnitro: Virtual reality: Taking an emerging technology mainstream. (2016). [online]. https://www.brandingmag.com/2016/11/16/virtual-reality-taking-an-emerging-technology-mainstream/

Shareef, M. A., Dwivedi, Y. K., Kumar, V., & Kumar, U. (2016). Reformation of public service to meet citizens' needs as customers: Evaluating SMS as an alternative service delivery channel. *Computers in Human Behavior, 61*, 255–270.

Violino, B. (2016). Virtual reality, augmented reality markets poised for growth spurt I ZDNet. [online]. http://www.zdnet.com/article/virtual-and-augmented-reality-systems-poised-for-growth-spurt/. Accessed 15 June 2017.

Virtual reality technology in China: Opportunities and challenges in an emerging market. (2016). *eMarketer*. [online]. https://www.emarketer.com/Report/Virtual-Reality-Technology-China-Opportunities-Challenges-Emerging-Market/2001843. Accessed 15 June 2017.

Wilson, S. (2017). Augmented and virtual reality devices to become a $4 billion-plus business in three years. *CCS Insight*. [online]. http://www.ccsinsight.com/press/company-news/2251-augmented-and-virtual-reality-devices-to-become-a-4-billion-plus-business-in-three-years. Accessed 17 June 2017.

Yim, M. Y. C., Chu, S. C., & Sauer, P. L. (2017). Is augmented reality technology an effective tool for E-commerce? An interactivity and vividness perspective. *Journal of Interactive Marketing, 39*, 89–103.

Zhang, X., Navab, N., & Liou, S. P. (2000). E-commerce direct marketing using augmented reality. In *Multimedia and expo, 2000. ICME 2000. 2000 IEEE international conference*, Vol. 1 (pp. 88–91). IEEE, New York, NY, USA.

Salma S. Abed is an assistant professor in the Management Information Systems Department at the College of Business in King Abdulaziz University, Rabigh, Saudi Arabia. She obtained her PhD from the management school at Swansea University, Wales, UK. She received her MSc in Business Information Technology from the College of Computing and Digital Media at DePaul University, Chicago, Illinois, USA.

Chapter 11
The Impact of Social Media on Internal Communications in the Tanzanian Telecom Industry

Shirumisha Kwayu, Banita Lal, and Mumin Abubakre

Abstract Social media, a new class of information technology (IT) that allows interaction and interoperability of users, is transforming organisational communication processes by offering affordances that were impossible to achieve with previous forms of IT. Social media affect knowledge transfer, socialisation and power processes within organisations. Likewise, it increases ambient awareness (knowledge of communication occurring amongst others in the organisation), metaknowledge (knowledge of who knows what and who knows whom), as well as increasing accountability. However, despite understanding potential effects of using social media within organisations, there is limited knowledge on how the internal use of social media within organisations influences structures and processes within an organisation. It is agreed that the interplay between people and technology within organisations enacts the structure of using technologies, consequently generating emergent processes and structures within organisations. Considering this, the chapter intends to explore how the internal use of social media within organisations influences the structure and process of communication within organisations. The chapter uses practice theory perspective, which considers the interplay between people and material in the process of organising. The study uses the case of the Tanzanian telecom industry to gather empirical evidence. Results of this initial study will advance our understanding of social media practices and the ways in which it affects structures and processes of communication within organisations. In particular, this will enable us to understand how people in organisations organise themselves when they engage with social media technologies and how such organisational processes produce communication structures and processes within the organisation. Furthermore, the results will assist management with insights on how to manage dynamic and fluid communication practices that are the essence of social media. Therefore, this will help organisations to moderate power dynamics, enhance knowledge management and socialisation through better management of social media practices.

S. Kwayu (✉) · B. Lal · M. Abubakre
Nottingham Trent University, Nottingham Business School, Nottingham, UK
e-mail: Shirumisha.kwayu2014@my.ntu.ac.uk; banita.lal@ntu.ac.uk; mumin.abubakre@ntu.ac.uk

Y. K. Dwivedi et al. (eds.), *Emerging Markets from a Multidisciplinary Perspective*, Advances in Theory and Practice of Emerging Markets,
https://doi.org/10.1007/978-3-319-75013-2_11

Keywords Social Media · Structure and Processes · Practice Perspective · Imbrication · WhatsApp

11.1 Introduction

Social media applications such as Facebook, Instagram, Twitter, YouTube and WhatsApp are new class information technologies (IT) that allow interaction and interoperability of users. The increasing use of social media within organisations is changing the communication dynamics as it offers affordances that previous sets of information technologies could not provide. For example, in a simultaneous and consistent manner, social media affords organisational communication with visibility, editability, association and persistence (Treem & Leonardi, 2012). The impact of communication facilitated by these affordances affects various aspects of the organisation such as knowledge management, socialisation and power relations. In addition, it is acknowledged that social media communication within organisations increases the ambient awareness (knowledge of communication taking place within the organisation), metaknowledge (knowledge of who knows who and who knows what) and accountability through making communication visible (Treem, 2015). Despite the understanding of these potential impacts of social media on organisational communication, Huang, Baptista, and Galliers (2013) suggest that little is known about the effects of social media on established and emerging communication practices (i.e. how people interact and engage with others) within the organisation. Thus, the aim of this chapter is to address this paucity through exploring the impact of social media on the structure and processes of communication practices within organisations. The aim is to enhance the prevailing theoretical discussion on the role of technology in influencing organisational structure and processes, especially with a contemporary technology (social media) that is fluid and dynamic.

Understanding the impact of social media on organisational structure and processes is somewhat complex because the effects of social media technology are highly influenced by social aspects (Treem, 2015). The complexity is stirred by the fact that people's behaviours and action vary depending on their sense-making (interpretation) of the use of social media. Thus, when people interact with social media, they produce new communication practices within the organisation. Communication practices, which are the interplay between people and technology (social media), enact emergent structures and processes within the organisation (Orlikowski, 2000). Thus, the focal lens of understanding the impact of social media on internal communication is to focus on the practices that emerge from the interplay between people and social media within the organisation. Considering this, this chapter is going to use the practice perspective to analyse the impact of social media on the internal communication of an organisation with the precise focus on the structure and processes of communication within the organisation. Thus, following this objective, this chapter seeks to answer the following research question: (1) how are new communication practices that are supported by social media affecting the structure and processes of communication within organisations? This question will be answered using an interpretivist philosophy which adopts a case study. Initial empirical evidence from a Tanzanian telecommunications organisation is gathered to provide an insight on social media communication practices and their influence on structure and processes. The chapter will contribute to information systems (IS) literature on how technology affects the structure and processes of communication within organisations as well as in practice, by offering evidence that may help managers to manage dynamic and fluid communication practices that emerge in organisation when members engage with social media. In doing so, this will help management to be in a better position in managing important organisational aspects such as power dynamics, socialisation and knowledge management.

11.2 Literature Review

Social media, which are explained as a group of Internet-based applications that are built on the ideological and technical foundations of web 2.0, have significantly transformed organisational communication by allowing the creation and exchange of user-generated content (Kaplan & Haenlein, 2010). As well as social media being Internet-based applications, they are also mobile-based which integrate technology, telecommunication and social interaction to enable the creation and dissemination of words, videos, images and audios (Dabner, 2012). Their ability to allow cheap and different forms of content creation and the exchange of information between users has enabled social media to soar within a relatively short space of time. Today most of the popular social media applications such as Facebook, YouTube, Instagram, Twitter, WhatsApp and Snapchat have more than a billion users (Piskorski, 2014). This has made the use of these platforms universal, and, within organisations, it has advanced to the mainstream level (Pillet & Carillo, 2016). Considering this rise and development of social media and their increasing influence on business organisations, a considerable interest in generating an understanding of the impact of social media and its role in organisations has emerged.

'Social media' is a very broad term that embodies various forms, which makes it difficult to apprehend. In an effort to explain it, some scholars have classified social media according to its characteristics, while others have classified it according to the functions that it supports. Kaplan and Haenlein (2010) categorised six forms of social media according to characteristics that are collaborative projects (i.e. Wikipedia), blogs, content communities (i.e. YouTube), social networking sites (i.e. Facebook), virtual game worlds (i.e. world of Warcraft) and virtual social worlds (i.e. Second Life). On the other hand, Kietzmann, Hermkens, McCarthy, and Silvestre (2011) explained social media through developing a framework of seven functional building blocks that are identity, conversation, sharing, relationships, presence, groups and reputations. Following the functional building blocks categorisation, social media activities are defined by the extent to which the social media application focuses on some or all functional blocks. Considering the categorisation of social media, this implies that each form of social media contains a form of affordances regarding the kind of communication that it supports and, thus, each form of social media applications will have a unique set of impacts on its users. For instance, Twitter enables users to associate with other users through following their activities; it also enables sharing through tweeting and retweeting. However, Twitter does not support functions such as groups (the extent to which users are ordered or form communities). Also, it does not show the presence of the user. Thus, one can observe how twitter can support certain forms of communication but will be unable to support others such as group conversations.

The advancement of social media as a new class of information technology has influenced organisational communication in various ways. For example, Gallaugher and Ransbotham (2010) argue that social media has changed how content is contributed, structured, organised as well as the flows of interaction between users. In addition, Kietzmann et al. (2011) suggest that these changes have an effect on different aspects of organisations such as reputation, sales, as well as its survival. Moreover, Scott and Orlikowski (2012) suggest that social media has presented organisations with complex information dynamics which propels organisations in unexpected directions, redrawing boundaries and shifting relationships. Considering these arguments, there is an increasing rationale to explore the way social media is influencing established structure and processes of communication as well as instituting new structures and processes of communication within organisations.

According to Harper (2015), structure is a clearly defined pattern of activity in which, ideally, every series of action is functionally related to the purpose of the organisation, whereas processes are a systematic series of actions directed by organisational members towards a goal (Harris, Kaefer, & Salchenberger, 2013). Following the descriptions of structure and processes, they suggest that the unit of analysis is the actions/activities taking place within an organisation. The nature and manner of activities within the organisation materialise to form the reality of the organisation. Thus, to understand the impact of social media on the structure and processes of an organisation, the focus is on the pattern of social media activities (the social media practice), which endure across space and time. Thus, to understand social media practice or the recursive pattern of social media activities in the organisation, one must consider the materiality of social media. Materiality of social media is a constitution of the material aspects of social media and the social aspects of members of the organisation. Leonardi (2013) defines materiality as the arrangement of artefacts – physical and/or digital materials – into a particular form that endures across different places and time. This means that materiality are the features of technology that do not change across space and time. Important to note is that although materiality is distinct from the social aspect of organisations, they simultaneously indicate their synergetic interaction, meaning that it is difficult to separate the two. This means that social and material agencies are separate, but once they interact, it is difficult to separate them.

Understanding how human (social agents) interact with material (technology) is central for discerning how technology affects the structure and processes within an organisation. This has been an ongoing discussion within the IS field: Orlikowski

(1992) provides an account of this discussion. In brief, earlier convention viewed technology as an external force with a deterministic effect on structure; this view was opposed by those who focused on the social aspect of technology who viewed the technology effect on structure as an intervention. This resorted to a softer view of determinism that views technology as an external object with an impact on structure but moderated by human actors and organisational context. Thereafter, it emerged another view that centred on the premise that technology is not an external object but a product of ongoing human action, design and appropriation. Following this emerged a view of technology as a trigger of structural change, whereby technologies influence organisational structures in an orderly way and that order depends on the historical processes in which they are embedded. Subsequently, Orlikowski (1992) discussed a view of structuration, which is a social process that involves the reciprocal interaction of human actors and structural features of organisations. With this view, technology is created and changed by humans, and humans accomplish an action using that technology. Thus, technology contains a structure which is embedded, and then it is appropriated within the organisation. Hence, the structuration view helps to see a technology as enacted by humans, and it is institutionalised in structure. Considering this, structuration is a dynamic process which is embedded historically and contextually.

Orlikowski (2000) advanced the structuration view to a practice perspective that views how people interact with technology in their ongoing practices to enact structures that shape their emergent and situated use of technology. This view advances the notion of embeddedness with emergent structures and the appropriation with enactment. The central focus of this view is to focus on practice, which is a focus on recursive interaction between people, technology and social action. Through focusing on practice, it enables us to understand the impact of technology when people engage with it in organisations. Given that the discussion on the role of technology in organisations is an ongoing endeavour, this chapter is going to set its premises by using the practice perspective as it considers the constitutive role of humans and technology in affecting the organisational structure. By doing so, this perspective will help us to understand the emerging structures and how they are enacted when people engage with social media in organisations.

Although the practice perspective is known for considering the constitutive role of humans and technology, there are still different views on how humans and technology come together. In other words, it is conventional wisdom that humans and technology are highly intertwined; however, there is a disagreement on how they become intertwined, which brings us onto an ontological debate on this matter. The agential realist believes that the interaction between humans and technology is ontological and, thus, inseparable, whereas the critical realist believes that humans and technology are two distinct agencies that interact and affect each other (Cecez-Kecmanovic, Galliers, Henfridsson, Newell, & Vidgen, 2014). Considering this difference between the agential and critical realist, Leonardi (2011), from the critical perspective, addresses the interweaving of human and technology (material) using an imbrication metaphor, which assumes the inherent separation between human and technology agency while simultaneously indicating their synergetic interaction. Given that materiality is independent on human agency, this means that

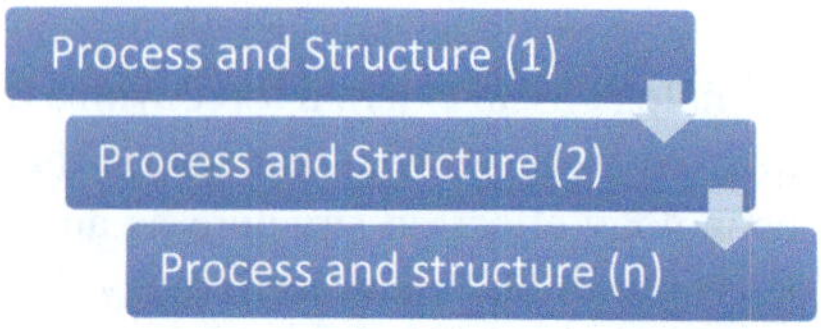

Fig. 11.1 Imbrication process

people react to the material (note: materiality is different to technology, independent of its use and the context that it is used within (Cecez-Kecmanovic et al., 2014)). Thus, from a critical perspective, people react to materiality, and this brings to 'affordances' (how people interpret or make sense on the use of technology) that people see on the technology. Therefore, although the material and social are separate from a critical perspective (Leonardi, 2011), the social and material impact and mutually shape each other through imbrication in social action. Since social agency and material agency interact in an imbrication manner, also the processes and structure occur in an imbrication manner, containing the elements of the past and the new ones in an overlapping way as seen in Fig. 11.1:

The above discussion on social media, which is fluid and dynamic in nature, presents a thought-provoking discussion on how it affects organisational structure and processes. Bearing in mind that structure and processes are concerned with the flows of activities in organisations, a practice perspective that considers the interplay between people and technology provides a suitable angle for studying the effect of social media effect within organisations. Understanding the established and emergent practices supported by social media helps to understand the influence of social media in the processes and structure of communication in organisations. A further insight on the way in which the structure and processes of organisation are affected is important for managing and predicting the emerging structure and processes within organisations.

11.3 Methodology

A case study method was selected after considering the aim of this chapter – understanding how the internal use of social media within organisations influences the structure and processes of communication within organisations. A case study method allows an in-depth exploration of what is going on in the life of an organisation, enabling us to understand the research phenomena and the context which gives insight to the context and process to which it is enacted (Yin, 2013). The guiding philosophy for this case study is interpretivist, which asserts that knowledge is socially constructed through language, shared meaning and consciousness (Orlikowski & Baroudi, 1991). The interpretivist philosophy supports studying phenomena in its natural setting, which removes researcher's predetermined views that may obscure gaining new knowledge, and, thus, it aims to remove bias.

The case organisation is a telecommunications company in Tanzania (Kijiko – a pseudonym used). Kijiko is a private company. It is one of the biggest telecom organisations in the country. It is a vibrant user of social media and a proponent of a digital lifestyle, making it a suitable case for this research. Moreover, given that the case company is in Tanzania, which is an emerging market, it makes the context of this research more interesting as the digital infrastructure is different to that of the western developed world, which has many studies done on social media in organisations in comparison. This study selected a telecom organisation, as telecom organisations are faster in adopting new technology (Belasen & Rufer, 2013). The selection of Kijiko also considered the size of the company as well as the use of social media. A large company was preferable as it provides a wider base for exploring the processes and structures of communication within organisation across its different departments and functions.

Data was collected through semi-structured interviews which allows the researcher to hear what the informant says about the topic as well providing the opportunity of probing more in areas which the researcher identifies (Parveen, Jaafar, & Ainin, 2015). The interviews were conducted with staff and management at Kijiko with the rationale that communication is carried out by all members of the organisation. Ten interviews were conducted with members from different functions within the organisation. The interviews were conducted in multilingual (mix of Swahili and English) languages.

The analysis was done through narrative structuring, which follows an inductive approach that concentrates on issues and themes extracted from the data collected (Glaser & Strauss, 1967). Narrative structuring provides a description of an experience that is told in a systematic way, indicating a flow of related events which, when compiled together, is significant to the narrators and conveys meaning to the researcher (Coffey & Atkinson, 1996). The narrative structuring is a powerful means of analysing data as it brings the context and social situation into the analysis of the events that occurred (Saunders et al., 2009). In addition, analysis using narrative structuring provides the ability to highlight points that were made and what they symbolise and how they explain specific issues within the organisation such as culture, politics and change. Thus, the analysis was done by creating a coherent story from the data collected through the interviews. By doing this, it enables researchers to take into account the social and organisational context of how the events occurred (Saunders et al., 2009). The analysis was done after transcription and translation of the recorded interviews.

11.4 Findings

Interviews with managers and other members of staff at Kijiko revealed that social media in the form of WhatsApp communication is widely used within the company. WhatsApp is a web and mobile application that allows calls, voice notes, text messages, video calls, groups and location service, and it allows attachment of files both audio and video. This section is going to present the key issues associated with WhatsApp use at Kijiko.

11.5 Uses of WhatsApp

There are various reasons why people prefer to use WhatsApp communication in Kijiko. The four main reasons that are associated with the use of WhatsApp are urgency, solving problems, sending reports and presenting evidence.

Urgent issues:

Urgent issues are normally done through WhatsApp. – Customer Service staff member

Solving problems:

I am a leader and I use WhatsApp, our group we are twelve with three leaders. If there is any challenge, we send it to the group. When they get a problem in the market, they send it to the group and we solve it – Marketing Team Leader

Sending reports:

With WhatsApp a boss can order me to send him a report, I take a photo within a minute I send him and it becomes easy – Sales Person

Evidence:

WhatsApp helps a lot on our communication. Our communication need evidence, if you move from here and you go marketing. I must take a photo that am on the market a certain area and send it to the group. Anything happens here in office I will need to send a photo. Therefore, it helps a lot in work but also shows evidence. – Manager Branch Y

11.6 Dynamics Around WhatsApp Use

Although people prefer to use WhatsApp, email and conference calls are the main means of communication in Kijiko. The zonal manager explains this as follows:

We use email and WhatsApp groups. Email is key, but we also have official WhatsApp groups. If there are matters that cannot be sent in email, they done through WhatsApp. Agent issues also are sent via *WhatsApp or through conference calls. These are the main communication technologies that we use* – Zonal Manager

Similarly, a branch manager from Branch X explains how they use WhatsApp at their branch as follows:

Our office uses WhatsApp. Our office has eight staff members and we have a [Whatsapp] group which we update each other. This is because not everything is shared on email. Not all the people are using email. We are customer service; we are eight and there are only two computers. That means other people are not connected to email but people are using WhatsApp because it is modern, attractive and easy to communicate anything concerning the office. – Manager Branch X

As observed from the explanation above, the use of WhatsApp is manifested in groups. The manager from Branch Y explains the WhatsApp groups as follows:

Every group has its process and structure depending on the objective of the group. For instance, in our northern zone, we have two groups, one for official and the other it's social. On social group, you will find everything concerning social, that group is social oriented.

People will talk jokes, football etc. *Through that group, you can know what someone likes and dislikes. Nevertheless, the official group is only about work, it is business oriented. Therefore, on social group is where you can be free as you like but on business is serious matters.* – Manager Branch Y

Although WhatsApp is widely used within Kijiko, it is still unknown whether it is an official or unofficial communication practice. The manager of Branch X explains this ambiguity as follows:

I cannot term WhatsApp as official communication because we are not official told. However, our leaders and we use it so we see it as official. Because when someone request you an information will either want you to reply through WhatsApp or through email. This is something that is official because the office depends on it because there are two kinds of groups ones that are business oriented and ones that are social. Therefore, when I say they are official I think am correct. Even when we ask each other, we look at the group and share. Therefore, it is something that we use officially. – Manager Branch X

11.7 Challenges of Using WhatsApp

Apart from the above-mentioned reasons, the use of WhatsApp at Kijiko is coupled by several challenges. The challenges associated with WhatsApp use include work-life balance, Internet access and disinterest of WhatsApp communication.

Work-life balance:

It brings destruction but it depends on yourself. I may decide not to respond until am back in the office. Then I weigh on how I spoke with the customer. For instance, if the service level agreement is 72 Hours and when I look the 72 hours have or are about to pass. I will feel guilty. Therefore, I will let him know I have receive the email. Therefore, I see its better I tell him to avoid complain. – Manager Branch Y

Internet access:

Sometimes, a group member does not have internet access and is supposed to solve the issue. Also, at times, someone may say he was in a location with no internet. Therefore, I can say the problem is internet access. – Marketing staff member

Disinterest:

Official groups have challenges; sometimes people do not give information on time. Then when you ask he takes it as not an official media of communication. Someone can find an excuse and say why you did not send me an email or call me. – Manager Branch X

11.8 Discussion

From the findings, we learn some details regarding the use of WhatsApp in internal communications at Kijiko. The use of WhatsApp is spread across the organisation from the management to the staff: they all use WhatsApp to communicate. WhatsApp is used alongside other communication channels like email and conference calls.

The use of WhatsApp substitutes and supplements other channels in fundamental ways. It is important to note that the use of WhatsApp has not diminished the use of other channels, but it has reinforced and introduced the purpose, interpretative meanings, norms and abilities for each communication channel (technology) in use within the organisation. For example, when the zonal manager asserts that '*If there are matters that cannot be sent in email, they done through WhatsApp. Agent issues also are sent* via *WhatsApp or through conference calls*', this suggests that each channel of communication is assigned with an interpretive meaning on their use. Furthermore, the distinction between the social group and the WhatsApp group emphasises the purpose and norms in the use of WhatsApp within the organisation.

In terms of structure and processes, the findings reveal ambiguity between interpretive and procedural aspects of communication. For example, when the branch manager at X states, '*I cannot term WhatsApp as official communication because we are not official told. However, our leaders and we use it so we see it as official.*', it shows that the use of WhatsApp communication is interpreted as an official means of communication, but the procedures have not set it as official. This ambiguity raises a challenge on the use of WhatsApp communication. For example, disinterest of communication sent via WhatsApp as some people claim it is not an official means of communication.

In a positive way, the use of WhatsApp at Kijiko influences processes and structure in various aspects such as urgent issues, problem-solving, evidence and reporting process. These are important aspects in any process; for example, reporting on the processes helps to know the status of an activity and helps to achieve better performance. Also, during crisis, WhatsApp communication becomes a handy tool to help the processes. The ability of WhatsApp to influence processes in this way is because of its influence on structure, for instance, the grouping which has structure and purpose. For example, separating the groups between social and work groups, this is arguably to enable urgency as work group communication is not diluted with information that does not need a quick response. Likewise, the groups help to fuse the synergy between different levels of management and within a sect.

One of the negative impacts of WhatsApp communication within Kijiko is work-life balance. WhatsApp communication challenges staff on drawing a boundary between their work and personal lives. WhatsApp has enabled the staff to work remotely as they can get the information on what is going on and through that some are obligated to engage. Although it can be argued that social WhatsApp groups help socialisation within Kijiko, it appears to intensify the conflation between work and home and, similarly, to the work groups.

Associating the findings with the literature, the staff at Kijiko have established the affordances of WhatsApp through group communication. Members of Kijiko have found affordances of WhatsApp, for example, the staff's use of camera and location services to provide evidence of their activities or to support their communication. Also, the ability to form social and work groups is afforded by the material aspects of WhatsApp. Thus, when the staff engage with WhatsApp, they form the groups, whereby through these groups, they can solve some problem. Extenuating this, one must differentiate between a normal work group and WhatsApp work group in their ability to function. The physical work group, even when formed by the same people, can only work and collaborate when they are physically present at a single location, whereas with the WhatsApp work group, they can work at a distance; for instance, if one is at the office and other members are in the field, i.e. marketing can get the support at a distance which is aided not just by text but also with videos, photos and audios.

Considering the example above which provides an analogy between the physical work group and WhatsApp work group, the fundamental question is how the interaction between the people and WhatsApp affects the structure and processes within the organisation. The findings indicate that people's social action (i.e. groups/teams) and WhatsApp's material features exist as separate, but once they interact, it becomes a WhatsApp group which the social media cannot be taken away from. Both agencies come together in an imbricate manner. The teams for executing processes within the organisation existed before WhatsApp, but with the emergence of WhatsApp groups, they contain elements of the former while introducing new elements. For example, the separation of the WhatsApp social group and WhatsApp work groups, where each WhatsApp group has its norms and purpose. Thus, it is through this imbrication process that new elements of structure and process are enacted and emerge.

11.9 Conclusion

Contemporary organisations such as Kijiko are embracing new social media technologies such as WhatsApp which are fluid and dynamic in nature. These technologies are influencing organisational communication to become significant communication channels. Social media technologies such as WhatsApp are spreading within organisations before procedural authorisation, leaving them to the interpretation of the users within organisation to establish new communication practices as with the case of Kijiko. For example, the ambiguity on whether WhatsApp is an official or unofficial means of communication is evidence that procedures are lagging behind the use of social media within the organisation. Putting procedures in place can assist in guiding the use of social media within organisation. Lack of procedures creates differences in interpretation on the use of social media, consequently leading to challenges such as disinterest of communication through the WhatsApp channel. Thus, it is essential for management to understand the dynamics of social media and manage them by allowing interpretive use of the technology which is balanced with procedures in order to harness the potential powers of social media into their structure and processes within organisation.

This research has shown how communication structure and processes within organisation are affected when members of organisation interact with WhatsApp. The interaction occurs in an imbrication manner, creating structures and processes which develop from previous ones to create a new emergent structure which contains elements of the former. Also this initial finding highlights how social media affects socialisation (i.e. the use of WhatsApp social group within the organisation), power dynamics (i.e. increase control power of managers through sourcing evidence via WhatsApp) and knowledge management (i.e. as members of the organisation, they can solve issue/challenges through WhatsApp) through emerging practices supported by WhatsApp communication. Finally, though this has shown how practices emerge from the interaction with WhatsApp at Kijiko and their impact, future research will benefit more on learning how to manage fluid and dynamic communication practices as it is certain that these types of communication practice have an effect on flows of activity within organisation.

References

Belasen, A., & Rufer, R. (2013). Innovation communication and inter-functional collaboration: a view from the competing values framework for corporate communication. In *Strategy and Communication for Innovation* (pp. 227–240). Springer Berlin Heidelberg. Germany

Cecez-Kecmanovic, D., Galliers, R. D., Henfridsson, O., Newell, S., & Vidgen, R. (2014). The sociomateriality of information systems: Current status, future directions. *MIS Quarterly, 38*(3), 809–830.

Coffey, A., & Atkinson, P. (1996). *Making sense of qualitative data: Complementary research* Glaser, B. and Strauss, A., 1967. The discovery of grounded theory. 1967. *Weidenfield & Nicolson, London* (pp. 1–19). *Strategies*. Sage Publications, Inc.

Dabner, N. (2012). 'Breaking ground' in the use of social media: A case study of a university earthquake response to inform educational design with Facebook. *The Internet and Higher Education, 15*(1), 69–78.

Gallaugher, J., & Ransbotham, S. (2010). Social media and customer dialog management at Starbucks. *MIS Quarterly Executive, 9*(4). 197–212

Glaser, B., & Strauss, A. (1967). The discovery of grounded theory. 1967 (pp. 1–19). London: Weidenfield & Nicolson.

Harper, C. (2015). *Organizations: Structures, processes and outcomes*. Routledge. New York

Harris, D. A., Kaefer, F., & Salchenberger, L. M. (2013). The development of dynamic capabilities through organisational and managerial processes. *International Journal of Business Environment, 5*(4), 398–412.

Huang, J., Baptista, J., & Galliers, R. D. (2013). Reconceptualizing rhetorical practices in organizations: The impact of social media on internal communications. *Information Management, 50*(2), 112–124.

Kaplan, A. M., & Haenlein, M. (2010). Users of the world, unite! The challenges and opportunities of Social Media. *Business Horizons, 53*(1), 59–68.

Kietzmann, J. H., Hermkens, K., McCarthy, I. P., & Silvestre, B. S. (2011). Social media? Get serious! Understanding the functional building blocks of social media. *Business Horizons, 54*(3), 241–251.

Leonardi, P. M. (2013). Theoretical foundations for the study of sociomateriality. *Information and Organization, 23*(2), 59–76.

Leonardi, (2011) When Flexible Routines Meet Flexible Technologies: Affordance, Constraint, and the Imbrication of Human and Material Agencies. MIS Quarterly *35*(1), 147

Orlikowski, W. J. (1992). The duality of technology: Rethinking the concept of technology in organizations. *Organization Science, 3*(3), 398–427.

Orlikowski, W. J. (2000). Using technology and constituting structures: A practice lens for studying technology in organizations. *Organization Science, 11*(4), 404–428.

Orlikowski, W. J., & Baroudi, J. J. (1991). Studying information technology in organizations: Research approaches and assumptions. *Information Systems Research, 2*(1), 1–28.

Parveen, F., Jaafar, N. I., & Ainin, S. (2015). Social media usage and organizational performance: Reflections of Malaysian social media managers. *Telematics and Informatics, 32*(1), 67–78.

Pillet, J. C., & Carillo, K. D. A. (2016). Email-free collaboration: An exploratory study on the formation of new work habits among knowledge workers. *International Journal of Information Management, 36*(1), 113–125.

Piskorski, M. J. (2014). *A social strategy: How we profit from social media*. Princeton University Press. New Jersey

Saunders, M., Lewis, P., & Thornhill, A. (2009). Research methods for business students, 5th ed. Edinburgh: Pearson Education.

Scott, S. V., & Orlikowski, W. J. (2012). Reconfiguring relations of accountability: Materialization of social media in the travel sector. Accounting, Organizations and Society, 37(1), 26–40. https://doi.org/10.1016/j.aos.2011.11.005.

Treem, J. W. (2015). Social media as technologies of accountability: Explaining resistance to implementation within organizations. *American Behavioral Scientist, 59*(1), 53–74.

Treem, J. W., & Leonardi, P. M. (2012). Social media use in organizations: Exploring the affordances of visibility, editability, persistence, and association. *Communication Yearbook, 36*, 143–189.

Yin, R. K. (2013). *Case study research: Design and methods*. Sage. London

Shirumisha Kwayu is a PhD student at Nottingham Trent University. His research topic explores the impact of social media on the alignment of strategies within organisations.

Banita Lal is a Senior Lecturer in Information Studies at the Nottingham University Business School, Nottingham Trent University. She gained her PhD in Information Systems from Brunel University. Her research interests revolve around the adoption and diffusion of technology, including broadband, mobile and e-Government technology. Banita has published in leading peer-reviewed conferences and journals in the field of Information Systems, including Information Systems Frontiers, Government Information Quarterly and Information Technology & People.

Mumin Abubakre is a Senior Lecturer in Management. He holds a PhD in Management Information Systems from Loughborough University. Mumin's research interests span culture and its interface with the implementation of e-business/IS strategies, global management of IT and digital entrepreneurship. Mumin has published articles in peer-reviewed scholarly journals such as Information & Management Journal, Information Technology & People and Journal Global of Information Management. He is currently on the editorial board of Journal Global of Information Technology Management.

Part IV
Information Systems and Communication Technologies

Chapter 12
Social Media Research in and of India: A Snapshot

P. Vigneswara Ilavarasan

Abstract Despite being a large and fastest emerging market, the existing landscape of social media research in and of India is not known. The literature is classified in two axes – level of analysis (people and society, platforms and firms) and activities (features, tactics, management and measurement). The review points out that computer scientists dominate the field, whose research is not Indian context specific. Adoption and impact studies are done in a considerable number. Other areas of research – platforms' business models and operations in India, management of social media strategy within organizations, usage of specific features of platforms and homegrown platforms – are still unexplored. The paper used rapid literature review to obtain the results from SCOPUS database and had analysed through Rayyan, a tool for systematic review.

Keywords Emerging markets · India · Literature review · Social media · Strategy

12.1 Emerging Markets, ICTs and Social Media

Using rapid literature review, the paper presents a quick state of the art of social media research in and of India. This section discusses the importance of studying emerging markets, especially India, what it takes to have a working information and communication technology (ICT) ecosystem and position of social media platforms. The second section presents India, status of social media and how they are being used by people and businesses. The third section introduces the methodology used by the review. The findings are presented in the fourth section. The fifth section offers areas for future research.

Emerging markets are those national economies that are not bigger than developed countries but progressing towards them with regulatory mechanisms maturing

P. V. Ilavarasan (✉)
Department of Management Studies, Indian Institute of Technology Delhi,
Hauz Khas, New Delhi, India
e-mail: vignes@iitd.ac.in

Y. K. Dwivedi et al. (eds.), *Emerging Markets from a Multidisciplinary Perspective*, Advances in Theory and Practice of Emerging Markets,
https://doi.org/10.1007/978-3-319-75013-2_12

to handle the required international market transactions. Those number of countries are clearly defined, and the concept creates a mention conception of countries like India, China, Brazil, Malaysia, Hungary, etc.[1] It is estimated that emerging markets are likely to contribute around 70% in the coming years. The balance of payments looks healthy, and long-term investments in emerging markets are outperforming the advanced economics.[2] From the research perspective, emerging economies are fascinating due to its dynamism and need for customization of successful formulae of the developed world. In these emerging economies, information and communication technologies (ICTs) play a major role in enabling the growth and linking the external global markets.

For an ICT ecosystem to operate, there is a need of symbiotic relationships across four different layers (Fransman, 2010): network hardware manufacturers, called as networked elements; network providers; platform, content and application providers; and consumers. For instance, consumers can take 'selfies' when manufacturers sell mobile phones with front camera. The photographs are enhanced and shared through applications like Instagram and Facebook. The telecom service providers and Internet service providers enable the data transmission of the applications. There is also a possibility that mobile phone manufacturers had introduced front cameras in their devices after realizing the consumers' demand. Some of the mobile manufacturers built the applications as part of the device or telecom service providers make their access free. Thus all four layers work together to produce the desired effect. The overall ecosystem is ably supported by the regulatory environment, like freeing up spectrum for service providers or enabling access to low-cost devices, etc. The economic capacity of the consumers is also important for the overall ecosystem to function.

Lack of symbiotic relationships across the layers affects the nature of functioning. Telecom service providers throttling speed of Internet[3] while accessing YouTube or at a particular time would result in poor use of applications. There are differences in technology use in the developing world when compared with the developed world. Discouraging developmental and regulatory environments limits the capacity of developing countries to adopt new technologies and gain from the subsequent innovations (Bergoeing, Piguillem, & Loayza, 2010). For instance, Internet banking in India needs to be completed with one-time password comes via SMS. Without having a valid mobile phone connection linked to bank accounts, one cannot perform Internet-based transactions.

Also the nature of usage shall differ, as the one or more layers of the ecosystem do not work properly and regulatory environment is not encouraging. There are instances in the developing world, where users avoid making calls but communicating only with missed calls to manage the higher cost of calling in mobile phones

[1] Please see for further details: http://www.investopedia.com/terms/e/emergingmarketeconomy.asp

[2] https://www.forbes.com/pictures/eglg45gdjd/why-invest-in-emerging-markets-2/#17f8219972e0are

[3] https://www.usatoday.com/story/tech/2017/07/26/verizon-slows-video-traffic-causing-concerns-net-neutrality-advocates/513248001/

(Donner, 2007). The low-resources environment in the developing world is resulting innovative use of technologies unheard in the developed world (Hellström, 2010; Ling & Horst, 2011).

The emerging and developing markets offer different challenges while deploying social media for various business functions. The ownership and usage of ICTs, especially social media platforms in these markets, differ significantly than the developed ones. Though the reasons are known – differential penetration rates, content availability, cost of broadband access, affordability of devices, weaker network externalities and regulatory frameworks and state of the art of social media strategies in the developing world are still emerging. The knowledge in this domain also seems to be sparse. Businesses, both local and multinationals, compete with each other in winning the emerging markets. The proven frameworks and social media strategies are from the developed markets of better wired consumers. They need to be customized or adapted and subsequently disseminated.

Macro-studies link ICTs, especially broadband to the national growth. For instance, a World Bank study (Minges, 2016) showed that there is positive causal relationship between broadband and GDP. A recent study showed that relationship between ICTs and economic growth is stronger in poorer countries (Cruz-Jesus, Oliveira, Bacao, & Irani, 2016). Despite the absence of conclusive evidence about the linkage between ICTs and productivity (Carr, 2004) or the developmental outcomes (Ilavarasan, 2017) at the micro level, governments continue with significant amount of ICT expenditures.[4] The governments are treating Internet as one of the essentials for their citizens. Recent initiatives of attempting to provide high-speed Internet by building national optical fibre networks (Gunaratne, Ilavarasan, Fernando, & Rohman, 2015) are extensions of the same.

As the ICTs continue to penetrate as mobile phones or high-speed Internet in the emerging markets, the usage of ICT applications is exploding. For instance, in Asia Pacific, with 4.1 billion people, 1.4 billion are active social media users which are 53% of global social media users.[5] As more number of people using social media, both academics and businesses are following them either to study (Dwivedi et al., 2016) or to convert them into customers.[6] Businesses use social media platforms in all the possible domains (Rathore & Ilavarasan, 2018) – marketing, customer relationship management, recruitment, brand management, market research and new product development, etc. It appears that the extant management research is predominantly focusing on the developed markets. Political activism has gained a lot more currency due to Arab Spring and other neo-social movements in the some of the developing world. The field needs to move beyond the developed world.

Social media can be explained as electronic technologies that enable two communication between users and populated predominantly by the user generated content (Kaplan & Haenlein, 2010). The research about social media be approached from three major perspectives: people, businesses and technology. Dwivedi, Kapoor

[4] https://ict4dblog.wordpress.com/2009/04/06/worldwide-expenditure-on-ict4d/

[5] https://wearesocial.com/sg/blog/2016/09/digital-in-apac-2016use

[6] https://www.umassd.edu/media/umassdartmouth/cmr/studiesandresearch/2013_Fortune_500.pdf

Table 12.1 Framework for social media research

		Activities			
		Design and features	Strategy and tactics	Management and organization	Measurement and value
Levels of analysis	Users and society	I	II	III	IV
	Platforms and intermediaries	V	VI	VII	VIII
	Firms and industries	IX	X	XI	XII

Source: Aral et al. (2013)

and Chen (2015) focused on social media marketing. They suggested that the future research could look at the different age groups, country contexts and marketing types for comparisons. Not surprisingly, this view is dominated by researchers from business schools and management discipline. Similar observations have been made by few other subsequent reviews on social media in marketing context (AlAlwan, Rana, Dwivedi, & Algharabat, 2017; Ismagilova, Dwivedi, Slade, & Williams, 2017; Plume, Dwivedi, & Slade, 2016). A review from people's perspective (Ngai, Tao, & Moon, 2015) formulated a causal chain model lineated sets of antecedents, moderators and mediators and outcomes. Brand equity and customer relationship are outcomes in the organizational context. Personal context had user intention and user behaviour. The rest of all variables or factors are from the society or individual orientation. This view seems to be coming more from psychologists and other social scientists. The third set of studies are coming from computer scientists who focus on the technical aspects of the platforms or development of an application that can be deployed on top of the platforms. They also contribute to the business and people domain of the literature, but predominant focus is on the methodology by which large scale of data can be handled.

Aral, Dellarocas and Godes (2013) combine these perspectives and come up with a matrix (Table 12.1) with areas that could be studied. The levels of analysis is about the focus of studies – whether it is about the consumers or individuals, organizations or platforms themselves. The activities include (p. 4) design and features (use of specific social media features, process of fixing standards of features by various stakeholders and how it benefits), strategy and tactics (how social media platforms are used to meet the goals), management and organization (process and structures to use social media are formed and executed) and measurement and value (measuring the efforts in social media and value generated).

The cells in the first row (1–4) and in the last row (9–12) are relatively easy to undertake by way of primary data, when compared to the middle row (5–8), where access to the social media platforms are required. Cell 5 requires a programming skill set as part of the study to be undertaken. This framework shall be used for further discussion of the literature.

In the light of above, the present paper makes a modest attempt to understand the Indian context.

12.2 India, Social Media, People and Businesses

India remains one of the attractive emerging markets for investment and growth for multiple reasons.[7] India is one of the fastest-growing economies in the world, with 7% in 2016–2017, and projected to have similar growth rate for next years.[8] Half of the present 1.2 billion people are expected to be below 26 years in 2020.[9] This demographic composition is attractive both as labour pool and the spending capacity. However, the gross national income per capita is low, US$ 1680 in 2016 compared to China's US$ 8260.[10]

Despite the impressive population of 1.3 billion, Internet penetration is very low with 32%.[11] The larger population, 24.3%, is accessing Internet through their mobile phones. The mobile Internet penetration is quite impressive with 262 million in urban and 109 million in rural locations. This is likely to grow as 88% of the households have mobile phones, when compared to only 18% that have access to tap water.[12] Smartphone ownership is catching up with only 17% and rest of them are still using basic feature phones.[13]

A large-scale survey of close to half million households done by Govt of India reports that there is not much difference between rural and urban areas when spending on communication services, including mobile recharges, 25%.[14] It appears that large percentage of population is skipping the personal computer phase to access and use Internet, through mobile phones. Decreasing cost of devices and Internet access are major reasons for the same. As the technologies evolve, particularly video streaming in low bandwidth, use of Internet is growing in a rapid pace. These trends indicate amplified use of social media by urban and rural customers alike. In a survey done by the American Express in three countries, Indians tend to use social media to get a customer response, 71% more than Japan (29%) and Hong Kong (29%).[15]

The data about social media users are not collected by Govt of India. The data are either reported by the platforms themselves or private agencies on the basis of survey or opinions of experts.[16] Out of an estimate of 216 million social media users in

---

[7] http://www.pwc.in/press-releases/2016/india-is-an-attractive-emerging-market-destination-for-foreign-portfolio-investors-pwc.html

[8] https://www.ibef.org/economy/indiasnapshot/about-india-at-a-glance

[9] https://blogs.thomsonreuters.com/answerson/indias-demographic-dividend/

[10] http://data.worldbank.org/indicator/NY.GNP.PCAP.CD

[11] https://www.statista.com/topics/2157/internet-usage-in-india/

[12] http://www.livemint.com/Politics/kZ7j1NQf5614UvO6WURXfO/88-of-households-in-India-have-a-mobile-phone.html

[13] http://www.livemint.com/Consumer/yT14OgtSC7dyywWSynWOKN/Only-17-Indians-own-smartphones-survey.html

[14] http://indiatoday.intoday.in/story/rural-india-technonology-mobile-phones-national-survey/1/710883.html

[15] http://lighthouseinsights.in/2015-american-express-indian-social-media-report.html/

[16] Sometimes data are aggregated by individual bloggers as well. Please see, http://www.soravjain.com/social-media-facts-and-stats-india-2016

India in Sept 2016, YouTube and Facebook lead (33% each), followed by Google Plus (24%), Twitter (24%), Instagram (22%), LinkedIn (21%) and Pinterest (15%). There are significant amount of mobile messenger users as well (Whatsapp, 28%, and FB messenger, 23%).[17]

A study by an industry association reported[18] that out of all social media users in the country, 33% are college students followed by 27% of young men, 12% of school kids, 11% of nonworking men and 10% of older men. By composition of locations, 47% of users are from top four metros, 25% are next four metros, 23% are from small metros, and only 4% are from non-metros. Among the activities done on social media, more than half of them update status in a social networking site or Twitter, comment on someone's blog, upload an audio-video content and maintain profile on social media networking sites. 47% of post reviews of products or services and 40% contribute to online forums/edit articles in Wikipedia.

The social media use by businesses in India is not very significant when compared to Fortune 500 firms. In 2015, a study (Ilavarasan & Rathore, 2015) looked at the top hundred listed firms in terms of revenue and found only 38% of them are using Twitter, followed by 36% of Facebook users, 32% YouTube users and 16% LinkedIn users. The usage is almost half of American firms' use of social media in 2010 (Culnan, McHugh, & Zubillaga, 2010). The penetration seems to be increasing in a rapid manner. In 2017, in a total of 50 NIFTY[19] firms in Indian stock exchange, 80% use Facebook, 76% use Twitter, 72% use YouTube and 66% use LinkedIn (Kaushik, Hemani, & Ilavarasan, 2017).

The scenario appears brighter when looks at a study done by EY (2016) using a non-probability sampling of 1250 industry representatives from more than 100 different companies. Some of the significant findings are home pages are still considered most effective means to engage with the customers; social media spending forms 16% or more of the marketing budget; three major challenges in social media marketing are sustaining or increasing engagement rates, content creation and measuring effectiveness; almost half of them do not have formal social media policy and governance structure; Instagram is becoming popular, with presence in 60% of surveyed; Facebook is used by all firms, Twitter by 96% and LinkedIn by 84%.

12.3 Rapid Literature Review

This paper is intended to provide a snapshot of research on social media in Indian context and has followed rapid literature review method. This can be operationalized in the lines of rapid evidence summaries or assessments followed in the field of health or medicine (Haby et al., 2016). This method is a diluted version of

[17] https://www.statista.com/statistics/284436/india-social-network-penetration/

[18] http://www.livemint.com/Politics/FqcL24fK5aQ68qC6KzohJO/Social-media-in-India.html

[19] https://www.nseindia.com/products/content/equities/indices/nifty_50.htm

Table 12.2 Rapid literature review search results

Search terms	Results	Subject area composition
India *AND* Facebook	138	Computer science (36.7%), social sciences (31.7%), engineering (26.6%), business and management (14.4%)
India *AND* LinkedIn	14	Business and management (50%), computer science (43%)
India *AND* YouTube	46	Computer science (43.5%), social sciences (39.1%), engineering (26.1%), arts and humanities (13%), business and management (8.7%)
India *AND* Twitter	152	Computer science (42%), social sciences (21.7%), engineering (42%), business and management (7.2%)
India *AND* 'social media'	368	Computer science (31%), social sciences (31.5%), engineering (23.6%), business and management (16.3%)

Note: There were no search results for India *AND* Google Plus, India *AND* Instagram, and India *AND* Pinterest

systematic review (Snilstveit, 2012), in terms of shortened timeframe, lessened databases to search for, exclusion of grey literature, etc.

We had selected *SCOPUS* database and searched for studies that were conducted in India. The database is used in review by other studies as well (for instance, Dwivedi et al., 2015). We had used the following sets of keywords while searching: India *AND* Facebook, India *AND* LinkedIn, India *AND* YouTube, India *AND* Google Plus, India *AND* Instagram, India *AND* Twitter and India *AND* Pinterest. We had picked up the platforms that are most used by Indians. We had included title, abstract and the keywords while searching. The search results are presented in Table 12.2.

Facebook and Twitter are most studied platforms, followed by YouTube and LinkedIn. Research in the domain of computer science tends to dominate when compared to social sciences. Business and management comes as a clear third or fourth. This inference needs to be treated with caution, as there could be multidisciplinary research and incorrect labelling. For instance, Ruhela, Bagchi, Mahanti and Seth (2015), using a large volume of tweets, attempted to understand the difference between popular and regular users and their role in information diffusion, especially related to events and their popularity.

The final results were fed into a tool used for systematic review, Rayyan (Ouzzani et al., 2016). Rayyan has an interface by which one can read the title and abstract of the search result and decide whether to include or exclude in further analysis. The software automatically detects the duplicates. Only 14 duplicates were found and removed. The number of published articles took a leap in 2015 with 158, from 88 in 2014. This is followed by 135 articles in 2016. In 2009, there are only two articles.

Out of the results, only 345 were included in the analysis, as others either did not focus on India or did not discuss anything related to social media (Table 12.3). Results that did not provide adequate information to make judgement were also excluded. There are some studies that focus on two or more domains.

Table 12.3 Classification of literature on social media

		Activities			
		Design and features	Strategy and tactics	Management and organization	Measurement and value
Levels of analysis	Users and society	(I) 20 [5]	(II) 95 [25]	(III) 9 [2]	(IV) 47 [14]
	Platforms and intermediaries	(V) 105 [30]	(VI) 6 [1]	(VII) 3 [0.8]	(VIII) 24 [7]
	Firms and industries	(IX) 4 [1]	(X) 44 [12]	(XI) 18 [5]	(XII) 53 [15]

Notes: Cells are identified in (). Number of results are presented without brackets and corresponding percentages out of 345 are given in []. Total percentage shall not be 100%, as there are studies contain multiple domains

12.4 Research Areas

The top two populated cells are II and V. Cell II talks about how users and society use social media and attempts to find out the antecedents and moderating factors. More number of technology adoption studies are present in this cell. The cell V is dominated by articles from the computer science background. These studies focus on one or two features of the platform. For instance, Agrawal and Velusamy (2016) reports about the unsupervised approach to detect spam content messages in social networking sites. These similar studies are universal in nature. In other words, the data used in the study are not India specific, and the findings can be used and applied by anyone. Another example can be designing of a novel advertisement recommendation system for video networking sites by Soundappan, Shajikumar, Ritwik, Satheedevi, and Vishanth (2015). Though efforts by these researchers are commendable, they cannot be clubbed under research on Indian context. Studies about pan India-based social media platforms is scarce, except about SMSGupShup (Rangaswamy & Cutrell, 2012).

The extant research on platforms and intermediaries on three activities – strategy and tactics, management and organization and measurement and value – is poor. For instance, there can be case studies on what Facebook is doing in the Indian market. Recently it has launched a programme which trains women entrepreneurs on Facebook marketing.[20] A study capturing this shall under cell VI. How the technology is developed and the role played by India development centres shall fall under cell VII.

The cell VIII has some studies that share the impact of local platforms present in specific locations. For instance, Roy and Ghosh (2013) present the benefits of e-learning platform for farmers, KissanKerala. Similar platforms are mostly projects tied to one location and are not pan India. Nevertheless, these studies move the boundaries of the field.

The cell I is about how articular feature of the platform is used by the users or society. For instance, Singh (2016) looked at only negative attitude towards advertisements in the platforms. But overall, the number of studies is also less. The extant

[20] https://yourstory.com/2017/03/facebook-launches-sheleadstech-programme-to-help-women-entrepreneurs/

adoption studies, in cell II, treat the platform as whole and ignore the specificities. For instance, comedy and entertainment, mostly Bollywood, is the most viewed category than education channels run by premier educational institutions in the country.[21] Similar lacuna is present for firms and industries, cell IX. We do not have much studies to illuminate how Indian businesses are using certain features of platforms.

The cell III talks about the how users and society are managing their social media activities as a part of their lives. For example, Menon (2013) shows that YouTube videos used by regional language Rap musicians to stand against the state and main stream music in a province. Jena (2015) showed how mandatory use of platforms as part of learning environment is creating stress among academicians. Again, the number of studies is less in this cell, 2%, clearly indicating need for further studies.

The cell IV is about the impact of the platforms or measuring about it and possible values they bring to people and society. Bharathi and Mala (2016) showed that platforms did not bring any value to work-life balance of the women programmers. Roy (2015) argues that social media is strengthening the democracy in India. Chakraborty and Banerjee (2013) highlight that post-disaster awareness is getting better with social media use. Twitter analytics is also used to gauge about the people's perception of Indian budget (Lakhiwal & Kar, 2016). Though there are studies, this cell also needs attention from future researches.

The literature is inadequate about how businesses are using different social media platforms. Some studies listed in cell X also double up for the users and society, as the data were collected from the managers and reported for the enterprises. For instance, Sawant (2014) collected data from instructors and showed that Web 2.0 tools are inadequately used by the library information science education offering universities.

There are some literature count studies or secondary data analysis where social media presence of the firms are found and analysed. Bakshi and Mishra (2014) lament that Indian firms have mere presence in the platforms but do not engage further or increase investment for better returns. Medhekar (2016) recommends that social media should be harnessed for medical tourism.

The cell XI is about what organizations align new social media personnel or experts with the existing resources. Chauhan and Pillai (2013) delineated the relationship between the content strategy and customer engagement by looking at the nature of posts in social media communities. English (2017) spoke multimedia gatekeeping in sports journalism from individual and magazine points of view. Other possible related questions can be: whether social media experts should be part of marketing department or communications unit, who responds to social media posts or who design the campaigns, whether the internal unit should handle it or should be outsourced, what kind of skill sets are required and how they be evaluated. Overall this cell is also underexplored by the existing literature.

---

[21] http://www.bgr.in/news/10-emerging-trends-from-indias-online-video-consumption-boom/

The last cell XII is similar to IV, but the impact is related to firms and industries. This cell also includes the government organizations and activities done by government like elections or health campaigns. Agnihotri (2014) found that firms' market valuation is enhanced by CEOs' social media reputation. Similar results are found related to twitter activities of firms and their stock prices (Deshmukh, Jain, Patwardhan, & Kulkarni, 2016). Digital India, a flagship programme of Govt of India, was found to be positive by half of population through sentiment analysis of twitter data (Mishra, Rajnish, & Kumar, 2017). Yadav and Rahman (2016) share how social media help during natural disasters using a case of Chennai floods in 2015. Twitter data is used by most of the studies when compared to other platforms.

12.5 Future Research

The rapid review of literature showed that computer scientists dominate this space in India. But their researches are not necessarily contributing the contractual knowledge of India. There is a need for multidisciplinary work. For instance, Samarajiva, Lokanathan, Madhawa, Kreindler and Maldeniya (2015)'s work on using telecom data for urban mobility showed how programming knowledge could be used for developmental research. This can be attempted for business practices as well. Social scientists including management researchers should think of applying results from computer scientists. For instance, spam detection results would be useful for fake news or scam-related domains.

In the earlier section, following gaps were identified: studies about pan India-based social media platforms are scarce; inadequate knowledge about what platforms as businesses are operating in Indian market and what are their plans; need for illuminating how Indian businesses are using certain features of platforms and are they different in different sectors; how do users and society manage their social media activities as a part of their lives; knowledge about platforms apart from the most popular ones being used by businesses is poor; how do organizations align new social media personnel or experts with the existing resources; and what is the subsequent organizational change.

There are many homegrown social media platforms. Zomato (www.zomato) is Indian equivalent of Yelp, a platform for crowd-sourced reviews of restaurants and other food joints. MouthShut (www.mouthshut.com) is a site for reviews of products and services written by consumers. PaGalGuy (www.pagalguy.com) is a networking site for management students and business school aspirants. Searching for these platforms did not yield any results. All these sites have content predominantly Indian and are context specific. Studying about them shall provide rich insights about the minds of users and possible usage by the customers.

There are platforms which are used by Indians in large number. For instance, Quora, a platform where users ask questions and answer, has larger number of Indians. In its membership base, 20% are Indians after 34% of US citizens.[22]

[22] http://www.alexa.com/siteinfo/quora.com

Searching for Quora in the literature did not yield any results. Similarly, Snapchat is a popular image messaging and networking mobile app among the teens in the world,[23] and India is no exception. The literature does not offer any clues about the use in India. Apart from academic studies, there seems to be lot of material from the trade press. For instance, Social Samosa, a digital advertising firm specializing in social media marketing publishes case studies regularly, covering all social media platforms.[24] The case studies lack the academic rigour but can be definitely used in the classrooms for teaching or leading discussions.

In summary, social media research in and of India is inadequate and is open for future explorations in almost all aspects of platforms. The research about Indian context has universal appeal as emerging market model. The time appears to be ripe for such researches.

References

Agnihotri, A. (2014). Mass-media-based corporate reputation and firms' market valuation – Evidence from emerging markets. *Corporate Reputation Review*, *17*(3), 206–218. https://doi.org/10.1057/crr.2014.10

Agrawal, M., & Velusamy, R. L. (2016). Unsupervised spam detection in hyves using SALSA. *Advances in Intelligent Systems and Computing*, *404*, 517–526. https://doi.org/10.1007/978-81-322-2695-6_43

AlAlwan, A., Rana, N. P., Dwivedi, Y. K., & Algharabat, R. (2017). Social media in marketing: A review and analysis of the existing literature. *Telematics and Informatics*. Available at http://www.sciencedirect.com/science/article/pii/S0736585317301077

Aral, S., Dellarocas, C., & Godes, D. (2013). Introduction to the special issue – Social media and business transformation: A framework for research. *Information Systems Research*, *24*(1), 3–13.

Bakshi, M., & Mishra, P. (2014). Social media marketing in emerging economies: Case study of three Indian firms. In *Digital arts and entertainment: Concepts, methodologies, tools, and applications* (Vol. 2). Hershey, PA: IGI Global. https://doi.org/10.4018/978-1-4666-6114-1.ch029

Bergoeing, R., Piguillem, F., & Loayza, N. V. (2010). *Why are developing countries so slow in adopting new technologies? The aggregate and complementary impact of micro distortions. Policy Research Working Papers*. The World Bank. https://doi.org/10.1596/1813-9450-5393.

Bharathi, S. V., & Mala, E. P. (2016). A study on the determinants of work–life balance of women employees in information technology companies in India. *Global Business Review*, *17*(3), 665–683. https://doi.org/10.1177/0972150916630847

Carr, N. G. (2004). *Does IT matter?: Information technology and the corrosion of competitive advantage*. Boston, MA: Harvard Business Press.

Chakraborty, B., & Banerjee, S. (2013). Modeling the evolution of post disaster social awareness from social web sites. In *2013 IEEE International Conference on Cybernetics, CYBCONF 2013* (pp. 51–56). Lausanne. https://doi.org/10.1109/CYBConf.2013.6617444.

Chauhan, K., & Pillai, A. (2013). Role of content strategy in social media brand communities: A case of higher education institutes in India. *Journal of Product and Brand Management*, *22*(1), 40–51. https://doi.org/10.1108/10610421311298687

[23] https://www.recode.net/2017/5/9/15584458/snapchat-teen-users-facebook-despite-size

[24] https://www.socialsamosa.com/category/indian-social-media-case-studies/

Cruz-Jesus, F., Oliveira, T., Bacao, F., & Irani, Z. (2016). Assessing the pattern between economic and digital development of countries. *Information Systems Frontiers*, (February), 1–20. https://doi.org/10.1007/s10796-016-9634-1

Culnan, M. J., McHugh, P. J., & Zubillaga, J. I. (2010). How large US companies can use Twitter and other social media to gain business value. *MIS Quarterly Executive*, *9*(4):243–259.

Deshmukh, B. G., Jain, P. S., Patwardhan, M. S., & Kulkarni, V. (2016). Spin-offs in Indian stock market owing to twitter sentiments, commodity prices and analyst recommendations. In B. S. K. Kuri M. Goar V. (Ed.), *ACM International Conference Proceeding Series* (Vol. 12–13–Augu). Association for Computing Machinery. https://doi.org/10.1145/2979779.2979856.

Donner, J. (2007). The rules of beeping: Exchanging messages via intentional "missed calls" on mobile phones. *Journal of Computer-Mediated Communication*, *13*(1), 1–22.

Dwivedi, Y. K., Kapoor, K. K., & Chen, H. (2015). Social media marketing and advertising. *The Marketing Review*, *15*(3), 289–309.

Dwivedi, Y. K., Mäntymäki, M., Ravishankar, M. N., Janssen, M., Clement, M., Slade, E. L., … Simintiras, A. C. (2016). Social Media: The Good, the Bad, and the Ugly: 15th IFIP WG 6.11 Conference on e-Business, e-Services, and e-Society, I3E 2016, Swansea, UK, September 13–15, 2016, Proceedings. Springer.

English, P. (2017). Social media boundaries in sports journalism: Individual and organisational gatekeeping in India and Australia. *Asian Journal of Communication*, 1–17. https://doi.org/10.1080/01292986.2017.1284876

EY. (2016). *Social media marketing: India trends study 2016.*

Fransman, M. (2010). *The new ICT ecosystem: Implications for policy and regulation.* Cambridge: Cambridge University Press.

Gunaratne, R. L., Ilavarasan, P. V., Fernando, S., & Rohman, I. K. (2015). National broadband networks of Malaysia, India, Indonesia and Australia: A comparative study. *Competition and Regulation in Network Industries*, *16*(1), 23–46.

Haby, M. M., Chapman, E., Clark, R., Barreto, J., Reveiz, L., & Lavis, J. N. (2016). What are the best methodologies for rapid reviews of the research evidence for evidence-informed decision making in health policy and practice: A rapid review. *Health Research Policy and Systems*, *14*(1), 83. https://doi.org/10.1186/s12961-016-0155-7

Hellström, J. (2010). *The Innovative Use of Mobile Applications in East Africa. Africa.* Retrieved from http://109.73.162.110/~humanito/sites/default/files/SR2010-12_SIDA_Hellstrom.pdf

Ilavarasan, P. V. (2017). Bridging ICTD research and policy-making: Notes from a systematic review on MSMEs in the low- and middle-income countries. *Information Technology for Development*, *0*(0), 1–11. https://doi.org/10.1080/02681102.2017.1315355

Ilavarasan, V., & Rathore, A. (2015). Social Media use in Indian Businesses: Inputs for Appropriateness. In *ECSM2015-Proceedings of the 2nd European Conference on Social Media 2015: ECSM 2015* (p. 218). Academic Conferences Limited.

Ismagilova, E., Dwivedi, Y. K., Slade, E. L., & Williams, M. D. (2017). *Electronic word of mouth (eWOM) in the marketing context: A state of the art analysis and future directions.* Cham, Switzerland: Springer International Publishing.

Jena, R. K. (2015). Technostress in ICT enabled collaborative learning environment: An empirical study among Indian academician. *Computers in Human Behavior*. https://doi.org/10.1016/j.chb.2015.03.020

Kaplan, A. M., & Haenlein, M. (2010). Users of the world, unite! The challenges and opportunities of Social Media. *Business Horizons*, *53*(1), 59–68.

Kaushik, B., Hemani, H., & Ilavarasan, P. V. (2017). *Does social media matter?* (No. NA). New Delhi.

Lakhiwal, A., & Kar, A. K. (2016). Insights from twitter analytics: Modeling social media personality dimensions and impact of breakthrough events. *Lecture Notes in Computer Science* (Including Subseries Lecture Notes in Artificial Intelligence and Lecture Notes in Bioinformatics), *9844*, 533–544. https://doi.org/10.1007/978-3-319-45234-0_47.

Ling, R., & Horst, H. A. (2011). Mobile communication in the global south. *New Media & Society*, *13*(3), 363–374. https://doi.org/10.1177/1461444810393899

Medhekar, A. (2016). The role of social media for knowledge dissemination in medical tourism: A case of India. In *Harnessing social media as a knowledge management tool*. Hershey, PA: IGI Global. https://doi.org/10.4018/978-1-5225-0495-5.ch002

Menon, B. (2013). The blazon call of hip hop: Lyrical storms in Kerala's musical cultures. *Journal of Creative Communications*, *8*(2–3), 231–250. https://doi.org/10.1177/0973258613512574

Minges, M. (2016). Exploring the relationship between broadband and economic growth. *World Development Report*, *1*. Retrieved from http://documents.worldbank.org/curated/en/2016/02/25851781/world-development-report-2016-digital-dividends-exploring-relationship-between-broadband-economic-growth

Mishra, P., Rajnish, R., & Kumar, P. N. (2017). Sentiment analysis of Twitter data: Case study on digital India. In *2016 International Conference on Information Technology, InCITe 2016 - The Next Generation IT Summit on the Theme - Internet of Things: Connect your Worlds* (pp. 148–153). Institute of Electrical and Electronics Engineers Inc. https://doi.org/10.1109/INCITE.2016.7857607.

Ngai, E. W. T., Tao, S. S. C., & Moon, K. K. L. (2015). Social media research: Theories, constructs, and conceptual frameworks. *International Journal of Information Management*, *35*(1), 33–44. https://doi.org/10.1016/j.ijinfomgt.2014.09.004

Ouzzani, M., Hammady, H., Fedorowicz, Z., Elmagarmid, A., Chalmers, T., Smith, H., … Yen, P. (2016). Rayyan—A web and mobile app for systematic reviews. *Systematic Reviews*, *5*(1), 210. https://doi.org/10.1186/s13643-016-0384-4

Plume, C. J., Dwivedi, Y. K., & Slade, E. L. (2016). *Social media in the marketing context: A state of the art analysis and future directions* (1st ed.). Oxford, UK: Chandos Publishing Ltd.

Rangaswamy, N., & Cutrell, E. (2012). Re-sourceful networks: Notes from a mobile social networking platform in India. *Pacific Affairs*, *85*(3), 587–606. https://doi.org/10.5509/2012853587

Rathore, A. K., & Ilavarasan, P. V. (2018). Social media and business practices. In *Encyclopedia of information science and technology* (Fourth ed., pp. 7126–7139). Hershey, PA: IGI Global.

Roy, D. (2015). Social media -the new weapon in indian democracy. *Journal of Interdisciplinary and Multidisciplinary Research*, *2*(7), 49–54. Retrieved from https://www.scopus.com/inward/record.uri?eid=2-s2.0-84947246957&partnerID=40&md5=99ec9e2a40534c4a335a43e3aa60e770

Roy, M., & Ghosh, C. K. (2013). The benefits of the e-learning agricultural project kissankerala to digital immigrants and digital natives. *Turkish Online Journal of Distance Education*, *14*(2), 150–164. Retrieved from https://www.scopus.com/inward/record.uri?eid=2-s2.0-84881638836&partnerID=40&md5=26ad825a9feac04c2c37b23b954254ce

Ruhela, A., Bagchi, A., Mahanti, A., & Seth, A. (2015). The rich and middle classes on twitter: Are popular users indeed different from regular users? *Computer Communications*. https://doi.org/10.1016/j.comcom.2015.07.024

Samarajiva, R., Lokanathan, S., Madhawa, K., Kreindler, G., & Maldeniya, D. (2015). Big data to improve urban planning. *Economic & Political Weekly*, *50*(22), 43.

Sawant, S. (2014). Open source and free e-learning tools useful in LIS education. In *Open source technology: Concepts, methodologies, tools, and applications* (Vol. 3–4). Hershey, PA: IGI Global. https://doi.org/10.4018/978-1-4666-7230-7.ch071

Singh, R. (2016). Monotony of social networking among millennial and its effect on social advertisement: A challenge to digital marketers. *Young Consumers*, *17*(4), 376–387. https://doi.org/10.1108/YC-05-2016-00605

Snilstveit, B. (2012). Systematic reviews: From "bare bones" reviews to policy relevance. *Journal of Development Effectiveness*, *4*(3), 388–408.

Soundappan, S., Shajikumar, R., Ritwik, M., Satheedevi, C., & Sakthie Vishanth, T. M. (2015). A novel advertisement recommendation system for online video portals. *International Journal of Applied Engineering Research*, *10*(11), 28903–28910. Retrieved from https://www.scopus.com/inward/record.uri?eid=2-s2.0-84937829066&partnerID=40&md5=500c7a05180a10ba48dae8f0a6d243fc

Yadav, M., & Rahman, Z. (2016). The social role of social media: The case of Chennai rains-2015. *Social Network Analysis and Mining*, *6*(1). https://doi.org/10.1007/s13278-016-0410-5

P. Vigneswara Ilavarasan (PhD, IIT Kanpur) is Associate Professor at the Dept. of Management Studies, Indian Institute of Technology Delhi. He researches and teaches about production and consumption of information and communication technologies (ICTs) with a special focus on India. His specific research interests are ICTs and development, Indian IT industry and social media. Dr. Ilavarasan has been a visiting research fellow at the United Nations University Institute on Computing and Society (Macau). He is a recipient of the Outstanding Young Faculty Fellowship Award at IIT Delhi and Prof. M.N. Srinivas Memorial Prize of the Indian Sociological Society. He has received large research grants from IDRC (Canada), Govt. of India, Oxford Analytica (UK), IPTS (European Commission) and IdeaCorp (Philippines). He is an active contributor to the international journals and conferences of repute. Further details: http://web.iitd.ac.in/~vignes/

Chapter 13
Evaluating the Current Situation of Mobile Services (M-Services) in the Kingdom of Saudi Arabia

Abdullah Mohammed Baabdullah, Ali Abdallah Alalwan, and Naim Salameh Al Qadi

Abstract The main aim of this study is to provide further understanding about the adoption of mobile services (mobile Internet and mobile government) over the context of Saudi Arabia. Through a careful evaluation of the current situation of mobile services in Saudi Arabia, researchers have noticed that the lower adoption of these services is the main barrier that could prevent citizens and service providers the full utilisation of these applications. It was also noticed that the related issues of mobile services have been rarely examined in Saudi Arabia as well as there is a necessity to select a theoretical foundation suitable for the perspective of Saudi customers. Therefore, the unified theory of acceptance and use of technology (UTAUT2) was adopted to propose the conceptual model of the current study. This is expanded by considering trust and awareness alongside UTAUT2 factors. Further, it was proposed that a survey questionnaire could be more appropriate to test the conceptual model and verify the research hypotheses. The main limitations and future research directions are discussed further in the last section of this study.

Keywords Mobile services · Mobile Internet · Mobile government · Saudi Arabia · UTAUT2

A. M. Baabdullah (✉)
Department of Management Information Systems, Faculty of Economics and Administration, King Abdulaziz University, Jeddah, Saudi Arabia
e-mail: baabdullah@kau.edu.sa

A. A. Alalwan · N. S. Al Qadi
Amman University College for Financial & Administrative Sciences, Al-Balqa' Applied University, Salt, Jordan
e-mail: alwan.a.a.ali@gmail.com; dr.naem@bau.edu.jo

Y. K. Dwivedi et al. (eds.), *Emerging Markets from a Multidisciplinary Perspective*, Advances in Theory and Practice of Emerging Markets,
https://doi.org/10.1007/978-3-319-75013-2_13

13.1 Introduction

Several countries worldwide are increasingly keen to utilise the technological revolution in the communication and mobile field to improve their quality of life for their own people. Indeed, mobile and telecommunication is one of the most valuable sectors for any country. For instance, in the Kingdom of Saudi Arabia (KSA), the largest share of investment and spending in the area of information and communication technology (ICT) is for the communication sector (80%). This means that there are a lot of opportunities in the KSA that are also available to expand the scope of mobile services (M-Services) provided to the Saudi citizens. Nevertheless, the adoption rate of the mobile Internet (M-Internet) by Saudi citizens is very low (less than 10%). This is in addition to the fact that such innovative services have never been used by about 8% of customers in the KSA. Accurately, the adoption rate of these services goes to the lowest level in the southern side of the KSA and for the age group of 55 years and more. According to a report published by the Communications and Information Technology Commission CITC (2007), M-Internet services are realised by more than half of Saudi users as substitute services for traditional platforms (i.e. landline phone and computers) of communication. The same situation of M-Internet services could also be noticed regarding Saudi private sector where the adoption rate of these services does not go more than 8%. As for the public sector, the Communications and Information Technology Commission CITC (2007) reported that only 5% of the public organisations have already adopted mobile government (M-Gov). Based on these statistics for the current situation of M-Services for either individuals or business customers, it could be concluded that the adoption of these services does not reach what has been planned and expected (Abanumy & Mayhew, 2005; Alhussain, Drew, & Von Hellens, 2010; Al-Khalifa, 2011; Almutairi, 2011; Alsenaidy & Ahmad, 2012; Baabdullah, Alalwan, Rana, Dwivedi, & Weerakkody, 2017). Accordingly, a lot of research and practical efforts are requested to accelerate the current understanding about the main reasons hindering or motivating the acceptance of such innovative services in the KSA among all kinds of users. Therefore, this study was motivated to analyse the current situation of two kinds of M-Services (M-Internet and M-Gov) as well as to identify the main factors that could shape the Saudi citizens' intention to adopt such services.

In fact, an understanding of the main reasons behind the customers' intention and adoption of M-Services will definitely help to move those potential adopters to be actual users of these services. Thus, the main concertation of this paper is to discover and identify the most important factor that could have an impact on the behavioural intention to adopt M-Services by Saudi citizens. The fundamental challenge to let M-Services get success in the KSA is to know how M-Services' providers and the Saudi government can effectively introduce such innovative applications in an attractive manner as well as motivate Saudi citizens to adopt such applications as more useful and productive channels in comparison with traditional human encounter (Alsenaidy & Ahmad, 2012). This, in turn, encourages a good number of researchers to examine and figure out the key factor that could play a critical role in hindering or motivating individuals' inclination to accept and adopt M-Services (see Abanumy & Mayhew, 2005; Alhussain et al., 2010; Al-Khalifa, 2011; Almutairi, 2011; Alsenaidy & Ahmad, 2012; Alwahaishi & Snášel, 2013a, 2013b; Analysys Mason, 2012; Venkatesh, Morris, Davis, & Davis, 2003; Weidong, Keyi, Linlin, & Likun, 2009).

In spite of the fact that these studies' efforts expand the current understanding about the adoption of M-Services, there is always a need to build a comprehensive conceptual model covering the main personal, perceptual, environmental and psychological dimensions from the perspective of citizens in the KSA. For the aim of this study, the new model of Venkatesh, Thong, and Xu (2012), the unified theory of acceptance and use of technology (UTAUT2), was adopted as a theoretical foundation of the current study model. In detail, the Saudi citizens' intention to adopt M-Internet and M-Gov is supposed to be predicted by performance expectancy (PE), effort expectancy (EE), social influence (SI), facilitating conditions (FC), perceived value (PV) and hedonic motivation (HM). This is in addition to two other factors – trust (TR) and awareness (AWA) – which are proposed to have a direct impact on the behavioural intention as well.

13.2 The Current State of Literature of M-Internet and M-Gov in the Saudi Arabian Context

As discussed in the prior section, the related issues of M-Internet have attracted a considerable interest for researchers and practitioners. This interest could be a return to the developments and expansions in the mobile and telecommunication industry in the KSA especially over the commercial and financial market (STC Group, 2011). As the customers' intention is the main challenge for moving potential adopters to be actual users of the M-Internet, there is a need to discover and identify the main factors that could have an influence on customers' intention and, accordingly, understand how the actual adoption of these services could be enhanced. Therefore, there are several researchers worldwide who have examined the related issues of adoption of the M-Internet services such as Das (2011), Hailin (2010), Hong, Thong, and Tam (2006), Hsu, Lu, and Hsu (2007), Venkatesh et al. (2003) and Weidong et al. (2009). However, over the Saudi context, there are quite a few researchers who have paid attention to examining the adoption of M-Internet services (see Alwahaishi & Snášel, 2013a, 2013b; Baabdullah, Nasseef, & Alalwan, 2016). From this perspective, current research aspires to expand the current understanding about the main factors that could predict the citizens' intention in the KSA as well as add a theoretical contribution to the existing literature in the KSA.

In their endeavours to explore factors that could predict Saudi citizens' adoption of the M-Internet, Alwahaishi and Snášel (2013a) expanded the UTAUT by considering the role of perceived value, attention focus and playfulness. Their empirical results supported the statistical impact of performance expectancy, facilitating conditions, social influences and perceived playfulness on the Saudi citizens' intention to adopt M-Internet services. In a different study, Alwahaishi and Snášel (2013b) were also able to prove that customers' inclination to use the M-Internet is significantly predicted by the impact performance expectancy and perceived playfulness. Earlier in 2005, Abanumy and Mayhew examined the acceptance of M-Gov. Abanumy and Mayhew (2005) indicated that the level of adoption of M-Gov is not as expected and this lowest level could be attributed to the lower level of adoption of overall E-Gov services. Accordingly, Abanumy and Mayhew (2005) claimed this situation to the fact that the Saudi government has not spent sufficient efforts to motivate Saudi citizens to adopt such innovative services.

In his study, Al-Khalifa (2011) asserted the importance of examining Saudi citizens' intention towards kinds of mobile phones and which new or traditional applications are available over these phones as well. By the same token, Al-Solbi and Mayhew (2005) focused on how technology readiness either in the public or private context could influence on the success of M-Gov applications in the KSA. One of the main outcomes reached by Al-Solbi and Mayhew (2005) is the importance of having a well-planned strategy by the Saudi government to firstly accelerate the level of technology readiness at the level of governmental organisations and secondly work hard to learn and educate people about the existing and importance of such innovative services in their daily life. Similarly, Alhussain and Drew (2010) empirically approved that customers in the KSA are more likely to be interested in using M-Gov services if they perceived that such services were well secured and protecting their privacy. Alhussain and Drew (2010) also concluded that the adoption of M-Gov is most likely to reach the highest level among those customers who have a higher willingness to use these emerging services. Alsenaidy and Ahmad (2012) presented a number of benefits that could be utilised from both perspectives: service providers (i.e. productivity, effectiveness, less paper work, cost reduction, feasibility) and customers (i.e. public information, quick and accurate service delivery, accessibility). Despite these benefits, customers in the KSA are still hesitating to actually adopt the M-Gov services. This is attributed by Alhussain and Drew (2010) and Alsenaidy and Ahmad (2012) to the fact that Saudi customers are not fully aware of these services positively; there is also distrust in using these services. Other obstacles of adoption of M-Gov in the KSA were mentioned by Almutairi (2011) such as M-authentication, M-payment, location-aware applications and the content display management. Later, Ahmad, Ansari, Akhtar, and Parveen (2014) attributed the lower level of customers' knowledge and awareness of M-Gov to the fact that these services are not commonly used and adopted by people in the KSA. Among the main reasons behind this level of adoption of M-Gov are the levels of perceived risk as well as that the main technical and informational facilities are not adequately available in the KSA (see Ahmad et al., 2014). One of the main solutions suggested to enhance the adoption of these services is biometric technology to decrease the level of customer risk as well as provide more secured and trustworthy services (see Alhussain et al., 2010; Alhussain & Drew, 2012; Baabdullah, Dwivedi, & Williams, 2015a, 2015b).

All things considered, it seems that the main challenge of success for such innovative services is not only related to introducing and implementing these services but also the extent of how much citizens in the KSA could be converted to be actual users. This is especially in the light of the fact that these services have recently been implemented in the KSA, and accordingly, the related issues of M-Internet and M-Gov have not been adequately examined and well covered in the KSA.

13.3 Research Gap

In fact, the related issues of the M-Internet and M-Gov have received less attention by researchers in the KSA (see Table 13.1). Practically, different research methods have been adopted by researchers to test the adoption of M-Internet and M-Gov. As M-Internet and M-Gov represent new issues to be discovered in the KSA, there are very few studies examining these applications. Thus, some researchers have employed the qualitative approach to discover the related issues of M-Internet and M-Gov in the KSA (see Table 13.1). To put it differently, theory building has been the main standpoint for these qualitative studies because of the absence of a solid theoretical foundation in the KSA for the adoption of M-Internet and M-Gov. On the other hand, quite a few studies have adopted the quantitative approach and theory testing standpoint. Noticeably, students were the main source of the empirical data for these quantitative studies. This, in turn, reflects negatively on the generalisability of these studies' results for other categories of people in the KSA.

Based on critical reviewing of the most studies in the KSA, it could be noticed that well-known models and theories (i.e. theory of reasoned action (TRA), theory of planned behaviour (TPB), innovation diffusion theory (IDT), motivational model (MM) or technology acceptance model (TAM)) have not been adopted or integrated to examine the related issues of M-Internet and M-Gov issues. Accordingly, one of the main challenges for the current study is to select a theoretical base covering the most important aspects from the Saudi citizens' perspective and provide a more accurate view regarding the adoption of such innovative systems in the KSA.

As such, this study recognises a need to propose a solid conceptual model based on a well-established theoretical foundation. This is in addition to the fact that there is a necessity to explore the related issues of M-Internet and M-Gov adoption based on a theoretical foundation focusing on the customers' perspective rather than an organisational perspective which has never happened prior to these studies being conducted in the KSA. Therefore, as the UTAUT2 proposed by Venkatesh et al. (2012) is fully focused on customer context, the decision was to select UTAUT2 as a theoretical base for the current study model. Also, to override the generalisability concern existing in the prior study over the KSA, this study in its proposed research methodology indicates that all categories of people will be presented and targeted in the current study sample.

Table 13.1 Examples of M-Internet/M-Gov studies within the context of Saudi Arabia

Technology	Study	Citation	Methodology, key findings, contributions, limitations and future research recommendations
M-Internet	M-Internet Diffusion	Alwahaishi and Snášel (2013c)	Quantitative and qualitative studies have been followed. The findings constitute a starting point for theoretical framework to identify the factors affecting the acceptance and use of mobile in a consumer context. Nevertheless, future research is demanded in order to increase the amount of collected data in order to establish robust theoretical framework
	M-Internet Acceptance/Use	Alwahaishi and Snášel (2013a)	
	M-internet adoption	Alwahaishi and Snášel (2013b)	
M-Gov	Adoption of Biometrics in M-Gov Applications	Alhussain and Drew (2012)	In these studies, a qualitative research with secondary data resources has been followed. The papers reviewed the M-Gov implementation in the KSA. There is a need for gradual transition from E-Gov to M-Gov services. Generally speaking, they did not investigate the factors that can have an effect on the implementation of M-Gov
	M-Gov Security	Alhussain et al. (2010)	
	M-Gov Websites	Al-Khalifa (2011)	
	A review of current state M-Gov	Ahmad et al. (2014); Alsenaidy and Ahmad (2012)	
	Challenges and Key Success Factors in M-Gov	Almutairi (2011)	

13.4 Conceptual Model

As discussed before, the selection of UTAUT2 was based on the fact that this model was especially proposed by Venkatesh et al. (2012) to address the innovation adoption from the customers' perspective. Besides that, the original model of Venkatesh et al. (2012) has been tested and supported by several researchers (i.e. Alalwan, Dwivedi, & Rana, 2017; Alalwan, Dwivedi, Rana, & Williams, 2016; Alalwan, Dwivedi, & Williams, 2016; Alwahaishi & Snášel, 2013c; Wang & Wang, 2010; Yfantis, Vassilopoulou, Pateli, & Usoro, 2013) in the context of M-Services. Thus, the main factors of UTAUT2 [PE, EE, SI, HM, PV, FC) are formulated as key predictors of the Saudi customers' intention to adopt M-Internet and M-Gov services (see Fig. 13.1). As the targeted respondents of the current study are potential users who have not yet used or adopted M-Internet and M-Gov, habit was dropped from the conceptual model of the current study.

Due to the fact that UTAUT2 does not cover all the dimensions that could have an impact on the customers' intention as stated by Alalwan et al. (2017), Alalwan, Dwivedi, Rana, Lal, and Williams (2015), Alalwan, Dwivedi, Rana, and Williams (2016), Alalwan, Dwivedi, and Williams (2016), Alalwan, Dwivedi, Rana, and Williams (2016), there was a need to expand the theoretical horizon of UTAUT2 by considering other constructs. This was highly recommended by Venkatesh et al.

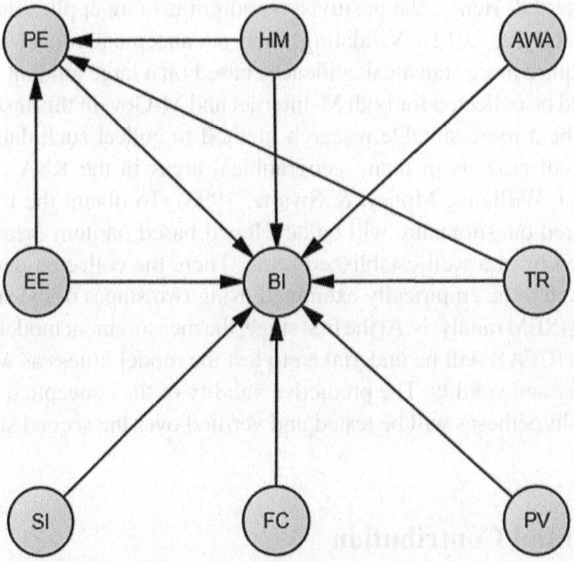

Fig. 13.1 Proposed research model (Adapted from: Gefen, Karahanna, & Straub, 2003; Venkatesh et al., 2012).

(2012) who assured the importance of expanding the UTAUT2 theoretically by considering different factors and practically by applying UTAUT2 in different countries and context and for different applications as well. Indeed, a closer scrutiny of the prior literature of M-Services leads to discovering two main factors; they are trust (TR) and awareness (AWA) as key predictors of the customers' intention over this area (i.e. Almutairi, 2011; Alsenaidy & Ahmad, 2012; Chong, Ooi, Lin, & Bao, 2012; Pedersen, 2005; Shareef, Kumar, Kumar, & Dwivedi, 2011; Shi, Wu, Zhou, & Chen, 2009; Zhang, Huang, & Chen, 2010), and therefore, both were considered over the conceptual model. Furthermore, as seen in Fig. 13.1, it was added as a new causal relationship among the UTAUT constructs. Therefore, PE was supposed to be predicted by three factors: EE as suggested by Davis, Bagozzi, and Warshaw (1989), TR as suggested by Gefen et al. (2003) and HM as recommended by Van der Heijden (2004).

13.5 The Proposed Research Methodology

It was mentioned above that the conceptual model of the current study was built and based on a strong theoretical foundation (UTAUT2), and accordingly, the nature of this study seems to be more theory testing rather than theory building (Bhattacherjee, 2012). According to Orlikowski and Baroudi (1991) and Straub, Boudreau, and Gefen (2004), this is in addition to the fact that the area of information system and technology acceptance is well-established and a lot of models and theories have been validated and tested. Hence, the positivist paradigm is more applicable to the current study (Bhattacherjee, 2012). Validating such a conceptual model and testing its hypotheses require more statistical evidences based on a large amount of quantitative data that should be collected for both M-Internet and M-Gov. In this instance, a survey was found to be a more suitable research method to collect such data from a large number of Saudi citizens in many geographical areas in the KSA (Bhattacherjee, 2012; Remenyi, Williams, Money, & Swartz, 1998). To obtain the required data, a self-administered questionnaire will be developed based on item measurements that will be selected from a well-established scale. Then, the collected data will be processed and saved to be empirically examined using two stages of the structural equation modelling (SEM) analysis. At the first stage, the measurement model (confirmatory factor analysis (CFA)) will be undertaken to test the model fitness as well as the construct reliability and validity. The predictive validity of the conceptual model and the main research hypotheses will be tested and verified over the second stage.

13.6 Potential Contribution

There is a considerable amount of theoretical contribution that could hopefully be captured by the current study. First of all, this study addresses the problem which has rarely been tested over the Saudi context. Accordingly, this will make a contribution to the current understanding for the related issues of M-Services over this emerging country. Further, this study will be a foundation for future empirical studies that will be undertaken in the KSA by extracting very critical factors from a very well-known theory (UTAUT2) and other M-Internet and M-Gov literature. By doing so, this study was also able expand the validity of UTAUT to a new emerging context (the KSA) as well as to test the Saudi citizens' intention to adopt new applications (M-Internet and M-Gov). Likewise, adding both trust and awareness in the conceptual model expands the theoretical scope of UTAUT2. This was largely suggested and recommended by Venkatesh et al. (2012). By the same token, other relationships were added over the conceptual model as well. For instance, the important role of intrinsic utilities (hedonic motivation) on performance expectancy will add a deep view on how customers could perceive such new systems as more useful and productive in their daily life. Also, according to Gefen et al. (2003), it will be an important contribution for the current study to see how the aspects of trust could shape the perception of Saudi citizens towards these innovative services.

13.7 Limitations and Future Research

Indeed, this study seems to be a more theoretical and conceptual attempt to understand how Saudi citizens could react and perceive M-Services. However, it does not provide empirical evidence about the main factors that could actually influence the

Saudi citizens' intention and adoption. Thus, it is important to empirically examine the proposition introduced in the current study by collecting empirical data from customers who are interested in such services in the KSA. Even though adding both trust and awareness could expand the theoretical horizon of the UTAUT2, it would be appropriate to conduct a construct relationships' analysis and mapping to identify other relevant factors for examining M-Services adoption. For example, some recent studies (Alenezi, Tarhini, Masa'deh, Alalwan, & Al-Qirim, 2017; Dwivedi et al., 2017; Dwivedi, Rana, Jeyaraj, Clement, & Williams, 2017; Rana, Dwivedi, Lal, Williams, & Clement, 2017; Rana, Dwivedi, Williams, & Weerakkody, 2016) have highlighted the need of reintroducing and examining the role of attitude in UTAUT and UTAUT2, which may also be appropriate for examining M-Services in Saudi Arabia. Likewise, Kapoor, Dwivedi, and Williams (2014a, 2014b, 2014c, 2014d, 2015a, 2015b) has highlighted the role of a number of innovation attributes for explaining consumer intention and adoption of mobile-based innovations in a developing country context, which may also be appropriate for explaining the adoption of a mobile-based innovation in Saudi Arabia. This could be the focus of attention by future researchers to consider. The current study model just presents the main causal paths between independent and dependent factors without any justification or explanations. Accordingly, future work should discuss these hypotheses more by providing more logical and theoretical justifications for each causal path.

References

Abanumy, A., & Mayhew, P. (2005). M-government implications for e-government in developing countries: The case of Saudi Arabia. *EURO mGOV, 2005*, 1–6.

Ahmad, T., Ansari, A. A., Akhtar, A., & Parveen, S. (2014). Current review of ICT and m-government services in Saudi Arabia. *International Journal of Computer and Engineering Applications, 7*(2):71–77.

Alalwan, A. A., Dwivedi, Y. K., & Rana, N. P. (2017). Factors influencing adoption of mobile banking by Jordanian bank customers: Extending UTAUT2 with trust. *International Journal of Information Management, 37*(3), 99–110.

Alalwan, A. A., Dwivedi, Y. K., Rana, N. P., Lal, B., & Williams, M. D. (2015). Consumer adoption of internet banking in Jordan: Examining the role of hedonic motivation, habit, self-efficacy and trust. *Journal of Financial Services Marketing, 20*(2), 145–157.

Alalwan, A. A., Dwivedi, Y. K., Rana, N. P., & Williams, M. D. (2016). Consumer adoption of mobile banking in Jordan: Examining the role of usefulness, ease of use, perceived risk and self-efficacy. *Journal of Enterprise Information Management, 29*(1), 118–139.

Alalwan, A. A., Dwivedi, Y. K., & Williams, M. D. (2016). Customers' intention and adoption of telebanking in Jordan. *Information Systems Management, 33*(2), 154–178.

Alenezi, H., Tarhini, A., Masa'deh, R. E., Alalwan, A., & Al-Qirim, N. (2017). Factors affecting the adoption of e-government in Kuwait: A qualitative study. *Electronic Journal of e-Government, 15*(2), 84–102.

Alhussain, T. O. M., & Drew, S. (2010). Towards secure m-gov applications: A survey study in the Kingdom of Saudi Arabia. In *International conference on intelligent network and computing* (ICINC 2010). IEEE. 26th to 28th November 2010 Kuala Lumpur, Malaysia

Alhussain, T. O. M., & Drew, S. (2012). *Developing a theoretical framework for the adoption of biometrics in m-gov applications using grounded theory*. INTECH Open Access Publisher. London, UK

Alhussain, T. O. M., Drew, S., & Von Hellens, L. A. (2010). Qualitative study on implementing biometric technology in m-gov security: A grounded theory approach. *In 5th international conference on qualitative research in IT and IT in qualitative research (QualIT2010)*. QUT, Griffith University and ANU. QualIT 2010 - Brisbane, QLD, Australia Duration: 29 Nov 2010 - 30 Nov 2010

Al-Khalifa, H. S. (2011). Development of m-gov websites: A functional design approach. In *Proceedings of the 13th international conference on information integration and web-based applications and services* (pp. 455–458). ACM. 5-7 December 2011 Ho Chi Minh City, Vietnam

Almutairi, M. S. (2011). M-gov: Challenges and key success factors. Saudi Arabia case study. In M. Almutairi & L. A. Mohammed (Eds.), *Cases on ICT utilization, practice and solutions: Tools for managing day-to-day issues* (pp. 78–96). Hershey, PA: IGI Global.

Alsenaidy, A., & Ahmad, T. (2012). *A review of current state m-Gov in Saudi Arabia*. Department of Biochemistry, King Saudi University. Hang Tuah Jaya, Melaka.

Al-Solbi, A., & Mayhew, P. J. (2005). *Measuring e-readiness assessment in Saudi organisations preliminary results from a survey study from e-government to m-government* (pp. 467–475). Brighton, UK: Mobile Government Consortium International LLC.

Alwahaishi, S., & Snášel, V. (2013a). Acceptance and use of information and communications technology: A UTAUT and flow-based theoretical model. *Journal of Technology Management and Innovation, 8*(2), 61–73.

Alwahaishi, S., & Snášel, V. (2013b). Factors influencing the consumers' adoption of mobile Internet. In *the third international conference on digital information and communication technology and its applications (DICTAP2013)* (pp. 31–39). The Society of Digital Information and Wireless Communication. 8th to 10th July 2013 OStrava, Czech Republic

Alwahaishi, S., & Snášel, V. (2013c). Modeling the determinants influencing the diffusion of mobile internet. *Journal of Physics: Conference Series, 423*(1), 012037. IOP Publishing.

Analysys Mason. (2012). Available on: http://www.gsma.com/spectrum/wp-content/uploads/2012/05/GSMA_ report_on_KSA_DD2_6GHz_2012-04-30.pdf. Accessed 10 Oct 2015.

Baabdullah, A. M., Alalwan, A. A., Rana, N. P., Dwivedi, Y., & Weerakkody, V. (2017). *Assessing consumers' intention to adopt mobile internet services in the Kingdom of Saudi Arabia*. Boston, MS: AMCIS.

Baabdullah, A. M., Dwivedi, Y. K., & Williams, M. D. (2015a). *Understanding the adoption of mobile internet in the Saudi Arabian context: Results from a descriptive analysis. Open and Big Data Management and Innovation* (pp. 95–106). Cham, Switzerland: Springer International Publishing.

Baabdullah, A. M., Dwivedi, Y. K., & Williams, M. D. (2015b). Towards examining factors influencing the adoption of mobile government (m-Gov) in Saudi Arabia. In *British Academy of management (BAM) conference proceedings, 08th–10th September 2014*. Portsmouth, UK: University of Portsmouth.

Baabdullah, A. M., Nasseef, O., & Alalwan, A. A. (2016). Consumer adoption of mobile government in the Kingdom of Saudi Arabia: The role of usefulness, ease of use, perceived risk and innovativeness. In *Conference on e-Business, e-Services and e-Society* (pp. 267–279). Cham, Switzerland: Springer International Publishing.

Bhattacherjee, A. (2012). *Social science research: Principles, methods, and practices* (2nd ed.). Tampa, FL: Anol Bhattacherjee.

Chong, A. Y. L., Ooi, K. B., Lin, B., & Bao, H. (2012). An empirical analysis of the determinants of 3G adoption in China. *Computers in Human Behavior, 28*(2), 360–369.

Communications and Information Technology Commission CITC. (2007). Available on: http://www.citc.gov.sa/ english/Pages/default.aspx. Accessed 19 Feb 2016.

Das, C. (2011). *A study on validity of modified technology acceptance model of mobile*. Nagpur, India: RTM Nagpur University.

Davis, F. D., Bagozzi, R. P., & Warshaw, P. R. (1989). User acceptance of computer technology: A comparison of two theoretical models. *Management Science, 35*(8), 982–1003.

Dwivedi, Y. K., Rana, N. P., Janssen, M., Lal, B., Williams, M. D., and Clement, R. M. (2017). An empirical validation of a unified model of electronic government adoption (UMEGA).

Government Information Quarterly. Available at http://www.sciencedirect.com/science/article/pii/ S0740624X1730103X

Dwivedi, Y. K., Rana, N. P., Jeyaraj, A., Clement, M., and Williams, M. D (2017). Re-examining the unified theory of acceptance and use of technology (UTAUT): Towards a revised theoretical model. *Information Systems Frontiers*. Available at https://link.springer.com/article/10.1007/s10796-017-9774-y

Gefen, D., Karahanna, E., & Straub, D. W. (2003). Trust and TAM in online shopping: An integrated model. *MIS Quarterly, 27*(1), 51–90.

Hailin, S. (2010). Mobile Internet experience research – Based on TAM. In *E-Product E-Service and E-Entertainment (ICEEE), 2010 international conference on* (pp. 1–4). IEEE. 07 Nov - 09 Nov 2010 Henan, China

Hong, S., Thong, J. Y., & Tam, K. Y. (2006). Understanding continued information technology usage behavior: A comparison of three models in the context of mobile internet. *Decision Support Systems, 42*(3), 1819–1834.

Hsu, H. H., Lu, H. P., & Hsu, C. L. (2007). Adoption of the mobile internet: An empirical study of multimedia message service (MMS). *Omega, 35*(6), 715–726.

Kapoor, K. K., Dwivedi, Y. K., & Williams, M. D. (2014a). Innovation adoption attributes: A review and synthesis of research findings. *European Journal of Innovation Management, 17*(3), 327–348.

Kapoor, K. K., Dwivedi, Y. K., & Williams, M. D. (2014b). Rogers' innovation adoption attributes: A systematic review and synthesis of existing research. *Information Systems Management, 31*(1), 74–91.

Kapoor, K. K., Dwivedi, Y. K., & Williams, M. D. (2014c). The interbank mobile payment acceptance in an Indian context. *International Journal of Indian Culture and Business Management, 8*(4), 473–494.

Kapoor, K. K., Dwivedi, Y. K., & Williams, M. D. (2014d). Conceptualizing the role of innovation-attributes for examining consumer adoption of mobile innovations. *The Marketing Review, 14*(4), 407–430.

Kapoor, K. K., Dwivedi, Y. K., & Williams, M. D. (2015a). Examining the role of three sets of innovation attributes for determining adoption of the interbank mobile payment service. *Information Systems Frontiers, 17*(5), 1039–1056.

Kapoor, K. K., Dwivedi, Y. K., & Williams, M. D. (2015b). An empirical examination of the role of three sets of innovation attributes for determining adoption of the IRCTC mobile ticketing service. *Information Systems Management, 32*(2), 153–173.

Orlikowski, W., & Baroudi, J. J. (1991). Studying information technology in organizations: Research approaches and assumptions. *Information Systems Research, 2*(1), 1–28.

Pedersen, P. E. (2005). Adoption of mobile internet services: An exploratory study of mobile commerce early adopters. *Journal of Organizational Computing and Electronic Commerce, 15*(3), 203–222.

Rana, N. P., Dwivedi, Y. K., Lal, B., Williams, M. D., & Clement, M. (2017). Citizens' adoption of an electronic government system: Towards a unified view. *Information Systems Frontiers, 19*(3), 549–568.

Rana, N. P., Dwivedi, Y. K., Williams, M. D., & Weerakkody, V. (2016). Adoption of online public grievance redressal system in India: Toward developing a unified view. *Computers in Human Behavior, 59*, 265–282.

Remenyi, D., Williams, B., Money, A., & Swartz, E. (1998). *Doing research in business and management: An introduction to process and method*. London, UK: Sage Publications Ltd..

Shareef, M. A., Kumar, U., Kumar, V., & Dwivedi, Y. K. (2011). E-government adoption model (GAM): Differing service maturity levels. *Government Information Quarterly, 28*(1), 17–35.

Shi, W., Wu, P. & Zhou, W., Chen, J. (2009). Gender differences in purchase intention on mobile data services. In *computational sciences and optimization, 2009.CSO 2009. International joint conference on* (Vol. 1, pp. 773–777). IEEE. Sanya, Hainan, China, 24–26 April 2009

STC Group. (2011). Saudi telecom company annual report. Available on: https://www.stc.com.sa/wps/wcm/connect/english/stc/resources/e/8/e82a0cad-43ca-4b7b-ab5c-50d333c77b88/AnnualReport-2011-en.pdf. Accessed 19 Feb 2016.

Straub, D., Boudreau, M. C., & Gefen, D. (2004). Validation guidelines for IS positivist research. *The. Communications of the Association for Information Systems, 13*(1), 63.
Van der Heijden, H. (2004). User acceptance of hedonic information systems. *MIS Quarterly, 28*, 695–704.
Venkatesh, V., Morris, M. G., Davis, G. B., & Davis, F. D. (2003). User acceptance of information technology: Toward a unified view. *MIS Quarterly, 27*(3), 425–478.
Venkatesh, V., Thong, J., & Xu, X. (2012). Consumer acceptance and use of information technology: Extending the unified theory of acceptance and use of technology. *MIS Quarterly, 36*(1), 157–178.
Wang, H. Y., & Wang, S. H. (2010). User acceptance of mobile internet based on the unified theory of acceptance and use of technology: Investigating the determinants and gender differences. *Social Behavior and Personality: An International Journal, 38*(3), 415–426.
Weidong, T., Keyi, W., Linlin, L. Likun, X. (2009). Study on consumer behavior of wireless music. In *Management and service science, 2009.MASS'09. International conference on* (pp. 1–6). IEEE.
Yfantis, V., Vassilopoulou, K., Pateli, A., & Usoro, A. (2013). The influential factors of m-gov's adoption in the developing countries. In *Mobile web and information systems* (pp. 157–171). Berlin/Heidelberg, Germany: Springer.
Zhang, J., Huang, J., & Chen, J. (2010). Empirical research on user acceptance of mobile searches. *Tsinghua Science and Technology, 15*(2), 235–245.

Baabdullah is an Assistant Professor of Information Systems at the Department of Management Information Systems, Faculty of Economics and Administration, King Abdulaziz University, Jeddah, Kingdom of Saudi Arabia. His academic qualifications include a PhD in Information Systems from Swansea University in Wales, MSc in Management Information Systems from University of Surrey and BSc in Management Information Systems from King Abdulaziz University. Dr. Baabdullah's research interests are in the area of information systems, analysis/development of IS theories/models, IT/IS adoption, diffusion of emerging ICTs, acceptance and use of E-services and M-applications, E-Government/M-Government and social media/social networking.

Ali Abdallah Alalwan is an Assistant Professor at Amman College of Banking and Finance at Al-Balqa' Applied University, Jordan. He holds a PhD from Swansea University in Wales. He also holds a Bachelor's Degree in Marketing and an MBA/Marketing Degree from the University of Jordan. His current research interest is in the area of information systems, technology acceptance, electronic marketing, social media, Internet of things, self-service technologies, Internet banking and mobile banking. A part of his work has been published in some refereed journals including *JFSM*, *JEIM*, *ISM* and *Dirasat: Administrative Sciences*.

Naim Salameh Al Qadi is an Associate Professor at Amman University College of Finance and Administrative Sciences, affiliated to Al-Balqa' Applied University, Jordan. His Bachelor's and Master's Degrees are in Finance and Credit from Donetsk State University of Management, USSR. Dr. Al Qadi is a PhD bearer from the Institute of Oriental Studies, USSR. His research field interests are finance and financial social capital; economics; electronic banking, Internet banking and mobile banking; and entrepreneurship and business skills. Dr. Al Qadi is the present dean of the abovesaid college, i.e. Amman University College.

Chapter 14
An Examination of the Role of National IT Development and Infrastructure in Models for Smartphone Adoption and Use: The Cases of Iraq, Jordan and the UAE

Nisreen Ameen and Robert Willis

Abstract This research aims to examine the effect of national IT development on Arab consumers' behavioural intention and their actual use of smartphones. This effect was compared to the effect of two factors: usefulness and ease of use. The study was conducted in three different countries, namely, Iraq, Jordan and the UAE. A total of 1264 questionnaires were collected from smartphone consumers aged 18–29 years old in the three countries. The collected data were analysed using partial least squares-structural equation modelling. The results revealed that the new proposed factor, national IT development, has a more significant effect on behavioural intention than the effect of perceived relative advantage (usefulness) and ease of use. The research provides information to academics, policy makers and mobile companies operating in Iraq, Jordan and the UAE, enabling them to understand the perceptions of their customers of the effects of ICT development and policies on smartphone adoption and use.

Keywords TAM · National IT development · Arab countries · Smartphone adoption

14.1 Introduction

The popularity of smartphones is continuing to increase as technology continues to advance. In the Arab region, the smartphone penetration rate is expected to reach 65% by 2020 (GSMA, 2015b). Young people under the age of 30 make up more than 60% of the Arab population (GSMA, 2013), meaning that this is a significant

---

N. Ameen (✉) · R. Willis
Lord Ashcroft International Business School, Anglia Ruskin University, Cambridge, UK
e-mail: nisreen.ameen@pgr.anglia.ac.uk; rob.willis@anglia.ac.uk

Y. K. Dwivedi et al. (eds.), *Emerging Markets from a Multidisciplinary Perspective*, Advances in Theory and Practice of Emerging Markets,
https://doi.org/10.1007/978-3-319-75013-2_14

market with great potential. The benefits of using mobile phones in the region extend to businesses and governments, in addition to contributing to GDP (4.4% in 2013), and mobile phone use is expected to contribute further in the years to come (GSMA, 2014). However, mobile companies in Arab countries have experienced a decline in revenue since 2013 (GSMA, 2015b). These companies are striving to build a strong customer base and increase profit. The GSMA (2016) report identified that it is unlikely that mobile companies in the Middle East will retain the same level of revenues they used to obtain in the past (GSMA, 2016). This makes understanding customers' needs and preferences even more important to try to maintain or increase their revenues. Therefore, it is necessary to identify the factors that may affect existing customers' adoption and use of the new generation of mobile phones – smartphones.

In Arab countries, the development of a fully working regulatory framework is considered to be taking longer than in other markets. Market competitiveness is also still behind in comparison with other markets (GSMA, 2014; Varoudakis & Rossotto, 2004). The regulatory framework varies widely in this region (International Telecommunication Union, 2013). Unless efficient information and communications technology (ICT) infrastructure and policies are put in place, Arab consumers will not be able to exploit the full potential of their smartphones. The effective use of smartphones and mobile applications requires effective ICT policies and an infrastructure that supports mobile Internet and mobile services.

From a theoretical perspective, the technology acceptance model (TAM) was developed in the 1980s by Davis (1989) to explore the fundamental determinants of user acceptance of computers. Based on the findings of the TAM, the main determinants of technology adoption were established to be perceived usefulness (PU) and perceived ease of use (PEOU). A substantial number of studies in the existing literature suggest that, along with user intention, the two main factors of the TAM can be applied successfully to explain the acceptance and use of mobile phones (Son, Park, Kim, & Chou, 2012; Tsai, Wang, & Lu, 2011). These two factors were found in many subsequent technology acceptance theories, for example, the decomposed theory of planned behaviour (TPB) (Taylor & Todd, 1995b), the augmented theory of planned behaviour (A-TPB) (Taylor & Todd, 1995c), diffusion of innovation (DoI) (Rogers, 2003), the model of PC utilisation (MPCU) (Thompson, Higgins, & Howell, 1991), the unified theory of acceptance and use of technology (UTAUT) (Alalwan, Dwivedi, & Rana, 2017; Alalwan, Dwivedi, Rana, Lal, & Williams, 2015; Alalwan, Dwivedi, Rana, & Simintiras, 2016; Alalwan, Dwivedi, Rana, & Williams, 2016; Dwivedi, Rana, Janssen et al., 2017; Dwivedi, Rana, Jeyaraj, Clement, & Williams, 2017; Rana, Dwivedi, Lal, Williams, & Clement, 2017; Rana, Dwivedi, Williams, & Weerakkody, 2016; Venkatesh, Morris, Davis, & Davis, 2003) and the extended unified theory of acceptance and use of technology (UTAUT2) (Alalwan et al., 2017; Venkatesh, Thong, & Xu, 2012). It can be argued that most technology acceptance theories, including the TAM (Davis, 1989), assume a high level of ICT infrastructure and the availability of technology products. This is not the case in developing countries.

There is a gap in the existing technology acceptance theories in terms of considering the macroenvironment surrounding the individual users of technological products, such as national IT infrastructure and policies. The reason behind this may be that the theories were created and tested in the developed world, where the ICT infrastructure is advanced and technology products are widely available and used. This does not apply in less developed countries, more specifically Arab countries. Applying models on technology adoption that were originally developed in western countries in non-western countries should be carried out carefully (McCoy, Galletta, & King, 2007; Straub, Keil, & Bernner, 1997).

The main aim of this study is to examine the effect of national IT development on Arab consumers' behavioural intention and their actual use of smartphones. This effect will be compared to the effects of two well-known factors: usefulness and ease of use. The research is cross national, as it studies the effects of national IT development and infrastructure on the adoption and use of smartphones in three Arab countries: Iraq, Jordan and the United Arab Emirates (UAE).

This cross national research informs a gap in the existing technology acceptance theories by examining the role of national IT development and infrastructure in smartphone adoption and use in three Arab countries. Furthermore, the research is important as it integrates the new factor – national IT development – into a conceptual model on smartphone adoption and tests its significance in the model in these countries. The research reveals the level of Arab consumers' awareness of the effect of ICT development and policies on their use of the latest generation of mobile phones – smartphones. The selection in this study of the three countries, Iraq, Jordan and the UAE, adds value to the research. These three countries are different in terms of their economic, social, political and technological advancement, which makes testing the proposed model in each of them important as it reveals how the new proposed factor fits into different countries with different characteristics. The UAE is considered the most technologically advanced country in the Arab region (GSMA, 2016), Iraq is considered to be technologically behind compared to other Arab countries (GSMA, 2016), and Jordan is in the middle in terms of technological advancement. The research also provides evidence for the ongoing debate about how appropriate it is to apply models of technology acceptance that were originally developed from a western perspective in a non-western context.

14.2 Mobile Telecom Development in Arab Countries

Diab (2010) contended that the case of telecommunications companies in the Middle East is unique compared to companies in any other region in the world for three main reasons: first, the majority of the population is young; second, the Arab culture is unique; and third, the high demand in this region leads to higher adoption rates. Smartphone penetration in Saudi Arabia alone exceeded smartphone penetration in the USA in 2011 (Alkuhunaizan & Love, 2012). However, there is a lack of recent studies that address the current situation of the telecommunications market in Arab countries (Ameen & Willis, 2016).

The GSMA (2015b) report revealed a decline in revenue for mobile companies in the Arab region. The report revealed that the reasons behind this could be the fierce competition between companies operating in the market and the unstable political and economic conditions in the region. Although it is expected that the revenue level will increase again, the increase is likely to be modest (GSMA, 2015b, 2016). There was a decline of 2.4% in revenues obtained by mobile operators in 2014 (GSMA, 2015b). In 2015, 54% of the total population of the Arab states were mobile subscribers. However, as subscriber growth has reached a high level, it is anticipated that it will slow significantly, leading to just 57% in 2020, below the global average (GSMA, 2015b). The slow growth is also a result of the unstable political and economic conditions in some countries in the region and the increased competition between mobile companies (GSMA, 2015b, 2016).

The liberalisation of the telecom market in the Middle East and North Africa (MENA) countries is still an issue due to government control (Ezzat, 2014). Ezzat (2014) described the situation of the telecom markets in the MENA countries as allowing some level of liberalisation and competition and controlling the regulators. In the majority of Arab countries, the government still has either full control or a major share in this sector (Abbasi, 2011), and it is mainly under government control (GSMA, 2014). In general, the regulatory framework is highly varied in the Arab region (International Telecommunication Union, 2013). Even with the presence of regulatory authorities, the development of ICT laws and policies is carried out by the sector's ministry in these countries, which creates inconsistency (International Telecommunication Union, 2013). Openness and competitiveness in the market are vital for increasing the usage of technology, due to their direct effect on price reduction (Varoudakis & Rossotto, 2004).

In Arab countries, developing a fully working regulatory framework is seen to be slower than in other markets. Market competitiveness is also still behind compared to other markets (Varoudakis & Rossotto, 2004). Hakim and Neaime (2014) contended that liberalisation is based on two steps, with the first being setting and implementing the right laws and regulations via an independent regulating body. This was also stated by the International Telecommunication Union (2013). The second step is the actual liberalisation process (Hakim & Neaime, 2014). Setting up the right policies remains problematic (Alrawabdeh, Salloum, & Mingers, 2012; International Telecommunication Union, 2013; UNDP, 2013). It took a long time to begin the process of liberalisation and issuing licences to more than one company in Arab countries.

Although competition is increasing in mobile markets in Arab countries, the key areas of telecoms such as international gateways and 'single wholesale networks' are still controlled by monopolists (GSMA, 2014). The process of privatisation on its own is insufficient. For privatisation to bring effective results, the presence of an independent regulatory body and competition in the market is required (Ezzat, 2014). When the government rules the regulatory body, and owns the largest telecom operator, competition cannot exist (Ezzat, 2014), and customers are at a disadvantage.

Within the context of the three countries included in this research, Iraq, Jordan and the UAE, the telecom environment and ICT policies are different. Mobile operators in Iraq have experienced the highest fall in revenues among all Arab countries, as they fell by 12% in 2014 in comparison with 2013 (GSMA, 2015b). The unemployment rate in Iraq increased from 20% in 2014 to 34% in 2015 among young people aged 15–24 years (GSMA, 2015b), which is a high increase. Smartphone penetration rate is 17% in Iraq (GSMA, 2015a). The roles of policy making and regulations have overlapped in Iraq (Best, 2011). The study conducted by Best (2011) revealed significant shortcomings in this market that are still present and need to be resolved. Overall, the country suffers from poor ICT policies and a poor regulatory environment (International Telecommunication Union, 2013). The Kurdistan Regional Government's (2011) report indicated that the Kurdistan government has set goals to make the best use of the frequencies available for mobile calls and services, to raise mobile network coverage to 90% and to increase regulations and support companies operating in the sector, in order to achieve further price reductions and an increase in service quality (Kurdistan Regional Government, 2011). However, in 2014, additional taxes on mobile and Internet usage were enforced, which significantly increased the price of using mobile phones and mobile services in the country.

Smartphones accounted for nearly a third of the total mobile connections in Jordan in 2015 (GSMA, 2015b). Jordan has a liberalised telecommunications market (Hakim & Neaime, 2014). The competition between telecommunications companies in Jordan has been high since 2005 (GSMA, 2015a). This has contributed to the fast penetration of technological products, even though Jordan is a middle-income Arab country. However, taxation is high in Jordan, with an average growth of tax burden on mobile services of 7.7% a year between 2008 and 2012 (GSMA, 2014). In fact, taxes on mobile phones and mobile services in Jordan are among the highest worldwide (GSMA, 2015b, 2016). In 2013 and 2015, new regulations for increasing taxes on mobile phones and services were launched (GSMA, 2015a). The taxes on mobile services are also high in Jordan, with an increase from 12% in 2010 on calls, SMS and mobile broadband to 26% specific taxes in 2013. Ten per cent are paid by mobile operators, in addition to the general sale tax of 16% which is applied to most products (GSMA, 2015a). This has led to a significant increase in prices, which adversely affects affordability, especially with the high unemployment level in Jordan (GSMA, 2015a).

The smartphone penetration rate in the UAE is 83%, which is among the highest worldwide (GSMA, 2015a). The telecom market in the UAE is a duopoly between two major companies (Ellam, 2008): Etisalat (Emirates Telecommunications Corporation), the dominant and major player, and du (Emirates Integrated Telecommunications Company PJSC), which started operating in 2005 (Diab, 2010; Kamli, 2012). In 2011, Etisalat had the larger mobile market share in the mobile market in the UAE (Kamli, 2012). The prices of mobile phones and their services are high. However, due to the high GDP level, a significant number of individuals own more than one mobile device (Sabri, Al-Nakeeb, & Alrawi, 2011). The Ministry of Finance owns 60% of Etisalat, the largest telecom company (Ellam, 2008). High fees are paid in taxes and regulatory aspects by Etisalat and du (Ellam, 2008). The country is still behind in terms of creating and implementing effective ICT policies (Alfaki & Ahmed, 2013). Although the UAE's ICT infrastructure has developed significantly in recent years, it is still behind compared to other developed countries (Alfaki & Ahmed, 2013).

There are restrictions on voice over internet protocol (VOIP) applications such as Skype and Viber for Etisalat and du to keep dominating the market (Freedomhouse, 2013). A deal took place between the UAE telecom companies and Apple to disable FaceTime from all iPhones in the UAE (Freedomhouse, 2015). In 2015, Etisalat decided to make 20% of its shares available for foreign companies to purchase (Freedomhouse, 2015). In the UAE, the International Telecommunication Union (ITU) recently allowed Etisalat and du to provide prepaid packages without obtaining regulatory approval. This will allow two mobile virtual network operators (MVNOs), Virgin and Axiom Telecom, to start offering their services in the future, which should result in increased competition. Nevertheless, Etisalat and du are still mainly owned by the government and dominate the market. Table 14.1 below provides a comparison between the three countries included in the study.

This section provided a background to the status of the mobile telecom development in the Arab region in general and in the three countries included in this study. It revealed the differences between the three countries in terms of their telecom environments.

14.3 Theoretical Background

14.3.1 The Technology Acceptance Model

The technology acceptance model (TAM) was developed in the 1980s by Davis (1989). The author explored the fundamental determinants of the user acceptance of computers. The work on TAM stemmed from the theory of reasoned action (TRA) which was related to individuals' behaviour (Alryalat, Rana, & Dwivedi, 2015; Kwon & Chidambaram, 2000). It has been used by a substantial number of academics (Hong, Hwang, Hsu, Wong, & Chen, 2011; Jan & Contreras, 2011; Shih, 2004; Tsai et al., 2011) and applied to different settings. During the study, Davis (1989) tested users' acceptance of using a computerised mail system and file editor, as well as IBM PC-based graphics systems for testing the variables. Two different methods of testing took place. The study was applied in an organisational setting. The first study included 112 staff members of an organisation with 6 months experience of using the system. The second study included 40 students using the two systems for the first time. Based on the findings, the main determinants of technology adoption were perceived usefulness (PU) and perceived ease of use (PEOU). Perceived usefulness was defined as the degree to which a person believed that using a particular system would enhance their job performance (Davis, 1989). PEOU was defined as the degree to which a person believed that using a particular system would be free

Table 14.1 Comparison of the countries included in the study

	Iraq	Jordan	UAE
Population(ASDA'A Burson-Marsteller, 2015)	34.8 m	7.5 m	9.4 m
GDP-PPP (ASDA'A Burson-Marsteller, 2015)	494.5 (USD billion)	80.2 (USD billion)	604.96 (USD billion)
Number of mobile cellular subscriptions (per 100 people) (World Bank, 2016)	95	148	178
Smartphone adoption (GSMA, 2015a)	17%	30%	83%
Development of new technologies	No	Yes	Yes
ICT infrastructure	3G – Iraq is behind compared to other countries included in the study as it has only been launched recently	4G – Jordan is advanced in terms of mobile networks	4G – UAE is advanced in terms of ICT infrastructure
Type of user (Brach, 2010)	Isolated users: They tend to have less interaction with technology. This is due to the several wars the country has been through and the severe political and economic situation in the country	Integrated users: They are more open to technology than isolated users, although not as open as the 'consumers' category of users in the UAE	Consumers: They are open to technological advancements
Competition	Competition	Competition	Duopoly
Policies	Poor ICT policies and regulatory environment. Compared to the other countries included in the study, Iraq is behind in terms of the regulatory environment. Major issues in the area of mobile taxation	High regulatory and legal framework. One of the most liberalised ICT markets compared to the other countries. However, there are gaps and major issues in the area of mobile taxation	The country is still behind in terms of creating and implementing effective ICT policies

of effort (Davis, 1989). The findings indicated that PU was a stronger driver of technology adoption. PU and PEOU affect an individual's attitudes towards using technology systems which, in turn, are a major determinant of actual system usage (Davis, 1989). Overall, TAM could explain 40% of the variance in use.

Davis, Bagozzi, and Warshaw (1989) compared TAM to TRA (Fishbein & Ajzen, 1975) in terms of intention prediction. The authors found that TAM can work better in terms of technology adoption, as it is less complex than TRA and less costly. TAM is one of the most robust models and has been validated by a significant number of studies due to its power for predicting technology adoption (Saloman &

Salman, 2013). Mathieson (1991) compared TAM to TPB (Ajzen, 1985), which was also similar to TRA (Ajzen & Fishbein, 1980; Fishbein & Ajzen, 1975) with minor differences. The results of the research showed that both models can explain and present intention to use the system. Whilst TAM is simpler and less costly, TPB can explain user intention further and provide more accurate information, due to its complexity (Mathieson, 1991).

PU is a significant determinant of technology adoption (Davis, 1989; Davis et al., 1989; Igbaria, Parasuraman, & Baroudi, 1996; Taylor & Todd, 1995a, 1995c). It was also found to be the most significant determinant of behavioural intention towards camera mobile adoption (Rouibah, Abbas, & Rouibah, 2011). In fact, it was found to be more significant than PEOU in many studies (e.g. Keil, Beranek, & Konsynski, 1995; Son et al., 2012). However, Igbaria, Zinatelli, Cragg, and Cavaye (1997) found that during the systems use life cycle, there are some points (precisely when starting to use the system) where PEOU has a more significant effect on usage than PU. Karahanna and Straub's (1999) findings were also consistent with these findings. The authors emphasised that training and support are important only at the beginning and then their effect starts to diminish gradually as experience increases. PU is certainly one of the most significant factors in TAM. However, the level of its significance in comparison with PEOU changes at the different points of system use. The two factors were constantly present in the main technology acceptance theories that were subsequent to TAM (as shown in Table 14.2 below).

TAM has been used extensively within the context of technology adoption in Arab countries; more specifically, it has been used within the context of mobile services adoption in Arab countries. Rouibah and Abbas (2010) studied the acceptance of camera mobile phones in Kuwait. The authors found that factors such as personal innovativeness, attachment motivation and subjective norms had a significant impact on the acceptance of camera mobile phones. Awwad and Ghadi (2010) investigated the factors affecting the adoption of mobile banking in Jordan using a sample of customers of Jordanian banks. The authors found that complexity, compatibility, trialability and perceived risk were vital factors for the adoption of mobile banking in Jordan. Surprisingly, usefulness was not important. The authors stated that the reason behind this may be that mobile banking adoption in Jordan is still relatively new so consumers were not yet aware of its advantages. Khraim, Al-Shoubaki, and Khraim (2011) explored the factors affecting mobile banking adoption in Jordan. The authors found that the factors including relative advantage, compatibility, complexity, trialability and risk and self-efficacy apply to the Jordanian consumers' adoption of mobile banking. Abbas (2014) investigated smartphone adoption in Kuwait. The author used the extended technology acceptance model (TAM2), which was developed by Venkatesh and Davis (2000), to develop the model. The author found that the factors PEOU and attachment motivation had a significant effect on behavioural intention, while subjective norms and PU did not have a significant effect on intention. However, the factors PU and PEOU were found to affect mobile phone technology adoption, and they were found to be related to the adoption of all mobile services in a study conducted by Nassuora (2013). TAM constituted the basis of theoretical models developed in many studies

Table 14.2 The presence of perceived usefulness and perceived ease of use in existing technology acceptance theories

Theory	Authors	Usefulness	Ease of use
Technology acceptance model (TAM)	Davis (1989)	Perceived usefulness: 'The degree to which a person believes that using a particular system would enhance his or her job performance' (Davis, 1989, p. 320)	Perceived ease of use: 'The degree to which a person believes that using a particular system would be free of effort' (Davis, 1989, p. 320)
Theory of planned behaviour (TPB)	Ajzen (1991)	No	No
Model of PC utilisation (MPCU)	Thompson et al. (1991), Thompson, Higgins, and Howell (1994)	Job fit (the level to which the use of PCs can help to support the performance of the individual's job): Defined as 'the extent to which an individual believes that using [a technology] can enhance the performance of his or her job' (Thompson et al., 1991, p. 129)	Complexity (negative relationship between complexity and usage), stemmed from Rogers and Shoemakers (1971): 'The degree to which an innovation is perceived as relatively difficult to understand and use' (Thompson et al., 1991, p. 128)
Motivational model (MM)	Davis, Bagozzi, and Warshaw (1992)	Extrinsic motivation 'is perceived to be instrumental in achieving valued outcomes that are distinct from the activity itself, such as improved job performance, pay, or promotions' (Davis et al., 1992, p. 1112)	No
Social cognitive theory (SCT)	Bandura (1986), Compeau and Higgins (1995)	Performance outcome expectations: (related to job outcomes) defined as 'the performance-related consequences to the behavior. Specifically, performance expectations deal with job-related outcomes' (Compeau & Higgins, 1995) Personal outcome expectations: (self-esteem and sense of accomplishment) defined as 'the personal consequences of the behavior. Specifically, personal expectations deal with the individual esteem and sense of accomplishment' (Compeau & Higgins, 1995)	Partially found in self-efficacy: 'Judgment of one's ability to use a technology (e.g., computer) to accomplish a particular job or task' (Compeau & Higgins, 1995)

(continued)

Table 14.2 (continued)

Theory	Authors	Usefulness	Ease of use
Decomposed theory of planned behaviour (DTPB)	Taylor and Todd (1995c)	Perceived usefulness: Adapted from the technology acceptance model (TAM) Davis (1989)	Perceived ease of use: Adapted from the technology acceptance model (TAM) Davis (1989)
Augmented technology acceptance model (A-tam)	Taylor and Todd (1995a)	Perceived relative advantage: Adapted from the diffusion of innovation theory (DoI) Rogers (2003)	Complexity: Adapted from the diffusion of innovation theory (DoI) Rogers (2003)
Extended technology acceptance model (TAM2)	Venkatesh and Davis (2000)	Perceived usefulness: Adapted from the technology acceptance model (TAM) Davis (1989)	Perceived ease of use: Adapted from the technology acceptance model (TAM) Davis (1989)
Diffusion of innovation (DoI)	Rogers (2003)	Relative advantage: 'The degree to which an innovation is perceived as being better than the idea it supersedes' Rogers (2003, p. 229)	Complexity: 'The degree to which an innovation is perceived as relatively difficult to understand and use' (Rogers, 2003, p. 257)
Unified theory of acceptance and use of technology (UTAUT)	Venkatesh et al. (2003)	Performance expectancy: 'The degree to which an individual believes that using the system will help him or her to attain gains in job performance' (Venkatesh et al., 2003, p. 447)	Effort expectancy: 'The degree of ease associated with the use of the system' (Venkatesh et al., 2003, p. 450)
Extended unified theory of acceptance and use of technology (UTAUT2)	Venkatesh et al. (2012)	Performance expectancy: 'The degree to which using a technology will provide benefits to consumers in performing certain activities' (Venkatesh et al., 2012, p. 159)	Effort expectancy: 'The degree of ease associated with consumers' use of technology' (Venkatesh et al., 2012, p. 159)

in the Arab region, for example, m-government in the UAE (Almuraqab, 2016), m-learning in Oman (Sarrab, Al Shibli, & Badursha, 2016), m-government in Saudi Arabia (Alotaibi, Houghton, & Sandhu, 2016) and m-banking in the UAE, in which the two factors usefulness and ease of use were found to be significant.

A substantial number of studies in the existing body of literature have suggested that the two main constructs of TAM, along with user intention, can be applied successfully to explain the acceptance and usage of mobile phones (Son et al., 2012; Tsai et al., 2011). The study conducted by Davis and Venkatesh (1996) concluded that PU and PEOU are valid and reliable. Adams, Nelson, and Todd (1992) and Davis et al. (1989) found that these two constructs are able to explain system acceptance among different applications, with PU having a stronger influence on behavioural intention (BI). This argument was supported by Davis (1993). Nevertheless, it can be argued that technology acceptance varies across different IT systems as well as between individuals (Straub et al., 1997). PU and PEOU remained significant and empirically validated in most of these studies.

14.3.2 Cultural Influence Model for Information Technology Transfer

Straub, Loch, and Hill (2001) developed the cultural influence model for IT transfer to the Arab region. A national IT policies and technological infrastructure construct was also included but not tested. This construct was defined as 'specific technology policies that guide the development of information systems in a specific country together with the existing structure of computing and communication capabilities and the ability of the population to operate and utilise these capabilities. The overall construct reflects the level of support for technological development within a given nation' (Straub et al., 2001, p. 9). Although this construct was not tested in their study, it may very well apply to the case of Arabs' use of smartphones. Without an efficient ICT infrastructure and policies in place, Arab individuals will not be able to adopt and exploit the full potential of using mobile phones. This is especially the case for the latest generation of mobile phones, smartphones, which require an effective ICT infrastructure for mobile Internet and mobile services. Loch, Straub, and Kamel (2003) provided the main measurements for the national IT policies/infrastructure construct in the model developed on cultural influence modelling and IT transfer, namely, privatisation of IT industries, perception of current demand for IT, perception of current supply of IT, software piracy enforcement, government IT initiatives, taxation of IT imports, other IT tariffs or restrictions and tax benefits for IT use.

14.4 Proposed Research Model

Despite the fact that the area of technology adoption is mature and well developed, there is a lack of theories that include national IT development as a construct that can affect customers' intention towards and use of technology. Perhaps the reason behind this is that these theories were developed and tested in the developed world where the level of ICT development and policies is well advanced. This is not the case in developing countries, in which the level of ICT development and policies is considered to lag behind. Therefore, analysing the effects of this factor on both behavioural intention and actual use is important in the case of smartphone adoption and use in Arab countries. Since the two factors PU and PEOU, which stemmed from TAM, were found significant in many subsequent theories and in studies that examined mobile application adoption, the proposed conceptual framework in this research integrated these two factors, along with behavioural intention (BI) and

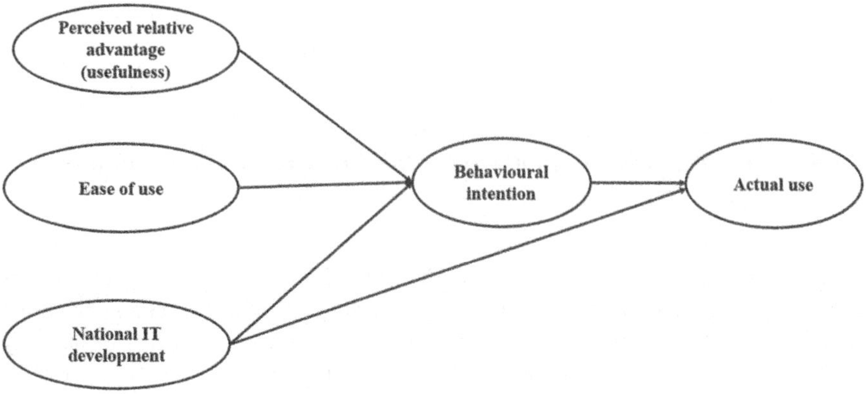

Fig. 14.1 Proposed research model

actual use (USE). In addition, this research proposes a new factor to be integrated into the proposed research model – national IT development (ND) – which was found in the studies conducted by Loch et al. (2003) and Straub et al. (2001). The literature review conducted in this research shows that this factor can be highly applicable to the case of smartphone adoption in Arab countries, more specifically, in the three countries included in the study. Figure 14.1 below shows the proposed research model.

The main factors in the proposed model and their hypothesised relationships are explained below.

14.4.1 Perceived Relative Advantage (Usefulness) (PRA)

Perceived relative advantage (PRA) usefulness stems from perceived usefulness, which proved to be important in previous technology acceptance studies (e.g. Alwahaishi & Snášel, 2013; Davis, 1989; Venkatesh et al., 2012). Previous studies showed that usefulness was found to be a significant determinant of BI (Adams et al., 1992; Davis, 1989; Davis & Venkatesh, 1996). Similarly, PRA adapted from Moore and Benbasat's (1991) study was expected to have a significant effect on BI in this study. Rogers (2003, p. 229) defined relative advantage as 'the degree to which an innovation is perceived as being better than the idea it supersedes'. Wang, Meister, and Wang (2011) studied the relationship between PRA and PU. They stated that the two terms are usually used interchangeably when studying the adoption of technology. However, relative advantage is more accurate, as it includes other competing technologies, too, especially the idea that smartphones and their services have other ICT rivals. Following the approach of Igbal and El-Gohary (2014), substituted perceived usefulness by perceived relative advantage (PRA) (usefulness) based on the findings of the previous research carried out by Moore and

Benbasat (1991), the authors suggested that the term 'relative advantage' is more detailed and perceptive to the user. In this research, the term 'perceived relative advantage' was used to represent usefulness as it is more specific. Therefore, the following hypothesis was developed:

H1 Perceived relative advantage (usefulness) has a positive significant effect on behavioural intention to use smartphones.

14.4.2 Ease of Use (EOU)

Ease of use (EOU) was found to be significant in previous studies (e.g. Davis, 1989; Davis et al., 1992; Rana & Dwivedi, 2016; Rana, Dwivedi, & Williams, 2013; Taylor & Todd, 1995a, 1995c; Venkatesh & Davis, 2000; Venkatesh et al., 2003, 2012). Within the context of young users in Arab countries, EOU was expected to be important. It was originally found in TAM as PEOU and complexity in MPCU (Thompson et al., 1991) and DoI (Rogers, 2003). Although EOU was not significant in some studies (e.g. Aboelmaged & Gebba, 2013; Terzis & Economides, 2011; Wu, Chen, & Lin, 2007), it proved to be significant in a high number of studies, in particular for mobile phone technology (Carlsson, Carlsson, Hyvönen, Puhakainen, & Walden, 2006; Jaradat & Al-Rababa, 2013). Complexity was considered as an obstacle to ICT adoption in many studies (e.g. Awwad & Ghadi, 2010; Khraim et al. 2011; Rogers, 2003; Thompson et al., 1991; Van Biljon & Kotze, 2008). Within the low level of education and technological awareness in the Arab countries, EOU was expected to be a significant factor that influences the individual user's current and future behaviour towards smartphone adoption. Within the existing body of literature related to technology adoption, EOU was found to be particularly important at the beginning of the system use, decreasing as the individual's level of experience of using the system increases (Davis et al., 1989; Karahanna & Straub, 1999). Thus, it was hypothesised that:

H2 Ease of use has a positive significant effect on behavioural intention to use smartphones.

14.4.3 National IT Development (ND)

The present framework included a new construct called national IT development (ND). The construct refers to national IT policies and technological infrastructure. This included the analysis of the effect of policies and development of ICT systems in an Arab country on consumers' BI towards usage. Straub et al. (2001, p. 10) stated 'The overall construct reflects the level of support for technological development within a given nation'. The items for this construct were added in Loch et al.'s (2003) study, namely, privatisation of IT industries, perception of current demand for IT, perception of current supply for IT, government IT initiatives, taxation of IT imports and other IT tariffs and restrictions, software piracy enforcement and tax benefits of IT use (Loch et al., 2003). Some of these items that apply to smartphone technology and the individual consumer were adopted in this research. We investigated some aspects of this construct that consumers could provide information about. We investigated the Arabs consumers' opinions about the tariffs, restrictions, taxations, privatisation and competition in IT industries and their perceptions of current supply and demand for IT. Also, the level of IT development, policies and infrastructure varies among Jordan, Iraq and the UAE. Therefore, these variations and their effect on smartphone adoption and use are expected to be revealed in more depth from the young Arabs' perspective. We hypothesised that national IT development would have a significant effect on both behavioural intention and actual use of smartphones. The reason for testing the effect of national IT development on actual use is that this construct was expected to affect how people use their smartphones, for example, the frequency of usage or the use of different mobile applications in terms of mobile tariffs or restrictions. It was hypothesised that:

H3 National IT development has a positive significant effect on behavioural intention to use smartphones.

H4 National IT development has a positive significant direct effect on actual use of smartphones.

14.4.4 Behavioural Intention (BI)

The research framework included behavioural intention (BI) to mediate between the independent variables in the model and actual use (USE). Behavioural intention was found to be significant in many theories related to technology acceptance including TRA (Ajzen & Fishbein, 1980; Fishbein & Ajzen, 1975), TAM (Davis, 1989; Rana & Dwivedi, 2015), TPB (Ajzen, 1991), DTPB (Taylor & Todd, 1995c), A-TAM (Taylor & Todd, 1995b), TAM2 (Venkatesh & Davis, 2000), UTAUT (Venkatesh et al., 2003), UTAUT2 (Venkatesh et al., 2012) and MOPTAM (Van Biljon & Kotze, 2008). Based on Ajzen's (1991) definition, we define behavioural intention within the context of our research as 'the Arab users' intention to continue to use smartphones'. Therefore, it was hypothesised:

H5 Behavioural intention to use smartphones has a positive significant direct effect on actual use of smartphones.

14.5 Methodology

As this research is concerned with the Arab region, we collected data from three Arab countries: Iraq, Jordan and the UAE. Iraq forms the third largest mobile market in the Arab region (GSMA, 2014). However, the country is lagging behind in terms of technology, and there is a lack of research on technology adoption in general, and smartphone adoption in particular, in Iraq. Furthermore, mobile companies in Iraq have experienced the highest drop in revenue in the Arab region (GSMA, 2015b). In terms of the level of mobile phone adoption, Jordan falls between Iraq and the UAE. Although there is a high level of unemployment among young people in Jordan, the level of mobile phone adoption is high in comparison with other Levant countries. Mobile operators in Jordan have also experienced a decline in revenue in the last few years (GSMA, 2015a). The UAE is the most advanced Arab country in terms of mobile phone adoption and penetration (GSMA, 2016). In fact, it has one of the highest mobile adoption levels and smartphone penetration rates in the world (GSMA, 2016). The inclusion of these three countries in the research made it possible to assess the significance of national IT development in different countries with different characteristics in terms of economic and technological development. To fully understand how the factor national IT development fits in the model, it is important to test its significance in Arab countries that vary in terms of advancement of ICT infrastructure and policies. Therefore, the three countries included in this research to test the model were different: Iraq, which is technologically behind; the UAE, which is the most advanced Arab country in terms of ICT infrastructure; and finally Jordan, which ranks in the middle in terms of ICT policies and infrastructure.

A total of 1599 questionnaires were distributed in the three countries to consumers aged between 18 and 29 years old. There were many reasons for selecting this particular age group. The segment '15–29 years old' (the youth segment) is the largest segment of the Arab population (Choueiki, 2010; Dhillon & Yousef, 2009; GSMA, 2013, 2014; Hayutin, 2009; Kronfol, 2011). The 2014 GSMA report stated that one out of five in the region is aged 15–24, and more than 60% of the population is less than 30 years old (GSMA, 2014). Another study, specifically focusing on social media via cell phone adoption and usage in Egypt (Kavanaugh et al., 2012), not only stated that 15–29-year-olds form the largest segment of the Arab population but that they also form a large segment of Internet users. The authors stated, 'There is a high percentage of young people (aged 15–29) among the total population in most Middle Eastern countries, and a high proportion of Internet and social media users among young people. These two factors allow this segment of the population to draw on many online sources of information besides the more widely used mainstream media of television and newspapers' (Kavanaugh et al., 2012, p. 8). In addition, young people form a large segment of the population in Iraq (UNDP, 2014a), Jordan (UNDP.org, 2013) and the UAE (UNDP, 2014b).

Multistage cluster sampling was used. This took place over five main stages:

Stage one: three Arab countries were selected – Iraq, Jordan and the UAE.

Stage two: a major city in each country was selected as an urban area.
Stage three: three districts from each selected city were selected randomly.
Stage four: all subdistricts of each district were included.
Stage five: households with an individual aged 18–29 years old were selected randomly.

The questionnaires were distributed face-to-face in households in major cities in each of the three countries: Erbil in Iraq, Amman in Jordan and Dubai in the UAE. Five hundred thirty-three questionnaires were distributed face-to-face in each of the three countries. A total of 1264 completed questionnaires (398 from Iraq, 429 from Jordan and 437 from the UAE) were included in the analysis after assessing the responses for missing data and unengaged responses. The response rate was 75% in Iraq, 80% in Jordan and 82% in the UAE. The face-to-face distribution of the questionnaires helped to reach a high response rate.

The collected data were analysed using partial least squares-structural equation modelling (PLS-SEM). There were two reasons for selecting PLS-SEM as a method of analysis. First, the collected data were not normally distributed. Being a non-parametric data analysis method, PLS-SEM was an appropriate choice. Second, the proposed model included two formative constructs including national IT development and actual use. The collected data were analysed using the newest version of SmartPLS (SmartPLS 3.0). The items of actual use were adopted from Venkatesh et al.'s (2012) study. This construct was acknowledged as being formative by Venkatesh et al. (2012). In addition, we applied Jarvis, MacKenzie, and Podsakoff's (2003) criteria for assessing the type of each construct – formative or reflective. The results of the assessment showed that while PRA, EOU and BI are reflective constructs, USE and ND are formative constructs.

The questionnaire included questions asking the participants about their demographic information. The second section asked the participants whether they owned a smartphone and the frequency of their use of smartphones and mobile applications; this was followed by the item for each construct. The use of a seven-point Likert scale, as a minimum, was recommended by Foddy (1994) as it increases the validity and reliability of the scale. Based on this recommendation and the extensive use of the seven-point Likert scale in previous studies including Davis (1989), Venkatesh et al. (2003, 2012), we used this scale in this research.

We assessed the model separately in each country, followed by a multigroup analysis conducted using partial least squares-multigroup analysis (PLS-MGA) to accurately test the differences between the three groups, in terms of how the model fits and the significance of the factor ND. The first stage of the analysis was assessing the measurement model including formative and reflective measurement models. The second stage assessed the structural model. Table 14.3 shows the measurement items for each construct in the proposed model and their sources. Some items were modified, and new items were added to be more applicable to the context of this research – smartphone adoption and use by Arab consumers.

14.6 Results

14.6.1 Samples Characteristics

All of the respondents were between 18 and 29 years old. In Iraq, 46.7% of the respondents were aged between 18 and 22, and 53.3% were aged between 23 and 29. The Iraqi sample was balanced in terms of gender (male, 51%; female, 49%). In Jordan, 38.9% were aged between 18 and 22, and 61.1% were aged between 23 and 29. In terms of gender, 46.9% were male, and 53.1% were female. In the UAE, the sample was distributed almost evenly among the two age groups: 51.7% were aged between 18 and 22, and 48.3% were aged between 23 and 29. In terms of gender, 52.9% were male, and 47.1% were female. All of the participants from Iraq, Jordan and the UAE owned a smartphone.

14.6.2 Reflective Measurement Model

The first stage was to assess the reflective measurement model in each of the three samples separately. This included the assessment of convergent and discriminant validity and factor loadings from each of the three samples.

In terms of the data collected from Iraq, Table 14.4 below shows that all average variance extracted (AVE) values were higher than the threshold value of 0.5 (Hair, Hult, Ringle, & Sarstedt, 2014). The AVE values ranged from 0.710 to 0.754. The Cronbach alpha (CR) values were higher than the threshold value of 0.70 (Hair et al., 2014). The CR values ranged from 0.864 to 0.909, and the composite reliability values were also higher than the threshold value of 0.70, ranging from 0.907 to 0.932.

Table 14.5 below shows the results of assessing both convergent and discriminant validities for the Jordanian sample. The AVE values ranged between 0.801 and 0.837. The CR values ranged between 0.915 and 0.942, and the composite reliability values ranged between 0.941 and 0.956.

In the UAE sample, the AVE values were higher than the minimum threshold value of 0.50, ranging from 0.802 and 0.886. The composite reliability values were higher than 0.70, ranging from 0.941 to 0.959, and CR values ranged from 0.915 to 0.946 (as shown in Table 14.6 below).

Discriminant validity was assessed by examining the cross loadings of each construct, as they should load higher on their own indicators than on the indicators of the other constructs (Chin, 1998). The second criterion for evaluating discriminant validity was the Fornell-Larcker criterion (Fornell & Larcker, 1981). In this assessment, a construct should share more variance with its own indicators than with the other constructs. The results showed that the square root of each construct's AVE was greater than its highest correlation with any other constructs in all three groups. The assessment of the discriminant validity in all three groups, using cross loadings

Table 14.3 Items for each construct and their sources, with modifications to fit the context of smartphone adoption and use

Item by variable	Source
Perceived relative advantage (usefulness) (PRA)	
PRA1. I find that a mobile phone is useful in my daily life	Davis (1989), Davis et al. (1989)
PRA2. Using a mobile phone helps me to achieve things more quickly	Davis (1989), Davis et al. (1989), Moore and Benbasat (1991)
PRA3. Using a mobile phone helps me to stay connected to people	Author's own
PRA4. Using a mobile phone makes it easier to carry out my daily activities	Davis (1989), Davis et al. (1989), Moore and Benbasat (1991), with minor modifications
Ease of use (EOU)	
EOU1. Learning how to use mobile phones is easy for me	Davis (1989), Davis et al. (1989)
EOU2. Learning how to use mobile applications is easy for me	Davis (1989), Davis et al. (1989)
EOU3. My interaction with mobile phones is clear and understandable	Davis (1989), Davis et al. (1989)
EOU4. I find mobile applications easy to use	Davis (1989), Davis et al. (1989)
EOU5. It is easy for me to become skilful at using mobile phones	Davis (1989); Davis et al. (1989)
National IT development (ND)	
ND1. I find that the current demand for IT is high	Loch et al. (2003)
ND2. I find that the current supply of IT is high	Loch et al. (2003)
ND3. Government IT initiatives in policy making are working well	Loch et al. (2003) (with adjustments)
ND4. I find current mobile tariffs acceptable	Loch et al. (2003)
ND5. I find that currently there are no restrictions to using different mobile applications	Based on Loch et al.'s (2003) study with some modifications to test restrictions on mobile applications
Behavioural intention to use the smartphone (BI)	
BI1. I intend to continue using mobile phones in the future	Venkatesh et al. (2012)
BI2. I will always try to use mobile phones in my daily life	Venkatesh et al. (2012)
BI3. I plan to continue to use mobile phones frequently	Venkatesh et al. (2012)
BI4. I envisage using mobile phones in the future	Author's own
Actual use of smartphones (USE)	

(continued)

Table 14.3 (continued)

Item by variable	Source
The usage frequency for each of the following: (a) Mobile phone (for making calls) (b) SMS (c) Mobile Internet (d) Games (e) Mobile e-mail (f) Mobile messaging apps (e.g. Viber, Skype or WhatsApp) (g) Mobile social media (h) Mobile banking (i) M-commerce	Initially adopted from Venkatesh et al.'s (2012) study. Additional items related to mobile services are the author's own

Table 14.4 Assessment of convergent validity and reliability of the Iraqi sample

	AVE	Composite reliability	Cronbach's alpha
BI	0.710	0.907	0.864
EOU	0.734	0.932	0.909
PRA	0.754	0.925	0.891

Table 14.5 Assessment of convergent validity and reliability of the Jordanian sample

	AVE	Composite reliability	Cronbach's alpha
BI	0.801	0.941	0.915
EOU	0.813	0.956	0.942
PRA	0.837	0.954	0.935

Table 14.6 Assessment of convergent validity and reliability of the UAE sample

	AVE	Composite reliability	Cronbach's alpha
BI	0.802	0.941	0.915
EOU	0.823	0.959	0.946
PRA	0.886	0.959	0.936

and the Fornell-Larcker criterion, showed that the data had no issues in terms of discriminant validity. Also, all factor loadings were higher than 0.7 (Hair et al., 2006) in all groups.

14.6.3 Formative Measurement Model

The assessment of the formative measurement model was conducted using the collinearity assessment and by assessing the significance and relevance of the formative indicators. In the Iraqi sample, all of the variance inflation factor (VIF) loadings were lower than the threshold value of 5, and the tolerance values were lower than the threshold value of 0.2 (Hair et al., 2014). The VIF values in the Iraqi sample ranged from 2.386 to 1.192, and the tolerance values ranged from 0.378 to 0.801. In the Jordanian sample, all VIF values were lower than 5, ranging from 1.353 to 3.574, and the tolerance values were higher than 0.20, ranging from 0.225 to 0.412 below. In the UAE sample, the VIF values were lower than 5, ranging from 1.153 to 3.038. Also, the tolerance values were higher than 0.20, ranging from 0.211 to 0.351.

The formative measurement model in each of the three samples was assessed in terms of the significance and relevance of the formative indicators. The outer weight is calculated using the *t* value. If the outer weight is significant, the indicator should be retained. When the indicator's outer weight is insignificant but the outer loading is high (more than 0.50), the indicator should be retained and can be considered as absolutely important rather than relatively important. On the other hand, if an indicator's weight is not significant and the outer loading is less than 0.50, the researcher should assess the significance of the indicator's outer loading. If it is significant, the researcher should decide whether to keep or delete the indicator, depending on the theory and how it supports the indicator's existence (Hair et al., 2014). If it is insignificant, the formative indicator should be deleted. The assessment of the significance and relevance of the formative indicators showed that the formative factors did not have any issues in terms of the significance of the items' weight, their loadings and the significance of their loadings in any of the three samples included in the study.

14.6.4 Structural Model

The structural model was assessed using the path analysis, effect size (f^2) and predictive relevance (q^2) (Hair et al., 2014). The structural model was calculated using the bootstrapping method (500 samples). The results in Table 14.7 below show the results of the structural model in Iraq. ND had the highest effect on BI, with a medium effect size and medium predictive relevance ($t = 4.702$, $p = 0.000$, $f^2 = 0.376$ and $q^2 = 0.200$). Therefore, H3 was supported. This was followed by EOU, with a small effect size and a small predictive relevance ($t = 3.780$, $p = 0.000$, $f^2 = 0.062$ and $q^2 = 0.090$). Thus, H2 was supported. PRA had the lowest significant effect on BI with a small effect size and a small predictive relevance ($t = 2.909$, $p = 0.004$, $f^2 = 0.036$ and $q^2 = 0.041$). Thus, H1 was supported. While BI had a significant effect on USE with a medium effect size and a medium predictive relevance ($t = 3.516$, $p = 0.000$, $f^2 = 0.208$ and $q^2 = 0.254$) and H5 was supported, ND did not have any significant effect on USE ($t = 1.698$, $p = 0.090$, $f^2 = 0.015$ and $q^2 = 0.011$). Therefore, H4 was not supported. All hypotheses were supported in the Iraqi sample, except H4 as the results showed that ND does not have a direct significant effect on USE. The R^2 for BI was 0.622 and 0.391 for USE. This indicates that the model in Iraq can explain 62% of the variance in BI and 39% of the variance in USE.

Table 14.7 Results of structural model in the Iraqi sample

	t statistics	*p* values	f^2 value	q^2 value	Hypothesis supported
BI -> USE (H5)	3.516	0.000	0.208	0.254	Yes
EOU-> BI (H2)	3.780	0.000	0.062	0.090	Yes
ND -> BI (H3)	4.702	0.000	0.376	0.200	Yes
ND -> USE (H4)	1.698	0.090	0.015	0.011	No
PRA -> BI (H1)	2.909	0.004	0.036	0.041	Yes

Table 14.8 Results of structural model in the Jordanian sample

	t statistics	*p* values	f^2 values	q^2 values	Hypothesis supported
BI -> USE (H5)	4.466	0.000	0.118	0.128	Yes
EOU-> BI (H2)	3.891	0.000	0.077	0.051	Yes
ND -> BI (H3e)	5.463	0.000	0.361	0.310	Yes
ND -> USE (H4)	3.946	0.000	0.094	0.041	Yes
PRA -> BI (H1)	3.999	0.000	0.094	0.062	Yes

In the Jordanian sample, ND had the most significant effect on BI with a high effect size and a medium predictive relevance ($t = 5.463$, $p = 0.000$, $f^2 = 0.361$ and $q^2 = 0.310$). Therefore, H3 was supported. This was followed by PRA, with a small effect size and small predictive relevance ($t = 3.999$, $p = 0.000$, $f^2 = 0.094$ and $q^2 = 0.062$). Therefore, H1 was supported. Then, EOU, with a small effect size and a small predictive relevance ($t = 3.891$, $p = 0.000$, $f^2 = 0.077$ and $q^2 = 0.051$). Therefore, H2 was supported. BI had a significant effect on USE, with a small effect size and a small predictive relevance ($t = 4.466$, $p = 0.000$, $f^2 = 0.118$ and $q^2 = 0.128$). Thus, H5 was supported. Also, ND had a significant effect on USE, with a small effect size and a small predictive relevance ($t = 3.946$, $p = 0.000$, $f^2 = 0.094$ and $q^2 = 0.041$). Thus, H4 was supported. The results in Table 14.8 below show the results of the structural model in Jordan. The results showed that all hypotheses were supported in the Jordanian sample. The R^2 for BI was 0.692 and 0.491 for USE. This indicates that the model in Jordan can explain 69% of the variance in BI and 49% of the variance in USE.

In the UAE sample, ND was the most significant factor affecting BI, with a high effect size and a medium predictive relevance ($t = 5.270$, $p = 0.000$, $f^2 = 0.347$ and $q^2 = 0.251$). Thus, H3 was supported. The second most significant factor affecting BI was PRA, with a medium effect size and a medium predictive relevance ($t = 4.423$, $p = 0.000$, $f^2 = 0.0221$ and $q^2 = 0.167$). Therefore, H1 was supported. This was followed by EOU, which had a significant effect on BI with a small effect

Table 14.9 Results of structural model in the UAE sample

	t statistics	*p* values	f^2 values	q^2 values	Hypothesis supported
Bi -> USE (H5)	5.289	0.000	0.149	0.151	Yes
EOU-> BI (H2)	3.120	0.002	0.063	0.054	Yes
ND -> BI (H3)	5.270	0.000	0.347	0.251	Yes
ND -> USE (H4)	3.558	0.000	0.071	0.041	Yes
PRA -> BI (H1)	4.423	0.000	0.221	0.167	Yes

size and a small predictive relevance ($t = 3.120, p = 0.002, f^2 = 0.063$ and $q^2 = 0.054$. Thus, H2 was supported. BI had a significant effect on USE, with a medium effect size and a medium predictive relevance ($t = 5.289$, $p = 0.000$, $f^2 = 0.149$ and $q^2 = 0.151$). Therefore, H5 was supported. ND had a significant effect on USE, with a small effect size and a small predictive relevance ($t = 3.558, p = 0.000, f^2 = 0.071$, $q^2 = 0.041$). Thus, H4 was supported. The results in Table 14.9 below show the results of the structural model in the UAE. These results showed that all hypotheses were supported for the UAE sample. The R^2 for BI was 0.694 and 0.473 for USE. This indicates that the model in the UAE can explain 69% of the variance in BI and 47% of the variance in USE.

14.6.5 Multigroup Analysis

The next stage was to critically assess the differences in terms of how the model fits in each of the three countries: Iraq, Jordan and the UAE. This was carried out using the partial least squares-multigroup analysis (PLS-MGA). The PLS-MGA is based on estimating the path model for each group which, in turn, is assessed based on a separate bootstrap analysis (Henseler, 2010). The analysis in this approach relies on assessing the observed distribution of the bootstrap outcomes instead of the distributional assumptions (Henseler, 2010). The centred bootstrap estimates of the groups are compared, and then the difference between the groups is divided by the total number of bootstrap samples to indicate the probability that the second group is greater than the first group; this is evaluated using the *p*-value (Henseler, 2010). *P*-values of 0.05 or lower and 0.95 or higher indicate significant differences between the paths in the groups.

The results of the PLS-MGA showed that there were no significant differences between the groups except differences in terms of the significance of national IT development between Iraq and Jordan ($p = 0.963$) and Iraq and the UAE ($p = 0.967$). The remaining relationships were not significantly different between the three groups (as shown in Table 14.10 below).

Table 14.10 Results of multigroup analysis using PLS-MGA

	Total effects-diff (Iraq – Jordan)	*p*-Value (Iraq vs Jordan)	Total effects-diff (Iraq – UAE)	*p*-Value (Iraq vs UAE)	Total effects-diff (Jordan – UAE)	*p*-Value (Jordan vs UAE)
BI -> USE (H5)	0.027	0.272	0.041	0.192	0.014	0.371
EOU-> BI (H2)	0.009	0.543	0.015	0.421	0.024	0.380
ND -> USE (H4)	**0.154**	**0.963**	**0.179**	**0.967**	0.075	0.176
ND -> BI (H3)	0.028	0.621	0.121	0.897	0.093	0.855
PRA -> BI (H1)	0.013	0.402	0.030	0.726	0.044	0.835

14.7 Discussion

The main aim of this research was to examine the effect of national IT development on Arab consumers' behavioural intention and actual use of smartphones and compare its significance to the significance of the two well-known factors usefulness and ease of use. The research was conducted in three different countries, namely, Iraq, Jordan and the UAE, to compare how the newly integrated factor, national IT development, would fit into the model in countries with different characteristics. The results revealed several interesting findings. The new proposed factor, national IT development, had a significant effect on behavioural intention in all three countries. This provides support to the studies conducted by Loch et al. (2003) and Straub et al. (2001).

The results of the data analysis showed that the newly integrated factor has a highly significant effect in the model in each of the three countries. In fact, national IT development was the most significant factor affecting behavioural intention and actual use of smartphones. Its significance was higher than the two TAM factors that are widely used in information systems adoption literature: usefulness and ease of use. Furthermore, the model's explanatory power was acceptable in all countries. The model's strongest explanatory power is in Jordan, in which the model is able to explain 69% of the variance in behavioural intention and 49% of the variance in actual use of smartphones. The effect of national IT development remained significant in the model in all three countries, despite the differences between them in terms of technological, economic and political factors.

Usefulness was repeatedly found as a highly significant determinant of technology adoption in previous studies (e.g. Adams et al., 1992; Alkuhunaizan and Love, 2012; Davis, 1989, 1993; Davis et al., 1989; Rouibah et al., 2011). In this research, perceived relative advantage (usefulness) was significant in the model in all three countries, but it was not the most significant factor affecting behavioural intention in any of the three countries. In addition, the findings of this research from all three countries showed that the effect of effort expectancy has become less significant for Arab smartphone users due to the increasing level of experience they have gained from using these devices. Furthermore, the participants in all three countries were actual users with good experience levels of using smartphones. In this research, although perceived relative advantage and effort expectancy were significant predictors of behavioural intention, they were not the most significant determinants of behavioural intention in the model in the three countries. These two factors were also found in TAM (Davis, 1989), and they were widely used to study technology adoption. The results of this research show that the inclusion of other factors, more related to young Arabs in Arab countries in terms of ICT development, overrides the importance of perceived relative advantage and ease of use among actual users of smartphones. This highlights the importance of ICT infrastructure-related factors when developing or extending existing technology acceptance models in Arab countries.

The hypothesised direct impact of national IT development on behavioural intention was supported in the results from the analysis of the data collected from the Iraqi sample. Previous studies including Straub et al. (2001) and Loch et al.'s (2003) studies stressed that because of the low technological infrastructure in Arab countries, investigating the effect of national IT development and ICT infrastructure is important in these countries. The literature showed that the technological infrastructure and policy making in Iraq are behind in comparison with other Arab countries (Sanati, 2005) as there is an absence of regulations as well as an absence of an independent regulatory authority (Best, 2011; Tawfeeq, Kheder, & Qadar, 2014). The political situation in Iraq has affected the telecommunications market (International Telecommunication Union, 2013). Iraqi respondents believed that national IT development is a significant factor that can affect behavioural intention towards smartphone use in Iraq. It was expected that national IT development would have a significant effect on both behavioural intention and actual use. Surprisingly, although national IT development had a significant effect on behavioural intention, the hypothesis testing did not support the statement that national IT development has a significant effect on actual use. This can be due to the poor policy making and ICT infrastructure in Iraq, which makes it a significant predictor of behavioural intention but not actual use. The possible explanation for this is that even with the problems young Iraqi users have faced in terms of the lack of ICT policies and infrastructure, they continued using smartphones for many years so they do not find it as an issue that would stop them from using smartphones. Nevertheless, the impact of national IT development if the country is behind in terms of ICT development can be negative, and it affects the users' experience when using a system (i.e. causing an unpleasant experience when using smartphones). In the original cultural influence model for information technology transfer, Straub et al. (2001) referred to ITT/system outcomes as the intention or the actual use of technology. Within the context of the research model in Iraq, national IT development had a significant effect on behavioural intention only. This can be because users in Iraq have mostly experienced poor levels of ICT infrastructure and policy environment (Tawfeeq et al., 2014), even with the slow improvements that have recently took place in terms of network strength and speed, and they became used to this level, which affected their views on the significance of national IT development on actual use. This indicates that the low level of ICT infrastructure and inefficiency in policy making does not necessarily mean that users will completely discontinue using smartphones in Iraq but it certainly affects their experience when using them.

National IT development was the most significant determinant of behavioural intention in the research model in Jordan. This finding indicates that young Jordanians are aware of the importance of ICT development and the policies related to ICT in smartphone adoption. Jordan is considered as one of the advanced Levant Arab countries in terms of ICT development and policy making, with high levels of competition in the market (Ezzat, 2014). The Jordanian telecommunications market is a liberalised market (Hakim & Neaime, 2014). The significance of national IT development in the model stresses the importance of improving ICT policies and development in Jordan. Competition was introduced into the market in 2005 (GSMA, 2015a), and the country enjoys fast network connectivity as 4G networks are currently in use (GSMA, 2015b). However, new rules were introduced in 2013 in terms of taxation, which led to an increase in the prices that consumers have to pay in relation to smartphones and services (GSMA, 2015a); this affects affordability.

In the model in the UAE, national IT development was the most significant predictor of behavioural intention and the second most significant predictor of actual use. The UAE is the most technologically advanced country in the Arab region (Alfaki & Ahmed, 2013). However, the country is not advanced in terms of developing ICT policies and creating real competition in the market (Alfaki & Ahmed, 2013). The two dominant companies in the mobile market are Etisalat and du (Ellam, 2008; TRA, 2014). There is a higher level of restrictions on some mobile applications in the UAE than in Jordan and Iraq. Promoting ICTs and network coverage is high in comparison with other countries in the world (TRA, 2014). The significance of national IT development on both behavioural intention (it was the most significant predictor of behavioural intention) and actual use within the model in the UAE shows that respondents are aware of the importance of national IT development in the adoption and use of smartphones both directly and via its effect on behavioural intention.

The results of this study showed that when studying technology adoption, more specifically, smartphone adoption in Arab countries, it is important to consider the macroenvironment surrounding the user. ICT development and policy making play a significant role in technology adoption in developing countries, and consumers in all three countries are aware of these effects. It confirms the significance of the new proposed factor, national IT development, on behavioural intention and actual use.

14.8 Research Limitations and Directions for Future Work

The context of this research is consumers in urban areas (major cities in three countries). Therefore, the findings cannot be generalised to include consumers in rural areas, as there are significant differences between consumers in urban areas and those in rural areas. However, this research opens a new path for conducting future studies in rural areas in these countries. In addition, due to the lack of accurate and up-to-date data on the population of young Arabs in each selected city and district in this research, the research did not have an accurate sampling frame.

The sample size selected in this research was equal among all three countries despite the differences between them in terms of the population size. The selected sample size was appropriate for the PLS-SEM analysis, and it was consistent with the sample sizes of the majority of previous studies. However, this sample still limits the possibility of generalising the results and findings of this research.

Attitude was found to be significant in a number of existing technology acceptance theories, for example, TRA (Ajzen & Fishbein, 1980; Fishbein & Ajzen, 1975), TAM (Davis, 1989), TPB (Ajzen, 1991), A-TAM (Taylor & Todd, 1995b) and DTPB (Taylor & Todd, 1995c). Venkatesh et al. (2003) found that attitude does not have a significant effect on intention. The authors stated that attitude can be found within the effects of performance expectancy (usefulness) and effort expectancy (ease of use). Our proposed model did not include attitude. However, a recent study conducted by Dwivedi, Rana, Jeyaraj et al. (2017) emphasised the significance of the inclusion of this factor in technology acceptance models. Therefore, future studies can integrate and test this factor as part of the proposed model.

In the light of both the findings and the limitations of this research, we recommend new paths for future research. We recommend that future studies should integrate our new proposed factor, national IT development, in models on technology adoption in the Arab region. This can also extend beyond the TAM. Also, future studies can add new items to the construct or amend the existing items to adapt to the technology being investigated and the country in which the research is taking place.

14.9 Implications

The findings of this research have important implications for academics, policy makers and mobile companies operating in Iraq, Jordan and the UAE. From the theoretical perspective, this research proposed and tested a theoretical model with national IT development as one of the constructs, along with the TAM model. The findings of this study advocate the importance of considering factors related to national IT development in models on technology adoption. Indeed, the high level of significance of this factor was consistent in the model in all three countries. This indicates that this factor remains important whether it is applied in a country that is considered to lag behind in technology (Iraq) or in a country that is technologically advanced (the UAE). This factor was more significant than usefulness or ease of use in all three countries. The research provides evidence that beyond the two well-known factors in the TAM, there are other, more significant, factors related to IT policies and infrastructure that should be studied and incorporated into technology acceptance models in developing countries – more specifically, Arab countries.

Williams, Rana, and Dwivedi (2015) recommended the inclusion of more than a single task when investigating technology adoption. This research included the mobile handset as well as its applications to understand how the new generation of mobile phones –smartphones – as a whole are adopted and used and to begin to understand how to adopt each single application as their uses are interlinked in various aspects. The adoption and use of the mobile handset can be affected by the mobile applications that can be accessed through it by the individual user and vice versa. Also, the adoption and use of different mobile applications and services, for example, mobile messaging applications, m-banking and m-commerce, are affected by the ICT infrastructure and policies, network strength and other factors included in this study. Therefore, the results of this research are important for researchers wishing to study the adoption of mobile applications.

From a practical perspective, this research provides important insights for policy makers and mobile companies that are operating or willing to operate in this region. The results of this research showed that young Arab consumers are highly aware of the impact of their country's IT policies and infrastructure on their adoption and use of smartphones and mobile applications. The findings of this research can assist telecommunications companies (mobile operators) in the countries included in the study to target their younger customers and increase customer satisfaction. Mobile companies, handset manufacturers and mobile application developers need to understand that beyond the two traditional factors in TAM (usefulness and ease of using smartphones), which are important, there are other, more important factors such as national IT development, which can affect smartphone and application adoption and use for young Arab users.

It is important for mobile companies, handset manufacturers and policy makers to ensure that the tariffs of mobile handsets, mobile Internet and applications are reasonable in comparison with the benefits they provide. New pricing policies related to tariffs are also required in all three countries in this research. There is a need to introduce further competition in the mobile market in the UAE. In the case of Jordan, tax reduction (in both general and specific taxes) is required. Removing any restrictions on mobile applications in the UAE is required from the consumers' perspective.

Policy makers need to ensure a transparent regulatory environment that is open and easy for consumers to understand and evaluate. These, in turn, will also contribute towards the enhancement of national IT development, which was found to be a significant factor affecting both behavioural intention and the actual use of smartphones.

14.10 Conclusion

This research proposed the integration of a new construct, national IT development, into the TAM. It also compared the significance of the new construct to the significance of the two constructs that emerged from the TAM: usefulness and ease of use.

Specifically, we modelled the national IT development construct in terms of demand of IT, supply of IT, government IT initiatives in policy making, mobile tariffs and restrictions on mobile applications. We tested the proposed model in three different Arab countries, namely, Iraq, Jordan and the UAE, using a sample of 1264 questionnaires. Our findings showed that it is important to consider the macroenvironment surrounding the individual user in terms of policy making and ICT development when the research is taking place in Arab countries. This is an important finding as such a factor has not been integrated into technology acceptance models in studies conducted in the Arab region or outside it. Our findings revealed that the new construct had a significant effect on behavioural intention in all the three countries included in the study and it had a direct significant effect on actual use in both Jordan and Iraq. The significance of national IT development exceeded the significance of both perceived relative advantage and ease of use in the model. Thus, our findings are important in terms of highlighting a new factor, more applicable to smartphone adoption in the Arab region.

References

Abbas, H. (2014). Antecedents of consumers' behaviour intentions to use smartphones in Arab World [online]. In *Proceedings of world business and social science research conference*, Paris, France, ISBN: 978-1-922069-47-4. http://www.wbiw orldconpro.com/uploads/paris-conference-2014/management/1396502112_404-Abbas.pdf. Accessed 23 Dec 2014.

Abbasi, J. (2011). Information and Communication Technology in the Middle East: situation as of 2010 and prospective scenarios for 2030. CASE Network Reports, 105, ISBN 978-83-7178-552-8.

Aboelmaged, M., & Gebba, T. (2013). Mobile banking adoption: An examination of technology acceptance model and theory of planned behaviour. *International Journal of Business Research and Development*, *2*(1), 35–50.

Adams, D. A., Nelson, R. R., & Todd, P. A. (1992). Perceived usefulness, ease of use and usage of information technology: A replication. *MIS Quarterly*, *16*(2), 227–247.

Ajzen, I. (1985). From intentions to actions: A theory of planned behaviour. In J. Kuhl & J. Beckman (Eds.), *Action-control: From cognition to behaviour*. Heidelberg, Germany: Springer.

Ajzen, I. (1991). The theory of planned behaviour. *Organizational Behavior and Human Decision Processes*, *50*(2), 179–211.

Ajzen, I., & Fishbein, M. (1980). *Understanding attitudes and predicting social behaviour*. Englewood Cliffs, NJ: Prentice-Hall.

Alalwan, A. A., Dwivedi, Y. K., & Rana, N. P. (2017). Factors influencing adoption of mobile banking by Jordanian bank customers: Extending UTAUT2 with trust. *International Journal of Information Management*, *37*(3), 99–110.

Alalwan, A. A., Dwivedi, Y. K., Rana, N. P., Lal, B., & Williams, M. D. (2015). Consumer adoption of internet banking in Jordan: Examining the role of hedonic motivation, habit, self-efficacy and trust. *Journal of Financial Services Management*, *20*(2), 145–157.

Alalwan, A. A., Dwivedi, Y. K., Rana, N. P., & Simintiras, A. C. (2016). Jordanian consumers' adoption of telebanking: Influence of perceived usefulness, trust and self-efficacy. *The International Journal of Bank Marketing*, *34*(5), 690–709.

Alalwan, A. A., Dwivedi, Y. K., Rana, N. P., & Williams, M. D. (2016). Consumer adoption of mobile banking in Jordan: Examining the role of usefulness, ease of use, perceived risk and self-efficacy. *Journal of Enterprise Information Management*, *29*(1), 118–139.

Alfaki, I., & Ahmed, A. (2013). Technological readiness in the United Arab Emirates towards global competitiveness. *World Journal of Entrepreneurship, Management and Sustainable Development, 9*(1), 4–13.

Alkuhunaizan, A., & Love, S. (2012). What drives mobile commerce? An empirical evaluation of the revised UTAUT model. *International Journal of Management and Marketing Academy, 2*(1), 82–99.

Almuraqab, N. A. S. (2016). M-government adoption factors in the United Arab Emirates: A partial least-squares approach. *International Journal of Business and Information, 11*(4), 404.

Alotaibi, R., Houghton, L., & Sandhu, K. (2016). Exploring the potential factors influencing the adoption of M-government Services in Saudi Arabia: A qualitative analysis. *International Journal of Business and Management, 11*(8), 56–71.

Alrawabdeh, W., Salloum, A., & Mingers, J. (2012). Key factors influencing the diffusion of information and communication technology (ICT) in the Arab world. A comparative study. *British Journals of Economics, Finance and Management Science, 5*(2), 45–59.

Alryalat, M., Rana, N. P., & Dwivedi, Y. K. (2015). Citizen's adoption of an e-government system: Validating the extended theory of reasoned action (TRA). *International Journal of Electronic Government Research, 11*(4), 1–23.

Alwahaishi, S., & Snášel, V. (2013). Consumers' acceptance and use of information and communications technology: A UTAUT and flow based theoretical model. *Journal of Technology Management & Innovation, 8*(2), 61–73.

Ameen, N., & Willis, R. (2016). Current and future challenges facing mobile phone use in the Arab world. *The Journal of Policy, Regulation and Strategy for Telecommunications, Information and Media, 4*, 1–6.

ASDA'A Burson-Marsteller. (2015). Arab youth survey [online]. http://arabyouthsurvey.com/media/wp-content/themes/arabyouth/english/downloads/2015-AYS-White-Paper-EN.pdf. Accessed 20 Mar 2016.

Awwad, M., & Ghadi, M. (2010). Investigation of factors influencing the intention to adopt mobile banking services in Jordan. *Administrative Sciences, 37*(2), 545–556.

Bandura, A. (1986). *Social foundations of thought and action: A social cognitive theory*. Englewood Cliffs, NJ: Prentice Hall.

Best, M. (2011). Chapter 2: Mobile phones in conflict-stressed environments: macro, meso and microanalysis. In M. Poblet (Ed.), *Mobile Technologies for conflict management online dispute resolution, Governance, Participation. Law, Governance and Technology, Series 2*. Dordrecht, The Netherlands: Springer Science and Business Media.

Brach, J. (2010). *Technological readiness in the Middle East and North Africa – Implications for Egypt* [online] (Working Paper, No: 155). http://www.giga-hamburg.de/en/system/files/publications/wp155_brach.pdf. Accessed 28 Mar 2014.

Carlsson, C., Carlsson, J., Hyvönen, K., Puhakainen, J., & Walden, P. (2006). Adoption of mobile devices/services: Searching for answers with the UTAUT. Proceedings of the 39th annual Hawaii international conference on system sciences (HICSS'06). *Track, 6*, 1–10.

Chin, W. W. (1998). The partial least squares approach to structural equation modelling. In G. A. Marcoulides (Ed.), *Modern methods for business research*. London, UK: Lawrence Erlbaum Associates.

Choueiki, A. (2010). Finding a foundation for peace: Engaging youth in the Middle East [online], Georgia Institute of Technology. http://www.google.co.uk/url?sa=t&rct=j&q=&esrc=s&source=web&cd=1&ved=0CCE. Accessed 24 Sept 2014.

Compeau, D. R., & Higgins, C. A. (1995). Computer self-efficacy: Development of a measure and initial test. *MIS Quarterly, 19*(2), 189–211.

Davis, F., Bagozzi, R., & Warshaw, P. (1989). User acceptance of computer technology: A comparison of two theoretical models. *Management Science, 35*(8), 982–1003.

Davis, F. D. (1989). Perceived usefulness, perceived ease of use, and user acceptance of information technology. *MIS Quarterly, 13*(3), 319–340.

Davis, F. D. (1993). User acceptance of computer technology: System characteristics user perceptions. *International Journal of Man-Machine Studies, 38*(3), 475–487.

Davis, F. D., Bagozzi, R. P., & Warshaw, P. R. (1992). Extrinsic and intrinsic motivation to use computers in the workplace. *Journal of Applied Social Psychology*, *22*(14), 1111–1132.

Davis, F. D., & Venkatesh, V. (1996). A critical assessment of potential measurement biases in the technology acceptance model: Three experiments. *International Journal of Human-Computer Studies*, *45*(1), 19–45.

Dhillon, N., & Yousef, T. (2009). *Generation in waiting. The unfulfilled promise of young people in the Middle East*. Washington, DC: Brookings Institution Press.

Diab, S. (2010). Telecommunication broadband explosion [online]. http://www.rasmala.com/equity_report/Rasmala_Telecommunications_Sector_Report_12May2010.pdf. Accessed 25 Mar 2014.

Dwivedi, Y. K., Rana, N. P., Janssen, M., Lal, B., Williams, M. D., & Clement, M. (2017). An empirical validation of a unified model of electronic government adoption (UMEGA). *Government Information Quarterly*, *34*(2), 211–230. https://doi.org/10.1016/j.giq.2017.03.001

Dwivedi, Y. K., Rana, N. P., Jeyaraj, A., Clement, M., & Williams, M. D. (2017). Re-examining the unified theory of acceptance and use of technology (UTAUT): Towards a revised theoretical model. *Information Systems Frontiers*. https://doi.org/10.1007/s10796-017-9774-y.

Ellam, I. (2008). UAE Telecom Sector [online]. Al Mal Capital. http://content.argaam.com.s3-eu-west-1.amazonaws.com/244db147-3f5c-41d0-a3be-e7aadcb5a6f5.pdf. Accessed 16 May 2014.

Ezzat, R. (2014). Regulation, ownership and competition in the telecommunication sector: Evidence from MENA countries [online]. Centre d'Economie de la Sorbonne. http://ces.univparis1.fr/membre/seminaire/S2I/18mois2014_article/Effect%20of%20regulation,%20ownership%20and%20competition%20on%20sector%20perfromance.pdf. Accessed 08 Jan 2015.

Fishbein, M., & Ajzen, I. (1975). *Belief, attitude, intention, and behaviour: An introduction to theory and research*. Reading, MA/Don Mills, Canada: Addison-Wesley.

Foddy, W. (1994). *Constructing questions for interviews and questionnaires: Theory and practice in social research*. Cambridge, UK: Cambridge University Press.

Fornell, C., & Larcker, D. (1981). Structural equation models with unobservable variables and measurement error: Algebra and statistics. *Journal of Marketing Research*, *18*(3), 328–388.

Freedomhouse. (2013). Freedom on the Net 2013′. A global assessment of internet and digital media [online]. https://freedomhouse.org/sites/default/files/resources/FOTN%202013_Full%20Report_0.pdf. Accessed 03 Dec 2015.

Freedomhouse. (2015). Freedom on the Net 2015, United Arab Emirates [online]. https://freedomhouse.org/sites/default/files/resources/FOTN%202015_United%20Arab%20Emirates.pdf. Accessed 03 Dec 2015.

GSMA. (2013). Arab States mobile observatory 2013 [online]. Available at: http://www.gsma.com/publicpolicy/wpcontent/uploads/2012/03/GSMA_MobileObservatory_ArabStates2013.pdf. Accessed 4 May 2014.

GSMA. (2014). The mobile economy: Arab States 2014 [online]. Available at: http://arabstates.gsmamobileeconomy.com/GSMA_ME_Arab_States_2014.pdf. Accessed 15 Mar 2015.

GSMA. (2015a). Digital inclusion and mobile sector taxation in Jordan [online] Deloitte. Available at: http://www.gsma.com/publicpolicy/wp-content/uploads/2015/05/GSMA_Jordan-Report_WEB.pdf. Accessed 9 Dec 2015.

GSMA. (2015b). The mobile economy: Arab States 2015 [online]. Available at: https://gsmaintelligence.com/research/?file=7910cff3a3e6f96219cd50e31d6d3e1c&download. Accessed 20 Dec 2015.

GSMA. (2016). The mobile economy Middle East and North Africa 2016 [online]. Available at:https://www.gsmaintelligence.com/research/?file=9246bbe14813f73dd85b97a90738c860&download. Accessed 29 June 2017.

Hair, J. Black, W., Babin, B., Anderson, R. & Tatham, R. (2006). *Multivariate Data Analysis*. (6th ed), New Jersey: Pearson Prentice Hall.

Hair, J. F., Hult, G. T. M., Ringle, C. M., & Sarstedt, M. (2014). *A primer on partial least squares structural equation modeling (PLS-SEM)*. Thousand Oaks, CA: Sage.

Hakim, S., & Neaime, S. (2014). The demand elasticity of mobile telephones in the Middle East and North Africa. *Research in International Business and Finance*, *32*, 1–14.

Hayutin, A. (2009). Critical demographics of the greater Middle East: A new lens for understanding regional issues [online]. Stanford Center on Longevity, Global Aging Program. http://longevity3.stanford.edu/wp-content/uploads/2012/10/Critical-Demographics-of-the-Greater-Middle-East.pdf. Accessed 24 Sept 2014.

Henseler, J. (2010). PLS-MGA: A non-parametric approach to partial least squares-based multi-group analysis. *Proceedings of the 34th annual conference of the Gesellschaft fur Klassifikation* e.V., Karlsruhe 2010.

Hong, J., Hwang, M., Hsu, H., Wong, W. & Chen, M., (2011). Applying the technology acceptance model in a study of the factors affecting usage of the Taiwan digital archives system. *Computers and Education, Journalism 57*(3), 2086–2094. http://www.sciencedirect.com.proxylib.anglia.ac.uk/science/article/pii/S0360131511000923. Accessed 02 July 2014.

Igbal, T., & El-Gohary, E. (2014). An attempt to understand E-marketing: An information technology prospective. *International Journal of Business and Social Science*, *5*(4), 234–256.

Igbaria, M., Parasuraman, S., & Baroudi, J. (1996). A motivational model of microcomputer usage. *Journal of Management Information Systems*, *13*(1), 127–143.

Igbaria, M., Zinatelli, N., Cragg, P., & Cavaye, A. (1997). Personal computing acceptance factors in small firms: A structural equation model. *MIS Quarterly*, *21*(3), 279–305.

International Telecommunication Union. (2013). Telecom/ICT regulatory reform evolution: Achievements and way forward ARAB region report [online]. Available at: https://www.itu.int/ITU-D/arb/Special_About/2013/Arab-Book/Arab-Book-PDF-E.pdf. Accessed 12 May 2014.

Jan, A. U., & Contreras, V. (2011). Technology acceptance model for the use of information technology in universities. *Computers in Human Behavior [e-journal]*, *27*(2), 845–851. http://www.sciencedirect.com.proxylib.anglia.ac.uk/science/article/pii/S0747563210003523 Accessed 01 Feb 2014.

Jaradat, M., & Al-Rababa, M. (2013). Assessing key factor that influence on the acceptance of mobile commerce based on modified UTAUT. *International Journal of Business and Management*, *8*(23), 102–112.

Jarvis, C. B., MacKenzie, S. B., & Podsakoff, P. M. (2003). A critical review of construct indicators and measurement model misspecification in marketing and consumer research. *Journal of Consumer Research*, *30*(2), 199–218.

Kamli, A. (2012). Arab ICT use and social networks adoption: Report [online]. http://www.kacst.edu.sa/en/about/publications/Other%20Publications/Arab%20ICT%20Use%20Report%202012.pdfMadar. Research and Development. Accessed 14 May 2014.

Karahanna, E., & Straub, D. W. (1999). The psychological origins of perceived usefulness and ease of use. *Information Management*, *35*(4), 237–250.

Kavanaugh, A., Sheetz, S., Hassan, R.,Yang, S., Elmongui, H., Fox, E., ... Shoemaker, D. (2012). Between a rock and a cell phone: Communication and information technology use during the 2011 Egyptian uprising [online]. *Proceedings of the 9th international ISCRAM conference* – Vancouver, Canada, April 2012. Rothkrantz, L., Ristvej, J. & Franco, Z. edshttp://www.iscram-live.org/ISCRAM2012/proceedings/185.pdf. May 04, 2014.

Keil, M., Beranek, P., & Konsynski, B. (1995). Usefulness and ease of use: Field study evidence regarding task considerations. *Decision Support Systems*, *13*(1), 75–91.

Khraim, H., Al-Shoubaki, Y., & Khraim, A. (2011). Factors affecting Jordanian consumers' adoption of mobile banking services. *International Journal of Business and Social Science*, *2*(20), 96–105.

Kronfol, N. (2011). The youth bulge: a demographic challenge for the region [online]. Human and Health, 17. http://www.wdaforum.org/fileadmin/ablage/wdaforum/publications/dp2011-08.pdf. Accessed on 24 Sept 2014.

Kurdistan Regional Government. (2011). Regional development strategy for kurdistan region 2012–2016 [online], Ministry of Planning. http://www.mop.krg.org/resources/MoP%20Files/PDF%20Files/gd_ps/regional_development_strategy.pdf. Accessed 26 Dec 2014.

Kwon, S. K., & Chidambaram, L. (2000). A test of the technology acceptance model: The case of cellular telephone adoption. In *Proceedings of the 33rd Hawaii international conference on systems sciences*, Hawaii.

Loch, K. D., Straub, D. W., & Kamel, S. (2003). Diffusing the internet in the Arab world: The role of social norms and technological culturation. *IEEE Transactions of Engineering Management, 50*(1), 45–63.

Mathieson, K. (1991). Predicting user intentions: Comparing the technology acceptance model with the theory of planned behaviour. *Information Systems Research, 2*(3), 173–191.

McCoy, S., Galletta, D., & King, W. (2007). Applying TAM across cultures: The need for caution. *European Journal of Information Systems, 16*(1), 81–90.

Moore, G. C., & Benbasat, I. (1991). Development of an instrument to measure the perceptions of adopting an information technology innovation. *Information Systems Research, 2*(3), 192–222.

Nassuora, A. (2013). Understanding factors affecting the adoption of M-commerce by consumers. *Journal of Applied Sciences, 13*(6), 913–918.

Rana, N. P., & Dwivedi, Y. K. (2015). Citizen's adoption of an e-government system: Validating extended social cognitive theory (SCT). *Government Information Quarterly, 32*(2), 172–181.

Rana, N. P., & Dwivedi, Y. K. (2016). Using clickers in a large business class: Examining use behavior and satisfaction. *Journal of Marketing Education, 38*(1), 47–64.

Rana, N. P., Dwivedi, Y. K., Lal, B., Williams, M. D., & Clement, M. (2017). Citizens' adoption of an electronic government system: Toward a unified view. *Information Systems Frontiers, 19*(3), 549–568.

Rana, N. P., Dwivedi, Y. K., & Williams, M. D. (2013). Evaluating alternative theoretical models for examining citizen centric adoption of e-government. *Transforming Government: People, Process, and Policy, 7*(1), 27–49.

Rana, N. P., Dwivedi, Y. K., Williams, M. D., & Weerakkody, V. (2016). Adoption of online public grievance Redressal system in India: Toward developing a unified view. *Computers in Human Behavior, 59*, 265–282.

Rogers, E.M., & Shoemaker, F. (1971). *Communication of Innovations: A Cross-Cultural Approach*. New York: Free Press

Rogers, E. M. (2003). *Diffusion of innovations* (5th ed.). New York, NY: The Free Press.

Rouibah, K., & Abbas, H. (2010). Effect of personal innovativeness, attachment motivation and social norms on the acceptance of camera mobile phones: An empirical study in an Arab country. *International Journal of Handheld Computing Research, 1*(4), 41–62.

Rouibah, K., Abbas, H., & Rouibah, S. (2011). Factors affecting camera mobile phone adoption before e-shopping in the Arab world. *Technology in Society, 33*(3), 271–283.

Sabri, K., Al-Nakeeb, A., & Alrawi, K. (2011). Mobile technology and the gulf society: Perception and attitude. In A. Abdel-Wahab & A. El-Masry (Eds.), Mobile information communication technologies adoption in developing countries' IGI global: Hershey. Chapter 13 (pp. 195–204).

Saloman, D., & Salman, R. (2013). E-commerce propagation in the Middle East economies: An application of a revised technology acceptance model. *Innovative Space of Scientific Research Journals International, Journal of Innovation and Applied Studies, 4*(1), 37–42.

Sanati, F. (2005). E-Commerce strategy for Southern Kurdistan region [online]. http://kurdishcongress.org/data/upimages/subfolders/PDF/computer-farzad-sanati-e-com-in-kurdistan-v3.pdf. Accessed 04 Apr 2014.

Sarrab, M., Al Shibli, I., & Badursha, N. (2016). An empirical study of factors driving the adoption of mobile learning in Omani higher education. *The International Review of Research in Open and Distributed Learning, 17*(4), 1–19.

Shih, H. (2004). Extended technology acceptance model of internet utilization behaviour. *Information and Management, [e-journal], 41*(6), 719–729. Available at: http://www.sciencedirect.com.proxylib.anglia.ac.uk/science/article/pii/S0378720603001216. Accessed 01 June 2014.

Son, H., Park, Y., Kim, C., & Chou, J. (2012). Toward an understanding of construction professionals' acceptance of mobile computing devices in South Korea: An extension of the technology acceptance model. *Automation in Construction, 28*, 82–90.

Straub, D., Keil, M., & Berner, W. (1997). Testing the technology acceptance model across cultures: A three country study. *Information Management*, *33*(1), 1–11.

Straub, D., Loch, K., & Hill, C. (2001). Transfer of information technology to the Arab world: A test of cultural influence modeling. *Journal of Global Information Management*, *9*(4), 6–28.

Tawfeeq, B., Kheder, M., & Qadar, N. (2014). Internet governance from the regional kurdistan of Iraq [online]. *International Journal of Multidisciplinary and Current Research*, *2*, ISSN: 2321-3124. http://ijmcr.com/wp-content/uploads/2014/05/Paper37399-406.pdf. Accessed 08 Jan 2015.

Taylor, S., & Todd, P. (1995a). Decomposition and crossover effects in the theory of planned behaviour: A study of consumer adoption intentions. *International Journal of Research in Marketing*, *12*(2), 137–155.

Taylor, S., & Todd, P. A. (1995b). Understanding information technology usage: A test of competing models. *Information Systems Research*, *6*(2), 144–176.

Taylor, S., & Todd, P. A. (1995c). Assessing IT usage: The role of prior experience. *MIS Quarterly*, *19*(4), 561–570.

Terzis, V., & Economides, A. A. (2011). Computer based assessment: Gender differences in perceptions and acceptance. *Computers in Human Behaviour*, *27*(6), 2108–2122.

Thompson, R., Higgins, C., & Howell, J. (1994). Influence of experience on personal computer utilization: Testing a conceptual model. *Journal of Management Information Systems*, *11*(1), 167–187.

Thompson, R. L., Higgins, C. A., & Howell, J. M. (1991). Personal computing: Toward a conceptual model of utilization. *MIS Quarterly*, *15*(1), 125–143.

TRA. (2014). UAE telecommunication sector development and indicators, 2010–2013 [online]. Fifth annual sector review https://www.tra.gov.ae/assets/I2cG5zVC.pdf.aspx. Accessed 25 Jan 2015.

Tsai, C., Wang, C., & Lu, M. (2011). Using the technology acceptance model to analyze ease of use of a mobile communication system [online]. *Social Behavior and Personality: An International Journal, [e-journal]*, *39*(1), 65. Available at: http://web.b.ebscohost.com.proxy-lib.anglia.ac.uk/ehost/detail?sid=40698a04-592b-430b-a02a-7fda0016f424%40sessionmgr198&vid=1&hid=121&bdata=JnNpdGU9ZWhvc3QtbGl2ZQ%3d%3d#db=s3h&AN=58034289. Accessed 24 Sept 2014.

UNDP. (2013). Mobile technologies and empowerment: enhancing human development through participation and innovation [online]. Available at: http://www.undp.org/content/undp/en/home/librarypage/democratic-governance/access_to_informationande-governance/mobiletechnologiesprimer.html. Accessed 6 May 2014.

UNDP. (2014a). Iraq human development report 2014 [online]. Available at: http://www.lse.ac.uk/middleEastCentre/publications/IraqNHDR2014-English.pdf. Accessed 27 Aug 2016.

UNDP. (2014b). Arab knowledge report 2014 youth and localisation of knowledge [online]. Available at: http://www.undp.org/content/dam/rbas/report/UNDP-GENERAL-REPORT-ENG.pdf. Accessed 27 Aug 2016.

UNDP.org. (2013). About Jordan [online]. Available at: http://www.jo.undp.org/content/jordan/en/home/countryinfo/. Accessed 27 Aug 2016.

Van Biljon, J., & Kotze, P. (2008). Cultural factors in a mobile phone adoption and usage model. *Journal of Universal Computer Science*, *14*(16), 2650–2679.

Varoudakis, A., & Rossotto, C. (2004). Regulatory reform and performance in telecommunications: Unrealized potential in the MENA countries. *Telecommunications Policy*, *28*(1), 59–78.

Venkatesh, V., & Davis, F. D. (2000). A theoretical extension of the technology acceptance model: Four longitudinal field studies. *Management Science*, *46*, 186–204.

Venkatesh, V., Morris, M., Davis, G., & Davis, F. (2003). User acceptance of information technology: Toward a unified view. *MIS Quarterly*, *27*(3), 425–478.

Venkatesh, V., Thong, J., & Xu, X. (2012). Consumer acceptance and use of information technology: Extending the unified theory of acceptance and use of technology. *MIS Quarterly*, *36*(1), 157–178.

Wang, Y. W., Meister, D., & Wang, Y. (2011). Reexamining relative advantage and perceived usefulness: An empirical study. *International Journal of Information and Communication Technology Education, 7*(1), 46–59.

Williams, M., Rana, N., & Dwivedi, Y. (2015). The unified theory of acceptance and use of technology (UTAUT): A literature review. *Journal of Enterprise Information Management, 28*(3), 443–488.

World Bank. (2016). Mobile cellular subscriptions (per 100 people) [online]. http://data.worldbank.org/indicator/IT.CEL.SETS.P2. Accessed 12 Mar 2016.

Wu, J., Chen, Y., & Lin, L. (2007). Empirical evaluation of the revised user computing acceptance model. *Computers in Human Behaviour, 23*(1), 162–174.

Nisreen Ameen is a researcher at Anglia Ruskin University/Cambridge and a lecturer in business information systems. Her major field of research is technology adoption and human-computer interaction.

Robert Willis is an academic and researcher at Anglia Ruskin University/Cambridge. Dr. Robert's research interests include public policy and the impact on public service delivery and innovation, sustainable business practices and strategic direction of organisations.

Chapter 15
Factors Influencing the Adoption of E-Ticketing in Arabic Frontier Markets: Conceptual Extension of UTAUT

Zainah Qasem

Abstract Recent years have witnessed a growing interest of researchers to examine e-commerce (EC) systems and mobile commerce (MC) role in different sectors. e-ticketing—a paperless, electronically recorded to merchant's system, electronic document used for ticketing travellers or event attendants—is one of the most important services in e-commerce.

This conceptual paper aims to investigate, understand, and improve e-ticketing adoption in Arabic frontier markets—Morocco, Tunisia, Bahrain, Jordan, Kuwait, Lebanon, and Oman. To achieve this goal, a revised unified theory of acceptance and use of technology (UTAUT) model was introduced. The introduced model emphasized the significant relationship between theory's main four independent variables—performance expectancy, effort expectancy, social influence, and facilitating conditions—and intention. Trust was incorporated into UTAUT, and nonempirical suggestion of a significant positive relationship between social influence and trust and facilitating conditions and trust were proposed.

Keywords UTAUT · E-Ticketing · Frontier markets · Trust · Social influence

15.1 Introduction

Marketing academic discipline and management activities have seen an apparent revolution during the past two decades. Many academics and practitioners agree that what once considered an effective marketing approach, such as mass communication, and focusing on benefit and utility, has become less effective (Constantinides, 2014). Much of this change is contributed to the evolution of information and communication technologies. Although the market has seen the emergence of different

Z. Qasem (✉)
School of Business, The University of Jordan, Amman, Jordan
e-mail: z.qasem@ju.edu.jo

Y. K. Dwivedi et al. (eds.), *Emerging Markets from a Multidisciplinary Perspective*, Advances in Theory and Practice of Emerging Markets,
https://doi.org/10.1007/978-3-319-75013-2_15

influential information and communication technologies, the Internet remains the most prominent among these technologies (Ayeh, Au, & Law, 2016).

The Internet use in business went through different phases of evolution; however, two phases are considered the most influential. First is the phase in which e-commerce systems—systems that facilitate "the process of buying, selling, or exchanging products, services, and information over the internet" (Turban et al., 2006, p. 4)—were introduced. These systems enabled order processing, online payment, and updating information on Web pages (Chan et al., 2001). As a result e-commerce led to the introduction of new and convenient marketing channel, and the exchange of value between producers of different products (goods, services, and ideas) and customers became less complicated and extra comfy (Abdullah & Kadhim, 2016). Following the introduction of e-commerce, the second phase is the integration of mobile computing technologies and mobile applications. This phase enabled universal access to the Internet and mobile e-commerce (Chan et al., 2001).

e-ticketing—a paperless, electronically recorded to merchant's system, electronic document used for ticketing travellers or event attendants (Alfawaer, Awni, & Al-Zoubi, 2011; Qteishat, Alshibly, & Al-ma'aitah, 2014)—is one of the most important applications of e-commerce. Nowadays, providing e-ticketing services is affecting the customer and the business. Modern customers are keen on saving time and effort, and modern businesses are keen on reducing the cost of ticket management (Lu, Chao, & Chen, 2014).

Due to e-ticketing increasing importance, this conceptual paper aims to investigate, understand, and improve e-ticketing adoption, specifically, in frontier collectivist culture markets. To achieve this goal, a revised unified theory of acceptance and use of technology (UTAUT) model is introduced.

This conceptual paper contributes to research in several ways. First, the study shows the important role of UTAUT's constructs in predicting customer intention to adopt new technologies generally and e-ticketing as a new technology specifically. Second, it adds to the literature that supports the need to incorporate trust in UTAUT as a fifth construct to predict adoption of new technology. Third, this study has a nonempirical suggestion to restudy social influence role in UTAUT.

The remainder of the paper is structured as follows. Section 15.2 summarizes the literature related to UTAUT and its constructs relationship. Section 15.3 introduces the research model and hypothesis development. Finally, conclusion and future work are given in Sect. 15.4.

15.1.1 Research Setting

Frontier markets are "smaller, less accessible, yet still investable countries in the developing world" (Berger et al., 2011, p. 227). There are different methods and indexes to classify frontier markets. However, this paper will use Morgan Stanley Capital International (MSCI) index. MSCI method of classification is based on economic development, size, liquidity, and market accessibility (MSCI, 2018) which matches the elements of Berger et al.'s (2011) definition of frontier markets.

Although still smaller than traditional emerging and developed stock markets, frontier markets are providing important investment opportunities for businesses (De Groot, Pang, & Swinkels, 2012). In spite of the important consideration to frontier markets among the investment community, very little research addresses those markets (Berger et al., 2011). Therefore, this paper will focus on understanding what encourages customers to adopt new technologies in frontier markets in order to provide investors and business owners with an insight into potential business.

According to MSCI, frontier markets are found in the Americas, Europe, the Middle East, and Africa. However, the Middle East and North Africa host seven Arabic frontier markets—Morocco, Tunisia, Bahrain, Jordan, Kuwait, Lebanon, and Oman.

There are two fundamental classifications for cultural differences: individualism and collectivism (Frost, Goode, & Hart, 2010). While individualism displays an independence from social influence, collectivism displays a great importance to group approval (Frost et al., 2010; Hofstede, 2001).

Hofstede's cultural index—a framework for cross-cultural communication—grouped the Arabic countries and provided a single score to the Arabic culture in general (Khanum et al., 2012). According to Hofstede's cultural index, the Arabic group culture is a collectivist culture.

15.2 Literature Review

15.2.1 E-Ticketing

e-ticketing is a form of e-commerce whereby customers reserve a seat at an event or in an airline and all reservations are recorded electronically when the purchase is made on firm's reservation database (Alfawaer et al., 2011; Hoosain et al., 2000; Lee & Wan, 2010; Qteishat et al., 2014).

Known e-ticketing service providers in Arabic frontier markets are very few. For example, in Jordan, there are only two known event registration and e-ticketing solution websites (Karasi.com and Sajilni.com), and also, there are five Jordanian domestic airlines with only three providing e-ticketing services. There is also no information regarding the number of e-ticketing users in Jordan. The previous indicate that e-ticketing is still in its early adoption stages as compared to the USA and Europe.

e-ticketing represents the future of operations for the user and the business itself; it makes customers' lives easier by saving their time and reducing the costs of ticket management for companies (Lu et al., 2014). Therefore, understanding what influences customer decision to adopt e-ticketing is a priority for organizations that benefit from providing services such as event management companies and airlines.

15.2.2 UTAUT and Technology Acceptance Models

e-ticketing is a technological innovation; hence, whether customers will adopt this technology depends on their assessment of the technology (Lee & Wan, 2010).

Previous studies on technology acceptance propose different theories and models that try to explain consumer adoption of different types of systems and technologies (e.g. Alalwan, Dwivedi, & Rana, 2017; Alalwan, Dwivedi, Rana, Lal, & Williams, 2015; Alalwan, Dwivedi, Rana, & Simintiras, 2016; Alalwan, Dwivedi, Rana, & Williams, 2016; Alryalat, Rana, & Dwivedi, 2015; Davis, 1989; Dwivedi et al., 2017; Dwivedi, Rana, Jeyaraj, Clement, & Williams, 2017; Karahanna, Straub, & Chervany, 1999; Mathieson, 1991; Rana & Dwivedi, 2015, 2016; Rana, Dwivedi, Lal, Williams, & Clement, 2017; Rana, Dwivedi, & Williams, 2013; Rana, Dwivedi, Williams, & Weerakkody, 2016; Venkatesh, Morris, Davis, & Davis, 2003; Williams, Rana, & Dwivedi, 2015). However, technology acceptance model (TAM), TAM2, and UTAUT are the most used models to explain customer's adoption of new technology.

TAM was introduced as a model that explains and predicts user acceptance of specific types of technology (Ngai, Poon, & Chan, 2007). TAM, which was based on theory of reasoned action (TRA), theorizes that perceived usefulness and perceived ease of use are the two key beliefs that determine person's intention to adopt a new technology (Davis, 1989). Venkatesh and Davis (2000) combined several external variables (subjective norms, voluntariness, image, job relevance, and output quality) to TAM and introduced TAM2 to accommodate for the continuous development in the technology field.

The success of TAM and TAM2, along with other theories and models in explaining technology acceptance and adoption behaviour, promoted the need to introduce a more holistic model (Qasem, 2014). Venkatesh et al. (2003) presented UTAUT as a holistic theory based on TAM. Variables in eight different models about users' technology acceptance and adoption, including TAM, UTAUT, TRA, motivational model, theory of planned behaviour (TPB), a combined TAM and TPB model, model of PC utilization, diffusion of innovation theory, and social cognition theory, were compared, tested, and integrated into the model. UTAUT consisted of four core variables—performance expectancy, effort expectancy, social influence, and facilitating conditions—and four moderating variables, gender, age, experience, and voluntariness of use (Venkatesh et al., 2003).

In UTAUT performance expectancy is defined as "the degree to which an individual believes that using the system will help him or her to attain gains in job performance" (Venkatesh et al., 2003, p. 447). Effort expectancy is "the degree of ease associated with the use of the system" (Venkatesh et al., 2003, p. 450). Facilitating conditions are defined as "the degree to which an individual believes that an organizational and technical infrastructure exists to support the use of the system" (Venkatesh et al., 2003, p. 453). Social influence is defined as "the degree to which an individual perceives that important others believe he or she should use the new system" (Venkatesh et al., 2003, p. 453).

UTAUT was described as a robust model, with the ability to describe users' intention to use a new technology up to 70% more than the eight models (Venkatesh et al., 2003, p. 453). Furthermore, model's viability, validity, and stability have been confirmed for technology adoption research studies in several contexts (Alharbi, 2014).

Although the applicability of TAM and UTAUT to predict technology acceptance and adoption was proven in many settings, there is still a general concern about their effectiveness in predicting consumer adoption of technology across different national cultures (Ayeh et al., 2016; Lee, 2016; McCoy et al., 2007). In this regard, substantial research has been conducted to understand the adoption of several online technologies across cultures.

15.2.3 UTAUT and Culture Relationship

Culture is "the collective programming of the mind which distinguishes the members of one group or category of people from others" (Hofstede, 1980, p. 5). Hofstede's index and its cultural dimensions have been the most used approach to define culture, explain the adoption of several technologies across cultures, and justify variation in results (Al-Gahtani, Hubona, & Wang, 2007; Im et al. 2011; Oshlyansky et al., 2007; Tarhini, El-Masri, Ali, & Serrano, 2016).

Straub et al. (1997) stated that cultural differences across countries affect international company's ability to adopt and use information technology. Hill, Loch, Straub, and El-Sheshai (1998) specified that difference in culture and society has an influence on how customers view, accept, and adopt new technologies. Therefore, it is very important to understand how customers in different cultures adopt new technologies.

TAM was described as culturally biased and criticized for being culturally limited (Anderson et al., 1988; McCoy et al., 2007; McCoy, Everard, & Jones, 2005). UTAUT has, also, been verified across cultures. Oshlyansky et al. (2007) described UTAUT is a robust model with the ability to predict user acceptance of technology; however, they have found that the influence of constructs varied among countries. For example, social influence factor was described as a significant factor in Saudi Arabia and had a higher weight than in the other sampled countries (the UK, Greece, Czech Republic, New Zealand, South Africa, India, and Malaysia). These results showed that although some of the tested cultures are all described by Hofstede's index as collectivist cultures (India and Malaysia), yet the effect of social influence varies on each country's customers, which brings attention to the need to investigate the effect of social influence and potential other variables related to the culture and population when interpreting customers' technology adoption across countries and cultures.

Dai and Palvi (2009) also reported similar results; in their findings, they reported that social influence had a higher influence on Chinese customers' decision to adopt MC than the American customers.

Social influence was not the only construct reported to have different significance variation among cultures. Im et al. (2011) reported a higher impact of performance expectancy on behavioural intention in the USA than in Korea. This suggests that the US users consider how easy the technology is to use as a vital variable in their decision on technology adoption compared to the Koreans (Im et al., 2011).

These differences in UTAUT variable significance and weight between different countries, specifically these that score on opposite sides of Hofstede's cultural dimension of collectivism and individualism, indicate that there is still a need to further investigate UTAUT and to systematically investigate and theorize the salient factors that would apply to consumer acceptance and adoption of new technology in different cultural context and new contexts, such as new technologies (Venkatesh et al., 2012).

15.2.4 Trust

Trust has always been an important factor in online communication and usage. However, the fast evolvement of technology and the need to submit personal information especially in personalized services such as e-ticketing have increased trust role significantly (Nwanekezie et al., 2016; Sreenivasan & Noor, 2010). Mayer, Davis, and Schoorman (1995) defined trust as "the willingness of a party to be vulnerable to the actions of another party based on the expectations that the other party will perform a particular action important to the trustor, irrespective of the ability to monitor or control that other party" (Mayer et al., 1995, p. 172). Grandison and Sloman (2000) suggested that trust is a solid belief in the ability of a thing to act consistently, securely, and dependably within a definite context. As these definitions suggest, uncertainty and risk of vulnerability are two critical conditions that are related directly to trust (Belanche, Casaló, & Flavián, 2012). Trust is believed to reduce vulnerability and assist the individual in comprehending social surrounding of the interchange (Pavlou, 2003), by providing an interpretation to what, when, why, and how others behave (Belanche et al., 2012; Gefen & Straub, 2003).

Trust in an online purchase is described as "an attitude of confident expectation in an online situation of risk that one's vulnerabilities will not be exploited" (Corritore, Kracher, & Wiedenbeck, 2003, p. 740). In the online context, there is no guarantee that the e-vendor will commit to his promises; there is also a high level of uncertainty and risk including conveying inaccurate information, financial fraud, violating of customer privacy, and unauthorized use of credit card information. Consequently, trust is a critical aspect of the online purchase and a key driver for adoption in the online context (Gefen, 2000; Gefen & Straub, 2003). Therefore, trust might be considered a key variable in explaining the adoption of e-commerce in general and online purchase.

15.3 Research Model and Hypothesis Development

15.3.1 Intention to Use E-Ticketing

Intention refers to the "anticipated or planned future behaviour of individuals and is also an immediate determinant of a behaviour" (Chen, 2007, pp. 110–111). In this conceptual paper, intention refers to individual acceptance to adopt e-ticketing.

Many studies have reported a sturdy and significant causal link between behavioural intention and targeted behaviour (Davis, 1989; Sheppard et al., 1988; Venkatesh & Davis, 2000; Venkatesh et al., 2003). As e-ticketing is still at its early stages in Arabic frontier markets, and customers' adoption of this technology is primitive, this conceptual paper will use intention as a commission for actual usage (Lee & Wan, 2010).

15.3.2 UTAUT and E-Ticketing

UTAUT proposes four independent variables as the core variables—performance expectancy, effort expectancy, social influence, and facilitating conditions. UTAUT assumes that there is a positive relationship between performance expectancy and intention to use and adopt new technologies. Performance expectancy refers to individual's expectation of how helpful is the new technology in performing the intended task (Venkatesh et al., 2003). In the case of e-ticketing, performance expectancy refers to the presence of advantages perceived by an individual when using the e-ticketing (Lee & Wan, 2010). The positive relationship between performance expectancy and intention to adopt and use new technology has been well established in the literature, and evidence of its existence and robustness has been reported in a different context and among countries and cultures (e.g. Madigan et al., 2016; Oliveira, Faria, Thomas, & Popovič, 2014). Therefore, a positive relationship between performance expectancy and intention to accept and use e-ticketing is hypothesized.

Hypothesis 1 Performance expectancy has a positive relationship with intention to adopt e-ticketing in frontier collectivist culture markets.

UTAUT also posits that effort expectancy which represents the perceived cognitive effort an individual needs to put in order to learn how to use and utilize the technology (Venkatesh et al., 2003) has a positive relationship with intention to adopt and use new technology. Similar to performance expectancy, effort expectancy and intention relationship has been reported significantly in different context and among countries and cultures. In the case of e-ticketing, effort expectancy represents the perceived cognitive effort put in order to learn how to use and utilize the interface used to purchase the e-ticket (Lee & Wan, 2010).

Hypothesis 2 Effort expectancy has a positive relationship with intention to adopt e-ticketing in frontier collectivist culture markets.

The third core independent variable of UTAUT is facilitating conditions. Venkatesh et al. (2003, p. 453) introduced this variable as "the degree to which an individual believes that an organizational and technical infrastructure exists to support the use of the system". Although this variable showed a significant relationship with intention, yet it was excluded in some online-related adoption studies. For example, Oshlyansky et al. (2007) excluded facilitating condition specifically because the chosen technology, websites, would be available and accessible to all participants. A known form of facilitating condition is the technical support provided for a technology (Im et al., 2011). In the field of e-ticketing, facilitating conditions refer to the perceived support provided by the e-ticketing system provider. Previous studies have posited a relationship between facilitating conditions and intention to adopt e-ticketing. For example, Zhao, Chen, Wang, and Wang (2016) reported that system support has an influence on predicting customer adoption of mobile ticketing. Based on the previous, this conceptual paper hypothesizes a significant positive relationship between facilitating condition and intention to adopt e-ticketing.

Hypothesis 3 Facilitating conditions have a positive relationship with intention to adopt e-ticketing in frontier collectivist culture markets.

Finally, social influence refers to "the degree to which an individual perceives that important others believe he or she should use the new system". (Venkatesh et al., 2003, p. 453). Previous studies reported mixed findings regarding social influence. Yet, the social influence was reported to significantly influence intention in collectivist cultures. This was interpreted to the higher concern of people opinion in collectivist cultures. Thus, in this study social influence is hypothesized to have a significant positive relationship with intention.

Hypothesis 4 Social influence has a positive relationship with intention to adopt e-ticketing in frontier collectivist culture markets.

15.3.3 UTAUT and Trust

There are numerous features and characteristics of electronic service delivery, such as the lack of face-to-face interaction and the dynamicity of the virtual environment that results in creating uncertainty and reluctance to purchase online (Mariani & Lamarauna, 2017). The latter have positioned trust, in e-commerce relations, in a critical position. Accordingly, trust is expected to hold a significant role in adopting any activity that involves purchase of online goods and services (De Ruyter, Wetzels, & Kleijnen, 2001; Flavián & Guinalíu, 2006; Harris & Goode, 2004). Therefore, it is relevant to assume a significant influence of trust in adopting new technology that involves online transactions such as online purchase and e-ticketing.

Previous studies which investigated online ticket purchase have produced mixed results. For example, Kamarulzaman (2007) reported a nonsignificant direct effect of trust on the adoption of online travel shopping. On the other hand, Wen (2010) reported a positive effect on intention to online travel shopping. Since purchasing e-tickets signifies an alteration of the behaviour of purchasing paper ticket, then it is possible to associate it with instability. Moreover, insecurity associated with the perceived risk of computer system error (Chen, 2007) is expected to lead to suspicion, which magnifies the importance of trust. Therefore, trust is designated as the fifth independent variable.

Hypothesis 5 There is a positive relationship between perceived trust and purchase intention in frontier collectivist culture markets.

15.3.4 Trust and Social Influence

Previous studies established an association between individualism and collectivism and psychological outcomes of interest (values, self-concept, relationality, cognitive processes) (Jarvenpaa, Tractinsky, & Saarinen, 1999). Collectivist culture is described as cultures where individuals' beliefs depend on the social norms of the group (Kluckhorn & Strodtbeck, 1961). Collectivists were also described as sensitive to the ingroup-outgroup boundary (Jarvenpaa et al., 1999; Triandis, 1989). Thus, they are more likely to trust someone who is part of their group or trusted by their group (Yamagishi & Yamagishi, 1994). In reference to the assumption of group influence on trust, it is hypothesized that social influence has an influence to enhance the trust in adopting e-ticketing in frontier collectivist culture markets.

Hypothesis 6 There is a positive relationship between social influence and perceived trust in frontier collectivist culture markets.

15.3.5 Trust and Facilitating Conditions

Ang, Dubelaar, and Lee (2001) proposed that to improve online trust, merchant should be able to deliver the product or service as promised, protect customers' privacy using adequate privacy policies, and, most importantly, have the willingness to rectify in case the purchase did not meet the customer expectations.

As mentioned previously, facilitating conditions are related to the available technical infrastructure to support the use of the system (Venkatesh et al., 2003). In e-ticketing field, facilitating conditions refer to the perceived support provided by the e-ticketing system, which is expected to deliver the product or service as promised, protect customers' privacy by saving any financial or personal information customers share, and rectify any wrong should the purchase not meet the customer expectations by helping them amend their order. Therefore, we propose that facilitating condition has a positive relationship with trust.

Hypothesis 7 There is a positive relationship between facilitating conditions and perceived trust in frontier collectivist culture markets.

15.4 Conclusion and Future Work

This conceptual paper aims to explore the related issues surrounding e-ticketing adoption in Arabic frontier markets, which is described as a collectivist culture. To achieve this goal, a revised UTAUT model was introduced. UTAUT is a robust theory that explains the adoption of new technology; however, the application of theory has generated contradictory findings (Abubakar & Ahmad, 2013).

To provide explanations to customers' technology acceptance in the frontier collectivist culture markets, such as e-ticketing industry, the proposed model incorporates the factors of the unique characteristics of e-commerce, collectivist culture, and frontier markets. In the revised model, trust is proposed as a fifth independent variable added to the model and posits a positive relationship with intention. In reference to Arabic consumer distinct characteristics which are associated with collectivist culture, the revised model hypothesized that social influence has a significant influence on trust. The model also suggested that facilitating conditions also have a significant relationship with trust.

Following theory establishment, a subsequent empirical test to the revised model must be accomplished. The empirical study should focus on developing a research instrument that signifies the proposed relationships cross-countries to validate the results.

References

Abdullah, M. N., & Kadhim, E. H. (2016). Airline mobile reservation development. *Development, 3*(10), 1–3.

Abubakar, F., & Ahmad, H. (2013). The moderating effect of technology awareness on the relationship between UTAUT constructs and behavioural intention to use technology: A conceptual paper. *Australian Journal of Business and Management Research, 3*(02), 14–23.

Alalwan, A. A., Dwivedi, Y. K., & Rana, N. P. (2017). Factors influencing adoption of mobile banking by Jordanian bank customers: Extending UTAUT2 with trust. *International Journal of Information and Management, 37*(3), 99–110.

Alalwan, A. A., Dwivedi, Y. K., Rana, N. P., Lal, B., & Williams, M. D. (2015). Consumer adoption of internet banking in Jordan: Examining the role of hedonic motivation, habit, self-efficacy and trust. *Journal of Financial Services Management, 20*(2), 145–157.

Alalwan, A. A., Dwivedi, Y. K., Rana, N. P., & Simintiras, A. C. (2016). Jordanian consumers' adoption of telebanking: Influence of perceived usefulness, trust and self-efficacy. *International Journal of Bank Marketing, 34*(5), 690–709.

Alalwan, A. A., Dwivedi, Y. K., Rana, N. P., & Williams, M. D. (2016). Consumer adoption of mobile banking in Jordan: Examining the role of usefulness, ease of use, perceived risk and self-efficacy. *Journal of Enterprise Information Management, 29*(1), 118–139.

Alfawaer, Z. M., Awni, M., & Al-Zoubi, S. (2011). Mobile e-ticketing reservation system for Amman International Stadium in Jordan. *International Journal of Academic Research, 3*(1), 848–852.

Al-Gahtani, S. S., Hubona, G. S., & Wang, J. (2007). Information technology (IT) in Saudi Arabia: Culture and the acceptance and use of IT. *Information Management, 44*(8), 681–691.

Alharbi, S. T. (2014). Trust and acceptance of cloud computing: A revised UTAUT model. In *Computational science and computational intelligence (CSCI), 2014 international conference on* Bhopal, India. (Vol. 2, pp. 131–134).

Alryalat, M., Rana, N. P., & Dwivedi, Y. K. (2015). Citizen's adoption of an e-government system: Validating the extended theory of reasoned action (TRA). *International Journal of Electronic Government Research, 11*(4), 1–23.

Anderson, J. C., & Gerbing, D. W. (1988). Structural equation modelling in practice: A review and recommended two-step approach. *Psychological Bulletin, 103*, 411–23.

Ang, L., Dubelaar, C., & Lee, B.-C. (2001). To trust or not to trust? A model of internet trust from the customers point of view. In *Proceedings of the 14th bled electronic commerce conference* (pp. 40–52), Bled, Slovenia.

Ayeh, J. K., Au, N., & Law, R. (2016). Investigating cross-national heterogeneity in the adoption of online hotel reviews. *International Journal of Hospitality Management, 55*, 142–153.

Belanche, D., Casaló, L. V., & Flavián, C. (2012). Integrating trust and personal values into the technology acceptance model: The case of e-government services adoption. *Cuadernos de Economía y Dirección de la Empresa, 15*(4), 192–204.

Berger, D., Pukthuanthong, K., & Yang, J. J. (2011). International diversification with frontier markets. *Journal of Financial Economics, 101*(1), 227–242.

Chen, F. C. Y. (2007). Passenger use intentions for electronic tickets on international flights. *Journal of Air Transport Management, 13*(2), 110–115.

Constantinides, E. (2014). Foundations of social media marketing. *Procedia-Social and Behavioral Sciences, 148*, 40–57.

Corritore, C. L., Kracher, B., & Wiedenbeck, S. (2003). On-line trust: Concepts, evolving themes, a model. *International Journal of Human-Computer Studies, 58*(6), 737–758.

Chan, H., Lee, R., Dillon, T., & Chang, E. (2001). E-Commerce, Fundamentals and Applications. Wiley, Pennsylvania State University.

Dai, H., & Palvi, P. C. (2009). Mobile commerce adoption in China and the United States: A cross-cultural study. *ACM SIGMIS Database, 40*(4), 43–61.

Davis, F. D. (1989). Perceived usefulness, perceived ease of use, and user acceptance of information technology. *MIS Quarterly, 13*(3), 319–340.

De Groot, W., Pang, J., & Swinkels, L. (2012). The cross-section of stock returns in frontier emerging markets. *Journal of Empirical Finance, 19*(5), 796–818.

De Ruyter, K., Wetzels, M., & Kleijnen, M. (2001). Customer adoption of e-service: An experimental study. *International Journal of Service Industry Management, 12*(2), 184–207.

Dwivedi, Y. K., Rana, N. P., Janssen, M., Lal, B., Williams, M. D., & Clement, M. (2017). An empirical validation of a unified model of electronic government adoption (UMEGA). *Government Information Quarterly, 34*(2), 211–230.

Dwivedi, Y. K., Rana, N. P., Jeyaraj, A., Clement, M., & Williams, M. D. (2017). Re-examining the unified theory of acceptance and use of technology (UTAUT): Towards a revised theoretical model. *Information Systems Frontiers*. https://doi.org/10.1007/s10796-017-9774-y

Flavián, C., & Guinalíu, M. (2006). Consumer trust, perceived security and privacy policy: Three basic elements of loyalty to a web site. *Industrial Management & Data Systems, 106*(5), 601–620.

Frost, D., Goode, S., & Hart, D. (2010). Individualist and collectivist factors affecting online repurchase intentions. *Internet Research, 20*(1), 6–28.

Gefen, D. (2000). E-commerce: The role of familiarity and trust. *Omega, 28*(6), 725–737.

Gefen, D., & Straub, D. W. (2003). Managing user trust in B2C e-services. *E-service Journal, 2*(2), 7–24.
Grandison, T., & Sloman, M. (2000). A survey of trust in internet applications. *IEEE Communications Surveys & Tutorials, 3*(4), 2–16.
Harris, L. C., & Goode, M. M. (2004). The four levels of loyalty and the pivotal role of trust: A study of online service dynamics. *Journal of Retailing, 80*(2), 139–158.
Hill, C. E., Loch, K. D., Straub, D., & El-Sheshai, K. (1998). A qualitative assessment of Arab culture and information technology transfer. *Journal of Global Information Management (JGIM), 6*(3), 29–38.
Hofstede, G. (1980). *Culture's consequences: International differences in work-related values.* Beverly Hills, CA: Sage.
Hofstede, G. (2001). *Culture's consequences: Comparing values, behaviors, institutions, and organizations across nations* (2nd ed.). Thousand Oaks, CA: SAGE Publications. ISBN 978-0-8039-7323-7. OCLC 45093960.
Hoosain, A, Khan, S., Kira, D. and Farhoomand, A. (2000). Japan Airlines: Impact of e-ticketing. In: Management information systems: Managing the digital firm (8th ed.). Laudon, K. C., Laudon, J. P., (Eds.), pp. 511–520, Englewood Cliffs, NJ: Prentice Hall.
Im, I., Hong, S., & Kang, M. S. (2011). An international comparison of technology adoption: Testing the UTAUT model. *Information and management, 48*(1), 1–8.
Jarvenpaa, S. L., Tractinsky, N., & Saarinen, L. (1999). Consumer trust in an internet store: A cross-cultural validation. *Journal of Computer-Mediated Communication, 5*(2), 0–0.
Kamarulzaman, Y. (2007). Adoption of travel e-shopping in the UK. *International Journal of Retail & Distribution Management, 35*(9), 703e719.
Karahanna, E., Straub, D. W., & Chervany, N. L. (1999). Information technology adoption across time: A cross-sectional comparison of pre-adoption and post-adoption beliefs. *MIS Quarterly, 23*, 183–213.
Khanum, M., Fatima, S., & Chaurasia, M. (2012). Arabic interface analysis based on cultural markers. arXiv preprintarXiv:1203.3660.
Kluckhorn, F., & Strodtbeck, F. L. (1961). Variations in value orientations. In R. Peterson (Ed.), Evanston, IL.
Lee, C. B. P., & Wan, G. (2010). Including Subjective Norm and technology trust in the Technology Acceptance Model: A case of e-ticketing in China. *ACM SIGMIS Database: The DATABASE for Advances in Information Systems, 41*(4), 40–51.
Lee, L. Y. S. (2016). Hospitality industry web-based self-service technology adoption model a cross-cultural perspective. *Journal of Hospitality & Tourism Research, 40*(2), 162–197.
Lu, S. P., Chao, C. W., & Chen, C. H. (2014). A study of electronic ticket verification methods. *International Journal of Computer Science and Network Security (IJCSNS), 14*(11), 27.
Madigan, R., Louw, T., Dziennus, M., Graindorge, T., Ortega, E., Graindorge, M., & Merat, N. (2016). Acceptance of automated road transport systems (ARTS): An adaptation of the UTAUT model. *Transportation Research Procedia, 14*, 2217–2226.
Mariani, M., & Lamarauna, A. M. I. (2017). The impact of social influence and trust on customer-to-customer online shoppers' purchase intention: An empirical study in indonesia. *GSTF Journal on Computing (JoC), 5*(3), 1.
Market Classification. (2018). Morgan Stanley Capital International (MSCI) index.[online] [accessed on 12.5.2017]. Available at the World Wide Web at: https://www.msci.com/market-classification
Mathieson, K. (1991). Predicting user intentions: Comparing the technology acceptance model with the theory of planned behavior. *Information Systems Research, 2*(3), 173–191.
Mayer, R. C., Davis, J. H., & Schoorman, F. D. (1995). An integrative model of organizational trust. *Academy of Management Review, 20*(3), 709–734.
McCoy, S., Everard, A., & Jones, B. M. (2005). An examination of the technology acceptance model in Uruguay and the US: A focus on culture. *Journal of Global Information Technology Management, 8*(2), 27–45.

McCoy, S., Galetta, D. F., & King, W. R. (2007). Applying TAM across cultures: The need forcaution. *European Journal of Information Systems, 16*(1), 81–90.

Ngai, E. W., Poon, J. K. L., & Chan, Y. H. C. (2007). Empirical examination of the adoption of WebCT using TAM. *Computers & Education, 48*(2), 250–267.

Nwanekezie, U., Choudrie, J., & Spencer, N. (2016). Public sector online communication channel adoption and usage amongst older adults: A UK local government perspective. In: *Proceedings of Twenty-Fourth European Conference on Information Systems*. İstanbul, Turkey.

Oliveira, T., Faria, M., Thomas, M. A., & Popovič, A. (2014). Extending the understanding of mobile banking adoption: When UTAUT meets TTF and ITM. *International Journal of Information Management, 34*(5), 689–703.

Oshlyansky, L., Cairns, P., & Thimbleby, H. (2007). Validating the Unified Theory of Acceptance andUse of Technology (UTAUT) tool cross-culturally. In Proceedings of the 21st British HCI Group Annual Conferenceon People and Computers: HCI... but not as we know it. 2. Pp. 83-86). British Computer Society.

Pavlou, P. A. (2003). Consumer acceptance of electronic commerce: Integrating trust and risk with the technology acceptance model. *International Journal of Electronic Commerce, 7*(3), 101–134.

Qasem, Z. A., (2014). *The role of website experience in building attitude and intention towards online shopping* (Doctoral dissertation), University of Leeds.

Qteishat, M. K., Alshibly, H. H., & Al-ma'aitah, M. A. (2014). The impact of e-ticketing technique on customer satisfaction: An empirical analysis. *JISTEM-Journal of Information Systems and Technology Management, 11*(3), 519–532.

Rana, N. P., & Dwivedi, Y. K. (2015). Citizen's adoption of an e-government system: Validating extended social cognitive theory (SCT). *Government Information Quarterly, 32*(2), 172–181.

Rana, N. P., & Dwivedi, Y. K. (2016). Using clickers in a large business class: Examining use behavior and satisfaction. *Journal of Marketing Education, 38*(1), 47–64.

Rana, N. P., Dwivedi, Y. K., Lal, B., Williams, M. D., & Clement, M. (2017). Citizens' adoption of an electronic government system: Toward a unified view. *Information Systems Frontiers, 19*(3), 549–568.

Rana, N. P., Dwivedi, Y. K., & Williams, M. D. (2013). Evaluating alternative theoretical models for examining citizen centric adoption of e-government. *Transforming Government: People, Process, and Policy, 7*(1), 27–49.

Rana, N. P., Dwivedi, Y. K., Williams, M. D., & Weerakkody, V. (2016). Adoption of online public grievance redressal system in India: Toward developing a unified view. *Computers in Human Behavior, 59*, 265–282.

Sheppard, H., Hartwick, J., & Warshaw, R. (1988). The theory of reasoned action: A meta-analysis of past research with recommendations for modifications and future research. *Journal of Consumer Research, 15*, 325–343.

Sreenivasan, J., & Noor, M. N. M. (2010). A conceptual framework on mobile commerce acceptance and usage among Malaysian consumers: The influence of location, privacy, trust and purchasing power. *WSEAS Transactions on Information Science and Applications, 7*(5), 661–670.

Straub, D., Keil, M., & Brenner, W. (1997). Testing the technology acceptance model across cultures: A three-country study. *Information and Management, 33*(1), 1–11.

Tarhini, A., El-Masri, M., Ali, M., & Serrano, A. (2016). Extending the UTAUT model to understand the customers' acceptance and use of internet banking in Lebanon: A structural equation modeling approach. *Information Technology & People, 29*(4), 830–849.

Triandis, H. C. (1989). Cross-cultural studies of individualism-collectivism. In J. J. Berman (Ed.), *Nebraska symposium on motivation: Cross-cultural perspectives*. Lincoln, NE: University of Nebraska Press.

Turban, E., King, D., Lee, J. K. and Viehland, D. (2006). Electronic Commerce: A Managerial Perspective. 4th Ed.Prentice Hall.

Venkatesh, V., & Davis, F. D. (2000). A theoretical extension of the technology acceptance model: Four longitudinal field studies. *Management Science, 46*(2), 186–204.

Venkatesh, V., Morris, M., Davis, G., & Davis, F. (2003). User acceptance of information technology: Toward a unified view. *MIS Quartirly*, *27*(3), 425–478.

Venkatesh, V., Thong,Y., & Xu, X. (2012). Consumer acceptance and use of information technology: Extending the unified theory of acceptance and use of technology. *MIS Quarterly*, *36*(1), 157–178.

Wen, I. (2010). Online travelers' decision makings: A new equation model to evaluate impacts of website, search intention, and trust. *Information Technology & Tourism*, *12*(2), 153e173.

Williams, M. D., Rana, N. P., & Dwivedi, Y. K. (2015). The unified theory of acceptance and use of technology: A systematic review. *Journal of Enterprise Information Management*, *28*(3), 443–488.

Yamagishi, T., & Yamagishi, M. (1994). Trust and commitment in the United States and Japan. *Motivation and Emotion*, *18*(2), 129–166.

Zhao, Q., Chen, C. D., Wang, J. L., & Wang, K. J. (2016). Study of factors influencing mobile ticketing adoption: Status quo bias perspective. *Journal of Marine Science and Technology*, *24*(5), 926–937.

Zainah Qasem is an assistant professor at the School of Business of the University of Jordan. She has received her B.A. degree in Marketing from the University of Jordan and her M.A. and Ph.D. degrees in Marketing from the University of Leeds-UK. Her active research are consumer behaviour, e-marketing, and e-retailing.

Chapter 16
Internet of Things (IoT) in Agriculture Supply Chain Management: A Developing Country Perspective

Sunil Luthra, Sachin K. Mangla, Dixit Garg, and Anil Kumar

Abstract Agriculture supply chain management (ASCM) faces specific challenges such as dependence on weather conditions, involvement of very large number of actors and lack of literacy in the majority of the workforce that lead to requirement of information and communications technologies (ICT). The aim of this chapter is to introduce Internet of things (IoT)-based technologies and to describe its applications in the agriculture supply chain context in a developing country such as India. Based on literature, a total of six IoT-based technologies in the context of ASCM have been identified in this work. The application of IoT in agri-food sectors in India can promote the development of agriculture supply chain by reducing the wastage considerably and fulfil the requirements of users in a most sustained way. IoT-based technology has a significant scope of integrating in various functions of ASCM in industrial contexts in a developing country like India.

Keywords Agriculture supply chain management (ASCM) · Information and communications technologies (ICT) · Internet of things (IoT) · Radio-frequency identification (RFID)

S. Luthra (✉)
Department of Mechanical Engineering, Government Engineering College, Nilokheri, Haryana, India

S. K. Mangla
Department of Mechanical Engineering, Graphic Era University, Dehradun, Uttarakhand, India

D. Garg
Department of Mechanical Engineering, National Institute of Technology, Kurukshetra, Haryana, India

A. Kumar
School of Management, BML Munjal University, Gurgaon, Haryana, India

Y. K. Dwivedi et al. (eds.), *Emerging Markets from a Multidisciplinary Perspective*, Advances in Theory and Practice of Emerging Markets,
https://doi.org/10.1007/978-3-319-75013-2_16

16.1 Introduction

Over the past few decades, agriculture supply chain management (ASCM) faces specific challenges such as dependence on weather conditions, involvement of very large number of actors, rural India-driven supply, lack of literacy and skills in the majority of the workforce, etc. that lead to requirement of information and communications technologies (ICT). ICT refers to the technologies that are used for interlinking information technology mechanisms and equipment, such as computers and sensors, grids with communication technologies and their telecommunication networks (Chapman & Slaymaker, 2002).

Due to uncertain characteristics of agriculture supply chain (ASC), the current status of ICT in the agri-food sector is greatly influenced by availability of large amount of data and information. However, there is a huge gap in integrating ICT with agri-food sector supply network and in providing support for accurate usage of available data or information (Lehmann, Reiche, & Schiefer, 2012; Verdouw, Sundmaeker, Meyer, Wolfert, & Verhoosel, 2013). Over the past three decades, the performance of ASC has been improved significantly due to ICT applications, particularly in food production and transportation to the customers (Murakami et al., 2007; Nikkilä, Seilonen, & Koskinen, 2010). In addition, the solutions provided by ICT have been slow because of a number of significant unresolved issues up to this date. Information management is one of the key challenges in the agri-food industry whether within a particular function or throughout the supply chain from farm to customer (Sørensen et al., 2010). One of the most major challenges that has been faced by the agri-food industry is the involvement of multiple stakeholders along the supply chain for its sustainability and their heterogeneity and their continuously changing business relations with respect to each other during food supplies. Due to this, the information flow is very poor over each and every member that exists along the supply chain. In the last few decades, it has been seen that the lack of information became a critical issue in the ASCM. Therefore, for improving the overall performance, there is a need for greater transparency in the ASC and employment of tracking and tracing of foods to avoid health and safety issues and enable the supply chain to prevent and respond to food emergencies.

The Internet of things (IoT) is one of the key technologies that has been used in the last few years for managing information in the ASC. The IoT works with the help of embedded devices like actuators, sensors and network connectivity. These devices enable real-time interaction and data sharing among different smart devices/objects in the supply chain for information sharing (Gubbi, Buyya, Marusic, & Palaniswami, 2013; Zhong & Zhong, 2013). The most used technology in IoT to track and trace the real-time status of food products is radio-frequency identification (RFID) technology (Lee & Lee, 2015; Tsai & Liu, 2011). The tracking of agricultural products is mainly based on the data collected from RFID readers and tags which are able to record the location and time when an event/behaviour of the products changes.

The key aim of this chapter is to introduce IoT-based technologies and to describe its applications in the agriculture supply chain context. This chapter has been organized into six sections. Section 16.1 provides the introduction and discusses the need of this work. Relevant literature on ASCM, ASCM in developed and emerging economies and smart agriculture supply chain management has been presented in Sect. 16.2. IoT-based technologies and ASCM have been covered in Sect. 16.3. Section 16.4 covers the analysis of the processes in ASCM based on the IoT. The applicability of the IoT-based technology in ASCM in a developing economy context has been discussed in Sect. 16.5. Finally, concluding remarks are provided along with the future research implications in Sect. 16.6.

16.2 Literature Review

This section presents literature on ASCM in developed and emerging country context and smart ASCM.

16.2.1 ASCM in Developed and Emerging Countries

In ASCM, various actors are involved from 'farm to customer' involving effective flow of agricultural products to fulfil the customer requirements. ASCM involves the flow of agro-based products right from growing seedlings to end consumers (Mariani, 2007). ASCM includes all actors of supply chain such as producers, collectors, packers, processors, transporters, marketers, wholesalers, retailers, customers, etc. (Duan, 2011). In today's scenario, the research on ASCM has achieved quite advanced levels in many developed countries such as the United States, Holland, Japan and the EU. In Europe, generally shorter food supply chain is preferred, i.e. delivering products directly to the customers so as to avoid complexities involved in supply chain like uncertainty and information asymmetry and ensure the freshness and safety of products. In Holland, agricultural value chain has been organized successfully through its high levels of research, information and knowledge on ASCM. By virtue of which, it is possible to achieve higher quality and stability in supply of agricultural products and global vision of market for increasing the sustainability of supply chain in agri-food sector in Holland (Tang et al., 2015).

In an emerging country context, like China, the research on ASCM starts at the end of the twentieth century and is still going on at present time. Unlike developed countries, Chinese ASCM consists of connecting or organizing the millions of small-scale farmers to form a value chain. The status of food supply chain management in China can be summarized in terms of a complex and unsustainable supply network, inappropriate policy structure, lack of infrastructure which leads to wastage of food grains, inefficient information and knowledge sharing which leads to bullwhip effect, poor internet facilities, etc. (Chen, Zhang, & Delaurentis, 2014).

The development of ICT, especially with the introduction of IoT technology, such as RFID, sensor, etc., offers a huge scope of research on ASCM by tracking and tracing of all the activities involved in SCM and proper information sharing and good internet facilities involved in ASCM and ensures modernization and development in recent scenario of agriculture sector (Bosona and Gebresen, 2013).

India with its predominant rural base is deliberated as one of the world's largest and oldest agrarian countries. In India, agriculture sector contributes to 25% of GDP and employs more than 70% of the country's labour force. India is one of three major agri-food producers of the globe; however it accounts for only 1.2% in the world food trade (WTO, 2004). The agriculture sector is one of the highly unorganized sectors in India as nearly 60% of food quality is wasted throughout the supply chain. This means that customers are paying higher for a comparatively low efficient supply chain. In this manner, farmers in India are also getting back less money for their food products, and 60–80% of the price paid by the customers goes to traders, agents, wholesalers, retailers, etc. (Singh, 2014).

The ASCM in India is now shaping to some new dimensions and market realities driven through globalization and changes in behaviour of consumption patterns of consumers and shifting to high-value products like fruits, vegetables, animal proteins, etc. To deal with this issue of agricultural food sector of the country, the government intervention is significant. Government agencies are needed to frame regulations to invite private investors/stakeholders to join hands to develop agricultural infrastructure and to promote coordinated efforts in ASCM.

16.2.2 Smart Agriculture Supply Chain Management

Smart supply chain management means "having the right product item in the right quantity at the right time at the right place for the right price in the right condition to the right customer" (Wu, Yue, Jin, & Yen, 2016). However, due to the complexity, uncertainty, poor coordination, insufficient information and other factors involved in ASC, there are supply-demand mismatch problems such as overstocking, understocking and late delivery which have long been popular research topics over the last few decades in the business management literature (Wong , Skipworth, Godsell, & Achimugu, 2012). Smart supply chain management has characteristics of being cheaper, faster and better. But nowadays, ASCs are becoming more complex, costly, uncertain and easily effected by outer environment. To deal effectively with the increasing challenges due to globalization and increasing demand of customer, supply chains must become a lot smarter (Butner, 2010). In smart agriculture supply chain management (SASCM), the efficiency and sustainability of supply chain improved by integrating several areas, like semiconductor computer applications and other engineering-based technologies; the new version of supply network needs to develop a highly intelligent infrastructure for managing data, information, physical objects, products and business processes together (Schuster, Allen, & Brock, 2007). The IoT is emerging as a promising research area, converting conventional

ASCM to SASCM. For example, the food processing factories are equipped with smart equipment and instruments that can fulfil orders placed by a customer with the help of global teams, intelligent analytics for situation handling and finally dynamic systems all across the supply chain (Hessman, 2013).

16.3 Internet of Things (IoT)-Based Technologies and ASCM

The IoT is basically a network that consists of software, hardware, devices, objects, databases and sensors, which are working within a system for fulfilling the community needs (Mims, 2013). IoT is a technological revolution in computing and communications, which leads to vision of communication at anytime and anywhere, through any media (Atzori, Iera, & Morabito, 2010; Li, Da Xu, & Zhao, 2015).

In today's scenario, many latest technologies are developed to have better and superior quality food and food products (Käferstein, 1999). Some modern technologies such as irradiation, ICT, genetic modifications, etc. are useful in dealing with probable challenges in the food industry, such as shortened shelf life of food products. To deal with this issue, radio-frequency identification (RFID)-based data is very useful (Kärkkäinen, 2003) and one of the keys of IoT applications. In recent years, the topic of RFID has been extensively researched in the literature in the last few years (Zhu, Mukhopadhyay, & Kurata, 2012). As such, IoT allows digital and physical entities to be interlinked together so that it can provide a whole new class of applications and services in ASCM. The network is basically based on the automatic identification of the food products and their location, tracking, monitoring and generating the corresponding event (Aung & Chang, 2014; Sundmaeker, Guillemin, Friess, & Woelfflé, 2010).

In addition to this, several other Internet-based technologies such as cloud computing, artificial intelligence, 3-D printing, biosensors, etc. are higher performance-focused mechanisms. The application of IoT is significant to reduce the food wastage (Sundmaeker et al., 2010). However, it is clearly a lack of adoption of these high efficient IoT-based technologies in AFSCM in India (Verdouw, Wolfert, Beulens, & Rialland, 2016). At the same time, there are few Internet-based technologies that have been used to improve the performance of Indian agri-food sector such as Skymet, Mitra, Eruvaka Technologies and Ekgaon Technologies.

There is a wide range of IoT applications that have emerged and were accepted by food enterprises in recent years. According to Bradley, Barbier, and Handler (2013), IoT applicability in ASCM can bring $14.4 trillion in value. IoT-based technologies are significant to assisting the food organization to trace their process or product at every level. The purpose of food traceability is to permit the full backward and forward track of a product and its life history. In this work, we identified six IoT-based technologies in the context of agri-food sector or ASCM as shown in Table 16.1.

Table 16.1 IoT-based technologies in the context of agri-food sector or ASCM

IoT-based technologies in the context of agri-food sector or ASCM	Description	Sources
Radio-frequency identification	RFID tags can be extensively used to categorize, identify and manage the flow of products in an industrial context. For example, Walmart is using RFID to enhance the security and safety of food product.	Bilgen and Ozkarahan (2004); Valdramidis and Koutsoumanis (2016)
Vibrational spectroscopy	Vibrational spectroscopy is an efficient method for both the assessment of food quality and food authenticity. This technique is highly preferred among food enterprises.	Li-Chan, Chalmers, and Griffiths (2011); Cozzolino (2012)
Bio/wireless sensors/ mechanisms	With the help of biosensors/wireless mechanism, food contamination problems can be recognized very effectively and thereby improving the quality of food products. Biosensors play an important role in detection of food pathogens.	Tothill (2001)
Traceability	Traceability is mainly used for the prevention or reduction of food hazards. In this process, the products are traced at each level for determining any contamination in food products.	Bosona and Gebresenbet (2013); Valdramidis and Koutsoumanis (2016)
Artificial intelligence	Artificial intelligence is significant to use during the food sorting stage of the production line in a food industry. This may involve the integration of expert system knowledge and database in executing artificial intelligence-based activities to help managers to secure safety of food products.	Eerikäinen, Linko, Linko, Siimes, and Zhu (1993); Zhang, Zhang, Liu, Fu, and Mu (2010)
High pressure processing	High pressure processing is crucial in improving the food quality. This process is a type of cold pasteurization technique, and products are subjected to high level of pressure applied to food during or before their packaging.	Buckow and Heinz (2008); Chen et al., (2012)

16.4 Evaluating the Processes in ASC Based on the IoT

As mentioned above, IoT involves many latest technologies such as RFID, sensor networks, artificial intelligence, cloud computing, etc. (Chow, Choy, Lee, & Lau, 2006; Tajima, 2007; Whitaker, Mithas, & Krishnan, 2007). ASCM involves movement of food products between different stages, such as supplier, production, distribution and sale, food authenticity and quality, etc. A brief detail for evaluating the processes in ASC based on the IoT is given as below:

16.4.1 Production Stage

There is a significant scope of IoT-based technology application in production stage. In the production process of agricultural products, the raw materials/semi-finished products and finished products are distinguished and tracked using RFID tags in conjunction with electronic product code (EPC) for a steady production. This RFID code helps to identify each agricultural product along with necessary information for the product like product name, manufacturer, grade, expiry date, shelf life and so on. High pressure processing is also useful in improving quality products by applying pressure to products prior/during the packaging.

16.4.2 Transportation Stage

Transportation also allows significant opportunities to use IoT-based technology in agri-food sector. In the transportation stage of agricultural products, organizations may use GPS system to the transportation mediums, i.e. on vehicle to know exactly the location and condition of the vehicles. This may avoid delays during transportation and helps to avoid any accident and wastage of food products.

16.4.3 Distribution and Sale Stage

IoT-based technology has also great applications in distribution and sale stage in the food industry. The application of the IoT can be seen in the statistics, security and validity monitoring forms. EPC, RFID and traceability can help farmers and manufacturers to determine the quality of product such as product expiry date, origin of problems, flaws in management of supply chain, etc.

16.5 IoT-Based Technology Applicability in the ASCM in a Developing Economy of India

IoT plays a vital role in ASCM in emerging economies. These are provided as below (Ramundo, Taisch, & Terzi, 2016; Satpute & Tembhurne, 2014; Wang & Liu, 2014).

16.5.1 Purify Agricultural Material Market

The ASC based on the technology of the IoT (RFID, biosensors/wireless sensors/traceability) is a chain that includes production, storage, distribution and retailing facility to fulfil the customer's requirements of higher quality and authenticity. The application of RFID and biosensors/wireless sensors/traceability enables managers to recognize exact information about the products and maintains the quality of products. This will further improve the food quality and reduce the food wastage as well.

16.5.2 Reduce the Burden on Farmers

IoT will improve the transparency of each step of supply chain to a large extent greatly. RFID tag can automatically record each and every operation of the whole supply chain of agricultural products. It will not only reduce the 'bullwhip effect' but also reduce various costs (inventory/labour costs), which leads to improved performance. This will further reduce the cost, and benefits may be passed to farmers.

16.5.3 Opportunity to Develop Efficient Supply of Agricultural Products

IoT will guarantee to serve each and every link of agricultural production supply chain on a most effective way. It will improve the capacity of supply chain of supplying agricultural products and meet the needs of agricultural products by adopting technology (high pressure processing/artificial intelligence/vibrational spectroscopy) and tracking-based distribution techniques. A major part of Indian population resides in rural areas that lack not only modern facilities but basic also. Their issues like health, employment, agriculture, women empowerment, education and gender equality can be resolved through the access of ICT tools and services.

16.6 Conclusions

In this new era of globalization, Indian agriculture sector is facing problems like the low level of industrialization, lack of supply chain efficiency, management inadequacy, distorted information sharing in the supply chain, etc. To deal with these issues, the application of new Internet technology, i.e. IoT, has been proposed to develop smart agriculture supply chains. IoT is a feasible method for improving the efficiency and sustainability of the ASC.

In this chapter, the emergence of the IoT applications, the analysis of the processes in ASC based on the IoT and the applications of the IoT to the agricultural products supply chain in the context of developing country such as India have been explained. The application of IoT in agri-food sector in India can promote the development of agriculture and fulfil the requirements of users in a most sustained way.

Based on literature, a total of six IoT-based technologies in the context of ASCM have also been identified in this work. However, a significant gap is available in employability of these techniques in developing countries as compared to developed countries. There are several challenges in employing the IoT-based technology in ASCM in India, such as costing issues, low research and development facilities and industry standards. To the end, the IoT-based technology has a significant scope of integrating in various functions of ASCM in industrial contexts, which may be investigated in the future studies.

References

Atzori, L., Iera, A., & Morabito, G. (2010). The internet of things: A survey. *Computer Networks, 54*(15), 2787–2805.

Aung, M. M., & Chang, Y. S. (2014). Traceability in a food supply chain: Safety and quality perspectives. *Food Control, 39*, 172–184.

Bilgen, B., & Ozkarahan, I. (2004). Strategic tactical and operational production-distribution models: A review. *International Journal of Technology Management, 28*(2), 151–171.

Bosona, T., & Gebresenbet, G. (2013). Food traceability as an integral part of logistics management in food and agricultural supply chain. *Food Control, 33*(1), 32–48.

Bradley, J., Barbier, J., & Handler, D. (2013). Embracing the internet of everything to capture your share of $14.4 trillion. *White Paper,* CISCO.

Buckow, R., & Heinz, V. (2008). High pressure processing– A database of kinetic information. *Chemie Ingenieur Technik, 80*(8), 1081–1095.

Butner, K. (2010). The smarter supply chain of the future. *Strategy & Leadership, 38*(1), 22–31.

Chapman, R., & Slaymaker, T. (2002). ICTs and rural development: Review of the literature. *Current interventions and opportunities for action.* London: Overseas Development Institute.

Chen, C., Zhang, J., & Delaurentis, T. (2014). Quality control in food supply chain management: An analytical model and case study of the adulterated milk incident in China. *International Journal of Production Economics, 152*, 188–199.

Chen, J. H., Ren, Y., Seow, J., Liu, T., Bang, W. S., & Yuk, H. G. (2012). Intervention technologies for ensuring microbiological safety of meat: Current and future trends. *Comprehensive Reviews in Food Science and Food Safety, 11*(2), 119–132.

Chow, H. K., Choy, K. L., Lee, W. B., & Lau, K. C. (2006). Design of a RFID case-based resource management system for warehouse operations. *Expert Systems with Applications, 30*(4), 561–576.

Cozzolino, D. (2012). Recent trends on the use of infrared spectroscopy to trace and authenticate natural and agricultural food products. *Applied Spectroscopy Reviews, 47*(7), 518–530.

Duan, Y. E. (2011). Research on integrated information platform of agricultural supply chain management based on Internet of Things. *Journal of Software, 6*(5), 944–950.

Eerikäinen, T., Linko, P., Linko, S., Siimes, T., & Zhu, Y. H. (1993). Fuzzy logic and neural network applications in food science and technology. *Trends in Food Science & Technology, 4*(8), 237–242.

Gubbi, J., Buyya, R., Marusic, S., & Palaniswami, M. (2013). Internet of Things (IoT): A vision, architectural elements, and future directions. *Future Generation Computer Systems, 29*(7), 1645–1660.

Hessman, T. (2013). The dawn of the smart factory. *Industry Week, 14*, 14–19.

Käferstein, F. K. (1999). Foodborne diseases – A global public health challenge. *BioScience and Microflora, 18*(1), 11–15.

Kärkkäinen, M. (2003). Increasing efficiency in the supply chain for short shelf life goods using RFID tagging. *International Journal of Retail & Distribution Management, 31*(10), 529–536.

Lee, I., & Lee, K. (2015). The Internet of Things (IoT): Applications, investments, and challenges for enterprises. *Business Horizons, 58*(4), 431–440.

Lehmann, R. J., Reiche, R., & Schiefer, G. (2012). Future internet and the agri-food sector: State-of-the-art in literature and research. *Computers and Electronics in Agriculture, 89*, 158–174.

Li, S., Da Xu, L., & Zhao, S. (2015). The internet of things: A survey. *Information Systems Frontiers, 17*(2), 243–259.

Li-Chan, E., Chalmers, J., & Griffiths, P. (2011). *Applications of vibrational spectroscopy in food science*. Wiley.

Mariani, M. (2007, June). Sustainable agri-food supply chains and systems. In *Forum China-Europe, Work in Progress* (Vol. 27, p. 12). Available online at: http://docs.china-europa-forum.net/doc_62.pdf

Mims, C. (2013). Here's the one thing someone needs to invent before the internet of things can take off. *Backbone Magazine, February–March*, 12–13.

Murakami, E., Saraiva, A. M., Ribeiro, L. C., Cugnasca, C. E., Hirakawa, A. R., & Correa, P. L. (2007). An infrastructure for the development of distributed service-oriented information systems for precision agriculture. *Computers and Electronics in Agriculture, 58*(1), 37–48.

Nikkilä, R., Seilonen, I., & Koskinen, K. (2010). Software architecture for farm management information systems in precision agriculture. *Computers and Electronics in Agriculture, 70*(2), 328–336.

Ramundo, L., Taisch, M., & Terzi, S. (2016, September). State of the art of technology in the food sector value chain towards the IoT. In *2016 IEEE 2nd International Forum On Research and Technologies for Society and Industry (RTSI): Leveraging a Better Tomorrow* (pp. 1–6).

Satpute, P., & Tembhurne, O. (2014). A review of: Cloud centric IoT based framework for supply chain management in precision agriculture. *International Journal of Advance Research in Computer Science and Management Studies, 2*(11), 14–23.

Schuster, E. W., Allen, S. J., & Brock, D. L. (2007). *Global RFID: The value of the EPC global network for supply chain management*. Springer Science & Business Media.

Singh, R. K. (2014). Coordination in food supply chain: A framework. *International Journal of Information Systems and Supply Chain Management, 7*(3), 104–117.

Sørensen, C. G., Fountas, S., Nash, E., Pesonen, L., Bochtis, D., Pedersen, S. M., … Blackmore, S. B. (2010). Conceptual model of a future farm management information system. *Computers and Electronics in Agriculture, 72*(1), 37–47.

Sundmaeker, H., Guillemin, P., Friess, P., & Woelfflé, S. (2010). Vision and challenges for realising the Internet of Things. *Cluster of European Research Projects on the Internet of Things, European Commission, 3*(3), 34–36.

Tajima, M. (2007). Strategic value of RFID in supply chain management. *Journal of Purchasing and Supply Management, 13*(4), 261–273.

Tang, Q., Li, J., Sun, M., Lv, J., Gai, R., Mei, L., & Xu, L. (2015). Food traceability systems in China: The current status of and future perspectives on food supply chain databases, legal support, and technological research and support for food safety regulation. *Bioscience Trends, 9*(1), 7–15.

Tothill, I. E. (2001). Biosensors developments and potential applications in the agricultural diagnosis sector. *Computers and Electronics in Agriculture, 30*(1), 205–218.

Tsai, H. C., & Liu, Y. Y. (2011). *U.S. Patent No. 8,013,744*. Washington, DC: U.S. Patent and Trademark Office.

Valdramidis, V. P., & Koutsoumanis, K. P. (2016). Challenges and perspectives of advanced technologies in processing, distribution and storage for improving food safety. *Current Opinion in Food Science, 12*, 63–69.

Verdouw, C. N., Sundmaeker, H., Meyer, F., Wolfert, J., & Verhoosel, J. (2013). Smart agri-food logistics: Requirements for the future internet. In *Dynamics in logistics* (pp. 247–257). Berlin, Heidelberg: Springer.

Verdouw, C. N., Wolfert, J., Beulens, A. J. M., & Rialland, A. (2016). Virtualization of food supply chains with the internet of things. *Journal of Food Engineering, 176*, 128–136.

Wang, X., & Liu, N. (2014). The application of internet of things in agricultural means of production supply chain management. *Journal of Chemical and Pharmaceutical Research, 6*(7), 2304–2310.

Whitaker, J., Mithas, S., & Krishnan, M. S. (2007). A field study of RFID deployment and return expectations. *Production and Operations Management, 16*(5), 599–612.

Wong, C., Skipworth, H., Godsell, J., & Achimugu, N. (2012). Towards a theory of supply chain alignment enablers: A systematic literature review. *Supply Chain Management: An International Journal, 17*(4), 419–437.

WTO. (2004). *World trade report*. Geneva: World Trade Organisation.

Wu, L., Yue, X., Jin, A., & Yen, D. C. (2016). Smart supply chain management: A review and implications for future research. *The International Journal of Logistics Management, 27*(2), 395–417.

Zhang, X., Zhang, J., Liu, F., Fu, Z., & Mu, W. (2010). Strengths and limitations on the operating mechanisms of traceability system in agro food, China. *Food Control, 21*(6), 825–829.

Zhong, Y. H., & Zhong, Y. C. (2013). Key impact factors of collaborative knowledge management in IoT-related low carbon supply chains. *International Journal of Digital Content Technology and its Applications, 7*(1), 126.

Zhu, X., Mukhopadhyay, S. K., & Kurata, H. (2012). A review of RFID technology and its managerial applications in different industries. *Journal of Engineering and Technology Management, 29*(1), 152–167.

Sunil Luthra is an assistant professor at the Government Engineering College at Nilokheri, Haryana in India. He has contributed over 100 research papers in international refereed and national journals and conferences of international and national reputes. He has shown his research aptitude by publishing several research papers in high-impact factor journals. He has an excellent research track record with more than 115 research impact points, more than 1350 citations on Google Scholar, h-index of 19 on Google Scholar and a score of 28.05 on ResearchGate. His research interests include production and operations management, green and sustainable supply chain management, sustainable consumption and production and renewable and sustainable energies.

Sachin K. Mangla works in the field of green supply chain, smart manufacturing, machine learning, risk management, simulation, optimization, reverse logistics, renewable energy and MCDM. He loves to do quality research. He is an assistant professor of supply and operations in a leading international university. He has published/presented several papers in repute international/national journals (e.g. RSER, TRE-D, ANOR, JCP, PPC, IJPR, IJPE, PPC, RCR, IJOR, JFSM) and conferences (POMS, SOMS, IIIE, GLOGIFT). He has an h-index of 13, i10-index of 17 and Google Scholar citations of around 450.

Dixit Garg is a professor of the Mechanical Engineering Department at the National Institute of Technology (Institute of National Importance as per Parliament act) at Kurukshetra, Haryana, India. He published more than 170 research papers to his credit, published in international and national journals. He acted as an editor and reviewer in international journals/conferences and short-term training programmes. His specific areas of interest are operations and quality management, just-in-time, (JIT), production planning and control, manufacturing processes, supply chain management, educational planning, industrial engineering, productivity, entrepreneurship and green supply chain management, etc.

Anil Kumar is a faculty of Decision Science in the School of Management at BML Munjal University, Gurgaon, India. He completed his Ph.D. in Management from Indian Institute of Information Technology and Management, Gwalior. He holds MBA, MSc (Mathematics) and undergraduate degree in Mathematics (honours). He also qualified for UGC-NET. He has more than 30 research papers/book chapters and 4 books to his credit. His research interest includes supply chain analytics, consumer analytics, multi-criteria decision-making, fuzzy multi-criteria decision-making, fuzzy optimization, application of soft computing and econometrics modelling in marketing and multi-criteria decision-making and fuzzy applications in e-commerce and m-commerce.

Chapter 17
Readiness of Smart City: Emerging Economy Perspective

Sheshadri Chatterjee and Arpan Kumar Kar

Abstract Urban settings have been changed by rapid inflow of rural people. Consequently, more improvements have become necessary for the cities to make them livable. This ignited the idea of creation of smart cities for improving urbanization in general. The developed economies long back adopted this idea, and now emerging economies are also adopting the idea of creation of smart cities. The cities of emerging economies are facing problems owing to rapid inflow of rural people there. It is essential that those people are to be kept aware of the modernity of smart cities so that there is unhindered adoption of technological advanced services to be provided to them. For this, studies are to be conducted to assess their behavioral and attitudinal patterns with the help of available relevant technology adoption theories or models. Besides, for shaping ideal smart cities, the emerging economies are improving their infrastructure with proper readiness to create smart cities. The purpose of this paper is to study these aspects including keeping the city authorities ready to handle any unforeseen eventuality. For achieving these goals, a conceptual model has been proposed for planning and successful implementation of future smart cities.

Keywords Emerging economies · Privacy · Readiness · Security · Smart city

17.1 Introduction

In our global agenda, rapid growth of population and scarcity of available resources are appearing as critical and crucial issues. More than 50% of the world's population now lives in urban areas (Dirks, Gurdgiev, & Keeling, 2010). For improvement of lifestyle, rural people are rapidly agglomerating in urban areas. Consequently, it

---

S. Chatterjee (✉) · A. K. Kar
Department of Management Studies, Indian Institute of Technology Delhi, New Delhi, India

Y. K. Dwivedi et al. (eds.), *Emerging Markets from a Multidisciplinary Perspective*, Advances in Theory and Practice of Emerging Markets,
https://doi.org/10.1007/978-3-319-75013-2_17

has become a dire need to improve the living conditions of urban areas so that the inhabitants there can live with availability of modern services, hence lies the need to shape cities smarter. Such rapid congregation of influx of people to urban areas would render the inhabitants in an unlivable condition. This has given rise to the conception of smart cities throughout the world (Johnson, 2008). The developed economies long back realizing the situation have taken the appropriate steps for creation of smart cities and have also created smart cities in the real sense of the term. But this is not the exact scenario so far as the emerging economies are concerned. Here because of this urban migration, new kinds of problems are generated because of insufficient, deteriorating, and aging infrastructure (Marceau, 2008). Thus, to achieve best results for the citizens of smart cities to be created in emerging economies, the infrastructural developments have become a dire necessity, and for this, proper plan and frameworks are needed to be available and regular validation as well as reconciliation of performance with global standard (ISO, 37120) to be augmented to improve the readiness of the smart cities in the emerging economies and to develop the infrastructure.

17.2 Conceptualization of Smart Cities

The concept of smart cities is still emerging having no universally acceptable standard definition. It is still in progress (Hollands, 2008). Some experts opined that smart cities are urban phenomenon powered by ICT. A few working definitions are given below. By the soothing collaboration among physical, IT, social, and business infrastructures, the collective intelligence can be achieved in a city which then may be called as a smart city (Harrison et al., 2010; Pancholi, 2014; Odendaal, 2003). The congenial integration of physical, digital, and human systems would ensure to deliver sustainable, prosperous, and inclusive future for the citizens of the smart cities (Department of Business Innovation and Skills (2013), BSI). Smart cities are those cities where there exists appropriate use of all interconnected updated information available which would help for better understanding and for better control over different operations as well as for better optimization of the use of limited resources (Cosgerove, 2011). Smart cities would be the cities of smart citizens (Falconer & Mitchell, 2012). The nineteenth century was a century of empires, the twentieth century was of nation-states, and the twenty-first century would be a century of cities (Kehoe & Nesbitt, 2011). Smart city contextually is an urbanized area where multiple sectors cooperate for achieving sustainable outcome by the help of analysis of contextual real-time information which have been shared among sector-specific information and operational technology systems (Ernst & Young, 2016). There are some definitions given from different sectors for providing a general conception regarding creation of smart city approach. This creation of smart city approach includes a holistic initiative by the concerned authorities of the concerned country to boost up economic growth which would help improve effectively and pragmatically the quality of life of the people inhabiting in that area including big data challenges since it would bring in local development with modern amenities. It would also harness updated technology (ICT) which would ensure eventually an effective smart outcome for the betterment of concerned citizens (Batty et al., 2012; Chauhan, Agarwal, & Kar, 2016).

17.3 Smart Growth Approach in Emerging Economies

Although emerging economies are growing in a rapid pace, they have many growth challenges especially building the required infrastructures to become competitive globally and establishing themselves in the global stage as a major destination of digital economy. Smart city is one of such growth approaches for emerging economies where majority of services will be based on digital transactions. The conception of smart city leads to the fact that smart cities are intimately associated with smart growth from all relevant angles (Koradag, 2013). These are as follows:

- Amalgamated utilization of available land
- To take advantage of compact building design for users' convenience
- To create a range of housing opportunities and options for the potential users
- To develop neighborhood accessibility through walk
- To foster distinctive communities for updating lifestyle
- Arrange to provide sufficient open space for proper utilization
- Arrange to create firmland and to ensure not to disturb natural beauty
- To provide critical environmental areas for sustainable growth
- To ensure overall developments from all corners toward the existing communities
- To arrange so that inhabitants have enough options toward the use of variety of transportation
- To ensure that decision for development should be pragmatic and cost-effective
- Arrange to get all stakeholders involved while taking developmental decisions to avoid unwanted complications in future

However, during the mid-2000s some firms like IBM, Cisco, Siemens, etc. for achieving rapid success in all aspects in smart cities arranged for integration of ICT with urban structures and services to be provided to the citizens rendering the services converted to digital services. However, these modern applications of ICT in the services to be provided in modern intelligent cities may not find the pace of advancement owing to the menace of privacy and security (Goodhue & Straub, 1991; Maeyer, 2007; Kolb & Abdullah, 2009; Kehoe et al., 2011) vulnerabilities as well as owing to the adoption issues by the potential users. For this the IT authorities to be working in the proposed smart cities of India are required to be very cautious in providing structured and methodical guidelines for the potential citizens expected to be living in proposed smart cities of India and to realize the behavioral and attitudinal patterns of the potential users to avoid adoption issues.

17.4 Pillars of Smart City in Emerging Economies

In most of the emerging economies, different kinds of smart cities are being developed or planned by the respective governments. Unlike in the developed economies, emerging economies have high growth rate, but there are lack of institutional infrastructure, physical infrastructure, etc. Here, in this section, the four common pillars of smart cities in emerging economies have been discussed. There are many features on which structure of smart city depends. Out of those features, four features are construed to be pillars for a smart city (Ernst & Young, 2016). These are as follows:

- Institutional infrastructure
- Physical infrastructure
- Social infrastructure
- Economic infrastructure

Institutional Infrastructure It includes mainly planning in a pragmatic way with a conception of tricks of implementation so that the plan in the circumstances can be safely executed. There must be good governance which should act as per need. Efficient management must be there for translating all the planning and governance into proper action.

Physical Infrastructure It includes urban mobility system, high-speed unobstructed network like 5G, sanitation, solid waste, energy, etc. which are digital services or IT-enabled services. Efficient usage of ICT ensures that these systems' flow is not interrupted in any way which may jeopardize the interest of the citizens.

Social Infrastructure It includes development of social as well as human capital like education, entertainment, sports, etc. Attention must be there by the authorities so that the facilities provided in these respects can be enjoyed by the potential users with ease, and they are to be made aware of these IT-enabled services to avoid any adoption issue.

Economic Infrastructure It includes effective and meaningful employment generation. It also includes creation of a congenial environment which might attract investments.

17.5 Digital Services in Smart Cities in Emerging Economies

Here now we shall discuss the key parameters of smart cities in emerging economy context (Carlino, 2011). These are as follows:

Smart Mobility Modern traffic management system with all updated technologies, proper and effective parking system, and transportation pricing system associated with automatic devices are required to be available.

Smart Energy Efficient and effective management connected with energy usage and audit, smart grid (modern networking), smart meters, and storage of energy for the future when in crisis are to be ensured.

Smart Buildings Modern ventilation system, air conditioning and hitting system with less consumption of energy, automated lighting and lock system, etc. are to be ensured rendering the buildings as automated intelligent buildings.

Modern Connectivity Free Wi-Fi with ease, 5G connectivity, and no broadband hazard for multichannel networks are to be ensured.

Smart Infrastructure The entire management system is to be digitalized with the help of ICT. Sensor-oriented activities are to be ensured to reduce wastage and to save energy.

Smart Education and Smart Governance E-education in all levels is to be implemented, and best e-governance activities are to be ensured.

Smart Healthcare Collected medical system is to be available. E-health and m-health systems should work properly.

Smart Citizens Well-trained citizens to digest all digitalized facilities are to be ensured, and there must be facilities for having ease of green mobility along with availability of lifestyle modernized option.

17.6 Security and Privacy Issues in Emerging Economy

Emerging economies have many challenges such as low level of literacy, lack of awareness of digital economy by the citizens, and issues on trustworthiness on digital transactions; few of the economies have language challenges, etc. Upon these several challenges faced by the emerging economies, security and privacy issues are two major concerns. With the development of smart cities in these emerging economies, ICT would play a vital role, and since ICT will have a major role in developing these smart cities, security and privacy vulnerabilities can be of major challenges. As already discussed in brief, the pace of growth of ICT-based services and activities in modern digitalized cities otherwise called as smart cities in the emerging economies is not accelerating in desired level due to challenges of privacy and security issues. Online activities are found vulnerable to personal data disclosure in some issues requiring special attention by the authorities lest those do not become rampant since in that case users would hardly be involved in those activities rendering the mission of creating modern cities in emerging economies infructuous (Anthony, Kacmar, & Perrewe, 2002; Carlino, 2011; Craig, 2011). In intelligent cities, secured and resilient cyberspace should be safely available to the citizens for their different ICT-based works for which security-based practices to be followed, and there must be proper periodical security audit (Solms & Solms, 2004; Osborne, 1998). In this way, all the checks and breaks are to be ensured for achieving safe and secured services so that security is not at stake and privacy is not compromised for the stakeholders. All the emerging economies have been using many modern devices to plug up these vulnerabilities; still we are to listen that almost 100 countries in 2017 have become unfortunate victims of Ransomware virus attack, especially Britain where the entire healthcare system was reported to have collapsed.

17.7 Smart City Development Approach in Emerging Economy

The international experience of developing smart cities mostly has two accepted urban planning approaches, that is, technological and complex. Both have their own guidelines, approaches, methods, advantages, and disadvantages. In most of the emerging economies, these approaches are being followed. The technological approach is first followed in most of the emerging economies while developing the smart cities, and information and communication technology plays a vital role while planning and developing these smart cities. For taking such approaches, almost in all the emerging economies have certain authorities responsible for developing the smart cities. To give proper shape of a smart city, for methodical and structured systematic steps of approach for targeting a goal, the authorities must be very cautious to proceed in a very calibrated manner, and the approach can be visualized in the following flowchart (Fig. 17.1).

17.8 Phases for Development of Smart Cities in Emerging Economies

An emerging economy is a nation's economy which is progressing at a rapid pace, and it is progressing toward becoming an advanced economy in the near future. These emerging economies, e.g., BRICS countries (Brazil, Russia, India, China, South Africa) are experiencing an expanding role in world economy, and they are also experiencing rapid urbanization. To develop new cities in a more planned way, most of the emerging economies are developing smart cities in different phases. Here, in this section, we shall now describe these phases (analysis, design,

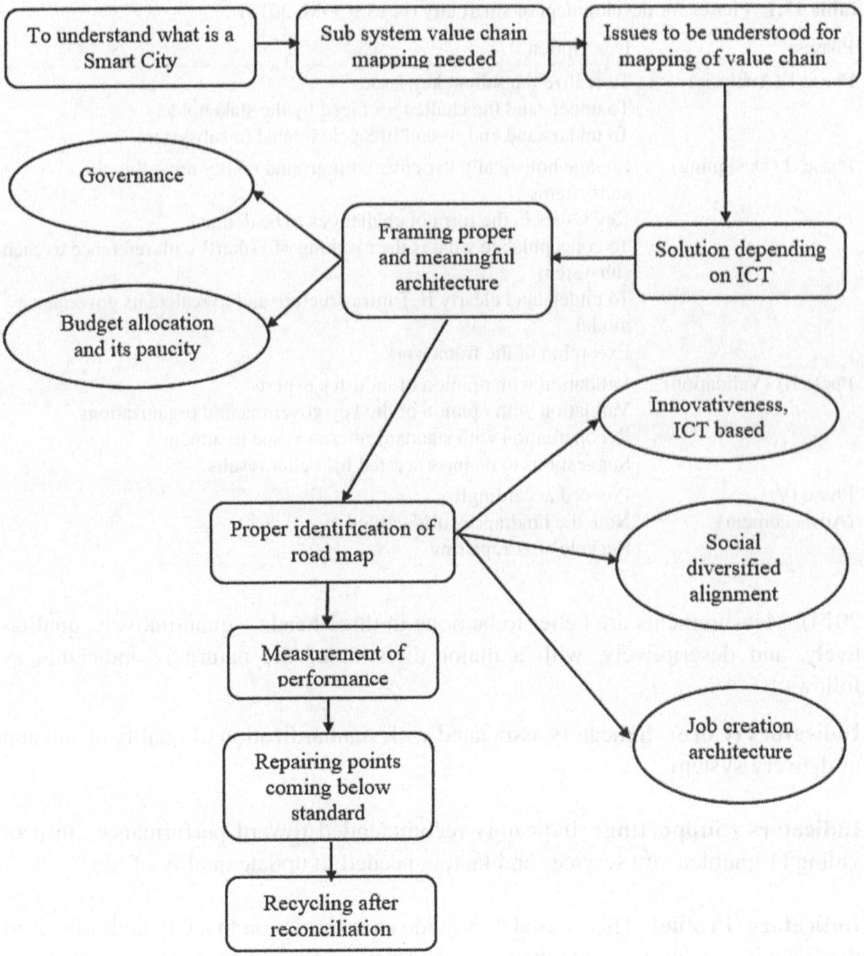

Fig. 17.1 Smart city development approach

validation, advancement) in a tabular form. Basically, there are four phases of development to shape ideal smart city which are depicted below (Table 17.1):

17.9 Assessment of Performances: Standardization

Periodical assessments of performances are of crying need because, besides validation, if those are also not done, it will be difficult to ascertain that the existing IT-enabled services provided for the utilization of the citizens would require any treatment to remove ailments if at all exist. The assessment process is obviously included to compare with the indicators having international standard (ISO 37120,

Table 17.1 Phases for development of smart city (NASSCOM, 2015)

Phases	Description
Phase 1 (Analysis)	To realize the salient key issues To understand the challenges faced by the stakeholders To understand end-to-end lifecycle related to subsystem
Phase II (Designing)	Engage holistically to define with ground reality regarding the subsystems Key issues in the form of challenges to be defined To conceptualize what is the meaning of "smart' with reference to each subsystem To understand clearly ICT infrastructure and to realize its governance model Execution of the framework
Phase III (Validation)	Validation with opinion of industry experts Validation with opinion of the key governmental organizations Reconciliation with standard reference and treatment Suggestions to be incorporated for better results
Phase IV (Advancement)	Proceed accordingly Note the hindrances if identified Recycle after repairing

2014). Measurements are better to be done in three heads – quantitatively, qualitatively, and descriptively, with a major division of the nature of indicators as follows:

Indicators (Core) Indicators associated with standardization of quality of life and of delivery system.

Indicators (Supporting) Indicators recommended toward performances in providing IT-enabled city services and factors needed to update quality of life.

Indicators (Profile) This is used to provide an information to a city authority as to the fact with which standard city their performances are required to be compared to. It acts as an informative reference. Some of the salient points mentioned here as major parameters for measurement of performance of the smart city are shown as follows:

Education Full-time enrolment and part-time enrolment including primary, secondary, and higher education including consideration of the number of dropout.

Natural Disaster Flood, hurricane, and earthquake – how the disaster response team would work in demanding situations and what are the standard operating procedures (SOP).

Waste Management Hazardous waste, solid waste, and tracheophytes – how they are managed with reference to standard laudable procedures.

IT System How the authorities in standardized manner are striving to address the threat of security and privacy issues.

Water, Energy, and Electricity How the standard methods are being applied for plugging up any weakness in the ICT system which is finding application in water, energy, and electricity management to keep wastage in check.

Be it mentioned here, other points are also needed to be focused on like economy, finance, environment, governance, health, recreation, shelter for people, transportation, urban planning, telecommunication, and networking systems. All these services if found not acting properly are to be measured with standard reference. If these are continuously done, the quality of checking and measuring devices involving IT would not be rusted, and it would get scope to improve devices with needs of time.

17.10 Conclusion

If all the steps mentioned earlier are properly dealt with and nurtured, a full-proof smart city may be achieved. In brief, the following benefits are to be ensured to understand the readiness of the smart city in the emerging economy (Karadag, 2013):

- Effective elasticity regarding data infrastructure is to be achieved rendering meaningful maintenance of agile and prompt services.
- Different subdepartmental activities are to be integrated appropriately.
- Task of prioritization for the city authority will be easier with the help of having information and with the help of analysis.
- According to the needs, appropriate regulations can be framed for better result and for plugging up pilferage.
- Resource management could help optimize the budgetary preparation.
- New value-added services to the citizens can be ensured.
- Proper training and awareness is to be imparted to the resources of the authority for their upgradation to face needs of time.
- Bureaucratic processes would be standardized, ensuring transparency and knowledge management would fetch better result.
- Involvement of citizens would help the process of execution to run in a smoother way.

Several empirical studies have been conducted to examine implementation, adoption, and the use of citizen-centric technologies and services such as common service centers and electronic government (see, e.g., Dwivedi, Rana, Janssen, Lal, Williams, & Clement, 2017; Rana, Dwivedi, Williams, & Weerakkody, 2016; Rana, Dwivedi, Lal, Williams, & Clement, 2017; Shareef, Dwivedi, Kumar, & Kumar, 2016) for gaining a better understanding of citizen's attitude and behavior leading to their widespread adoption and use. However, such studies are limited in the context of smart cities. For involving citizens with smart city-related initiatives and encouraging their acceptance and adoption and the use of smart city-related applications and services, it is important to conduct empirical studies using established theories and models (Dwivedi et al. 2017; Kapoor, Dwivedi, & Williams, 2014a, 2014b; Venkatesh, Morris, Davis, & Davis, 2003; Venkatesh, Thong, & Xu, 2012) for facilitating wider diffusion of such emerging technologies.

References

Anthony, W. P., Kacmar, K. M., & Perrewe, P. L. (2002). *Human resource management: A strategic approach* (4th ed.). New York, NY: South-Western.

Batty, M., Axhausen, K. W., Giannotti, F., Pozdnoukhov, A., Bazzani, A., Wachowicz, M., & Portugali, W. (2012). Smart cities of the future. *The European Physical Journal, Special Topics, 214*, 481–518.

Carlino, G. A. (2011). Three keys of the city: Resources, agglomeration economies, and sorting. *Business Review Quarterly, 3*, 1–13. Available at https://www.philadelphiafed.org/-/media/research-and-data/publications/business-review/2011/q3/brq311_three-keys-to-the-city.pdf

Chauhan, S., Agarwal, N., & Kar, A. K. (2016). Addressing big data challenges in smart cities: A systematic literature review, info: Digital policy. *Regulation and Governance, 18*(4), 73–90.

Cosgrove, V. (2011). *Smart cities: Introducing the IBM city operations and management solutions*. IBM.

Craig, G. (2011). Introduction: Community development in the United Kingdom. In G. Craig, M. Mayo, K. Popple, M. Shaw, & M. Taylor (Eds.), *The community development reader: History, themes and issues*. Bristol, UK: Polity Press.

Department of Business Innovation and Skills (BSI). (2013). *Smart Cities: Background Paper*. London, BIS/13//1209.

Dirks, S., Gurdgiev, C., & Keeling, M. (2010). *Smarter cities for smarter growth: How cities can optimize their systems for the Talent – Based – Economy*. IBM Global Business Services New York, 1–24. Available at https://www.zurich.ibm.com/pdf/isl/infoportal/IBV_SC3_report_GBE03348USEN.pdf

Dwivedi, Y. K., Rana, N. P., Janssen, M., Lal, B., Williams, M. D., & Clement, R. M. (2017). An empirical validation of a Unified Model of Electronic Government Adoption (UMEGA). *Government Information Quarterly, 34*(2), 211–230

Ernst & Young. (2016). Cyber Security: A necessary pillar of smart cities. Indian Security Conference, ASSOCHEM, India. Available at http://www.ey.com/Publication/vwLUAssets/ey-cyber-security-a-necessary-pillar-of-smart-cities/$FILE/ey-cyber-security-a-necessary-pillar-of-smart-cities.pdf

Falconer, G., & Mitchell, S. (2012). Smart City framework: A systematic process for enabling Smart Connected Community. 1–11. Available at http://www.cisco.com/c/dam/en_us/about/ac79/docs/ps/motm/Smart-City-Framework.pdf

Goodhue, D. L., & Straub, D. W. (1991). Security concerns of system users: A study of perception of the adequacy of security. *Information Management, 20*(1), 13.

Harrison, C., Eckman, B., Hamilton, R., Hartswick, P., Kalagnanam, J., Paraszczak, J., & Williams, P. (2010). Foundations for Smarter Cities. *IBM Journal of Research and Development, 54*(4), 1–16.

Holland, R. G. (2008). Will the real smart city please stand up? *City, 2*(3), 303–320.

International Standard ISO 37120. (2014). Sustainable development of communities – Indicators for city services and quality of life. *International Organization for Standardization: Great Things Happen When the World Agrees, 13*(1), 1–85.

Johnson, B. (2008). Cities, systems of innovation and economic development. *Innovation Management Policy and Practice, 10*(2/3), 146–155.

Kapoor, K. K., Dwivedi, Y. K., & Williams, M. D. (2014a). Innovation adoption attributes: A review and synthesis of research findings. *European Journal of Innovation Management, 17*(3), 327–348.

Kapoor, K. K., Dwivedi, Y. K., & Williams, M. D. (2014b). Rogers' innovation adoption attributes: A systematic review and synthesis of existing research. *Information Systems Management, 31*(1), 74–91.

Karadag, T. (2013). An evolution of the smart city approach. The graduate school of natural and applied sciences of Middle East Technical university. Available at http://citeseerx.ist.psu.edu/viewdoc/download?doi=10.1.1.633.3072&rep=rep1&type=pdf

Kehoe, M., Meegan, J., & Nesbitt, P., Cosgerove, M., Harthoom, W., Hogan, J., Jabbar, R. (2011). *Smart Cities: Introducing the IBM city operations and management solutions*. 4733, IBM Corp., 1–32.

Kehoe, M., & Nesbitt, E. (2011). *Smarter Cities services: A foundation of understanding IBM Smarter Cities*. IBM Redbooks. Available at https://pdfs.semanticscholar.org/55e0/c011168f3993f79cdf367980be56b5edb5b7.pdf

Kolb, N., & Abdullah, F. (2009). Developing an information security awareness program for a non-profit organization. *International Management Review, 5*(2), 103–107.

Maeyer, D. D. (2007). Setting up an effective information security awareness program. In ISSE/SECURE Securing Electronic Business Process Highlights of the Information Security Solutions, Europe/SECURE: 2007 Conference (pp. 126–349).

Marceau, J. (2008). Introduction: Innovation in the city and innovative cities. *Management Policy and Practice, 10*(2/3), 136–145.

NASCOMM. (2015). *Smart City ICT Framework*. Available at https://www.niua.org/sites/all/files/consultationworkshop/Nasscom_TechnologyArchitectureFramework.pdf

Odendaal, N. (2003). Information and communication technology and local governance: Understanding the difference between cities in developed and emerging economies. *Computers, Environment and Urban Systems, 27*(6), 585–607.

Osborne, K. (1998). Auditing the IT security function. *Computers and Security, 17*(1), 34–41.

Pancholi, V. S. (2014). Measuring decentralization in reforms era: A case of Kalyan-Dombivi, India. *Scientific Research, 2*(2), 116–126.

Rana, N. P., Dwivedi, Y. K., Lal, B., Williams, M. D., & Clement, M. (2017). Citizens' adoption of an electronic government system: Towards a unified view. *Information Systems Frontiers, 19*(3), 549–568.

Rana, N. P., Dwivedi, Y. K., Williams, M. D., & Weerakkody, V. (2016). Adoption of online public grievance redressal system in India: Toward developing a unified view. *Computers in Human Behavior, 59*, 265–282.

Solms, B.V. & Solms, R.V. (2004). The 10 deadly sins of information security management. *Journal of Computer & Security, 23*(5), 371–376.

Shareef, M. A., Dwivedi, Y. K., Kumar, V., & Kumar, U. (2016). Reformation of public service to meet citizens' needs as customers: Evaluating SMS as an alternative service delivery channel. *Computers in Human Behavior, 61*, 255–270.

Venkatesh, V., Thong, J., & Xu, X. (2012). Consumer acceptance and use of information technology: Extending the unified theory of acceptance and use of technology. *MIS Quarterly, 36*(1), 157–178.

Venkatesh, V., Morris, M. G., Davis, G. B., & Davis, F. D. (2003). User acceptance of information technology: Toward a unified view. *MIS Quarterly, 27*(3), 425–478.

Sheshadri Chatterjee is a management practitioner presently working at Microsoft Corporation in India. Academically he has an engineering and management background and has completed MTech and MBA. His is currently working as a research scholar at IIT Delhi. Professionally Sheshadri has worked as a management consultant in several MNCs in different capacities like package solution consultant, business program manager, learning and development manager, etc. Few of the organizations he was associated with are IBM Global Business Services (Consulting Division), Hewlett-Packard Company (Enterprise Services), Microsoft Corp for Asia Pacific region, etc. Sheshadri' s current interests are in the areas of smart cities, security, trust and privacy issues in IT governance, Internet of things, artificial intelligence and machine learning, culture and its influence in IT industry, customer relationship management, cyber security and assurance, end-user experience, etc.

Arpan Kumar Kar teaches in the Department of Management Studies in Indian Institute of Technology Delhi, India. His research interests are in the domain of e-business, social media, e-governance, data analytics, and technology management. He has published over 70 articles in reputed journals and conferences which are available in Elsevier, IEEE, Springer, Taylor & Francis, and Emerald. He is a managing editor of Global Journal of e-Business and Knowledge Management and an associate editor of Global Journal of Flexible Systems Management. He has earlier worked for the Indian Institute of Management Rohtak, IBM Research Laboratory, and Cognizant Business Consulting. He has handled multiple major research and consulting projects for private and public organizations under Government of India. He has also received multiple awards and recognitions for his research from reputed organizations like Association of Indian Management Schools, Tata Consultancy Services, Project Management Institute, and IIM Rohtak.

Chapter 18
Integration of Public Sector Healthcare Information Systems with Private Sector Healthcare Providers in Pakistan: Challenges, Opportunities and Solutions

Khalil Khoumbati, Munir Abbasi, Syed Ghulam Sarwar Shah, and Lampros K. Stergioulas

Abstract Globally the implementation of information and communication technology (ICT) in the healthcare sector has brought about significant improvement in the delivery of healthcare services, yet such transformation is still under way or in its infancy in many developing countries. Pakistan is a lower middle-income country (LMIC) where the health status of population and management of health systems data are very poor. In Pakistan, healthcare services are being provided by public and private sector organisations as well as by individual practitioners. Healthcare delivery and disease monitoring and evaluation are supported by health information systems (HISs) and district health information systems (DHIS). However, like in many other LMICs, implementation of HIS and DHIS is under-deployed in Pakistan mainly due to non-integration of public and private healthcare providers' information systems. Thus there is a pressing need for exploring and facilitating the effective use and integration of public sector DHIS with the private healthcare sector in Pakistan (as well as other similar LMICs) – not only for the diagnosis, monitoring and healthcare delivery in general but also for planning and decision-making processes. Such a systemic change will usher in a new era of increased availability of high-quality accessible and relevant health information, which will be of great benefit to the population's health.

Keywords Integration of health information systems · Public healthcare providers · Private healthcare providers · Pakistan · Lower middle-income countries

K. Khoumbati (✉)
Institute of Information and Communication Technology, University of Sindh, Jamshoro, Pakistan

M. Abbasi · L. K. Stergioulas
Surrey Business School, University of Surrey, Guildford, UK

S. G. S. Shah
Department of Clinical Sciences, Brunel University London, Uxbridge, UK

Y. K. Dwivedi et al. (eds.), *Emerging Markets from a Multidisciplinary Perspective*, Advances in Theory and Practice of Emerging Markets,
https://doi.org/10.1007/978-3-319-75013-2_18

18.1 Introduction

The implementation of information and communication technology (ICT) in the healthcare sector plays an important role in the delivery of healthcare services (Khoumbati, Themistocleous, & Irani, 2005). In addition, the latest ICT tools and applications are supporting the integration of healthcare service processes (Khoumbati, Themistocleous, & Irani, 2006) enabling the availability of clinical- and drug-related information to doctors, healthcare professionals and decision makers at the right time, place and form and to the right people. As a result, a reduction in medical errors has been reported (Khoumbati et al., 2006). Thus, research and development (R&D) projects involving large-scale investments are under way for the improvement and enhancement of ICT infrastructure and implementation in healthcare organisations in many countries, especially the developed countries such as the UK (Catwell & Sheikh, 2009) and the US (Catwell & Sheikh, 2009). In addition, different ICT applications and tools such as clinical information systems, electronic medical records, benefit-risk tools, telemedicine services and mobile health applications are being implemented in healthcare organisations in several countries (Chandwani, De, & Dwivedi, 2017; Chandwani & Dwivedi, 2015; Dwivedi, Shareef, Simintiras, Lal, & Weerakkody, 2016). However, the adoption and use of ICT infrastructure, decision support systems, tools and applications are very low in developing countries such as Pakistan.

In Pakistan, healthcare services are being provided through public and private sector healthcare providers. The public healthcare services are being provided at three levels, i.e. primary healthcare, secondary healthcare and tertiary healthcare providers. The private healthcare is provided through 'for-profit' hospitals, clinics and self-employed practitioners and 'not-for-profit' non-government providers, such as charities and faith organisations.

In Pakistan, most of the population live mainly in rural areas where people have limited access to primary healthcare facilities, which suffer from the shortage of staff, faulty equipment and deficient supply of medicines and poor referral system (Ahmed & Shaikh, 2011). In addition, poverty and sociocultural factors exacerbate inequalities in accessing and utilising of healthcare especially by women (Majrooh et al., 2013). The situation of healthcare provision can be worsened due to inadequate and inaccessible essential health information, which could lead to increase in avoidable morbidity and mortality (Sundari, 1992). Most of the health indicators for Pakistan are poor. For example, mortality rate under 5 is 80/1000 (highest in the world), maternal mortality ratio is 170/100,000 live births and 63% of the total expenditure on health is private in the country (World Bank, 2015). The majority of patients seek healthcare from the private sector, especially in primary healthcare (Anwar, 2008), and the private sector has taken over government basic health units in the country (Shaikh et al., 2010).

In Pakistan, a nationwide health management information system (HMIS) was adopted in 1993 to support evidence-based decision-making and management of healthcare (Qazi & Ali, 2009). The main objective of the project was to assist middle and senior health managers to use the patient data in the decision-making process (Health System Profile Report, 2007). In 2001, under the *devolution of power* taking place at the time, the health portfolio was transferred from the federal government to the provincial governments resulting in a revamp of the HMIS.

In addition, after the 18th Amendment bill in Pakistan in April 2010, several issues such as data management, integration and control created new management issues affecting the implementation of the HMIS. According to Health Facility Assessment Sindh Provincial Report (2012, 63) 'HMIS is badly neglected as it is only implemented in 83 HFs (health facilities) out of 275 (belonging to Health department in Sindh province)'. Moreover, the information from the public sector DHIS is untimely and unreliable (Gething et al., 2006), inefficient and under-reported (Kumar et al., 2012). One of the main reasons of under-reporting of health information, including disease burden, is the lack of data from the private healthcare sector, which plays a significant role in providing healthcare to a large part of the population in the country. Thus, the exclusion of the private healthcare providers from the implementation of DHIS leads to inadequate health information gathering and utilisation and limits the realisation of benefits from the DHIS. In addition, health policies are formulated based on health information collected through only public sector DHIS, which does not fully represent the whole patient population in the country. Thus, the current implementation arrangements of DHIS are not supporting adequately the decision-making processes in healthcare (Government of Sindh, 2013).

The current situation demands that decision makers of the healthcare organisations should take certain steps for the further improvement and enhancement of the system (Ahmed & Shaikh, 2011). Therefore, crucial improvements to health systems in general, and DHIS in particular, are needed in Pakistan for effective decision-making about patient care, diagnosis, treatment and preventative measures. This will further help for the development of integrated health record systems.

This paper, therefore, proposes a possible solution for integrated healthcare infrastructure where the public sector healthcare information systems could be integrated with the private sector healthcare information systems. The proposed health information system integration model is aimed to help decision makers to better understand the challenges and issues involved, which can be essential for preparing and devising the appropriate solutions.

18.2 Enterprise Application Integration

The most widely reported definition of enterprise application integration (EAI) technology is as follows:

> Unrestricted sharing of information between two or more enterprise applications. A set of technologies that allow the movement and exchange of information between different application and business process within and between organisations. (Linthicum, 1999, p. 345)

According to Themistocleous et al. (2000), EAI leading to the integration of different applications can reduce cost by 50%. In addition, the integrated applications can communicate freely with each other through a common integration infrastructure/platform rather than through point-to-point integration, compared to the traditional interconnection approaches (Linthicum, 1999). The above evidence supports that EAI can provide better solutions by integrating various applications being used by public and private healthcare providers.

18.3 Integration of Public Sector Healthcare Information Systems With Private Sector Healthcare Providers

The integration of healthcare information systems (HIS) is considered very complicated, but the potential of using it has enormous advantages. The literature shows that several organisations have deployed various integration technologies such as electronic data interchange (EDI) (Erasala, David, & Rajkumar, 2002), enterprise resource planning (ERP) (Bradford & Florin, 2003), enterprise application integration (EAI) (Linthicum, 1999) and Web services (Estrem, 2003) to integrate their disparate systems. In addition to these general-purpose integration systems, there have been many efforts by different countries, organisations and individuals to integrate various approaches adopted by healthcare organisations, such as Health Level 7 (HL7) (Beeler, 1998); CEN/TC251 (Ceusters et al., 1997); Synergy Extranet (SynEx) (Spyrou et al., 2002); Synapses, DICOM (Ferrara, 1998); and Common Object Broker Architecture in Medicine (CORBAmed).

In the context of HIS, information sourcing/collection, integration, transformation, storage, analysis and usage can be achieved at various levels. The literature (e.g. Khoumbati et al., 2005 amongst others) reports that the integration of healthcare information can be achieved internally at public sector hospital levels and externally at the public or private healthcare providers or private hospital, clinic and general practitioner (GP) levels. Figure 18.1 presents our proposed model for possible integration of various healthcare information systems that can be integrated at different levels.

The integration of HIS of public sector healthcare providers and the HIS of private sector healthcare providers (including clinics, hospitals and general practitioners) with the EAI can provide several benefits to the healthcare organisations, healthcare professionals, decision makers and other stakeholders such as patients. Khoumbati et al. (2006) have reported various benefits that can be achieved when the public and private healthcare providers' HISs are integrated: for example, the EAI could provide the following benefits:

- Systems integration can save patients' lives.
- Hospitals will be interconnected with each other.
- The records including the medical history of all patients can be viewed from anywhere in real time by the authorised persons.

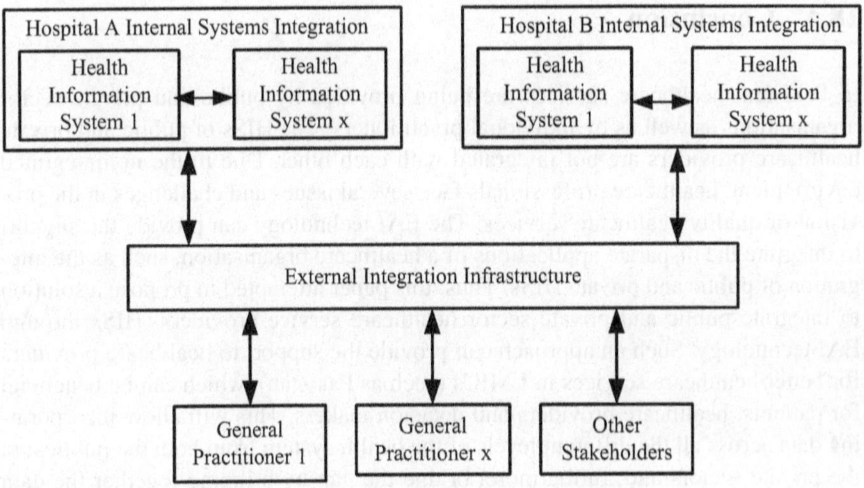

Fig. 18.1 Healthcare information system integration (Source: Khoumbati, 2005)

- The life of patients can be saved by providing appropriate and timely diagnosis and treatment.
- Healthcare processes benefits including medical treatment, insurance and medical cost claims and revenue cycle.
- Real-time monitoring of clinical and businesses process.
- Healthcare planning and policy making (Khoumbati et al., 2006).

In addition, the healthcare organisations need to take a holistic approach to connect their enterprises together to reduce the costs; improve the quality of care; reach consumers, employers and suppliers; and adapt quickly to their highly regulated, increasingly complex and competitive environment (Grimson et al., 2000). Moreover, each patient may have a specific condition that requires customised care, especially patients with complex/chronic medical conditions or co-morbidities where several clinical measurements and information need to be captured at various intervals. As such, additional measurements may also be required; thus, the measurement intervals in data collection need to be adapted to specific care pathways. Currently diagnosing and monitoring a set of patients in the public hospitals are available for newly admitted patients, but the integrated facility is not available at the private hospitals, clinics and healthcare providers. Our proposed integration model may provide solutions that will help to diagnose, monitor, plan, deliver and provide a high-quality and integrated healthcare services to patients and communities, particularly those living in the rural areas.

18.4 Conclusion

In Pakistan, healthcare services are being provided by public and private sector organisations as well as by individual practitioners. The HISs of public and private healthcare providers are not integrated with each other. Due to the nonintegrated environment, healthcare professionals face several issues and challenges in the provision of quality healthcare services. The EAI technology can provide the support to integrate the disparate applications of a healthcare organisation, such as the integration of public and private HISs. Thus, this paper attempted to propose a solution to integrate public and private sector healthcare service providers' HISs through EAI technology. Such an approach can provide the support to healthcare providers for better healthcare services in LMICs (such as Pakistan), which can be beneficial for patients, healthcare providers and decision makers. This will allow incorporating data across all the different levels of the health system from both the public and the private sectors and, furthermore, bridge the gap by bringing together the data from various disparate databases, which will help to generate reliable and accurate information about patients' medical history and treatment, and hospital records which can not only be used by the health practitioners but also by the decision makers, enabling them to plan and monitor health interventions across all levels of the health system. The result of such systemic change would be the well-structured and uniform provision and distribution of health facility. This will further help to devise a dedicated health strategy for chronic diseases such as diseases in the heart, kideny, and mental health, cancer, diabetes, arthritis, dementia, etc. The proposed system can also help patients to become active participants in their own care by combining further information, knowledge and software tools in the future. Further research topics to be addressed in the future can include the evaluation of the proposed infrastructure on the usability, acceptability, accessibility, effectiveness, security, transparency and interoperability issues.

References

Ahmed, J., & Shaikh, B. (2011). The state of affairs at primary health care facilities in Pakistan: Where is the state's stewardship? *Eastern Mediterranean Health Journal, 17*(7), 619–623.

Anwar, S. (2008). Health care delivery in Karachi – The worst of both worlds. *The Journal of the Pakistan Medical Association, 58*(11), 595–596.

Beeler, G. (1998). HL7 version 3-an object-oriented methodology for collaborative standards development. *International Journal of Medical Informatics, 48*(1–3), 151–161.

Bradford, M., & Florin, J. (2003). Examining the Role of Innovation Diffusion Factors on the ImplementationSuccess of Enterprise Resource Planning systems, *International Journal of Accounting Information Systems, 4*(3), 205–225.

Catwell, L., & Sheikh, A. (2009). Evaluating eHealth interventions: The need for continuous systemic evaluation. *PLoS Medicine, 6*(8), e1000126. https://doi.org/10.1371/journal.pmed.1000126

Ceusters, W., Buekens, F., DeMoor, G., Bernauer, J., Dekeyser, L., & Surjan, G. (1997). TSMI: A CEN/TC251 standard for time specific problems in healthcare informatics and telematrics. *International Journal of Medical Informatics, 46*(2), 87–101.

Chandwani, R., De, R., & Dwivedi, Y. K. (2017). Telemedicine for low-resource settings: Exploring the generative mechanisms. *Technological Forecasting and Social Change*, 127, 177–187.

Chandwani, R., & Dwivedi, Y. K. (2015). Telemedicine in India: Current state, challenges and opportunities. *Transforming Government: People, Process and Policy, 9*(4), 393–400.

Dwivedi, Y. K., Shareef, M. A., Simintiras, A. C., Lal, B., & Weerakkody, V. (2016). A generalised adoption model for services: A cross-country comparison of mobile health (m-health). *Government Information Quarterly, 33*(1), 174–187.

Erasala, N., David, C., & Rajkumar, M. (2002). Enterprise application integration in the electronic commerce world. *Computer Standards & Interfaces, 25*(2), 69–82.

Estrem, W. A. (2003). An evaluation framework for deploying web services in the next generation manufacturing enterprise. *Robotics and Computer-Integrated Manufacturing, 19*(6), 509–519.

Ferrara, F. (1998). The CEN healthcare information systems architecture standard and the DHE middleware. A practical support to the integration and evolution of healthcare systems. *International Journal of Medical Informatics, 28*(1–3), 173–182.

Gething, P., et al. (2006). Improving imperfect data from health management information systems in Africa using space-time geostatistics. *PLoS Medicine, 3*(6), e271.

Government of Sindh (2012). *Sindh Health Sector Strategy 2012–2020.* Health Support Reforms Unit, Department of Health, Karachi, Pakistan.

Government of Sindh (2013). *Health profile of Sindh (District wise) as on 01–01-2013. Bureau of Statistics, Planning Development Department* Karachi.

Grimson, J., Grimson, W., & Hasselbring, W. (2000). The SI Challenge in Health Care. *Communications of the ACM, 43*(6), 49–55.

Health System Profile Report. (2007). http://apps.who.int/medicinedocs/documents/s17305e/s17305e.pdf

Khoumbati, K. (2005). Evaluation the adoption of enterprise application integration in healthcare organaizations' (PhD Thesis). Department of Information Systems and Computing, Brunel University, London.

Khoumbati, K., Themistocleous, M., & Irani, Z. (2005). *Integration technology adoption in healthcare organisations: A case for enterprise application integration*, 38th Hawaii International Conference on Systems Sciences HICSS, [CD-Proceedings].

Khoumbati, K., Themistocleous, M., & Irani, Z. (2006). Integration technology adoption in healthcare organisations: A case for enterprise application integration. *Information Management, 41*(2), 117–187.

Kumar, R., et al. (2012). Role of health management information system in disease reporting at a rural district of Sindh. Pakistan. *Journal of Public Health, 2*(2), 10–12.

Linthicum, D. (1999). *Enterprise application integration*. Boston, MA: Addison-Wesley.

Majrooh, M., et al. (2013). Accessibility of antenatal services at primary healthcare facilities in Punjab, Pakistan. *The Journal of the Pakistan Medical Association, 63*(4, S-3), S60–S66.

Qazi, M., & Ali, M. (2009). Pakistan's health management information system: Health managers' perspectives. *The Journal of the Pakistan Medical Association, 59*(1), 10–14.

Shaikh, B., et al. (2010). Contracting of primary health care services in Pakistan: Is up-scaling a pragmatic thinking? *The Journal of the Pakistan Medical Association, 60*(5), 387–389.

Spyrou, S., Bamidis, P., Chouvarda, I., Gogou, G., Tryfon, M., & Maglaveras, N. (2002). Healthcare information standards: Comparison of the approaches. *Health Informatics Journal, 8*(1), 14–19.

Sundari, T. (1992). The untold story: How the health care systems in developing countries contribute to maternal mortality. *International Journal of Health Services, 22*(3), 513–528.

Themistocleous, M., Irani, Z., & Sharif, A. (2000). Evaluating Application Integration, 7th European Conference on Evaluation of Information Technology, CITE, pp. 193–202.

World Bank (2015). Data. http://data.worldbank.org/ Health expenditure, public (% of GDP).

Khalil Khoumbati received his Ph.D. in 'Evaluation the Adoption of Enterprise Application Integration in Healthcare Organisations' from the School of Information Systems, Computing and Mathematics, Brunel University, UK, and MSc in Computer Technology and BSc in Electronics from IICT, University of Sindh, Jamshoro, Pakistan. Currently, he is a Professor in IICT, University of Sindh, Jamshoro, Pakistan. His current research focus is on enterprise systems, e-health and e-government applications. He is on the editorial board of several international journals such as ***Transforming Government: People, Process and Policy***. He has published more than 30 research papers in internationally refereed journals such as Journal of Management Information Systems and Journal of Computer and Information Systems. He has presented more than 20 papers in international conferences such as HICSS, AMCIS, ECIS and EMCIS. He has edited a book for IGI group of publisher USA on ***Handbook of Research on Advances in Health Informatics and Electronic Healthcare Applications: Global Adoption and Impact of Information Communication Technologies, 2009***. He is also a member of several professional organisations.

Dr. Munir Abbasi is a senior researcher and project manager. He received his first degree in electrical engineering and his PhD from Brunel University, London, UK. He has a broad range of experience (more than 25 years) working on various 'state-of-the-art' national and international programmes, projects and products' full life cycles from ideation to completion. He has worked for public and private sectors which include communications, defence and academia. He has been working and contributing to several EU-funded projects including Base 2, Dyrect, TEL-MAP, HOTEL, FET-Art, Open Discovery Space, CRe-AM, ADVANCE and Designscapes projects. He has authored/co-authored more than 25 publications appearing in scientific journals and conference proceedings. His research interests are technologies and tools for creativity and innovation, healthcare, hybrid networks, design innovation, technology roadmaps, decision support systems, analytics, evaluation frameworks, impact, business models and sustainability strategy.

Dr. Syed Ghulam Sarwar Shah is a trained medical doctor and is currently working as a postdoctoral research fellow at the Guy's and St. Thomas' NHS Trust, London. He has studied in Pakistan, Germany, the Netherlands and the UK. He holds a bachelor of medicine and bachelor of surgery (MBBS) degree from the University of Sindh, Pakistan. He holds MSc and Ph.D. from Brunel University London. He has worked in primary health and civil services in Pakistan and at Brunel University London, UK. His research interests include health study research, public health, patient experiences, (public) health intelligence, electronic medical records and medical device technologies. He has published several articles in peer-reviewed journals and presented papers at international conferences held in Brazil, Canada, Malaysia, Spain and the UK. He is a manuscript reviewer for a number of academic journals

Lampros K. Stergioulas is professor of business analytics at the University of Surrey, UK. He has studied Informatics and Physics in his first degree and received MSc and Ph.D. in electrical engineering from the University of Liverpool, UK. He has published over 150 scientific publications and has supervised and examined numerous PhD dissertations in information systems and computer science. He has held many national and EU Grants in information systems, technology-enhanced learning, human-centred communications and computing, medical and health informatics, information processing and intelligent systems. He has been the principal investigator in numerous EU projects, including UNIVERSAL (FP5), TIME2LEARN (FP5), PROLEARN (FP6), BASE2 (FP6), HoTEL, OpenScout, iCOPER, ODS and ADVANCE, and he is the coordinator of the e-Start, TEL-Map, CRe-AM and European research projects.

Part V
Marketing

Chapter 19
Adoption of Pro-poor Innovations in the Context of the Base of the Pyramid and Subsistence Marketplaces: Challenges, Opportunities and Research Agenda

Ben Lowe and Md. Rajibul Hasan

Abstract In countries such as Bangladesh, some innovations have diffused rapidly and been taken up by large segments of the population (e.g. mobile phones). However, some innovations which offer the promise of time saving, greater efficiency and better economy have been slower in their take-up (e.g. gas stoves). What explains these contrasting examples? The study of consumer innovation adoption is vast. However, the majority of research in this area has been written about economically developed economies where consumers have excess disposable income to spend on the latest gadgets. Yet, innovations benefit economically less wealthy consumers too (e.g. mobile banking, information communication technologies, etc.). Such innovations have been termed pro-poor innovations by some (Ramani, SadreGhazi, & Duysters, Technological Forecasting and Social Change 79(4):676–687, 2012) and are innovations which offer some developmental benefit within the so-called Base of the Pyramid markets. The literature in this area is fragmented and scattered across numerous disciplines such as business, health, development, economics and others. Given this, researchers interested in this area have great opportunities to expand our knowledge base and contribute to an area of societal importance. This chapter reviews literature in this area, presents some challenges (opportunities!) for doing research in this context and provides a future research agenda.

Keywords Adoption · Consumer · Base of the Pyramid · Pro-poor innovations · Subsistence marketplaces

---

B. Lowe (✉)
Sibson Building, Kent Business School, University of Kent, Canterbury, UK
e-mail: b.lowe@kent.ac.uk

Md. R. Hasan
Rennes School of Business, Rennes, France
e-mail: rajibul.hasan@rennes-sb.com

Y. K. Dwivedi et al. (eds.), *Emerging Markets from a Multidisciplinary Perspective*, Advances in Theory and Practice of Emerging Markets,
https://doi.org/10.1007/978-3-319-75013-2_19

19.1 Introduction

The work of CK Prahalad and colleagues (Hart & Prahalad, 2002) established the business case for multinational organisations marketing their products to the so-called "Bottom of the Pyramid" (BOP) and identified them as a lucrative market segment with needs and wants that were not being fulfilled by existing offerings. The rationale was that these markets had different characteristics – poor road networks, unreliable electricity, lack of connectivity, low income, high inflation, low literacy, etc. – and because of this, required products and services were carefully designed for this context. Providing products and services at reduced prices with reduced functionality was not sufficient to meet the needs and wants of this growing market. Though margins are smaller, volumes are higher than in conventional markets, leading to profitability and an incentive for companies to continue to serve the needs of this underserved market.

One interesting and often cited characteristic of this market segment is the speed at which some innovations have diffused, despite income restrictions. For example, countries like Bangladesh surpassed fixed line telecommunications and rapidly adopted mobile telephones and related technologies, even amongst the poor (Donner, 2008). However, on the other hand, there are a plethora of examples where innovative new products designed for the needs of the poor have failed. For example, cooking with gas offers many advantages over wood fuelled stoves including a more reliable source of fuel, cheaper and easier fuel supply and broader environmental benefits. However, such innovations have exhibited slower levels of adoption in BOP segments than might be expected even in light of their objective economic and societal benefits (Kanagawa & Nakata, 2007; Panwar, Kurchania, & Rathore, 2009). It would appear that even though such segments are economically constrained, other factors are important in determining the speed at which an innovation is adopted; for example, compatibility with existing lifestyles and social mores (Miller & Mobarak, 2014). These contrasting examples raise questions about what we know of innovation adoption within the BOP. What are the factors that are important in understanding the adoption of such innovative new products in these markets? Perhaps an understanding of these consumers from the "bottom up" might shed some light on the answer to this question. Researchers argue for developing a greater understanding of these consumers from the bottom up, and such an approach complements and adds richness to the literature on the BOP (e.g. Viswanathan & Rosa, 2007; Viswanathan, Sridharan, & Ritchie, 2010). This chapter proceeds by defining what an innovation is within the BOP and subsistence marketplace context. It then goes on to look at what we know of consumer innovation adoption in other contexts and the extent to which this knowledge might be transferred over to the BOP. Taking the broad qualitative versus quantitative classification, it then looks at the advantages and disadvantages of these research methodologies for the context here. The chapter then concludes by offering a future research agenda for those researchers interested in defining new frontiers in the area of pro-poor innovation adoption.

19.2 Pro-poor Innovations: Perception Is Reality

A crucial question around this theme is "What is meant by an innovation?". An innovation can be defined as "an idea, practice, or object that is *perceived* [emphasis added] as new by an individual or other unit of adoption" (Rogers, 2003, p. 12). Thus, it is one's perception which is what matters rather than some objective notion of innovativeness. This is consistent with the view of other researchers in the field such as Danneels and Kleinschmidt (2001, p. 362) who state "…customers themselves are the only proper informants regarding how new they perceive a new product to be, and in what ways it is new to them…". In the context of the BOP and subsistence marketplaces, a new product or service is innovative if perceived as such by its customers, and so a phone, although not innovative in one geographic market, may well be considered as innovative in another market; something that is perceived to be new but also superior to what currently exists (Lowe & Alpert, 2015).

The central idea behind marketing to the BOP is that businesses can assist in alleviating poverty by ensuring access to innovations for the BOP (Prahalad, 2005). However, some innovations have a greater development impact on consumers and improve the life of the poor. For example, the long-term effects of using shampoo in mini sachets (a commonly quoted "innovation") are unlikely to be the same as the long-term effects of clean water because clean drinking water has a greater bearing on the wellbeing of poor consumers. By looking at the developmental aspects of innovations, Ramani, SadreGhazi, and Duysters (2012) and Mendoza and Thelen (2008) define these types of innovations as "pro-poor innovations" and argue that pro-poor innovation is characterised by new products and services that satisfy the essential needs of the poor. This includes improved food, water, healthcare, housing and sanitation or innovations which enhance productivity and income generation capacity. Mendoza and Thelen (2008) also emphasise that the delivery system of pro-poor innovations must ensure accessibility to the targeted BOP consumers along with positive reputational or financial returns to suppliers in order for them to be sustainable. For instance, mobile banking services such as bKash (Bangladesh) and M-Pesa (Kenya) have replaced traditional payment systems but also provide an increase in wellbeing to consumers (e.g. lower cost, easier accessibility, etc.).

19.3 Consumers and Innovation Adoption

To help provide some insight about the factors likely to affect adoption in this context, an obvious angle for enquiry is literature in the area of consumer innovation adoption. The literature in this area is rich and has a long history in business and sociological research (Arts, Frambach, & Bijmolt, 2011). Indeed, a good deal of initial research in the area was done amongst poor rural farmers in countries like Bangladesh (Rahim, 1961), and research here gave rise to theory about the diffusion of innovations (Rogers, 1962) which has remained significant for many decades (e.g. Rogers, 2003). Rogers' DOI asserts that diffusion is a function of a product's innovation characteristics, including its *perceived* relative advantage, complexity, compatibility, observability and trialability. Other research (Chau & Hu, 2001; Davis, Bagozzi, & Warshaw, 1989) which has looked at innovation adoption has utilised models from social psychology such as the Theory of Reasoned Action (TRA) and the Theory of Planned Behaviour (TPB). The TRA suggests that consumers' behaviours are determined by their intentions, which are in turn determined by their attitudes towards the action and subjective norms (Fishbein & Ajzen, 1975). Extending the TRA, the TPB was developed to acknowledge the importance of an individual's self-efficacy over a behaviour through the inclusion of perceived behavioural control (Ajzen, 1991). Later, the TAM was derived from the Theory of Reasoned Action, which was used as a guiding framework (Davis, 1989). Specifically, the TAM predicts that an individual's adoption of an innovation is a function of perceived ease of use (PEU) and perceived usefulness (PU).

Other competing models such as the Consumer Acceptance of Technology (CAT) model (Kulviwat, Burner II, Nasco, & Clark, 2007) have also been developed to take account of consumers' affective reactions to new products. The CAT integrates constructs such as pleasure, arousal and dominance (PAD) with the TAM in light of the TAM's focus on utilitarian and rational evaluation of innovations. Another recent consumer-based innovation adoption model is the Value-Based Adoption Model (VAM), proposed by Kim, Chan, and Gupta (2007). The VAM explains consumers' adoption from the value maximisation perspective, showing that all belief antecedents (e.g. usefulness, enjoyment, technicality, perceived fee) are mediated through perceived value.

However, within this research stream, the majority of research has been conducted amongst consumers from economically wealthy countries. Some research has looked at developing countries (but typically focuses on wealthier consumers within such countries; e.g. Alalwan, Dwivedi, Rana, Lal, & Williams, 2015; Alalwan, Dwivedi, Rana, & Simintiras, 2016; Alalwan, Dwivedi, & Rana, 2017; Dwivedi, Khan, & Papazafeiropoulou, 2007). Other research has looked at poorer consumers within these countries but typically picks a model from the innovation adoption literature and uses that model with little modification for the context (Pick, Gollakota, & Singh, 2014). The BOP and subsistence marketplaces are different because of the unique restrictions that these consumers face (e.g. poor road networks, unreliable electricity, lack of connectivity, low income, high inflation, low literacy, etc.). As such, research in these markets may reveal that (i) existing and known antecedents have differing effects and degrees of importance (e.g. antecedents such as compatibility may well be more significant than suggested by past research) or (ii) that new and less well-explored antecedents might become more important. Consequently, research in this area seems to require a two-pronged approach to move forward.

19.4 Quantitative Methods for Understanding Pro-poor Innovation Adoption: Existing Models and Antecedents

To address the first point above, systematic meta-analysis and other quantitative model comparison approaches offer much promise in light of the large amount of literature that already exists in this area (Arts et al., 2011). Perennial concepts such as "relative advantage" or "ease of use" would seem to have much relevance to a range of different contexts. So rather than reinventing the wheel, researchers might first look at which existing innovation adoption concepts have a statistically and substantively significant effect and the order of magnitude of their effects. One might expect, for example, that concepts such as perceived value would become of paramount importance to markets constrained by income, yet concepts such as excitement might take more of a back seat; in essence, the theory here is strong and well established, albeit not in this context, so scholars might first make use of this existing knowledge base and establish its boundaries.

Meta-analysis approaches are well established in social science research and need little introduction in this paper (interested readers are referred to Stanley & Doucouliagos, 2012 for a good review on the subject). A key benefit of such an approach is the ability to quantitatively assess the effect of existing constructs on dependent variables like adoption and to see how other research design artefacts (e.g. nature of the sample, type of product, methodology) impact these effects. However, by definition, such approaches are historical in nature and do not take account of the present.

Model comparison approaches have a rich history in the information systems and marketing literature (e.g. Davis et al., 1989; Dwivedi et al., 2017; Dwivedi, Rana, Jeyaraj, Clement, & Williams, 2017; Mathieson, 1991; Taylor & Todd, 1995; Venkatesh, Morris, Davis, & Davis, 2003) and can be used to look at existing consumers. Venkatesh et al. (2003) provide a framework through which existing knowledge about innovation adoption can be quantitatively evaluated in a new context, taking account of multiple products/services and large sample sizes for generalisability. Beyond its timeliness, the advantage of such an approach is that it can take account of the complexity of information processing in the innovation adoption decision by examining intervening psychological processes and other moderating effects. With large sample sizes, this can also provide a certain level of generalisability. In recent years, such approaches have gained attraction and been used to look at innovation adoption in a variety of contexts (e.g. Chau & Hu, 2001; Plouffe, Hulland, & Vandenbosch, 2001). However, though such an approach offers much promise, it cannot identify new concepts which may be important or overlooked.

Therefore, meta-analysis and model comparison approaches offer a great deal of promise to the study of innovation adoption in this context. However, they are unable to uncover *new* antecedents and less likely to uncover new processes which affect the adoption decision. Though we would anticipate some level of overlap and a degree of consistency in key innovation adoption antecedents, we would also anticipate the different context may well reveal other important antecedents more applicable to the BOP and subsistence marketplaces. For example, is social influence a more powerful influencer and what moderates this relationship? Is affect important in the BOP or is it all about price/quality ratios and utilitarian motivations? What are the key influencers of compatibility and complexity?

19.5 Qualitative Methods for Understanding Pro-poor Innovation Adoption: New Models and Antecedents

To address the second point above and overcome the limitations of the different quantitative approaches, useful insights might be gleaned from exploratory qualitative research procedures. Exploratory qualitative research procedures are appropriate when there is a limited knowledge of the subject matter (Zikmund, D'Alessandro, Winzar, Lowe, & Babin, 2016) and when new insights are sought. Such research is characterised by loosely defined research questions that allow exploration of the phenomenon in more depth. The concern is not about testing specific hypotheses or measurement but exploring the phenomenon and its complexity using rich data sources (Blumberg, Cooper, & Schindler, 2014; Denzin & Lincoln, 2005). In light of these objectives, careful sampling procedures are not so important here. Instead it is important to ensure that a skilful, fluent and culturally au fait moderator is used to open up the discussion. This is particularly the case in situations where sensitive issues are discussed or when the participant is new to involvement in such research procedures.

A range of methods are possible here from the more traditional in-depth interviews and focus groups to more involved methods such as ethnography and participant observation. Newer techniques such as video ethnography offer some promise with the development and pervasiveness of mobile technology. What is perhaps most promising is the ability to observe such participants in their natural setting, using mobile cameras and recording their behaviours where appropriate. Research in this area is beginning to develop rapidly with the pervasiveness of such devices (Spinney, 2011) and is expected to contribute in this context through its ability to observe complex interactions (Farrington-Darby & Wilson, 2009) and social relations which prior research seems to suggest come into play. Extending conceptual research by Nakata and Weidner (2012) recent research by Hasan, Lowe, and Rahman (2017) used qualitative techniques to uncover how visual cues on new products helped low-literate BOP consumers to understand product use and create product meaning. Though such techniques are novel, they may provide a first step in understanding this market segment better due to their flexibility and adaptability.

19.6 Understanding Pro-poor Innovation Adoption in the BOP and Subsistence Marketplaces: A Research Agenda

Currently, given the paucity of research in the area, research and knowledge development should not be hindered by a narrow focus or methodological approach and pluralism should a key aim. For researchers who wish to get off the beaten track, research in the area of pro-poor innovation adoption in the BOP and subsistence marketplaces is wide open to explore and opens up many possibilities. However, exploration has its perils, and researchers should be aware of these. For example, this may not be a research area for researchers who take comfort in psychometrically developed and validated scales (of which there are few) or who wish to do research at arm's length through online panel providers (sampling frames often do not exist and participants are typically not "online" to take part in research). Consequently we offer the following research priorities to develop our knowledge within this area.

19.6.1 No Need to Reinvent the Wheel

Research about consumer innovation adoption is not new. Consequently research efforts might first be directed at showing how existing knowledge can be utilised most effectively. There are three main ways researchers could approach this. One way is through systematic literature review across multiple disciplines (e.g. health, development, international business, marketing, etc.) where numerous studies already exist which seek to explain how BOP consumers react to new ideas, new technologies and new interventions. The process here needs to be systematic rather than ad hoc, and the synthesis can be qualitative in nature taking account of the distinctions between studies at a qualitative level (e.g. country, consumer type, methods used, etc.). However, the amount of literature here is extensive, and other more quantitative review approaches might assist in synthesising this data. Therefore, taking the same systematic approach to literature search research might use statistical methods to perform a meta-analysis on the existing research across disciplines. This would take the subjectivity out of the analysis process and would allow effect sizes to be estimated quantitatively and with respect to different moderating factors. Another way in which existing research could be utilised is through taking the collective wisdom of existing highly cited and relevant consumer innovation adoption models (e.g. DOI, TPB, TAM and others) and following existing model comparison approaches (e.g. Venkatesh et al., 2003) in order to assess the relative statistical and substantive importance of different antecedents in this new context. While such approaches provide a good deal of promise to enhancing our knowledge and understanding of this phenomenon, they can only reorganise what we already know. So, while reinventing the wheel may not necessary, strengthening it may well be an efficient strategy here.

Prior to performing survey research of this nature, a few words of caution are in order. Given existing psychometrically developed scales are less common, researchers should be concerned about developing scales where needed or translating those scales effectively into new languages (see, e.g. Brislin, 1980; Maneesriwongul & Dixon, 2004). Access to respondents also differs markedly from traditional research contexts where the conduct of research is more common and more familiar to consumers. This seems to have its pros and cons. On the one hand, consumers in the BOP are surveyed far less frequently. As a consequence, such consumers might find the research process interesting and fun (on the basis of some surveys conducted, we found particularly high response rates, and it seemed this could be attributed to the novelty of being part of the survey process). However, the researcher also has to put in place mechanisms to ensure more representative samples given the lack of appropriate sampling frames. In one survey we conducted, the response rate was heavily skewed towards male respondents, perhaps because of gender roles in the country where the survey took place and the nature of the products being investigated. Because of the lack of familiarity consumers have with the research process, this also has the potential to affect response quality. Therefore, we recommend surveys are conducted face-to-face to overcome misunderstandings and avoid ambiguity and confusion which seemed common. Furthermore, questions can be designed to take account of subjects' low literacy skills through the use of pictures and other carefully designed visual representations for scales. Literacy is a well-known issue within such marketplaces. To account for this, the usual prescriptions about careful pretesting apply. However, pretesting should be particularly thorough and rigorous and should also include a range of community members. We found this assists in gaining community acceptance to undertake the survey and increases consumer willingness to respond, effectively acting as an endorsement by community leaders. This process also has the added benefit of developing better measures by taking account of language and colloquialisms. So, research could also develop through a careful assessment of the literature on research methods in subsistence marketplace contexts.

... but a couple of extra spokes might help to strengthen it...

To overcome the inherent limitations of quantitative research, qualitative research will be important to add new insight to this literature domain. A number of possibilities exist here, but, given the importance of context, priority might be given to inquiry that is naturalistic (Lincoln & Guba, 1985) and involves participants within their natural environment where cues and context are more salient to them and where the researcher is better able to understand the complexities and subtleties of the social relations, constraints and decisions that need to be made. Using video ethnographic techniques has particular appeal because of what Spinney (2011) refers to as "Seeing there and feeling there". This is of particular importance to BOP researchers where such subjects might be less accessible or accessible sporadically.

So technology provides advantages to consumers in subsistence marketplaces but also to researchers. It is also less costly and more readily available.

19.6.2 Conceptual Issues

Beyond methodological issues, there are a number of conceptual priorities that require further thought and evidence. The literature remains unclear on these, and further research will help to clarify our understanding.

What segments exist within the BOP? So far the BOP has been largely assumed to be a homogeneous mass of consumers (Ramani et al., 2012). Some have gone into more depth here and broadly define segments geographically as either rural or urban. These classifications may well transcend country boundaries but remain fairly broad. What is the nature of BOP adopter segments and what are their psychological characteristics?

What role does price play in the adoption decision? So far, the assumption of most research has been that lower prices are more beneficial and more socially acceptable. However, recent research from development economics seems to suggest that this relationship may not be linear (Ashraf, Berry, & Shapiro, 2010). In this research, the researchers found that a development intervention was more widely adopted and *used* if participants within a field experiment paid a positive price for the intervention in comparison to if they were given it for free. The small, positive price seems to act as a signal of quality and may provide a "sunk cost" that is noticed by consumers who then attribute greater value towards it as a consequence. Therefore, how should psychological concepts in pricing research be used to enhance adoption of pro-poor innovations and increase their usage?

Is the adoption decision all "rational" with a heavy emphasis on the cost to benefits ratio equation or does affect play a role too? Recent models of innovation adoption have started to take account of emotions and affect in the adoption decision (e.g. Wood & Page Moreau, 2006). It might be expected that such concepts are less important in the BOP where consumers are constrained by a range of resources and that rational evaluations take priority. However, some indications from research in this market suggest that affect and emotion may well be important factors to these consumers (Jebarajakirthy & Lobo, 2015).

The research priorities noted above are not meant to be exhaustive. However, based on our experience, they seem to be areas where research efforts are needed in order to make a contribution.

19.7 Conclusion

This research area is wide open to exploration and raises a plethora of questions that systematic research efforts can shed light on. Consistent with other researchers in the area (Prahalad, 2005; Viswanathan & Rosa, 2007), we feel that BOP consumers should be provided with better-quality products and services that meet their needs more effectively. Prahalad's (2005) seminal work in this area makes the business case for this, and work by Viswanathan and Rosa (2007) provides a process through which this increased understanding can take place at a micro level and from the bottom up through systematic and careful research at the consumer level. Compared to research in non-BOP markets, there seems to be a mountain to climb given the lack of research that exists. This presents its challenges but also provides the motivated researcher with an excellent opportunity to beat the path less trodden.

References

Ajzen, I. (1991). Theories of cognitive self-regulation the theory of planned behavior. *Organizational Behavior and Human Decision Processes*, *50*(2), 179–211.

Alalwan, A. A., Dwivedi, Y. K., & Rana, N. P. (2017). Factors influencing adoption of mobile banking by Jordanian bank customers: Extending UTAUT2 with trust. *International Journal of Information Management*, *37*(3), 99–110.

Alalwan, A. A., Dwivedi, Y. K., Rana, N. P., Lal, B., & Williams, M. D. (2015). Consumer adoption of internet banking in Jordan: Examining the role of hedonic motivation, habit, self-efficacy and trust. *Journal of Financial Services Marketing*, *20*(2), 145–157.

Alalwan, A. A., Dwivedi, Y. K., Rana, N. P., & Simintiras, A. C. (2016). Jordanian consumers' adoption of telebanking: Influence of perceived usefulness, trust and self-efficacy. *International Journal of Bank Marketing*, *34*(5), 690–709.

Arts, J. W., Frambach, R. T., & Bijmolt, T. H. (2011). Generalizations on consumer innovation adoption: A meta-analysis on drivers of intention and behavior. *International Journal of Research in Marketing*, *28*(2), 134–144.

Ashraf, N., Berry, J., & Shapiro, J. M. (2010). Can higher prices stimulate product use? Evidence from a field experiment in Zambia. *The American Economic Review*, *100*(5), 2383–2413.

Blumberg, B. F., Cooper, D. R., & Schindler, P. S. (2014). *Business research methods*. New York, NY: McGraw-hill education.

Brislin R.W. (1980). Cross-Cultural Research Methods. In: Altman I., Rapoport A., Wohlwill J.F. (eds) Environment and Culture. Human Behavior and Environment (Advances in Theory and Research), vol 4. Springer, Boston, MA.

Chau, P. Y. K., & Hu, P. J.-H. (2001). Information technology acceptance by individual professionals: A model comparison approach. *Decision Sciences*, *32*(4), 699–719.

Danneels, E., & Kleinschmidtb, E. J. (2001). Product innovativeness from the firm's perspective: Its dimensions and their relation with project selection and performance. *Journal of Product Innovation Management*, *18*(6), 357–373.

Davis, F. D. (1989). Perceived usefulness, perceived ease of use, and user acceptance of information technology. *MIS Quarterly*, *13*(3), 319–340.

Davis, F. D., Bagozzi, R. P., & Warshaw, P. R. (1989). User acceptance of computer technology: A comparison of two theoretical models. *Management Science*, *35*(8), 982–1003.

Denzin, N. K., & Lincoln, Y. S. (2005). *The sage handbook of qualitative research* (pp. 695–728). Thousand Oaks, CA: Sage.

Donner, J. (2008). Research approaches to mobile use in the developing world: A review of the literature. *The Information Society, 24*(3), 140–159.

Dwivedi, Y. K., Khan, N., & Papazafeiropoulou, A. (2007). Consumer adoption and usage of broadband in Bangladesh. *Electronic Government, an International Journal, 4*(3), 299–313.

Dwivedi, Y. K., Rana, N. P., Janssen, M., Lal, B., Williams, M. D., & Clement, R. M. (2017). An empirical validation of a unified model of electronic government adoption (UMEGA). *Government Information Quarterly. 34*(2), 211–230. Available at http://www.sciencedirect.com/science/article/pii/S0740624X1730103X.

Dwivedi, Y. K., Rana, N. P., Jeyaraj, A., Clement, M., & Williams, M. D. (2017). Re-examining the unified theory of acceptance and use of technology (UTAUT): Towards a revised theoretical model. *Information Systems Frontiers*. https://doi.org/10.1007/s10796-017-9774-y.

Farrington-Darby, T., & Wilson, J. R. (2009). Understanding social interactions in complex work: A video ethnography. *Cognition, Technology & Work, 11*(1), 1–15.

Fishbein, M., & Ajzen, I. (1975). *Belief, attitude, intention and behavior: An introduction to theory and research*. Reading, MA: Addison- Wesley.

Hart, S., & Prahalad, C. K. (2002). The fortune at the bottom of the pyramid. *Strategy+ Business, 26*, 54–67.

Hasan, M. R., Lowe, B., & Rahman, M. (2017). Visual cues and innovation adoption among bottom of the pyramid consumers. *Qualitative Market Research, 20*(2), 147–157.

Jebarajakirthy, C., & Lobo, A. (2015). A study investigating attitudinal perceptions of microcredit services andtheir relevant drivers in bottom of pyramid market segments, *Journal of Retailing and Consumer Services,* 23(March), 39–48.

Kanagawa, M., & Nakata, T. (2007). Analysis of the energy access improvement and its socio-economic impacts in rural areas of developing countries. *Ecological Economics, 62*(2), 319–329.

Kim, H. W., Chan, H. C., & Gupta, S. (2007). Value-based adoption of mobile internet: An empirical investigation. *Decision Support Systems, 43*(1), 111–126.

Kulviwat, S., Bruner Burner, G. C., II, Nasco, S. A., & Clark, T. (2007). Toward a unified theory of consumer acceptance. *Psychology and Marketing, 24*(12), 1059–1084.

Lincoln, Y. S., & Guba, E. G. (1985). *Naturalistic inquiry* (Vol. 75). Thousand Oaks, CA: Sage.

Lowe, B., & Alpert, F. (2015). Forecasting consumer perception of innovativeness. *Technovation, 45*, 1–14.

Mathieson, K. (1991). Predicting user intentions: Comparing the technology acceptance model with the theory of planned behavior. *Information Systems Research*, 2(3), 173–191.

Mendoza, R. U., & Thelen, N. (2008). Innovations to make markets more inclusive for the poor. *Development Policy Review, 26*(4), 427–458.

Miller, G., & Mobarak, A. M. (2014). Learning about new technologies through social networks: Experimental evidence on nontraditional stoves in Bangladesh. *Marketing Science, 34*(4), 480–499.

Maneesriwongul, W. and Dixon, J.K. (2004). Instrument translation process: a methods review, *Journal of Advanced Nursing, 48*(2), 175–186.

Nakata, C., & Weidner, K. (2012). Enhancing new product adoption at the base of the pyramid: A contextualized model. *Journal of Product Innovation Management, 29*(1), 21–32.

Panwar, N. L., Kurchania, A. K., & Rathore, N. S. (2009). Mitigation of greenhouse gases by adoption of improved biomass cookstoves. *Mitigation and Adaptation Strategies for Global Change, 14*(6), 569–578.

Pick, J. B., Gollakota, K., & Singh, M. (2014). Technology for development: Understanding influences on use of rural telecenters in India. *Information Technology for Development, 20*(4), 296–323.

Plouffe, C. R., Hulland, J. S., & Vandenbosch, M. (2001). Research report: Richness versus parsimony in modelling technology adoption decisions—Understanding merchant adoption of a smart card-based payment system. *Information Systems Research, 12*(2), 208–222.

Prahalad, C. K. (2005). *Fortune at the bottom of the pyramid: Eradicating poverty through profits*. Upper Saddle River, NJ: Wharton School Publishing.

Rahim, S. A. (1961). *The diffusion and adoption of agricultural practices: A study in a village in East Pakistan*. Comilla, Bangladesh: East Pakistan Academy of Village Development.
Ramani, S. V., SadreGhazi, S., & Duysters, G. (2012). On the diffusion of toilets as bottom of the pyramid innovation: Lessons from sanitation entrepreneurs. *Technological Forecasting and Social Change*, *79*(4), 676–687.
Rogers, E. M. (1962). *Diffusion of innovations* (1st ed.). New York, NY: Free Press.
Rogers, E. M. (2003). *Diffusion of innovations* (5th ed.). New York, NY: Free Press.
Spinney, J. (2011). A chance to catch a breath: Using mobile video ethnography in cycling research. *Mobilities*, *6*(2), 161–182.
Stanley, T. D., & Doucouliagos, H. (2012). *Meta-regression analysis in economics and business*. New York, NY: Routledge.
Taylor, S., & Todd, P. A. (1995). Understanding information technology usage: A test of competing models. *Information Systems Research*, *6*(2), 144–176.
Venkatesh, V., Morris, M. G., Davis, G. B., & Davis, F. D. (2003). User acceptance of information technology: Toward a unified view. *MIS Quarterly*, *27*(3), 425–478.
Viswanathan, M., Sridharan, S., & Ritchie, R. (2010). Understanding consumption and entrepreneurship in subsistence marketplaces. *Journal of Business Research*, *63*(6), 570–581.
Viswanathan, M., & Rosa, J. A. (2007). *Product and market development for subsistence marketplaces: Consumption and entrepreneurship beyond literacy and resource barriers*. Amsterdam, Netherlands: Elsevier.
Wood, S. L., & Page Moreau, C. (2006). From fear to loathing? How emotion influences the evaluation and early use of innovations. *Journal of Marketing*, *70*(3), 44–57.
Zikmund, W., D'Alessandro, S., Winzar, H., Lowe, B., & Babin, B. (2016). *Marketing research: 4th Asia Pacific edition*. Melbourne, VIC: Cengage Learning.

Ben Lowe is professor of marketing at Kent Business School, University of Kent, UK. He does research into consumers, their adoption of innovations and their interaction with technology. He has published over 30 refereed journal articles in journals such as ***Psychology & Marketing***, ***Technovation***, ***International Marketing Review***, ***European Journal of Marketing***, ***Journal of Interactive Marketing***, ***Journal of Marketing Management***, ***the American Journal of Agricultural Economics*** and others and has co-authored a book on marketing research which is in its fourth edition.

Md Rajibul Hasan is assistant professor of marketing at Rennes School of Business, France. Much of his thesis focuses on the Bottom of the Pyramid market and subsistence marketplaces. In this context, his research interests include branding, diffusion of innovations, technology acceptance models, ethics in marketing, finance and poverty alleviation. He has published in journals such as *Strategic Change*, *Qualitative Market Research: An International Journal* and the *Review of Enterprise and Management Studies*.

Chapter 20
Branding for Bottom of the Pyramid: A Case of Branded Footwear Consumer in Indian Rural Setting

Ashish Gupta and Anushree Tandon

Abstract The fortune at the bottom of the pyramid (BOP) has been a major direction for organizations vying to expand/tap into the vast consuming base of rural India. In order to attract and retain these specific consumers, it is critical to understand their psyche, attitudes, motives and expectations as they offer the key to building a brand image. The paper attempts to understand the implications of maintaining a loyal consumer base in rural markets of India by building a sustainable brand image through understanding the dimensions of perceived quality, product promotion and brand trust. It also attempts to study the significant impact of such brand images on brand loyalty for the chosen product category of sports shoes. The formulated hypotheses were tested empirically through regression analysis to validate the proposed research framework for the present study. The study holds importance for brand marketers attempting to penetrate or establish a presence in the Indian rural markets.

Keywords Bottom of pyramid · Quality · Brand image · Brand trust · Rural market · India

20.1 Introduction

Acknowledged as one of the world's largest consumer markets (BCG, 2017), the growth of India's economy has captured the attention of multiple stakeholders at both national and international levels. A significant contributor to this expected growth is the development of India's rural markets and consumers belonging to the

---

A. Gupta (✉)
Department of Business Management, Dr. Hari Singh Gour Central University, Sagar, Madhya Pradesh, India

A. Tandon
Amity School of Business, Amity University, Noida, Uttar Pradesh, India

Y. K. Dwivedi et al. (eds.), *Emerging Markets from a Multidisciplinary Perspective*, Advances in Theory and Practice of Emerging Markets,
https://doi.org/10.1007/978-3-319-75013-2_20

'bottom of the pyramid (BoP)'. Since the acknowledgement of the commercial potential of consuming populace in these segments, organizations have been exploring ways to tap its tremendous potential (Gupta & Srivastav, 2016).

The substantial transformation of India's rural socio-demographic panorama has been a cumulative effect of the continual economic growth, increasing discretionary incomes, growing aspirations of consumers and synchronous development of rural markets (BCG, 2017; IFMR, 2011; McKinsey Global Institute, 2007). Growing at the rate of 7–8% per annum, the number of rural Indian consumers earning over five dollars a day is expected to increase from 50 million to 150 million (IFMR, 2011), and the rural market is expected to add US$ 100 billion in consumption demand by the end of 2017 (IBEF, 2017). This consumer segment is a significant component of India's BoP population, and its significant growth will have a definitive impact on the composition of India's income pyramid. With over 291 million people expected to shift from poverty to a more sustainable life (McKinsey Global Institute, 2007), BoP populace in India is also set to shrink significantly, from 379 million adults in 2015 to 145 million adults in 2030 (Euromonitor, 2017). These figures hold manifold connotations for organizations hoping to capture or maintain a slice of this market, especially in context of attracting and retaining rural consumers, as they shift to more affluent sections of the economy (Agarwal & Xavier, 2015). One way of achieving this objective would be to establish strong brand loyalties amongst rural consumers – creating future opportunities for new product introduction, up-selling and cross-selling sales strategies. As urban markets become increasingly saturated with similar and competing products, organizations are focusing on developing this potentially profitable segment of Indian consumers by understanding the determinants which drive product consumption and incite brand loyalty amongst them.

20.2 Bottom-of-Pyramid Consumers: Marketing and Branding Initiatives

Marketing initiatives for bottom-of-pyramid (BoP) consumers have seen appreciation as well as criticism from academia in the years since its emergence as a research area. Though this consumer segment has been lauded as possessing vast commercial potential for organizations, concerns have arisen over the marketing techniques used towards these consumers. Such techniques have been criticized as aggressive, even exploitative, by researchers who believe that prevailing low levels of education, economic and experiential deprivation, as well as information accessibility, severely limit rational decision-making by BoP consumers, leading to harmful consequences (Davidson, 2009; Jaiswal, 2008; Jaiswal & Gupta, 2015; Karnani, 2009).

Conversely, the emergence of Transformative Consumer Research has recalled focus to the equal rights of BoP consumers to consume products that enhance their individual potential and improve their quality of life and social and cultural conditions (Blocker et al., 2013; Mick, Pettigrew, Pechmann, & Ozanne, 2012). BOP consumers, especially in low-income and emerging economies (Agarwal & Xavier, 2015; Jaiswal & Gupta, 2015; Subrahmanyan & Tomas Gomez-Arias, 2008), exhibit complex shopping behaviour which is often impacted by aspirational needs (Agarwal & Xavier, 2015; Gupta & Srivastav, 2016; Jaiswal & Gupta, 2015; Prahalad & Hammond, 2002), self-expression (Dalton, 2009) and conspicuous consumption (Batra, Ramaswamy, Alden, Steenkamp, & Ramachander, 2000). In order to develop this market segment and profitably serve its consumers, industry and academic practitioners need to develop innovative products as well as alternative models of distribution, marketing mix and branding strategies, etc. that are suited to their unique needs and constraints (Agarwal & Xavier, 2015; Chikweche & Fletcher, 2010; Jaiswal & Gupta, 2015; Simanis, 2012; Viswanathan, 2007).

20.2.1 *Branding Initiatives for BoP*

Due to the intensive competition in urban markets (Sinha et al., 2017; Vasavada-oza, Nagraj, & Krishna, 2012), specific brands are being targeted at large BoP consumer groups in context of their small per capita purchases (Rajagopal, 2009) and brand awareness (Jaiswal & Gupta, 2015). However, the segregation of consumer behaviour between urban and rural markets (Cruickshank, 2009; Vasavada-oza et al., 2012) requires organizations to redefine their branding philosophies for the BoP consumers found primarily in rural markets to accommodate their unique consumption behaviour.

Researchers like Hamilton (2009) and Hamilton and Catterall (2007, 2008) have proposed that BoP consumers may fulfil familial needs with branded products to diminish effects of poverty and improve social status of selves and family members (Gupta & Srivastav, 2016; Kumar, Vohra, & Dangi, 2016). Thus, building aspirational brand images amongst BoP consumers is a critical task as these consumers are extremely value-conscious (Omar & Williams, 2009) and save a fraction of their incomes for consumption of conspicuous products (Gupta & Srivastav, 2016). Even though BoP consumers have smaller disposable incomes, they are strongly driven by their aspirational consumption and end up spending relatively more on globally known brands due to their low awareness of lesser known brands (Elliot & Leonard, 2006; Kumar et al., 2016).

It is thereby necessary for organizations to understand BoP consumers in context of their different shopping styles (Kumar et al., 2016), motivations (Kolk, 2014; Subrahmanyan & Tomas Gomez-Arias, 2008), competitive environment (Rajagopal, 2009), macro-environmental constraints (Chikweche & Fletcher, 2011; Ersado, 2006), brand awareness and perception (Chikweche & Fletcher, 2011), influence of cultural values and individual personality traits (Rajagopal, 2009) as well as marketing programmes implemented by organizations for BoP consumers (Rajagopal, 2009). Gaining a deeper insight into BoP consumer behaviour by understanding these issues can help organizations understand what drives brand loyalty for this segment, critically filling a gap in existing body of knowledge (Chikweche & Fletcher, 2011; Kumar et al., 2016).

20.3 Branded Footwear Purchase by BoP Consumers

Global sports market, including events, infrastructure, training, manufacturing and retail, is estimated by KMPG-CII (2016) to be approximately INR 37.8 to 44.2 lakh crore or USD 600–700 billion. In India too, the Footwear sector has seen continual growth in the recent years with sales reaching up to INR 553 billion in 2016 (Euromonitor, 2017). The demand for branded footwear is expected to further increase to potentially reach sales of INR 778 billion in 2021, through aspirational consumer purchases in Tier III and Tier IV cities of India (KPMG-CII, 2016).

Footwear, for Indian BoP consumers, is not only a necessity; it also holds symbolic value as a consumer's conspicuous projection of self-image. For this study, the authors focus on the consumption of branded sports shoes amongst BoP consumers since these products have gained popularity due to their not only utilitarian as well as hedonic value. Sportswear has become a universally purchased category amongst the younger consumers in India due to perceived benefits of comfort, projection of a relaxed lifestyle and personal style (Singh and Pattanayak, 2014). Amongst BoP consumers, consumption of products like footwear is strongly driven by extrinsic goals, such as peer acceptance, enhancement of social status, projection of a desirable image etc. (Dreze & Nunes, 2009; Gupta & Srivastav, 2016; Thakur & Kaur, 2015) and intrinsic goals like comfort and sense of hedonic well-being (Ryan, Huta, & Deci, 2008).

As one of the most trusted and well-known footwear brands in the Indian subcontinent (Brand Trust Report, 2017), Bata has been riding high on this demand, leading the sector with a retail share of 5% in 2016 and operational plans to add 100 stores to its impressive distribution channel (Euromonitor, 2017). Due to its widespread awareness and presence in semi-urban as well as urban cities of India, the authors have focused on consumers of Bata's sports shoes for this study.

20.4 Brand Loyalty Amongst the BoP

Measured in behavioural and attitudinal context, brand loyalty is as a multidimensional construct affected by consumers' culture (Parida & Sahney, 2017), value perceptions and benefits of the brand (Bennur & Jin, 2017) as well as cognitive variables related to brand awareness and identity (Wu & Anridho, 2016). Brand loyalty is defined as the degree to which a consumer consistently purchased the same brand within a product class despite competitors' efforts (Ogba & Tan, 2009; Sriram, Balachander, & Kalwani, 2007). The concept has been intensely studied in the recent past due to the increasing focus on consumer-brand relationships and its impact an organization's market as well as financial performance (Cengiz and Akdemir-Cengiz, 2016). However, majority of the research has concentrated on urban populace, leaving the brand loyalty of rural and BoP consumers a mostly unexplored area, especially in context of emerging economies (Paninchukunnath, 2010; Parida & Sahney, 2017). Understanding this area holds significant connotations for organizations in emerging markets with large instances of BoP population as researchers seem to be at a consensus pertaining to the proclivity of BoP consumers to purchase brands (perceived as value bargains) as a way of inducing self-confidence and attempt to attain a better quality of life (Rahman et al., 2013; Ghuman & Krishnamacharyulu, 2008; Mahajan & Banga, 2005). The few studies that have undertaken to understand the brand consciousness and loyalty of these consumers have unequivocally asserted on the potential of cultivating their loyalty to reap better returns than from urban consumers (Chikweche & Fletcher, 2011; D'Andrea, 2006; Gupta & Srivastava, 2016; Prahald, 2005; Rahman et al., 2013). This study is an attempt to gain insight into brand loyalty and its antecedents in Indian BoP consumers and add to the existing body of knowledge and aid marketers in developing viable BoP-oriented branding strategies. Towards this objective, the authors theorize that factors impacting consumer loyalty towards such branded products may relate to brand trust, product promotion and perceived quality leading to creation of a positive brand image and, subsequently, brand loyalty.

20.4.1 *Perceived Quality*

Defined as a consumer's perception of a product's consistent specifications, product benefits, quality and value additions (Aaker, 1991; Bhuian, 1997; Chi et al., 2009; Dodds & Grewal, 1991; Zeithaml, 1988), perceived quality acts as a salient differentiator for a brand (Aaker, 1991; Wu & Anridho, 2016). It is a dimension which significantly impacts the level of consumer's brand trust (Chi et al., 2009; Ghalandari, Nazarian, & Norouzi, 2016; Laluyan, Pangemanan, & Worang, 2017). However it cannot be fairly described since it is a summary construct (Aaker, 1991, pp. 85–86; Severi & Ling, 2013) and is based on the consumers' subjective evaluation of a product/brand (Chi et al., 2009; Severi & Ling, 2013), contributing to consumers' image of a brand.

H_1 Perceived quality is a predictor of brand image.

20.4.2 *Brand Trust*

The concept of trust explains an individual's characteristic – a belief in an institution (Khan and Rahman, 2016; Rotter, 1967) or reliance on a partner in whom confidence is placed (Moorman, Deshpande, & Zaltman, 1993; Pentina, Zhang, &

Basmanova, 2013) in face of uncertainty (Beccera & Badrinarayanan, 2013; Chaudhuri & Holbrook 2001; Delgado –Ballester & Munuera-Aleman, 2001; Habibi, Laroche, & Richard, 2014). Brand trust, an extension of such characteristic, has been an element on which the perspective on which relationship marketing has been based (Pentina et al., 2013). Strong trust in a brand is an indicator of consumers' confidence in brand competence and integrity (Hegner & Jevons, 2016) as well as a sense of security in consumption of the particular brand (Habibi et al., 2014; Lock, 2016) and influences consumer attitudes pertaining to purchase, commitment and even referrals (Beccera & Badrinarayanan, 2013). It thus acts as an antecedent of brand loyalty (Bennur & Jin, 2017; Habibi et al., 2014; Khan and Rahman, 2016; Pongpaew, Speece, & Tiangsoongnern, 2016), which makes it imperative for marketers to inculcate brand trust, especially amongst BoP consumers who have higher needs for low uncertainty in purchase of brands due to their various constraints.

H_2 Brand Trust is the predictor of brand image.

20.4.3 Product Promotion

Brand awareness is precursor to consumers' contextual and behavioural loyalty elements of purchase intentions, brand image, referrals and trust. Through provision of learning advantages to the brand and establishing linkages with consumers, brand awareness influences decision-making, allowing a brand to be a consistent member of a consumer's consideration set (Hoyer & Brown, 1990; Huang & Sarigollu, 2012). Research suggests that product promotion enhances brand awareness and influences consumers' brand choice (Singh and Pattanayak, 2014; Weng & De run, 2013) by creating a positive brand image and lowering consumers' risk perception. Whether through appealing to consumers' conscious desires for esteem or lowest prices, though advertisements as well as trade promotions, a cleverly designed promotional strategy may hold the key to inculcating consumer loyalty. However, to create influential promotional strategies, it is imperative for organizations to understand the consumers' personal values and characteristics (Weng & De run, 2013) in order to induce constructive changes in consumers' motives and lower perceived psychic costs and efforts associated with product purchase (Aydinli, Bertini, & Lambrecht, 2014). For BoP consumers, who are limited by resources and therefore more risk averse, product promotion could be a way to enhance their value perception of a purchase.

H_3 Product promotion is a predictor of brand image.

20.4.4 Brand Image

American Marketing Association (2017) defines brand image as the perception of a brand in the minds of persons. The brand image is a mirror reflection (though perhaps inaccurate) of the brand personality or product being. It is what people believe about a brand – their thoughts, feelings and expectations. A critical consequence branding strategists aim for, brand image is a reflection of the associations and symbolic value that consumers attach to the attributes and benefits of a branded product or service (Khan & Jalees, 2016; Ogba & Tan, 2009). Brand image is a cumulative perception of a consumer's awareness and perception of a brand's quality, benefits, attributes and values. Created from a consumer's direct as well as indirect knowledge of and interaction with a brand, brand image is often a result of concentrated marketing efforts focused towards creating a unique brand personality, enhancing brand awareness and establishing benchmarks for perceived quality in minds of the targeted audience. These efforts allow marketers to create functional and emotional connections and develop a strong consumer-brand relationship (Thakur & Kaur, 2015). Since consumers' consumption of a brand is an expression of their self-image through its associated, symbolic values, the development of a strong relationship between the two indicates consumers' strong brand identification (Ogba & Tan, 2009; Thakur & Kaur, 2015). Thus, a positive brand image holds significant implications for consumer purchase behaviour and attitudinal loyalty (Ogba & Tan, 2009; Thakur & Kaur, 2015).

H_4 Brand Image is a predictor of brand loyalty.

Based on the literature review, the authors propose to study the following relationships in context of branded footwear purchase of Indian BoP consumers.

20.5 Research Methodology

The study used a mix of descriptive and causal research to identify significant relationships between the dimensions chosen for the study. The variables used for the measurement of chosen dimensions have been adapted through an exhaustive literature review pertaining to brand usage by rural consumers. They have been tested for validity and reliability in the current context for building the conceptual framework through factor analysis and Cronbach's Alpha test. Regression analysis has been used to test the significance of proposed relationships between the dimensions in the study.

The unit of analysis for the present research was a specific collaborative brand loyalty and dimensions of brand image. Here the dimensions of brand image that play an important role in the further generation of brand loyalty are served as perceived quality, product promotion and brand trust. The methodology has been framed wherein a sample of 210 respondents has been taken from the Sagar region

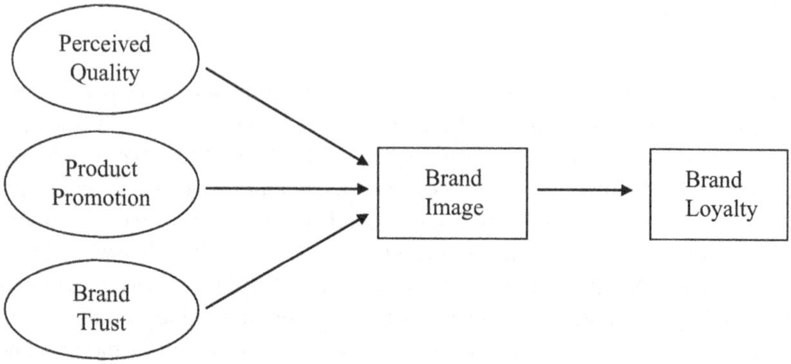

Fig. 20.1 Proposed framework for study

for the data collection in regard to footwear. The research design is a combination of exploratory and descriptive research design wherein the researcher has described the variables and their interrelations through literature review (descriptive analysis). Also, the researcher has tried to explore the new dimensions effecting the brand image and loyalty of customers for sportswear through primary data analyses. A structured questionnaire was developed to test and validate the model by collecting data from the respondents. A total of 30 items were asked, out of which 23 items were reliable and are part of the study at present.

Participants were influential decision-makers involved in selecting, managing and monitoring purchase decision for the sports shoes they prefer wearing. Participants of all the age groups and from different socio-economic backgrounds were invited to participate in the study so that diverse opinions could be gathered in relation to the development of brand image and loyalty for sports shoe brands.

The final sample comprised of respondents who are wearing branded sports shoes and are from different socio-economic backgrounds and different age groups. The participating respondent's economic background varied from the average monthly income of Rs. 5000 to almost up to Rs. 10,000 per month. The selected age bar for the respondents was between 20 and 50 years. The final sample consisted of 210 participants.

A self-administered, structured questionnaire was developed to collect data through a survey. In order to measure the identified variables in the study, the researcher used a number of constructs and a Likert (1 to 5 point) response scale. Pilot testing was done to test the reliability of the constructs.

Based on the preceding discussion, a research framework has been proposed (see Fig. 20.1) showing an interrelation between the different variables which will be tested with the help of different statistical tools. The premise of the framework is the brand loyalty which indicates the successful marketing strategies if adopted by marketers may achieve the competitive edge over other competitor in the market.

20.6 Data Analysis and Interpretation

Reliability analysis was carried out using Cronbach's coefficient alpha, which indicates the internal consistency of a multiple-item scale for various constructs (variables), used for the purpose of data collection. The minimum cutoff value of Cronbach's coefficient alpha should be $\alpha = 0.6$ (Hair, Black, Babin, Anderson, & Tatham, 2010). The values of Cronbach's coefficient alpha for the selected variables were found to be significant. For the perceived quality as one of the constructs, the value of alpha (α) comes out to be *0.707*, similarly for product promotion, brand trust and brand image, the α value derived is *0.785*, *0.848* and *0.765* which is considered as highly significant. For brand loyalty α value comes out to be *0.665* which is accepted and considered significant for the present study (Table 20.1).

20.7 Hypothesis Testing

Regression analysis was used to test the various hypotheses. The value of $R = 0.679$ signifies a good relationship between the brand image and the predictors of brand image, i.e. perceived quality, product promotion and brand trust (see Table 20.2); this amounted to a proportion of $R^2 = 0.460$. The Durbin–Watson value that is derived to test the serial correlation between the errors comes out to be *1.952* which is almost close to 2 and thus helps in proving that the residuals are not correlated (Field, 2009).

Individually, the correlation for the predictors of brand image (independent variables) and the brand image itself (dependent variable) also signified a moderate degree of positive correlation between them (see Table 20.3). The Karl Pearson's coefficient of correlation between brand image and perceived quality showed a moderate degree of positive correlation $(R = 0.480)$. Similarly the value of R between brand image and product promotion comes out to be *0.459* that again depicts a moderate degree of positive correlation. Finally, the value of R between brand image and brand trust comes out to be *0.651* that too depict a moderate degree of positive correlation between the two variables. Therefore, it can be concluded that the value of R (Karl Pearson's coefficient of correlation) signifies a good relation between the brand image and its predictors, i.e. perceived quality, product promotion and brand trust.

The beta values tell the degree of each predictor affecting the outcome. Here the t-values help in measuring the significant contribution of each and every predictor to the model. All the variables made a significant contribution to the model. The values of beta for all predictors, i.e. perceived quality, product promotion and brand trust, are $p \leq 0.05$.

The formulated hypotheses were tested empirically through regression analysis. It was done to test and validate the proposed research framework for the present

Table 20.1 Reliability and validity analysis

Construct	Item code	Items	Item loading	Cronbach's alpha
Perceived quality	PQ_1	I feel good about the material used in sports shoes I wear	0.518	0.707
	PQ_2	Colours of sports shoes are very attractive offered by my company	0.754	
	PQ_3	I feel good about the design of the sports shoes I wear	0.819	
	PQ_4	Sports shoes of my company are very comfortable	0.580	
Product promotion	PP_1	Advertisement of my sports shoe brand is very popular	0.614	0.785
	PP_2	Advertisement of my sports shoe is seen frequently on TV or other media	0.735	
	PP_3	My friends too mention about the sports shoe brand I wear	0.591	
	PP_4	My sports shoe brand is popular amongst my family and friends	0.516	
	PP_5	My company selects the best celebrity for promoting sports shoe brand	0.702	
	PP_6	My company puts best promotional efforts in promoting sports shoe brand	0.726	
Brand trust	BT_1	My sports shoe brand has fulfilled my expectations	0.689	0.848
	BT_2	The promises made by my sports shoe company are reliable	0.712	
	BT_3	I am satisfied with my decisions of buying the sports shoe brand I wear	0.733	
	BT_4	Using the sports shoe brand I wear has been a good experience	0.760	
	BT_5	I have been delighted with the sports shoe brand I wear	0.688	
Brand image	BI_1	My sports shoe company has good brand in the mind of the customer	0.604	0.765
	BI_2	Reputation of my sports shoe company is high	0.546	
	BI_3	My sports shoe company holds a good market value	0.591	
	BI_4	My sports shoe brand is very popular amongst different generations	0.651	
Brand loyalty	BL_1	I buy the same sports shoe brand over a loyalty period of time	0.550	0.665
	BL_2	I would not buy other brand, if my favourite sports shoe brand is not available at the store	0.765	
	BL_3	I would still love to buy my favourite sports shoe brand if other brands are on sale	0.727	

(continued)

Table 20.1 (continued)

Construct	Item code	Items	Item loading	Cronbach's alpha
	BL_4	I will continue with the same sports shoe brand if company significantly charges high prices than other brands	0.561	

Total variance extracted: 57.75%

Table 20.2 Regression analysis – model summary

Model summary[b]					
Model	R	R square	Adjusted R square	Std. error of the estimate	Durbin-Watson
1	.679[a]	0.461	0.453	0.46404	1.952

[a]Predictors: (Constant), BRAND_TRUST, PRODUCT_PROMOTION, PERCEIVED_QUALITY
[b]Dependent Variable: BRAND_IMAGE

study. Therefore, it is clearly concluded that all proposed null hypotheses are accepted (Table 20.4).

The results of hypotheses testing are shown in Table 20.5. The results of hypotheses testing clearly depict the relationship between and amongst the variables of the proposed framework. The results suggest strong support for hypotheses H1, H2 and H3. Here, perceived quality, product promotion and brand trust are identified as the predictors of brand image.

For predicting the relationship between the brand image and the brand loyalty, the Karl Pearson's coefficient of correlation was depicted in Table 20.6.

The value of $R = 0.30$ which signifies a moderate degree of relationship between the two variables. The reason behind is because with the outcome of new and competitive brands in the market place, teenagers, generation Y and even the elders up to the age of 50 years prefer sports shoes that provide comfort from all dimensions whether it includes price, quality and value. Because of the presence of different varieties of brands, and the dynamic nature of the customer group which includes the changing tastes and preferences at fast pace, people prefer trying new things which at large affects the loyalty towards a particular brand. Therefore, the value of R in this case too is moderate for the brand loyalty towards the sports shoe wear.

20.8 Discussion, Conclusions and Limitations

Gaining the loyalty of BoP consumers in India is a feat most organizations would tremendously benefit from. However, it is also an uphill task due to the comparatively lower levels of brand awareness, resources and accessibility constraints that these consumers face. While marketers would benefit from designing products specifically targeting the needs of these consumers, they would more importantly need to address these needs in their marketing and branding strategies.

Table 20.3 Karl Pearson's coefficient of correlation analysis – model summary

Correlations		BRAND_IMAGE	PERCEIVED_QUALITY	PRODUCT_PROMOTION	BRAND_TRUST
BRAND_IMAGE	Pearson correlation	1	.480[a]	.459[a]	.651[a]
	Sig. (2-tailed)		0.000	0.000	0.000
	N	210	210	210	210
PERCEIVED_QUALITY	Pearson correlation	.480[a]	1	.378[a]	.628[a]
	Sig. (2-tailed)	0.000		0.000	0.000
	N	210	210	210	210
PRODUCT_PROMOTION	Pearson correlation	.459[a]	.378[a]	1	.462[a]
	Sig. (2-tailed)	0.000	0.000		0.000
	N	210	210	210	210
BRAND_TRUST	Pearson correlation	.651[a]	.628[a]	.462[a]	1
	Sig. (2-tailed)	0.000	0.000	0.000	
	N	210	210	210	210

[a]Correlation is significant at the 0.01 level (2-tailed)

Table 20.4 Regression analysis – coefficients

Coefficients[a]

Model		Unstandardized coefficients		Standardized coefficients		
		B	Std. Error	Beta	t	Sig.
1	(Constant)	0.757	0.257		2.950	0.004
	PERCEIVED_QUALITY	0.173	0.082	0.194	2.121	0.015
	PRODUCT_PROMOTION	0.162	0.053	0.178	3.058	0.003
	BRAND_TRUST	0.489	0.075	0.468	6.543	0.000

[a]Dependent variable: BRAND_IMAGE

Table 20.5 Summary of hypotheses testing

Hypotheses	Description	Result
H1	Perceived quality → Brand image	Supported
H2	Product promotion → Brand image	Supported
H3	Brand trust → Brand image	Supported

Table 20.6 Karl Pearson's coefficient of correlation – summary

Correlations

		BRAND_LOYALTY	BRAND_IMAGE
BRAND_LOYALTY	Pearson correlation	1	.300[a]
	Sig. (2-tailed)		0.000
	N	210	210
BRAND_IMAGE	Pearson correlation	.300[a]	1
	Sig. (2-tailed)	0.000	
	N	210	210

[a]Correlation is significant at the 0.01 level (2-tailed)

For Indian BoP consumers, branded purchases are a validation of their aspirations for a better quality of life and a better future not only for themselves but also for their familial circle. However, due to their resource constraints, such consumers are careful of their purchases, expecting a quality standard which is perhaps higher than their urban counterparts. BoP consumers show a comparatively extended usage of branded products in an effort to derive maximum value from them, especially in cases of apparel, footwear and accessories. For these consumers, who come from varying occupations, sports shoes are not only a hedonic product for sport-based occasions but a functional and highly utilitarian purchase that often finds use in everyday life. Due to this propensity of BoP consumers, their sports shoe purchases are significantly driven by their awareness of and trust in a brand, as is also evident in the results of the study.

The significance of perceived quality for BoP consumers' evaluation of a brand's image is a validation of previous researches in the area. For a brand to generate loyalty amongst the BoP consumers, it has to maintain an image that lowers their risk perception in terms of performance, functionality and even social acceptance. For a BoP consumer to repurchase a brand, it has to measure up in all three aspects making it imperative for marketers to measure negating associated risks while developing their marketing strategies. Furthermore, the study surprisingly shows that for these consumers, product promotion holds a higher level of importance than perceived quality. This behaviour may be due to their penchant for purchasing the best 'value' deal and save as much as they can even as they spend. Thus such consumers would be drawn to a brand which not only has a socially acceptable brand image in their aspirational groups but also an acclaimed quality standard amongst their peers and associative reference groups. Thus marketers would need to go beyond traditional methods of promotions and adopt methods that grant them greater access to this consumer segment in order to generate and maintain a brand image that appeals to the majority of them.

The study was limited in its design to BoP consumers in only one Indian city. The results may be indicative of the consumer behaviour in the region that was studied but would need further testing to generate more generalized results.

References

Aaker, D. A. (1991). *Managing brand equity: Capitalizing on the value of a brand name*. New York: Free Press.

Agarwal, S., & Xavier, M. J. (2015). Consumers in Emerging Economies. In *Encyclopedia of consumption and consumer studies* (pp. 1–5.) https://doi.org/10.1002/9781118989463.wbeccs258

American Marketing Association. (2017). AMA Dictionary. https://www.ama.org. Retrieved 09 August 2017, from https://www.ama.org/resources/Pages/Dictionary.aspx?dLetter=B

Aydinli, A., Bertini, M., & Lambrecht, A. (2014). Price promotion for emotional impact. *Journal of Marketing*, *78*(4), 80–96.

Batra, R., Ramaswamy, V., Alden, D. L., Steenkamp, J. B. E., & Ramachander, S. (2000). Effects of brand local and nonlocal origin on consumer attitudes in developing countries. *Journal of Consumer Psychology*, *9*(2), 83–95.

BCG. (2017). The new indian: The many facets of a changing consumer. https://www.bcg.com. Retrieved 6 July 2017, from https://www.bcg.com/en-in/publications/2017/marketing-sales-globalization-new-indian-changing-consumer.aspx

Becerra, E. P., & Badrinarayanan, V. (2013). The influence of brand trust and brand identification on brand evangelism. *Journal of Product & Brand Management*, *22*(5), 371–383. https://doi.org/10.1108/JPBM-09-2013-0394

Bennur, S., & Jin, B. (2017). The mediating role of brand trust and affect in clothing brand loyalty formation: A cross-cultural examination of US and India. *The Journal of The Textile Institute*, *108*(1), 1–9.

Bhuian, S. N. (1997). Marketing cues and perceived quality: Perceptions of Saudi consumers toward products of the U.S., Japan, Germany, Italy, U.K. and France. *Journal of Quality Management*, *2*(2), 217–235.

Blocker, C. P., Ruth, J. A., Sridharan, S., Beckwith, C., Ekici, A., Goudie-Hutton, M., & Varman, R. (2013). Understanding poverty and promoting poverty alleviation through transformative consumer research. *Journal of Business Research*, *66*(8), 1195–1202.

Brand Trust Report. (2017). The brand trust report 2017. https://www.trustadvisory.info. Retrieved 11 August 2017, from http://www.trustadvisory.info/categoryBTR17.php

Chaudhuri, A., & Holbrook, M. (2001). The chain of effects from brand trust and brand affect to brand performance: The role of brand loyalty. *Journal of Marketing*, *65*(2), 81–93.

Chikweche, T., & Fletcher, R. (2010). Understanding factors that influence purchases in subsistence markets. *Journal of Business Research*, *63*(6), 643–650.

Chikweche, T., & Fletcher, R. (2011). Branding at the base of pyramid: A Zimbabwean perspective. *Marketing Intelligence & Planning*, *29*(3), 247–263.

Cruickshank, J. A. (2009). A play for rurality–modernization versus local autonomy. *Journal of Rural Studies*, *25*(1), 98–107.

Cengiz, H., & Akdemir-Cengiz, H. (2016). Review of Brand Loyalty Literature: 2001–2015. Journal of Research in Marketing, 6(1), 407–434.

Chi, H. K., Yeh, H. R., & Yang, Y. T. (2009). The impact of brand awareness on consumer purchase intention: The mediating effect of perceived quality and brand loyalty. The Journal of International Management Studies, 4(1), 135–144.

D'Andrea, G. (2006). *Breaking the paradox of emerging markets: Strategies for reaching consumers at the base of the pyramid*. Working Paper, Universidad Austral, Buenos Aires.

Dalton, A. (2009). Look on the bright side: Self-expressive consumption and consumer self-worth. *Advances in Consumer Research*, *36*(1), 131–132.

Davidson, K. (2009). Ethical concerns at the bottom of the pyramid: Where CSR meets BOP. *Journal of International Business Ethics*, *2*(1), 22.

Dodds, W. B., & Grewal, D. (1991). Effect of price, brand and store information on buyer's product evaluation. *Journal of Marketing Research*, *28*(3), 307–319.

Dreze, X., & Nunes, J. C. (2009). Feeling superior: The impact of loyalty program structure on consumers' perception of status. *Journal of Consumer Research*, *35*(6), 890–905.

Delgado-Ballester, Elena, and José Luis Munuera-Alemán. "Brand trust in the context of consumer loyalty." European Journal of marketing 35, no. 11/12 (2001): 1238–1258.

Elliott, R., & Leonard, C. (2006). Peer pressure and poverty: Exploring fashion brands and consumption symbolism among children of the 'British poor'. *Journal of Consumer Behaviour*, *3*(4), 347–359.

Ersado, L. (2006). *Income Diversification in Zimbabwe: Welfare Implications from Urban and Rural Areas* (Vol. 3964). World Bank Publications. Washington, DC.

Euromonitor. (2017). Top 5 bottom of the pyramid markets: Diverse spending patterns and future potential. Retrived July 10, 2017, from http://blog.euromonitor.com/2017/03/top-5-bottom-pyramid-markets-diverse-spending-patterns-future-potential.html

Ghalandari, K., Nazarian, M., & Norouzi, A. (2016). Developing a model to predict Intentions customers of sport shoes : The role of consumer values , Involvement , the perceived quality and overall satisfaction with product. *The IIOAB Journal*, *7*(4), 252–259.

Ghuman, K., & Krishnamacharyulu, C. (2008). *Rural marketing: Concepts and practices*. New Delhi: Tata McGraw-Hill.

Gupta, S., & Srivastav, P. (2016). An exploratory investigation of aspirational consumption at the bottom of the pyramid. *Journal of International Consumer Marketing*, *28*(1), 2–15.

Habibi, M. R., Laroche, M., & Richard, M. O. (2014). The roles of brand community and community engagement in building brand trust on social media. *Computers in Human Behavior*, *37*, 152–161. https://doi.org/10.1016/j.chb.2014.04.016

Hair, J. F., Jr., Black, W. C., Babin, B. J., Anderson, R. E., & Tatham, R. L. (2010). *Multivariate data analysis with readings* (7th ed.). Englewood Cliffs, NJ: McGraw-Hill.

Hamilton, K. (2009). Those left behind: Inequality in consumer culture. *Irish Marketing Review*, *20*(2), 40.

Hamilton, K., & Catterall, M. (2007). Love and consumption in poor families headed by lone mothers. *Advances in Consumer Research*, *34*, 559–564.

Hamilton, K. L., & Catterall, M. (2008). I can do it! consumer coping and poverty. *Advances in Consumer Research*, *35*, 551–556.

Hegner, S. M., & Jevons, C. (2016). Brand trust: A cross-national validation in Germany, India, and South Africa. *Journal of Product & Brand Management*, *25*(1), 58–68.

Hoyer, W. D., & Brown, S. P. (1990). Effects of brand awareness on choice for a common, repeat-purchase product. *Journal of Consumer Research*, *17*(2), 141–148.

Huang, R., & Sarigöllü, E. (2012). How brand awareness relates to market outcome, brand equity, and the marketing mix. *Journal of Business Research*, *65*(1), 92–99.

IBEF. (2017). Indian rural market. https://www.ibef.org. Retrieved 10 August 2017, from https://www.ibef.org/industry/indian-rural-market.aspx

IFMR. (2011). The Base of Pyramid distribution challenge: Evaluating alternate distribution models of energy products for rural Base of Pyramid in India, Retrieved 8 July 2017, from https://www.microfinancegateway.org/sites/default/files/mfg-en-paper-the-base-of-pyramid-distribution-challenge-evaluating-alternate-distribution-models-of-energy-products-for-rural-base-of-pyramid-in-india-2011.pdf

Jaiswal, A. K. (2008). The fortune at the bottom or the middle of the pyramid. *Innovations: Technology, Governance, Globalization*, *3*(1), 85–100.

Jaiswal, A. K., & Gupta, S. (2015). The influence of marketing on consumption behavior at the bottom of the pyramid. *Journal of Consumer Marketing*, *32*(2), 113–124.

Karnani, A. (2009). Romanticising the poor harms the poor. *Journal of International Development*, *21*(1), 76–86.

Khan, S. K., & Jalees, T. (2016). Antecedents to Brand Image. *Market Forces*, *11*(2), 11–24.

KPMG and CII. (2016, September). The business of sports: Playing to win as the game unfurls. Retrieved July 10, 2017, from https://assets.kpmg.com/content/dam/kpmg/in/pdf/2016/09/the-business-of-sports.pdf

Kumar, A., Vohra, A., & Dangi, H. K. (2016). Consumer decision-making styles and post purchase behaviour of poor for Fast Moving Consumer Goods. *International Journal of Consumer Studies*, *41*(2), 121–137.

Kolk, A., Rivera-Santos, M., & Rufin, C. (2014). Reviewing a decade of research on the "base/bottom of the pyramid" (BOP) concept. Business & Society, 53(3), 338–377.

Khan, I., & Rahman, Z. (2016). E-tail brand experience's influence on e-brand trust and e-brand loyalty: the moderating role of gender. International Journal of Retail & Distribution Management, 44(6), 588–606.

Laluyan, W. N., Pangemanan, S. S., & Worang, F. G. (2017). The effect of advertising, perceived quality and brand awareness on consumer purchase intention (Case study: Adidas sport shoes). *Jurnal EMBA*, *5*(2), 267–278.

Lock, A. C. (2016). Impact of brand knowledge on brand trust in Private Higher Education Institutions : How do word of mouth sources intervene ? *Sarjana*, *31*(2), 13–32.

Mahajan, V., & Banga, K. (2005). *The 86 percent solution: How to succeed in the biggest market opportunity of the next 50 years*. Upper Saddle River, NJ: Pearson Prentice-Hall.

McKinsey Global Institute. (2007, May). The 'Bird of Gold': The rise of India's consumer market. Retrieved July 10, 2017, from https://www.mckinsey.com/~/media/McKinsey/Global%20Themes/Asia%20Pacific/The%20bird%20of%20gold/MGI_Rise_of_Indian_Consumer_Market_full_report.ashx

Mick, D. G., Pettigrew, S., Pechmann, C. C., & Ozanne, J. L. (Eds.). (2012). *Transformative consumer research for personal and collective well-being*. New York, NY: Routledge.

Moorman, C., Deshpande, R., & Zaltman, G. (1993). Factors affecting trust in market research relationships. *Journal of Marketing*, *57*, 81–101.

Ogba, I. E., & Tan, Z. (2009). Exploring the impact of brand image on customer loyalty and commitment in China. *Journal of Technology Management in China*, *4*(2), 132–144.

Omar, M., & Williams, R. L., Jr. (2009). Marketing to the bottom of the pyramid: Opportunities in emerging markets. *International Journal of Services, Economics and Management*, *1*(4), 427–446.

Paninchukunnath, A. (2010). 3P framework: Rural marketing in India. *SCMS Journal of Indian Management, 7*(1), 54–67.

Parida, R. R., & Sahney, S. (2017). Cultural influence on brand loyalty of rural consumers in the Indian context. *Journal of Asia Business Studies, 11*(1), 60–72.

Pentina, I., Zhang, L., & Basmanova, O. (2013). Antecedents and consequences of trust in a social media brand: A cross-cultural study of Twitter. *Computers in Human Behavior, 29*(4), 1546–1555. https://doi.org/10.1016/j.chb.2013.01.045

Pongpaew, W., Speece, M., & Tiangsoongnern, L. (2016). Customer brand engagement , perceived social presence , and brand trust and loyalty in corporate Facebook. In Annual Conference of the Emerging Markets Conference Board. https://doi.org/10.2139/ssrn.2727178

Prahalad, C. K. (2005). *Fortune at the bottom of the pyramid: Eradicating poverty through profits*. Upper Saddle River, NJ: Wharton School Publishing.

Prahalad, C. K., & Hammond, A. (2002). Serving the world's poor, profitably. *Harvard Business Review, 80*(9), 48–59.

Rajagopal. (2009). Branding paradigm for the bottom of the pyramid markets. *Measuring Business Excellence, 13*(4), 58–68. https://doi.org/10.1108/13683040911006792

Rotter, J. B. (1967). A new scale for the measurement of interpersonal trust. *Journal of Personality and Social Psychology, 35*(4), 651–665.

Ryan, R. M., Huta, V., & Deci, E. L. (2008). Living well: A self-determination theory perspective on eudaimonia. *Journal of Happiness Studies, 9*, 139–170.

Rahman, M., Hasan, M. R., & Floyd, D. (2013). Brand orientation as a strategy that influences the adoption of innovation in the bottom of the pyramid market. *Strategic Change,* 22(3–4), 225–239.

Severi, E., & Ling, K. C. (2013). The mediating effects of brand association, brand loyalty, brand image and perceived quality on brand equity. *Asian Social Science, 9*(3), 125–137. https://doi.org/10.5539/ass.v9n3p125

Sinha, P. K., Sinha, P. K., Gupta, S., Gupta, S., Rawal, S., & Rawal, S. (2017). Brand adoption by BoP retailers. *Qualitative Market Research: An International Journal, 20*(2), 181–207.

Sriram, S., Balachander, S., & Kalwani, M. U. (2007). Monitoring the dynamics of brand equity using store-level data. *Journal of Marketing, 71*, 61–78.

Subrahmanyan, S., & Tomas Gomez-Arias, J. (2008). Integrated approach to understanding consumer behavior at bottom of pyramid. *Journal of Consumer Marketing, 25*(7), 402–412.

Simanis, E. (2012, June). Reality Check at the Bottom of the Pyramid. Retrieved 04 17, 2017, from www.hbr.org: https://hbr.org/2012/06/reality-check-at-the-bottom-of-the-pyramid.

Singh, P. K., & Pattanayak, J. K. (2014). Linking of Customer Satisfaction with Shareholders' value: A Review. Global Journal of Finance and Management, 6(5), 403–412.

Teck Weng, J., & Cyril de Run, E. (2013). Consumers' personal values and sales promotion preferences effect on behavioural intention and purchase satisfaction for consumer product. *Asia Pacific Journal of Marketing and Logistics, 25*(1), 70–101.

Thakur, A., & Kaur, R. (2015). Relationship between self-concept and attitudinal brand loyalty in luxury fashion purchase: A study of selected global brands on the Indian market. *Management: Journal of Contemporary Management Issues, 20*(2), 163–180.

Vasavada-oza, F., Nagraj, A., & Krishna, Y. (2012). Marketing to rural women : How various leading brands are doing it ? *The IUP Journal of Brand Management, 9*(2), 7–18.

Viswanathan, M. (2007). *Understanding product and market interactions in subsistence marketplaces: A study in South India. In Product and market development for subsistence marketplaces* (pp. 21–57). Emerald Group Publishing Limited, United Kingdom.

Wu, W. Y., & Anridho, N. (2016). The antecedents of brand loyalty: A meta-analysis study. *International Journal of Services and Standards, 11*(3), 242–260.

Zeithaml, V. A. (1988). Consumer perceptions of price, quality and value: A means-end model and synthesis of evidence. *Journal of Marketing, 52*, 2–22.

Ashish Gupta is an Assistant Professor at the Department of Business Management in Dr. Hari Singh Gour Central University, Sagar, Madhya Pradesh, India. He completed his PhD in Management from Motilal Nehru National Institute of Technology Allahabad, India, and his research area includes relationship marketing, customer retention and consumer behaviour. He has presented several research papers in international and national conferences. He has more than 20 research papers to his credit published in international and national journals like ***Asia Pacific Journal of Marketing and Logistics, Emerald, UK***; ***International Journal of Customer Relationship Marketing and Management, USA***; ***International Journal of Electronic Customer Relationship Management, UK***; International ***Journal of Indian Culture and Business Management, UK***; and ***Journal of Direct, Data and Digital Marketing Practice, USA.***

Anushree Tandon is an Assistant Professor in Amity School of Business, Amity University. She holds a degree in Management from IBS, Kolkata, is UGC-NET-qualified and completed her doctoral research at Motilal Nehru National Institute of Technology Allahabad. Her area of research is related to customer experience, retailing and value co-creation and has published in national and international journals of repute along with presenting several research papers in national and international conferences.

Chapter 21
Rurality in Flux: A Perspective on Rural Tourism Enterprise

Gunjan Saxena

Abstract This study underlines how a reordering of rural space has made rurality into a complex symbol of identity encompassing a broad range of meanings that both unite and split community on how they are applied in packaging and promoting places. In fact, it can be argued that rurality is in flux given the ambivalence it evokes – some take it seriously, arguing for a need to conserve, and others regard the conservation efforts as a joke, more of a gimmick in the light of the dissipation of sociocultural and natural attributes they have witnessed in their community. Thus it is fair to say that rurality no longer embodies static meanings and traits. In fact, whilst on one hand, there is a predominance of urban interests in the countryside, on the other rurality is boxed and presented for consumption in urban localities. In illustrating how creative enterprise is bringing about an innovative use of the rural ethos and space, this work will present case insights from India and Mexico. Findings underline how rurality acts as a tool for thinking about and reassembling local identity, mediating distinctions between insiders and outsiders, fact and fiction and inverting ways in which places are consumed.

Keywords Rural tourism · Creative · Enterprise · Rurality

21.1 Introduction

Whilst rurality matters both as a setting and an ethos for creative ventures that rely upon it as a driver for economic gains, there is limited research on how it is packaged and promoted in a multi-faceted manner to perform creatively for tourism markets. This work calls for a strong research emphasis on a holistic understanding of how rurality is transformed into a tourism product via particular processes that engender material and imaginary rural spaces. The potential of the creative sector in

G. Saxena (✉)
Faculty of Business, Law and Politics, The University of Hull, Hull, UK
e-mail: g.saxena@hull.ac.uk

Y. K. Dwivedi et al. (eds.), *Emerging Markets from a Multidisciplinary Perspective*, Advances in Theory and Practice of Emerging Markets,
https://doi.org/10.1007/978-3-319-75013-2_21

generating sustainable high-quality enterprise and employment opportunities and contributing to rural diversification remains an under-researched area as the focus is more on urban regions and their capacity to accommodate innovative clusters. However, unique 'place' strengths (e.g. natural resources and the quality of life) that exist in rural areas spur creative enterprise. In fact, my contention is that creativity-driven entrepreneurs can bring about innovative uses of rurality in uncertain and sometimes surprising manner, simultaneously estranging and engaging local community and consumers. Whilst their dynamism is embedded in place narratives fashioned by discourses on deprivation, peripherality (see Shucksmith & Brown, 2016), cultural capital and social cohesion (Saxena, 2016), their creative activities are often led by canny recognition of opportunities for innovation and market demand for unique, 'off-the-beaten-path' experiences. In fact, I argue that idealist rural imaginaries (re)produced through the ingenuity of entrepreneurs or what Lund and Jóhannesson (2016) call the 'poetics of making' (p. 653) provide means of grasping actor narratives – embedded in their imagination, emotions and performance – that are instrumental in creating and enhancing the image of a locality as visit-worthy. Thus the purpose of this work is twofold: (i) examine the 'stories of a place' that connect an assortment of elements to bring it alive and (ii) present 'the everyday acts' of place-making through which rurality is infused with unique meanings, commodified and marketed. I now discuss the ways in which selective representations of rurality, its materiality plus myths, memories and traditions, embedded in a place, become resources for tourism. In Sect. 21.3, I introduce the case study context and discuss the qualitative methodology employed in collecting data. My findings in Sect. 21.4 focus mainly on how rural ethos and space is (re)worked through the ingenuity of providers in delivering a memorable interface with experiential and material aspects of rurality. Section 21.5 brings the discussion to a close by underlining how the (re)use of rural imageries together with an element of risk-taking and experimenting can engender lasting marketing narratives and unique tourism experiences.

21.2 Packaging and Promoting Rurality

The classification of rurality as such is contrived, fashioned through metaphors and geographical imaginations that engender specific knowledges about 'rural' and provide the premise for a range of interpretations that appear to have been applied in defining rural (Halfacree, 1993; Hidle, Cruickshank, & Nesje, 2006). For instance, within the context of the potent imaginary of spatially integrated Europe, rural space is conceived and framed as a shrinking entity in the face of rapid growth in new telecommunications and information technology infrastructure (Hadjimichalis, 2003). In Central Asian economies like Uzbekistan and Kyrgyzstan, rural economy is viewed as means to ensure social stasis and the steady flow of rents to the elite (Markowitz, 2016). In general, rurality is employed to address an overall desire in Western society's longing for '…security, stasis and nostalgia in an uncertain, changing and globalising world' (Short, 2006, p. 143). Attractive rural living plus material and symbolical representations, such as gardens, foods or communal harmony, constitute an essential ingredient in '...a staged and co-performed production of rural places' (Jonasson, 2012, p. 28). Indeed, the policy emphasis is on stimulating sustainable, responsible and high-quality tourism in rural areas with a pro-poor agenda (EU, 2010; Dayananda & Leelavathi, 2016).

However, the use, indeed manipulation, of rurality for tourism gains is neither always a consensual affair nor a definitive representation of its socio-economic and cultural attributes. In fact, conflict is inherent in the very conceptualisation of rurality as a tourism commodity given that personal perhaps sacred sites and histories are selected for packaging and promotion. Moreover, as the process of its appropriation for tourism purposes is quite selective, certain elements and attributes are inevitably excluded and meaning(s) created to which not all may relate. It is not simply that rural localities symbolise particular values and beliefs, but their shift towards tourism entails that site consumption is determined more by the skill and experiences of entrepreneurs. Yet, this process whereby the identity of a place is defined and landscape assets intertwined with the business ethos is fraught with tension as 'individual notions of the rural' (Kordel, 2016, p. 216) compete with and contradict each other. In fact, as Thirumaran, Dam, &Thirumaran, (2014) point out in their study on Vietnamese souvenirs, that often it is the poor and traditional craftsmen who tend to be pushed back or neglected in the wake of commercialisation that the tourism industry stimulates. Similarly, Gao and Wu's (2017) study points out how residents have an inadequate say in government-led tourism initiatives in rural China.Thus in a bid to offer an understanding of how community voices and landscape assets are utilised/discarded in the process of redefining space and identity, this chapter underlines the emergence of atypical application of rural persona and the very notion of rurality for commercial gains.

21.3 Study Context

21.3.1 Case Study Areas

To reflect how the place character and local specificities (i.e. material and symbolic aspects of rurality) of everyday rural living are mobilised and reconfigured as a tool to generate custom, two firms – Chokhi Dhani in Jaipur, the capital of the state of Rajasthan, India, and Parque EcoAlberto (located in the municipality of Ixmiquilpan) in Mexico's Valle del Mezquital region – are included. The five-starrated Chokhi Dhani Resort & Hotel (see Fig. 21.1) illustrates how 'location alone' is an inadequate parameter for defining the 'rural' character of an enterprise. Rather, it stems from the business ethos of this firm that is directed at overseeing the transition of Rajasthani cuisine and handcrafts (via its support to the Kalagram initiative which facilitates sustained livelihood for local craftsmen) from the traditional domain into mainstream tourism circuits. The commercial success of this firm

Fig. 21.1 Chokhi Dhani, Jaipur (Source: Author)

elucidates how rurality, especially the cultural traits of rural living, constructed as 'out of place' within urban conurbations, has become not only saleable but an upmarket commodity. Within this carefully crafted rural space, one which is far removed from both the geography and the actuality of everyday life in rural areas, tourism experience is produced, marketed and consumed on the strength of its commercial appeal rather than 'authenticity'. Central to this context of what I term as 'contrived rurality' (Saxena, 2016, p. 31) is actors' conscious engagement in creating a sense of place through managing an impression of themselves as rural people – with their bodies, discursive practices and material artefacts. On one hand, these strategies determine how staff and artists who perform at the venue and display their craft define themselves in accordance with the rigorous customer-service-oriented dictum. On the other, they mask with success the exploitative setup, characterised by long hours and low pay, within which staff operate. Also, as I gathered from my informal conversations, they live on the periphery of the town in squalid conditions with few facilities and in 'out of sight' settings that are not available for the tourist gaze. The real ownership of the venture lies in the hands of Jaipur-based corporate group which owns similar enterprises in other Indian cities.

In contrast, the ownership of Parque EcoAlberto (see Fig. 21.2), located 100 kilometres from the US border, and about 2 hours away from Mexico City, lies in the hands of the Hñähñu community, an indigenous group.

Fig. 21.2 Parque EcoAlberto (Source: Author)

Unlike Chokhi Dhani that celebrates the idyllic aspects of rurality (e.g. 'traditional heritage hospitality of Rajasthani culture' as is marketed on its website (www.chokhidhani.com)), stark aspects of rural living have been commodified at EcoAlberto. It forms the backdrop for the staging of Caminata Nocturna (Night Walk) which simulates the experience of illegal border-crossing on the US-Mexico border during which participants pay an admission fee to be chased, shot at and verbally abused as they are rushed through streams, brambles and rugged land whilst being pursued by sirens, dogs and men masquerading as border patrol guards. Sarat (2010) contends that Caminata Nocturna is '…the shared product of a diverse and changing religious landscape in El Alberto. Over half of the town's residents are Pentecostal. For Pentecostals, the border is a space of divine encounter where hardship of crossing sometimes serves as a catalyst for conversion. Submitting themselves to the authority of a God for whom there are no borders, Pentecostals embrace migration as their right and travel with a sense of divine protection' (p. 9). Thus Caminata Nocturna has altered the stigma associated with the undocumented migrant journeys into a catalyst for reflection on deep-seated questions about negativtiy associated with rural communities. The initiative provides an avenue to developing sustainable alternatives to migration through tourism.

In general, via these two enterprises, I intend to illustrate how the notion of rurality, in particular its material and symbolic aspects, is utilised in framing particular discourses about place and inducing audiences to undertake both physical and imaginary journeys into its mystique (see Salazar, 2010; Bredvold & Skålén, 2016). The emphasis is on illustrating how creative enterprise is central in adding texture and unique meanings to a place, adding to its intrinsic value and the saleability of its everyday aspects.

21.3.2 *Methodology*

Data were collected via participant observation, informal conversation with visitors (3–4) and semi-structured interviews (5) lasting for 60–90 min at each site. An important characteristic of semi-structured interviews was that '...they incorporated features of both conversation and narrative' (Mills, 2001, p. 285). The research questions at the outset focused on the following issues:

- What were respondents' perceptions about making use of rural attributes in their locality?
- What stories did they share which were employed in enhancing the touristic appeal of their enterprise?

As the study progressed, the research question came to concentrate more precisely on the relationship between their sense of self and varied values/interpretations inscribed upon rural landscape accordingly. Overall, respondents who were selected for an inclusion in the study were chosen through a combination of 'purposive and snowball sampling', handpicked on the basis of their typicality (Cohen & Manion, 1994). The analysis presented in the next section focuses on those aspects of their narratives which illustrate how they utilise their individual life stories as a key ingredient in crafting momentous, experiential episodes for tourists. In general, in shaping the case-based discussion in chapter, I draw upon my own experience to reflect on what Kniazeva and Belk (2007) term as 'narrative vehicles' (p. 51) consisting of autobiographical accounts that reflect the everyday attributes of actors' lives as they enliven aspects of rurality.

21.4 Discussion and Analysis

21.4.1 *Enacting the Lived, Sensual Dimension of Rurality*

Essentially, at first glance, the place character and local specificities present at Chokhi Dhani make it appear like a microcosm of rural India – utopian, colourful space that invokes the feel of an Indian village and offers a sanitised experience. The enterprise is designed very much like the *Dilli Haat*, a retail plaza in Delhi that is planned like a miniature village where produce from different states of India is sold and where:

> Traffic, pollution, flyovers, street hawkers, urban slums, poverty, refuse, public urination, growing suburbanism, itinerant animals, and noise: all are filtered out ... through the mechanisms of the gate and ... entry ticket, which limit access to the urban middle class and elite. (Sethi, 2013, p. 53–77)

Further, the manner in which rurality is packaged at the site follows the structure of a fairy tale narrative (Grayson, 1997) seeking to transport consumers from the din and toil of their routine into a world:

… where nature is alive, natural scenic views are ready to serve you and where you can feel the fresh air of Indian rustic villages. (www.chokhidhani.com)

As cultural construction, this promise is full of mythic archetypes as it makes use of culturally familiar symbols and values, namely, the 'vibrant spirit of Rajasthan… Bani Thani art, the wall decorations, Dipak wall,[1] the fresh air, the evening performances, the enthusiasm, the 'manuhar' (a delicate request to eat till your heart's desire), the traditions, the costumes and at last but not least the Feelings' (ibid).

In marketing itself in this manner, this enterprise purports to fulfil the urban middle-class audiences' quest for belonging to an egalitarian, small-scale community and traditional living, the memory of which is embedded in collective consciousness. Thus when speaking to one of the front office managers, it was apparent that the emphasis was on creating an (in)tangible sense of place through effecting 'naturalness':

Because Rajasthani culture belongs to everybody, you don't have to teach people anything technical, just encourage them to be natural – humble, hospitable and honourable which Rajputana[2] is famous for anyway. Those are our three Hs of marketing if you like. (male, 40s)

However, Kniazeva and Belk (2007) argue that from a marketing perspective, being natural is an emotionally charged classification and not a product attribute as such for the marker 'natural' is a myth that is constantly (re)created by marketers and consumers for it lacks any certified definition and distinctive requisites. In fact, from the private tropes that I gathered and which tend to be bypassed in mainstream marketing communications about the site, the enterprise keeps artists and other members of staff confined in an unnatural setting as is evident from the following accounts:

My friends and I run the camel rides here. We have no education, little money. This business is our life bread. I am not from Jaipur, but cannot go home … *Majboori hai (am restrained).* (Male, 30s)

After a point, you stop thinking and just do what you are doing. What is the point? Life is not going to be any better or worse. It has been the same for me always. I am too busy to notice anyone or anything … (laughs). (Female, 50s, applies mehandi (henna) at the site at no cost)

Also, I could not help but notice the muddied feet and sweaty, tired faces of performers trying to pull a smiley demeanour plus their incessant pestering for tips, all of which combine to disrupt the myth 'natural'. My observations find resonance with some of the comments posted on TripAdvisor about this enterprise.

---

[1] Wall decorated with earthen lamps.

[2] Before the partition of India, Rajputana or the Land of the Rajputs (members of the warrior class, Kshatriya) was a princely state that included mainly the present-day Indian state of Rajasthan along with parts of Madhya Pradesh, Gujarat and some adjoining areas of Sindh in modern-day Southern Pakistan (www.britannica.com, accessed 01/08/2017/).

> From the time you enter, everywhere you see boards stating "Do not encourage tips". But guess what!! All the dancers and performers run behind you begging "*Mann se kuch do na*" (please give something which you please). We sat on the cots to watch a ghoomar performance and when it finished we got up to go. The dancer came running up and asked to give something. We refused. So basically the point is you pay for every damn thing you even just see! We were fed up with the begging everywhere and we lost interest in seeing the other things. (Female, Reviewed April 3, 2017, travelled with family in March 2017)

> My experience was horrible. Staff at reception is so rude. No hospitality. No feeling of *Padharo Mhare Desh* - Welcome to my Land. (Female, Reviewed May 17, 2017, travelled as a couple in May 2017)

Further, what is remarkable is the apparent failure of this business to confront the problems of rapidly expanding city making its narrative of rurality, culture and belonging quite farcical and redundant given that in its own right, it unsettles civic, urban life by contributing to an increase in traffic, noise and overcrowding, pushing the limits of patience, tolerance and generosity for customers as they jostle for a place and a seat inside the premises. In general, symbolic cultural performances enacted at the site are embedded in imaginary notions of community and communal life and have neither the relevance nor the social significance in contemporary urban living. Thus it will not be unfair to regard them as '… simply an expression of boosterism' (Gabbert, 2011, p. 39), as is often the case with commodified tourist events. Nevertheless, overwhelmingly positive consumer response (evident from customer reviews on TripAdvisor) and which I observed at the site is a testimony of the success of symbols, stories and rituals used in varying configurations in the making of 'The real Rajasthan' persona. In fact, this 'free-floating signifier' (after Hopkins, 1998) of symbolic country-living is used in giving meaning and character to other places with an appetite for flavours of 'rural Rajasthan'. Thus burgeoning Chokhi Dhani outlets are fast becoming common place in major cities of India.

In general, this case well illustrates how the materiality or the physical landscape is rendered subordinate to the aesthetics or signs of rurality. The enterprise provides its consumers (especially domestic visitors) with what can be described as a ritual space that allows them to remember and perform traditional practices (e.g. wear *pagdi* or turban, sit on the floor to eat with hands), rooting them deeper in the genealogy of place. For foreign visitors, their understanding of local culture (albeit commodified) and its symbolism is enhanced by partaking in the sensual dimension of rurality through music, dance, food and crafts. It was evident from their narratives how they experienced feeling 'out of place' and uncertain initially but slowly gave in to the 'swing of things' (male, 20s, visiting from Australia). Indeed, authors contend that themed settings, even if contrived, have their own form of authenticity which derives from their ability to engage consumers' attention in a multisensory fashion (Lukas, 2007; Waysdorf & Reijnders, 2016). Thus Chokhi Dhani's enclosed space is ideal in not only showcasing the desirable aspects of rurality in their vividness, but also forging an intimacy between the viewer and the 'subject' (i.e. staff, performers and artists) who, hands folded in a welcoming and willing to please or serve gesture, cement the sense of an interface with the 'exotic other' (O' Barr, 1994).

21.4.2 Enlivening Rurality Through a Narrated Kinaesthetics

This process of 'othering' (see Nelson, 2005), whereby attributes of rurality are presented as distinct with the promise to be unlike anything a tourist might encounter in his or her everyday life, is evident at Parque EcoAlberto as well. However, here the emphasis is on the body and memory as the basis of an intricate engagement with country. The manner in which rurality is commodified at Chokhi Dhani is founded on the picturesque engagement with the ambiance. In contrast, the interface with rurality that Caminata offers is more of '… a pulsational and gestural experience - that is, one concerned with the times and speeds of movement, rather than with form or geometry…' (Tawa, 2002, p. 49). The vision of migration embodied in Caminata Nocturna comes alive via narratives that locals (including former illegal migrants to the USA) provide and which populate the trajectories and itineraries of travel visitors undertake in the course of reliving the experience of border-crossing. For instance, for tour guides, most of whom have had first-hand experience of crossing the border illegally, Caminata serves as a means to consolidate their cultural identity and varied meanings they derive from the landscape that embodies the promise of the *American Dream*, as is evident from these accounts:

> Caminata is fun and a nightmare, all depends on my frame of mind … for someone like me who spent all his childhood in America. My parents and sister are there, but I was tricked into signing some documents by the police and here I am. They deported me despite my protests. Now, I sometimes assume the role of a *coyote*,[3] other times I am impersonating as the US border patrol agent. I can fake pretty good American accent you know, having lived there for almost fifteen years … in a way it is good I returned for this is where I belong … this water, these mountains, they are of the same blood as I am … you know what I mean …. (Male, 40s, lives alone but has the support of his extended family now that he is in Mexico)

> I have never dared cross the border so far, but since I have seen so many do it successfully, boys I have grown up with … now they own nice cars and fancy things in America, I want to try it myself and be like them. What is the harm? I don't see any wrong. People have always gone across, it is our way of life. (Female, 20s)

> I have tried once and was unsuccessful, but not to worry … it is not a case of if I will cross the border, but when. There is very little here to hold me back. (Male, 20s)

Thus Caminata not only serves as a means of transcending marginal rural living for a community immersed deeply in a migration lifestyle but also becomes a dichotomous medium through which people consolidate their identities on one hand and 'cross boundaries' in space and time on the other. Serat (2010) rightly regards it as 'a sincere, grass-roots effort through which a community strained by migration has come together to convey the hardship of border passage to their well-heeled fellow citizens' (p. 35). However, narratives of border-crossing which glorify the act

[3] *Coyote*, a canid native to North America, is the term given to paid guides who help illegal migrants emigrate to the USA as they know the track and are at times, I was informed, even able to strike a deal with the US border patrol agents (Saxena, 2016).

can also confine identity construction as they are also intertwined intrinsically with forgetting or downplaying less favourable experiences. What I found noticeable was the muted nature of the voices of dissent that argue in favour of 'moving away from the border' (making a living through art and craft plus farming as opposed to reliving the ugliness of the border – the violence and ignominy of encounter with border patrol agents). However, in general, Caminata Nocturna induces a shared sense of ownership of the enterprise unlike the sense of displacement I observed at Chokhi Dhani which is also grounded in the structure of collective labour, but one which is far removed from the sociocultural dynamics within which staff are embedded. Also, it is apparent how different types of bodies and voices (rather than the ones that are aesthetically pleasing at Chokhi Dhani) support and sustain the choreography of visitor encounters of rurality in Mexico dismantling the preconceived divisions between desirable and undesirable.

21.5 Conclusions

In sum, I underline that at both localities, careful management of marketing narratives ensures that the allure of rurality as a myth is employed effectively to shape place-making processes. Importantly, as the discussion illustrates, the main focus of Chokhi Dhani is on selling the visual, olfactory and sonic aspects of rurality, the experience Parque EcoAlberto provides is '... choreographic—in the sense that space and place are elaborated kinesthetically through practices of walking and speaking stories associated with country' (Tawa, 2002, p. 45). If consistency is a mark of success, both enterprises surely deserve credit for being steadfast in capturing visitors' imagination for a number of years. Interestingly, they have done this without any enduring institutional structure but simply through a trial and error method. The ideas they embrace have left tangible traces on the landscapes within which they are situated. In fact, rurality attains the quality of an artwork, crafted carefully and like an object inscribed in space and time, and becomes 'a world apart from the real thing' (visitor, 30s, male, describing Chokhi Dhani). On a more subtle level, I observed that 'voices of dissent' are subdued as traditional notions of group harmony and relationships become central to the successful functioning of the two enterprises.

Further, whilst the tension between fact and fiction created by stories that render the physicality of the site meaningful is apparent to both narrators and audiences, selective narratives still manage to bring about a merging of real and imagined episodes, enhancing the experiential quality of products and services offered. Thus narrators aim at inviting consumers to believe their accounts at some level, or temporarily suspend disbelief, or at least consider the possibility of truth even if they immediately reject it. In other words, the most important aspect of the experience Chokhi Dhani and Caminata Nocturna offer is not so much the final product but the process of co-creating the unique experience embodying tourists' sensibilities and narratives. Hence, it is fair to say that the storied world that the two enterprises package and present '... becomes immersive because it feels inhabitable – as detailed as the "real world" and shared with others as a sort of imaginary habitus' (Waysdorf & Reijnders, 2016, p. 5). It is brought alive through providers' efforts and narration plus the dynamic energy of visitors who co-create it through their experiences. In this respect, a key emphasis of the discussion has been to underline the potential of local creativity and ingenuity and its capacity in generating new and alternative forms of social and cultural expression and provide thought-provoking interface with facets of rurality. Further, visitors' subjective experiences are central in (re)making of the sites in defiance of the 'logic of market' which fixes the meaning of a place and its history rendering it as a commodity. Current frameworks of rural tourism are focused largely on tangible dimensions of rurality (e.g. place attributes), an approach that excludes its 'experiential dimension' which piques tourist interest due to compelling storytelling and creative place-making. In this sense, this chapter serves as a call for undertaking a concerted revision of rural tourism frameworks to account for the different dimensions of rurality (including the ones that are intangible and imperceptible) and how they are made saleable.

References

Bredvold, R., & Skålén, P. (2016). Lifestyle entrepreneurs and their identity construction: A study of the tourism industry. *Tourism Management, 56*, 96–105.

Cohen, L., & Manion, L. (1994). *Research methods in education*. London: Routledge.

Dayananda, K. C., & Leelavathi, D. S. (2016). Evolution of tourism policy in India. *IOSR Journal of Humanities and Social Science, 21*(11), 26–32.

EU. (2010). *Communication from the commission to the European Parliament, the council, the European economic and social committee and the Committee of the Regions – Europe, the world's no 1 tourist destination – A new political framework for tourism in Europe COM/2010/0352*, Brussels: European Commission.

Gabbert, L. (2011). *Winter carnival in a western town: Identity, change and the good of the community*. University Press of Colorado USA.

Grayson, K. (1997). Narrative theory and consumer research: Theoretical and methodological perspectives. *Advances in Consumer Research, 24*, 67–70.

Gao, J. and Wu, B. (2017) Revitalizing traditional villages through rural tourism: A case study of Yuanjia Village, Shaanxi Province, China, Tourism Management 63, 223–233.

Hadjimichalis, C. (2003). Imagining Rurality in the New Europe and Dilemmas for Spatial Policy. *European Planning Studies, 11*(2), 103–113.

Hidle, K., Cruickshank, J., & Nesje, L. M. (2006). Market, commodity, resource, and strength: Logics of Norwegian rurality. *Norsk Geografisk Tidsskrift – Norwegian Journal of Geography, 60*(3), 189–198.

Hopkins, J. (1998). Signs of the post-rural: Marketing myths of a symbolic countryside. *Geografiska Annaler. Series B, Human Geography, 80*(2), 65–81.

Halfacree, K. H (1993). 'Locality and social representation: space, discourse and alternative definitions ofthe rural', Journal of Rural Studies, 9(1), 23–37.

Jonasson, M. (2012). Co-producing and co-performing attractive rural living in popular media. *Rural Society, 22*(1), 17–30.

Kniazeva, M., & Belk, R. W. (2007). Packaging as vehicle for mythologizing the brand. *Consumption Markets & Culture, 10*(1), 51–69.

Kordel, S. (2016). Selling ruralities: How tourist entrepreneurs commodify traditional and alternative ways of conceiving the countryside. *Rural Society, 25*(3), 204–221.
Lukas, S. (2007). *The themed space: Locating culture, nation, and self.* Plymouth, KY: Lexington.
Lund, K. A., & Jóhannesson, G. T. (2016). Earthly substances and narrative encounters: Poetics of making a tourism destination. *Cultural Geographies, 23*(4), 653–669.
Markowitz, L. P. (2016). Rural economies and leadership change in Central Asia. *Central Asian Survey, 35*(4), 514–530.
Mills, J. (2001). Self-construction through conversation and narrative in interviews. *Educational Review, 53*(3), 285–301.
Nelson, V. (2005). Representation and images of people, place and nature in Grenada's tourism. *Geografiska Annaler. Series B, Human Geography, 87*(2), 131–143.
O'Barr, W. M. (1994). *Culture and the ad: Exploring otherness in the world of advertising.* Boulder, CO: Westview Press.
Salazar, N. B. (2010). *Envisioning Eden: Mobilising imaginaries in tourism and beyond.* New York, NY: Berghahn Books.
Sarat, L. M. (2010). The God without Borders and the Mexican dream: religion, space, and migration in El Alberto, Hidalgo, Unpublished Ph.D. Thesis, University of Florida.
Saxena, G. (2016). *Marketing rural tourism: Experience and Enterprise.* Cheltenham, UK: E-Elgar.
Short, B. (2006). Idyllic ruralities. In P. Cloke, T. Marsden, & P. Mooney (Eds.), *Handbook of rural studies* (pp. 133–148). London: Sage.
Shucksmith, M., & Brown, D. L. (2016). *Routledge international handbook of rural studies.* London: Routledge.
Sethi, C. M. (2013). 'Mapping craft in Contemporary India: Dilli Haat and Dastkari Haat Samiti's crafts maps, TheJournal of Modern Craft, 6(1), 49–77.
Tawa, M. (2002). Place, country, chorography: Towards a kinesthetic and narrative practice of place. *Architectural Theory Review, 7*(2), 45–58.
Thirumaran, K., Dam, M. X., & Thirumaran, C. M. (2014). Integrating souvenirs with tourism development: Vietnam's challenges. *Tourism Planning & Development, 11*(1), 57–67.
Waysdorf, A., & Reijnders, S. (2016). Immersion, authenticity and the theme park as social space: Experiencing the Wizarding world of Harry potter. *International Journal of Cultural Studies*, 1–16.

Gunjan Saxena (Marketing) works at the University of Hull, Faculty of Business, Law and Politics. She has published extensively on rural tourism. Her current research focuses on rural tourism marketing and small enterprises.

Chapter 22
Factors Affecting Jordanian Consumers' Attitudes Towards Facebook Advertising: Case Study of Tourism

Dina Hesham Abu-Ghosh, Hani Al-Dmour, Ali Abdallah Alalwan, and Rand Hani Al-Dmour

Abstract This research aims to examine factors affecting Jordanian consumers' attitude towards Facebook advertising (entertainment, informativeness, irritation, credibility, peer influence and privacy concerns). In order to test the proposed conceptual framework, an online web-based survey was employed, and data was collected from 380 university students in Jordan. Simple linear regression and multiple regression analysis, using the Statistical Package for the Social Sciences (SPSS) version 17, were employed to analyse the collected data. Results showed that entertainment, informativeness, interactivity, credibility and privacy concerns have a direct positive effect on Jordanian consumers' attitude towards Facebook advertising in tourism. However, entertainment has the most significant effect, while credibility has the lowest significant effect. The study recommends tourism companies to take into consideration the importance of these variables when designing their ads on Facebook in order to be able to benefit from this huge new virtual world of marketing opportunities in an ethical way.

Keywords Jordan · Facebook · Advertising · Social media

D. H. Abu-Ghosh (✉) · H. Al-Dmour
Marketing Department, Business School, University of Jordan, Amman, Jordan

A. A. Alalwan
Amman University College for financial & administrative sciences, Al-Balqa' Applied University, Salt, Jordan

R. H. Al-Dmour
Management Information Systems Department, Business School, The University of Jordan, Amman, Jordan
e-mail: Rand.aldmour@ju.edu.jo

Y. K. Dwivedi et al. (eds.), *Emerging Markets from a Multidisciplinary Perspective*, Advances in Theory and Practice of Emerging Markets,
https://doi.org/10.1007/978-3-319-75013-2_22

22.1 Introduction

Social media has become an essential part of our everyday lives (Alalwan, Rana, Algharabat, & Tarhini, 2016; Alalwan, Rana, Dwivedi, & Algharabat, 2017; Plume, Dwivedi, & Slade, 2016).We are now posting information about ourselves, posting photos and sending messages for friends about events. By the same token, social media has changed the ways in which businesses interact and communicate with consumers. This is because social media enables people around the world to interact and share information about products and brands with each other in a much easier and effective way using electronic word of mouth (eWOM) in comparison with traditional communication tools (Dwivedi, Kapoor, & Chen, 2015; Dwivedi et al., 2016; Ismagilova, Dwivedi, Slade, & Williams, 2017; Mir & Zaheer, 2012). Social media is defined as 'a group of Internet-based applications that builds on the ideological and technological foundations of Web 2.0 and allows the creation and exchange of User Generated Content' (Kaplan & Hanlein, 2010). Facebook is the top social network on the web that has been developed very fast (Alryalat, Rana, Sarma, & Alzubi, 2016). It's a thriving beast of a social networking site on the web with over 1.65 billion monthly active users as of the first quarter of 2016 and over one billion that log on daily (Facebook, 2016). These numbers are growing every second especially in the tourism industry. Social media plays an important role to gain more customers' involvement and increases their purchase intention (Khuong & Huong, 2016).

Online advertising is essential and is a powerful element that propels the Internet economy today, subsidising many websites, services and social networking sites like Facebook (Bannister, Kiefer, & Nellums, 2013). Marketers have recognised this new potential way to reach customers directly in a personal and social environment and have thus been keen to advertise in this new medium (Kornias & Halalau, 2012). Facebook is considered as the most social network that is used in the field of online tourism because of its role in bringing agencies and tourists closer through photographs, videos, wall posts and surveys; it allows continuous and direct interactivity. Therefore, the digital environment is a 'requirement' to achieve better results in the tourism industry. Facebook advertisements allow users to target people by location, age, gender, job title, keyword, relationship status, workplace or college, and as a user selects their target audience, Facebook provides information on an approximate number of users that their targeting will cover (Curran, Graham, & Temple, 2011). All this information shows that social media and specifically Facebook would be a new and important tool for the advertisers to grab the consumers' attention in the tourism sector.

Many previous research studies have showed that attitude is one of the most important variables that measure the advertising response. Attitude can be defined as 'a person's consistently favourable or unfavourable evaluations, feelings, and tendencies toward an object or idea' (Kotler & Armstrong, 2012), whereas attitude towards advertising is defined as 'a learned predisposition to respond in a consistently favourable or unfavourable manner towards advertising in genera' (MacKenzie

& Lutz, 1989). Usually, people form attitudes towards advertising that influence their decision-making processes to purchase a particular product from an advertiser (Pyun, 2006). Furthermore, the most important way of understanding users and their perceptions and acceptance of advertising messages is by studying attitudes (Hadija, 2008). In order to understand the attitudes towards social networking advertising, it is necessary to examine the factors that affect attitudes towards the ads.

With the very strong impact of globalisation, digitalisation and social media, advertising is changing. Many companies and advertising role players are forced to implement new consumer and business models and apply innovative business strategies. Social media marketing has become a norm for most companies. Nowadays, the process of marketing is used through social media sites like Twitter, Facebook and YouTube. By utilising the social aspect of the web, social media marketing is able to connect and interact on a much more personalised and dynamic level than through traditional marketing (Naidoo, 2011). Also, there are a limited number of researches that discuss the importance of Facebook advertising and measure attitudes towards Facebook advertising, especially in the tourism sector. Previous studies have focused on the consumers' attitudes towards traditional advertising media, Internet advertising and mobile phone advertising.

Tourism, like other industries, always faces many challenges. Today, tourism is one of the largest and most diverse industries in the world. Due to the economic impacts of this industry, good management of the sector will generate great economic prosperity. However, there is not much knowledge on how tourism companies should use Facebook and even less on how they actually use it. There has been some research on how to use social media for marketing (Zamani, 2016). Furthermore, according to the literature of previous studies, most of the studies that were conducted previously on measuring the attitude towards Facebook advertising were conducted in the West; therefore, it is important to study the attitude towards Facebook advertising in Jordan. As such, the focus in this study lies in identifying the factors affecting the Jordanian consumers' attitudes towards tourism advertisements on Facebook.

The overall aim of this research is to propose a conceptual framework for testing the factors affecting the attitude of Jordanian consumers towards Facebook advertising in the tourism sector.

22.2 Theoretical Foundation

The social networking site (SNS) has become a significant component of people's daily lives, which can be described as a platform to build relations and share information among people (Xu, Ryan, Prybutok, & Wen, 2012). Therefore, the use of social networking sites has attained development dramatically as the users have gained friendships, new knowledge and businesses through these new methods of communication. Barnes and Lescault (2011) provided a definition to the social network service as the 'online social network promotes a link among people to easily communicate with persons who are available in their sites using the web as their interface'. Murray and Waller (2007) also defined social network sites as 'virtual communities for people interested in a particular subject or just to "hang out" together.' Moreover, Smith (2009) classifies social networking as a global phenomenon that is spreading around the world and becoming an important marketing tool. The growth of social networking sites (SNS) such as Facebook, LinkedIn, Twitter and Google Plus has changed the way users interact with businesses and has also captured the attention of organisations because they create business opportunities for both e-business and traditional companies (Xu et al., 2012).

Business organisations are placing their advertisements on Facebook in order to create awareness and influence the customers' buying behaviour. All of that is due to Facebook's popularity (Rehman, Ilyas, Nawaz, & Hyder, 2014). Also, we should not forget to mention that the social network has generated 17.08 billion US dollars in ad revenues. Advertising accounts for the vast majority of Facebook's revenue (Facebook, 2016).

Theoretically, there have been different models studying attitude towards the advertising construct (Ducoffe, 1996; Kornias & Halalau, 2012; MacKenzie & Lutz, 1989). For instance, MacKenzie and Lutz (1989) proposed their model by adding the credibility factor and suggested the importance of a trust and credibility factor in the creation of attitudes towards the ad. The Ducoffe (1996) model found that attitudes towards web advertising were directly dependent on advertising value and consisted of three different factors: entertainment, informativeness and irritation; this initial model suggested building the basis in the creation of attitudes towards an ad.

Credibility and consumer demographics were added to the Ducoffe (1996) model as a complement, because it offered an additional explanation of the attitude towards the advertising construct. Wang, Zhang, Choi and D'Eredita (2002) believed that there are more factors that may be used to distinguish the Internet environment from traditional media. Wang et al. (2002) also identified interactivity and consumer motives as additional dimensions to those proposed by Ducoffe (1996). Interestingly, Kornias and Halalau (2012) used both the Ducoffe (1996) model and the MacKenzie and Lutz (1989) model together to provide a greater foundation for understanding the attitude towards display advertising on Facebook.

In the present study, the attitude towards Facebook advertising is measured by Ducoffe's (1996) model and includes credibility, interactivity, peer influence and privacy concerns in the same conceptual model as it will be discussed in the following section.

22.3 Conceptual Model

The conceptual model (Fig. 22.1) is developed based on the literature review of online advertising, Facebook, social media, networking sites and attitude. Attitude is considered to be one of the key variables that research studies (e.g. Dwivedi et al.,

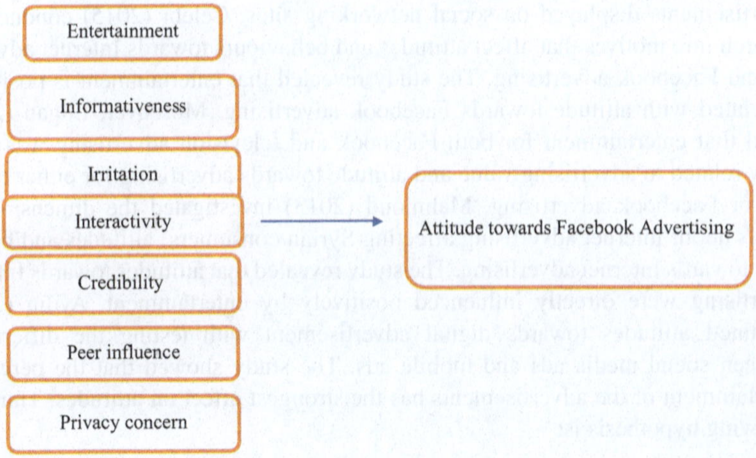

Fig. 22.1 Conceptual model (Sources: Adapted from Celebi, 2015; Deraz, 2016; Ducoffe, 1996; Ekstrom & Gustafsson, 2012; Kornias & Halalau, 2012; Yaakop, Anuar, & Omar, 2013)

2017; Dwivedi, Rana, Jeyaraj, Clement,& Williams, 2017; Rana, Dwivedi, Lal, Williams, & Clement, 2017; Rana, Dwivedi, Williams, & Weerakkody, 2016) tend to measure for understanding users' intention and behaviour towards information systems/information technology (IS/IT) adoption. In this study, we seek to measure the main factors that influence attitude towards Facebook advertising in the tourism sector which are entertainment, informativeness, irritation, credibility, interactivity, peer influence and privacy concerns, as explained below. Seven main variables are presented in Fig. 22.1: entertainment, informativeness, irritation, credibility, interactivity, peer influence and privacy concerns; these are proposed to have a direct influence on attitude towards Facebook advertising.

22.3.1 *Entertainment*

According to Taylor, Lewin, and Strutton (2011), the information that SNS advertising provided and how entertaining it was would result in affecting the acceptance of it. Furthermore, Wang and Sun (2010) considered the ability of advertisement to entertain as one of the major factors that may affect the effectiveness of advertising in creating an emotional link between a brand message and the consumer. Moreover, consumers like and prefer to see ads that have pleasurable and entertaining elements which consequently result in a favourable positive attitude towards advertising (Pollay & Mittal, 1993). Ma and Noichangkid (2011) showed that the entertainment of advertising indicates to the concept that the message of advertising should be amusing. Saxena and Khanna (2013) found that SNS advertisements which provided information and entertainment content result in accessing the value of advertisements displayed on social networking sites. Celebi (2015) conducted a research into motives that affect attitudes and behaviours towards Internet advertising and Facebook advertising. The study revealed that entertainment is positively associated with attitude towards Facebook advertising. Moreover, Logan (2013) found that entertainment for both Facebook and television advertising was positively related to advertising value and attitude towards advertising for either television or Facebook advertising. Mahmoud (2013) investigated the dimensions of beliefs about Internet advertising affecting Syrian consumers' attitudes and behaviours towards Internet advertising. The study revealed that attitudes towards Internet advertising were directly influenced positively by entertainment. Aydın (2016) examined attitudes towards digital advertisement with testing the differences between social media ads and mobile ads. The study showed that the perceived entertainment of the advertisements has the strongest effect on attitudes. Thus, the following hypothesis is:

H1 Entertainment could have a significant positive influence on the Jordanian consumers' attitudes towards Facebook advertising in tourism.

22.3.2 Informativeness

The information delivered is considered one of the important roles of advertising, which has a great effect on determining consumers' attitude towards advertising (Petrovici, Marinova, Marinov, & Lee, 2007). Based on the results of a study conducted by Van-Tien Dao et al. (2014), informativeness has a positive effect on consumers' perceived value of social media advertising, which results in positively influencing their online purchase intention. Interestingly, the informativeness factor has found to be the greatest influence on the behaviour of Facebook users that they have towards display advertising on Facebook (Algharabat, Alalwan, Rana, & Dwivedi, 2017; Kornias & Halalau, 2012). Li and Lai (2015) investigated the factors that affect the perceived value of advertisements in social networking sites. The results showed that the value of an SNS advertisement can be mainly influenced by informativeness. Moreover, Taylor et al. (2011) proved that there is a positive relationship between the informativeness factor and the attitudes of consumers towards SNS advertising. Thus, the following hypothesis is:

H2 The informativeness could have a significant positive influence on the Jordanian consumers' attitudes towards Facebook advertising in tourism.

22.3.3 Irritation

The consumers' feelings of irritation play a critical role in their perceptions towards the online advertisements (Rodgers & Thorson, 2000). Feelings of irritation would reduce if there is a trust on a brand which, in turn, leads to trust on brand posts such as ads (Deraz & Awuah, 2015). According to Logan (2013), an irritation variable did not predict the assessment of social networking advertisements. Conversely, Deraz and Awuah (2015) found that the irritation variable had a great negative effect on social networking advertisements. Saxena and Khanna (2012) asserted that the irritation value had a negative significant effect on the consumers' assessment of social networking advertisements. The ads are perceived as being irritating when people see advertising as interfering with their goal-oriented task for which they are present on Facebook (Kornias & Halalau, 2012). Consumers are likely to perceive advertising as undesirable and irritating when advertising uses techniques that confuse, annoy, offend, insult, or are excessively manipulative (Ogba, Saul, & Coates, 2012). In the same study, they suggested that creating a negative attitude towards the ad or brand is a result of advertising's intrusiveness which is described as a root for consumers' dissatisfaction. Thus, the following hypothesis is:

H3 Irritation could have a significant negative influence on the Jordanian consumers' attitudes towards Facebook advertising in tourism.

22.3.4 Credibility

Asn advertisements' credibility has been introduced as one of the critical variables for the assessment of social network advertisements (SNAs) (Deraz, Awuah, & Gebrekidan, 2015). That, however, has been contradicted by the findings of Yaakop et al. (2013); they have stated that the credibility of SNAs did not affect the consumers' assessment of SNAs. Moreover, indicated that the credibility of Facebook advertising is strong and positively related to the consumers' attitude towards Facebook advertising. As well as a number of different past-related advertising studies, they have identified a positive relationship between consumer perceptions of the credibility of an advertisement and consumer attitudes towards the advertisement (Van-Tien Dao et al., 2014). As well as, and according to Jung and Yoon (2015), privacy concerns were significantly associated with attitudes and behavioural intention towards social networking advertising on the most popular social network platform, Facebook. Also, a relevant previous research by Yaakop et al. (2013) demonstrated that privacy positively correlated with the dimension of attitude towards the advertisements on Facebook. Thus, the following hypothesis is:

H4 Credibility could have a significant positive influence on the Jordanian consumers' attitudes towards Facebook advertising in tourism.

22.3.5 Interactivity

Facebook is considered as an interactive media which enables users to use text, videos and images as interactive contents as ways to follow and share new products (Yaakop et al., 2013). Also, fans can interact with brand posts when they like it or write a comment on the brands timeline (De Vries, Gensler, & Leeflang, 2012). The interactivity value has been identified as a factor that contributes to consumers' attitude towards online advertisements (Wang et al., 2002), and this was confirmed by Yaakop et al. (2013) who found that perceived interactivity is one of the three factors that has positively influenced consumers' attitude towards advertising on Facebook. Also, El Ashmawy (2014) showed that interactivity of the advertisements has a significant positive relationship with attitudes towards advertising on Facebook. Thus, the following hypothesis is:

H5 Interactivity could have a significant positive influence on the Jordanian consumers' attitudes towards Facebook advertising in tourism.

22.3.6 *Peer Influence*

Taylor et al. (2011) suggested that peer influence is one of the important factors that had positively related to attitude towards social networking advertising (SNA). Jung and Yoon (2015) also found that peer influence had the most significant effect on attitude and behavioural intention at all types of SNA in a case of Facebook users. Bakshy, Eckles, Yan, and Rosenn (2012) explained how social advertising uses information about customers' peers to target ads and also to study their display which resulted in ad efficacy to be increased. Similarly, Iyengar (2009)) examined the impact of friends on users' purchases in the context of social media; there was a significant and positive influence of friends' purchasing activity among social media. Thus, the following hypothesis is:

H6 Peer influence could have a significant positive influence on the Jordanian consumers' attitudes towards Facebook advertising in tourism.

22.3.7 *Privacy Concerns*

Privacy concerns in SNS refer to the consumers' willingness to control the acquisition and subsequent use of information through online activity. Privacy and its related variables are important determinants of customer behaviour in the electronic market (Castañeda & Montoro, 2007). The online privacy discussion has existed since the creation of the Internet (Roberts, 2010). Privacy concerns are also defined as SNS user feelings such as worried about loss of privacy due to the set of information by SNS providers and/or SNS advertisers. When SNS users link privacy concerns with viewing SNS ads, they are likely to have a negative tendency towards SNA acceptance (Taylor et al., 2011). There is evidence that if a website has a privacy policy, individuals are more likely to share their personal data with the website (Cranor, 2000). On Facebook, it enables an access to user information and creates profile privacy settings in order to overcome the concern of privacy (Ragan, 2009).

According to Jung and Yoon (2015), privacy concerns were significantly associated with attitudes and behavioural intention towards social networking advertising on the most popular social network platform, Facebook. Also, relevant previous research such as Yaakop et al. (2013) demonstrated that privacy positively correlates with the dimension of attitude towards the advertisements on Facebook. According to the above arguments, and based on extant scholarly findings, the current research posits the following regarding advertisements in Facebook's tourism sector. Accordingly, this study hypothesised that:

H7 Privacy concerns have a significant positive influence on the Jordanian consumers' attitudes towards Facebook advertising in tourism.

22.4 Research Methodology

The target population of this study consisted of university students in Jordan at all levels (Bachelor's, Master's or PhD). This population was selected because university students have remarkably high Facebook memberships. Indeed, there are many examples from previous literature that have utilised a sample of university students to examine attitudes towards social networking advertising (Deraz, 2016; El Ashmawy, 2014; Kornias & Halalau, 2012; Yaakop et al., 2013). Therefore, a convenience sample of university students in Jordan was selected to collect the requested data. The final sample size was 380 university students from multiple universities in Jordan. Primary data was collected in this study by a web-based survey with a 5-point Likert scale questionnaire which was created through (www.surveymonkey.com).The questions that measured each variable in the questionnaire were obtained from previous related studies, and the questionnaire was adjudicated by several marketing professors in the University of Jordan. The source of items used in the questionnaire was also based on previous related studies, supported with literature reviews, and was proven to be reflective to the constructs that are being measured in this research (Table 22.1).

Table 22.1 Measurement of research constructs

Construct	Sources
Attitude towards advertising	Mahmoud (2013), Wang & Sun (2010)
Entertainment	Ducoffe (1996), Mahmoud (2013), Wang & Sun (2010)
Informativeness	Deraz (2016), Ducoffe (1996), Mahmoud (2013)
Irritation	Deraz (2016), Ducoffe (1996), Mahmoud (2013)
Credibility	El Ashmawy (2014)
Interactivity	El Ashmawy (2014), Yaakop et al. (2013)
Peer Influence	Jung (2015)
Privacy concerns	Jung (2015), Yaakop et al. (2013)

22.5 Results

The sample of respondents consisted of 56.3% males and 43.7% females. There were 263 respondents within the age group ranging from 18 to 25. All the respondents achieved university degrees: a Bachelor's degree (56.3%), a Master's degree (39.2%) and PhDs (4.5%). Additionally, the results showed that most of the respondents used their smartphone to log into Facebook; whereas, some of them used their own laptop (17.1%) and a few of them used their tablet to log into Facebook (5.8%).

Regarding the construct reliability, it can be seen from Table 22.2 that all values are greater than 0.60 which is statistically good since it is greater than the accepted percent (0.60) (Hair, Black, Babin, Anderson, & Tatham, 1998). The internal consistency reliability was very good and acceptable and can be considered to be reliable to achieve the research objectives.

In order to examine the study's hypotheses, the simple linear regression analysis was applied.

As seen in Table 22.3, entertainment can account for 33.6% of the variation of the attitude towards tourism featured in Facebook advertising. The table above also shows the probability of F-value which is significant at 0.05 as well as the t-calculated (13.827) which is higher than the t-tabulated (1.96). This indicates that entertainment has a direct effect on the attitude towards tourism seen in Facebook's advertisements, and this direct effect is positive with beta (0.580). Informativeness can account for 16.8% of the variation of the attitude towards tourism in Facebook advertising. Additionally, the table above shows the probability of F-value which is significant at 0.05, and t-calculated (8.744) is higher than t-tabulated (1.96). This indicates that informativeness has a direct effect on the attitude towards tourism in Facebook advertising, and this direct effect is positive with beta (0.41). Irritation can account for 17.6% of the variation of the attitude towards tourism in Facebook advertising. Additionally, the table above shows the probability of F-value which is significant at 0.05, and t-calculated (8.999) is higher than t-tabulated (1.96). This indicates that irritation has a direct effect on the attitude towards tourism featured in Facebook advertising, and this direct effect is negative with beta (−0.420). Interactivity can account for 29% of the variation of the attitude towards tourism in

Table 22.2 Cronbach's alpha coefficients

Study construct	Number of items	Cronbach's alpha values
Attitude towards advertising	5	0.788
Entertainment	4	0.864
Informativeness	4	0.702
Irritation	5	0.866
Credibility	5	0.851
Interactivity	6	0.802
Peer influence	4	0.780
Privacy concerns	3	0.749

Table 22.3 Results of the simple linear regression analysis

H#	R square	Std. error of the estimate	F-value	Sig	Standardised coefficient beta	T-value	P-value
H1: entertainment	0.336	3.62	191.189	0.000[a]	0.580	13.827	0.000[a]
H2: informativeness	0.168	4.053	76.462	0.000[a]	0.410	8.744	0.000[a]
H3: irritation	0.176	4.034	80.826	0.000[a]	−.420	−8.999	0.000[a]
H4: credibility	0.262	3.819	134.002	0.000[a]	0.512	11.576	0.000[a]
H5: interactivity	0.290	3.745	154.469	0.000[a]	0.539	12.429	0.000[a]
H6: peer influence	0.094	4.231	39.060	0.000[a]	0.306	6.250	0.000[a]
H7: privacy concerns	0.026	4.387	10.055	0.000[a]	0.161	3.171	0.002[a]

Facebook advertising. Additionally, the table above shows the probability of F-value which is significant at 0.05, and t-calculated (12.429) is higher than t-tabulated (1.96). This indicates that interactivity has a direct effect on the attitude towards tourism seen in Facebook advertising, and this direct effect is positive with beta (0.539).The peer influence can account for 9.4% of the variation of the attitude towards tourism in Facebook advertising. Additionally, the table above shows the probability of F-value which is significant at 0.05, and t-calculated (6.250) is higher than t-tabulated (1.96). This indicates that peer influence has a direct effect on the attitude towards tourism shown in Facebook advertising, and this direct effect is positive with beta (.306). Privacy concerns can account for 2.6% of the variation of the attitude towards tourism presented in Facebook advertising. Additionally, the table above shows the probability of F-value which is significant at 0.05, and t-calculated (3.171) is higher than t-tabulated (1.96). This indicates that privacy concerns have a direct effect on the attitude towards tourism contained in Facebook advertising, and this direct effect is positive with beta (0.161).

22.6 Discussion

In this study, the researchers were trying to find out (1) which variables of the proposed model would most likely affect Jordanian consumers' attitudes towards tourism featured in Facebook advertising, (2) which variables would least affect their attitudes towards tourism in Facebook advertising and (3) which variables wouldn't affect their attitudes at all. Data was collected from university students in Jordan (Bachelor's, Master's and PhD students) through the survey instrument. This can be explained as young consumers are more technology-oriented and have more willingness to accept new forms of technology. The hypotheses were tested by simple linear regression analysis.

The results showed that all Facebook-related variables are supported. Accurately, entertainment, informativeness, credibility, interactivity, peer influence and privacy concerns have a positive relationship with attitudes towards Facebook advertising in tourism, while the irritation variable has a negative relationship. Moreover, when simple linear regression analyses were run between the independent variables and the dependent variable, which is the attitude towards tourism in Facebook advertising, all of the supported variables proved to be significant as shown in Table 22.3. The variable with the highest contribution to the variance in attitude towards the tourism ad was entertainment followed by interactivity; the variable with the least contribution was irritation.

The variable with the highest contribution to attitude towards the Facebook advertising in tourism was entertainment. This comes in conformity with the findings of previous researches (e.g. Alalwan, Dwivedi, & Rana, 2017; Celebi, 2015). These results indicate that entertainment value is an important variable when evaluating attitude towards advertising tourism in Facebook; thus it would immediately draw the consumers' attention. This means that entertainment value is crucial for the success of advertising tourism in Facebook. In this line, Ducoffe (1996) identifies entertainment value as a factor contributing to the consumers' evaluations of ad values and thus an attitude towards ads.

Interactivity is the second most significant variable in the attitude towards tourism being advertised in Facebook. This conforms to the results of Deraz (2016) who indicates that the interactivity value of SNAs is an important dimension of the assessment of SNAs which had the second highest positive relationship. This finding is also supported by Yaakop et al. (2013) who found interactivity was positively correlated with the dimension of attitude towards the advertisement on Facebook. The results of this study also indicate that the respondents were counted to interact with tourism featured in Facebook's advertisements. Also, this confirms the results of Ma and Noichangkid (2011) who indicate that interactivity positively correlates with attitude towards social media advertising.

The result also revealed that credibility, informativeness, peer influence and privacy concerns, respectively, have positive significant relationships with attitude towards tourism shown in Facebook advertising. This is confirmed by the findings of previous researches, such as Kornias and Halalau (2012) who revealed that credibility influences the attitudes towards display advertising by Facebook users. Likewise, El Ashmawy (2014) identified credibility as an important factor that has made a contribution to attitude towards Facebook advertising. However, this result contradicts the results of Yaakop et al. (2013) who stated that credibility had no effect on the consumers' perception towards SNAs.

Moreover, informativeness findings were supported by Deraz et al. (2015), Logan (2013) and Saxena and Khanna (2012). By the same token, peer influence conforms to the results of Jung (2015) who identified peer influence as having the most significant impact on attitude and behavioural intention across all types of SNA as well as Celebi (2015) who found that peer influence positively associated itself with attitudes towards Facebook advertising. Finally, privacy concerns' findings were also consistent with Yaakop et al. (2013) who found that privacy has a great effect on the attitudes towards advertising in Facebook. The variable with the least contribution and the least significance in attitude towards Facebook advertising is irritation which had the highest negative beta value (−0.420); this finding conforms with the results of El Ashmawy (2014) and Saxena and Khanna (2012) but is contradicted by the results of Deraz et al. (2015) and Logan (2013)) that irritation had no effect on the consumers' assessment of SNAs.

22.6.1 Theoretical Implications

The theoretical framework of this study has shown a good understanding of the factors that influence Jordanian consumers' attitude towards Facebook advertising in tourism. This is the first study, to the best of author's knowledge, that provides an examination of the attitude towards Facebook advertising in the tourism sector; previous studies have examined some of these factors but not all of them together; and it also measured its influence on SNS or Facebook advertising in general. Furthermore, the current research presents a model that has been examined in Jordan which makes a significant contribution to existing knowledge by enhancing our understanding of the factors that influence Jordanian consumers' attitude towards Facebook advertising in tourism.

22.6.2 Managerial Implications

The study findings provide important evidence for marketers and online advertisers in the tourism sector. It also helps them to reach their existing and potential customers easily; Facebook advertising can offer several advantages for tourism companies as it is easy and inexpensive. As mentioned in the discussion part, the most significant variable for the consumer is entertainment; consumers are more likely to create a favourable attitude towards an ad when the content that is delivered through advertising is entertaining. Accordingly, marketers have to provide amusing techniques of advertising in order to entertain more users and make them feel that the ads are not boring. Interactivity is the second important and significant variable; Facebook in general offers simple ways to let people interact with each other, such as sending private messages, writing on the wall, sharing photos and videos and the like and/or comment on features. Marketers have to know that through Facebook advertisements, they communicate with their consumers without any barriers, so they have to focus on these features in the design of Facebook advertising.

According to the study's findings, credibility is the third factor for the consumers. Thus, marketers have to provide the consumers with credible and trustworthy information on which the consumer can depend. Therefore, the tourist companies who would like to adopt such a marketing strategy must first strengthen and develop their brand image and position themselves in the minds of their consumers. The fourth important factor that has to be considered by marketers is informativeness; the results show that consumers consider Facebook as a good source of information. Thus, marketers have to be cautious about the information they send over Facebook ads, and this information has to be checked and updated regularly.

The fifth important and significant factor is peer influence. When users join Facebook advertising because of a recommendation, a comment or feedback from friends, they are more likely to have a favourable attitude towards Facebook advertising. Marketers have to pay more attention about this influential factor. The sixth factor is privacy concerns. When users feel secure in providing personal information to online advertisers, they will have more favourable attitude towards Facebook advertising. Marketers always have to make consumers feel secure when they provide personal and sensitive information to Facebook. The least factor that has to be seriously taken into consideration by Facebook is irritation. Therefore, marketers should know that when they advertise on Facebook, its users are as annoyed as they are by the traditional ways of advertising.

22.7 Research Limitations and Future Directions

The study has several limitations, which proposes some guidance for future researches. First, the study examined factors that influenced an attitude towards Facebook advertising in tourism. Therefore, the findings of this study cannot be generalised on other social media platforms. Thus, the most possible expansion for this study would be to extend the investigations of this research to include social media networks other than Facebook, in order to be able to generalise the results on other social media networks. Second, the authors depended on a questionnaire (quantitative method) as the only method of collecting data; individuals may read differently into each question, and their answer was based on their understanding of the question. Accordingly, future researches should be qualitative and developing a new factor that can influence attitude towards Facebook advertising. Third, the study was conducted in Jordan, which means that the findings of this research cannot be generalised on all users, since factors affecting attitude towards Facebook advertising may vary from one culture to another. Thus, further researches must take place in other countries to generalise the results. Hence, this study model should be conducted in countries other than Jordan to be able to generalise the results, since factors influencing attitude towards Facebook advertising may vary from one country to another. Fourth, the study focuses on the tourism sector, so the authors cannot generalise the findings of this study to other sectors such as fast food, fashion, education and healthcare. Therefore, another expansion would be to examine factors influencing attitude towards Facebook advertising in different sectors. Finally, the study sample only included university students from different educational levels (Bachelor's, Master's, and PhDs).They are well-educated users, and most respondents from the study sample were young (69.2% between 18 and 25 years of age). This means that the results of the study cannot be fully generalised on older and less educated users. Consequently, further research must be done on diverse categories of users in order to get a better understanding of the attitude towards Facebook advertising in tourism. Hence, another expansion would be to examine the research hypotheses on different categories of users in Jordan who are older and/ or less educated to be able to understand more professionally the users' attitude towards Facebook advertising.

References

Alalwan, A. A., Rana, N. P., Dwivedi, Y. K., & Algharabat, R. S. (2017). Social Media in Marketing: A Review and Analysis of the Existing Literature. *Telematics and Informatics*. https://doi.org/10.1016/j.tele.2017.05.008

Alalwan, A. A., Rana, N. P., Algharabat, R., & Tarhini, A. (2016). A systematic review of extant literature in social media in the marketing perspective. In *Conference on e-Business, e-Services and e-Society* (pp. 79–89). Springer International Publishing. Swansea, UK

Alalwan, A. A., Dwivedi, Y. K., & Rana, N. P. (2017). Factors influencing adoption of mobile banking by Jordanian bank customers: Extending UTAUT2 with trust. *International Journal of Information Management, 37*(3), 99–110.

Algharabat, R., Alalwan, A. A., Rana, N. P., & Dwivedi, Y. K. (2017). Three dimensional product presentation quality antecedents and their consequences for online retailers: The moderating role of virtual product experience. *Journal of Retailing and Consumer Services, 36*, 203–217. Chicago.

Alryalat, M.A.A., Rana, N.P., Sarma, H.K.D., & Alzubi, Z.A. (2016). An empirical study of facebook adoption among young adults in a North-Eastern State of India: Validation of extended technology acceptance model (TAM). I3E2016, Swansea University, UK.

Aydın, G. (2016). Attitudes towards digital advertisements: Testing differences between social media ads and mobile ads. *International Journal of Research in Business Studies and Management, 3*(2), 1–11.

Bakshy, E., Eckles, D., Yan, R., & Rosenn, I. (2012). Social influence in social advertising: Evidence from field experiments. In *Proceedings of the 13th ACM Conference on Electronic Commerce* (pp. 146–161). ACM.

Bannister, A., Kiefer, J., & Nellums, J. (2013). College students' perceptions of and behaviors regarding Facebook© advertising: An exploratory study. *The Catalyst, 3*(1), 2.

Barnes, N. G., & Lescault, A. M. (2011). *Social media adoption soars as higher-ed experiments and reevaluates its use of new communications tools*. North Dartmouth, MA: Center for Marketing Research. University of Massachusetts Dartmouth.

Castañeda, J. A., & Montoro, F. J. (2007). The effect of Internet general privacy concern on customer behavior. *Electronic Commerce Research, 7*(2), 117–141.

Celebi, S. I. (2015). How do motives affect attitudes and behaviors toward internet advertising and Facebook advertising? *Computers in Human Behavior 51*, 312–324

Cranor, J. R. (2000). Beyond concern: understanding net users' attitudes about online privacy. In *The internet upheaval: Raising questions, seeking answers in communication policy* (pp. 47–70). Cambridge, MA: The MIT Press.

Curran, K., Graham, S., & Temple, C. (2011). Advertising on Facebook. *International Journal of E-business Development, 1*(1), 26–33.

De Vries, L., Gensler, S., & Leeflang, P. S. (2012). Popularity of brand posts on brand fan pages: An investigation of the effects of social media marketing. *Journal of Interactive Marketing, 26*(2), 83–91. Ducoffe (1995).

Deraz, H., & Awuah, G. B. (2015). The assessments of social networking advertisements; as perceived by brand communities' consumers. *International Journal of Current Research, 7*(8), 19787–19796.

Deraz, H., Awuah, G. B., & Gebrekidan, D. A. (2015). *Assessing the value of social network sites' advertisements* (pp. 89–101). In The Third International Conference on E-Technologies and Business on the Web, Paris, France 2015.

Deraz, H. (2016). *Assessments of advertisements on social networking sites.* PhD diss., Halmstad University Press.

Ducoffe, R. H. (1996). Advertising value and advertising on the web. *Journal of advertising research, 36*(5), 21–21.

Ducoffe, R. H. (1996). Advertising value and advertising the web. *Journal of Advertising Research, 36*(5), 21–35.

Dwivedi, Y. K., Rana, N. P., Janssen, M., Lal, B., Williams, M. D., & Clement, M. (2017). An empirical validation of a unified model of electronic government adoption (UMEGA). *Government Information Quarterly.* https://doi.org/10.1016/j.giq.2017.03.001

Dwivedi, Y. K., Rana, N. P., Jeyaraj, A., Clement, M., & Williams, M. D. (2017). Re-examining the unified theory of acceptance and use of technology (UTAUT): Towards a revised theoretical model. *Information Systems Frontiers.* https://doi.org/10.1007/s10796-017-9774-y

Dwivedi, Y. K., Mäntymäki, M., Ravishankar, M. N., Janssen, M., Clement, M., Slade, E. L., Rana, N. P., Al-Sharhan, S., & Simintiras, A. C. (Eds.) (2016). Social media: The good, the bad, and the ugly: 15th IFIP WG 6.11 Conference on e-Business, e-Services, and e-Society, I3E 2016, Swansea, UK, September 13–15, 2016, Proceedings (Vol. 9844). Springer. URL: http://www.springer.com/gb/book/9783319452333

Dwivedi, Y. K., Kapoor, K. K., & Chen, H. (2015). Social media marketing and advertising. *The Marketing Review, 15*(3), 289–309.

Ekstrom, A., & Gustafsson, N. (2012). Consumers' attitudes towards printed green advertising. Master thesis, Jonkoping University, Sweden., pp.18–24.

El Ashmawy, M. (2014). Measuring the University Students' Attitude toward Facebook Advertising (Doctoral dissertation), Arab Academy for Science.

Facebook. (2016). Available at: http://www.statista.com/statistics/264810/number-of-monthly-active-facebook-users-worldwide/.

Hadija, Z. (2008). *Perceptions of advertising in online social networks: In-depth interviews.* The Rochester Institute of Technology, Department of Communication, College of Liberal Arts.

Hair, J. F., Black, W. C., Babin, B. J., Anderson, R. E., & Tatham, R. L. (1998). Multivariate data analysis (Vol. 5, No. 3, pp. 207–219). Upper Saddle River, NJ: Prentice hall.

Ismagilova, E., Dwivedi, Y. K., Slade, E. L., & Williams, M. D. (2017). *Electronic word of mouth (eWOM) in the marketing context: A state of the art analysis and future directions.* Springer International Publishing. Inggris Available at http://www.springer.com/us/book/9783319524580

Jung, S. W. (2015). Factors affecting attitudes and behavioural intention towards social networking advertising: A case of Facebook users in South Korea. *International Journal of Advertising, 36*(2), 248–258.

Jung, H. S., & Yoon, H. H. (2015). The impact of employees' positive psychological capital on job satisfaction and organizational citizenship behaviors in the hotel. *International Journal of Contemporary Hospitality Management, 27*(6), 1135–1156.

Kaplan, A. M., & Hanlein, M. (2010). Users of the world, unite! The challenges and opportunities of social media. *Busiss Horizons, 53*(1), 59–68.

Kelty Logan, (2013) And now a word from our sponsor: Do consumers perceive advertising on traditional television and online streaming video differently?. Journal of Marketing Communications 19 (4):258-276

Khuong, M. N., & Huong, T. T. (2016). The Influence of social media marketing on Vietnamese traveller's purchase intention in tourism industry in Ho Chi Minh City. *Journal of Economics, Business and Management, 4*(4), 280–285.

Kornias, G. and Halalau, R. (2012). Factors influencing users' attitude towards display advertising on Facebook.

Kotler, P., & Armstrong, G. (2012). *Principles of marketing* (15th global ed.). Pearson.

Li, J., & Lai, J. (2015). Identifying factors affecting value of social network advertising. *Advanced Science and Technology Letters, 120*, 843–849.

Logan, K. (2013). And now a word from our sponsor: Do consumers perceive advertising on traditional television and online streaming video differently? *Journal of Marketing Communications, 19*(4), 258–276.

Ma, Y. and Noichangkid, P. (2011). Bored with Ads? A study investigating attitude towards social media advertising. Master's degree at UMEA University.

MacKenzie, S. B., & Lutz, R. J. (1989). An empirical examination of the structural antecedents of attitude toward the ad in an advertising pretesting context. *The Journal of Marketing*, 48–65.

Mahmoud, A. (2013). Syrian consumers: Beliefs, attitudes, and behavioral responses to Internet advertising. *Verslas: Teorijairpraktika, 14*(4), 297–307.

Mir, I., & Zaheer, A. (2012). Verification of social impact theory claims in social media context. *Journal of Internet banking and commerce, 17*(1), 1.

Murray, K. E., & Waller, R. (2007). Social networking goes abroad. *International Educator, 16*(3), 56.

Naidoo, T. (2011). The effectiveness of advertising through the social media in Gauteng. Doctoral dissertation, North-West University.

Ogba, I. E., Saul, N., & Coates, N. F. (2012). Predicting students' attitudes towards advertising on a university Virtual Learning Environment (VLE). *Active Learning in Higher Education, 13*(1), 63–75.

Petrovici, D., Marinova, S., Marinov, M., & Lee, N. (2007). Personal uses and perceived social and economic effects of advertising in Bulgaria and Romania. *International Marketing Review, 24*(5), 539–562.

Plume, C. J., Dwivedi, Y. K., & Slade, E. L. (2016). *Social media in the marketing context: A state of the art analysis and future directions* (1st ed.). Oxford, UK: Chandos Publishing Ltd. Available athttps://www.elsevier.com/books/social-media-in-the-marketing-context/plume/978-0-08-101754-8

Pollay, R. W., & Mittal, B. (1993). Here's the beef: factors, determinants, and segments in consumer criticism of advertising. *The Journal of Marketing, 27*(1993), 99–114

Pyun, D. Y. (2006). Proposed model of attitude toward advertising through sport. PhD thesis, Florida State University.

Ragan, S. (2009). Privacy issues plague Facebook users. *The Tech Herald*.

RaghuramIyengar, S. H. (2009). Do friends influence purchases in a social network? *Social Science Research Network, 27*(4), 2–29.

Rana, N. P., Dwivedi, Y. K., Lal, B., Williams, M. D., & Clement, M. (2017). Citizens' Adoption of an Electronic Government System: Toward a Unified View. *Information Systems Frontiers, 19*(3), 549–568.

Rana, N. P., Dwivedi, Y. K., Williams, M. D., & Weerakkody, V. (2016). Adoption of Online Public Grievance Redressal System in India: Toward Developing a Unified View. *Computers in Human Behavior, 59*, 265–282.

Rehman, F., Ilyas, M., Nawaz, T., & Hyder, S. (2014). How Facebook advertising affects buying behavior of young consumers: The moderating role of gender. *Academic Research International, 5*(4), 395–404.

Roberts, K. K. (2010). Privacy and perceptions: How Facebook advertising affects its users. *The Elon Journal of Undergraduate Research in Communications, 1*(1), 1–10.

Rodgers, S., & Thorson, E. (2000). The interactive advertising model: How users perceive and process online ads. *Journal of interactive advertising, 1*(1), 41–60.

Saxena, A., & Khanna, U. (2012). Advertising on social network sites: A structural equation modelling approach. *Vision: The Journal of Business Perspective, 17*(1), 17–25.

Saxena, A., & Khanna, U. (2013). Advertising on social network sites: A structural equation modelling approach. *Vision*, *17*(1), 17–25.

Smith, C. (2009). The social media revolution. *International. Journal of Marketing Research*, *51*(4), 559–561.

Taylor, D. G., Lewin, J. E., & Strutton, D. (2011). Friends, fans, and followers: Do ads work on social networks? *Journal of Advertising Research*, *51*(1), 258–275.

Van-Tien Dao, W., Nhat Hanh Le, A., Ming-Sung Cheng, J., & Chao Chen, D. (2014). Social media advertising value: The case of transitional economies in Southeast Asia. International Journal of Advertising, 33(2), 271–294. Deraz (2016).

Wang, C., Zhang, P., Choi, R., & D'Eredita, M. (2002). Understanding consumers' attitude toward advertising. AMCIS 2002 Proceedings, p.158.

Wang, Y., & Sun, S. (2010). Examining the role of beliefs and attitudes in online advertising: A comparison between the USA and Romania. *International Marketing Review*, *27*(1), 87–107.

www.surveymonkey.com

Xu, C., Ryan, S., Prybutok, V., & Wen, C. (2012). It is not for fun: An examination of social network site network. *Information & Management, 49(5),* 210–217.

Yaakop, A., Anuar, M. M., & Omar, K. (2013). Like it or not: Issue of credibility in Facebook advertising. *Asian Social Science*, *9*(3), 154.

Zamani. (2016). Examining the role of marketing models based on social networking in the tourism industry in Iran. *International Journal of Humanities and Cultural Studies*,4(2), 115–116.

Dina Hesham Abu-ghosh was born in Amman in 1989. She received a bachelor's degree in Marketing from Al-Hussein Bin Talal University and a Master's degree in Marketing from University of Jordan in Amman, Jordan. She has over 3 years of human resources experience and she currently works as hr. officer in Housing Bank for trade and finance (HBTF). She is interested in e-marketing and social media research.

Hani Al-Dmour 's background is in international marketing, and his particular research interests surround the export marketing behaviour and services marketing. He completed university education and received Bachelor's Degree in Business Management from the University of Jordan in 1983 and MBA degree from the University of Edinburgh in 1986. In 1985, he gained his PhD degree from the University of Sheffield in export marketing behaviour in 1993. In addition of being author of more than 80 scientific articles and 8 books, he is known as an expert in the fields of marketing and quality management of higher education institutions.

Ali Abdallah Alalwan is an assistant professor at Amman Collage of Banking and Finance at the Al-Balqa Applied University, Jordan. He holds a Bachelor's Degree in Marketing and an MBA/Marketing degree from the University of Jordan. He also holds a PhD from Swansea University. His current research interest is in the area of information systems, technology acceptance, electronic marketing, social media, Internet of things, self-service technologies, Internet banking and mobile banking. A part of his work has been published in some refereed journals including JFSM, JEIM, ISM and ***Dirasat*: *Administrative Sciences***.

Rand Hani Al-Dmour is an assistant professor at the Management Information System Department, School of Business at the University of Jordan. She holds a Bachelor's Degree in Management Information System and MBA/Management degree from the University of Jordan. She also holds a PhD degree from the Brunel University, London, UK. Her current research interest is in the area of information system, innovation, human resources information system and management information system.

Chapter 23
Factors Affecting Consumers' Pro-environmental Behaviours in Saudi Arabia

Hawazin Alzubaidi

Abstract Major environmental issues are considered to be partly rooted in consumer overconsumption. Although pro-environmental behaviours (PEBs) have been examined extensively in developed, Western countries, researchers recommend future studies to investigate consumers' PEBs in developing countries. Responding to these calls, this research contributes to the marketing literature from a non-Western perspective. Review of the concepts associated with consumers' PEBs highlights numerous factors connected with consumers' PEBs in Saudi Arabia including materialism, social norms, and perceived consumer effectiveness (PCE). The extensive review of relevant literature provides a useful first glimpse to inform marketing strategies harnessing PEBs in the emerging markets and offers a starting point for further qualitative and quantitative research.

Keywords Pro-environmental behaviour (PEBs) · Materialism · Social norms · Perceived consumer effectiveness (PCE) · Saudi Arabia

23.1 Introduction

Current patterns of unsustainable consumption mean growing demand for the natural resources of our planet. The recent economic growth in developing countries, triggered by technological revolution and globalisation, has led to market-driven growth in consumption patterns, leading in turn to unsustainable consumption (Biswas & Roy, 2016). A range of environmental issues that threaten the planet can be seen to have resulted from this, including climate change, air pollution, and scarcity of safe drinking water (Biswas & Roy, 2015; Steg & Vlek, 2009). This study

H. Alzubaidi (✉)
Emerging Markets Research Centre (EMaRC), School of Management,
Swansea University Bay Campus, Swansea, Wales, UK
e-mail: 807199@swansea.ac.uk

Y. K. Dwivedi et al. (eds.), *Emerging Markets from a Multidisciplinary Perspective*, Advances in Theory and Practice of Emerging Markets,
https://doi.org/10.1007/978-3-319-75013-2_23

aims to contribute to knowledge in terms of presenting an initial understanding of factors that play an important role in encouraging consumer pro-environmental behaviours (PEBs) in Saudi Arabia as a response to the call by several studies to achieve an understanding of consumers' PEBs from different cultural perspectives (Hurst, Dittmar, Bond, & Kasser, 2013; Strizhakova & Coulter, 2013). This paper presents a review of the relevant concepts associated with consumers' PEBs and related theories as well as discusses the importance of, and the need to, explore factors influencing PEBs in Saudi Arabia. The paper goes on to illustrate factors identified in the literature that influence Saudi consumers' intentions towards PEBs, including materialism, social norms, and perceived consumer effectiveness (PCE).

23.2 The Importance of Studying PEBs in Saudi Arabia

PEBs can be referred to as 'behaviour that harms the environment as little as possible, or even benefits the environment' (Steg & Vlek, 2009, p. 309). It is crucial to gain an understanding of concepts relevant to consumers' PEBs in developing countries to provide useful information for marketers to develop strategies to target these consumers (Y. Kim & Choi, 2005; Laroche, Bergeron, & Barbaro-Forleo, 2001; Mariadoss, Tansuhaj, & Mouri, 2011; Pickett-Baker & Ozaki, 2008). A thorough understanding of the literature through 62 academic publications, in journals or conference proceedings, concentrating on the antecedents of consumers' PEBs, indicates the importance of PEBs research. This section will now proceed to unpick the gaps and document limitations in existing research to determine possible avenues for future research in the context of PEBs.

Different cultures exist as a result of different social environments, norms, religions, regulations, and infrastructure. Far exceeding all other countries, Europe has been the subject of numerous PEBs studies (Bamberg, 2003; Bockarjova & Steg, 2014; J. I. De Groot & Steg, 2009; J. I. M. de Groot & Steg, 2008; De Leeuw, Valois, Ajzen, & Schmidt, 2015; Harland, Staats, & Wilke, 1999, Harland, Staats, & Wilke, 2007; Jansson, 2011; Moser, 2015; Noppers, Keizer, Bolderdijk, & Steg, 2014; Onwezen, Antonides, & Bartels, 2013; Vermeir & Verbeke, 2006), as well as the UK (Gatersleben, Murtagh, & Abrahamse, 2014; Ozaki & Sevastyanova, 2011; Pickett-Baker & Ozaki, 2008; Whitmarsh & O'Neill, 2010) and the USA (Gleim, Smith, Andrews, & Cronin, 2013; Kalamas, Cleveland, & Laroche, 2014; Kilbourne & Pickett, 2008; Y. Kim & Choi, 2005). China has also been the subject of PEBs research (Chan, 2001; Polonsky, Kilbourne, & Vocino, 2014; Thøgersen, de Barcellos, Perin, & Zhou, 2015) as well as Korea (Cho, Thyroff, Rapert, Park, & Lee, 2013; Lee, Kim, Kim, & Choi, 2014). However, there is only one paper focusing on Saudi Arabia in the context of PEBs (Abdul-Muhmin, 2007). Given that PEBs research has largely been limited to the location of the researchers, this is usually considered a limitation, thus suggestions for future research include presenting an understanding of the factors encouraging consumer PEBs in other geographical contexts.

The effect of constructs such as attitude, social norms, and PCE on behavioural intention to adopt PEBs among consumers has stood strong across different countries. For instance, almost every study including PCE as an influencing factor on consumers' PEBs has found it to have a significant effect (Pam Scholder Ellen, Wiener, & Cobb-Walgren, 1991; Gleim et al., 2013; Huang, 2016; Y. Kim & Choi, 2005). Furthermore, other than Harland et al. (1999); Kumar, Manrai, and Manrai (Kumar, Manrai, & Manrai, 2017); and Yazdanpanah and Forouzani (2015), all of the studies considering social influence as an antecedent of PEBs have found its effect to be significant in Europe and the UK (Bamberg, 2003; De Leeuw et al., 2015; Hynes & Wilson, 2016; Onwezen et al., 2013; Vermeir & Verbeke, 2006; Whitmarsh & O'Neill, 2010), demonstrating the validity of this relationship in a variety of countries. Research in Saudi Arabia and other emerging markets will uncover the generalisability of such findings in different contexts.

23.3 Theories Used to Underpin the Antecedence of Consumers PEBs

Analysis of the 62 articles related to the focus of this study revealed the theory of planned behaviour (TPB) had been adopted by several studies (Bamberg, 2003; Chan, 2001; De Leeuw et al., 2015; Hsu, Chang, & Yansritakul, 2017; Kalamas et al., 2014; Kumar et al., 2017; Moser, 2015; Polonsky et al., 2014; Whitmarsh & O'Neill, 2010; Yazdanpanah & Forouzani, 2015). Other studies used the norm activation theory (NAT) as the basis of a conceptual model of consumer PEBs (J. I. De Groot & Steg, 2009; Harland et al., 2007). Several studies combined both TPB and NAT (Bamberg & Möser, 2007; Gatersleben et al., 2014; Gleim et al., 2013; Onwezen et al., 2013).

According to the TPB (I Ajzen, 1991), it is necessary to understand individuals' intentions, attitudes, perceived behavioural control, and subjective norm, as they play a significant role in predicting and understanding individuals' behaviours (Icek Ajzen, 2011). The intention construct is central to the TPB. Intentions 'represent a person's motivation in the sense of her or his conscious plan or decision to exert effort to enact the behaviour' (Conner & Armitage, 1998, p. 1430). Attitudes towards the behaviour 'refer to the degree to which a person has a favourable or unfavourable evaluation or appraisal of the behaviour in question' (I Ajzen, 1991, p. 188). Attitudes hold individuals' behavioural beliefs in relation to any given behaviour (Icek Ajzen, 2011). Subjective norm is a social factor that refers to 'the perceived social pressure to perform or not to perform the behaviour' (I Ajzen, 1991, p.188). Finally, perceived behavioural control is defined as 'the perceived ease or difficulty of performing the behaviour and it is assumed to reflect past experience as well as anticipated impediments and obstacles' (I Ajzen, 1991, p.188). Evidence suggests that TPB has been used regularly in the field of PEBs research (Armitage & Conner, 2001; Bamberg, 2003; Bamberg & Möser, 2007), although the model accounts for only 27% and 39% of the variance in intention and behaviour (Armitage & Conner, 2001).

Offering a different perspective, NAT (Schwartz, 1977) proposes that personal norms predict individuals' behaviours and that both awareness of consequences and ascription of responsibility are antecedents of personal norms (J. I. De Groot & Steg, 2009). Personal norms are defined as self-expectations that are based on individuals' values. These are experienced as feelings of personal obligation to carry out a particular behaviour (Harland et al., 1999). According to NAT, personal norms can result in altruistic behaviours under two conditions: awareness of the consequences of individuals' behaviours on others and the environment and the ascription of responsibility, which is the individual's responsibility for the consequences of their behaviour (Hynes & Wilson, 2016).

The NAT considers the role of personal norms as an influence on PBEs (Hynes & Wilson, 2016), which are considered a form of altruistic behaviour whereby individuals give up personal benefits for the sake of the environment. NAT focuses on altruism or helping behaviours, so some studies integrate the model with variables from TPB, as NAT focuses on moral drivers of PBE, ignoring non-moral motivations. These non-moral factors, such as perceived behavioural control, could be captured by the use of TPB (Klöckner, 2013). Empirical evidence suggests that combining variables from both TPB and NAT could enhance understanding of individuals' PEBs (Bamberg & Möser, 2007; Harland et al., 1999; Klöckner, 2013; Park & Ha, 2014). As a result, NAT was extended in one particular study (Stern, 2000) that introduced the value-belief-norm theory (VBN) by building on the main assumptions of NAT. Both NAT and VBN are commonly used in the field of environmental psychology (Klöckner, 2013). NAT focuses only on the influencing values on individuals' PEBs and ignores cultural differences, social altruistic components, and egoistic components (Schultz & Zelezny, 1999). An extended model of NAT was needed to overcome its limitations; therefore the VBN theory was introduced. Stern (2000) has suggested that predicting PEBs could be difficult due to the broad range of influencing factors, and the VBN theory could better predict individuals' PEBs if combined with different values that could influence individual personal norms to do the behaviour (Stern, 2000). However, adding values such as altruistic, biospheric, and egoistic values, as well as personal norms, would have made the model more complex, so these were not considered in this study. With this analysis in mind, the TPB model was deemed most appropriate for this study, as the present research focuses on emphasising the influence of both internal and external factors on consumers' intentions to adopt PEBs in Saudi Arabia.

23.4 Relationships Previously Validated in Consumer PEBs Research

A multitude of relationships have been explored in the 62 articles relating to the adoption of PEBs. As some constructs were given different labels in different studies while retaining a similar meaning, these were merged and are used here under the most common name among the various studies, for example, the terms

Table 23.1 Frequently examined relationships in consumers PEBs research

Independent variable	Dependent variable	Significant	Not significant
Attitudes	Intentions towards PEBs	Bamberg (2003), Bamberg & Möser (2007), Chan (2001), Cho et al. (2013), De Leeuw et al. (2015), Fransson & Garling (1999), Gatersleben et al. (2014), Harland et al. (1999), Hsu et al. (2017), Klöckner (2013), Kumar et al. (2017), Nguyen, lobo, & Greenland (2016), Vermeir & Verbeke (2006), Whitmarsh & O'Neill (2010), Yazdanpanah & Forouzani (2015)	–
Intentions	PEBs	(Bamberg, 2003; Bamberg & Möser, 2007; Chan, 2001; De Leeuw et al., 2015; Fransson & Garling, 1999; Gatersleben et al., 2014; Gleim et al., 2013; Harland et al., 1999; Klöckner, 2013; Kumar et al., 2017; Lee et al., 2014; Minton & Rose, 1997; Nguyen et al., 2016; Onwezen et al., 2013; Polonsky et al., 2014; Vermeir & Verbeke, 2006; Whitmarsh & O'Neill, 2010)	–
Subjective norms	Intentions towards PEBs	(Bamberg, 2003; De Leeuw et al., 2015; Gatersleben et al., 2014; Gleim et al., 2013; Hsu et al., 2017; Hynes & Wilson, 2016; Klöckner, 2013; Minton & Rose, 1997; Nguyen et al., 2016; Onwezen et al., 2013; Vermeir & Verbeke, 2006; Whitmarsh & O'Neill, 2010)	(Harland et al., 1999; Kumar et al., 2017; Yazdanpanah & Forouzani, 2015)
PCE	PEBs	(P. S. Ellen et al., 1991; Huang, 2016; Kim, Jeong, & Hwang, 2013; Y. Kim & Choi, 2005; McCarty & Shrum, 2001; Straughan & Roberts, 1999)	–
PCE	Intentions towards PEBs	(Antonetti & Maklan, 2014; Bockarjova & Steg, 2014; Cho et al., 2013; Gleim et al., 2013; Harland et al., 1999; Y. Kim, 2011; Lee et al., 2014; Vermeir & Verbeke, 2006)	–
Materialism	PEBs	(Banerjee & McKeage, 1994; Dermody, Hanmer-Lloyd, Koenig-Lewis, & Zhao, 2015; Hurst et al., 2013; Hynes & Wilson, 2016)	–

'pro-environmental behaviours', 'pro-environmental purchasing', 'green consumption behaviour', 'environmentally conscious behaviour', and 'environmentally responsible behaviour' are grouped under the umbrella term pro-environmental behaviours. 'Subjective norm', 'social norms', and 'social influence' are all presenting the same construct. Also, the construct 'perceived self-efficacy' was found under different names such as 'self-efficacy', 'perceived consumer effectiveness', and 'locus of control'. Table 23.1 documents the most examined relationships in the field of PEBs, highlighting where these have been reported as significant or not significant.

Table 23.1 shows that among previous studies on PEBs, several constructs have been suggested as factors influencing consumers' PEBs, including attitudes (Bamberg, 2003; Bamberg & Möser, 2007; De Leeuw et al., 2015; Gatersleben et al., 2014; Harland et al., 1999; Hsu et al., 2017; Kumar et al., 2017; Vermeir & Verbeke, 2006; Whitmarsh & O'Neill, 2010), materialism (Kilbourne & Pickett, 2008; Polonsky et al., 2014), social norms (Bamberg, 2003; De Leeuw et al., 2015; Hynes & Wilson, 2016), and PCE (Antonetti & Maklan, 2014; Bockarjova & Steg, 2014; Cho et al., 2013; Gleim et al., 2013; Harland et al., 1999; Huang, 2016; Y. Kim, 2011; Lee et al., 2014; Vermeir & Verbeke, 2006). This study considers factors that might be related to consumers' PEBs in Saudi Arabia based on the TPB, as this theory is more related to the most influential factors suggested in Table 23.1. The following three subsections discuss each factor in more detail.

23.4.1 Materialism

Materialism is often suggested in the literature as an influential factor affecting consumers in the direction of higher consumption patterns (Gatersleben, White, Abrahamse, Jackson, & Uzzell, 2010; Hurst et al., 2013; Kilbourne & Pickett, 2008). Materialism is defined as a value system that determines individual happiness and influences behaviour (Marsha L Richins, 2004). On the other hand, Belk (1984) defined materialism as a set of personality traits related to consumers' obsession for owning objects. According to Belk (1984), materialism includes possessions, non-generosity, and envy. Possessions refer to the relationship between individuals and objects after purchasing; non-generosity refers to individuals' unwillingness to share items with others; envy is based on self-concern over concern for others. It is argued that consumers with these personality traits exercise greater control over owning and borrowing goods, and they experience a fear of losing their possessions (Belk, 1984).

The current research adopted Richins and Dawson's (1992) conceptualisation of materialism, whereby consumers with highly materialistic values are more likely to purchase products, as materialism is considered as a factor contributing to higher consumption, which potentially conflicts with the notion of environmental consumption (Banerjee & McKeage, 1994; Hurst et al., 2013; Hynes & Wilson, 2016; Kilbourne & Pickett, 2008; Polonsky et al., 2014). Consumers who acquire satisfaction and happiness by acquisition and consumption are more self-centred and less likely to be fulfilled by engaging in environmental activities (Kilbourne & Pickett, 2008; Polonsky et al., 2014). It has been found that consumers with highly materialistic values purchase products in search of a sense of identity, happiness, self-image, and social recognition or status (Nepomuceno & Laroche, 2015; Marsha L Richins, 2004; M. L. Richins & Dawson, 1992; Tsang, Carpenter, Roberts, Frisch, & Carlisle, 2014; Ward & Wackman, 1971). Materialistic values are growing in developing countries as consumers imitate patterns of Western consumption and lifestyles (Kilbourne & Pickett, 2008). It is argued that individuals in developing countries experience higher levels of materialistic values because of the rapid economic growth and social media activities experienced in those nations (Ger & Belk, 1996; Kasser, Ryan, Couchman, & Sheldon, 2004; Strizhakova & Coulter, 2013). Thus, several studies confirmed the negative influence of materialism on individuals' PEBs (Banerjee & McKeage, 1994; Hurst et al., 2013; Hynes & Wilson, 2016; Kilbourne & Pickett, 2008; Polonsky et al., 2014).

However, some inconsistencies are reported in the literature, suggesting that materialism may be considered differently by consumers in developing countries. It is confirmed that there is a positive influence of materialism on individuals' PEBs, suggesting that individuals may focus on the idea of being 'green' as a new trend, which has encouraged individuals to develop PEBs (Strizhakova & Coulter, 2013). Consumers with highly materialistic values may purchase products to display their status and such status could be gained by the use of environmentally friendly products (Martin & Schouten, 2012). These consumers are generally concerned about social rejection and usually define themselves by what they own. In addition, more materialistic consumers are motivated to consume based on judgement from others (Strizhakova & Coulter, 2013). Taking the above into consideration and following the majority of previous literature, the following can be hypothesised:

H1 Materialism has a negative impact on consumers' PEBs.

23.4.2 Social Norms

'Social norms' refers to 'the perceived social pressure to perform or not to perform [a] behaviour' (Ajzen, 1991, p.188). In collectivist cultures, individual behaviours are usually driven by social norms (Leonidou, Leonidou, & Kvasova, 2010). It has been argued that individuals in collectivist cultures could be influenced by social comparison and the imitation of peers and reference groups, which causes people to focus on their decision-making process in reference to the behaviours of others (Janssen & Jager, 2002). Social influence is therefore considered a critical factor in changing purchasing patterns that could influence consumers to adopt PEBs in predominantly collectivist cultures (Gleim et al., 2013; Hynes & Wilson, 2016; Vermeir & Verbeke, 2006). Saudi behaviours are heavily driven by social norms that emphasise sharing resources with others such as families and friends (Al-Kandari & Gaither, 2011); therefore it can be argued that individuals in collectivistic cultures are more likely to develop positive environmental attitudes because they show care for their relationships with others, and they would rather give priority to the group rather than themselves (Al-Kandari & Gaither, 2011; Laroche et al., 2001). Collectivism stresses group goals over personal ones and has a positive effect on consumers' PEBs (McCarty & Shrum, 2001). Several studies have concluded that subjective norms have a significant effect of individuals' PEBs (Bamberg, 2003; De Leeuw et al., 2015; Hynes & Wilson, 2016; Klöckner, 2013; Onwezen et al., 2013; Vermeir & Verbeke, 2006; Whitmarsh & O'Neill, 2010). Thus, it is hypothesised that:

H2 Social norms have a positive influence on individuals' PEBs.

23.4.3 *Perceived Consumer Effectiveness (PCE)*

PCE is defined 'as a domain-specific belief that the efforts of an individual can make a difference in the solution to a problem' (P. S. Ellen et al., 1991, p. 103), which 'examine[s] the extent to which any one consumer can have an impact on the environment' (Gilg, Barr, & Ford, 2005, p.484). To motivate behavioural changes, consumers need to be convinced that their behaviours have an influence on the environment and an impact on solving environmental issues. It is believed that PCE can significantly contribute to predicting individuals' environmental behaviours (P. S. Ellen et al., 1991). Consumers with a strong belief that their environmentally conscious behaviours can have a positive effect of the environment will be more likely to engage in PEBs. It has been argued that if individuals believe that environmental issues must be solved, this belief must influence their actual behaviour. Therefore, understanding consumers' PCE might be useful for predicting consumers' PEBs (Huang, 2016; Y. Kim & Choi, 2005). Several studies have observed a significant effect of PCE on individuals' PEBs (Bockarjova & Steg, 2014; Cho et al., 2013; P. S. Ellen et al., 1991; Gilg et al., 2005; Gleim et al., 2013; Kalamas et al., 2014; Y. Kim & Choi, 2005; McCarty & Shrum, 2001; Vermeir & Verbeke, 2006). Therefore, the following can be hypothesised:

H3 PCE has a positive influence on individuals' PEBs.

23.5 Conclusion

Substantial growth in consumption has followed the recent general economic growth triggered by technological revolution, and globalisation has led to market-driven growth in consumption patterns in the Middle East. This conflicts with the notion of sustainable development and requires alternative consumption patterns to decrease depletion of the resources of our planet. This study has provided insight into the key factors that could influence consumers' PEBs in Saudi Arabia, and identified current gaps in knowledge pertaining to their adoption, and has highlighted the most influential factors underlying PEBs in order to provide further information for future studies. For this purpose, more qualitative and quantitative studies are needed that could use the variables viewed and examine their influence on consumers' intentions towards PEBs in the emerging markets.

Acknowledgement Grateful thanks go to my supervisors, Dr. Emma Slade and Professor Yogesh K. Dwivedi, who kindly gave me their time to make this chapter possible. I am really thankful for their valuable guidance, feedback, and advice that helped me in improving the content of this chapter.

References

Abdul-Muhmin, A. G. (2007). Explaining consumers' willingness to be environmentally friendly. *International Journal of Consumer Studies, 31*(3), 237–247.

Ajzen, I. (1991). *The theory of planned behavior organizational behavior and human decision processes: Milton Keynes*. England: Open University Press.

Ajzen, I. (2011). Theory of planned behavior. *Handb Theor Soc Psychol Vol One, 1*(2011), 438.

Al-Kandari, A., & Gaither, T. K. (2011). Arabs, the west and public relations: A critical/cultural study of Arab cultural values. *Public Relations Review, 37*(3), 266–273. https://doi.org/10.1016/j.pubrev.2011.04.002

Antonetti, P., & Maklan, S. (2014). Feelings that make a difference: How guilt and pride convince consumers of the effectiveness of sustainable consumption choices. *Journal of Business Ethics, 124*(1), 117–134.

Armitage, C. J., & Conner, M. (2001). Efficacy of the theory of planned behaviour: A meta-analytic review. *British Journal of Social Psychology, 40*, 471–499. https://doi.org/10.1348/014466601164939

Bamberg, S. (2003). How does environmental concern influence specific environmentally related behaviors? A new answer to an old question. *Journal of Environmental Psychology, 23*(1), 21–32.

Bamberg, S., & Möser, G. (2007). Twenty years after Hines, Hungerford, and Tomera: A new meta-analysis of psycho-social determinants of pro-environmental behaviour. *Journal of Environmental Psychology, 27*(1), 14–25.

Banerjee, B., & McKeage, K. (1994). How green is my value – exploring the relationship between environmentalism and materialism. In C. T. Allen & D. R. John (Eds.), *Advances in consumer research., Vol Xxi* (Vol. 21, pp. 147–152).

Belk, R. W. (1984). Three scales to measure constructs related to materialism: Reliability, validity, and relationships to measures of happiness. *Advances in Consumer Research, 11*(1) 291–297.

Biswas, A., & Roy, M. (2015). Green products: An exploratory study on the consumer behaviour in emerging economies of the east. *Journal of Cleaner Production, 87*, 463–468.

Biswas, A., & Roy, M. (2016). A Study of Consumers' Willingness to Pay for Green Products. *Journal of Advanced Management Science, 4*(3), 211–215.

Bockarjova, M., & Steg, L. (2014). Can protection motivation theory predict pro-environmental behavior? Explaining the adoption of electric vehicles in the Netherlands. *Global Environmental Change, 28*, 276–288.

Chan, R. Y. (2001). Determinants of Chinese consumers' green purchase behavior. *Psychology & Marketing, 18*(4), 389–413.

Cho, Y.-N., Thyroff, A., Rapert, M. I., Park, S.-Y., & Lee, H. J. (2013). To be or not to be green: Exploring individualism and collectivism as antecedents of environmental behavior. *Journal of Business Research, 66*(8), 1052–1059.

Conner, M., & Armitage, C. (1998). Extending the theory of planned behavior: A review and avenues for further research. *Journal of Applied social Psychology, 28*(15), 1429–1464.

De Groot, J. I., & Steg, L. (2009). Morality and prosocial behavior: The role of awareness, responsibility, and norms in the norm activation model. *The Journal of Social Psychology, 149*(4), 425–449.

de Groot, J. I. M., & Steg, L. (2008). Value orientations to explain beliefs related to environmental significant behavior - how to measure egoistic, altruistic, and biospheric value orientations. *Environment and Behavior, 40*(3), 330–354. https://doi.org/10.1177/0013916506297831

De Leeuw, A., Valois, P., Ajzen, I., & Schmidt, P. (2015). Using the theory of planned behavior to identify key beliefs underlying pro-environmental behavior in high-school students: Implications for educational interventions. *Journal of Environmental Psychology, 42*, 128–138.

Dermody, J., Hanmer-Lloyd, S., Koenig-Lewis, N., & Zhao, A. L. (2015). Advancing sustainable consumption in the UK and China: The mediating effect of pro-environmental self-identity. *Journal of Marketing Management, 31*(13–14), 1472–1502. https://doi.org/10.1080/0267257x.2015.1061039

Ellen, P. S., Wiener, J. L., & Cobb-Walgren, C. (1991). The role of perceived consumer effectiveness in motivating environmentally conscious behaviors. *Journal of Public Policy & Marketing, 10*(2), 102–117.
Fransson, N., & Garling, T. (1999). Environmental concern: Conceptual definitions, measurement methods, and research findings. *Journal of Environmental Psychology, 19*(4), 369–382. https://doi.org/10.1006/jevp.1999.0141
Gatersleben, B., Murtagh, N., & Abrahamse, W. (2014). Values, identity and pro-environmental behaviour. *Contemporary Social Science, 9*(4), 374–392.
Gatersleben, B., White, E., Abrahamse, W., Jackson, T., & Uzzell, D. (2010). Values and sustainable lifestyles. *Architectural Science Review, 53*(1), 37–50.
Ger, G., & Belk, R. W. (1996). Cross-cultural differences in materialism. *Journal of Economic Psychology, 17*(1), 55–77. https://doi.org/10.1016/0167-4870(95)00035-6
Gilg, A., Barr, S., & Ford, N. (2005). Green consumption or sustainable lifestyles? Identifying the sustainable consumer. *Futures, 37*(6), 481–504.
Gleim, M. R., Smith, J. S., Andrews, D., & Cronin, J. J. (2013). Against the green: A multi-method examination of the barriers to green consumption. *Journal of Retailing, 89*(1), 44–61.
Harland, P., Staats, H., & Wilke, H. A. (1999). Explaining proenvironmental intention and behavior by personal norms and the theory of planned behavior1. *Journal of Applied Social Psychology, 29*(12), 2505–2528.
Harland, P., Staats, H., & Wilke, H. A. (2007). Situational and personality factors as direct or personal norm mediated predictors of pro-environmental behavior: Questions derived from norm-activation theory. *Basic and Applied Social Psychology, 29*(4), 323–334.
Hsu, C.-L., Chang, C.-Y., & Yansritakul, C. (2017). Exploring purchase intention of green skincare products using the theory of planned behavior: Testing the moderating effects of country of origin and price sensitivity. *Journal of Retailing and Consumer Services, 34*, 145–152.
Huang, H. (2016). Media use, environmental beliefs, self-efficacy, and pro-environmental behavior. *Journal of Business Research, 69*(6), 2206–2212.
Hurst, M., Dittmar, H., Bond, R., & Kasser, T. (2013). The relationship between materialistic values and environmental attitudes and behaviors: A meta-analysis. *Journal of Environmental Psychology, 36*, 257–269. https://doi.org/10.1016/j.jenvp.2013.09.003
Hynes, N., & Wilson, J. (2016). I do it, but don't tell anyone! Personal values, personal and social norms: Can social media play a role in changing pro-environmental behaviours? *Technological Forecasting and Social Change, 111*, 349–359.
Janssen, M. A., & Jager, W. (2002). Stimulating diffusion of green products. *Journal of Evolutionary Economics, 12*(3), 283–306.
Jansson, J. (2011). Consumer eco-innovation adoption: Assessing attitudinal factors and perceived product characteristics. *Business Strategy and the Environment, 20*(3), 192–210.
Kalamas, M., Cleveland, M., & Laroche, M. (2014). Pro-environmental behaviors for thee but not for me: Green giants, green gods, and external environmental locus of control. *Journal of Business Research, 67*(2), 12–22.
Kasser, T., Ryan, R. M., Couchman, C. E., & Sheldon, K. M. (2004). Materialistic values: Their causes and consequences. *Psychology and consumer culture: The struggle for a good life in a materialistic world*, 11–28.
Kilbourne, W., & Pickett, G. (2008). How materialism affects environmental beliefs, concern, and environmentally responsible behavior. *Journal of Business Research, 61*(9), 885–893. https://doi.org/10.1016/j.jbusres.2007.09.016
Kim, S., Jeong, S.-H., & Hwang, Y. (2013). Predictors of pro-environmental behaviors of American and Korean students: The application of the theory of reasoned action and protection motivation theory. *Science Communication, 35*(2), 168–188.
Kim, Y. (2011). Understanding green purchase: The influence of collectivism, personal values and environmental attitudes, and the moderating effect of perceived consumer effectiveness. *Seoul Journal of Business, 17*(1), 65.
Kim, Y., & Choi, S. M. (2005). Antecedents of green purchase behavior: An examination of collectivism, environmental concern, and PCE. In G. Menon & A. R. Rao (Eds.), *Advances in consumer research., Vol 32* (Vol. 32, pp. 592–599).

Klöckner, C. A. (2013). A comprehensive model of the psychology of environmental behaviour—A meta-analysis. *Global Environmental Change, 23*(5), 1028–1038.

Kumar, B., Manrai, A. K., & Manrai, L. A. (2017). Purchasing behaviour for environmentally sustainable products: A conceptual framework and empirical study. *Journal of Retailing and Consumer Services, 34*, 1–9.

Laroche, M., Bergeron, J., & Barbaro-Forleo, G. (2001). Targeting consumers who are willing to pay more for environmentally friendly products. *Journal of Consumer Marketing, 18*(6), 503–520.

Lee, Y.-k., Kim, S., Kim, M.-s., & Choi, J.-g. (2014). Antecedents and interrelationships of three types of pro-environmental behavior. *Journal of Business Research, 67*(10), 2097–2105.

Leonidou, L. C., Leonidou, C. N., & Kvasova, O. (2010). Antecedents and outcomes of consumer environmentally friendly attitudes and behaviour. *Journal of Marketing Management, 26*(13–14), 1319–1344.

Mariadoss, B. J., Tansuhaj, P. S., & Mouri, N. (2011). Marketing capabilities and innovation-based strategies for environmental sustainability: An exploratory investigation of B2B firms. *Industrial Marketing Management, 40*(8), 1305–1318. https://doi.org/10.1016/j.indmarman.2011.10.006

Martin, D., & Schouten, J. (2012). *Sustainable marketing*. Boston, MA: Prentice Hall.

McCarty, J. A., & Shrum, L. (2001). The influence of individualism, collectivism, and locus of control on environmental beliefs and behavior. *Journal of Public Policy & Marketing, 20*(1), 93–104.

Minton, A. P., & Rose, R. L. (1997). The effects of environmental concern on environmentally friendly consumer behavior: An exploratory study. *Journal of Business Research, 40*(1), 37–48.

Moser, A. K. (2015). Thinking green, buying green? Drivers of pro-environmental purchasing behavior. *Journal of Consumer Marketing, 32*(3), 167–175.

Nepomuceno, M. V., & Laroche, M. (2015). The impact of materialism and anti-consumption lifestyles on personal debt and account balances. *Journal of Business Research, 68*(3), 654–664. https://doi.org/10.1016/j.jbusres.2014.08.006

Nguyen, T. N., Lobo, A., & Greenland, S. (2016). Pro-environmental purchase behaviour: The role of consumers' biospheric values. *Journal of Retailing and Consumer Services, 33*, 98–108.

Noppers, E. H., Keizer, K., Bolderdijk, J. W., & Steg, L. (2014). The adoption of sustainable innovations: Driven by symbolic and environmental motives. *Global Environmental Change, 25*, 52–62.

Onwezen, M. C., Antonides, G., & Bartels, J. (2013). The norm activation model: An exploration of the functions of anticipated pride and guilt in pro-environmental behaviour. *Journal of Economic Psychology, 39*, 141–153.

Ozaki, R., & Sevastyanova, K. (2011). Going hybrid: An analysis of consumer purchase motivations. *Energy Policy, 39*(5), 2217–2227.

Park, J., & Ha, S. (2014). Understanding consumer recycling behavior: Combining the theory of planned behavior and the norm activation model. *Family and Consumer Sciences Research Journal, 42*(3), 278–291.

Pickett-Baker, J., & Ozaki, R. (2008). Pro-environmental products: Marketing influence on consumer purchase decision. *Journal of Consumer Marketing, 25*(5), 281–293.

Polonsky, M., Kilbourne, W., & Vocino, A. (2014). Relationship between the dominant social paradigm, materialism and environmental behaviours in four Asian economies. *European Journal of Marketing, 48*(3/4), 522–551.

Richins, M. L. (2004). The material values scale: Measurement properties and development of a short form. *Journal of Consumer Research, 31*(1), 209–219.

Richins, M. L., & Dawson, S. (1992). A consumer values orientation for materialism and its measurement - scale development and validation. *Journal of Consumer Research, 19*(3), 303–316. https://doi.org/10.1086/209304

Schultz, P. W., & Zelezny, L. (1999). Values as predictors of environmental attitudes: Evidence for consistency across 14 countries. *Journal of Environmental Psychology, 19*(3), 255–265. Retrieved from <Go to ISI>://WOS:000083090200004.

Schwartz, S. (1977). Normative influences on altruism. *Advances in Experimental Social Psychology, 10*(1), 221–279.

Steg, L., & Vlek, C. (2009). Encouraging pro-environmental behaviour: An integrative review and research agenda. *Journal of Environmental Psychology, 29*(3), 309–317. https://doi.org/10.1016/j.jenvp.2008.10.004

Stern, P. C. (2000). New environmental theories: Toward a coherent theory of environmentally significant behavior. *Journal of Social Issues, 56*(3), 407–424.

Straughan, R. D., & Roberts, J. A. (1999). Environmental segmentation alternatives: A look at green consumer behavior in the new millennium. *Journal of Consumer Marketing, 16*(6), 558–575.

Strizhakova, Y., & Coulter, R. A. (2013). The "green" side of materialism in emerging BRIC and developed markets: The moderating role of global cultural identity. *International Journal of Research in Marketing, 30*(1), 69–82. https://doi.org/10.1016/j.ijresmar.2012.08.003

Thøgersen, J., de Barcellos, M. D., Perin, M. G., & Zhou, Y. (2015). Consumer buying motives and attitudes towards organic food in two emerging markets: China and Brazil. *International Marketing Review, 32*(3/4), 389–413.

Tsang, J. A., Carpenter, T. P., Roberts, J. A., Frisch, M. B., & Carlisle, R. D. (2014). Why are materialists less happy? The role of gratitude and need satisfaction in the relationship between materialism and life satisfaction. *Personality and Individual Differences, 64*, 62–66. https://doi.org/10.1016/j.paid.2014.02.009

Vermeir, I., & Verbeke, W. (2006). Sustainable food consumption: Exploring the consumer "attitude - behavioral intention" gap. *Journal of Agricultural & Environmental Ethics, 19*(2), 169–194. https://doi.org/10.1007/s10806-005-5485-3

Ward, S., & Wackman, D. (1971). Family and media influences on adolescent consumer learning. *American Behavioral Scientist, 14*(3), 415–427.

Whitmarsh, L., & O'Neill, S. (2010). Green identity, green living? The role of pro-environmental self-identity in determining consistency across diverse pro-environmental behaviours. *Journal of Environmental Psychology, 30*(3), 305–314.

Yazdanpanah, M., & Forouzani, M. (2015). Application of the theory of planned behaviour to predict Iranian students' intention to purchase organic food. *Journal of Cleaner Production, 107*, 342–352.

Hawazin Alzubaidi is a PhD student at Swansea Business School, Swansea University, UK. Her main research focuses on investigating the concepts associated with consumers' pro-environmental behaviours, with a specific focus on values, attitudes, and cultural factors.

Chapter 24
Do you Like to be an Aspirational Referee to Promote a Product? Act Like a Celebrity in Emerging Market

Mahmud A. Shareef, Vinod Kumar, Uma Kumar, and Mohammad Abdallah Ali Alryalat

Abstract Since in emerging market, social network like Facebook is a common platform to generate collective opinion as an opinion leader, viral advertisement promoted by any member and shared among peers of their network has potential contribution in shaping favorable attitude. This study is designed to understand attitude of members of social network to be persuaded by any promotional marketing-related messages in terms of its effectiveness and ability to pursue them to be motivated. Precisely, it is aimed to derive the factors which have an influence in perusing attitude toward any message generated, distributed, and shared among the members of a common social loop. Five interdependent factors, namely, message initiator (identity), message language (informality), message content (logic and counter logic), message entertainment (hedonic motivation), and message reliability (experience based), are constructed as the independent variables to understand attitude of members of social media toward any promotional message in an emerging market context.

Keywords Emerging market · Facebook · Viral marketing · Product promotion · Advertisement · Consumer attitude

---

M. A. Shareef (✉)
School of Business & Economics, North South University, Dhaka, Bangladesh
e-mail: mahmud.shareef@northsouth.edu

V. Kumar · U. Kumar
Sprott School of Business Carleton University, Ottawa, ON, Canada
e-mail: vinod_kumar@carleton.ca; uma_kumar@carleton.ca

M. A. A. Alryalat
Al-Balqa' Applied University, Salt, Jordan

Y. K. Dwivedi et al. (eds.), *Emerging Markets from a Multidisciplinary Perspective*, Advances in Theory and Practice of Emerging Markets,
https://doi.org/10.1007/978-3-319-75013-2_24

24.1 Introduction

From the conceptual understanding of the social identity theory (Tajfel & Turner, 1986), it can be referenced that consumers' perception of social association is an important motivation to perform group behavior in decision-making. Social affiliation helps to form group opinion for making decision to purchase. Consumers, as social members, collectively interact, pursue, cross-examine, and ultimately develop a consensus decision that will be persuasive for them as the determinant of a favorable attitude. Hogg & Vaughan (2002) suggested that consumers having the consistent and compatible personality show a pattern of similar attitude and expect to develop a connected group in social behavior that represents the symbol of that group. Consequently, in recent phenomenon of virtual social network, any opinion generated among the members of a connected group is substantially shared as the collective peer opinion (Kim & Ko, 2012). This pattern of social media behavior ultimately creates the scope for creating an opinion leader similar to aspirational reference and engages to be persuasive among group members (di Pietro & Pantano, 2012; Lee, Kim, & Kim, 2011; Schulze, Scholer, & Skiera, 2014).

When consumers purchase any product, selection of distribution channel depends on how they want to buy the product and what product they want to buy. Associated elements with how they want to buy the products are termed as service output demand (SOD). Like SOD, to receive product promotional information, members of social network are also concerned of how they want to receive the message. Therefore, source of generation and distribution of message about any product in a social network like Facebook among the members of a group is the classic root of either accepting or rejecting message (Akar & Topcu, 2011; Chu, 2011; Kim & Ko, 2012). Informal source like a peer of any group in a social network can be the most sensitive and widely accepted reference for promotional message of a product. Heuristically, streamlining consumers' favorable attitude toward a product through viral advertisement in any social network is enormously facilitated by the authentication of the message. In other words, it can be said that derogation of the message about product promotion largely depends on whether it is generated and passed on by any informal peer or formal advertising source (di Pietro & Pantano, 2012; Schulze et al., 2014; Shareef, Dwivedi, & Rana, 2015).

In social network like Facebook, for acceptance of viral marketing, source of marketing is an important criterion for the promotional effort to be successful (Hayes & King, 2014). And, for a connected group in social network, the source is naturally authenticated, hence likely to be cordially accepted if it is any member from them (Chu, 2011; Kim & Ko, 2012; Logan et al., 2012; di Pietro & Pantano, 2012; Schulze et al., 2014). This phenomenon has created a new marketing pattern through social network. Now, marketing companies while promoting a product through social network (like Facebook) do not need any external and formal aspirational reference as any peered member from the group can informally distribute the promotional message of the product among their connected members and that may have wide acceptance. So, it is a potential opportunity of any general members from any group of a social network to act like a traditional aspirational reference to promote a product through that network.

Researchers analyzing promotional marketing in social network (Lee et al., 2011; Taylor, Lewin, & Strutton, 2011) also acknowledged that in these network consumers' beliefs, perception, and communication pattern are significantly different from that of regular advertising media. Shedding light on the conceptual root of gratification theory (LaRose, Mastro, & Eastin, 2001) and media richness theory (Daft & Lengel, 1986), we can find logical underpinning for this unique communication and persuasive behavior. In social network, for any general communication, basically members develop a cohesive group like a structured organization with uniform culture and exchange views to share and form a collective opinion and decision process (Akar & Topcu, 2011; Chu, 2011). Therefore, members' satisfaction process in social media has distinct characteristics that resembles to any social organization having enthusiasm to form a bonded structure. Consequently, investigating impact of product promotional message generated by a general member of any group in social network media has enormous merit.

Many scholarly studies (Akar & Topcu, 2011; Pietro and Pantano, di Pietro & Pantano, 2012; Schulze et al., 2014) revealed that viral marketing in social media has substantial impact in emerging or developing market, because emerging market structure is changing rapidly due to the proliferation of information and communication technology (ICT) particularly mobile-enabled services and applications. Therefore, the purpose of this study is to explore and conceptualize the underlying factors in creating impact of any product-related message among the members of a social network as prospective consumers in the context of emerging markets.

The next section explains the recent trend of viral marketing via social networks. The following section then formulates a number of relevant hypotheses as a basis for conducting an empirical investigation. Then, the conclusion of this study is outlined and future research direction is delineated.

24.2 Promotional Marketing in Social Network

Tools and techniques related to digital and social media marketing is increasingly being utilized for promoting product and services as well as for engaging customers with brands and citizens with government and political processes (AlAlwan, Rana, Dwivedi, & Algharabat, 2017; Dwivedi et al., 2016; Dwivedi et al., 2017; Dwivedi, Kapoor, & Chen, 2015; Dwivedi, Rana, & Alryalat, 2017; Ismagilova, Dwivedi, Slade, & Williams, 2017; Kapoor & Dwivedi, 2015; Kapoor, Dwivedi, & Piercy, 2016; Plume, Dwivedi, & Slade, 2016). Several researchers working on understanding practice of viral marketing using social networks such as Facebook (di Pietro & Pantano, 2012; Schulze et al., 2014) suggest such marketing approaches have strong potential particularly in the context of emerging or developing markets. This is because consumers there, in absence of any well-structured message distribution channel, are socially, technologically, and behaviorally connected through social network. Researchers engaged in identifying marketing scopes through social network have explored and revealed many potential issues of viral marketing like adoption and acceptance of viral marketing (Akar & Topcu, 2011; Logan et al., 2012; di Pietro & Pantano, 2012), appropriateness of products for viral marketing (Schulze et al., 2014), value perception of advertisement in Facebook in comparison to television (Logan et al., 2012), attitude toward Facebook advertisement (Chu, 2011), effect of brand relationships for viral marketing (Hayes & King, 2014), etc. However, impact of source derogation and origin of generation of message in Facebook for product promotion is yet to be investigated. However, researchers revealed that for social network advertisement, consumers like members of social network may have different attitudes about the promotional message (Hayes & King, 2014).

Theoretically an aspirational reference group is anyone who can represent and influence a particular segment of a society due to his/her phenomenal social status (Escalas & Bettman, 2005). Rhetorically, any peer of a connected social network group in Facebook represents the status of associative reference, i.e., any surrounding members who have an influence to shape peers opinion (Lessig & Park, 1978). As per conceptual paradigm, associative referees are personally known and socially connected people who have psychological influence among their surroundings to set some attitudinal standards (Singer, 1981). However, there are some people who are socially popular due to their celebrity image and can create certain social value and standard among their social networks (Escalas & Bettman, 2005). Many people have intrinsic motivation to follow these social celebrities as they perceive them as their standard. Like these celebrities, if any member interacting among the peers of their social network group can generate, distribute, communicate, and influence through message, ultimately that member creates an image of societal ambassador. This way, social network like Facebook offers the opportunity of a general member to become aspirational referee from associative referee.

According to the observational learning theory (Rothschild, 1981), in any displayed advertisements, prospective consumers try to keenly follow the models' behavior acting in the advertisement or generating the message of promotional marketing as their ideal. Through observation, if consumers perceive that they can perform the same behavior, typically they are attempted to streamline their attitude to implement the displayed behavior. Viral marketing studies (Chu, 2011; di Pietro & Pantano, 2012; Taylor et al., 2011) investigated several special characteristics of users of social network. They recognized that in social network, consumers' group behavior and involvement in forming common opinion are extremely important. Members of any social network like Facebook pursue their intention to be consumers and make purchase decision in the alignment of other members in their common network loop (Kim & Ko, 2012; Logan et al., 2012). Therefore, when any message containing product information is generated and circulated among them, they feel their involvement in passing on that message and are willing to contribute their own opinion to share. This way, this message ultimately represents their group opinion, and they are emotionally persuasive to that message. Following the fundamental concept of social identity theory (Tajfel & Turner, 1986), members of a society who believe in similar social concept are attempted to formulate similar decision-making through a common social structure. As per self-categorization theory (Turner, Hogg,

Oakes, Reicher, & Wetherell, 1987), social cohesion and polarization occur when a group of members find their association through very similar attitudinal congruence. Now researchers of social network (Chu, 2011; Logan et al., 2012; di Pietro & Pantano, 2012) revealed that those people who form a connected loop through interacting and exchanging their views pragmatically conceive and express asymmetric self-concept. Consequently, they are very eager, interested, and actively participative in forming, passing, and communicating through collective decision or opinion to share. They also are psychologically motivated to form group decision and be persuaded on that opinion (Chu, 2011; Schulze et al., 2014). Again, it has been found that around 70% members of any social network are intended to form their purchasing opinion through sharing information among their group members (Kim & Ko, 2012). As a result, in social media like Facebook, when any members first initiate any message to share information about their purchasing experience, other members of that loop actively participate to share, contribute, exchange, and pass on that message among other members which finally leads to represent a collective opinion of that group about a product or service (Hughes & Palen, 2009; Hayes & King, 2014).

Shedding light on cognitive response model (Nicosia, 1966), source derogation and its logical consequence are important predictors whether any advertisement containing a message would be influential or not. According to this concept, consumers before developing their favorable attitude toward any message of advertisement primarily examine the authenticity of the source of the message embedded in any product promotion. Prospective consumers also analyze the underlying concept and logical consequences of the product message to justify its authenticity and final acceptance (Shareef et al., 2015). Now integrating this concept with theoretical approach of social behavior extracted from social identity and self-categorization theory, we can infer that social network members who are prospective consumers can pursue their attitudes favorably toward any message circulated in their network loop, if it is generated and initiated through any member of the same group. This happens because member who generated that message has similar self-concept. Rhetorically, any member of social network has that scope to initiate and distribute a product promotional message, and if that message is persuasive, that member may act as an aspirational member of that social network.

24.3 Theoretical Background and Hypothesis Development

This study is conceptual in nature and aimed at identifying and discussing the underlying factors important for persuading prospective consumers of asocial loop for circulating messages initially generated by another peer of same social loop. In order to achieve that, this study invited 200 social network members of Facebook to gather their views. This helped to identify five issues or factors that Facebook users considered important and relevant for persuading decision-making about purchasing any product when that product-related message is initiated by and circulated among them through their social network loop. At point, the study was not intended to reveal the pursuing factors through any established psychological, behavioral, or technological model of consumers' behavioral prediction to shape favorable attitude about any product information generated and circulated in their social loop of Facebook. This is because it is argued that consumers' social network behavior is a new phenomenon and members of a social network are highly congruent to formulate their cohesive decision as a group to purchase any product uniquely. This study did not utilize any prescribed questionnaire to identify paradigm of conceptual model; rather, respondents were given freedom to articulate criteria from the scratch reflecting their self-concept to be persuaded to any message initiated, generated, and communicated among them through any peer of their same network loop. The active members of Facebook representing different social groups were asked to provide their own opinion reflecting self-judgment and perception.

The study was conducted in Bangladesh as an emerging market. We have invited 200 university students as active Facebook users and who had experience in purchasing product through receiving product information from their social network loop. This country as an emerging market and the respondents as the sample of the population were chosen for the following reasons:

1. More than 160 million people are living in this small country, and around 3.75 million people are actively using Facebook for sharing views.
2. Around 85% members of Facebook in Bangladesh actively collect information about any product to take purchase decision.
3. University students represent the majority members in Bangladesh who actively use Facebook to generate, share, and distribute messages related to any product before purchase.

All the respondents are MBA students in a leading private university in Bangladesh. They were physically contacted and were asked to answer the following question about their past experience in receiving product-related message from their social media group: "Suppose in your Facebook account, you got information related to any product promotion from your connected group. You do not know the originator or initiator of the message, i.e. source derogation is not verified. Please mention 5 most important criteria to be persuaded and develop favorable attitude toward that product promotional information which is being communicated among your group members."

The respondents were provided with email address of the researcher, so that they can return their perception about the subject through email.

Respondents were given 3 days to respond. Out of 200 students, 186 students responded based on their experience in purchasing product through sharing information from their Facebook. Forty-two respondents were students with no job, 51% are industry-related professionals having different educational and professional backgrounds, and the rest 7% were self-employed. The average age of all the respondents was 28 years. Among the respondents, 64% were male and 36% were female. Reflecting educational background, job experience, age, and professional position, it can be predicted that respondents represented lower middle-class, middle-class, and higher middle-class people. The average experience to involve actively in Facebook is 5.7 years.

The respondents addressed and recommended several issues related to marketing, technology, virtual medium, peer evaluation, group cohesiveness, self-concept, trustworthiness, and social media behavior. However, quite expectedly, as a similar and systematic behavioral pattern for social media network, there were considerable commonalities in respondents' preferences. Their behavioral pattern and evaluative expectation denoted enough similarities in choosing any keywords. To present the qualitative data obtained from the 186 respondents, the information gathered was rearranged according to the principles of matrix thinking, which is a strong statistical technique to organize and categorize qualitative information (Patton, 1981). Several respondents expressed their perception through long sentences. Those sentences were broken down into small keywords and contrasted with recognized attributes. The common attributes or parameters identified and recommended by the respondents were then categorized as per their frequency of appearance. Only those factors were chosen in developing a conceptual model as the persuading reasons for social network members to accept any circulating message containing product promotional information which are mentioned by at least 50% of the respondents. By this way, this study was able to postulate a parsimonious yet comprehensive model. Based on the recommendations by the survey respondents, the following five constructs were selected as driving factors important for developing favorable attitude toward any product promotional message initiated and circulated among the connected loop members of Facebook where the source derogation is not verified.

24.3.1 Message Initiator (Identity)

Researchers of promotional marketing regarding effectiveness of advertisement (Chu, 2011; Pelling & White, 2009) have acknowledged that authenticity of source of the advertisement has significant impact whether the consumers would be persuaded with a message or not. Studies related to consumers' trust disposition attitude (McKnight, Choudhury, & Kacmar, 2002) have also recognized that if the source of any information is reliable and authenticated, consumers feel motivated to accept that message. In this context, if the source or the originator of the message is known or familiar to them, it is more trustworthy to them, as they do not find any commercial intention from the source. Social media experts admitted through studies on prospective consumers (Kim & Ko, 2012; Logan et al., 2012) that if the message is initiated by their peers from the same network loop, members' perception about that message is reliable. Under this context, this study proposes that:

H_1 Identity of the message initiator has significant positive influence on social network members to find intrinsic motivation to accept that message.

24.3.2 Message Language (Informality)

Language of the advertisement in mobile advertisement has been found very important (Ducoffe, 1996; Jarad, 2014; Mallat, 2007). Researchers on social media like Facebook (Hughes & Palen, 2009; Hayes & King, 2014) have investigated the impact of language in terms of informality and revealed that in social media, members of any network loop do not like any commercial promotional message in their network to be persuaded. This identification clearly opens up a new agenda of promotional marketing research. Typically, consumers are familiar to evaluate any promotional advertisement offered commercially. Studies investigating the effect of advertisement argued that important predictors in this aspect are personalization, compatibility with own personality, and noncommerciality of the content (Shareef, Dwivedi, & Kumar, 2016). However, social marketing researchers postulated that Facebook members' behavior to initiate, share, and distribute any message generated in their loop is quite distinct (Hughes & Palen, 2009; Hayes & King, 2014, Mittal & Lassar, 1996). Peers of any network loop fundamentally, due to their bonding and cohesiveness, perceive themselves as a collective group with common opinion (Shareef, Dwivedi, & Kumar, 2016). Therefore, they have extreme inclination toward the noncommercial nature of the message. If they find the circulated message contains informal language, they feel more congruence with the message. Under this context, we can argue:

H_2 Language of the message whether commercial or informal has significant positive influence on social network members to find intrinsic motivation to accept that message.

24.3.3 Message Content (Logic and Counter Logic)

Viral marketing researchers (Akar & Topcu, 2011; Chu, 2011; Kim & Ko, 2012) have found that argument of the content of the message related to promotional marketing is very important for users of social network (such as Facebook) to be exposed, attentive, and perceived positively. Considering observational learning theory (Rothschild, 1981), consumers feel intrinsically motivated toward any message of an advertisement if they believe that they can perform the same behavior which is expressed in the message. According to self-identity theory (Tajfel & Turner, 1986), if consumers' self-concept is compatible with the content of the message, they feel urged to accept the message. On the other hand, social network researchers identified that members of social network are more eager to accept any message in their network if they find the content of the message is justified reflecting their personality and is based on strong logical expression. Consumers while analyzing any promotional advertisement keenly evaluate its merit through logic and counter logic (Shareef, Dwivedi, & Kumar, 2016; Shiau & Luo, 2012). Based on this argument, promotional marketing through social media, we can postulate that:

H_3 Logical argument of the message has significant positive influence on social network members to find intrinsic motivation to accept that message.

24.3.4 *Message Entertainment (Hedonic Motivation)*

Information- and communication technology-related research studies have found that entertainment has significant impact in pursuing favorable attitude of consumers toward the virtual media (Shareef et al., 2015; Shareef, Kumar, Dwivedi, & Kumar, 2016). In any virtual media, while consumers like to interact through self-service, they are very interested to get enjoyment from their lonely interaction and affiliation in the virtual environment (Akar & Topcu, 2011;Chu, 2011 ; Kim & Ko, 2012). Studies on social media have acknowledged that if consumers do not find entertainment, they will not be motivated to interact in that media (Logan et al., 2012; di Pietro & Pantano, 2012). Shedding light on behavioral theory like unified theory of acceptance and the use of technology (UTAUT) (Dwivedi, Rana, Jeyaraj, Clement, & Williams, 2017; Venkatesh, Thong, & Xu, 2012), it can be argued that hedonic motivation has substantial impact on consumers' behavior to find value of an advertisement. Many mobile marketing researchers (Chu, 2011; Lu, Yao, & Yu, 2005; Shareef, Dwivedi, & Kumar, 2016) have found that consumers in a social media environment are inclined to get hedonic motivation while choosing any media or accepting any viral advertisement. Therefore, we can propose:

H_4 Entertainment of the message has significant positive influence on social network members to find intrinsic motivation to accept that message.

24.3.5 *Message Reliability (Experience Based)*

In social media environment, sometimes, it is difficult to identify the source of the message. Any message in any social loop can be generated from their own members, or it can be injected externally from the media administrators. As a result, it is a serious challenge to understand and evaluate the credibility of the message (Shareef, Dwivedi, & Kumar, 2016). But in social media, reliability of the message has substantial impact on the members who are prospective buyers to believe and accept information regarding the product (di Pietro & Pantano, 2012). If consumers find the message generated from any of their peers reflecting their own consumption experience, other members would feel enough inclination to accept the content of the message (Chu, 2011; Kim & Ko, 2012). Therefore, reliability of the message has significant impact on the social network members to generate favorable attitude toward the message, and thus, we can propose:

H_5 Reliability of the message has significant positive influence on social network members to find intrinsic motivation to accept that message.

24.4 Conclusion

This study is attempted to understand attitude of members of a social network to be persuaded by any promotional marketing-related messages in terms of its effectiveness and ability to pursue them to be motivated. It was particularly focused on understanding the effect of any social member as an aspirational reference to pursue other network members regarding any promotional message initiated, shared, and distributed among members of the common social network through Facebook. This study is engaged in revealing the driving factors of social network members to be persuaded by any product promotion-related message generated, shared, and distributed among the members of the network loop, which is utmost important for emerging market. Since in emerging market, social network like Facebook is a common platform to generate collective opinion as an opinion leader, viral advertisement promoted by any member and shared among peers of their loop has potential contribution in shaping favorable attitude.

In any social media like Facebook, connected members of any network loop initiate, pass on, share, contribute, and distribute messages within the network frequently. Many scholarly articles that have examined behavioral aspects of social media members (Logan et al., 2012; di Pietro & Pantano, 2012; Schulze et al., 2014) articulated that prospective consumers are enthusiastic to learn about product-related attributes and its advantages and disadvantages from their social media where they are strongly affiliated. In the light of behavioral theory (Lieber & Syverson, 2011; Michael & Becker, 1973; Rothschild, 1981), we can also claim that any groups of a social media are interested to develop a collective opinion through a common message regarding product promotional information. In this aspect, social media can be an effective premise where marketers can shape prospective consumers' attitude through shared values and opinion. Therefore, this study was engaged in deriving the factors which have an influence in persuading attitude toward any message generated, circulated, distributed, and shared among the members of a common social loop.

Theory of planned behavior (Ajzen, 1991) addressed different beliefs pertained to develop human attitude toward any behavior. As per this theory, human psychology differs significantly considering their sources of beliefs for a particular issue. Researchers of human behavior in social media (Akar & Topcu, 2011; Chu, 2011; Kim & Ko, 2012) analyzed human psychology derived and shaped by certain beliefs from some unique perspectives like group cohesiveness, virtual interactions, communication of information, technological orientation, scope and opportunity, group dynamic and flexibility, and decision-making process. They acknowledged that for social media like Facebook, group members who are also prospective consumers develop and shape their attitude based on certain beliefs which are compatible with social media characteristics. This identification can be analyzed shedding deeper understanding on media richness theory (Daft & Lengel, 1986). According to this theory, different media utilize different techniques and ability to reach and communicate with users. As per their structure, channel network, association, and properties, they distribute information and image to their prospective users. Accordingly, users use their different senses to pursue attitude; however, ability of different media to effectively communicate and motivate differs significantly. As a result, in case of promotional marketing, communication type and its effectiveness vary substantially (Shareef, Dwivedi, & Kumar, 2016). Marketing managers evaluate different types of media for their effectiveness to launch any advertisement. Under the above assumption and argument, this study, through literature review and theoretical analysis, has postulated a total of five hypotheses to understand value of a message in pursuing consumers' favorable attitude toward any promotional advertisement inside asocial loop. Five interdependent factors, namely, message initiator (identity), message language (informality), message content (logic and counter logic), message entertainment (hedonic motivation), and message reliability (experience based), are constructed as independent variables to understand social media members' attitude toward any promotional message.

24.5 Future Research Direction

Future researchers can empirically test this parsimonious model to identify the validity of the model. However, demographic variables like age, gender, income, and profession can have moderating effect on consumers' attitude. Therefore, future researchers can also explore the moderating effects of any demographic variables. This study is particularly focused toward emerging market as viral marketing has significant implications in such contexts. However, for generalizability, this study should also be experimented in developed countries.

Reference

Ajzen, I. (1991). The theory of planned behavior. *Organizational Behavior & Human Decision Processes*, *50*(2), 179–211.

Akar, E., & Topcu, B. (2011). An examination of the factors influencing consumer's attitudes toward social media marketing. *Journal of Internet Commerce*, *10*(1), 35–67.

AlAlwan, A., Rana, N. P., Dwivedi, Y. K., & Algharabat, R. (2017). Social media in marketing: A review and analysis of the existing literature. *Telematics and Informatics*. Available at https://doi.org/10.1016/j.tele.2017.05.008.

Chu, S.-C. (2011). Viral advertising in social media: Participation in Facebook groups and responses among college-aged users. *Journal of Interactive Advertising*, *12*(1), 30–43.

Daft, R. L., & Lengel, R. H. (1986). Organizational information requirements, media richness and structural design. *Management Science.*, *32*(5), 554–571.

di Pietro, L., & Pantano, E. (2012). An empirical investigation of social network influence on consumer purchasing decision: The case of Facebook. *Journal of Direct, Data and Digital Marketing Practice*, *14*(1), 18–29.

Ducoffe, R. H. (1996). Advertising value and advertising on the web. *Journal of Advertising Research*, *36*(5), 21–35.

Dwivedi, Y. K., Kapoor, K. K., & Chen, H. (2015). Social media marketing and advertising. *The Marketing Review, 15*(3), 289–309.

Dwivedi, Y. K.,Mäntymäki, M., Ravishankar, M. N., Janssen, M., Clement, M., Slade, E. L., Rana, N. P., Al-Sharhan, S. &Simintiras, A. C. (Eds.) (2016). *Social media: The good, the bad, and the ugly*: 15th IFIP WG 6.11 Conference on e-Business, e-Services, and e-Society, I3E 2016, Swansea, UK, September 13–15, 2016, Proceedings (Vol. 9844). Springer. URL: http://www.springer.com/gb/book/9783319452333.

Dwivedi, Y. K., Rana, N. P., & Alryalat, M. A. A. (2017). Affiliate marketing: An overview and analysis of emerging literature. *The Marketing Review, 17*(1), 33–50.

Dwivedi, Y. K., Rana, N. P., Jeyaraj, A., Clement, M., & Williams, M. D. (2017). Re-examining the unified theory of acceptance and use of technology (UTAUT): Towards a revised theoretical model. *Information Systems Frontiers*, 1–16. Available at https://link.springer.com/article/10.1007/s 10796-017-9774-y.

Dwivedi, Y. K., Rana, N. P., Tajvidi, M., Lal, B., Sahu, G. P., & Gupta, A. (2017), Exploring the role of social media in e-Government: an analysis of emerging literature. In *Proceedings of the 10th International Conference on Theory and Practice of Electronic Governance* (pp. 97–106). ACM, 7th to 10th March 2017, New Delhi, India.

Escalas, J. E., & Bettman, J. R. (2005). Self-construal, reference groups, and brand meaning. *Journal of Consumer Research, 32*(3), 378–389.

Hayes, J. L., & King, K. W. (2014). The social exchange of viral ads: Referral and coreferral of ads among college students. *Journal of Interactive Advertising, 14*(2), 98–109.

Hogg, M. A., & Vaughan, G. M. (2002). *Social psychology* (3rd ed.). London, UK: Prentice Hall.

Hughes, A. L. & Palen, L. (2009). Twitter Adoption and Use in Mass Convergence and Emergency Events. In Proceedings of the 6th International ISCRAM Conference, Sweden.

Ismagilova, E., Dwivedi, Y.K., Slade, E.L. & Williams, M.D. (2017). *Electronic Word of Mouth (eWOM) in the Marketing Context: A State of the Art Analysis and Future Directions*. Springer International Publishing. Available at http://www.springer.com/us/book/ 9783319524580.

Jarad, G. A. (2014). Marketing over social media networks. *European Journal of Business and Management, 6*(13), 114–118.

Kapoor, K. K., & Dwivedi, Y. K. (2015). Metamorphosis of Indian electoral campaigns: Modi's social media experiment. *International Journal of Indian Culture and Business Management, 11*(4), 496–516.

Kapoor, K. K., Dwivedi, Y. K., & Piercy, N. C. (2016). Pay-per-click advertising: A literature review. *The Marketing Review, 16*(2), 183–202.

Kim, A. J., & Ko, E. (2012). Do social media marketing activities enhance customer equity? An empirical study of luxury fashion brand. *Journal of Business Research, 65*(10), 1480–1486.

LaRose, R., Mastro, D. A., & Eastin, M. S. (2001). Understanding internet usage: A social cognitive approach to uses and gratifications. *Social Science Computer Review, 19*(4), 395–413.

Lee, D., Kim, H. S., & Kim, J. K. (2011). The impact of online brand community type on consumer's community engagement behaviors: Consumer-created vs. marketer-created online brand community in online social-networking web sites. *Cyber Psychology, Behavior & Social Networking, 14*(1/2), 59–63.

Lessig, V. P., & Park, W. (1978). Promotional perspectives of reference group influence: Advertising implications. *Journal of Advertising, 7*(2), 41–47.

Lieber, E., & Syverson, C. (2011). Online vs. offline competition. In M. Peitz & J. Waldfogel (Eds.), *Oxford handbook for the digital economy* (pp. 189–223). New York, NY: Oxford University Press.

Logan, K., Bright, L. F., & Gangadharbatla, H. (2012). Facebook versus television: Advertising value perceptions among females. Journal of Research in Interactive Marketing, 6(3), 164–179.

Lu, J., Yao, J. E., & Yu, C.-S. (2005). Personal innovativeness social influences and adoption of wireless internet services via mobile technology. *Journal of Strategic Information Systems, 14*(3), 245–268.

Mallat, N. (2007). Exploring consumer adoption of mobile payments – A qualitative study. *Journal of Strategic Information Systems, 16*(4), 413–432.
McKnight, D. H., Choudhury, V., & Kacmar, C. (2002). Developing and validating trust measures for e-commerce: An integrative typology. *Information Systems Research, 13*(3), 334–359.
Michael, R. T., & Becker, G. S. (1973). On the new theory of consumer behavior. *The Swedish Journal of Economics, 75*(4), 378–396.
Mittal, B., & Lassar, W. M. (1996). The role of personalization in service encounters. *Journal of Retailing, 72*(1), 95–109.
Nicosia, F. (1966). *Consumer decision processes*. Englewood Cliffs, NJ: Prentice Hall.
Patton, M. Q. (1981). *Creative evaluation*. San Anselmo, CA: Sage Publications, USA.
Pelling, E., & White, K. M. (2009). The theory of planned behavior applied to young people's use of social networking websites. *Cyber psychology & Behavior, 12*(6), 755–759.
Plume, C. J., Dwivedi, Y. K., & Slade, E. L. (2016). *Social Media in the Marketing Context: A state of the art analysis and future directions* (1st ed.). Oxford, UK.: Chandos Publishing Ltd. Available athttps://www.elsevier.com/books/social-media-in-the-marketing-context/plume/978-0-08-101754-8
Rothschild, M. L. (1981). Behavioral learning theory: Its relevance to marketing and promotions. *Journal of Marketing, 45*. (Spring, 70–78.
Schulze, C., Scholer, L., & Skiera, B. (2014). Not all fun and games: Viral marketing for utilitarian products. *Journal of Marketing, 78*, 1–19.
Shareef, M. A., Dwivedi, Y. K., & Kumar, V. (2016). *Mobile Marketing Channel: Mobile Phone SMS & Online Consumer Behavior*. USA: Springer.
Shareef, M. A., Dwivedi, Y. K., & Rana, N. P. (2015). Consumer behavior in the context of SMS-based marketing. *The Marketing Review, 15*(2), 135–160.
Shareef, M. A., Kumar, V., Dwivedi, Y. K., Kumar, U. (2016), Service delivery through mobile-government (mGov): Driving factors and cultural impacts. *Information Systems Frontiers*, 18(2), 315–332.
Shiau, W. L., & Luo, M. M. (2012). Factors affecting online group buying intention and satisfaction: A social exchange theory perspective. *Computers in Human Behavior, 28*(6), 2431–2444.
Singer, E. (1981). Reference Groups and Social Evaluations. In M. Rosenberg & R. H. Turner (Eds.), *Social Psychology* (pp. 66–93). New York, NY: Basic Books.
Tajfel, H., & Turner, J. C. (1986). The social identity theory of inter-group behavior. In S. Worchel & L. W. Austin (Eds.), *Psychology of intergroup relations*. Chicago, IL: Nelson-Hall.
Taylor, D. G., Lewin, J. E., & Strutton, D. (2011). Friends, fans, and followers: Do ads work on social networks. *Journal of Advertising Research, 51*(1), 258–275.
Turner, J. C., Hogg, M. A., Oakes, P. J., Reicher, S. D., & Wetherell, M. S. (1987). *Rediscovering the social group: A self-categorization theory*. Oxford, UK: Blackwell.
Venkatesh, V., Thong, J., & Xu, X. (2012). Consumer acceptance and use of information technology: Extending the unified theory of acceptance and use of technology. *MIS Quarterly, 36*(1), 157–178.

Mahmud A. Shareef is a professor of school of business, North South University, Bangladesh. He was a visiting faculty in DeGroote School of Business, McMaster University, Canada, during his postdoctorate research. He has done his PhD in Business Administration from Sprott School of Business, Carleton University, Canada. He received his graduate degree from both the Institute of Business Administration, University of Dhaka, Bangladesh, in Business Administration, and Carleton University, Ottawa, Canada, in Civil Engineering. His research interest is focused on online consumer behavior and virtual organizational reformation. He has published more than 60 papers addressing consumers' adoption behavior and quality issues of e-commerce and e-government in different refereed conference proceedings and international journals. He was the recipient of more than ten academic awards including three Best Research Paper Awards in the UK and Canada.

Vinod Kumar is a professor of Technology and Operations Management of the Sprott School of Business (Director of School, 1995–2005), Carleton University. He received his graduate education from the University of California, Berkeley, and the University of Manitoba. Vinod is a well-known expert sought in the field of technology and operations management. He has published over 150 papers in refereed journals and proceedings. He has won several Best Paper Awards in prestigious conferences, Scholarly Achievement Award of Carleton University for the academic years 1985–1986 and 1987–1988, and Research Achievement Award for the years 1993 and 2001. Vinod has given invited lectures to professional and academic organizations in Australia, Brazil, China, Iran, and India, among others.

Uma Kumar is a full professor of the Management Science and Technology Management and director of the Research Centre for Technology Management at Carleton University. She has published over 140 papers in journals and refereed proceedings. Ten papers have won best paper awards at prestigious conferences. She has won Carleton's prestigious Research Achievement Award and, twice, the Scholarly Achievement Award. Recently, she won the teaching excellence award at the Carleton University. She has been the director of Sprott School's Graduate Programs. She has consulted DND, CIDA, the Federal partners of technology transfer, and the Canadian association of business incubators. Uma has taught in executive MBA program in Hong Kong and in Sprott MBA in Ottawa, Iran, and China. Over the last 20 years, she has supervised more than 70 MBA, MMS, and EMBA student's projects. She has also given invited lectures to academics and professionals in Brazil, China, Cuba, and India.

Part VI
Management and International Business

Chapter 25
Institutional Export Barriers on Exporters from Emerging Markets: Evidence from China

Jia Li and Ling Liu

Abstract The emerging markets have become the increasingly important trading nations in the global economy. Given its significance to practitioners and policy-makers, export barriers has been the popular topic in the international business studies. However, research about export barriers caused by the local institutions are under developed, though institutional voids and institutional inefficiency are reported as the major determinants for business development in emerging markets. This paper aims to fill in this gap by exploring the institutional export barriers in emerging markets. Based on existing studies on export barriers and institutional perspective, a conceptual framework is initially developed by separating formal and informal institutional export barriers. Then three specific institutional export barriers are identified, including government policy, weak legal system and informal and personal networks. In the meanwhile, this paper sheds light on how the institutional export barriers are developed and obstruct exporting in emerging markets.

Keywords Institutional export barriers · Exporting · Emerging markets · China

25.1 Introduction

Emerging markets have become an increasingly important source for the world's growth in the last two decades (Cavusgil, Ghauri, & Agarwal, 2002), with rapid integration into global production networks as well as successful exporting

J. Li (✉)
Emerging Markets Research Centre, School of Management,
Swansea University, Swansea, UK
e-mail: Jia.li@swansea.ac.uk

L. Liu
University of Edinburgh Business School, Edinburgh, UK
e-mail: ling.liu@ed.ac.uk

Y. K. Dwivedi et al. (eds.), *Emerging Markets from a Multidisciplinary Perspective*, Advances in Theory and Practice of Emerging Markets,
https://doi.org/10.1007/978-3-319-75013-2_25

performance. In 2015, the share of international trade from developing countries accounted for approximately 43% of the global total (WTO, 2016).

Export barriers, defined as "all those constraints that hinder the firm's ability to initiate, to develop, or to sustain business operation in overseas markets" (Leonidou, 2004, p. 281), are discussed in existing literature. Firms must take account of export barriers in their exporting decisions and subsequent exporting activities. These export barriers can be both internal factors such as lack of physical resources and managerial and marketing knowledge and external factors derived from home/host countries' business environment (Kahiya, 2013; Leonidon, 1995).

Firms from emerging markets are more likely to be affected by the external barriers associated with distinctive institutional environments, where institutional voids (Miller, Lee, Chang, & Le Breton-Miller, 2009), uncertainty of institutional change (Child & Tse, 2001) and misalignment between institutional supply and firm demand (Witt & Lewin, 2007) jointly exist. Export barriers display highly country-specific characteristics (Leonidon, 1995). However, to our knowledge, studies on export barriers for emerging market firms are limited and fail to identify such variances associated with emerging economies.

This article aims to fill the gap by identifying the specific institutional export barriers confronted by emerging market exporters. Specifically, what are the institutional export barriers that Chinese exporters and foreign buyers encounter when undertaking exporting activities in China? The identification and understanding of export barriers may not only help firms to respond to the obstacles and enhance exporting performance but also help policymakers to identify and develop appropriate simulation and assistance for exporters (Leonidou, 2004). We use China as a case to investigate the question as one of the most representative of emerging markets. It is widely acknowledged that China's 35-year economic reform and export-orientated development strategy have considerably contributed to substantial economic growth, yet less is known about how China has overcome the huge challenges that obstructed international business activities and made itself the leading trading nation (Li & Liu, 2012). By echoing the statement in existing literature that institutions have played the most important role for business in emerging markets (Meyer & Peng, 2016; Peng, Wang, & Jiang, 2008), we make two contributions to the field: conceptualising institutional export barriers as the most important export barriers for firms from emerging markets and identifying three major institutional export barriers in China, considering how they are developed and obstruct exporting.

25.2 Institutional Export Barriers

Exporting is an effective entry strategy for firms' international expansion, because it incurs lower costs, risks and resource commitment compared with other market entry modes (Katsikeas, Leonidou, & Samiee, 2009). There are many existing studies on export, including export stimulation (Leonidou, 1995), exporting process (Leonidas C. Leonidou & Katsikeas, 1996), determinants of export performance (Shoham, 1998; Zou & Stan, 1998), relationship between the exporter and importer

(Leonidou, Barnes, & Talias, 2006) and export intermediaries (Peng & Ilinitch, 1998). However, the existing conceptual classifications pay less attention to the dynamics, and are less likely to find the key barriers and original cause of these barriers. For instance, the shortage of certain resources for exporters may come from ill-developed environmental factors.

Institutions, as the rules of the game, constrain and shape individual interactions (North, 1990). Some institutions help to reduce uncertainty and benefit market transactions and business, while others can constraint market entry, raise transaction costs and damage business transactions. In the real business world, the imperfect market gives rise to both types of institution (North, 1990). For emerging markets, institutions have turned out to be the most important business characteristic, as they impact and construct unique business practices (Meyer & Peng, 2016). Moreover, the negative impacts from institutions on business are more significant. Different from developed economies with stable and effective institutions, emerging markets experience a special period of mixed institutions (Nee, 1992) and result in a series of institution-related problems, such as institutional instability (Hitt, Ahlstrom, Dacin, Levitas, & Svobodina, 2004), restrictive legislation (Meyer, 2001) and institutional voids (Khanna & Palepu, 2000). The exporters from these emerging markets are confronted with different export barriers related to institutions. In this study, we define those export barriers, which are considerably related to local institutions and impede firms' exporting ability, as *institutional export barriers*.

Building on existing literature on institutional theory and emerging markets, this study proposes a framework that separates formal and informal institutions. Formal institutions contain political, legal and economic rules (North, 1990). In emerging markets, it is widely reported that formal institutions, like government policy and legislation, turn out to be problematic for business (Hitt et al., 2004). Informal institutions refer to culture, customs, traditions and codes of conduct, which "come from socially transmitted information" (North, 1990, p. 37). They are usually enforced by business and social groups, family or private entities and can substitute and supplement formal institutions (Keefer & Shirley, 2000, p. 96). The informal institutions,

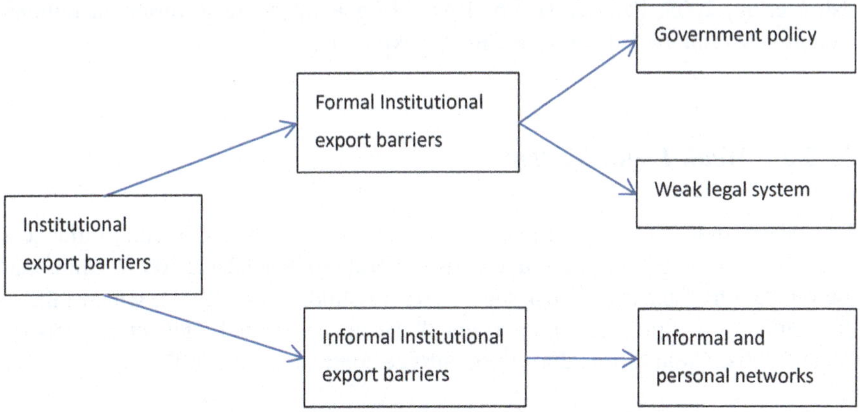

Fig. 25.1 Institutional export barriers in Chinese exporting market

such as Chinese guanxi and Russian blat, are quite unique and hard-to-master for foreign and even domestic firms, as their complexity is rooted in local social and cultural factors over time (Hitt et al., 2004). Figure 25.1 displays a framework of *formal and informal institutional export barriers*. Under it, we identify three important formal and informal institutional export barriers in China, and the next section demonstrates how these barriers are developed and obstruct exporting.

25.3 Formal Institutional Export Barriers

25.3.1 Government Policy

Government policy, as a formal institution, is often labelled as an important institutional barrier for international companies (Kahiya, 2013), which is true for Chinese exporters. With continuous influence from the former central-planned economy, the government is still playing an important role in the emerging market economy in China (Child & Yuan, 1996). One serious problem is the superfluous business licenses and permits. Li and Liu (2012) reported that Chinese exporters had to obtain many export-related approvals and permits from different government departments for each export transaction. The application and process of such licences and permits inevitably incur inefficient and opaque bureaucratic administrative procedures (Estrin, Meyer, & Bytchkova, 2008), which increase Chinese exporters' costs of money and time and make them less competitive. Moreover, it results in uncertainty for Chinese exporters. Similar to other emerging markets, fundamental and continuous institutional transition towards market economy is a major characteristic of the business environment in China (Buck, Filatotchev, Nolan, & Wright, 2001; Peng, 2003). It leads to unstable and changing government policy and hence notable uncertainty. Many studies confirm that unstable and changing government policies with institutional change largely raise uncertainty and problems for business in emerging markets (Bevan, Estrin, & Meyer, 2004; Estrin et al., 2008; Peng & Heath, 1996). In general, these government policies increase uncertainty and costs for Chinese exporters.

25.3.2 Weak Legal System

The legal system is a major formal institution (North, 1990) and directly influences transaction enforcement and related costs (Furubotn & Richter, 2005). China has the reputation of having a weak legal system (Child & Tse, 2001), which fails to efficiently protect property rights (Peng & Heath, 1996) and intellectual property (Beata, 2004; Child & Tse, 2001) and enforce contracts (Luo, 2002).

Exporting involves many different organizations, including manufacturers, suppliers, middlemen, exporting intermediaries, shipment companies and forwarders, and requires efficient cooperation among them. Inevitably such kinds of cooperation are based on variable contracts and their enforcement. A weak legal system incurs a number of problems for exporting, including product quality and timely delivery, most of which are reported as key barriers for foreign buyers' purchasing from China (LFRC, 2010; Nassimbeni & Sartor, 2006). In other words, many of the current problems with exporting from China are actually contributed by a main institutional exporting barrier, weak legal system.

25.4 Informal Institutional Export Barriers

25.4.1 *Informal and Personal Networks*

The common use of informal and personal networks is a remarkable business phenomenon in emerging markets (Ahlstrom & Bruton, 2006). Significant cultural and social characteristics in the Chinese business environment (Park & Luo, 2001) mean networks have an important role in international trade (Rauch, 2001; Rauch & Trindade, 2002). Generally, networks considerably reduce matching and enforcing costs in exporting (Rauch & Trindade, 2002). As stated above, exporting involves many different organizations. Without an effective market mechanism, including legal system, searching for business partners and monitoring contract enforcement among these organizations are costly in emerging markets. In turn, networks are able to reduce these costs by mitigating information asymmetry and opportunistic behaviours (Rauch & Trindade, 2002).

With long-established networks, Chinese exporters are able to find reliable business partners with appropriate products and services and informally enforce contracts to secure quality and time. However, the popularity of networks has turned out to be a barrier for Chinese exporters, especially those small exporters. First, the involvement of such networks requires skill, time and resources, which make these exporters less capable of exporting. It can also cause additional costs for Chinese exporters, as exporters from developed countries can easily rely on market mechanisms with effective contract enforcement. In addition, these personal networks are established on long-term commitment (Cavusgil, Ghauri, & Akcal, 2012), which is another disadvantage for Chinese exporters. Chinese exporting and relevant industries also experience institutional transition from central-planned to market-based economy in China (Li & Liu, 2012). Most networks are still in the hands of former managers of state-owned trading companies. With economic reform and privatization in China, these network assets become rare for most emerging private exporters. It is not uncommon that a considerable number of entrepreneurs of the export intermediaries are former employees of state-owned trading companies who took away their clients and suppliers.

25.5 Conclusion

The studies on export barriers are significant for research and practice. They can benefit exporting managers to identify, reduce and overcome these obstacles and improve exporting performance. They are also able to help policymakers to identify barriers and develop appropriate stimulations and assistances for exporters (Leonidou, 2004).

References

Ahlstrom, D., & Bruton, G. D. (2006). Venture capital in emerging economies: Networks and institutional change. *Entrepreneurship Theory and Practice*, *30*(2), 299–320.

Beata, S. J. (2004). The composition of foreign direct investment and protection of intellectual property rights: Evidence from transition economies. *European Economic Review*, *48*(1), 39–62.

Bevan, A., Estrin, S., & Meyer, K. (2004). Foreign investment location and institutional development in transition economies. *International Business Review*, *13*(1), 43–64.

Buck, T., Filatotchev, I., Nolan, P., & Wright, M. (2001). Different paths to economic reform in Russia and China: Causes and consequences. *Journal of World Business*, *35*(4), 379–400.

Cavusgil, S. T., Ghauri, P. N., & Agarwal, M. R. (2002). *Doing business in emerging markets: Entry and negotiation strategies*. Thousand Oaks, CA: Sage.

Cavusgil, S. T., Ghauri, P. N., & Akcal, A. A. (2012). *Doing business in emerging markets*. London, UK: Sage.

Child, J., & Tse, D. K. (2001). China's transition and its implications for international business. *Journal of International Business Studies*, *32*(1), 5–21.

Child, J., & Yuan, L. (1996). Institutional constraints on economic reform: The case of investment decisions in China. *Organization Science*, *7*, 60–77.

Estrin, S., Meyer, K. E., & Bytchkova, M. (2008). Entrepreneurship in transition economies. In Mark Casson, The Oxford Handbook of Entrepreneurship (pp. 693–725). Oxford: Oxford University Press.

Furubotn, E. G., & Richter, R. (2005). *Institutions and economic theory: The contribution of the new institutional economics*. Ann Arbor, MI: University of Michigan Press.

Hitt, M. A., Ahlstrom, D., Dacin, M. T., Levitas, E., & Svobodina, L. (2004). The institutional effects on strategic alliance partner selection in transition economies: China vs. Russia. *Organization Science*, *15*(2), 173–185.

Kahiya, E. T. (2013). Export barriers and path to internationalization: A comparison of conventional enterprises and international new ventures. *Journal of International Entrepreneurship*, *11*(1), 3–29.

Katsikeas, C. S., Leonidou, L. C., & Samiee, S. (2009). *Research into exporting: Theoretical, methodological, and empirical insights*. Sage London.

Keefer, P., & Shirley, M. M. (2000). Formal versus informal institutions in economic development. In C. Ménard (Ed.), *Institutions, contracts, and organizations: perspectives from new institutional economics*. Cheltenham, UK: Edward Elgar Publishing.

Khanna, T., & Palepu, K. (2000). Is group affiliation profitable in emerging markets? An analysis of diversified Indian business groups. *The Journal of Finance*, *55*(2), 867–891.

Leonidon, L. C. (Writer). (1995). Empirical research on export barriers: Review, assessment, and synthesis [Article]. *Journal of International Marketing: American Marketing Association*. *3*(1), 29–43.

Leonidou, L. C. (1995). Export stimulation research: Review, evaluation and integration. *International Business Review*, *4*(2), 133–156.

Leonidou, L. C. (2004). An analysis of the barriers hindering small business export development. *Journal of Small Business Management, 42*(3), 279–302.

Leonidou, L. C., Barnes, B. R., & Talias, M. A. (2006). Exporter-importer relationship quality: The inhibiting role of uncertainty, distance, and conflict. *Industrial Marketing Management, 35*(5), 576–588.

Leonidou, L. C., & Katsikeas, C. S. (1996). The export development process: An integrative review of empirical models. *Journal of International Business Studies, 27*(3), 517–551.

LFRC. (2010). *China purchasing development report.* Hong Kong, China: Li & Fung Research Centre & China Federation of Logistics & Purchasing.

Li, J., & Liu, L. (2012). The exporting trading companies from China: An institution-based view. In S. Harris, O. Kuivalainen, & V. Stoyanova (Eds.), *International business: New challenges, new forms, new perspectives* (p. 97). Basingstoke, UK: Palgrave Macmillan.

Li, J., & Liu, L. 2012. The Exporting Trading Companies from China: An Institution-based View. In S. Harris, O. Kuivalainen, & V. Stoyanova (Eds.), International Business: New Challenges, New Forms, New Perspectives: 97 (pp. 97-115). Palgrave Macmillan, London.

Luo, Y. (2002). Partnering with foreign firms: How do Chinese managers view the governance and importance of contracts? *Asia Pacific Journal of Management, 19*(1), 127–151.

Meyer, K. E. (2001). Institutions, transaction costs, and entry mode choice in Eastern Europe. *Journal of International Business Studies, 32*(2), 357–367.

Meyer, K. E., & Peng, M. W. (2016). Theoretical foundations of emerging economy business research. *Journal of International Business Studies, 47*(1), 3–22.

Miller, D., Lee, J., Chang, S., & Le Breton-Miller, I. 2009. Filling the institutional void: The social behavior and performance of family vs non-family technology firms in emerging markets. *Journal of International Business Studies, 40*(5): 802–817

Nassimbeni, G., & Sartor, M. (2006). International purchasing offices in China. *Production Planning & Control, 17*(5), 494–507.

Nee, V. (1992). Organizational dynamics of market transition: Hybrid forms, property rights, and mixed economy in China. *Administrative Science Quarterly, 37*(1), 1–27.

North, D. C. (1990). *Institutions, institutional change and economic performance.* Cambridge: Cambridge university press.

Park, S. H., & Luo, Y. (2001). Guanxi and organizational dynamics: Organizational networking in Chinese firms. *Strategic Management Journal, 22*(5), 455–477.

Peng, M. W. (2003). Institutional transitions and strategic choices. *The Academy of Management Review, 28*(2), 275–296.

Peng, M. W., & Heath, P. S. (1996). The growth of the firm in planned economies in transition: Institutions, organizations, and strategic choice. *The Academy of Management Review, 21*(2), 492–528.

Peng, M. W., & Ilinitch, A. Y. (1998). Export intermediary firms: A note on export development research. *Journal of International Business Studies, 29*(3), 609–620.

Peng, M. W., Wang, D. Y. L., & Jiang, Y. (2008). An institution-based view of international business strategy: A focus on emerging economies. *Journal of International Business Studies, 39*(5), 920–936.

Rauch, J. E. (2001). Business and social networks in international trade. *Journal of Economic Literature, 39*, 1177–1203.

Rauch, J. E., & Trindade, V. (2002). Ethnic Chinese networks in international trade. *Review of Economics and Statistics, 84*(1), 116–130.

Shoham, A. (1998). Export performance: A conceptualization and empirical assessment. *Journal of International Marketing, 6*, 59–81.

WTO. (2016). World Trade Statistical Review 2016: The World Trade Organization.

Witt, M. A., & Lewin, A. Y. 2007. Outward foreign direct investment as escape response to home country institutional constraints. Journal of International Business Studies, 38(4): 579–594.

Zou, S., & Stan, S. (1998). The determinants of export performance: A review of the empirical literature between 1987 and 1997. *International Marketing Review, 15*(5), 333–356.

Dr. Jia Li is a lecturer of international business at the School of Management, Swansea University. He obtained his PhD from University of Edinburgh Business School. His research focuses on firms' exporting behaviours and the influence from institutions in China. He is particularly interested in the topics of the interplay between institutions and international companies in emerging markets from the perspectives of institutional theories, transaction costs economics and resource-based view.

Dr. Ling Liu obtained her doctoral degree at the Judge Business School, Cambridge. She worked as an international business consultant in China before joining the academic community, and her research interests include globalization, industrial strategy, FDI spillovers and corruption in emerging markets.

Chapter 26
What Caused the Shortage of Labour: Examining the Recruitment and Selection in the Internet Financial Industry in China

Jingyi Liu and Yujie Cai

Abstract Since the recent rapid development of the Internet financial industry in China, the human resource management department has been required to provide strong support through recruiting and selecting suited employees based on industry development needs. The labour shortage in human resource management (HRM) may seem more severe than before, and some of the problems of recruitment and the selection process may have been exposed more than ever. However, researchers consider that this finding may have important implications for human resource recruitment theory and practice in the emerging industry. By summing up the interview results from 11 HR practitioners in the Internet financial company recruitment, this paper has examined the reality of the recruitment and selection in the Chinese Internet financial industry and analysed the reasons caused by this organisational phenomenon. Results reveal that there are four main factors which could affect the recruitment of the Internet financial industry, including the recruitment channel, staffing structure, management policies and industry background. It is suggested that the Internet financial industry should actively expand and diversify its recruitment channels, while continue paying close attention to the changes of relevant talent markets in order to obtain the required personnel.

Keywords Recruitment · Selection · Internet finance · Human resource management · China

J. Liu
Neri & Hu Design and Research Office, Shanghai, China
e-mail: yvonne_777@126.com

Y. Cai (✉)
Centre for People and Organisation, Swansea University, Bay Campus, Swansea, Wales, UK
e-mail: yujie.cai@swansea.ac.uk

Y. K. Dwivedi et al. (eds.), *Emerging Markets from a Multidisciplinary Perspective*, Advances in Theory and Practice of Emerging Markets,
https://doi.org/10.1007/978-3-319-75013-2_26

26.1 Introduction

The Internet financial industry is inseparable from the progress of social needs and the rise of science and technology; it plays a key role in the development of the financial industry at large (Yao, 2014). The rise of Internet finance were the results of the developments made due to the social demand, and the characteristics of the industry which relied on the Chinese cultural, social and technical background.

First, advances in information and network technology have facilitated the rapid development of the Internet financial industry in providing the technical foundation. Technical breakthroughs have encouraged a sudden growth in the development of the Internet finance industry because a new generation of information technology, including cloud computing, search engines, social networking, big data and mobile payment, continue to enable the rise of the Internet financial industry (Yao, 2014).

Second, the virtual economy, especially the rapid development of e-commerce for Internet financial development, provides an economic background. The development of electronic commerce has penetrated deep into Chinese industrial and agricultural production, business trade and community service (Schneider, 1952). At the same time, electronic commerce has noticed the uninterrupted amalgamation of the network economy, showing a clear trend of cross-border cooperation and global expansion. The sudden development of electronic commerce has caused an urgent need for a convenient way to pay online, and this has facilitated opportunities for Internet financial development to diversify.

Finally, the accumulation of innovative financial services models, such as third-party payment, P2P, crowd funding and others, provides a historical background for the rapid development of Internet finance (Yao, 2014). A large number of Internet innovation companies have accelerated their integration between traditional financial institutions and Internet companies, setting off the Internet finance era.

The financial industry considers talent as its primary resource, and personnel development plays an important and crucial role in the construction of this industry. With mobile Internet permeating into the traditional financial sector, cross-industry and innovative financial talent is very scarce in the talent market. At the 13th China International Talent Exchange Conference, researchers announced that the talents of the traditional financial industry have greater mobility, but the labour shortage for product research and development as well as risk control was evident in the emerging Internet industry. The talents for new product development, professional web promotion and wind control aspects are very scarce, and Internet finance companies face constant difficulties in hiring professionals. Currently, this talent shortage is a challenge that the Internet financial industry needs to deal with. The common approach is for the Internet financial personnel, generally from the traditional financial sector and e-commerce industry to switch over; however, these people generally lack the Internet thinking mode, and it is difficult to adapt to the new financial products which are exploited in this new situation. Thus, the Internet financial industry requires better development in the future, and the recruitment and selection of the right talent has become a very important step.

According to the above, the recruitment and selection of Internet financial sector talent is important for, and relevant to, promoting this industry's development. This dissertation therefore focuses on analysing the labour shortage in this industry: from the perspective of industrial strategic development to the possible impact of human resource recruitment and selection, to whether the industry talent demand in the labour market will become an important reserve resource of industry development or not. While addressing the development of the emerging industry, this paper will look at the reasons behind the recruitment difficulty in the Internet financial industry and hopefully establish its causes.

26.2 Literature Review

26.2.1 The Recruitment Status of the Internet Financial Industry in China

With China's economic development, its peoples' material and cultural life and values in the country have shifted, which is directly reflected in the major changes in the demands of work. People have undertaken a conceptual transition from "work equates to livelihood" to "people want to gain a higher quality of life and to realise the value of life". Therefore, in order to adapt to this change, the Internet financial industry needs to improve its employer image (Zhongpin Inc., 2007). In China, the employment relationships are now based on corporate policies and practices, which include paying more attention to building new relationships between employers and employees, encouraging enterprises to be more open and providing more humane treatment of employees; changing this employment relationship is a result of business development process. The best employers should not only give employees the material aspects of rich rewards but also should keep up with the times in order to give employees a better workplace environment and promote harmonious and healthy workplace relation (Zhongpin Inc., 2007).

More and more enterprises entering the field make for an increasingly competitive industry, so lack of professionals is a serious problem being faced by many Internet companies. A large number of high-paying job advertisements confirm the extent of the shortage of Internet financial professionals (Liu, 2015). A "One Securities Daily" correspondent reports that at present, three kinds of professionals are needed in Internet financial firms. The first category is the network technician. Their work is mainly responsible for the development of PC clients and mobile clients, while practitioners need to have a strong network expertise. The second category is the professional financial staffs. They are responsible for the quantitative data analysis and financial product design. The third category has the greatest demand: These are the operating officers in this industry (Liu, 2015). According to the "2014 Internet Financial Industry Talent Shortage Report" from Puxin Research Institute (PRI), product managers and operations managers are the most in demand;

other industries just have a few scarce jobs around 70%. Nevertheless, there is more than a 70% scarcity rate for 10 positions in emerging Internet financial industry (Puxin Research Institute, 2014).

Although the Internet financial industry originated from the traditional financial sector, there is a big gap between the talent recruitment requirements. In China, the financial industry wages are far higher than those of other industries; furthermore, the Chinese financial salary growth rate is much higher than the level of developed countries. In the United States, the salary growth rate of the financial industry was 2.85% in 2013, while the growth rate of China's financial industry pay was 11.04%, almost four times that of the US salary growth rate. China's financial sector salary growth level slowed in 2014 to only 8.65%, but this was still nearly 2.6% greater than the US financial sector pay growth (CFA Institute, Roland Berger Strategy Consultants, & LinkedIn, 2016). High-wage industries encourage primary employees into the financial industry, but the talent demand is mainly among the high-end complex talent and creative professionals. From the view of the talent type, the traditional financial industry practitioners pay more attention to local experience, while the Internet financial industry prefers returning talent. Through an interview survey, it was found that Internet financial companies prefer to recruit employees who have completed undergraduate studies in China and then studied abroad (CFA Institute et al., 2016), because these employees are better at adapting to the local corporate culture compared to the overly Westernised returnee personnel and they also have an international perspective and overseas experience.

26.2.2 *The Influencing Factors of Recruitment on the Internet Financial Industry*

Personnel recruitment is an important process for every organisation. Staff recruitment refers to the scientific methods applied by organisations to find and attract candidates and to choose the personnel to be hired for the enterprise process (Parry, 1994). In accordance with the requirements of the business strategic planning excellence, organisations should be recruiting the right people into the business, putting the right people in the right positions (Bratton & Gold, 2012). There are three crucial stages in the recruitment process (Still, 1985): In the first phase, companies need to engage the attention of potential applicants through job applications or interviews by undertaking a series of propaganda. Companies need to fill the reserve pool of talent resources, helping the organisation gain more options in the next phase (Still, 1985). In the second phase, the organisation can make choices based on the actual capacity and career-matching rate. During the third stage, according to the ability of the admitted employees, organisations need to implement talent management.

Traditional approaches of recruitment and selection tend to attract a lot of candidates to fill the talent pool before selecting applicants who match the job descriptions and personnel specifications according to the formulated standard (Bratton & Gold, 2012). The Internet financial industry also needs to learn from these methods. The enterprise should consider local conditions in the job recruiting process, including external and internal factors.

The external factors include national laws and regulations, external labour market, and competitors. Laws and regulations not only play a regulatory role in terms of citizens' behaviours on a daily basis, but they also have the function of limiting the enterprise recruitment process (Rashmi, 2010); this normally defines the outer boundary of the corporate recruitment activities (Monowar, 2015). For example, there are legal provisions in Western countries that outline that enterprise recruitment information cannot be related to the special provision of gender, race and age, unless there is a proven professional need. An example from China shows that the Beijing municipal government have regulations stressing that companies cannot impose unfair conditions. For example, "only Beijing registered permanent residence" in their recruitment information. These kinds of conditions can hinder business recruitment activities.

Job recruitment, especially external recruitment, is mainly in the external labour market. Hence, the situation of supply and demand in the labour market will affect the result of recruitment. When demand exceeds supply in the labour market (Rashmi, 2010), companies find it more difficult to attract prospective employees (Hayton, 2015). Contrary to this, when supply exceeds demand in the labour market, companies find it relatively easy to attract talent. In order to analyse the impact of the external labour market, organisations need to divide candidates depending on specific job levels and types of jobs. From the available information, analysis of the external labour market is still not perfect in the Internet financial sector.

During the recruitment process, competitors are a very important factor (Rashmi, 2010). Candidates often make the final decision after undertaking comparison; if the recruitment condition of the organisation is very different from its competitors, this will affect the organisation's attraction level. Therefore, organisations need to undertake a comprehensive comparison between their strengths and those of rivals before recruitment, seeking to maximise their comparative advantages (Zaharie & Osoian, 2013).

The internal factors include enterprise brand image, recruitment budget and enterprise policy. Some companies from traditional industries with a preferred image and position have certain advantages in human resource recruitment (Rashmi, 2010). Employer branding, as a term of recruitment and selection, is a very essential factor in the recruiting process (Bratton & Gold, 2012). Jeff Gold considers that "good employers" (Chartered Institute of Particular and Development [CIPD], 2005) can attract more talents to work for their industries and companies (2012). For example, in 2000, the US *Fortune* magazine created a ranking system, and Cisco Systems was elected the most attractive employee in the information industry. Therefore, most jobseekers will prioritise their choice based on the corporate image of the company when they are applying.

Recruitment activities entail certain costs; the corporate recruiters' budget also has an important impact on the result of recruitment (Rashmi, 2010). Enterprises with adequate recruitment funding can select more recruitment methods and expand the scope of recruitment. The recruitment method of the business also reflects the payment of salaries. Higher salaries and better benefits will attract even more talented inflow of people into this industry. Insufficient funds, on the other hand, will limit the capacity to choose high-calibre talent in the recruitment process.

Enterprise policy also has a direct impact on the business of recruitment activities (Rashmi, 2010). Generally, enterprises always have two recruitment channels in the hiring process, internal recruitment and external recruitment. Recruitment channels will be selected depending on their enterprise policy. Some companies tend to use internal recruitment, but other companies are more inclined to use the external recruitment. If organisations focus on external recruitment, they will still need to consider two aspects: the campus recruitment and the social recruitment.

Admittedly, recruitment problems exist in many companies due to various different factors. For example, companies require workforce planning as much as possible to attract a large number of candidates to ensure differences in talent. In the case of posting unexpected vacancies in the organisation, the human resource manager should ensure adequate labour conditions and avoid wasting the cost of hiring the "wrong" employees (Newell, 2005).

26.2.3 The Problems of Recruitment and Selection in China's Internet Financial Industry

In recent years, the news that the Internet financial sector hires professional administrative and technical personnel is often reported in newspapers. P2P network loan companies have paid more than three hundred thousand pounds to hire product managers and risk control personnel. In this regard, the Internet financial industry needs new talent to inject into the current talent gap (Oliver Wyman, 2014). PPmoney, Zhongguancun Internet Finance Institute and Beijing University Internet Financial Research Institute are research leaders in the Internet financial industry; they have issued a circular expressing their willingness to pay higher salaries and offer a good welfare policy in order to recruit senior management personnel and research staff. With the development of the Internet financial industry, the problem of talent shortage has become increasingly serious. In this respect, recruitment via various recruitment channels has become the strategy that Internet financial companies cannot ignore. Recruitment in the Internet financial sector is divided among the use of four channels: campus recruitment, poaching, online recruitment and social recruitment. However, the actual effect of these recruitment channels highlights several recruitment problems.

In the early days of the Internet financial industry, candidates did not fully understand the concept of Internet finance during the campus recruitment process (Deloitte, 2016). In 2015, the government of China made a significant effort to support this industry, and as a result, the Internet financial industry entered a golden period of development. Subsequently, college graduates have come to understand the concept of Internet finance. However, there are still some scholars who believe that Internet finance reflects some potential unstable factors. These scholars believe that Internet finance may be out of the real economy; although high-level technology is used to realise the innovative business model, there are still regulatory loopholes (Jeffery, 2015). The P2P network lending platform doesn't have a review of information security, which leads to the presence of illegal fund-raising. Therefore, the police have reminded people to be prudent in verifying the reliability of Internet financial companies. As a result, in the Internet industry, the risk factors have become an obstacle to practitioners entering the industry. The Internet financial industry needs a stable financial profitability and return rate; at the same time, it also needs to improve its business model. The industry needs to repair its unflattering reputation and establish its own brand image. The new model for this industry must ensure that talented professionals are proud to work in these companies (Oliver Wyman, 2014).

The supply of professionals and an incomplete training system have not been able to meet the rapid development of the industry; therefore, most Internet finance companies used poaching in the early phase. This involves the use of high salaries and equity incentives to attract talents from traditional banking, insurance, Internet and other industries (Deloitte, 2016). Therefore, many bank executives and Internet industry professional managers have quit emerging Internet finance companies. Furthermore, as a new industry, the overall high-pay levels have led to too much pressure from higher labour costs. The core position pay depends on negotiations between the parties, and this often leads the company to undertake passive recruitment. Therefore, hiring executives from other industries is a complementary talent strategy. With the development of the Internet financial industry, the industry needs to establish a healthy talent echelon.

26.3 Research Methodology

In order to explore the reasons for recruitment difficulty among the Internet financial sector, and considering the industry development status in China and social reasons, some particular in-depth information needs to be collected from those involved. The eleven respondents selected are all relevant personnel who are familiar with the procedure of recruitment and are selected from the three Internet financial companies in China; five of the respondents currently work in human resource recruitment and selection, and the remaining six respondents are jobseekers who have applied for Internet financial companies. They all come from cities across China with a well-developed Internet financial industry, and they all have a good educational background; they can accurately express their views on the industrial recruitment and selection according to their own experiences and observations.

The three Internet financial companies referred to in this research are companies who have a certain social influence in the Chinese Internet financial industry. What follows are the specific conditions of these three companies. First, Alibaba Group's Ali Finance Company is a microfinance business division of small microfinancial services, which is responsible for financing all its subsidiary platforms. This company was founded in 2009, mainly for small and microenterprises and individual entrepreneurs to provide micro-credit business. In less than a year after its establishment, the company's total lending was more than 10 billion RMB (about 1.14 billion pounds). It has more than 300 employees, and the scope of work is related to product development, marketing, risk assessment, etc.

Second, PPmoney is a P2P net loan platform launched in December 2012 and based in Guangzhou; it has 450 employees and is operated by Guangzhou Wanhui Investment Management Co., Ltd. It has a registered capital of 30 million RMB (about 3.4 million pounds). Founded more than 3 years ago, the cumulative turnover has reached 24.2 billion RMB (about 2.7 billion pounds) and its registered users exceed 500 million. The company helps users earn an income of over 400 million RMB (about 45 million pounds) and does not appear to have any bad debts; it was named in the national top three platforms in this industry. It's worth noting that PPmoney's average daily turnover accounts for 70% of the Guangzhou market turnover, and the mobile terminal transactions account for 80% of overall turnover.

Third, Rong 360 (Beijing Rong Century Information Technology Co., Ltd.) is a new online financial services company using big data and search technology to provide recommendations and application services for financial products to individual consumers and small and microenterprises. Rong 360 also provides users with convenient, cost-effective and secure financial information services at no charge. Hundreds of bank financial products can be visually presented to the user on this platform. From October 8, 2011, to the present, the number of employees has grown from the original Rong 360. It started with ten people and has now nearly seven hundred people. The company has developed into the largest platform for financial products "recommended + search + service", covering nearly 300 cities in China and providing PCs and mobile terminal services for free. The number of users has amounted to 12.3 million in 4 years, and the approved amount of credit application is nearly 3000 billion RMB (about 340 billion pounds). The number of searches is nearly one billion each month, and as a result, Rong 360 has successfully created the first entry-level financial search service.

The interview framework is designed around nine open-ended questions (*see Appendix 1*) and provides ample space for interviewees to express their own opinions on the human resource recruitment issue. These interview questions are designed to be dependent on the results of the literature review, and the purpose is to explore the experiences and ideas of industrial stakeholders. According to these nine questions, interviews are conducted with related recruiting personnel and candidates who have been involved in the hiring process in the Internet financial industry. Recruitment-related personnel are interviewed in order to gain more information about the firm's recruitment policy and team-building strategies, while interviews with candidates provide a deeper understanding of the candidates' psychology with regard to the actual recruitment process and the specific challenges. Therefore, the interviews are divided into two parts, in order to conduct a comprehensive analysis of this social problem from the talent supply and the talent demand perspective. The respondents selected are from different Chinese Internet financial companies and different positions related to recruitment. Therefore, their views and experiences reflect the authentic situation of recruitment in the Internet financial sector.

26.4 Results

26.4.1 *Recruitment Channels*

Ali Finance relies on her parent company, Ali Group. Having a good reputation helps; the company has therefore rarely been short of jobseekers; however, there has also been some confusion in the human resource recruitment. When asked about the recruitment channels of Ali Finance, one HR recruiter said:

> There are two main reasons that can influence the recruitment effect: recruitment channels and recruitment needs. Almost all companies are not satisfied with any recruitment channels, so companies' human resources departments often lament recruitment difficulties. More candidates are bullish on the prospects for Alibaba group, and therefore companies' campus recruitment and online recruitment usually receives a lot of application materials, but the recruitment effect is not very good. Although the campus recruitment is in favour of long-term development and updated knowledge of human resources, they lack work experience, and do not know their career self-positioning. Campus recruitment may lead companies to take the risk of larger job mobility.

From this perspective, despite the fact that the good reputation of the company can attract a large number of jobseekers through the Internet and campus recruitment, screening the outstanding candidates is still a challenge that HR needs to face. Although many jobseekers bring more choice to companies, there is also an increase in the time cost of the recruitment process. One suggestion by a HR recruiter, in this regard, said:

> The method of recruiting candidates' needs to be adjusted from the traditional way of thinking of a buyer's market mirroring selection of personnel like, marketing "positioning". The recruitment process needs to consider recruitment requirements, not only be concerned with the number of candidates.

For Rong 360, HR staff member Mr. Chen suggested that recruitment mainly depended on unified social recruitment in spring and autumn. Graduate recruitment and summer temps can get through campus recruitment; this recruitment channel is adapted to recruit for some professional staff positions and special technical posts. These employees have a strong plasticity when they are in the workplace; they quickly become familiar with the business and adapt to the environment. If the company wants to recruit some senior positions, Mr. Chen said that Rong 360 usually carried out such recruitment with the cooperation of professional head-hunters:

> Recruitment occupied most of the work time in the human resources department, this process takes time and energy, but the effect is not obvious. Hence, HR likes to maintain a cooperative relationship with professional head-hunters, thus enabling the recruitment

> efficiency to improve a lot. The characteristics of employees who are headhunted have rich work experience in management or professional skills, or they are relatively rare talent in the industry, and even in the corresponding position. In addition, the company's senior positions are generally on-job employees; open recruitment will affect their enthusiasm for work.

Although recruitment through headhunting saves time and improves the quality of the candidates, effective access to personnel requires higher recruitment costs. This is generally entrusted to professional headhunting firms; the principle cost is 30% of the hunted talent's annual salary. Therefore, Mr. Chen did not consider this recruitment channel suitable for a wide range of applications.

For PPmoney, social recruitment and campus recruitment are still the main recruitment channels. Its co-founder Hu said:

> Social recruiting is a common recruitment channel, the approach of employee referral has been more widely used in domestic and foreign enterprises, and the Microsoft Company has said that 40% of the employees are obtained through the method of employee referrals.

The main reason why the employee referral method is popular is that there is often a similarity between the candidates recommended and the existing employees. The quality and ability of recommended talents are more reliable, and after a referral by two-way communication, some rigid requirements of professionals and the status and development prospects of enterprises will have a very comprehensive understanding (Nilsson et al., 2016). As a result, this saves a lot of communication and contrast costs and will bring a relatively high success rate of recruitment. Mr. Sun, who is responsible for employee recruitment at PPmoney, said:

> Our PPmoney internet platform has also introduced 'Million hunting talents' recruitment plan, as long as recommended talents were selected by the company, the referrer will get a lot of money as a bonus – 30,000 RMB top prize. The reward focuses on product category, technology type, operational class and other talent gap larger positions.

It can be seen that the recruiting directors of PPmoney are more inclined to use this method; they think this approach can save costs, leading to recruiting personnel of high quality and a relatively low turnover rate. However, they did not discuss some of the negative impacts of employee referral channels, for example. And the actual cultural background of Chinese society will affect human resource recruitment. Some internal staff may just want to seek a job opportunity for their friends and family members; they do not necessarily consider whether the recommended person is qualified or not. Even worse is that some employees or senior leadership in the company just want to cultivate secret support; hence they arrange for their friends to be in some important positions in the company. The formation of several small groups will affect the company's organisational structure and normal functioning.

26.4.2 *Staffing Structure*

The rationality of staffing structure not only affects the entire teamworking efficiency as well as each employee's working attitude but also the motivation of potential employees to join in this industry (Wood, 2013). Ali Finance's management staff member Mr. Zhang provided a specific answer to this problem about employee structure rationality:

> There are currently more than 300 employees in Ali Finance, more than one-third are IT technology developers, nearly one-third are the data analysts, and the remaining one-third are client managers, financials and other positions like traditional banks. This kind of personnel structure cannot be seen in the traditional financial institutions. Certainly, traditional bank also cannot surpass the daily lending of on average nearly ten thousand times more in Ali Finance.

The job is split into several steps, each independently undertaken by one person, so that the job achieves specialisation. Employees engaged in specialised work will increase their productivity (Wood, 2013). Internet finance is more competitive in work efficiency than traditional banks; the main reason for this is the unreasonable industry employees assigned. Ali Finance is very aware of this. In addition, the echelon of talents is also very important, providing strong support for the improvement of personnel structure. Mr. Zhang commented further about Ali Finance's practices in talent echelon building:

> Adjusting the structure of Ali Finance is a reformation that we must go through when we face development in the future, but it also means the beginning of young Ali's era. We have seven younger managers who were born after the 80s hold key management positions.

Mr. Zhang's answer may identify that Ali Finance has a good plan for talent, but when the company has a vacancy for whatever reason, Ali Finance can ensure the right person will take over this position. Quickly resolving the issue of talent change is not only good for carrying out work but also builds a good company image of fresh talent, which will help to hire first-class talent. When asked about what kind of staffing structure is used in Rong 360, its co-founder Mr. Lu said:

> Nowadays the talent proportion between financial professionals and Internet talents is 1:1 in Rong 360. Of the department leaders who report work to me, almost all have experience working for banking operations for over 10 years. Therefore, we do not rush to find top talents in the banking industry.

Although the Internet financial industry is an emerging industry, it is clear that a wealth of relevant work experience is still a necessary part for the talent composition of Rong 360. Furthermore, the proportion of each type of talent is relatively balanced in the entire company. PPmoney reveal similarities to this:

> PPmoney currently have 450 employees, including 32 people in operations centres, 40 people in air control centres, 81 people in business centres and 95 people in technical centres. The internal staffing arrangement of our company is balanced very well.

26.4.3 *The Policy of Human Resource Management*

The company's policies for human resource management directly affect recruitment (Collings, 2012). Therefore, if the enterprise wants to attract more talents, they have to adjust their policies of human resource management. When asked about the management policies of Ali Finance, Ali Finance staff member Yong Zhang said:

> Ali Finance will use 40% of the shares to motivate all employees from Ali Finance and Ali Group, serving employees will receive shares of Ali Finance. Alibaba founder Jack Ma as one of all employees, will hold certain shares, but his stake will not exceed 7.3%.

This management style of the employees having stock ownership is rare in Chinese enterprises. With regard to the company's main reasons for all employees having stock ownership, Ali considers it a healthy, efficient and sustainable shareholding structure that is shared together with its employees, partners and customers. When the interests of stakeholders are met, this is more conducive to maintaining a long-term development and stability of talents (Longenecker & Fink, 2015).

In addition to some positive human resource management policies, the recruitment of Ali Finance has been affected by other management policies which are known to be controversial. It is understood that Ali Group announced that it would cut 2016 fresh graduate posts, from the original 3000 people to just 400 people. Ali Finance is a subsidiary, and it was inevitably affected by the new personnel management policies. The decision caused great controversy; a human resource recruiter noted that:

> Recruitment of some posts has slowed in the whole Ali Group because of a limited number of available posts; the company is more focused on the experienced talents.

There were a lot of complaints from interns of Ali Finance because they were not satisfied with changes in the policies of the company personnel management. Ali Finance intern Yixuan Zhang said:

> Ali's policies of talent strategy adjustment have sacrificed the interests of our interns; the recruitment reduction means we work hard for more than a year, but we cannot get the last entry offer. And what is more, HR even encourages us to recommend other friends to become interns. From the company's point of view, the company reduces employment costs and ensures the work is completed.

We can deduce that Ali Finance's interns have had a negative attitude to the results of the company's latest issue. Even though Ali Finance's management team considered the interests of the entire company before undertaking the strategic change in recruitment, the effect has not been viewed well at all. Interns, as potential employees, suspect the integrity of Ali Finance because the company has harmed the interests of its employees. Consequentially, they have had to find new working opportunities during the period of non-recruitment. As a result, the grievances of all interns and complaints have a bad effect on the employer brand of the Ali Group. Another intern, Wei Cheng, held a similar opinion; he said:

> Ali dealt with this issue very irresponsibly. Although acknowledging that the company's strategic reasons brought some losses to interns, Ali did not provide any compensation,

except for a few departments who gave a recommendation letter and a USB to them as an apology gift.

26.4.4 *The Challenges with the Recruitment Process*

The problem with recruitment is attributed by two issues. First, Internet financial companies find it difficult to attract talents. Second, existing candidates barely come up to the company's standard. In order to get a balanced perspective on these two aspects, Jun Chen, the general manager of Harbin Bank Shenyang Branch Product Innovation Centre, and Zheng Li, who went to an Ali Finance interview, shared their thoughts about the challenges of recruiting talents from traditional banking to the Internet financial industry; Jun Chen said:

> Internet financial companies always have talent pool characteristics of flattening, and the quantity demand of credit approval employees and risk control professionals are less than the traditional bank industry, but they are still indispensable positions. And furthermore, Internet financial companies have to face a difficult challenge in that they are recruiting risk control talents who reach the high-level stated requirements of the Internet financial industry.

Jun Chen analysed the main causes of this issue according to his working experience; he suggested that:

> There are two aspects related to this; one is that these people must have a wealth of experience, and this experience can only be found from the traditional banking system. Because of the corporate culture and the social orientation of traditional banks over the years, risk control talents have a high quality of experience in a universal role placed in an important prime leadership position, but they lack motivation for job-hopping. Another reason is to do with emolument: risk control directors of Internet financial companies get 300-400 thousand RMB as an annual income, which is almost no difference, and may not even be better than traditional banks.

Due to the lack of risk control talents in the Internet financial industry, the community widely suspects the risk control ability of Internet financial companies (Walet, 2015), providing inadequate incentives as compared with conventional banking. Nonetheless, this argument is not entirely correct. In the mobile Internet era, risk management methods and tools are both changing, so we should consider this issue depending on the respective development. In addition, it needs to be noted that the income of Internet financial companies is unsatisfactory for traditional bank employees. Another perspective suggests that candidates are attracted by Internet finance companies often less than the company's job requirements. One candidate, Zheng Li, shared his recruitment experience of Ali Finance. He said:

> My interviewer was working in creditor's right management, he required candidates to have a breadth of knowledge about macroeconomic theory and experience. I feel that only those people who possess economics PhDs or hold high-level posts in the asset management industry can perform this job. Obviously, my professional skills and abilities do not match.

The Internet financial industry is still in its early stages of development and companies are not willing to invest in talent training. Hence, access to personnel relies on the traditional financial industry or the Internet industry recruiting experienced personnel. People who meet these conditions generally already have a high occupational status and they do not want to risk job-hopping. Another point worth mentioning is that the higher standard requirements expected of graduating candidates undermine the construction of echelon personnel.

26.5 Discussion and Conclusion

Due to the rapid development of the Internet financial industry, the shortage of qualified personnel in this industry should be treated as a challenge. According to a traditional Chinese cultural background, analysing the reasons for recruitment problems in a new emerging field makes human resource management an interesting problem. In this essay, qualitative research methods, as well as secondary data research, helped explore some real issues dealing with the human resource practices in the Internet financial recruitment process. Conducting interviews with professionals and evaluating employee viewpoints about recruitment problems, the hope is that these findings and some recorded cases will help provide an answer of sorts to the issue.

The recruitment channel is the most important factor that affects the results of recruitment. Selected recruitment channels will significantly impact filling a vacancy in the Internet financial industry, which is always further affected by three factors (Sabatier, 2010). First, the selected recruitment channels based on the characteristics of the Internet financial companies concerned. Second, companies arrange multiple channels of recruitment, rather than just selecting one recruitment channel. A combination of recruitment channels is useful for improving the effectiveness of the company's recruitment. Third, the probability of filling a vacancy is strongly influenced by the recruitment strategies of the company (Sabatier, 2010). According to the actual situation of the Chinese Internet financial industry, the research result showed some differences from previous literature. Almost all Internet finance companies are dissatisfied with the recruitment channels; campus and online recruitment can lead to a lot of applications, but the candidate level may not meet the company requirements, which in turn, leads to a lot of wasted time and energy. Some firms recruit talents through headhunting companies in order to save time and get highly qualified professionals. However, there is a problem. They have to pay more recruitment costs. Interviewees expressed that the employee referral method is the most effective way to recruit suitable employees, because this method can attract some candidates who are similar to existing employees. The employee referral method is economical and high-efficiency; nonetheless, *guanxi* in Chinese culture easily affects the objectivity of this method (Cai & Yu, 2014). For example, existing employees may recommend some unsuitable candidates just because they are friends or family members. Hence, companies need to be on their guard against this in the process of recruitment.

The rationale of the staffing structure affects teamworking efficiency and the working attitude, which is a key element in developing the Internet financial industry. Along with the development of the entire industry, this assignment is split into many working steps, which will improve working efficiency and make it more specialised (Wood, 2013). From the results of the interviews, interviewees expressed that IT technology developers, data analysts and client managers are recruited in almost an equal number. Therefore, department balance is advantageous for the stability of employees' structure. In addition, Internet financial industry is an emerging industry, which tends to employ younger managers who were born after the 1980s and who held key management positions. This cannot only build a healthy talent echelon, but it also creates a good company image of fresh talent, helping Internet financial companies recruit more high-quality talents.

The human resource management policies of Internet financial companies influence recruitment effectiveness. Companies can attract more jobseekers through adjusting their human resource policies; for example, Ali Group intended to recruit 3000 employees in 2016 from graduate interns; this human resource policy attracted a lot of applicants to choose Ali and give up their other options in the workplace. However, a company's negative policies will also have a negative influence; for example, after attracting so many interns, Ali Group instituted a new HR policy that reduced the recruitment amount from 3000 people to 400 people. Ali interns complained about this unfair decision, and later some interns gave up this job opportunity. As a result, the integrity of Ali has been called into question. In this case, it provides a warning to companies that they should be cautious when they decide on human resource policies and consider emergency solutions in order to prevent damaging the employer brand image.

Research findings have highlighted some challenges. One of the main problems of recruitment is that it is difficult to attract talents while not ignoring the low quality of candidates, too. Internet financial companies need to pay more attention to risk control, so the industry has a higher standard for risk control practitioners in the recruitment processes. A higher standard requirement, which includes rich working experience or professional business knowledge with a certification of industry recognition, is hard to find through campus recruitment and general social recruitment. Consider the fact that companies do not like to invest in training, so they tend to recruit potential target employees from traditional banking backgrounds. In fact, interviewees reflected that people who do meet the company's standard requirement already have a good salary and a high professional position, and in most cases, they do not want to change to a new job. Other candidates, like new graduates or general employees, have not the deep macroeconomic theoretical knowledge and rich working experience required. These issues reflect the main difficulties in the recruitment process and it leaves unanswered questions.

Interviewees provided some suggestions for the future according to their own experiences. On the macro level, potential talents have not enough confidence in the Internet finance industry. Some negative information affects the judgment of talents;

it is suggested that relevant government departments should take forceful measures to strengthen the administration on laws and regulations, an approval system and risk management analysis. For instance, a clearly defined supervisory organisation provides a comprehensive institutional system in order to control the risk of bad debts. On the micro level, companies should invest in training their employees to reduce the capital of the company in the short term. This is good for long-term talent team construction. At the same time, people who want to work in this industry should undertake self-career planning and constantly improve their professional ability.

26.6 Limitations and Future Research Directions

Some limitations of the current research were discussed. The first limitation lies in the limited sample and the nature of qualitative research. Without additional quantitative research, the number of samples was limited to the 11 interviewees, so the finding represented is limited in this case. Although attempts were made to collect more information, the data collection may not be comprehensive enough.

The second limitation is that the interviews were conducted in Chinese Mandarin, so there is a problem of translation in the data collection stage. The Chinese often express their views in implied meanings; therefore the interviewer required a good comprehension ability and translation skills during the process of the interview. Although Chinese Mandarin is the interviewer's mother tongue and the interviewer has only been learning English for a couple of years, this still cannot guarantee that all the information is translated or understood accurately. In the translation process, the cultural background of the investigator will likely affect the objectivity of the survey result.

The third limitation is that the investigating media may have led to some disadvantages. Using the Internet as the survey method saved a lot of time and resources, but this approach still has drawbacks. Firstly, compared to the face-to-face interview, an online interview makes it more difficult to establish a trust relationship with respondents (Bryman & Bell, 2011). Therefore, investigators need to spend more time on the initial communication. Secondly, the interview relies mainly on plain text records, and any research cannot be fact-check with any accuracy based on the information obtained through eye contact and body language. Finally, some of the older respondents are not good at using computers for interviews. Despite the popularity of personal computers in China being relatively high, many of her citizens still cannot use computers (ibid). Therefore, the investigator had to commission a third party as a representative to complete the interview.

In this research, the researchers discussed some of the main reasons that obstruct the employee recruitment process. Different companies may have these issues due to other reasons. Hence, the subsequent research in this field refers to employee performance and development, reward management and employee training. In addition, the aim of this research only focused on the problems facing the Internet financial industry, and it didn't make comparisons with companies in different areas. Determining the reasons of recruitment difficulties between the developed and developing cities still needs further research, but for the moment, this paper presents suggestions in maximising performances in those areas.

In this Internet Age, you would think that the social attribute of people is increasing; on the contrary, the attributes of organisations are weakening. Companies need talent, but talent is less dependent on companies. In essence, companies no longer hold the initiative in the recruitment process; they have to change their attitudes. The development of the whole industry needs employees with professional backgrounds and good technical knowledge as well as an extensive working experience in the relevant industry. Hence, the Internet financial companies prefer to recruit talents from traditional banking and Internet companies. As a result, personnel recruited have vast stores of knowledge and experience and save the administrative cost of training and recruiting. But this recruitment model is not good for building a team of talents. A company without staff training will suffer, and there will be turbulence in the process of organising staff turnover.

Therefore, Internet financial companies need to provide multiple growth space and incentive mechanism for talent development (LinkedIn, 2016). First, companies need to establish a comprehensive internal promotion channel. Internet financial companies should have a full understanding of talent flows in order to identify talent needs of career development. Establishing a fair internal professional promotion system provides a career opportunity for existing employees and improves the efficiency of internal talent. Second, companies need to establish a staff training system in order to improve employees' sense of belonging. At the same time, companies should communicate actively with staff and give their employees a clear understanding of the organisational development planning in the future. With the purpose of pursuing flat organisation, managers can authorise the grass-roots talents, letting each employee gain experience of being respected. Third, companies should offer a multi-incentive system to meet the demands and expectations of existing employees. This helps to enhance the competitive advantage of Internet financial industry in the talent market.

Appendix

Interview Questions

For the HR practitioners who have participated in recruitment in the Internet finance companies:

1.	Why do you want to work in the Internet financial industry?
2.	What challenges did you encounter during the recruitment process?
3.	In your opinion, in what areas can the candidates improve?

4.	With regard to the recruitment process of the Internet financial companies, what would you like them to improve?
5.	Are you bullish about the prospects for the industry? Why? Why not?

For the key employees who understand the hiring process of Internet financial companies:

1.	Are there any recruitment difficulties in your company?
2.	Which channels for recruitment have been applied in your company?
3.	What kind of employees do you think are needed in the Internet financial industry?
4.	Which position is the most difficult to recruit at the present stage? Do you know why?
5.	What method do you think is most effective in the talent team construction of the Internet financial industry? Internal training or external employment?
6.	What are the human resource management policies for recruitment in your company?
7.	How do you think the Internet financial industry practitioners should undertake their own career planning?

References

Bratton, J. and Gold, J. (2012) Human Resource Management: Theory & Practice. New York: Palgrave Macmillan. 5th edition.

Bryman, A., & Bell, E. (2011). *Business research methods*. Oxford: Oxford University Press.

Cai, Y. & Yu, M. (2014). Examining Cross-Cultural HR Practices in Family Firms: Based on Three Taiwan Family Firms in Mainland China. International Journal of Global Management Studies 5(1), 51–66.

CFA Institute, Roland Berger Strategy Consultants and LinkedIn. (2016). Financial talent development in China 2016. *CFA Institute Report.* Retrieved from: http://www.cfainstitute.cn/media/89953/financial-talent-development-report-2016-final_en.pdf

Chartered Institute of Personnel and Development. (2005). *Recruitment, retention and turnover*. London, UK: CIPD.

Collings, G. D. (2012). International human resource management: Policies and practices for multinational enterprises. *The International Journal of Human Resource Management., 23*(7), 1509–1511.

Deloitte (2016). Banking industry disruptors: Banking reimagined. Retrieved from:https://www2.deloitte.com/us/en/pages/financial-services/articles/banking-industry-disrupter.html

Hayton, C. J. (2015). *Human resource management*. Online ISSN: 1099-050X.

Jeffery, P. (2015). *The next leading club*. London Business School. Retrieved from: https://www.london.edu/faculty-and-research/lbsr/the-next-lending-club#.V5VBclfMHUo

LinkedIn (2016) "Internet finance", the financial revolution for all people? Retrieved from:https://www.linkedin.com/pulse/internet-finance-financial-revolution-all-people-k-l-/

Liu, Q. (2015). Internet financial professionals will be hard to find: a CEO the highest annual salary of 10 million Yuan. *People.cn*. Retrieved from: http://money.people.com.cn/stock/n/2015/0815/c67815-27467050.html (In Chinese).

Longenecker, C., & Fink, L. S. (2015). Ten questions that make a difference for HR leadership. *Human Resource Management International Digest, 23*(3), 20–22.
Monowar, M. (2015). Strategy, structure, and HRM policy orientation: Employee recruitment and selection practices in multinational subsidiaries. *Asia Pacific Journal of Human Resources, 53*(3), 331–350.
Newell, S. (2005). Recruitment and selection. In S. Bach (Ed.), *Managing human resources*. Oxford: Blackwell.
Nilsson, I., Löjdqvist, M., Hoppe, M., Maaninen-Olsson, E., Mälardalens, H., Akademin, E., & Samhälle, T. (2016). *Recruiting through the grapevine: The relevance of employee referral programs within the field of employer branding*. Mälardalen University.
Oliver Wyman (2014) The challenges ahead the state of the financial services industry 2014. Retrieved from:http://www.oliverwyman.com/content/dam/oliver-wyman/global/en/files/insights/financial-services/2014/Jan/Oliver%20Wyman_State%20of%20Financial%20Services%20Industry%202014.pdf
Parry, J. (1994). *Recruitment*. London, UK: Library Association Publishing. ISBN: 1856041069.
Puxin Research Institute. (2014). *2014 Salary status of financial industry Internet*. Puxin Research Institute.
Rashmi, T. K. (2010). *Recruitment management*. Publisher: Himalaya Publishing House. (In Chinese).
Sabatier, M. (2010). Filling vacancies: Identifying the most efficient recruitment channel. *Economics Bulletin*. Retrieved from: https://hal.archives-ouvertes.fr/file/index/docid/825991/filename/EB-10-V30-I4-P310.pdf?frbrVersion=7
Schneider, P. G. (1952). *E-business* (8th ed.). Basingstoke, UK: Palgrave Macmillan. ISBN: 140391348X.
Still, M. (1985). *Technical recruitment*. London, UK: New Opportunity Press.
Walet, L. (2015). Internet finance and China will banking innovation promote growth and reform? *CFA Institute Magazine*. Retrieved from: http://www.lapres.net/cfa.pdf
Wood, E. (2013). New staffing structure builds on success of specialty team model. *OR Manager, 29*(7), 1–9.
Yao, L. (2014). *Policy discussion of Internet finance in China*. Bank of Finland – Institute for Economies in Transition. ISSN 2342-205X. Retrieved from: http://www.suomenpankki.fi/bofit/tutkimus/tutkimusjulkaisut/policy_brief/Documents/2014/bpb1314.pdf
Zaharie, M., & Osoian, C. (2013). Job recruitment and selection practices in small and medium organisations. *Studia Universitatis Babes-Bolyai.Serie Oeconomica, 58*(2), 86–94.
Zhongpin Inc. (2007). *Zhongpin awarded 'most competitive brand china 2006' and 'CCTV 2006 best employer of henan province'*. PR Newswire. Retrieved from: http://search.proquest.com/docview/451035141?accountid=14680

Ms. Jingyi Liu works in the HR department in Neri & Hu Design and Research Offices, an interdisciplinary architectural design practice based in Shanghai, China, with an additional office in London, UK. Her work role involves summarising and analysing cross-cultural human resource management methods in practice. Jingyi's research interests include cross-cultural human resource management, emerging industry management, employee participation, etc.

Dr. Yujie Cai is Lecturer in Human Resource Management in Swansea University, School of Management, UK. He is Honorary Fellow in University of Liverpool, Management School, and Research Fellow at the Institute of Leadership and Educational Advanced Development (ILEAD) at XJTLU. Dr. Cai's research interests include high-performance work systems, occupational safety, cross-cultural management, employee participation, volunteer workforce, etc.

Chapter 27
Advances in Talent Management Research: A Review of Extant Literature

Adel Alferaih

Abstract This paper aims to provide a selective literature review of articles published in the last decade on talent management (TM), specifically on aspects of TM implementation in particular sectors, and to explore the methodological and theoretical limitations of emerging research in this area. The review identified a total of 64 relevant articles related to the following 8 sectors: tourism and hospitality, education, banking and finance, business process outsourcing and information technology-enabled services, pharmaceuticals, healthcare, real estate and telecommunications. Among the most frequently occurring methodological limitations discovered were limited generalisability, context-specific subject or biased sample, insufficient sample size and a snapshot approach to data collection. The review also found that this research lacked a theoretical underpinning and that more research studies are needed to empirically validate some of the key variables emerging in this area of research. The study concludes with a literature synthesis and recommendations for future research.

Keywords Literature review · Talent · Talent management · Sector · Methodological limitations · Theoretical limitations

27.1 Introduction

Talent management (TM) is one of the most important human capital challenges faced by the twenty-first-century organisations (De Vos & Dries, 2013). Since a group of McKinsey consultants coined the phrase 'War for Talent' in 1997, the topic of TM has received a remarkable degree of interest from both practitioners and academics (Collings & Mellahi, 2009; Iles et al., 2010). It is essential to define 'talent' before studying TM, because it could influence how talents are recognised and how TM approaches are reinforced. The McKinsey report refers to talent as

A. Alferaih (✉)
Ministry of Education, Riyadh, Saudi Arabia

Y. K. Dwivedi et al. (eds.), *Emerging Markets from a Multidisciplinary Perspective*, Advances in Theory and Practice of Emerging Markets,
https://doi.org/10.1007/978-3-319-75013-2_27

'the best and brightest' and the 'A-level' employees of an organisation, who are ranked in the top 10–20% of its overall employee base (Beechler and Woodward, 2009). Alternatively, it has been argued that talent could be seen as the top performers, employees with high potential, senior managers suitable for directorships or other people apt for critical roles in the organisation (Blass, 2007). Taking a more analytical approach, Ulrich (2006) argues that talent is the multiplication of '3Cs', namely, the competence of an individual, commitment to the work and the organisation and contribution through the meaning and purpose of the work.

As with talent, TM has no agreed precise definition. Lewis and Heckman (2006) cite the practitioner-oriented literature as describing TM as 'a mindset' (Creelman, 2004), a key component of effective succession planning (Cheloha & Swain, 2005) and an effort to make sure that 'everyone at all levels works to the top of their potential' (Redford, 2005, p.20). They go on to identify three distinct strains of thought regarding TM. The first defines TM as typical human resource management (HRM) practices, functions, activities or specialist areas including recruitment, selection, development and career and succession management (Byham, 2001; Chowanec & Newstrom, 1991; Heinen & O'Neill, 2004; Hilton, 2000; Mercer, 2005; Olsen, 2000). A second perspective on TM focuses on the concept of the talent pool, which refers to the resource of high-potential and high-performing incumbents that the organisation can draw upon to fill critical positions (Collings & Mellahi, 2009). TM, for these authors, is a set of processes designed to ensure an adequate flow of employees into jobs throughout the organisation (Kesler, 2002; Pascal, 2004). A third perspective on TM focuses on talent in general without looking at the organisational boundaries or specific positions. Reviewing the three schools of thought, it is clear that TM is not only a perspective on managing the human resources of an organisation but also the act of doing everything to take the organisational workforce to its highest levels of capability and performance.

TM is the key to survivability and sustainability for every organisation. It is seen as a multifaceted compilation of associated HR processes that delivers a simple basic benefit for any organisation (Areiqat, Abdelhadi, & Al-Tarawneh, 2010). TM's best practices deliver extensive benefits to both organisations and professionals, including financial benefits, skills, capabilities and competence, boosting performance in both public and private sectors (Ahmadi et al., 2012). The use of talent management reduces the time spent hiring replacements for leaders and specialists (Cappelli, 2008; Hills, 2009). TM practices ensure that the right people are recruited to the workforce, so that a maximally talented workforce is identified, valued and retained with the appropriate incentives (Brundage & Koziel, 2010; Ringo et al., 2008). Similarly, in today's swiftly moving, uncertain and extremely competitive global environment, organisations across the world are facing a number of global talent challenges (Schuler et al., 2011; Scullion et al., 2010; Tarique & Schuler, 2010). Despite its significance for today's organisation, very few studies (e.g. Lewis & Heckman, 2006; Scott & Revis, 2008; Tarique & Schuler, 2010; Thunnissen et al., 2013; Vaiman et al., 2012) have reviewed the literature on this topic. Some (Scott & Revis, 2008) have reviewed literature on TM linked to particular sectors, while others have reviewed it under dominant themes (e.g. Thunnissen et al., 2013;

Vaiman et al., 2012) or specific types of TM, such as global talent management (e.g. Tarique & Schuler, 2010), emerging from the literature. However, none of the existing studies has had a scope extending to all possible sectors where TM has been implemented or to the theoretical and methodological limitations of the existing TM research. To fill this research gap, there are two main aspects of the present review, namely, a brief overview of the literature on TM implementation in various sectors and consideration of the methodological and theoretical limitations of existing TM research.

The remaining sections of the paper are structured as follows: Sect. 27.2 describes the literature search approach. Section 27.3 offers a brief overview of literature on TM implementation across various sectors. Section 27.4 discusses the methodological and theoretical limitations of existing TM research, and then Sect. 27.5 delivers a brief literature synthesis and recommendations for future research. Section 27.6 concludes this study by considering its limitations and suggesting future research directions.

27.2 Literature Search Approach

This study identifies and reviews all research articles on TM implementation in specific sectors which explicitly address their methodological and theoretical limitations, published during the years 2007–2017 and listed in the Google Scholar and Scopus databases. The decision to limit selection to the last decade was largely motivated by the fact that TM research has grown strongly and consistently during that time. Titles, keywords and abstracts were searched using the terms 'talent', 'talent management' and 'human capital', with logical OR, resulting in the identification of 95 studies. Further investigation found that 31 of these either did not specify their methodological or theoretical limitations or were not directly related to the key theme of TM implementation in a specific sector; some were concerned with generic private and/or public sector contexts or with the European context, for example. Excluding these 31 resulted in a final selection of 64 articles that fully matched the above inclusion criteria.

27.3 Literature Review

27.3.1 Talent Management in Various Economic Sectors

This section reviews the literature exploring the various TM-related challenges, such as those to attracting and retaining talent, turnover, commitment, satisfaction, performance and engagement, faced by diverse public and private organisations in the following eight sectors: hospitality and tourism, banking and finance, education, business process outsourcing (BPO) and IT-enabled services (ITES),

Table 27.1 Economic sectors and TM research

Economic sector	# of studies	Example source(s)
Hospitality and tourism	11	Barron (2008), Baum (2008), D'Annunzio-Green (2008), Deery (2008), Deery and Jago (2015), Grobler and Diedericks (2009), Hughes and Rog (2008), Maxwell and MacLean (2008), Scott and Revis (2008), Walsh and Taylor (2007), Watson (2008)
Education	8	Behrstock (2010), Davies and Davies (2010), Hoff (1999), Olson (2008), Peet et al. (2010), Stewart and Harte (2010), Sun (2012), van den Brink et al. (2013)
Banking and finance	5	Al Ruwaili et al. (2013), Kamil and Salleh (2013), Sparrow et al. (2013), Tajuddin, Ali, and Kamaruddin (2015), Tansley and Tietze (2013)
BPO and IT-enabled services	2	Bhatnagar (2007), Chadee and Raman (2012)
Pharmaceuticals	2	Garavan (2012), Sharma and Bhatnagar (2009)
Healthcare	2	Groves (2011), Macfarlane et al. (2012)
Telecommunications	1	Oehley and Theron (2010)
Real estate	1	Phillips and Roper (2009)

pharmaceuticals, healthcare, telecommunications and real estate. Table 27.1 then lists the studies identified within each category.

Hospitality and Tourism

Barron (2008) investigates a major issue facing the hospitality and tourism industry: how to attract and retain a critical group of talented people. The author reviews the current state of employment issues in the hospitality industry and presents an overview of the generations who at the time of publication were currently completing or had just completed higher education qualifications in hospitality and tourism. The study found that this generation had considerably different demands and preferences for education and careers from those of previous generations. The image of careers in industry among the young generation remained poor, so both education and industry must focus on addressing this issue. That is, the career aspirations of hospitality students are negatively influenced by exposure to the industry and the reality of working life. This remains a key responsibility of educators, who are responsible for addressing students' expectations of the realities of work in the industry; but the industry must, for its part, explore a complete student placement process and aim to provide opportunities that not only develop skills and knowledge but also ensure long-term career opportunities and positively encourage students to join the industry on graduation. Walsh and Taylor (2007) acknowledge high levels of employee turnover as a key challenge to the hospitality industry. Also using a sample of university graduates, they identify the job features that were found to strengthen managers' commitment to particular organisations and to the industry.

Their findings suggest that hospitality managers take a responsible attitude to their careers, seeking challenging jobs that provide growth opportunities with able leadership and reasonable remuneration.

Baum (2008) identifies the development and vital features of the hospitality and tourism labour markets, exploring how these have advanced and been transformed at both macro and micro levels insofar as the recognition, recruitment, growth and retention of talent are concerned. The study concludes that talent is a somewhat problematic concept in the tourism and hospitality context, where training and development are fundamental to TM, recommending adequate investment in training for all staff, not only for selected executives. The author also argues that despite the prevalent view that hospitality and tourism work requires only low skills, there is a need to analyse talent and its development within the sector.

D'Annunzio-Green (2008) explores the views of managers concerning the challenges and opportunities affecting the TM pipeline in the hospitality and tourism industry. The findings indicate a clear commitment to the value of TM but also reveal that some policy areas remain underdeveloped. The research addresses the senior management perspective on TM and its unique insight into the complexities of managing talent in hospitality and tourism, revealing the difficulties of attracting, retaining, developing and transitioning employees' talent as major issues facing organisations in the sector. While these findings are deep and rich, they are based rather narrowly on interviews with senior managers in a number of sub-sectors of the industry (e.g. hotels, bars, restaurants, contract catering and events management), a range of small- and medium-sized enterprises, large multinational corporations (MNCs), charities and government-funded bodies. The author suggests that further research should solicit the opinions of middle managers, to broaden understanding of the processes of managing talent.

Deery (2008) reviews studies published in hospitality and tourism journals examining the retention of good employees and the role of work-life balance (WLB) issues in their decisions to stay or quit. The key findings concentrate on job attitudes, including job satisfaction and organisational commitment, personal traits including positive and negative affectivity, the part of WLB in workforce turnover and strategies offered to reduce high turnover rates. The author suggests a number of actions to retain good staff, including providing flexible working hours, allowing flexible work arrangement such as job sharing and work at home, providing training opportunities during working hours, determining the right staff levels, allowing enough breaks during the working day, providing health and well-being opportunities and encouraging sound management practices. Grobler and Diedericks (2009) examine the extent to which TM practices are implemented in the hotel sector in South Africa. Despite the negative findings of the Travel and Tourism Competitiveness Report 2008 concerning hiring and firing practices in this sector, the general results of this study regarding human capital management are strongly positive. The authors also make recommendations for some of the problem areas. The research explores various factors related to talent development and these are analysed qualitatively using SPSS, whereas a quantitative analysis would arguably provide a better picture of the factors and their associations.

Maxwell and MacLean (2008) examine the operational and strategic implications of TM in hospitality and tourism in Scotland. Based on a literature review and focus group interviews with members of the Board of the Scottish Tourism Forum, they report that the sector had high employee turnover and an adverse public image as an employer. They argue that TM (in terms of attracting, developing and retaining talent) has significant potential to manage and develop opinions on careers in this sector. This research allows academics and practitioners to gain rich insight into the practices and perspectives of TM. However, its overall implications are largely restricted to the Scottish context.

Scott and Revis (2008) present a review of selected literature in the area of career and talent management relating to graduate employment in the hospitality industry. They propose a framework to aid an in-depth understanding of implications and practical applications, concluding that there is a need for committed, professional, motivated and developed graduates in order to combat immediate and long-term retention issues. The themes emerging from the selected literature include focusing on the graduate as talent, managing and developing talent for the hospitality industry, and hospitality graduate management. However, the development of these themes is largely based on the existing literature and does not cover any other aspects. Therefore, further empirical research is needed to validate the framework.

Having reviewed literature in the field of hospitality and tourism management development, Watson (2008) draws inferences from findings in the area of TM and from a review of the constituents of management development and factors affecting them. Four key areas of focus emerge from the review: factors influencing management development, hospitality management skills and competencies, hospitality work as a career and hospitality management development practices. The paper concludes with a model of key characteristics and influences on management and talent development in the tourism and hospitality industry.

Banking and Finance

Kamil and Salleh (2013) conducted preliminary research to clarify the requirements for effectual talent management practices such as how to attract, develop and retain talent among Islamic financial institutions in Malaysia. The literature indicates that human capital has become so costly that it can serve as a critical power resource to ensure the sustainability of the industry. A review of previous studies shows that leading firms with TM practices have considerably outperformed other organisations on key financial metrics. The weakness of this research is that it provides insight into TM practices only on the basis of a review and discussion of the available literature in this area, thus offering no empirical findings. Nevertheless, it can be considered to make a contribution to the literature on the subject of TM in the context of Islamic finance.

Al Ruwaili, Bright, and Alhameed (2013) examine the application of TM in Saudi banks, the data being collected through interviews with 18 HRM officials at four banks. Their key finding is that TM is a reality in Saudi banks, as evidenced by the success they have achieved. HRM in Saudi banks has also moved away from a traditional framework and has become increasingly focused on the management of talent. Sparrow, Farndale, and Scullion (2013) provide empirical justification of a theory-focused framework of corporate human resource (CHR) roles in global talent management (GTM). In particular, they explore knowledge of the process of GTM in the finance and professional services sectors. Based on data gathered through interviews with the leaders of two organisations, BankCo and AdviceCo, the study identifies four different roles for CHR in facilitating successful GTM, the interdependencies between these roles, the level to which they are contingent on strategic factors such as the business model and its level of centralisation or decentralisation and the influence of external factors such as business crises. Since the findings are based on interview data alone, the empirical analysis of quantitative data would be useful in providing statistical evidence of the relationship between CHR and successful GTM.

Tansley and Tietze (2013) conducted a case study to explore the experiences of talented accountancy professionals in a global management consultancy as they moved through the different levels of a TM programme. The findings indicate that successful transitions through such 'rites of passage' are necessary preconditions of talent progression. Secondly, the process of identity work is an associated element of these particular phases of TM. Thirdly, at the highest level of management, 'appropriate identities' of the firm need to be developed and demonstrated. The authors suggest an agenda for future research investigating the nexus of associations between the development of identities and decision-making behaviour. Moreover, as their study is limited to the case of a single major accountancy consultancy, there is a need to generalise the data by collecting it from a number of firms in the financial services sector.

Education

A literature review by Behrstock (2010) explores the efficiency of TM practice in education and other private sector activities with an emphasis on ways to attract members of Generation Y (Gen Y), i.e. those born roughly between 1977 and 1995. There is a body of business literature on Gen Y and its implications for TM. Research indicates that those managing talent in the private sector are focused on Gen Y. Although the groundwork has been done to identify the policies and practices that are likely to attract and retain the best teachers, the education sector would benefit from investment in and investigation of effective TM, particularly for Gen Y talent. Referring to a study conducted jointly by IBM and the Human Capital Institute, the author argues that the education sector has been given little attention as far as 'enlightened talent management practices' are concerned. The study found that the education and government sectors lagged behind industries such as banking, retail, financial markets, healthcare, telecommunications, professional services, industrial products, electronics/technology and consumer products, because they were not as knowledge-intensive as these other industries. Olson (2008) claims that no system exists to attract, train and support 'the best people for the job' in the area of education. The research was primarily restricted to the talent management policies and practices being followed by the Gen Y workforce in education and the private sector. The researcher concludes that the education sector lags behind in leveraging strategic TM approaches and addressing the requirements of Gen Y teachers. The strength of this research lies in its exploration of a wide range of literature including reports of MNCs and articles in business journals, while its major weakness is its restricted focus on a specific group of professionals, in the Generation Y category.

Davies and Davies (2010) explore talent identification, talent development and instituting a talent culture, based on case studies of academies, and provide an innovative and useful framework for developing TM in academies. They conclude that long-term sustainability requires academies to address the major concern of enhancing leadership talent and claim that their research contributes to this debate. In an article on agriculture-focused universities in China and Australia, Sun (2012) considers the differences between undergraduate studies in these countries in terms of their talent cultivation mode (TCM). To improve the Chinese higher education system and to advance its TCM, the author suggests not simply copying what others have done but making changes to teaching methods and approaches. It is also very important to change the notion of education to develop students' growth and imagination.

Peet, Walsh, Sober, and Rawak (2010) validated an innovative method of tacit knowledge retrieval with a small group of fundraising experts at the University of Michigan. Their findings indicate that the tacit knowledge of a retiring leader can be successfully regained, documented and fully reassigned to new leaders in various interview sessions. Stewart and Harte (2010) explore the need for research to address the links between TM and managing diversity to achieve better integration and less separation in academic HR research. The authors describe their research as at an early stage, so do not claim the findings to be generalisable. A study by van den Brink, Fruytier, and Thunnissen (2013) critically examines the recruitment and selection processes for junior and senior academic talent in the Netherlands. The researchers found three major predicaments in talent and performance management for universities: transparency versus autonomy, power of HR versus power of academics and equality versus homogeneity. Their paper challenges the view of academia whereby the allocation of rewards and resources is governed by the normative principles of transparency and objective performance systems.

Hoff (1999) provides an overview of valuable skills and attributes needed by the leaders and managers of higher education institutions in the USA, such as giving positive feedback; foresight; the roles (e.g. figurehead, leader and liaison) and relationships (both internal and external to the institution) of leaders' engagement; the culture, values and vision of the organisation; and the strategic planning and financial management processes. The focus of the study is limited to the leadership and managerial skills required for running higher education institutions in the USA. Based on reviews of the available scholarly literature in this area, it suggests appropriate ways for these leaders and managers to act in accordance with the requirements of such institutions.

Business Process Outsourcing and IT-Enabled Services

Bhatnagar (2007) studied talent management and its relationship to the degree of employee engagement in the context of the Indian BPO/IT-enabled services (ITES) sector. Low factor loadings in the initial phase of employees' careers indicated low engagement with the organisation, whereas high factor loadings later indicated high engagement at intermediate levels of employment. In the second phase, factor loadings indicated three distinct factors: corporate culture, career planning and encouragement and organisational support. The study captures the views of a small sample, so its findings cannot be generalised to the entire BPO/ITES sector.

A worldwide shortage of IT professionals has been recognised as one of the most serious threats to the ongoing development of offshore IT service providers (OSPs). Chadee and Raman (2012) surveyed a sample of 68 OSPs from India and found that factors such as external knowledge and talent management had a positive influence on organisational performance, while TM played a strong mediating role between external knowledge and firm performance. This is one of the very few TM studies to have developed a theoretical model and validated it with empirical data. However, the sample for validating the model was very small and limited to Indian OSPs, so caution must be applied to the generalisation of the results.

Pharmaceuticals

Garavan (2012) examined GTM in science-based firms during the global downturn. Literature on the resource-based view, the best-fit context and theory of resource dependence were used to develop a qualitative study of nine global pharmaceutical firms, examining how various actors visualised GTM during the worldwide downturn. GTM was found to play a significant role in organisations' ability to manage downsizing, expansion and structural alignment for their future development.

Based on the case study of a pharmaceutical organisation, Sharma and Bhatnagar (2009) draw lessons on how building a talent management strategy on the basis of competency profiling can become a critical impact area within the field of strategic HRM. They report that the talent mindset helped the organisation to recruit the best talent from the best pharmaceutical organisations. The strength of the paper is that it offers HR practitioners insights into how to attract, acquire and manage talent in fixed internal and external labour markets. It also provides empirical support for the theoretical understanding of the TM theme.

Healthcare

Groves (2011) researched the ways in which national healthcare systems deal with challenges through best-practice TM systems. Having identified significant gaps in talent management theory (e.g. the early development stage and the deficiencies of TM theory) and practice (e.g. the limited number of high-quality graduate programmes in healthcare administration and a general lack of sustained investment in TM compared with other industries), the researcher proposes a best-practice model of TM rooted in the contextual challenges facing healthcare professionals. The strength of the research is that it is based on a qualitative case study of 15 nationwide healthcare systems, using data gathered in semi-structured interviews with 30 executives and from document analysis. However, the model would have been better tested by quantitative analysis, which the author recommends for future research. Growing interest in TM is one of the reasons for effective leadership in the UK public sector. Applying HRM theory to an empirical case study, Macfarlane, Duberley, Fewtrell, and Powell (2012) examine the evolution of processes used for supervising talent and growing leaders in the UK National Health Service (NHS). Case studies of the NHS from the 1950s–2011 show a steady shift from soft to hard talent management. However, a more specific analysis of the 5 years before the study indicates an acceleration of the logic and values of hard TM.

Telecommunications

Oehley and Theron (2010) analyse the determinants of turnover intention and thus the intention to quit of talented employees of a telecommunications organisation in South Africa. Their partial TM structural model is validated using the LISREL software, which reveals reasonably good model-fit indices. The research provides clear evidence that TM proficiencies are causally associated among themselves and provides support for relationships between intention to quit and factors such as commitment and job satisfaction. The research concludes that to contribute to successful positive action through the retention of talented employees, a coherent and integrated array of HR actions will have to be concurrently performed, targeting variables which influence turnover intention such as job satisfaction and commitment. The strength of this study lies in the fact that it is one of very few offering an empirical analysis of TM dimensions and that it demonstrates 10 significant relationships from a total of 24 hypotheses. However, the authors acknowledge that it would have been preferable for the sample on which the structural model was validated to be larger.

Real Estate

Phillips and Roper (2009) found TM to be critical to organisational success in today's competitive marketplace, where real estate firms have started recognising the value of attracting and retaining their best workforce. Based on a review of available literature and expert panel interviews, the study found that innovative recruiting techniques (e.g. recruiters' ability to source and screen for bright talent, developing a creative recruitment strategy, offering competitive or above-market compensation packages) must be deployed to attract a new generation of workers.

27.4 Limitations of Talent Management Research

27.4.1 Methodological Limitations

Table 27.2 lists major limitations of the TM studies explicitly expressed by their authors. The analysis indicates that the majority reported that the outcomes of the research were difficult to generalise. The limitations include a sample drawn from only one or specific contexts, a limited or small sample size, a cross-sectional or snapshot approach to data collection, self-selection bias or a convenience sampling approach, lack of empirical research, the lack of more specific variables and exploratory or ongoing research. For example, having investigated the process of GTM in an MNC, McDonnell et al. (2011) acknowledge the limitations of their findings, which are based on a single case study.

Similarly, Sparrow et al. (2013) state that their work is based on only two case studies with a limited view of stakeholders. Hartmann, Feisel, and Schober (2010) likewise suggest that their research, using interviews with managers from seven companies, be treated as only exploratory. Some authors (e.g. Festing, Schäfer, & Scullion, 2013; Kamil & Salleh, 2013; Kim & Scullion, 2011; Malaeb & Chanaron, 2010; McDonnell & Collings, 2011; Nankervis, 2013; Sparrow et al., 2013) report conducting no empirical research or having limited empirical findings. This underlines the need for more empirical TM research.

The future research can address the limitations including small sample size, limited empirical research, exploratory analysis and lack of suitable variables. For example, the issue of sample size is addressed by collecting data from a relatively large number of respondents working in the hospitality industry across Saudi Arabia. The limited extent of empirical research can be dealt with by using quantitative analysis to understand the turnover intention of talent using structured equation modelling via AMOS 20.0. Moreover, as this research is based on a comprehensive review of the available literature on TM, it can be said to have overcome the issue of identifying the most suitable variables.

27.4.2 Theoretical Limitations

This review of academic literature on TM indicates that the field is in its infancy in terms of theory development, concentrating on the broader aspects of TM, including literature reviews (Collings & Mellahi, 2009; Tarique & Schuler, 2010), TM

Table 27.2 Methodological limitations

Limitations	Meaning	Example sources
Limited generalisability	Difficult to generalise or diversify the results or findings	Bethke-Langenegger, Mahler, and Staffelbach (2010, 2011), Bhatnagar (2007), Burbach and Royle (2010), Chadee and Raman (2012), Festing et al. (2013), Garavan (2012), Groves (2011), Hartmann et al. (2010), Kim and Scullion (2011), McDonnell et al. (2011), Moeller, Maley, Harvey, and Kiessling (2016), Poorhosseinzadeh and Subramaniam (2012), Skuza, Scullion, and McDonnell (2013), Sparrow et al. (2013), Sripirom, Jhundra-Indra, and Raksong (2017), Stewart and Harte (2010), Tansley and Tietze (2013), Tymon, Stumpf, and Doh (2010)
Context-specific subject/biased sample	Sample taken from only one, specific or limited organisations, regions, communities, cultures, countries, case studies, age groups, genders, skilled professionals, users, technologies	Boussebaa and Morgan (2008), Burbach and Royle (2010), Chadee and Raman (2012), De Vos and Dries (2013), Höglund (2012), Kim and Scullion (2011), Kucherov and Zavyalova (2012), Macfarlane et al. (2012), McDonnell et al. (2011), Singh, Jones, and Hall (2012), Sparrow et al. (2013)
Small/inadequate sample size	Very limited sample size	Bethke-Langenegger et al. (2010, 2011), Bhatnagar (2007), Chadee and Raman (2012), Oehley and Theron (2010), Poorhosseinzadeh and Subramaniam (2012), Shi and Handfield (2012)
Snapshot approach to data collection	Data collected at only one point in time	Bethke-Langenegger et al. (2010, 2011), De Vos and Dries (2013), Hartmann et al. (2010), Höglund (2012), Sheehan (2012), Skuza et al. (2013)
Self-report/ self-selection bias	Survey suffering from self-selecting opinion/ convenience sampling	Oehley and Theron (2010), Oltra and Vivas-López (2013), Skuza et al. (2013), Tymon et al. (2010)
Lack of or limited empirical research	Facts and figures not based on statistical findings	Festing et al. (2013), Kamil and Salleh (2013), Kim and Scullion (2011), Malaeb and Chanaron (2010), McDonnell et al. (2011), Nankervis (2013), Sparrow et al. (2013), Vaiman, Haslberger, and Vance (2015)
Exploratory analysis	Initial or broader level of analysis	Festing et al. (2013), Garavan (2012), Hartmann et al. (2010), Hejase, Hejase, Mikdashi, and Bazeih (2016), Kim and Scullion (2011), Stewart and Harte (2010)
Lack of more suitable variables	Only limited variables were used, leaving out some suitable ones	De Vos and Dries (2013), McDonnell et al. (2010), Poorhosseinzadeh and Subramaniam (2012)

conceptualisation (e.g. Baum, 2008; Boussebaa & Morgan, 2008; Burbach & Royle, 2010; Collings, Scullion, & Dowling, 2009), the shift from HRM to TM (Areiqat et al., 2010), exploring challenges and opportunities (Balaji, 2011; Barron, 2008; Boussebaa & Morgan, 2008) and developing early stage theoretical models (Bhatti, Waris, Zaheer, & Ur-Rehaman, 2011). Limited research has been undertaken on systematically developing a theoretical perspective specifically dedicated to analysing the different individual organisational aspects of using TM, such as employee engagement and retention, organisational performance and individual satisfaction with the organisation.

The review indicates that none of the studies has systematically examined the variables of TM based on the prior literature in the field concerned. For example, Sheehan (2012) examines the link between management development and perceived subsidiary performance for 143 UK-owned MNCs. However, the authors propose a framework for measuring this relationship without providing adequate theoretical justification. Similarly, the design of the research model developed by Vural, Vardarlier, and Aykir (2012) to evaluate how TM influences employee commitment is based entirely on the random selection of variables including the moderator (i.e. company type), with no theoretical underpinning. Although the research model presented by Oehley and Theron (2010) is based on an exhaustive literature review, it is too complex to be treated as a representative model to evaluate employees' commitment, job satisfaction and intention to quit. Poorhosseinzadeh and Subramaniam (2012) claim that their theoretical framework to establish relationships between TM initiatives and successful TM is based on the related literature and prior findings. However, only 49 questionnaires were distributed to gather data from MNCs in Malaysia. A survey with such a small sample size is unlikely to offer a complete picture of the performance of the model.

The review of a range of empirical studies indicates that even though initiatives have been taken to build and test theoretical models of TM, these efforts have not been based on a solid theoretical underpinning and a comprehensive review of the relevant literature.

27.5 Literature Synthesis and Recommendations for Future Research

The review of literature on TM indicates that only a handful of studies (e.g. Barron, 2008; Baum, 2008; D'Annunzio-Green, 2008; Deery, 2008; Maxwell & MacLean, 2008; Scott & Revis, 2008; Walsh & Taylor, 2007; Watson, 2008) have explored it in the context of the hospitality and tourism sector. Some of these (e.g. Maxwell & MacLean, 2008; Scott & Revis, 2008; Watson, 2008) are based on reviewing the literature, whereas others (e.g. Barron, 2008; Walsh & Taylor, 2007) explore the issues and challenges affecting the tourism and hospitality industry, such as attracting and retaining talent, minimising employee turnover, etc. However, there is a notable lack of empirical exploration of the various aspects of TM in this sector. Such research would help academics to understand the position and relevance of TM in hospitality and tourism and would help the government to utilise the various aspects of talent management to improve the development and performance of the organisations involved.

Some studies (e.g. Al Ruwaili et al., 2013; Kamil & Salleh, 2013; Sparrow et al., 2013; Tansley & Tietze, 2013) have also analysed TM in the context of banking and finance. However, these provide only an initial understanding of the role of talented human capital in the sector. A study by Al Ruwaili et al. (2013) found that culture had a major impact on TM in Saudi banks. Only the study by Sparrow et al. (2013) sheds some light on the roles of CHR in GTM using empirical findings. Hence, the review of literature in this sector also reveals a significant opportunity to explore TM in the context of banking and finance. The growing number of banking and financial organisations throughout the world, both public and private, and the increasing competition among them also warrant more research on TM in this sector.

A few studies (e.g. Behrstock, 2010; Davies & Davies, 2010; Olson, 2008; Peet et al., 2010; Stewart & Harte, 2010; Van den Brink et al., 2013) have examined the role of TM in the education sector. Analysis indicates that these are primarily literature reviews (Behrstock, 2010), exploratory research (Stewart & Harte, 2010), research drawing conclusions from the empirical findings of existing projects (Van den Brink et al., 2013), qualitative research (Peet et al., 2010) or conceptual studies (Davies & Davies, 2010) and that none provides either theoretical foundations or quantitative outcomes on the different dimensions of TM. This again leaves a significant space for future research to occupy.

Moreover, while some TM research has been undertaken in the areas of BPO/ITES (e.g. Bhatnagar, 2007; Chadee & Raman, 2012), pharmaceuticals (e.g. Garavan, 2012; Sharma & Bhatnagar, 2009), healthcare (e.g. Groves, 2011; Macfarlane et al., 2012), telecommunications (e.g. Oehley & Theron, 2010) and real estate (e.g. Phillips & Roper, 2009), none of these studies has worked towards developing a theoretical model of TM. This shows that irrespective of the sector in which TM research has been undertaken, there is a notable lack of quantitative empirical research based on the development of theoretical models.

A number of studies (e.g. Bethke-Langenegger et al., 2010, 2011; Bhatnagar, 2008; Bhatti et al., 2011; Hartmann et al., 2010; Holland et al., 2007; Sheehan, 2012; Tymon Jr. et al., 2010; Zheng, 2009) have analysed TM in the context of MNCs in general, rather than being limited to a specific sector. Some of these (e.g. Hartmann et al., 2010) have taken a qualitative empirical approach to explore how MNCs are able to recognise, develop and retain talents. Although initial efforts (e.g. McDonnell et al., 2010, 2011; Oltra & Vivas-López, 2013; Sabado, 2012; Tymon Jr. et al., 2010) have been made to develop and test theoretical models to address the issues of TM across MNCs, scholars have acknowledged the lack of theoretical underpinning and quantitative analysis in this area of research (Huanga and Tansley, 2012; McDonnell et al., 2010) and the need for much more work to be undertaken (Festing et al., 2013).

Some authors (e.g. Boudreau and Ramstad, 2005, 2007; Collings & Mellahi, 2009; Lewis and Hackman, 2006; Scullion and Collings, 2010; Thunnissen et al., 2013; Vaiman et al., 2012) have reviewed the TM literature. Some among these (Boudreau and Ramstad, 2005, 2007; Collings & Mellahi, 2009; Collings et al., 2009; Lewis and Heckman, 2006) also note a clear lack of theoretical underpinning to the TM studies reviewed. These observations concerning the lack of theoretical development and innovation in published studies emphasise the need to undertake more research into theoretical models and their testing using appropriate data. Moreover, existing reviews of TM literature have not been comprehensive in terms of exploring the demographic characteristics of the TM studies reviewed, such as lists of journals publishing articles on TM, chronological lists of published articles on TM, authors' background, the institutions most prolific in publishing TM articles or the countries in which TM work has been published. Thus, future research is required in this area to undertake a review of extant literature in a systematic and exhaustive manner.

In summary, it is clear that research in the area of TM significantly lacks theoretical rigour and conceptual development. The very few studies which have addressed theoretical development have not been very rigorous, nor have models been well tested with diverse datasets. The present review also suggests that this lack of theoretical development and rigour exists independently of the implementation of TM in any particular sector. Given the importance of talented human capital in any organisation, further empirical research in this area would be timely and significant, but before undertaking it, future researchers should comprehensively review the literature available to understand the overall development of prominent models and constructs emerging in this area. Such a review will help to guide future scholars through the process of selecting the appropriate research models and/or set of constructs. It is therefore recommended that future researchers undertake the weight- and meta-analysis of existing empirical studies to deepen insight into those models and constructs with potential to be used further. The keyword analysis might also help future researchers to dig deeper into any such underdeveloped or developing potential areas of research.

The review of methodological limitations indicates that future studies of TM should overcome the issues of limited generalisability, small and biased samples, snapshot data collection, bias due to self-selection or convenience sampling, lack of empirical research, the exploratory nature of research and limited variables. Some of the findings emerging on methodological limitations, including a lack of empirical research and the exploratory nature of TM research, are broadly aligned with the review of TM literature across various sectors. Such findings clearly indicate that despite a number of research studies being published in this area, the research on TM does not seem to be very rich in terms of its focus on empirical findings (Festing et al., 2013; Vaiman et al., 2015). The authors of some empirical studies (e.g. McDonnell et al., 2010; Poorhosseinzadeh & Subramaniam, 2012) that have used variables have suggested the inclusion of more suitable ones to analyse the various aspects of talent management. For example, McDonnell et al. (2010) identify the limited existing empirical work in the area of GTM and ignorance of contextual factors as limitations of the current literature on GTM practices. In essence, the authors suggest the inclusion in a future conceptual model of factors related to national institutional contexts, such as government systems and training and development systems.

The review of theoretical models in TM literature clearly indicates a paucity of research in this area. The empirical research is largely based on the random selection of variables, and there has not been any comprehensive effort made towards developing a framework based on a review of the existing literature. Only Oehley and Theron (2010) present a research model based on a review of the existing literature, but it is too complex to become a representative model for TM research. The theoretical review of literature in this area indicates a need to explore empirical research using weight- and meta-analysis, including meta-analytic structural equation modelling (MASEM) of the constructs to propose a possible conceptual model for TM.

27.6 Conclusion

The main focus of this literature review has been on three major aspects of TM research. Firstly, the studies to be reviewed have been categorised as related to eight broad categories, namely, hospitality and tourism, education, banking and finance, BPO/ITES, pharmaceuticals, healthcare, telecommunications and real estate. Secondly, this study has identified the methodological limitations of existing TM research and made recommendations for future researchers to address gaps in this area. Lastly, given that TM research is not yet quite mature, this study analyses the theoretical limitations of the existing research and outlines potential ways forward for theoretical research. However, like any other research, the present study has its own limitations. Firstly, it does not provide a comprehensive review of the literature and fails to address aspects such as the demographic characteristics of existing studies, weight- and meta-analysis of the available empirical research and the use of MASEM to identify possible frameworks for progress in this field. Secondly, it has not taken into consideration any studies seeking a generic understanding of TM concepts or those where TM analysis took place in nonspecific sectors. Future research should review all such studies to achieve a comprehensive review of literature in this area.

References

Ahmadi, A. A., Ahmadi, F., & Abbaspalangi, J. (2012). Talent management and succession planning. *Interdisciplinary Journal of Contemporary Research in Business, 4*(1), 213–224.

Al Ruwaili, N. F., Bright, D., & Alhameed, A. (2013). To what extent talent management in Saudi Arabian banks? *International Journal of Advances in Management Sciences, 1*(1), 9–15.

Areiqat, A. Y., Abdelhadi, T., & Al-Tarawneh, H. A. (2010). Talent management as a strategic practice of human resources management to improve human performance. *Interdisciplinary Journal of Contemporary Research in Business, 2*(2), 329–341.

Balaji, G. (2011). Exporting leadership talent: Challenges and opportunities in MNC subsidiaries in India. *Journal of Indian Business Research, 3*(4), 283–288.

Barron, P. (2008). Education and talent management: Implications for the hospitality industry. *International Journal of Contemporary Hospitality Management, 20*(7), 730–742.

Baum, T. (2008). Implications of hospitality and tourism labour markets for talent management strategies. *International Journal of Contemporary Hospitality Management, 20*(7), 720–729.

Beechler, S., & Woodward, I. C. (2009). Global talent management. *Journal of International Management, 15*, 273–285.

Behrstock, E. (2010). *Talent management in the private and education sectors: A literature review*. Naperville, IL: Learning Point Associates.

Bethke-Langenegger, P., Mahler, P., & Staffelbach, B. (2010). Effectiveness of talent management strategies in Swiss companies. *Universität Zürich Diskussionspapier Nr, 16*, 1–20.

Bethke-Langenegger, P., Mahler, P., & Staffelbach, B. (2011). Effectiveness of talent management strategies. *European Journal of International Management, 5*(5), 524–539.

Bhatnagar, J. (2007). Talent management strategy of employee engagement in Indian ITES employees: Key to retention. *Employee Relations, 29*(6), 640–663.

Bhatnagar, J. (2008). Managing capabilities for talent engagement and pipeline development. *Industrial and Commercial Training, 40*(1), 19–28.

Bhatti, W., Waris, S., Zaheer, A., & Ur-Rehaman, K. (2011). The effect of commitment and motivation on human talent and its contribution to organizational performance. *Management & Marketing Challenges for the Knowledge Society, 6*(3), 471–482.

Blass, E. (2007). *Talent management: Maximising talent for business performance*. London/Hertfordshire: Chartered Management Institute and Ashridge Consulting.

Boudreau, J. W., & Ramstad, P. M. (2005). Talentship, talent segmentation, and sustainability: A new HR decision science paradigm for a new strategy definition. *Human Resource Management, 44*(2), 129–136.

Boudreau, J. W., & Ramstad, P. M. (2007). *Beyond HR: The new science of human capital*. Boston, MA: Harvard Business School Press.

Boussebaa, M., & Morgan, G. (2008). Managing talent across national borders: The challenges faced by an international retail group. *Critical Perspectives on International Business, 4*(1), 25–41.

Brundage, H., & Koziel, M. (2010). Retaining top talent still a requirement for firms: Focus on people now to keep turnover costs down when the economy improves. *Journal of Accountancy, 209*(5), 38.

Burbach, R., & Royle, T. (2010). Talent on demand? Talent management in the German and Irish subsidiaries of a US multinational corporation. *Personnel Review, 39*(4), 414–431.

Byham, W. C. (2001). Are leaders born or made? *Workspan, 44*(12), 56–60.

Cappelli, P. (2008). Talent management for the twenty-first century. *Harvard Business Review, 86*(3), 74–81.

Chadee, D., & Raman, R. (2012). External knowledge and performance of offshore IT service providers in India: The mediating role of talent management. *Asia Pacific Journal of Human Resources, 50*(4), 459–482.

Cheloha, R., & Swain, J. (2005). Talent management system key to effective succession planning. *Canadian HR Reporter, 18*(17), 5–7.

Chowanec, G. D., & Newstrom, C. N. (1991). The strategic management of international human resources. *Business Quarterly, 56*(2), 65–70.

Collings, D. G., & Mellahi, K. (2009). Strategic talent management: A review and research agenda. *Human Resource Management Review, 19*(4), 304–313.

Collings, D. G., Scullion, H., & Dowling, P. J. (2009). Global staffing: A review and thematic research agenda. *The International Journal of Human Resource Management, 20*(6), 1253–1272.

Creelman, D. (2004). *Return on investment in talent management: Measures you can put to work right now*. Available from Human Capital Institute, 2121 K Street, N.W., Suite 800, Washington, DC 20037 USA.

D'Annunzio-Green, N. (2008). Managing the talent management pipeline: Towards a greater understanding of senior managers' perspectives in the hospitality and tourism sector. *International Journal of Contemporary Hospitality Management, 20*(7), 807–819.

Davies, B., & Davies, B. J. (2010). *Talent management in education*. London: Sage Publications.

De Vos, A., & Dries, N. (2013). Applying a talent management lens to career management: The role of human capital composition and continuity. *The International Journal of Human Resource Management, 24*(9), 1816–1831.

Deery, M. (2008). Talent management, work-life balance and retention strategies. *International Journal of Contemporary Hospitality Management, 20*(7), 792–806.

Deery, M., & Jago, L. (2015). Revisiting talent management, work-life balance and retention strategies. *International Journal of Contemporary Hospitality Management, 27*(3), 453–472.

Festing, M., Schäfer, L., & Scullion, H. (2013). Talent management in medium-sized German companies: An explorative study and agenda for future research. *The International Journal of Human Resource Management, 24*(9), 1872–1893.

Garavan, T. N. (2012). Global talent management in science-based firms: An exploratory investigation of the pharmaceutical industry during the global downturn. *The International Journal of Human Resource Management, 23*(12), 2428–2449.

Grobler, P. A., & Diedericks, H. (2009). Talent management: An empirical study of selected South African hotel groups. *Southern African Business Review, 13*(3), 1–27.

Groves, K. S. (2011). Talent management best practices: How exemplary health care organizations create value in a down economy. *Health Care Management Review, 36*(3), 227–240.

Hartmann, E., Feisel, E., & Schober, H. (2010). Talent management of western MNCs in China: Balancing global integration and local responsiveness. *Journal of World Business, 45*(2), 169–178.

Heinen, J. S., & O'Neill, C. (2004). Managing talent to maximize performance. *Employment Relations Today, 31*, 67–82.

Hejase, H. J., Hejase, A. J., Mikdashi, G., & Bazeih, Z. F. (2016). Talent management challenges: An exploratory assessment from Lebanon. *International Journal of Business Management & Economic Research, 7*(1), 504–520.

Hills, A. (2009). Succession planning – or smart talent management? *Industrial and Commercial Training, 41*(1), 3–8.

Hilton, D. M. (2000). Hiring and retaining top talent. *Credit Union Executive Journal, 40*(5), 12–16.

Hoff, K. S. (1999). Leaders and managers: Essential skills required within higher education. *Higher Education, 38*(3), 311–331.

Höglund, M. (2012). Quid pro quo? Examining talent management through the lens of psychological contracts. *Personnel Review, 41*(2), 126–142.

Holland, P., Sheehan, C., & De Cieri, H. (2007). Attracting and retaining talent: Exploring human resources development trends in Australia. *Human Resource Development International, 10*(3), 247–262.

Huang, J., & Tansley, C. (2012). Sneaking through the minefield of talent management: The notion of rhetorical obfuscation. *The International Journal of Human Resource Management, 23*(17), 3673–3691.

Hughes, J. C., & Rog, E. (2008). Talent management: A strategy for improving employee recruitment, retention and engagement within hospitality organizations. *International Journal of Contemporary Hospitality Management, 20*(7), 743–757.

Iles, P., Preece, D., & Chuai, X. (2010). Talent management as a management fashion in HRD: Towards a research agenda. *Human Resource Development International, 13*(2), 125–145.

Kamil, B., & Salleh, M. (2013). The need for effectiveness talent management practices among Islamic financial institution in Malaysia. In *4th International Conference on Business and Economic Research* (pp. 296–305).

Kesler, G. C. (2002). Why the leadership bench never gets deeper: Ten insights about executive talent development. *Human Resource Planning, 25*, 32–44.

Kim, C. H., & Scullion, H. (2011). Exploring the links between corporate social responsibility and global talent management: A comparative study of the UK and Korea. *European Journal of International Management, 5*(5), 501–523.

Kucherov, D., & Zavyalova, E. (2012). HRD practices and talent management in the companies with the employer brand. *European Journal of Training and Development, 36*(1), 86–104.

Lewis, R. E., & Heckman, R. J. (2006). Talent management: A critical review. *Human Resource Management Review, 16*(2), 139–154.

Macfarlane, F., Duberley, J., Fewtrell, C., & Powell, M. (2012). Talent management for NHS managers: Human resources or resourceful humans? *Public Money & Management, 32*(6), 445–452.

Malaeb, R. C., & Chanaron, J. J. (2010). *Talent management DNA*. Grenoble, France: Grenoble École de Management.

Maxwell, G. A., & MacLean, S. (2008). Talent management in hospitality and tourism in Scotland: Operational implications and strategic actions. *International Journal of Contemporary Hospitality Management, 20*(7), 820–830.

McDonnell, A., & Collings, D. G. (2011). The identification and evaluation of talent in MNEs. In H. Scullion & D. G. Collings (Eds.), *Global talent management* (pp. 56–73). London & New York: Routledge.

McDonnell, A., Lamare, R., Gunnigle, P., & Lavelle, J. (2010). Developing tomorrow's leaders - evidence of global talent management in multinational enterprises. *Journal of World Business, 46*(2), 150–160.

Mercer, S. R. (2005). Best-in-class leadership. *Leadership Excellence, 22*(3), 17.

Moeller, M., Maley, J., Harvey, M., & Kiessling, T. (2016). Global talent management and inpatriate social capital building: A status inconsistency perspective. *The International Journal of Human Resource Management, 27*(9), 991–1012.

Nankervis, A. R. (2013). 'Building for the future?' Government and industry responses to the challenges of talent management in China following the GFC. *Asia Pacific Business Review, 19*(2), 186–199.

Oehley, A. M., & Theron, C. C. (2010). The development and evaluation of a partial talent management structural model. *Management Dynamics, 19*(3), 2–28.

Olsen, R. (2000). Harnessing the internet with human capital management. *Workspan, 43*(11), 24–27.

Olson, L. (2008). Quality counts: Tapping into teaching – Human resources a weak spot. *Education Week, 27*, 18.

Oltra, V., & Vivas-López, S. (2013). Boosting organizational learning through team-based talent management: What is the evidence from large Spanish firms? *The International Journal of Human Resource Management, 24*(9), 1853–1871.

Pascal, C. (2004). Foreword. In A. Schweyer (Ed.), *Talent management systems: Best practices in technology solutions for recruitment, retention, and workforce planning*. Canada: Wiley.

Peet, M. R., Walsh, K., Sober, R., & Rawak, C. S. (2010). Generative knowledge interviewing: A method for knowledge transfer and talent management at the University of Michigan. *International Journal of Educational Advancement, 10*(2), 71–85.

Phillips, D. R., & Roper, K. O. (2009). A framework for talent management in real estate. *Journal of Corporate Real Estate, 11*(1), 7–16.

Poorhosseinzadeh, M., & Subramaniam, I. D. (2012). Determinants of successful talent management in MNCs in Malaysia. *Journal of Basic and Applied Scientific Research, 2*(12), 12524–12533.

Redford, K. (2005). Shedding light on talent tactics. *Personnel Today*, 20–22.
Ringo, T., Schweyer, A., DeMarco, M., Jones, R., & Lesser, E. (2008). *Integrated talent management, Part 3: Turning talent management into a competitive advantage*. Somers, NY: IBM.
Sabado, A. V. G. (2012). Global talent management of multinational companies. *European Journal of Business and Management, 4*(21), 117–124.
Schuler, R. S., Jackson, S. E., & Tarique, I. (2011). Global talent management and global talent challenges: Strategic opportunities for IHRM. *Journal of World Business, 46*(4), 506–516.
Scott, B., & Revis, S. (2008). Talent management in hospitality: Graduate career success and strategies. *International Journal of Contemporary Hospitality Management, 20*(7), 781–791.
Scullion, H., Collings, D. G., & Caligiuri, P. (2010). Global talent management. *Journal of World Business, 45*(2), 105–108.
Sharma, R., & Bhatnagar, J. (2009). Talent management-competency development: Key to global leadership. *Industrial and Commercial Training, 41*(3), 118–132.
Sheehan, M. (2012). Developing managerial talent: Exploring the link between management talent and perceived performance in multinational corporations (MNCs). *European Journal of Training and Development, 36*(1), 66–85.
Shi, Y., & Handfield, R. (2012). Talent management issues for multinational logistics companies in China: Observations from the field. *International Journal of Logistics Research and Applications, 15*(3), 163–179.
Singh, A., Jones, D. B., & Hall, N. (2012). Talent management: A research based case study in the GCC region. *International Journal of Business and Management, 7*(24), 94.
Skuza, A., Scullion, H., & McDonnell, A. (2013). An analysis of the talent management challenges in a post-communist country: The case of Poland. *The International Journal of Human Resource Management, 24*(3), 453–470.
Sparrow, P., Farndale, E., & Scullion, H. (2013). An empirical study of the role of the corporate HR function in global talent management in professional and financial service firms in the global financial crisis. *The International Journal of Human Resource Management, 24*(9), 1777–1798.
Sripirom, K., Jhundra-Indra, P., & Raksong, S. (2017). Strategic talent management and firm success: Evidence from electronic and electrical appliance businesses in Thailand. *AU-GSB e-Journal, 9*(2), 31–52.
Stewart, J., & Harte, V. (2010). The implications of talent management for diversity training: An exploratory study. *Journal of European Industrial Training, 34*(6), 506–518.
Sun, M. (2012). Case study of talent cultivation mode for undergraduate study in China and Australia. *Interdisciplinary Journal of Contemporary Research In Business, 4*(5), 384.
Tajuddin, D., Ali, R., & Kamaruddin, B. H. (2015). Developing talent management crisis model for quality life of bank employees in Malaysia. *Procedia: Social and Behavioral Sciences, 201*, 80–84.
Tansley, C., & Tietze, S. (2013). Rites of passage through talent management progression stages: An identity work perspective. *International Journal of Human Management, 24*(9), 1799–1815.
Tarique, I., & Schuler, R. S. (2010). Global talent management: Literature review, integrative framework, and suggestions for further research. *Journal of World Business, 45*(2), 122–133.
Thunnissen, M., Boselie, P., & Fruytier, B. (2013). A review of talent management: 'Infancy or adolescence'? *The International Journal of Human Resource Management, 24*(9), 1744–1761.
Tymon, W. G., Jr., Stumpf, S. A., & Doh, J. P. (2010). Exploring talent management in India: The neglected role of intrinsic rewards. *Journal of World Business, 45*(2), 109–121.
Ulrich, D. (2006). The talent trifecta. *Workforce Management*, 32–33.
Vaiman, V., Scullion, H., & Collings, D. (2012). Talent management decision making. *Management Decision, 50*(5), 925–941.
Vaiman, V., Haslberger, A., & Vance, C. M. (2015). Recognizing the important role of self-initiated expatriates in effective global talent management. *Human Resource Management Review, 25*(3), 280–286.

van den Brink, M., Fruytier, B., & Thunnissen, M. (2013). Talent management in academia: Performance systems and HRM policies. *Human Resource Management Journal, 23*(2), 180–195.

Vural, Y., Vardarlier, P., & Aykir, A. (2012). The effects of using talent management with performance evaluation system over employee commitment. *Procedia: Social and Behavioral Sciences, 58*, 340–349.

Walsh, K., & Taylor, M. S. (2007). Developing in-house careers and retaining management talent what hospitality professionals want from their jobs. *Cornell Hotel and Restaurant Administration Quarterly, 48*(2), 163–182.

Watson, S. (2008). Where are we now? A review of management development issues in the hospitality and tourism sector: Implications for talent management. *International Journal of Contemporary Hospitality Management, 20*(7), 758–780.

Zheng, C. (2009). Keeping talents for advancing service firms in Asia. *Journal of Service Management, 20*(5), 482–502.

Dr. Adel Alferaih completed his PhD at the School of Management at Swansea University in the UK. The author holds a bachelor's degree in English literature and a master's degree in Business Administration. His research interests lie in the area of talent management, entrepreneurship and emotional intelligence. Dr. Alferaih currently serves as an Assistant Professor in the Ministry of Education in Saudi Arabia; also he has over 7 years of diverse administrative experience in the capacity of Director of Administrative Development at the Ministry of Education and as a Deputy General Manager of Alferaih Hospital in Saudi Arabia. Adel Alferaih can be contacted at adel75ksa@hotmail.com.

Chapter 28
Networking and Entrepreneurial Activity in Kuwait

Antonis C. Simintiras and Yusif M. Al-Hajji

Abstract This study examines socializing and networking practices in Kuwait known as the *diwaniyas*. *Diwaniyas* are physical spaces where people gather regularly to discuss, among other things, politics, business, history, and/or matters of everyday life. The thesis put forward is that participation in the social establishment of *diwaniyas* favors the acquirement of social, cultural, and symbolic capital. This, in turn, fosters entrepreneurialism and increases opportunities and activities that can be converted into economic capital. The importance of this social infrastructure as a vehicle to help deliver the capital required for entrepreneurial activity is also highlighted.

Keywords Entrepreneurship · Social capital · Diwaniyas · Kuwaiti culture

28.1 Introduction

A recurring topic in the contemporary literature is how different types of capital – i.e., social, cultural, and symbolic – influence entrepreneurial activity. These three types of capital are prominent in Kuwaiti society and manifest in the form of *diwaniyas*. In brief, a *diwaniya* is a physical space where people meet. It is a traditional phenomenon that used to be a male-dominated activity but in modern times has widened to include female *diwaniyas* (Chay, 2016). These social hubs play a critical role in the processes of building networks, establishing relationships, gaining access to information, and other key activities that could influence entrepreneurialism.

A. C. Simintiras (✉)
Gulf University for Science and Technology, Mubarak Al-Abdullah, Kuwait

Swansea University, Swansea, UK
e-mail: Simintiras.A@gust.edu.kw

Y. M. Al-Hajji
Gulf University for Science and Technology, Mubarak Al-Abdullah, Kuwait
e-mail: y.alhajji@gmail.com

Y. K. Dwivedi et al. (eds.), *Emerging Markets from a Multidisciplinary Perspective*, Advances in Theory and Practice of Emerging Markets,
https://doi.org/10.1007/978-3-319-75013-2_28

This study examines the potential role of *diwaniyas* in promoting entrepreneurial activity. More specifically, it examines three elements of capital (social, cultural, and symbolic) to assess the role of *diwaniyas* using Pret, Shaw, and Dodd's (2016) framework pertinent to the convertibility of such capital into entrepreneurial practices. Research in this area will shed light onto the usefulness of local practices (i.e., *diwaniyas*) in propelling entrepreneurial activity and decipher how these social infrastructures link and reinforce capital required for entrepreneurship.

28.2 Background

28.2.1 Entrepreneurship

The concept of entrepreneurship has developed over time. It was originally coined as *disrupting* (Schumpeter, 1911), *forming new firms* (Knight, 1921), *equilibrating* (Kirzner, 1973), or *creating markets* (Casson, 1982). It has also been described as a choice one makes between being an employee and being self-employed (Lucas, 1978). The basic notion is that entrepreneurs start firms such that they can actualize their perceived opportunities (Holmes & Schmitz, 1990). This was further solidified later by Acs, Lee, and Florida (2004) and Audretsch et al. (2006) who added that entrepreneurs search through available knowledge supply and extract "knowledge bits" that could help encourage the development of new products and/or processes.

28.2.2 Types of Capital

As suggested by Bourdieu (1986), there are four types of capital. These are *social*, *cultural*, *symbolic*, and *economic*. *Social capital* is defined as "the actual and potential resources embedded within, available through, and derived from the network of relationships possessed by an individual or social unit" (Nahapiet & Ghoshal, 1998, p. 243). It is considered to be "the goodwill that is engendered by the fabric of social relations and that can be mobilized to facilitate action" (Adler & Kwon, 2002, p. 17). Social capital also refers to (a) the "connections among individuals — social networks and the norms of reciprocity and trustworthiness that arise from them" (Putnam, 2000, p. 19) and/or (b) a "collection of resources owned by the members of an individual's personal social network, which may become available to the individual as a result of the history of these relationships" (Van der Gaag & Snijders, 2004, p. 200). Some scholars consider social capital a *private good* that individuals possess which could lead to personal benefits like career advancement and which network members gain directly (Belliveau, O'Reilly, & Wade, 1996; Burt, 1997; Useem & Karabel, 1986). Other scholars identify social capital as being a *public good* (e.g., Bourdieu, 1986; Coleman, 1988; Putnam, 1993) equivalent to a social network that is available and beneficial to those who create it and group members at large (Kostova & Roth, 2003).

Symbolic capital relates to the possession of prestige, status, and positive reputation (Terjesen & Elam, 2009); it can stimulate belief in the quality of products, generate trust, and legitimize the actions of entrepreneurs (De Clercq & Voronov, 2009; Harvey, Maclean, Gordon, & Shaw, 2011). *Cultural capital*, as put forth by Bourdieu (1986), includes long-lasting personal dispositions (embodied form), cultural goods (objectified form), and academic qualifications. *Economic capital* refers to the business and financial assets, both tangible and intangible.

The dynamic nature of the different types of capital is depicted by the convertibility framework, suggested by Pret et al. (2016), and based on the works by Adler and Kwon (2002), Coleman (1988), and Nahapiet and Ghoshal, (1998). The convertibility of the types of capital depends on the facilitators and inhibitors of capital conversion. For example, social, cultural, and symbolic capital can be converted into economic capital which can take the form of generating income and additional tangible and intangible financial assets (Bourdieu, 1986; Jonsson & Lindbergh, 2013). Converting economic capital into social, cultural, and symbolic capital, however, is more complicated and time consuming (Greve & Salaff, 2003). Furthermore, cultural capital and social capital can generate symbolic capital (Bourdieu, 1986). Symbolic capital is an especially malleable capital form, readily interchangeable into the other three forms of capital (Pret et al., 2016). For example, prestige can be converted into social and cultural capital by enabling access to social networks and exclusive education (Lawrence, 2004; McLeod, O'Donohoe, & Townley, 2009). Regarding the conversion of social capital into symbolic capital, it has been argued that affiliation with reputable others can create a spill-over effect (Reuber & Fischer, 2005), whereas association with unreliable partners can impede reputation-building (Lange, Lee, & Dai, 2011). These are some examples of the way all four types of capital are interlinked and can be converted from one to another. The likely impact of these different types of capital on entrepreneurial activity is discussed below.

28.3 Types of Capital and Entrepreneurship

The literature presents a growing body of work on the relationship between the different types of capital and entrepreneurship. As suggested by Bourdieu (1986), all four types of capital are interlinked, implying that one type or form of capital can be converted into another. This section analyzes the relationship between social, cultural, and symbolic capital and entrepreneurial activity. This is a prerequisite for analyzing social gatherings, i.e., *diwaniyas*, where all forms of capital may coexist in a fertile environment for entrepreneurial activity.

Figure 28.1 depicts the relationship between different forms of capital and entrepreneurial activity. The suggested relationships are based on Pret et al.'s (2016) empirical study on capital convertibility. This conceptualization will be used below to explain the role of *diwaniyas* in fostering entrepreneurial activity through the

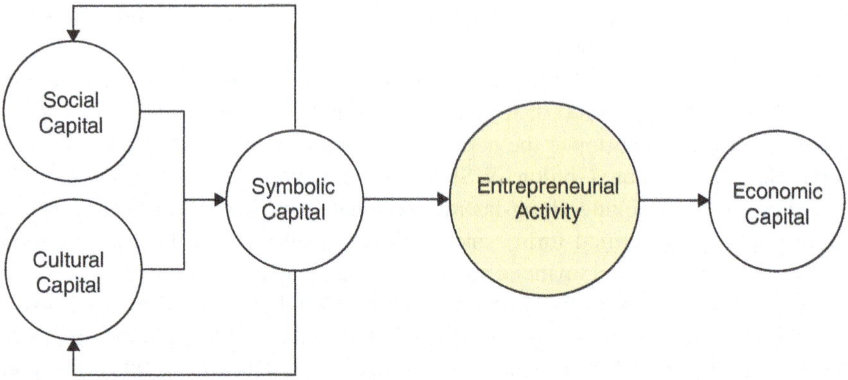

Fig. 28.1 Relationships between types of capital and entrepreneurial activity (Source: Adapted from Bourdieu, 1986 and Pret et al., 2016)

dynamic existence and convertibility of different types of capital. The literature pertinent to the relationship between social capital and entrepreneurship indicates that a critical factor in deciding to become an entrepreneur is one's involvement in social networks (Aldrich & Fiol, 1994; Jack & Anderson, 2002). Social network membership is usually considered a source of information regarding business opportunities that may provide entrepreneurs access to additional resources (funding or business experience). Moreover, experienced entrepreneurs already embedded in networks often serve as reference models, playing a key role in motivating others to engage in entrepreneurial activity. According to Neira, Portela, Cancelo, and Calvo (2013), access to social networks and entrepreneurial intention are positively related. In other words, networks give entrepreneurs the benefit of collectively owned and shared capital (Bowey & Easton, 2007; Rooks, Klyver, & Sserwanga, 2014). As social capital is a precondition for entrepreneurship, social network theory asserts that social capital of potential entrepreneurs could predict who will try to start their own business and who will move on to making it a success (Cousins, Handfield, Lawson, & Petersen, 2006; Hunt & Dennis, 2003).

Regarding cultural capital, it should be noted that it is indivisible from social capital, as cultural capital gives access to symbolic capital, which, in turn, gives rise to social capital (Fig. 28.1). Cultural capital takes the form of an individual's habitus and the opportunity for them to flaunt their knowledge (Bourdieu, 1993: 103). A lack of cultural capital can thus limit ability to "fit in" with accepted norms and can restrict access to social networks, therein impeding status enhancement (De Clercq & Voronov, 2009; Lounsbury & Glynn, 2001). Anderson and Miller (2003) proposed that high socioeconomic status (embodied cultural capital) allows entrepreneurs to develop wider social networks. Similarly, skills and industry experience – also a manifestation of cultural capital – can facilitate reputation-building (Beverland, 2005; Bitektine, 2011).

Moreover, both social and cultural capital feed into symbolic capital (Fig. 28.1). Once either of these two types of capital (social and/or cultural) are recognized, they can generate symbolic capital (Bourdieu, 1986), including *reputation* and *prestige*. This form of capital is particularly powerful as it can engender beliefs, generate trust, and legitimize the actions of entrepreneurs (De Clercq & Voronov, 2009; Harvey et al., 2011). Conversely, a lack of symbolic resources can impede entrepreneurial processes and have a negative long-term effect on entrepreneurial activity (Fischer & Reuber, 2007). Symbolic capital, such as prestige, can be converted back into social and cultural capital by further facilitating access to additional social networks (Lawrence, 2004; McLeod et al., 2009). In summary, social, cultural, and symbolic capitals in combination have a positive effect on, and lead to, entrepreneurial activity. These three types of capital along with resulting entrepreneurial activity enhance the fourth type: economic capital (Arregle et al., 2015; Light & Gold, 2000; Orban & Szanto, 2005), as economic capital is considered a bundle of tangible and intangible business assets, income, and reductions of transaction costs.

28.4 The Nature of Diwaniyas

The *diwaniya* is a long-standing Kuwaiti social institution (Alhajeri, 2010). It is a sociological phenomenon, and a prime example of a built environment – a man-made space. The term *diwaniya* "refers to both the actual space of the room, and the practice of gathering, and *diwaniyas* are places of social gathering where Kuwaiti men sit together to discuss issues relevant to them" (Chay, 2016). Numerous foreign diplomats to Kuwait have commented on the important role that *diwaniyas* play in Kuwaiti society. For instance, the French ambassador Christian Nakhla praised the rich diversity enjoyed by *diwaniyas* in Kuwait that include friendly people of different ages and culture (Kuwait News Agency, 2016). The Egyptian ambassador to Kuwait Yasser Atef also emphasized the opportunities these social gatherings offer in establishing connections and meet different personalities of Kuwait (Kwait News Agency, 2016).

The atmosphere of *diwaniyas* is similar to that of a social club where the members have refreshments, and many watch television, play cards, discuss business and neighborhood affairs, or sit in companionable silence. They usually begin in the early evening and sometimes last until late at night, with attendance being flexible depending on personal schedules (Scarce, 1985). *Diwaniya* gatherings have traditionally been a male activity, where business matters and the resolution of neighborhood disputes were discussed, and a way of socialization that remains popular even with the rise of oil wealth and modernization. Most *diwaniyas* are held at Kuwaiti homes; alternatively, separate building are renovated and converted into *diwaniyas* (Chay, 2016). Today, these social institutions maintain their historical traditions and contemporary values, despite the modernization of the State of Kuwait; in fact it has been argued that *diwaniyas* have been a fundamental driver for modernization (Al-Ghabrā, 1995).

28.5 Diwaniyas: Types of Capital and Entrepreneurship

28.5.1 Diwaniyas: A Form of Social and Cultural Capital

The French sociologist Henri Lefebvre conceived *space* as a social product (Lefebvre, 1992). The fact that *diwaniyas* are built environments – a type of *space* – renders them a social product, where social networks exist or can be formed. Through the numerous social interactions and networking opportunities available at *diwaniyas*, it could be argued that a degree of goodwill is created from all these interactions which can be used to facilitate action, whether for the benefit of individual members, i.e., social capital as a private good (personal benefits such as career advancements), or the benefit of the social institution at large, i.e., social capital as a public good (Belliveau et al., 1996; Bourdieu, 1986; Burt, 1997; Coleman, 1988; Putnam, 1993; Useem & Karabel, 1986). An additional link between *diwaniyas* and the notion of social capital is the suggestion that the amount of resources available at *diwaniyas*, such as industry connections, potential investors, and knowledge, can be capitalized on by individual members as a source of social capital (Van der Gaag & Snijders, 2004). These resources when utilized could therefore enhance reciprocity and trustworthiness, possibly further strengthening the social institution (Putnam, 2000).

In *diwaniyas* there is plenty of opportunity for individuals to display their knowledge. Bourdieu (1993) described this as a form of cultural capital as skills and industry experience are a manifestation of cultural capital (Beverland, 2005; Bitektine, 2011). This moreover allows individuals to "fit in" with accepted norms, which can possibly expand their access to other *diwaniyas* and enhance their status (De Clercq & Voronov, 2009). This is particularly beneficial to entrepreneurs as they can further grow their network (Anderson & Miller, 2003) and enjoy the benefits accruing from their participation in *diwaniyas*. As shown by Pret et al. (2016), this gives access to symbolic capital, which can in turn raise social capital.

28.5.2 Diwaniyas and Symbolic Capital

Attending *diwaniyas* is often perceived as a form of prestige, especially if the *diwaniyas* one attends are highly reputable and attract people of a high socioeconomic class. Being a member of such *diwaniyas* results in symbolic capital, as put forth by Terjesen and Elam (2009). Moreover, the more one attends these *diwaniyas*, the more symbolic capital – in the form of prestige and positive reputation – they obtain. In addition, symbolic capital stemming from *diwaniyas* can instill trust in the actions of its members (De Clercq & Voronov, 2009; Harvey et al., 2011). Such symbolic capital is not only used to increase other types of capital such as social and cultural capital, but it can also be a prerequisite for sustaining high levels of social capital (Deephouse & Carter, 2005).

28.5.3 Diwaniyas and Entrepreneurship

A critical and determining factor in entrepreneurial activity is, among others, the access to social, cultural, and symbolic capital, hence one's involvement in social networks (Aldrich & Fiol, 1994; Jack & Anderson, 2002). *Diwaniyas* offer a platform for gathering and social network flourishing in Kuwait. *Diwaniyas* offer almost unlimited access to social and cultural capital that is a rather rare contemporary social networking infrastructure. If the key factor for entrepreneurs is their access to different types of capital, hence their participation in social networks (Aldrich & Zimmer, 1986), and their participation is subject to the existence of social networks, then Kuwait has a highly social infrastructure. Whether *diwaniyas* with their social, cultural, and symbolic capitals remain distant from entrepreneurial activity or are embedded in entrepreneurial thinking and acting will determine, to a great extent, entrepreneurial activity in the country.

28.6 Conclusions

The level of entrepreneurship in Kuwait has grown significantly in recent years. The Kuwait government enacted a law in 2013 to establish a National Fund for small- and medium-sized enterprise (SME) development. This SME Fund intends to significantly support the efforts of Kuwaiti entrepreneurs (The National Fund, 2017) and is predicted to increase the number of entrepreneurs in the country by encouraging people to consider entrepreneurship as an alternative to public sector employment (Forbes, 2015). It is believed that mobilizing a cultural capital (i.e., *diwaniyas*) so prevalent in Kuwait, and converting it into social and symbolic capital, could become the driver for propelling entrepreneurial activity and meeting the national targets for new business. *Diwaniyas* could evolve further to become the forums for individuals to meet entrepreneurs. According to Arenius and Minniti (2005), individuals meeting other people working as self-employers (entrepreneurs) are more than twice as likely to become entrepreneurs as well.

The ultimate purpose of this short article has been to provide an overview of the relationship between different types of capital put forth by Bourdieu (1986) – social, cultural, and symbolic – and the culturally bound and widespread socializing phenomenon in Kuwait known as the *diwaniya*. An attempt has also been made to assess the role of *diwaniyas* in fostering entrepreneurial activity. We hope this study will propel more work into the nature and the crucial role of *diwaniyas* in delivering the capital required for entrepreneurial activity.

References

Acs, Z. J., Lee, S. Y., & Florida, R. (2004). Creativity and entrepreneurship. *Regional Studies, 38*, 879–891.

Adler, P. S., & Kwon, S.-W. (2002). Social capital: Prospect for a new concept. *Academy of Management Review, 27*, 17–40.

Aldrich, H., & Fiol, M. (1994). Fools rush in? The institutional context of industry creation. *Academy of Management Review, 19*(4), 645–670.

Aldrich, H., & Zimmer, C. (1986). Entrepreneurship through social networks. In D. L. S & Smilor (Eds.), *The art and science of entrepreneurship* (pp. 3–23). New York, NY: R. Cambridge.

Al-Ghabrā, S. (1995). *Al-Kuwayt: Dirāsa fī Aliyāt al-Dawla al-Qutrīya 51*. Cairo, Egypt: Dar Alamin.

Alhajeri, A. (2010). The development of political interaction in Kuwait through the "Dīwānīyas" from their beginnings until the year 1999. *Journal of Islamic Law and Culture, 12*(1), 24–44.

Anderson, A. R., & Miller, C. J. (2003). 'Class matters': Human and social capital in the entrepreneurial process. *The Journal of Socio-Economics, 32*(1), 17–36.

Arenius, P., & Minniti, M. (2005). Perceptual variables and nascent entrepreneurship. *Small Business Economics, 24*(3), 233–247.

Arregle, J. L., Batjargal, B., Hitt, M. A., Webb, J. W., Miller, T., & Tsui, A. S. (2015). Family ties in entrepreneurs' social networks and new venture growth. *Entrepreneurship Theory and Practice, 39*(2), 313–344.

Audretsch, D.B., Keilbach, M.C. and Lehmann, E.E. (2006). *Entrepreneurship and Economic Growth*, New York:Oxford Universitry Press.

Belliveau, M. A., O'Reilly, C. A., III, & Wade, J. B. (1996). Social capital at the top: Effects of social similarity and status on CEO compensation. *Academy of Management Journal, 39*, 1568–1593.

Beverland, M. B. (2005). Crafting brand authenticity: The case of luxury wines. *Journal of Management Studies, 42*(5), 1003–1029.

Bitektine, A. (2011). Toward a theory of social judgments of organizations: The case of legitimacy, reputation, and status. *Academy of Management Review, 36*(1), 151–179.

Bourdieu, P. (1986). The forms of capital. In J. G. Richardson (Ed.), *The handbook of theory and research for the sociology of education*. New York, NY: Greenwood Press.

Bourdieu, P. (1993). The field of cultural production, or: The economic world reversed. In R. Johnson (Ed.), *The field of cultural production: Essays on art and literature* (pp. 29–73). Cambridge: Polity Press.

Bowey, J. L., & Easton, G. (2007). Entrepreneurial social capital unplugged: An activity-based analysis. *International Small Business Journal, 25*(3), 273–306.

Burt, R. S. (1997). The contingent value of social capital. *Administrative Science Quarterly, 42*, 339–365.

Casson, M. C. (1982). *The entrepreneur: An economic theory*. Oxford, UK: Martin Robertson.

Chay, C. (2016). The dīwāniyya tradition in modern Kuwait: An interlinked space and practice. *Journal of Arabian Studies., 6*(1), 1–28.

Coleman, J. (1988). Social capital in the creation of human capital. *American Journal of Sociology, 94*(Supplement), S95–S120.

Cousins, P., Handfield, R., Lawson, B., & Petersen, K. J. (2006). Creating supply chain relational capital: The impact of formal and informal socialization processes. *Journal of Operations Management, 24*(6), 851–863.

De Clercq, D., & Voronov, M. (2009). Toward a practice perspective of entrepreneurship: Entrepreneurial legitimacy as habitus. *International Small Business Journal, 27*(4), 395–419.

Deephouse, D. L., & Carter, S. M. (2005). An examination of differences between organizational legitimacy and organizational reputation. *Journal of Management Studies, 42*(2), 329–360.

Fischer, E., & Reuber, R. (2007). The good, the bad, and the unfamiliar: The challenges of reputation formation facing new firms. *Entrepreneurship Theory and Practice, 31*(1), 53–75.

Forbes. (2015). Silicon Gulf? Kuwait moves beyond oil to nurture entrepreneurs. Available from: https://www.forbes.com. Accessed 5 June 2017.

Greve, A., & Salaff, J. W. (2003). Social networks and entrepreneurship. *Entrepreneurship Theory and Practice, 28*(1), 1–22.

Harvey, C., Maclean, M., Gordon, J., & Shaw, E. (2011). Andrew Carnegie and the foundations of contemporary entrepreneurial philanthropy. *Business History, 53*(3), 425–450.

Holmes, T. J., & Schmitz, J. A. (1990). A theory of entrepreneurship and its application to the study of business transfers. *Journal of Political Economy, 98*, 265–294.

Hunt, S., & Dennis, B. A. (2003). Resource-advantage theory and Embeddedness: Explaining RA Theory's explanatory success. *Journal of Marketing Theory and Practice, 11*(1), 1–17.

Jack, S., & Anderson, A. (2002). The effects of embeddedness on the entrepreneurial process. *Journal of Business Venturing, 17*(5), 467–487.

Jonsson, S., & Lindbergh, J. (2013). The development of social capital and financing of entrepreneurial firms: From financial bootstrapping to bank funding. *Entrepreneurship Theory and Practice, 37*(4), 661–686.

Kirzner, I. M. (1973). *Competition and entrepreneurship*. Chicago, IL: University of Chicago Press.

Knight, F. H. (1921). *Risk, uncertainty, and profit*. New York, NY: Augustus M. Lelley.

Kostova, T., & Roth, K. (2003). Social capital in multinational corporations and a micro-macro model of its formation. *Academy of Management Review, 28*, 297–317.

Kuwait News Agency. (2016). [Online]. Diplomats: Kuwait Diwaniyas are Mini Parliaments. Available from: http://alqabas.com. Accessed 20 May 2017.

Lange, D., Lee, P. M., & Dai, Y. (2011). Organizational reputation: A review. *Journal of Management, 37*(1), 153–184.

Lawrence, T. B. (2004). Rituals and resistance: Membership dynamics in professional fields. *Human Relations, 57*(2), 115–143.

Lefebvre, H. (1992). *The Production of Space* (trans: Nicholson-Smith). United Kingdom: Editions Anthropos.

Light, I. H., & Gold, S. J. (2000). *Ethnic economies*. San Diego, CA: Academic Press.

Lucas, R. E. (1978). On the size distribution of firms. *Bell Journal of Economics, 9*, 508–523.

Lounsbury, M. and Glynn, M.A. (2001). Cultural entrepreneurship: Stories, legitimacy, and the acquisition of resources. *Strategic Marketing Journal*, 22(6-7), 545–564.

McLeod, C., O'Donohoe, S., & Townley, B. (2009). The elephant in the room? Class and creative careers in British advertising agencies. *Human Relations, 62*(7), 1011–1039.

Nahapiet, J., & Ghoshal, S. (1998). Social capital, intellectual capital and the organizational advantage. *Academy of Management Review, 23*, 242–266.

Neira, I., Portela, M., Cancelo, M., & Calvo, N. (2013). Social and human capital as determining factors of entrepreneurship in the Spanish regions. *Investigaciones Regionales, 26*, 115–139.

Orban, A., & Szanto, Z. (2005). Társadalmi tőke. *Erdélyi Társadalom, 3*(2), 55–70.

Pret, T., Shaw, E., & Dodd, S. (2016). Painting the full picture: The conversion of economic, cultural, social and symbolic capital. *International Small Business Journal, 8*, 1004–1027.

Putnam, R. (1993). The prosperous community: Social capital and public life. *American Prospect, 13*, 35–42.

Putnam, R. (2000). *Bowling alone: The collapse and revival of American community*. New York, NY: Simon and Schuster.

Reuber, A. R., & Fischer, E. (2005). The company you keep: How young firms in different competitive contexts signal reputation through their customers. *Entrepreneurship Theory and Practice, 29*(1), 57–78.

Rooks, G., Klyver, K., & Sserwanga, A. (2014). The context of social capital: A comparison of rural and urban entrepreneurs in Uganda. *Entrepreneurship Theory and Practice*. Epub ahead of print 21 April. https://doi.org/10.1111/etap.12107.

Scarce, J. (1985). *The evolving culture of Kuwait* (p. 48). Edinburgh, Scotland: Royal Scottish Museum.

Schumpeter, J. A. (1911). *Theory of economic development. An investigation entrepreneur winning over, capital, credit, interest rate and the business cycle*. Berlin, Germany: Duncker and Humblot.

Terjesen, S., & Elam, A. B. (2009). Transnational entrepreneurs' venture internationalization strategies: A practice theory approach. *Entrepreneurship Theory and Practice, 33*(5), 1093–1120.

The National Fund. (2017). Vision and Mission. Available from: http://nationalfund.gov.kw. Accessed 5 June 2017.

Useem, M., & Karabel, J. (1986). Pathways to top corporate management. *American Sociological Review, 44*, 184–200.

Van der Gaag, M. and Snijders, T. (2004). Proposals for the measurement of indvidual social capital. In Flap, H. and Volker, B Eds., *Creation and returns of social capital. A new research program*. Routledge, London.

Professor Antonis C. Simintiras is the Dean of the College of Business Administration at 'Gulf University for Science and Technology' GUST, Kuwait, and a PT research professor at Swansea University, UK. His research interests are in the areas of business negotiations, education disequilibria, sociocultural infrastructures, and research methodology.

Mr. Yusif M. Al-Hajji holds a BSc in Accounting from Kuwait University and an MSc in International Business from the University of Leeds, UK. This work has been produced while he was on a research placement at Gulf University for Science and Technology, Kuwait. Currently, his research interests are in the areas of economics of social infrastructures and sociological bases of entrepreneurship.

Chapter 29
The Ethics and Governance of an Emerging Technology in an Emerging Market: The Case of Private Umbilical Cord Blood Banking in India

Shashank S. Tiwari

Abstract This chapter discusses the proliferation of private cord blood banking in India. It explores (a) the pattern of commercialisation, (b) the hope rhetoric, (c) the ethical and social issues raised and (d) the governance of cord blood banking and the problems facing the existing system of oversight. The study shows that hope and hype associated with an emerging technology in an emerging market such as India raise significant social, ethical and governance issues and concerns. Finally, the chapter argued that "hype bubbles" can damage both the market and the technological innovation in the absence of effective regulations.

Keywords Emerging market · Emerging technology · Private cord blood banking · India

29.1 Introduction

Stem cell technologies have emerged as one of the key emerging biomedical technologies worldwide including emerging markets such as India. It promises to address a wide range of clinical conditions (e.g. Parkinson's disease, Alzheimer's disease, retinal degeneration, muscular dystrophy, spinal cord injuries, diabetes mellitus, etc.) for which no effective treatment has yet been developed. Stem cells are unspecialised cells, which have a potential to develop into any kind of cells, tissues and organs. This unique property makes them an important medical tool in

S. S. Tiwari (✉)
Institute for Science and Society (ISS), School of Sociology and Social Policy, University of Nottingham, Nottingham, UK
e-mail: shashank17t@gmail.com

Y. K. Dwivedi et al. (eds.), *Emerging Markets from a Multidisciplinary Perspective*, Advances in Theory and Practice of Emerging Markets,
https://doi.org/10.1007/978-3-319-75013-2_29

health care. There is an excitement that stem cells will be able to boost the biotechnology and pharmaceutical industries in the future.

Countries across the world have evolved their own programmes and policies to take early advantage from stem cells. The global stem cell market is expected to reach USD 15.63 billion by 2025 (WBRC, 2017); as a result, stem cell research is becoming increasingly competitive. Research in the USA, the UK, the European Union, Asia and Asia-Pacific regions is highly supported by both public and private players (Gottweis, Salter, & Waldby, 2009; Sipp, 2011).

In this global context, India is rapidly becoming established as one of the key players in the stem cell field, having significant activities in basic research and clinical applications. India has started its stem cell programmes in the early 2000s, largely with the support of government-funded laboratories. The major activities are confined to adult stem cells followed by umbilical cord blood stem cells and embryonic stem cells (Bharadwaj & Glasner, 2009; Sharma, 2009; Tiwari & Desai, 2011).

In recent years, India has seen a significant rise in the preservation of umbilical cord blood. The driving force is that, from preserved cord blood, stem cell can be retrieved whenever a patient needs stem cell intervention. There are basically two types of cord blood banking: (a) public cord blood banking, which can be used by anyone, i.e. analogous, and there are no storage fees; and (b) private cord blood banking where the purpose of banking is only for the self, i.e. autologous, though it can also be used by siblings or other family members, and for this, service banking firms charge expectant parents to preserve their child's cord blood. The market of private umbilical cord blood (UCB) banking is worth millions of dollar in India. However, there are concerns about the safety and claims made for the benefits of UCB banking and regenerative therapies that might arise from them, none of which are proven at present. The risk of infection from cord blood transplantation is also a major concern (Agarwal, 2006). These issues have been the subjects of considerable public debate. Altogether, the proliferation of private cord blood banking in India raises important social ethical and governance issues.

This chapter, against this backdrop, analyses the commercial development of cord blood banking in India and will explore (a) the pattern of commercialisation, (b) the hope rhetoric, (c) the ethical and social issues raised and (d) the governance of cord blood banking and the problems facing the existing system of oversight. The chapter will show how a strict regulation is required for a successful innovation in emerging markets such as India, especially in the case of emerging technologies.

29.2 Emerging Technologies in Emerging Markets

Markets, which are in various stages of development and in the process of stabilisation in terms of its shape and size including rules and regulations, are characterised as emerging markets (EMs). Geographically, they are largely confined to "middle- and low-income" countries, and India is one of them (Hoskisson, Wright, Filatotchev, & Peng, 2013). The scholarships in EMs have noted political, economic and institutional uncertainty including hype as one of the key characteristics of these markets (Heinz & Tomenendal, 2012; Tracey & Phillips, 2011). The uncertainty and hype act as barriers; they, however, also provide opportunity. The Indian government at the time of launching the *Make in India* initiatives acknowledged that the unrealistic hype led to India's low growth rate. It was stated that the "*Make in India* was a timely response to a critical situation: by 2013, the much-hyped emerging markets bubble had burst, and India's growth rate had fallen to its lowest level in a decade. The promise of the BRICS Nations (Brazil, Russia, India, China and South Africa) had faded, and India was tagged as one of the so-called 'Fragile Five'" (Kant, 2015, p. 18).

Similar to emerging markets, hype, hope and visions are inherent features of emerging technologies. They play an important role in shaping of the particular research areas or technology. Scholarship in sociology of expectations has argued that a strong vision in terms of potential capability of a particular technology is necessary to draw attention of the public, funders and policymakers for social and financial support and a favourable policy regime (Borup, Brown, Konrad, & Van Lente, 2006; Brown & Michael, 2003). Furthermore, a "future" is deliberately created to marshal resources and the support of different actors for the development of a particular technoscientific venture and the direction of research especially for emerging technologies where actual products or services are yet to be manifested (Brown & Michael, 2003).

The studies have shown that expectation discourse is not only limited to attracting various resources and the alignment of various actors, in the form of "hope" rhetoric, but it also helps in the generation of capital, even when there is no actual product. The proliferation of cord blood banking, especially those that are private in nature, appears to be a good example for the same. It is observed that "the creation of commercial cord blood banks...marks the capitalization of human tissues within a future-oriented "regime of hope" (Martin, Brown, & Turner, 2008, p. 127). This development is viewed as a shift from the "regime of truth" (proven evidence and established practice) to the "regime of hope" in present bio-economy, where hope itself becomes a marketable product, termed "capitalization of hope" (Martin et al., 2008). The interesting thing about this "regime of hope", which has been observed by Paul Martin and his colleagues, is that, it is not geographically confined and it has a tendency to capture different countries and locations, which is conceptualised as a new "geography of promises" (Martin et al., 2008). Arguably, "this geography illustrates the spatiality of a regime of hope focused initially on the US and the UK, but with Asia and the near East closely following" (Martin et al., 2008, p. 134). For instance, private blood banking had been established during the 1990s in the West (Brown & Kraft, 2006; Martin et al., 2008) and has spread in countries such as in India in the beginning of the 2000s.

The majorities of studies in the sociology of expectations discussed above have concentrated on Western settings and do not pay attention to the nature of expectations in different cross-cultural settings. In addition, these studies limit their analysis of expectation discourse at the level of specific actors, viz. only scientists, clinicians and entrepreneurs, and overlook the role of nation states and governments in expectation rhetoric. Only a few studies have compared the nature of vision and hype in different cross-cultural settings, most notably the comparative study of bio-capital in the USA and India (Rajan, 2006) which attempted to investigate the varied nature of expectations in these two countries. In the USA, it is largely the corporate sector that engaged in the articulation of vision and hype, while in the case of India, it is the state itself, for the major part, playing a leading role in the creation of expectations. In India, the majority of biotechnology R&D is supported through government-funded laboratories; therefore, it is quite natural for the Indian state to actively participate in expectation discourse. However, the study of Sunder Rajan illuminates a fundamental difference between the vision and hype of the USA and India. The vision and hype in the former case are embedded in "salvation" rhetoric, i.e. a particular biomedical research has the capability to "save life"; while in the latter case, it is dominated by "nationalist" discourse where there is a desire to be a global player. Sunder Rajan further argues that, in contrast to the USA, "the speculative capitalism in India is far less developed in relation to manufacturing capitalism, which suggests that sales and profit, rather than the conjuration of futures, are likely to be the driving dynamic of the Indian biotech and pharmaceutical industries" (Rajan, 2006, p. 126). More clearly this argument reflects that the future vision circulates in the generation of capitalism (speculative) in the USA. Drawing on the observation of Paul Martin and his colleagues in the case of proliferation of cord blood banking (Martin et al., 2008), it can be argued that the "regime of truth" is dominant in India compared to the "regime of hope". However, the concept of "geography of promises" reflects that this regime has now started to change. Similarly, Sunder Rajan also illustrated that, in the desire to go global, India has started to lean towards the speculative/hope regime, which is a more market-oriented approach (Rajan, 2006).

It is noted that though hope, hype and vision are essential for a successful innovation, it might have serious implications for a technology if it fails to materialise. The unrealistic hype allows the proliferation of immature and unproven technologies, for instance, stem cell, and raises significant ethical and governance issues (Petersen, 2009, 2011).

It is clearly evident that unrealistic hype and hope are deliberately being generated in both emerging markets and in the case of emerging technologies as well as to marshal resources. However, this hype bubble is subject to burst, which can have serious implications on market, technology and society. Against this backdrop, this chapter analyses the proliferation of cord blood banking in India.

29.3 Methods

The chapter is an excerpt of my own PhD dissertation (2013) at the University of Nottingham (UK). To analyse and understand the proliferation of cord blood banking in India, a qualitative study of documents in different media (news and opinion, scientific literature, policy reports) and interviews with key stakeholders was

Table 29.1 Details of licensed private umbilical cord blood banks in India

Sl no.	Name	Location	Category
1.	Best Wellcare Management Services Pvt. Ltd	Vadodara, Gujarat	Private
2.	Cryo-Save (India) Pvt. Ltd.	Bangalore, Karnataka	Private
3	Cryobanks International India Pvt. Ltd.	Gurgaon, Haryana	Private
4.	LifeCell International Pvt. Ltd.	Chennai, Tamil Nadu	Private
5.	LifeCell International Pvt. Ltd.	Gurgaon, Haryana	Private
6.	Narayana Hrudayalaya Tissue Bank and Stem Cells Research Centre	Bangalore, Karnataka	Private
7.	Path Care Labs Pvt. Ltd.	Hyderabad, Telangana	Private
8.	Ree Laboratories Pvt. Ltd.	Mumbai, Maharashtra	Private
9.	Reliance Life Sciences Pvt. Ltd.	Navi Mumbai, Maharashtra	Private
10.	StemCyte India Therapeutics Private Limited	Gandhinagar, Gujarat	Private
11.	TotipotentRX Cell Therapy Pvt. Ltd.	Gurgaon, Haryana	Private
12.	Unistem Biosciences Pvt. Ltd.	Gurgaon, Haryana	Private
13.	Regenerative Medical Services Pvt. Ltd.	Mumbai, Maharashtra	Private
14.	Cord Life Sciences India Pvt. Ltd.	South 24, Parganas, West Bengal	Private

Source: Ministry of Health and Family Welfare, May 08 2015

undertaken. In total, I conducted 27 semi-structured interviews that include 5 scientists, 11 clinicians, 7 firms' representatives and 4 policymakers. The interviews were lasting between 45 min and an hour (with one exception, where the interview finished in 15 min). Interviews were conducted after ethical approval from the University of Nottingham during June 2010–January 2011, and again during September–October 2011, in various cities in India including New Delhi, Mumbai, Pune, Chennai, Bangalore, Hyderabad, Tirupati, Kolkata and Chandigarh where most of the research and clinical activities in stem cells are being carried out. The majority of the interviews were recorded with the informants' permission and transcribed. However, three interviewees refused permission to record the conversation. In that case, I noted down their response. Finally, to update this chapter, current news items, recent journal publications and policy documents were included to take on board recent developments in cord blood banking in India.

29.4 The Emergence of UCB in India

The majority of UCB banking in India is of private in nature except a few public cord blood banks. Compared to the West, UCB banking is rather a new phenomenon in India, which started in the early 2000s. Reliance Life Sciences (RLS) is credited to establish the first public cord blood bank in 2002; however, at RLS, the main focus is private banking (Patra & Sleeboom-Faulkner, 2016). Over the years, many

UCB banks were established in India. Currently, as per government document, there are 14 licensed/registered UCB banks in India (Table 29.1).

However, a recent media report noted 21 registered UCB banks and more than 500 unregistered banks in India (Bedi, 2017). The high birth rate is one of the major factors to attract many national and international players towards this venture. Majority of the banks in India have foreign in origin. India is seen as an emerging market for cord blood banking business. Private banks promise to treat a large number of disease conditions using stem cell derived from umbilical cord blood. They claim to freeze stem cell in liquid nitrogen so that it can be used up to 21 years from the date of preservation, if required. For the preservation, on an average, private banking of stem cells derived from cord blood costs USD 1000–USD1500. With the birth rate of 27 million births per year, the projected market for cord blood banking is worth millions of US dollars. In 2013, it was estimated to US$32 million, which is projected to US$430 million by 2020 (Patra & Sleeboom-Faulkner, 2016).

There is no doubt that cord blood banking is currently a big business in India. For instance, as per recent media report, India's LifeCell has preserved 2,00,000 units of cord blood so far and continues to collect 50,000 units of cord blood every year (The Hindu Business Line, 2017). However, their claims to address various disease conditions and marketing strategies including hope rhetoric have raised legitimate ethical and governance issues.

29.5 Hope, Hype and Visions

Since most of the leading firms in India are multinational, their strategies are more or less similar to what they adopt to create high expectations in the West. These firms advertised their banking services directly to the expectant parents through various workshops, seminars or via clinicians and the Internet. Expectant parents are being encouraged to "invest" their money for a "healthy and happy future" of their child in the name of "biological insurance" (Patra & Sleeboom-Faulkner, 2016). The advertisement leaflets of companies are making big promises of the benefits of stored cord blood such as "your child and families can [have] access to potential treatments for over 75 serious ailments such as leukaemia, thalassemia, brain injury, juvenile diabetes and many more" (Srinivasan, 2010).

In the beginning, the Government of India was also influenced by the hype of cord blood banking. An ex-policymaker stated that: "that was the time [in 2002] having the slow development of cord blood banks in India and it is also suggested that, yes, cord blood stem cell is a good source, and a country like India where you produce combined Australia and New Zealand every year...OK...that's our annual population is 25 million which is more than the combined population of Australia and New Zealand...Australia is 22 million, New Zealand is 2 million...24 million but we produced more than 25 million per year...so we have enough source material and if we effectively use it probably we can do lot of wonders" (Ex-policymaker).

However, compared to firms, the Government of India appears to be more aligned towards public cord blood banking. An official of the Indian Council of Medical Research (ICMR) illustrated that: "I belong to the lobby that nobody should store their cord blood for future use...unless family, where siblings are suffering or can be used for those siblings...but otherwise it is very important to have public banking" (Policymaker 2).

The private cord blood banking firms create expectations/hope on the basis that if parents can afford it, then they should preserve their child's cord blood, and also some of the banking firms stressed that people themselves want to go for private cord blood banking. A firm's representative illustrated that: "There is a lot of hope and hype in the cord blood banking business; there is something which is good about it...there are people who have money who say why not ...my child is precious I want to save it; whether it is 100% proven or not, there is some justification in saving a child's cord blood and I can afford it, then why shouldn't I do it...people want it ...they come up to us and say I want to store it" (Firm's representative, 5).

Over the years, cord blood banking firms have been able to influence expectant parents through their claims to treat large numbers of ailments and have created a demand amongst expectant parents, where affordable parents do not even question the legitimacy of private cord blood banking. They also take advantage of the largely joint family system in India while putting their claims in favour of private cord blood banking. As a firm's representative argued: "If there is an indication in the family it is a very good option ...it is a very good option ...you never know when it might come in handy" (Firm's representative, 4). It is also reflected from the above statement that not only "certain future" but "uncertain future" can also have the capacity to mobilise individuals in a particular direction. "You never know when it might come in handy" is somewhat speaking about a "speculative future". The representative of firm argues that, at the moment, there might be no benefit from cord blood banking, but in the future, we can take advantage from it. However, the firm's representative is not sure about the future prospects of private cord blood banking.

The other private cord blood banking firms argued that cord blood stem cells have potential to replace bone marrow transplantation, and on this basis, they are attracting expectant parents. A firm's representative of cord blood banking opined that: "We are of the opinion that cord blood banking is useful in terms of regenerative medicine...there is a lot of debate as to how useful cord blood banking is... whether it is worth spending that money for saving your child's cord blood...the opinion we have is that, if you can use these cells for a particular use...cord blood banking originally started as a replacement for bone marrow transplantation...it's very difficult to get bone marrow and to store bone marrow and to source bone marrow is difficult because we need donors...cord blood itself could be a useful alternative for bone marrow" (Firm's representative, 5). The idea here is that stem cells are viewed as a novel form of therapy having the capability to replace those existing therapies which are unable to tackle various debilitating disease conditions. In sum, the expectations around private cord blood banking are created on two key ways. First, it is useful for the self including other familiy members and second it can be used as a replacement for bone marrow.

The various studies, in both the science and social science domains, have shown that private storage is rarely used for the self and is basically based on "future promises" and "capitalising hope" (Kaimal, Smith, Laros Jr, Caughey, & Cheng, 2009; Martin et al., 2008). The chances that a particular child will develop a condition requiring cord blood transplantation are very slim. It has been observed that 0.04% (1/2500) of cord blood units stored would ever be used for autologous transplantation. The reason is that the occurrence of diseases currently treated with cord blood is small, and many patients would not be eligible for autologous cord blood, including those with genetic disorders and leukaemia (Kaimal et al., 2009). The key stakeholders in India have highlighted key ethical issues linked with the business of private cord blood banking.

29.6 Ethics

The data from the interviews in India have shown that the mushrooming of private cord blood banking potentially exploited expecting parents. The representative of a hybrid (both public and private in nature) UCB firm in India clearly stated that: "Private banking is rarely used for the self. It is very often ... this is something that people are being kind of promoting ... saying ... it can be used for the child from whom it is collected and this is rarely the case at all because, if the child has got the genetic problem and it has not been known at birth, the stem cells collected from the child would also be affected with the same problem and, unless you get involved in some sort of manipulation of those stem cells and then try to introduce them, only then will it be useful to the child from whom it has been taken. The only instance when it can be used for the child from whom it's taken is if it is an acquired illness of some kind or something which is not genetic, in those instances yes ... when you talk about private banking it is more likely to be used only by somebody else in the family ... maybe an older sibling or maybe somebody else" (Firm's representative, 1).

A scientist who is involved in research using cord blood stem cells opined that it is more useful in the case of allogenic transplantation (i.e. a patient receives stem cells from his own blood) in contrast to autologous transplantation (i.e. a patient receives stem cells from a donor): "The cord blood cells if at all, it can be used in an allogenic set up, it will be wonderful cells but for somebody used for autologous and the boy will be or kid will be grown and then he or she will have some problem and then the cell will be transplanted in that way it has no impact...impact will be less than .0001%, but if it is allogenic it will have tremendous potential" (Scientist, 1).

In spite of the rare chance of self-use, cord blood banking firms in India are attracting patients in the name of "biological insurance" (Mascarenhas, 2009), i.e. "an insurance for their child's future wellbeing" (Sullivan, Browett, & Patton, 2005). However, a scientist feels that it is a kind of insurance where one will not get anything and it is only a money-making endeavour: "This is a short-time business strategy that some people have decided...I don't want to sound too harsh but in some way I really feel that this is a yuppie phenomenon okay... somebody has one lakhs (~US$1500) to spend and they decide that wow! nothing is too good for my child so I am going to spend the lakhs, essentially on liquid nitrogen charges for preserving something. It sounds like a good idea but actually speaking there is not that much benefit to cord blood banking. It's like an insurance policy except in the case of an insurance you are going to use it at some point of time...whereas in cord blood...you know after the age of 21 you can give an autologous bone marrow transplant, why you need to have cord blood" (Scientist, 3).

The main criticism here is that private cord blood banking has a very limited use for the self. It is already documented through various studies that there are very low chances that a child will need his/her cord blood in the future. Furthermore, cord blood banking firms at the moment only preserve cord blood till the age of 21; then the question arises, what would happen if a child needed any transplantation after that age? The scientist argued that there is not much clinical benefit of preserving cord blood. Patients are being charged for only preserving materials such as liquid nitrogen. It does not deliver what it promises in the name of "biological insurance". A similar opinion has been also expressed by some other studies in the West, as Nelson argued "insurance provides a certain benefit for an uncertain future"; however, in the case of stem cell banking, there is "an uncertain benefit combined with uncertain future" (Nelson, 2008).

Scientist 3 is of the view that the cord blood banking is more beneficial for firms themselves rather than the child of expectant parents. She stated that: "To charge people for a low probability event sounds more like a business plan than a necessity" (Scientist, 3).

The private cord blood banking is even criticised by the representative of a firm, who himself engaged in the "cord blood banking business". He expressed his opinion against the preservation of cord blood, if any genetic disease affects a child: "The problem is that you can't use your own cord blood if you have a genetic disease. If you have a blood disorder later in life then you can't use your own cord blood because the stem cells in the cord blood may also have the same genetic disease or the same problem which you have now, so that really makes life difficult for cord blood banking companies because how do you justify this?" (Firm's representative, 5).

The European Commission's Group on Ethics in Science and New Technologies' (EGE) report on the ethics of private cord blood banking also questions the legitimacy of private cord blood banks for self-use. This report argues that, "they [private cord blood banks] promise more than they can deliver" (Puigdomench-Rosell & Virt, 2004). The representative of a hybrid cord blood banking firm argues along the same lines: "They do give a lot of false claims. There is a long list of 70 diseases that everybody keeps counting...I think, there needs to be more serious studies that go on before one can actually say it can be used for late year illness...their tall claims really frightened me...if you go to the website you feel that every disease under the sun can be cured" (Firm's representative, 1).

It is argued that the cord blood banking firms are playing with the emotion of parents. An ICMR official stated that: "Private banking, I find playing with the emotions of people who are donating or storing their cord blood...after 18...21 years its maintaining them for so long is of no use...I don't think so...Unless and until in family you need somebody requires then definitely one should store that" (Policymaker, 2).

The statement of the policymaker echoes the similar observation highlighted by Brown and Kraft while studying the role of expectations in the proliferation of cord blood banking in the UK where emotion plays an important role. It was reflected by this study that, at the time of birth, mothers are more emotional and also quite vulnerable and they can be easily influenced by any promises if it is for the future of their child (Brown & Kraft, 2006).

The other main ethical concern is that most of the firms in India do not possess enough scientific expertise to retrieve the stored cord blood. A stem cell clinician raised this issue during the field visit: "My experience with one of the cord blood banking was, they have saved it but they don't know how to retrieve it. They don't know a standardised way to remove [that] preservative and in a patient who had an autologous cord blood store we could not use her stem cell because the company did not know how to use it" (Clinician, 3).

The representative of another firm has similar opinion that it is practically impossible to retrieve stem cells from frozen cord tissue: "Some companies are saying okay...you pay us a small amount…and we will save the tissue for you. We will take the umbilical cord tissue and we will save it for you; whenever you need cells, we will remove it and we will derive cells from it and we will give it to you, which is hoggish because if you see the umbilical cord it is the complex tissue, it is thick sometimes and the thickness makes it difficult to freeze it ... if you take cord tissue and just freeze it you will kill all the cells which are there in the cord; you can't derive any cell from it later on but it is a marketing gimmick" (Firm's representative, 5).

It is clear from the above discussion that private cord blood banking in India is a business, which is based on promises rather than any tangible products or services. Expectant parents are being mobilised on "emotional grounds". The notion of "biological insurance" is also playing a major role in attracting expectant parents. However, there are very slim chances that a child would ever use his/her preserved cord blood in the future. Furthermore, some firms claim to treat various genetic disorders by using a child's own cord blood, which is again not valid since stem cells in the cord blood may contain same genetic defects. It was argued by some of the informants that firms do not even know how to retrieve stem cells from the preserved cord blood, which raises concerns in terms of the legitimacy of banking firms.

The development of private cord blood banking in India, which is similar to the development in the West, reflects the universal nature of bio-economies, which "depend on a promissory future economic value and potential rather than present use" (Martin et al., 2008, p. 128). In an emerging market where already there are uncertainties at the level of regulations, this business can be more exploitative.

The above stakeholders' perspective clearly suggests that the proliferation of promissory private UCB business has raised significant ethical and social issues and informed to examine the existing governance regime in India.

29.7 Governance

The Indian FDA, i.e. the Central Drugs Standard Control Organization (CDSCO), is designated to issue license and monitor cord blood banks in India. However, not all banks are registered with the CDSCO (Bedi, 2017). This suggests that the cord blood business in India is largely unregulated. It is also observed that there is no effective mechanism to regulate the exacerbated claims of benefits of private banking.

The national stem cell guidelines 2013 and the newly launched 2017 stem cell guidelines discourage private storage of cord blood. In the guidelines, it is stated that there are ethical and social concerns about the promotional advertisements. Such advertisements are often misleading and lack comprehensive and accurate information to the consumer. The National Apex Committee for Stem Cell Research and Therapy (NACSCRT), which was constituted in 2010, recently started monitoring advertisements related to stem cell including cord blood banking. With the help of Advertising Standards of Council of India (ASCI), the NACSCRT has put many private cord blood banks under scanner. Though many websites have already started amending their contents, this step is not effective enough to prevent misleading advertisements (Tiwari, 2015). Moreover, there is an ambiguity in governing private cord blood banking. On the one hand, the stem cell guidelines do not recommend private storage of cord blood; on the other hand, the Health Ministry asked the Finance Ministry in 2014 to exempt service tax on cord blood banking services (Tiwari, 2014). The exemption is to be continuing in the newly launched Goods and Services Taxes starting from July 1, 2017.

It appears that the hype surrounding emerging markets and cord blood banking services have also influenced the Government of India, which despite significant ethical and social concerns could not formulate strict regulations for private cord blood banking business. In the absence of effective governance in place, this hype can be burst any time as highlighted in the *Make in India* document. However, it should not be assumed that having a strict regulation would force people to behave as per mandate. In the case of India, implementation is a major issue (Tiwari & Raman, 2014).

29.8 Conclusions

In India, the majority of foreign origin stem cell firms are engaged in private cord blood banking. The future market of the private cord blood banking is worth millions of dollar, having millions of births per year in India. It seems that, for this potential market, multinational firms are attracted towards India. The firms create hope and hype amongst expectant parents on the basis that it is not only useful for the self but also for the other family members, and it has the capacity to replace bone marrow blood cells. However, there is no enough scientific evidence in the favour of self-use of the preserve cord blood.

The private blood banking business is largely seen as a money-making endeavour without having a tangible product. The key players such as scientists, clinicians, policymakers and a few firms' representatives are of the opinion that, in the name "biological insurance", expectant parents are being exploited since there is a rare chance for a child to use his/her own cord blood in the future. This raises significant ethical and social concerns. However, the Government of India has been unable to formulate an effective policy to regulate private banking; in contrast, indirectly the government supports this exploitative business by providing tax exemption.

It can be inferred that the "hype bubbles" are largely responsible for lax regulations. In the name of innovation and development, India appears to allow "controversial technologies" to flourish (Tiwari & Tiwary, 2015). The technology roadmap on medical science and health care under Technology Vision 2035 has acknowledged that emerging technologies, such as but not limited to genomics and stem cells, will be major drivers in health care in India. The visionary document also accepts that these technologies have many ethical and moral issues for which there is a need to have a robust regulatory environment. The document equally emphasises that regulation should not stifle innovation. However, in innovation studies, there is a greater thrust on rules and regulations. They are viewed as a key for a successful innovation. Regulations help in managing uncertainty at various levels. It is argued that rules and regulations are one of the constitutive elements of innovation (Borrás & Edquist, 2014).

The analysis in the chapter shows that hype and hope are inherent characteristics of both emerging markets and emerging technologies using the case study of private cord blood banking business in India. The unrealistic hope raises significant social, ethical and governance issues and concerns. In the long term, lax regulation and ambiguous policy against the backdrop of "hype bubbles" can damage both the market and the technological innovation.

Acknowledgements The chapter is the part of a Wellcome Trust Studentship (grant number: WT087867MA) awarded to Shashank Tiwari at the Institute for Science and Society, School of Sociology and Social Policy, University of Nottingham, Nottingham (UK). The Trust is not responsible for views expressed in this letter. The author is grateful to Paul Martin, Sujatha Raman and Pranav Desai for support and guidance.

References

Agarwal, M. (2006). Umbilical cord blood transplantation: Newer trends. *JAPI, 54*, 143–147.

Bedi, A. (2017, July 24). Cord blood firms turn Astrologers. *Outlook*.

Bharadwaj, A., & Glasner, P. (2009). *Local cells, global science: The proliferation of stem cell technologies in India*. New York, NY: Routledge.

Borrás, S., & Edquist, C. (2014). Institutions and regulations in innovation systems: Effects, problems and innovation policy design. Retrieved from. http://wp.circle.lu.se/upload/CIRCLE/workingpapers/201429_Borras_Edquist.pdf

Borup, M., Brown, N., Konrad, K., & Van Lente, H. (2006). The sociology of expectations in science and technology. *Technology Analysis & Strategic Management, 18*(3–4), 285–298.

Brown, N., & Kraft, A. (2006). Blood ties: Banking the stem cell promise. *Technology Analysis & Strategic Management, 18*(3–4), 313–327.

Brown, N., & Michael, M. (2003). A sociology of expectations: Retrospecting prospects and prospecting retrospects. *Technology Analysis & Strategic Management, 15*(1), 3–18.

Gottweis, H., Salter, B., & Waldby, C. (2009). The global politics of human embryonic stem cell science: Regenerative medicine in transition. In *Basingstoke*. New York, NY: Palgrave Macmillan.

Heinz, D. B., & Tomenendal, M. (2012). The emerging market hype–putting market size and growth in BRIC countries into perspective. *Critical Perspectives on International Business, 8*(3), 241–258.

Hoskisson, R. E., Wright, M., Filatotchev, I., & Peng, M. W. (2013). Emerging multinationals from mid-range economies: The influence of institutions and factor markets. *Journal of Management Studies, 50*(7), 1295–1321.

Kaimal, A. J., Smith, C. C., Laros, R. K., Jr., Caughey, A. B., & Cheng, Y. W. (2009). Cost-effectiveness of private umbilical cord blood banking. *Obstetrics & Gynecology, 114*(4), 848–855.

Kant, A. (2015). Transforming India into a global manufacturing hub. *Yojna, 59*(March), 18–22.

LifeCell launches community stem cell bank. (2017, March 10). *The Hindu Business Line*.

Martin, P., Brown, N., & Turner, A. (2008). Capitalizing hope: The commercial development of umbilical cord blood stem cell banking. *New Genetics and Society, 27*(2), 127–143.

Mascarenhas, A. (2009, October 2). Biological insurance: Cord blood banking on the rise in city. *The Indian Express*.

Nelson, B. (2008, March 13). Stem-cell banking: life line or sub-prime? *Nature Reports Stem Cells*

Patra, P. K., & Sleeboom-Faulkner, M. (2016). Following the banking cycle of umbilical cord blood in India: The disparity between pre-banking persuasion and post-banking utilization. *New Genetics and Society, 35*(3), 267–288.

Petersen, A. (2009). The ethics of expectations. *Monash Bioethics Review, 28*(1), 22–33.

Petersen, A. (2011). *The politics of bioethics*. New York, NY: Routledge.

Puigdomench-Rosell, P., & Virt, G. (2004). Ethical aspects of umbilical cord blood banking. *European Group on Ethics in Science and New Technologies, European Commission*.

Rajan, K. S. (2006). *Biocapital: The constitution of postgenomic life*. Durham, CA: Duke University Press.

Sharma, A. (2009). Stem cell research and policy in India: Current scenario and future perspective. *Journal of Stem Cells, 4*(2), 133–140.

Sipp, D. (2011). Global challenges in stem cell research and the many roads ahead. *Neuron, 70*(4), 573–576.

Srinivasan, S. (2010, August 18). The Wilde West of stem cell procedures. *Infochange*.

Sullivan, M., Browett, P., & Patton, N. (2005). Private umbilical cord blood banking: A biological insurance of dubious future benefit! *The New Zealand Medical Journal (Online), 118*(1208), 1–6.

Tiwari, S. S. (2014, November 5). Cord blood banking: Ambiguous policy. *Deccan Herold*.

Tiwari, S. S. (2015, June 9). Proliferation of stem cell therapies: Regulatory challenges. *Pharmabiz*.

Tiwari, S. S., & Desai, P. N. (2011). Stem cell innovation system in India: Emerging scenario and future challenges. *World Journal of Science Technology and Sustainable Development, 8*(1), 1–23.

Tiwari, S. S., & Raman, S. (2014). Governing stem cell therapy in India: Regulatory vacuum or jurisdictional ambiguity? *New Genetics and Society, 33*(4), 413–433.

Tiwari, S. S., & Tiwary, E. (2015). India: Assess social impact of technology. *Nature, 522*(7557), 419–419.

Tracey, P., & Phillips, N. (2011). Entrepreneurship in emerging markets. *Management International Review, 51*(1), 23–39.

World $15.63 Billion Stem Cells Market Analysis 2014–2025. (2017, July 13). *WBRC*.

Shashank S. Tiwari PhD is a scholar of Science and Technology Studies (STS) and Innovation Studies. He did his PhD in STS from the University of Nottingham, United Kingdom. He has an MPhil in science policy studies from Jawaharlal Nehru University, India. Dr. Tiwari specialises in the social studies of life sciences, biomedicine and biomedical technology.

Chapter 30
Institutional Voids and Indian Automotive Industry: Challenges and Reflection

Maneesh Kumar

Abstract Postliberalization period has seen significant growth in the Indian automotive industry, hosting majority of the big automobile giants of the world. In spite of significant growth in the last two decades, automotive industry has not managed to achieve its true potential due to the presence of 'institutional voids' in the area of product market, capital market, labour market, and macro context, as classified by Khanna and Palepu (Winning in emergent markets: A road map for strategy and execution. Harvard Business Press, Boston, MA, 2010). India is considered as a mid-range emerging economy (Hoskisson et al. J Manag Stud 50(7):1295–1321, 2013), thereby is considered to lack across the four areas of institutional voids, that presents challenges to multi-national corporations (MNCs) and large domestic firms when establishing or managing their supply chain in the emerging economies context. This chapter presents some of the voids faced by Indian automotive sector and countermeasures developed by industry and industry associations to address those voids.

Keywords Institutional voids · Automotive industry · India · Emerging economy

30.1 Introduction

Operations and supply chain management researchers need to shift focus from efficiency and effectiveness measures to understanding of factors affecting the growth of industries in emerging economies. Majority of the study within operations management domain focus at micro or meso levels, i.e. the boundary spanner is between internal operations and supply network. The macro perspective goes beyond firm or supply chain levels to include factors such as intermediaries, regulatory systems,

M. Kumar (✉)
Logistics & Operations Management Section, Cardiff Business School,
Cardiff University, Cardiff, UK
e-mail: kumarm8@cardiff.ac.uk

Y. K. Dwivedi et al. (eds.), *Emerging Markets from a Multidisciplinary Perspective*, Advances in Theory and Practice of Emerging Markets,
https://doi.org/10.1007/978-3-319-75013-2_30

contract-enforcing mechanism, skilled workforce, capital markets, to name a few factors responsible for creating fragile institutional environment, herein called *institutional voids*, affecting the functioning and performance of any industry in the emerging economies (Khanna & Palepu, 1997). Institutional voids are created due to the absence or weakness of *formal and informal institutions*, as mentioned above, that severely impact on market formation, economic growth, and development of an economy (Khanna & Palepu, 1997; Mair, Martí, & Ventresca, 2012). In the past decade, the concept of institutional voids has attracted attention from researchers in the field of international business and strategic management in particular (e.g. Khanna & Palepu, 1997, 2000; Mair et al., 2012; Miller, Lee, Chang, & Le Breton-Miller, 2009). Here, operations management researchers need to borrow theoretical insights from international business field to understand and explain how emerging market firms can compete in the global value chain, in spite of the presence of institutional voids, via constant improvement in their product and processes to support the operations of multi-national corporations (MNCs) and large domestic assemblers (Corredoira & McDermott, 2014; Khan, Shenkar, & Lew, 2015) in emerging economies.

This chapter presents findings from the research conducted in the automotive sector of India by following the institutional context framework proposed by Khanna and Palepu (2010: 27–50) that focuses on four areas – *product markets*, *capital markets*, *labour markets*, *and macro context* – and the absence or gap in these areas creates institutional voids. Data was collected by interviewing ten members of three industry associations – Society of Indian Automobile Manufacturers (SIAM, http://www.siamindia.com), Automotive Component Manufacturers Association of India (ACMA, https://www.acma.in/), Confederation of Indian Industries (CII, http://www.cii.in/), and a government body. Data triangulation was achieved by comparing the findings from primary research with industry reports and secondary literature.

As per Hoskisson, Wright, Filatotchev, and Peng (2013) classification, India can be considered as mid-range emerging economies, between newly developed economy and traditional emerging economy, that is characterized by high institutional development and low infrastructure and factor market development. While factor market can be considered as transformational activities to produce goods and services, institutions act as a facilitator for production and distribution of those goods and services through better contractual assurance (Hoskisson, Eden, Lau, & Wright, 2000; Hoskisson et al., 2013). The low-developed factor market and institutions will create *institutional voids* that affect the growth of industry within emerging economies. This chapter will discuss institutional voids affecting one of the highest performing industries in India, i.e. automotive sector, and reflect on alternative strategies that this sector will take forward by addressing those voids.

30.2 Indian Automotive Industry: Performance Statistics

The economic liberalization and delicencing of the automobile industry in India in 1991 provided significant boost to this industry with government granting permission for 100% foreign direct investment (FDI) in the sector (Kumaraswamy, Mudambi, Saranga, & Tripathy, 2012; Saranga, 2009). This attracted the attention of all the prestigious global brands including Ford, General Motors, Toyota, Hyundai, Volkswagen, Honda, and other MNCs that have established their manufacturing base, operations, and joint ventures in India. Today, this sector offers an immense potential for growth in India and also provides a platform for the synergistic growth of other sectors including auto components and machine, electronic, electrical, and plastic tools, etc. The growth of the automotive industry has also provided boost to the service industry including IT and software, banking, insurance, repair and maintenance, and transport and logistics industries.

The statistics of Indian automobile industry is sourced from SIAM and ACMA websites. The industry accounts for 7.1% of the country's gross domestic product (GDP) and provides employment, directly or indirectly, to over 32 million people in India. The industry produced a total of 25.316 million vehicles including passenger vehicles, commercial vehicles, three-wheelers, and two-wheelers in the financial year April 2016–March 2017, registering a growth of 5.41% over the same period last year, i.e. April 2015–March 2016. The domestic sales of automobile vehicles were 21.86 million in 2016–2017 compared with production figures of 25.316 million. Domestic sales have three types of vehicles, passenger (+9.23%), commercial (+4.16%), and two-wheelers (+6.89%), increased in the financial year April 2016–March 2017 compared with the same period in the last year. In the financial year of 2015–2016, two-wheelers occupied 80% of the market share, followed by passenger vehicle (14%), commercial vehicles (3%), and three-wheelers (3%). The two segments, passenger vehicles and commercial vehicles, also witnessed an increase in export by 16.20% and 4.99%, respectively. The world ranking figure of Indian automobile industry itself reflects on the strength of this sector and growth potential the sector possesses – top ranking in manufacturing of two-wheelers, three-wheelers, and tractor, 4th position in light commercial vehicles (LCVs) and 5th in heavy commercial vehicles (HCVs), and 5th largest in the world and third in Asia for exporting passenger cars.

Factors resulting in the growth of this industry include 100% FDI, no localization requirement, no minimum R&D spend required, quality focus, strong component and ancillary industry, government focus to make India an automotive manufacturing hub, to name a few factors (Kumaraswamy et al., 2012; Shashtry & Pradhan, 2013). This has helped MNCs to establish their production plant in India and follow the route of 'localization' by working closely with local suppliers and minimize dependence on import of technology or raw materials (Kumaraswamy et al., 2012). The Government of India has simplified many regulatory policy framework for ease of doing business in India, with a commitment of 'minimum government and maximum governance' (http://www.siamindia.com).

India is one of the favoured destinations for low-price automobile and low-cost sourcing options for auto components. In spite of strong performance of this industry, there are several inhibiting factors, termed in this paper as *institutional voids*, that do not allow this industry to achieve its true potential and climb further in the global ranking. Findings from the research study are presented in the next section of this chapter.

30.3 Findings

This section presents findings from the research conducted with three industry associations and a government body to report the institutional voids identified affecting the automotive sector performance. The findings are structured across the four areas of institutional context framework proposed by Khanna and Palepu (2010: 27–50) – product markets, capital markets, labour markets, and macro context.

30.3.1 Product Markets

There is a well-established communication mechanism such as established dealer networks, auto expo, and consumer information organization including JD Power survey that gives information on rankings, price, quality, and performance of car. However, given the size of the country, these dealer networks are not at reachable distance from the local population to help them take informed decision on the product to buy. More issues are faced in the part supply of the network. Indian Tier 1 and Tier 2 suppliers have developed their operational and technical capability in the last two decades but still face issues of quality, developing in-house R&D capability, matching the expectations of MNCs, and having the skilled workforce to supply the quality parts or components to the Original Equipment Manufacturer (OEM).

As a countermeasure, the non-market institutions (Corredoira & McDermott, 2014) such as industry associations including ACMA and CII have developed several formal socialization programmes (Khan et al., 2015) for Tier 2 suppliers in order to enhance comprehension and speed of knowledge transfer to these Tier 2 suppliers and develop their operational and technical capabilities for sustaining long-term growth. ACMA hosts several regional and national cluster programmes involving eight to ten companies in a cluster for a year to 18 months, where the focus is on developing in-house operations and technical capabilities of Tier 2 suppliers through joint learning from Gemba (shop-floor)-based activities for developing sustainable competitive advantage over western Tier 1 and 2 suppliers. The cluster programmes developed by ACMA are influenced from Toyota Production System but customized to the requirement of Indian automotive sector. Similarly, CII cluster programme is also Gemba-based long-term group project where OEMs, Tier 1, and Tier 2 join hands to learn and share best practices from each other. But given the size of this industry, it will take many years to involve all Tier 1 and 2 automotive suppliers covering all geographic region of India.

Auto component suppliers are slowly mastering the process technology from Japan, Europe, or America. The next step in the ladder is to graduate to more innovations and R&D capability by establishing centre for technology that can help industry suppliers for testing and validation. Auto Expo for automobile and auto components conducted on yearly basis in India and abroad has raised awareness on the operational, design, and technical capabilities of the Indian OEMs and part suppliers. This has helped the industry in general and part suppliers in particular to win new contracts for part supply. The industry also has 35 International Procurement Offices (IPO) to meet the requirements of the OEM in international markets. However, these offices are not fully integrated with each other to better respond to the OEM requirements.

30.3.2 Capital Markets

The MNEs investing in India have range of options to raise capital including banks, private equity provider, insurance firms, venture capital firm, mutual fund, and auditor. In order to have a strong financial regulatory system that protects the interests of investors, bring professionalism in the working of intermediaries in the capital markets, and create good financial environment in the market, the Government of India had set up Securities and Exchange Board of India (SEBI), a statuary body with wide regulatory powers. Intermediaries such as credit rating agency work under SEBI to provide rating to the issue of securities in the primary markets. It is also mandatory for companies to disclose all material facts and risk factors associated with their projects. Similar to issue highlighted in product markets, lack of communication of these complex regulations coupled with bureaucracy involved in paperwork create difficult environment for investors to do business in India. In addition, interest rates to borrow short-term or long-term loans are very steep in India (12%–13%) compared with Japan (practically nil or 1%), China, or Thailand (where it is about 3%) that dissuade investors from investing in India.

30.3.3 Labour Markets

The automotive workforce doing shop-floor job is either school drop-outs or high school graduate or have diploma from Industrial Training Institute (ITI). The vocational institutes like ITI are used to upgrade the technical skills of the workforce, though the content and quality of technical training provided in these institutes are questionable as they have struggled to update the syllabus based on the introduction of fast-changing upgraded technology in the automobile sector. Given the size of the automobile sector, more ITI is required to develop sectorial skilled workforce for the automotive industry. Thus, Automotive Skills Development Council (ASDC) was set up in 2010 to work in collaboration with industrial associations in automotive sector such as SIAM and ACMA and other government bodies such as National Skill Development Council (NSDC) for sectorial skill development of the workforce, scoping and designing of curriculum for ITI that fits with the requirement of the automotive industry. In the pilot project, around 800 people including welders, service technicians, and drivers were trained, most of which are either high school graduates or school drop-outs. The biggest challenge is the ambitious target set up by ASDC to scale up this initiative and reach out to twenty million people by 2020. The current infrastructure in ASDC and NSDC is significantly lower to reach out to that population, but with the support of the Government of India, ASDC is recruiting NGOs and other accredited training providers to cover wider geographic area across the automotive cluster in India.

Rationalization and flexibility in labour norms are critical to the growth and competitiveness of this industry and also to keep pace with the global markets. At the moment, the labour laws in India are very complex and inflexible. There are 44 central labour laws, 150 state labour laws, and numerous standing orders often having divergent definitions of terms such as wages and workers. Moreover, labour laws and reforms are very politically sensitive topic as labour unions have strong power and very close affiliation to political parties. Labour is a very huge vote bank in India, and the government does not want to tinker with the issues of labour reform.

30.3.4 Macro Context

Changes in Indian government policies in postliberalization period allowed 100% foreign ownership in the automobile and auto components market without the need to involve local players and no requirement of minimum investment in setting up the operations (Kumaraswamy et al., 2012). All these factors attracted the big automobile giants from Japan, the USA, Korea, and Europe to set up their production facilities in India.

In spite of having favourable conditions, there are several deficits that have an impact on the output of this sector. One of the key deficits that is pulling back automotive industry is the infrastructure deficit. The infrastructure deficit is the result of slow industrialization including underdeveloped road network, logistics solution, power supply, and sea ports, undersized manufacturing industries, and infrastructure projects burdened with bureaucratic delays and corruptions. One of the key issues faced by MNCs or domestics firms is environmental and land clearances that delay the project significantly. These are classic examples of institutional voids faced by domestic firms and MNCs in India. According to interviewees in ACMA, there are several factors that have resulted in negative growth lane of passenger vehicle industry including a challenging macroeconomic environment; high fuel prices, interest rates, and inflation; and weak income growth. However, some of these challenges or voids could be tackled by developing strong parts or component suppliers that can meet the requirement of MNCs or domestic firms.

There is also an issue of power outage for 8–10 h even in the industrial belt that forces companies to rely on industrial generators. A unit production cost from generator is INR 14–16, whereas the cost per unit from the distribution centre of the government is INR 6–8. The power outage and expensive power is a huge disadvantage that has an impact on communication channel as well as production cost.

In order to ease the business conditions in India, recommendations have been recently submitted by CII and SIAM to the Government of India on easing business regulations for bringing policy reforms related to land acquisition, taxation, starting new business, and contract enforcements. The example of Indian government commitment to 'minimum government and maximum governance' is the introduction of Goods and Services Tax (GST) to have uniform taxation policy across India. Previously the non-uniform GST across different states of India not only increased the overall operational cost but also introduced uncertainty in the delivery time of products to the destination. Uniform GST will ensure rationalisation of the taxation structure across India (amalgamating several central and state taxes into one tax), reduce uncertainty in delivery time and also operational costs, and thereby bring it at par with the practices in other emerging nations. However, it is too early to comment on the benefits of GST and the impact of increase in GST rates in the future on the automobile manufacturer and auto component suppliers.

A summary of key findings related to the four areas of institutional voids and strategies required to address those voids is presented in Table 30.1.

Indian government has also launched policies that replicate practices in the western world including decision to adhere to BS-VI emission norms, followed in Europe for environmental regulations, for all types of vehicles from April 2020. This will have big impact on reducing the emissions from vehicles, thereby contributing to the global effort of controlling climate change and improving human health. However, the benefits of such policy implementation can only be realised if standards are established and implemented for the inspection and maintenance of in-service vehicles and end-of-life vehicle, dismantling, and recycling management across the country. The government's commitment to have 100% electric vehicles in public sector and 40% in private sector by 2030 is an ambitious target that presents several challenges in terms of technology upgradation, investment and finance, affordability, implementation, infrastructure, etc. before the government, industry, regulatory bodies, and financial institutions, which require joining up hands by these stakeholders for joint R&D and innovative thinking. There are other challenges faced by sector when developing electric vehicles (EVs) which include development of charging infrastructure, lithium mining, and low-cost battery and disposal of discarded lithium batteries. The government needs to think beyond EVs and promote automobile manufacturers and other stakeholders to invest in other fuel technologies that are more effective in dealing with climate change and human health issues.

Table 30.1 Institutional voids and void-filling strategies in the Indian automotive sector

Institutional dimensions	Issues creating institutional voids (IVs)	Strategies to address IVs
Product market	Lack of effective communication channels between buyers and sellers Issues at the part supply level: limited availability of good quality and technologically advance suppliers	Industry associations helping to develop the operational and technical skills of part suppliers Auto expo helps to raise the awareness of availability of skilled workforce and technical capability of part suppliers to attract foreign customers
Capital market	High Interest rates for lending loans compared to other countries like Japan and China Complex regulations coupled with bureaucracy involved in paperwork create difficult environment for investors to do business in India	Existence of statuary body like SEBI to protect the interest of investors Companies to disclose all material facts and risk factors associated with their projects
Labour market	Limited availability of skilled workers to meet the needs of the automobile and auto component industry Out of date curricula used in vocational institutes such as ITI Labour laws are very complex and inflexible	Industry associations in the automotive sector working very closely with government bodies, ASDC and NSDC to revise the curricula of ITI, scale up the sectorial-based training to meet the needs of industry Innovative programme developed by ACMA and CII involving Tier 1 and Tier 2 suppliers to develop the operational and technical capabilities of part suppliers
Macro context	Infrastructure deficits including road, sea, and rail network; poor logistics management; power outage Delay in environmental and land clearances	Uniform GST Government focusing on policies related to infrastructure development to create conducive business environment for investors Proposal submitted to government on 'ease of doing business' to minimize the institutional voids affecting the performance of the manufacturing industry and in particular automotive industry

30.4 Conclusion

The advantages possessed by Indian automotive sector over other countries, which include reasonable manufacturing infrastructure, low-cost technology, reformed policies conducive for doing business in India, low-cost labour, rising middle class, and increasing demand from rural areas, have supported the growth of automotive sector to newer heights. In spite of several factors supporting the growth of this sector, the sector has not managed to achieve its true potential due to the presence of institutional voids in the mid-range emerging economy of India. Given the institutional contexts in which this industry exists and operates, it is imperative to understand how different business groups, including domestic firms and MNCs, are managing their supply chain to facilitate the creation of positive institutional environment and addressing the institutional voids created due to gaps in product, capital, labour markets, and macro context. It is also important to develop the non-market institutions (Corredoira & McDermott, 2014) such as industry associations and government bodies that develop innovative solutions to address the issues generated from institutional voids in emerging economy context. Automotive sector should focus on formal socialization programmes such as joint training, scheduled plant visit, and systematic sharing of technological designs between MNCs/large domestic firms/non-market institutions and Tier 1/Tier 2 suppliers to enhance the comprehension and speed of knowledge transfer to local suppliers (Corredoira & McDermott, 2014; Khan et al., 2015) for creating long-term competitive advantage.

References

Corredoira, R. A., & McDermott, G. A. (2014). Adaptation, bridging and firm upgrading: How non-market institutions and MNCs facilitate knowledge recombination in emerging markets. *Journal of International Business Studies, 45*, 699–722.

Hoskisson, R. E., Eden, L., Lau, C. M., & Wright, M. (2000). Strategy in emerging economies. *Academy of Management Journal, 43*, 249–267.

Hoskisson, R. E., Wright, M., Filatotchev, I., & Peng, M. W. (2013). Emerging multinationals from mid-range economies: The influence of institutions and factor markets. *Journal of Management Studies, 50*(7), 1295–1321.

Khan, Z., Shenkar, O., & Lew, Y. K. (2015). Knowledge transfer from international joint ventures to local suppliers in a developing economy. *Journal of International Business Studies, 46*, 656–675.

Khanna, T., & Palepu, K. (1997). Why focused strategies may be wrong for emerging markets. *Harvard Business Review, 75*(4), 41–51.

Khanna, T., & Palepu, K. (2000). The future of business groups in emerging markets: Long run evidence from Chile. *Academy of Management Journal, 43*, 268–285.

Khanna, T., & Palepu, K. (2010). *Winning in emergent markets: A road map for strategy and execution*. Boston, MA: Harvard Business Press.

Kumaraswamy, A., Mudambi, R., Saranga, H., & Tripathy, A. (2012). Catch-up strategies in the Indian auto components industry: Domestic firms' responses to market liberalization. *Journal of International Business Studies, 43*(4), 368–395.

Mair, J., Martí, I., & Ventresca, M. J. (2012). Building inclusive markets in rural Bangladesh: How intermediaries work institutional voids. *Academy of Management Journal, 55*(4), 819–850.

Miller, D., Lee, J., Chang, S., & Le Breton-Miller, I. (2009). Filling the institutional void: The social behavior and performance of family versus non-family technology firms in emerging markets. *Journal of International Business Studies, 40*(5), 802–817.

Saranga, H. (2009). The Indian auto component industry – Estimation of operational efficiency and its determinant using DEA. *European Journal of Operational Research, 196*(2), 707–718.

Shastry, T. L., & Pradhan, J. (2013). Indian foreign trade with reference to automobile industry-an analysis. *International Journal of Business and Management Invention, 2*(9), 62–71.

Dr. Maneesh Kumar is a reader in service operations and programme director of Executive MBA at Cardiff Business School, Cardiff University. He conducts cross-disciplinary research in the area of Operational Excellence including topics such as Lean Six Sigma (LSS), process/service innovation and knowledge management within SMEs, automotive industry, service industries, and public sector organizations. This has resulted in publications of over hundred journals and conferences papers, edited books, and conference proceedings. He has been involved in delivering LSS training up to black belt level and delivered several workshops on LSS application in different types and sizes of industries. He is also a regular speaker at international conferences and seminars on LSS and process excellence.

Index

A
Aadhaar Enabled Payment System (AEPS), 63
Advertisement/advertising
  credibility, 291
  defined, 286
  Facebook, tourism sector, 289, 318
  informativeness, 290
  interactivity, 292
  internet and mobile phone, 287
  language, 322
  models, 288
  online, 286
  promotional marketing, 318, 321
  social network, 316
Agriculture supply chain management (ASCM)
  agri-food sector supply network, 210
  agro-based products, 211
  burden on farmers, 216
  developed countries, 211
  food supply chain management, China, 211
  government agencies, 212
  ICT, 210
  India, 212
  information management, 210
  information sharing and internet facilities, 212
  IoT (*see* Internet of things (IoT))
  material market, 216
  multiple stakeholders, 210
  products supply, 216
  SASCM, 212
  value chain, 211
  weather conditions, dependence, 210
Ambidexterity
  digital enterprises, 51–52
  organizational, 50–51
Arab countries, mobile telecom development, 164–167
Attitude, 286
Augmented reality (AR)
  Botta Design, 108
  content management challenges, 114
  customized selections, 113
  definition, 108, 109
  display device challenges, 114
  diverse fields, 108
  3D see-through head-worn display, 109
  educators and designers, 109
  emerging markets, 110
  engaging buyer experience, 113
  environmental challenges, 113–114
  garment shopping, 112
  item-related information, 112
  leverage product visualization, 111
  'mixed reality' concept, 109
  mobile coupons, 111
  next-generation reality-based interfaces, 108
  novel applications, 107
  personal and daily use of, 111
  personal platforms, 111
  photorealistic computer-generated images, 109
  products and features, 113
  product shopping, 112
  user challenges, 114
  web-based social content, 112
Augmented theory of planned behaviour (A-TPB), 162
Automated teller machines (ATMs), 28

Y. K. Dwivedi et al. (eds.), *Emerging Markets from a Multidisciplinary Perspective*, Advances in Theory and Practice of Emerging Markets,
https://doi.org/10.1007/978-3-319-75013-2

Automotive industry, 410
Awaaz.De, a venture, 31

B

Banking sectors
and big data, 81–82
cloud computing, 81
Bank of England (BoE), 9
Behavioural intention (BI), 170, 174
Bharat Interface for Money (BHIM), 63
Big data, banking sectors, 81–82
"Big tent" organizations, 11
Biological insurance, 396
Bioscope instrument, 53
"Book-keeping", 65
Bottom of pyramid (BoP)
branding initiatives, 257–258
characteristics, 244
coefficients, 267
consumers and synchronous development, 256
Cronbach's coefficient alpha, 263
footwear purchase, 258
hypotheses testing, 267
India's rural markets and consumers, 255
industry and academic practitioners, 257
Karl Pearson's coefficient, correlation analysis, 266, 267
low-income and emerging economies, 257
lucrative market segment, 244
marketing initiatives, 256
mobile telephones and technologies, 244
objective economic and societal benefits, 244
product consumption, 256
regression analysis, 263, 265
reliability and validity analysis, 264–265
researchers, 244
research methodology, 261–263
See also Brand loyalty
Brand image, 261
Brand loyalty
image, 261
consumers' culture and value perceptions, 258
defined, 258
perceived quality, 259
product promotion, 260
self-confidence and quality of life, 259
Brand trust, 259–260
Brexit and UK economy
'austerity programs' and deficit reduction plan, 40
anxiety, 43
CGE model, 40
Commonwealth countries, 42
dramatic adjustment costs, 37
2030 economic impact assessment, 38
economic models, 39
FDI, 41
financial contribution, 38
financial services, energy and creative industries, 42
forecasts, 39
low-income household 2014, 40
medics/doctors, 39
multinational firms and domestic SMEs, 41
NIESR estimation, 39
private sector knowledge-intensive services, 43
'single pass porting' loss, 41
tariffs and non-tariff barriers, 42
trading arrangements, 43
wage inequality, 41
Bureaucratic processes, 229
Business process outsourcing (BPO), 361

C

Capital markets, 409
Central Drugs Standard Control Organization (CDSCO), 401
Centered on trust-building mechanisms, 50
China, institutional export barriers, 331–336
Chinese Holiday, Singles' Day, 92–93
Cloud computing, 81
Coercive pressures, 101
Common services centers, 30
Communications and Information Technology Commission (CITC), 150
Community manager, 32
Computable general equilibrium (CGE) model, 40
Conceptual model
credibility, 291
description, 288, 289
entertainment, 289–290
informativeness, 290
interactivity, 291–292
irritation, 290–291
peer influence, 292
privacy concerns, 292–293
Confirmatory factor analysis (CFA), 156
Consultative Group to Assist the Poor (CGAP), 28
Consumer attitude, 324, 325
Consumer protection
financial products and services, 18

India, 17
regulations and enforcement actions, 22
Consumers and innovation adoption, 245–246
Consumers' PEBs
antecedence, 305–306
economic growth, developing countries, 303
Middle East, 310
materialism, 308–309
PCE, 310
research, 306–310
Saudi Arabia, 304–305
social norms, 309
Cord blood banking, 392, 395, 397
Credibility, 291
Critical success factors (CSFs)
corporation's activities, 66
DPS adoption, 67–68
EC, 62
ISM, 62
"network of networks", 62
noncash payments method, 62
"payment system", 62
top-level management, 66
Cronbach's alpha coefficients, 294
Cultural capital, 383
Cultural influence model, 171
Culture relationship, 199, 200
Customer service point (CSP) agents, 32

D
Data protection and privacy, 80
Designing augmented reality environments workshop, 109
Developing economies, 9
Diffusion of innovation (DOI) theory, 100, 162
Digital enterprises, 51–52
Digital entrepreneurship
borrower repayments, 53
data analysis, 54
digital technologies, 50
effective delivery of loans, 55
fieldwork, 54
financial inclusions, 49
financial services, 52
fintech, 52
formal financial services, 49
harmonization, 50
impact detailing, 56
interest rate breakup, 53
low-income households, 54
mechanisms, 50
microfinance model, 49
narratives, 56
operations, 56
poverty premium, 52
Rang De model, 52
social investors, 52
Swabhimaan project, 53
Digital intermediaries, 30, 31
Digital literacy, 29, 30
Digital payment system (DPS)
AEPS, 63
BHIM, 63
"book-keeping", 65
characteristics, 64
electronic payment channels, 64
E-payment, 63
IMPS, 63
mobile banking access, 63
M-wallets, 63
NEFT and RTGS, 63
offline merchants, 64
online tools, 65
plastic money, 63
research paper objectives, 64
traditional cash-based instruments, 63
UPI, 63
USSD, 63
Digital services
modern connectivity, 225
smart buildings and citizens, 225
smart education and governance, 225
smart energy, 225
Smart Healthcare, 225
smart infrastructure, 225
smart mobility, 225
Discriminant validity assessment, 177
District health information systems (DHIS), 235
Diwaniyas, 385, 386
entrepreneurship, 387
symbolic capital, 386
Downs-Hotelling models, 11

E
Ease of use (EOU), 173
E-Business
adoption of, 98
competitive pressure, 101
contingent role models, 98
customers and business partners, 101
economy assimilation, 96
Indian economy change, 96
modern technologies, 96
NASSCOM, 97
OECD countries, 97
online procurement and selling, 97

E-Business (*cont.,*)
owner-manager, 99
technological factors, 100
third-party portals organization, 97
type III innovation, 100
E-Collaboration, 98
E-Commerce strategy, 98
consumer nationalistic feelings, 90
ECCs, 90
ethnocentric tendencies, 89
internet and facilitation, 90
local resources, 91
mobile apps, 91–92
multinationals' cross-border trade/ investment, 89
E-Communication, 98
Economic capital, 383
Economic sectors, 362
Economist Intelligence Unit's democracy index, 10
Effort expectancy, 198, 202
E-intelligence, 98
Eko, alternative design system, 32, 33
Electronic commerce (EC), 62
Electronic data interchange (EDI), 236
Electronic product code (EPC), 215
Electronic word of mouth (eWOM), 286
Emerging economies
digital transactions, 223
economic infrastructure, 224
institutional infrastructure, 224
phases development, 228
physical infrastructure, 224
security and privacy issues, 223, 225–226
smart cities conception, 223
social infrastructure, 224
See also Digital services
Emerging market multinationals (ECCs), 90–92
Emerging markets (EMs), 43, 108, 392, 393
AR, 110
Bangladesh, 320
business, 332
China, 334
economic capacity, consumers, 136
economies, 5, 8, 9, 11
emerging technologies, 392–394
export barriers, 332
external global markets, 136
Facebook, 324
ICT, 135, 317
institutional theory, 333
international market transactions, 136
internet banking, 136
local and multinationals business, 137
low-resources environment, 137
macro-studies link ICTs, 137
network hardware manufacturers, 136
political activism, 137
shopping and marketing, 111
telecom and internet service providers, 136
Emerging technology
biological insurance, 396, 398
cord blood banking, 392, 393, 396
cross-cultural settings, 393
emerging markets, 394
ethical concern, 400
ICMR official, 400
NACSCRT, 401
science and social science domains, 398
stem cell programs, 392
UCB in India, 395–396, 398
Employees, 10
Enterprise
consumers, 280
employment opportunities, 274
group harmony and relationships, 282
'rural' character, 275
urban middle-class audiences, 279
Enterprise application integration (EAI) technology
definition, 235
integration infrastructure/platform, 236
Enterprise resource planning (ERP), 236
Entertainment, 289–290
Entrepreneurs, 10
Entrepreneurship
concept, 382
cultural capital, 384
Diwaniyas, 385
reputation and prestige, 385
types of capital, 382, 383
E-payment systems (EPS), 62, 63
E-ticketing
adoption of, 196
costs of ticket management, 197
cultural differences, 197
culture relationship, 199, 200
description, 196, 197
e-commerce, 196
frontier markets, 196
Hofstede's cultural index, 197
intentional use, 201
investment opportunities, businesses, 197
Jordanian domestic airlines, 197
research studies, 196
social influence, 198
systems and technologies, 198
TAM, 198

technological innovation, 198
trust, 200, 202–203
UTAUT performance expectancy, 198
variables, 201
European Economic Area (EEA), 39

F
Facebook
social loop, 320
value perception, advertisement, 318
Facilitating conditions, 202–204
Financial development
adverse selection problem, 4
bankruptcy law reform in 1945, 5
corporate governance mechanisms, 4, 10
"corporatist" equilibrium, 11
de facto ability of courts, 4
economic and political elites, 10
economists, 3
electoral and policy coalitions, 12
firms, 4
government and private agents, 10
government's revenues and expenditures, 9
investors' rights, 5
legal origin influences structure, 4
liberalization, 8
"limited access" and "open access", 8
market economies, 9
Mexican governments, 8–9
minority shareholders, 10
nonincumbents, 5
policy reversals, 4 (*see also* Political economy)
political influence, 11
primary equity markets, 4
private sector lending, 8
resources mobilization, 4
shareholder and weak employment protection, 11
SLR, 9
two-way causality, 4
Financial inclusions, 49, 57
barriers, mobile phone usage, 29
description, 28
ICT design and implementation, 33
poverty reduction, 28
technology-based intermediaries, 30
Financial Redressal Agency (FRA)
constant regulatory interventions, 18
consumer protection, 17
empirical evidence, 18
financial products and services, 18 (*see also* Financial Regulation in India)
FSLRC and IFC, 18, 22
market integration, 22
Nachiket Mor Committee Report, 18
operational design, 22–23
policy documents and reports, 18
The Report of the Task Force, 22
retail consumers, 18, 22
Financial Regulation in India
frameworks, 19
interest and shadow financial services, 19
regulatory gaps and oversight, 19
Financial Sector Legislative Reform Commission (FSLRC), 18, 22
Foreign direct investment (FDI), 41, 407
Formal institutional export barriers
government policy, 334
weak legal system, 334–335
Formative measurement model, 179–180
Forward Markets Commission (FMC), 19
Frontier markets, 196, 197, 201, 204
F-value probability, 295

G
Garment shopping, 112
Generation Y category, 365, 366
Global e-commerce, 90
Globalization, 89
Goods and Services Tax (GST), 411
Google Scholar and Scopus databases, 361
Governance, 401
Gratification theory, 317
Grievance redressal
inconsistencies, 21
under sectorial regulation, 20
Gross domestic product (GDP), 407

H
Health management information system (HMIS), 234, 235
Hofstede's cultural index, 197
Human intermediary system, 30
Human resource management (HRM) practices, 360
company's policies, 350
internet financial companies, 353
Hyper-localization approach, 90, 91

I
Imbrication process, 123, 124, 129
Immediate Payment Service (IMPS), 63
Impact partners, 52

Indian automotive industry, 407–408
Indian context, social media
  classification of literature, 142
  information diffusion, 141
  rapid literature review search, 141
  SCOPUS database, 141
  summaries/assessments, 140
  systematic review, 141
Indian Council of Medical Research (ICMR), 397
Indian Financial Code (IFC), 18, 22
Informal institutional export barriers and personal networks, 335
Information and communication technologies for global development (ICT4D) projects, 30
Information and communication technology (ICT), 317
  agri-food sector supply network, 210
  applications, 234
  clinical- and drug-related information, 234
  healthcare sector, 234
  information technology mechanisms and equipment, 210
  tools and services, 216
Information technology transfer, 171
Informativeness, 290
Innovation diffusion theory (IDT), 153
Institutional export barriers, 334–335
  China, 332
  definition, 332
  distinctive institutional environments, 332
  emerging markets, 331
  formal (*see* Formal institutional export barriers)
  informal (*see* Informal institutional export barriers)
  institutions, 333
Institutional influences
  coercive pressure, 101
  macroenvironment, 101
  mimetic pressure, 101
  normative pressures, 102
  organizations, 101
Institutional voids, 408
  formal and informal institutions, 406
  and void-filling strategies, 412
Insurance Regulatory and Development Authority (IRDA), 19
Integration of health information systems
  complex/chronic medical conditions/co-morbidities, 237
  EAI, 236
  healthcare organizations, 236
  integration technologies, 236
  maternal mortality ratio, 234
  public sector hospital levels, 236
  supply of medicines and poor referral system, 234
Intermediaries
  Awaaz.De venture, 31
  barriers, 29
  CGAP, 28
  Common Services Centers, 30
  digital intermediation, 30
  Eko, alternative design system, 32, 33
  financial access, lack of, 28
  financial inclusion, 28
  financial literacy, 29
  human, 30
  Indian banking sector, 28
  'learning process' phenomenon, 33
  low-literate communities, 29
  microfinance institutions, 30
  mobile banking, 28
  Reserve Bank of India (RBI), 28
  role of, 29
  technology-based interventions, 30
International Symposium on Mixed and Augmented Reality, 109
International Workshop and Symposium on Augmented Reality, 109
Internet-based companies, 90
Internet financial industry
  bank executives, 345
  Beijing University Internet Financial Research Institute, 344
  challenges, 351–352
  characteristics of, 340
  company's policies, human resource management, 350–351
  deep macroeconomic theoretical knowledge, 353
  emerging industry, 353
  employee referral method, 352
  external and internal factors, 342–344
  financial sector and e-commerce industry, 340
  financial services models, 340
  higher standard requirement, 353
  HR practitioners, 355
  human resource policies, 353
  information and network technology, 340
  labour market, 341
  recruitment channels, 347–348, 352
  recruitment status, 341–342

research, 345–347, 354–355
scholars, 345
staffing structure, 349–350
teamworking efficiency, 353
13th China International Talent Exchange Conference, 340
virtual economy, 340
Zhongguancun Internet Finance Institute, 344
Internet of things (IoT)
description, 210
distribution and sale stage, 215
embedded devices, 210
food wastage reduction, 213
production stage, 215
RFID technology, 210, 213
technologies, 213, 214
transportation stage, 215
Interpretive structural modeling (ISM), 62
description, 66
digital payment adoption, CSFs, 69
problem domain, 65
reachability, antecedent and intersection set, 68
search engines, 66
Irritation, 290–291
IT-enabled services (ITES), 361
IT system, 229

K
Karl Pearson's coefficient of correlation analysis, 266
Kingdom of Saudi Arabia (KSA), *see* Mobile Services (M-Services)
Kuwaiti culture, 381, 385

L
Labour laws, 410
Labour markets, 409–410
Licensed umbilical cord blood banks, 395
Light commercial vehicles (LCVs), 407
Linear regression analysis, 295
Lower middle-income countries (LMICs), 238

M
Macro context, 410–411
Materialism, 308–309
M-authentication, 152
Media richness theory, 317
Message content, 322–323
Message entertainment, 323
Message initiator, 321
Message language, 322
Message reliability, 323
Methodological limitations, 370
M-Government (M-Gov)
adoption of, 151
biometric technology, 152
KSA, 152
public/private context, 152
researchers and practitioners, 151
service providers and customers, 152
UTAUT, role of, 151
Mimetic pressures, 101
Mobile apps, 91–92
Mobile banking (m-banking), 63
authentication, 80
Bank Muscat, flagship financial service provider, 77
confidentiality, 80
data protection and privacy, 80
defined, 76
enhanced data security, 78
3G and 4G services, 77
GigaOM survey, 77
increased efficiency, 78
information and communication technology, 77
instant access, 78
Juniper Research, 76
mobile/handheld devices, 75
network security, 80
Oman, 82–83
privacy and security concerns, 79
products and services, access of, 78
quality of infrastructure, 79
saves time and money, 78
scalability and reliability, 79
telebanking and automated teller machines, 76
traditional transactions, 76
user-friendly, 79
virus and SMS spoofing attack, 80
Mobile coupons, 111
Mobile Internet (M-Internet), 151
M-Gov (*see* Mobile government (M-Gov))
Saudi citizens, 150
Mobile Services (M-Services), 151–153
adoption rate of, 150
CITC, 150
hedonic motivation, performance expectancy, 156
innovative services, 150
limitations, 156–157

Mobile Services (M-Services) (*cont.*,)
M-Gov (*see* M-Government (M-Gov))
models and theories, 153
proposed research model, 154, 155
researchers in KSA, 153, 154
SEM and CFA, 156
and telecommunication, 150
theoretical foundation, customer's perspective, 153
traditional human encounter, 150
Mobile telecom development, 163–167
Model of PC utilization (MPCU), 162
Modern connectivity, 225
Morgan Stanley Capital International (MSCI) index, 196
Motivational model (MM), 153
MouthShut, social media platform, 144
M-payment, 152
Multinational corporations (MNCs), 363, 406
M-wallets, 63

N

Nachiket Mor Committee Report, 18
Narrated kinaesthetics, 281–282
National Apex Committee for Stem Cell Research and Therapy (NACSCRT), 401
National Capital Region (NCR), 32
National Electronic Fund Transfer (NEFT), 63
National Institute of Standards and Technology (NIST), 81
National IT development, 166, 172–173
Arabs consumers' opinions, 174
behavioural intention, smartphones use, 174
cultural influence model, 171
IT policies and technological infrastructure, 173
PRA, 172–173 (*see* Perceived relative advantage (PRA))
proposed research model, 171, 172
smartphone adoption, Arab countries, 163
TAM (*see* Technology acceptance model (TAM))
UAE, 163
usefulness and ease of use, 163
National IT development (ND)
effort expectancy, 184
explanatory power in countries, 183
formative measurement model, 179–180
ICT development and policy making, 185
independent regulatory authority, 184
ITT/system outcomes, 184
Jordanian telecommunications market, 185
methodology, 175–179
multigroup analysis, 182–183
reflective measurement model, 177–179
research limitations, 185–186
sample characteristics, 177
structural model assessment, 180–182
National Skill Development Council (NSDC), 410
Network security, 80
New East Indian Company (NEIC), 9
Non-cash payments, 62
Normative pressures, 102

O

Offshore IT service providers (OSPs), 367
Online advertising, 286
Operations and supply chain management, 405
Organizational ambidexterity, 50–51
Organizational factors, 100–101
Organizational readiness, 101
Organization for Economic Cooperation and Development (OECD) countries, 97
Original Equipment Manufacturer (OEM), 408
Owner-manager
characteristics, 99–100
E-Business, 99
organizational capability, 100
technology adoption decisions, 99

P

PaGalGuy, social media platform, 144
Partial least squares-multigroup analysis (PLS-MGA), 176, 182
Partial least squares-structural equation modeling (PLS-SEM), 176
Peer influence, 292
Pension Fund Regulatory Authority, 19
Perceived consumer effectiveness (PCE), 310
Perceived ease of use (PEU), 162, 246
Perceived quality, 259
Perceived relative advantage (PRA)
behavioural intention, smartphones use, 173
BI, 174
EOU, 173
relative advantage, defined, 172
technology acceptance studies, 172
Perceived usefulness (PU), 162, 166, 246
Performance expectancy, 201
Performances assessment
core indicators, 228
education, 228

IT-enabled services, 227
IT system, 229
natural disaster, 228
profile indicators, 228
quantitatively, qualitatively and descriptively measurement, 228
supporting indicators, 228
waste management, 228
water, energy and electricity, 229
Personal digital assistants (PDA), 76
Pharmaceuticals, 367
Plastic money, 63
Pleasure, arousal and dominance (PAD), 246
Political activism, 137
Political economy
cross-border capital flows, 7
equity market development, 5
extent and trends, financial development, 5
French civil law countries, 5
imports and foreign multinationals, 7
incumbent firms, 6
lawmaking and institutional building, 6
maximum interest rate, 6
nonlinear and non-monotonic trends, 6
PCM, 7
postentry environment, 6
prima facie explanation, 8
resources allocation, 6
trade liberalization, 7
Practice perspective
humans and technology, role of, 123
social media effect, 124
Pradhan Mantri Jan Dhan Yojana programme, 53
Price-cost margin (PCM), 7
Privacy concerns, 292–293
Privacy, emerging economies, 225–226
Private cord blood banking, 397–400
Private healthcare services, 'profit' and 'not-for-profit' non-government providers, 234
Private sector healthcare providers, 236–237
Product markets, 408–409
Product promotion, Facebook, 260, 318
Product shopping, 112
Profile indicators, 228
Promotional marketing
research, 322
social network, 317–319
Pro-poor innovations
BOP and subsistence marketplaces, 245
consumers and innovation adoption, 245–246
mobile banking services, 245
perceived adoption, 245
qualitative methods, 248
quantitative methods, 247–248 (*see also* Subsistence marketplaces)
types, 245
Proposed research model, 154, 155
Public healthcare services, 234
Public sector healthcare providers, 236–237

Q

Quasi-Beckerian paradigm, 11
Quora, social media platform, 144

R

Radio-frequency identification (RFID) technology, 210, 212–216
Rang De model, 52
Rang De's ambidextrous strategy, 57
Readiness, smart cities, 229
Real-time gross settlement (RTGS), 63
Reflective measurement model, 177–179
Regulatory framework, 19
Regulatory gaps, 23
Rentiers, 10
Reserve Bank of India (RBI), 19
Retail consumers, 17–19, 21–23
Retail investor protection, 18
Rurality
Chokhi Dhani, Jaipur, 276
creativity-driven entrepreneurs, 274
customer-service-oriented dictum, 276
firms, 275
lived, sensual dimension, 278–280
methodology, 278
narrated kinaesthetics, 281–282
'off-the-beaten-path' experiences, 274
packaging and promoting rurality, 274–275
Parque EcoAlberto, 277
rural diversification, 274
tourism markets, 273
town's residents, 277
urban conurbations, 276

S

Samwad, digital learning platform, 31
Saudi Arabia, consumer PEBs, 303–310
Security, emerging economies, 225–226
Self-help groups (SHGs), 30
Service output demand (SOD), 316
Shopping, *see* Augmented reality (AR)

Small and medium enterprises (SMEs)
classification, 97
drivers and inhibitors, 99 (*see also* E-Business)
employment
investment/sales, 97
turnover and assets, 97
exogenous and endogenous factors, firm, 99
institutional influences, 101–102
organizational factors, 100–101
owner-manager characteristics, 99–100
and researchers, 102–103
technological factors, 100
Smart buildings, 225
Smart cities
conceptualization, 222–223
critical and crucial issues, 221
emerging economies, 222 (*see also* Emerging economies)
inhabitants, 222
Smart citizens, 225
Smart city development approach, 226, 227
Smart education, 225
Smart energy, 225
Smart governance, 225
Smart healthcare, 225
Smart infrastructure, 225
Smart mobility, 225
Smartphone adoption
businesses and governments, 162
customers' adoption and use, 162
ICT policies, 162
market competitiveness, 162
non-western countries, 163
65% penetration rate by 2020, 161
Smart supply chain management (SASCM), 212
Smooth delivery of loans, 50
Snapchat, image messaging and networking mobile app, 145
Social capital, 382, 384
Social influence, 198, 202, 203
Social media
applications, 120, 121
attitude, defined, 286
brand equity and customer relationship, 138
business organizations, 121
businesses and communication with consumers, 286
communication practices, 120 (*see also* Conceptual model)
Cronbach's alpha coefficients, 294
definition, 121
determinism, 123
electronic technologies, 137
embeddedness, 123
eWOM, 286
Facebook advertisements, 286
framework for, 138
functional building blocks, 121
group of Internet-based applications, 121
humans and technology, role of, 123
imbrication process, 124
information technology, 122
knowledge management, socialization and power relations, 120
managerial implications, 297–298
marketing, 138, 287
materiality of, 122
methodology, 124–125
online advertising, 286
people and businesses, 139–140
personal context, 138
purchase intention, 286
research areas, 142–144
research constructs measurement, 293
research limitations, 298–299
simple linear regression analysis, 295
theoretical implications, 297
tourism, 287 (*see also* WhatsApp communication)
Social networking advertising (SNAs), 291, 292
Social networking site (SNS)
business organizations, 288
credibility and consumer demographics, 288
growth of, 288
people's daily lives, 287
trust and credibility factor, 288
Social network, promotional marketing, 317–319
Social norms, 309
Statutory liquidity requirement (SLR), 9
Stem cell technologies, 391
Structural equation modeling (SEM), 156
Structural model assessment, 180–182
Structural self-interaction matrix (SSIM), 66
Structure and processes
communication practices, 120
information systems (IS) literature, 121
interpretive and procedural aspects, communication, 128
social media activities, 122
Subsistence marketplaces
conceptual priorities, 251
consumer innovation adoption models, 249
description, 249
language and colloquialisms, 250
researchers, 249
sampling frames, 250
video ethnographic techniques, 250
Swabhimaan project, 53
Symbolic capital, 383

T
Talent cultivation mode (TCM), 366
Talent management (TM)
  academic literature, 369
  approaches, 359
  banking and finance, 364–365
  BPO/ITES sector, 367, 372
  economic sectors, 361–369
  education, 365–367
  hospitality and tourism management, 362–364
  HRM in Saudi banks, 365
  HR processes, 360
  limitations, 369
  literature, 364
  literature review, 365
  methodological limitations, 373
  national healthcare systems, 368
  OSPs, 367
  pharmaceutical organization, 367
  phases, 365
  pipeline, 363
  review of literature, 371
  telecommunications organization, 368
  theoretical models, 374
  WLB, 363
Tanzanian Telecom Industry, 121
Technology acceptance model (TAM), 153
  BI, 170
  IBM PC-based graphics systems, 166
  implications, 186–187
  perceived usefulness and ease, 166, 168–170
  robust models, 167
  TAM2, 168
  technology adoption, 168
  user acceptance of computers, 166
Theory of planned behaviour (TPB), 153, 162, 246
Theory of reasoned action (TRA), 153, 246
Travel and Tourism Competitiveness Report 2008, 363
Trust
  defined, 200
  e-commerce relations, 202
  and facilitating conditions, 203–204
  online purchase, 200, 203
  online communication and usage, 200
  online context adoption, 200
  social influence, 203

U
UCB banking, 395
Umbilical cord blood (UCB) banking, 392
Unified Payments Interface (UPI), 63
Unified theory of acceptance and use of technology (UTAUT), 162, 323
  e-commerce, 196 (*see also* E-ticketing)
  internet use, business, 196
  marketing academic discipline and management activities, 195
Unified theory of acceptance and use of technology 2 (UTAUT2)
  customer context focus, 153
  proposed research model, 154
  trust and awareness, 156, 157
Unstructured Supplementary Service Data (USSD), 63
UTAUT performance expectancy, 198

V
Value-Based Adoption Model (VAM), 246
Value-belief-norm theory (VBN), 306
Variance inflation factor (VIF), 179
Viral marketing
  acceptance of, 316
  issues of, 317
  social media, 317
Virtual reality (VR), 108
Virus and SMS spoofing attack, 80

W
Waste management, 228
WhatsApp communication
  agent issues, 128
  disinterest, 127
  evidence, 126
  internet access, 127
  interpretive and procedural aspects, communication, 128
  normal work group, 129
  official/unofficial communication practice, 127
  sending reports, 126
  solving problems, 126
  urgent issues, 126
  web and mobile application, 125
  WLB, 127
  work and personal lives, 128
  zonal manager, 126
Work-life balance (WLB), 363
World Trade Organization (WTO), 39

Z
Zomato, social media platform, 144

The manufacturer's authorised representative in the EU is Springer Nature Customer Service Centre GmbH, Europaplatz 3, 69115 Heidelberg, Germany. If you have any concerns regarding our products, please contact ProductSafety@springernature.com

Printed and bound by CPI Group (UK) Ltd, Croydon, CR0 4YY
30/09/2026
02225643-0013